Acclaim for Elaine Showalter's

A JURY OF HER PEERS

"Impressively researched. . . . Generous, thought-provoking. . . . [Showalter is] less polarized and more nuanced than other feminist critics of her generation . . . She is a lively and incisive guide, the perfect Virgil for our quest." —*The Washington Post*

"Enlightening. . . . The book may be dipped into at any chapter with much reward. . . . Showalter captures so well, often in just a few paragraphs, the image of the women she writes about. . . . Reading *A Jury of Her Peers* is not only an education in literary history, it is eminently satisfactory intellectual nourishment. Four out of four stars." —*Free Press*

"[A] vast democratic volume. . . . Vivid . . . extremely readable and enlightening. . . . Her short, incisive biographies offer a glimpse into the exotic travails of the past and the eternal concerns of female experience. . . . [A] ranging, inclusive history . . . likely to become an important and valuable resource for anyone interested in women's history."
—*The New York Times Book Review*

"Clear-sighted, ambitious . . . minutely researched and rich with opinion, anecdotes, samples, and interpretation. . . . Monumental." —*Elle*

"Absorbing . . . excellent . . . insightful. . . . The prose is so good that the 500-plus-page book also works as an absorbing cover-to-cover read. . . . Showalter does not try to force any of these writers into uncomfortable slots in any kind of artificial female pantheon. These writers are all individuals, and Showalter treats them as such."

—*The Christian Science Monitor*

"Elaine Showalter has delivered the first literary history of American women ever published, and the result is a riveting journey with scarcely a becalmed page. . . . Rich, readable . . . an immensely valuable work . . . vibrant regardless of where one dips in."

—*The Seattle Times*

"Accessible and readable. Brimming with wit and insight. . . . This monumental book will greatly enrich our understanding of American literary history and our culture."

—*Tuscon Citizen* (Recommended New Title)

"Showalter may have written the perfect book-group book: Not only is it fascinating on its own, but it also opens up possibilities for decades of further reading. . . . Like a raucous party, with some squabbling going on in the darker corners . . . Showalter's prose is lively, and she has no problem expressing her opinions."

—*The Columbus Dispatch*

"A breathtaking overview of the intersections of gender and genre in American letters. . . . With its frank assessments, impressive research and expansive scope, *A Jury of Her Peers* belongs on the shelf of any reader interested in the development of women's writing in America."

—*Ms. Magazine*

Elaine Showalter

A JURY OF HER PEERS

Elaine Showalter, a professor emerita at Princeton University, is the author of numerous books, including the groundbreaking *A Literature of Their Own: British Women Novelists from Brontë to Lessing*. A frequent radio and TV commentator in the United Kingdom, she has chaired the Man Booker International Prize jury and judged the National Book Awards and the Orange Prize. She divides her time between Washington, D.C., and London.

Also by

ELAINE SHOWALTER

A JURY OF HER PEERS

American Women Writers
from Anne Bradstreet
to Annie Proulx

Elaine Showalter

Vintage Books

A DIVISION OF RANDOM HOUSE, INC.

NEW YORK

FIRST VINTAGE BOOKS EDITION, JANUARY 2010

Grateful acknowledgment is made to the following for permission to reprint previously
published and unpublished material: *Copper Canyon Press*: Excerpt from "It's Me, I'm Not Home"
from *World Hotel* by Reetika Vazirani, copyright © 2002 by Reetika Vazirani. Reprinted by
permission of Copper Canyon Press, www.coppercanyonpress.org; *Farrar, Straus and Giroux, LLC*:
"Several Voices Out of a Cloud" from *The Blue Estuaries* by Louise Bogan, copyright © 1968 by
Louise Bogan. Copyright renewed 1996 by Ruth Limmer. Reprinted by permission of
Farrar, Straus and Giroux, LLC; *Roman Catholic Diocese of Tucson*: Excerpt from a letter from
Sophie Treadwell to Gerald Brenan dated August 16, 1969. The rights to Sophie Treadwell's
works are owned by the Roman Catholic Church Diocese of Tucson, a corporation
solely from whom rights must be obtained. Reprinted by permission of the Roman Catholic
Diocese of Tucson; *University of Pittsburgh Press*: Excerpt from "The Language of the Brag"
from *Satan Says* by Sharon Olds, copyright © 1980 by Sharon Olds. Reprinted by permission
of the University of Pittsburgh Press; *Viking Penguin*: Excerpt from "Resume" from
The Portable Dorothy Parker, edited by Marion Meade, copyright © 1926, 1928 and renewed 1954,
1956 by Dorothy Parker. Reprinted by permission of Viking Penguin,
a division of Penguin Group (USA) Inc.

The Library of Congress has cataloged the Knopf edition as follows:
Showalter, Elaine.
A jury of her peers : American women writers from Anne Bradstreet to Annie Proulx /
by Elaine Showalter. —1st ed.
p. cm.
Includes bibliographical references and index.
1. American literature—Women authors—History and criticism. 2. American literature—Women
authors—Bio-bibliography. 3. Women and literature—United States—History.
4. Women—United States—Intellectual life. 5. Women in literature. I. Title.
PS147.S46 2009
810.9'9287—dc22
2008042312

Vintage ISBN: 978-1-4000-3442-0

Author photograph © Claudio Vazquez
Book design by Anthea Lingeman

www.vintagebooks.com

Printed in the United States of America
10 9 8 7 6 5 4 3 2 1

To Diane Middlebrook

in loving memory

Contents

Introduction

In 1900, while she was a fledgling newspaper reporter in Des Moines, Iowa, Susan Glaspell covered a sensational murder case in which a farm woman was accused of murdering her husband. Glaspell was so haunted by the trial that she turned it into a one-act play, *Trifles*, in 1916, and then into a short story, "A Jury of Her Peers," in 1917. In both versions, two other farm women, Mrs. Hale and Mrs. Peters, are summoned away from their household chores to accompany their husbands, the county attorney and the sheriff, to an isolated house where the miserly and reclusive John Wright has been found strangled in his own bed with a rope around his neck. His wife, Minnie, has been arrested for the crime, which she denies committing; and the sheriff and his party have come to the farmhouse to search for clues, while their wives pack some clothes to take to Minnie in the county jail where she awaits trial.

Minnie herself, in fact, never appears in either the story or the play, which are less about her innocence or guilt than about the ways the men and the women who are thinking about the murder reach conclusions and judgments. What's needed for a conviction, the men explain, is a motive, "something to show anger or sudden feeling." But as hard as they search the chilly farmhouse, they are unable to find the sort of clear physical evidence they need. Their wives, however, notice domestic details and the "trifles" that signify Minnie's mental distress—a half-filled sack of sugar from the bin; a half-cleaned kitchen table; a piece of patchwork sewn with wild stitches. Taking in the desolation of the childless house, the women haltingly begin to express their own remorse at having failed in friendship to Minnie and perhaps colluded in the isolation that finally drove her mad. Their mounting identification with Minnie's hard life is intensified by the men's loud laughter and mockery of women's trivial concerns as they come through the kitchen on their way to search the barn. When Mrs. Hale and Mrs. Peters discover a strangled canary in Minnie's sewing box, and see the twisted door of its cage, they arrive at a mutual but unspoken conclusion: that John Wright wrung the bird's neck, that he violently silenced the one source of pleasure, music, and joy in his wife's bleak life, and that with the strength of madness, she retaliated by strangling him with a rope, as if executing him by hanging. Wordlessly, the women conspire to conceal or destroy the evidence they have found, and to protect Minnie from the patriarchal system of the Law. In effect, they constitute themselves as a jury of her peers, and they acquit her of the crime of murder.

Legal Juries and Literary Juries

Since it was rediscovered and reprinted in the 1970s, "A Jury of Her Peers" has been widely discussed in law school courses, law review articles, and symposia on civil procedure and criminal law. It is often cited in discussions of jury selection and analyses of the meaning of the term "peer." Legally and politically, women were not the peers of men in 1917, when feminists were engaged in the final years of effort to secure the vote. In 1893, the suffrage activist Lucy Stone had demanded a "jury of her peers" for the accused murderer Lizzie Borden, contending that only women could understand Borden's actions and motivations. No state in 1893, however, and few in 1917, permitted women to serve on juries. Utah was the first to grant the right in 1898, but not until 1968 did Congress pass legislation guaranteeing it to women in the entire United States. As law professor Patricia L. Bryan has commented, many legal experts have come to recognize "what Susan Glaspell suggests . . . that the patriarchal norms and expectations of those who stood in judgment, both as jury members and as members of the community, prevented the legal system from doing justice."[1]

Feminist critics have also interpreted "A Jury of Her Peers" as a parable of the fate of the American woman writer in a literary culture organized around patriarchal norms, values, judgments, and laws. Just as women were not allowed to serve on juries, so, too, were they left out of the scholarly editorial boards, panels of consultants, and academic leadership posts that established authoritative critical judgments. Histories of American literature traditionally excluded women from their boards of editors. The first such survey was written in 1879 by Moses Coit Tyler, a professor at the University of Michigan who thanked fourteen "men of letters" and "working-brothers" for help in his preface.[2] Tyler noted the contributions of Anne Bradstreet, but gave women writers in general short shrift. Paradoxically, although the poet, short-story writer, and literary critic Ellen Mackay Hutchinson coedited the eleven-volume

Library of American Literature (1888–90) with the critic Edmund Clarence Stedman, she concealed her identity and gender so effectively as "E. M. Hutchinson" that not even contemporary reviewers of the volumes noted her contributions. In 1917, the four male editors of *The Cambridge History of American Literature* set out to "enlarge the spirit of American literary criticism and render it more energetic and masculine." Two women, the scholar Louise Pound and the novelist Mary Austin, contributed essays to the *CHAL,* but the marginality of women's status to the undertaking was suggested at the end of the preface, where the editors thanked "Mrs. Carl Van Doren, who has prepared the index." Meanwhile, Mr. Carl Van Doren, one of the editors, made fun of the "amiable ladies" steeped in sentiment and religion, who wrote the earliest American novels.[3] In 1948, the year Glaspell died, the *Literary History of the United States* was edited by fifty-four men and one woman. Although she won a Pulitzer Prize for drama in 1931 and was ranked in her lifetime with Eugene O'Neill, Glaspell herself quickly dropped out of the literary canon.

Why did this woman disappear from literary history? Repeatedly, in looking at studies and biographies of individual American women writers, I came upon the same question. How could Lydia Maria Child, "a woman so influential in her own day and so perceptive about issues still relevant to ours have just disappeared from literary and historical textbooks?" "What has happened to Constance Fenimore Woolson's reputation? Why is it that a writer who was numbered among the country's best has been forgotten?" "Why didn't Mary Austin become the Owen Wister of the woman's Western?" "Why is Zona Gale still such an obscure figure?" "If *The Time of Man* [by Elizabeth Roberts] . . . is as good as I think it is, how did it happen to disappear so soon, almost without a bubble to mark the spot?"[4] Why don't Americans know about such landmark books as Julia Ward Howe's *Passion-Flowers* (1854), Pauline Hopkins's *Of One Blood* (1903), or Nella Larsen's *Quicksand* (1928)? Perhaps these women, and others like them, came of age at the wrong moment, between two literary movements. Perhaps they were too contaminated by sentimentalism or too radical. Perhaps they were too narrow and intense. Perhaps they didn't explore their inner life; perhaps they explored it too insistently. Or perhaps these women writers, among many others, needed a critical jury of their peers to discuss their work, to explicate its symbols and meanings, and to demonstrate its continuing relevance to all readers.

Glaspell's story asks us to consider what we mean by a peer. Is it someone of the same sex? The same race? The same age or class or region? Someone who shares a common language or cultural code? Nothing in U.S. law or in the Constitution defines or guarantees such fine-tuned rights, although an elaborate "science" of jury selection has developed to find jurors likely to agree with a lawyer's case.[5] Women are not always sympathetic to a woman defendant, and nothing prevents men from understanding women's stories when they are taught how to read them. Clearly the sheriff and the county attorney in Glaspell's story could be taught to recognize Minnie's clues and to interpret them as motives; otherwise Mrs. Hale and Mrs. Peters would not need to conceal and destroy the evidence. My experience in teaching "A Jury of Her Peers" is that men understand the story, and women's writing in general, perfectly well. When I have taught the story to federal judges, they have asked whether Mrs. Hale and Mrs. Peters genuinely do justice to Minnie Wright by destroying evidence that sheds light on her motives. Or do they actually suppress her chance to have a public hearing and bring out the details of domestic abuse that might sway the verdict in her favor? Are they her saviors or her accomplices? Legal experts who study Glaspell's story point out that all-male juries in 1900 were very reluctant to convict a woman of a serious crime, because of their chivalrous ideas about gentle womanhood. Indeed, in the real murder case upon which Glaspell based "A Jury of Her Peers," the defendant was ultimately set free. Is the best defense and the fairest trial a full airing of the evidence to an informed public? For the broader benefit of society, might a trial even lead to changes in public attitudes and laws?

I believe that American women writers no longer need specially con-stituted juries, softened judgment, unspoken agreements, or suppres-sion of evidence in order to stand alongside the greatest artists in our literary heritage. Indeed, we need the vigorous public debate of a critical trial, with witnesses for the prosecution as well as the defense, to ensure that American women writers take their place in our literary heritage. What keeps literature alive, meaningful to read, and exciting to teach isn't unstinting approval or unanimous admiration, but rousing argu-ment and robust dispute.

A Literary History of American Women Writers

This book is intended to begin that spirited debate in the twenty-first century. Surprisingly, it is the first literary history of American women writers ever written. From the learned and devout Puritan poet Anne Bradstreet, whose first book was published in 1650 and hailed for its excellence, to the contemporary novelist and short-story writer Annie Proulx, whose gritty tales of Wyoming cowboys published in 1999 revised the Western genre and entered popular culture as an Oscar-winning movie, American women have been authors for more than 350 years. They have come from every one of the fifty states, from every race and religion, and every class and ethnic background. So it's even more astonishing that no one before me has tried to trace their contribution to our national literature. Apart from a very few celebrated figures such as Louisa May Alcott, Emily Dickinson, and Harriet Beecher Stowe, most of the women writers before 1900 may be unfamiliar to readers, although several are enshrined in American cultural history as the invisible authors of well-known hymns like Anna B. Warner's "Jesus Loves Me," holiday songs like Lydia Maria Child's "Over the River and Through the Woods," nursery rhymes like Sarah Josepha Hale's "Mary Had a Little Lamb," patriotic anthems like Julia Ward Howe's "Battle Hymn of the Republic" and Emma Lazarus's inscription for the Statue of Liberty. Some women writers have stressed their femininity, and written about female experience and a mother's heart. Others have rejected the idea that there is anything distinctive or special about a female literary voice, and written about adventure, war, or sex from the perspective of male characters. But by the close of the twentieth century, American women writers had achieved literary fame and two, Pearl Buck and Toni Morrison, had received the Nobel Prize for literature. As we begin the twenty-first century, we need to understand how they were connected to each other and to their times, and to integrate their careers and contributions into our narrative of American literary history overall.

Since the 1970s, scholars of American literature have set out to change the literary canon by rediscovering and reprinting hundreds of lost, forgotten, or neglected works by women writers. We now have primary texts by scores of women writers from the seventeenth to the twentieth centuries, as well as biographies, editions of letters, anthologies, and pathbreaking collections of critical essays. Many scholarly journals now regularly publish research on American women writers, and one journal, *Legacy,* is completed devoted to them. There is a Society for the Study of American Women Writers, which hosts a biannual conference; and many societies dedicated to the study of individual women writers, from those as famous as Edith Wharton to those as obscure as Evelyn Scott.

So why no literary history up to now? One reason may be that the enterprise seemed too huge. When I set out on this project, my major concerns were its daunting size and its cultural, racial, and even geographical diversity. American women writers were so numerous, and their papers and manuscripts were scattered in so many libraries, that the task of traveling to carry out the necessary research seemed too great for any one person. Moreover, they were so productive, and published so many books, that reading them all seemed impossible in a lifetime. That's why national literary histories are usually huge team efforts, with a board of editors, a village of consultants, an army of research assistants; and even then, many scholars have died before finishing their own contributions to the whole. I worried whether I would have the stamina, longevity, and chutzpah to complete the book. To my relief, thanks to twenty-first-century technology, the research part of the task has become much more manageable, if not easy or short. Of course, I still needed to consult library holdings from Boston to Los Angeles, including trips to collections as far-flung as Tulsa and Tucson. I needed to read vast numbers of books, for which I chiefly depended on the splendid resources of the Firestone Library at Princeton University and the Huntington Library in San Marino, California. But the proliferation of reprints, the accessibility of rare and out-of-print books for sale online, and the ever-increasing digitalization of library holdings and archives made it possible for me to assemble my own research collection and to access thousands of texts and documents from my desk. The twenty-first century must be the best of times for doing American literary historical research.

Yet, ironically, the twenty-first century is also the worst of times for actually *writing* American literary history. Philosophical debates about whether literary history in general is theoretically possible or intellectually valid have discouraged the attempt to write histories like this one.[6] Academic doubts that Americans still have "a unifying vision of national identity" have added to the complicated theoretical problems. By the end of the twentieth century, even scholarly authorities admitted they were no longer certain "we know what American literature is or what history is, and whether we have the authority to explain either."[7] Some self-flagellating critics have argued that *all* literary judgments are relative, subjective, and political, depending on the sex, race, intellectual affiliations, and submerged agendas of the judges, and should therefore be avoided.

Feminist critics have also wondered if women writers could be fairly judged as artists by such traditional and possibly male-defined standards as intellectual quality, imaginative force, originality, formal and technical mastery, and literary influence. Rather than risk creating hierarchies among women writers, judging them as "major" or "minor," many feminist scholars preferred to abolish literary history altogether. They emphasized cultural importance rather than aesthetic distinction, and moved away from literary judgment or comparison toward social history. For example, as one critic has confessed, among feminist literary scholars there has been "an unspoken agreement not to submit nineteenth-century American women's novels to extended analytical evaluation," for fear of prematurely undoing the patient work of recovery.[8] In women's studies, the encyclopedic anthology of women's writing has replaced the literary history, which inevitably makes selections, distinctions, and judgments.

The American Female Tradition

In this book, however, I tell a story of American women's writing with a beginning, middle, and end, and I make selections, distinctions, and judgments. In my view, the female tradition in American literature is not the result of biology, anatomy, or psychology. It comes from women's relation to the literary marketplace, and from literary influence rather than essential sexual difference. It comes from pressures on women to lead private rather than public lives, and to conform to cultural norms and expectations. Therefore I have chosen to discuss women who wrote for publication, rather than women who wrote diaries, letters, recipes, or wills. I am asking how American women negotiated the act of writing professionally, how they were changed by committing themselves to writing as a vocation, how they reconciled their public selves with their private lives, and how changes in the status of women affected their lives and careers. Obviously, there are some special cases or exceptions; Emily Dickinson cannot be left out of literary history although she refused to publish more than a few of her poems during her lifetime. I focus on traditional literary genres—poems, plays, fiction—but I also look at popular fiction, girls' books, hit plays, and satiric verses. I trace the development of open treatment of female experience, but I am also interested in women writers' efforts to move beyond female experience, to create male characters, and to write outside of their own race and place, and I take those efforts as positive signs of ambition, compassion, imagination, and craft. Throughout the book, I have looked at what women actually wrote. I have no theoretical, political, or visionary idea of what women ought to write.

We can see American women writers' consciousness of social pressures and expectations in the signatures they chose for their publications, which usually concealed their identities but not their sex. In the seventeenth century, Bradstreet was credited for her publication as "a Gentlewoman." Eighteenth-century women writers tended to use classical pseudonyms, such as "Theodosia," "Portia," "Marcia," "Sylvia," "Philenia," or "Constantia." In the early nineteenth century, American women writers published anonymously and used both pseudonyms and signatures such as "A Lady of Massachusetts"; Lydia Maria Child signed her first book "By an American." But by mid-century a vogue for flowery and hyperfeminine pen names had sprung up, following the fashion of Sara Payson Willis Parton, who signed her popular newspaper column and best-selling novels as "Fanny Fern." In 1853, Fern advised aspiring women writers: "In choosing your signature, bear in mind that nothing goes down, now-a-days, but *alliteration*. For instance, Delia Daisy, Fanny Foxglove, Harriet Honeysuckle, Lily Laburnam, Paulena Poppy, Minnie Mignonette, Julia Jonquil, Seraphina Sunflower, etc."[9] In the twentieth century, women writers usually published under their own names, but in the 1970s, seeking to contribute to the male-dominated field of science fiction, Alice Sheldon signed her work "James Tiptree, Jr." and persuaded everyone that she was a man.

I have organized this history chronologically, discussing a writer when she began her career or made her most important contributions, but not every writer can be neatly catalogued by decade or in a single chapter. Where careers changed dramatically over a longer period of time, as with Harriet Beecher Stowe or Gwendolyn Brooks, I've come back to the writers at different moments; I've decided each case on its own terms. Edith Wharton and Willa Cather, major and pivotal figures whose careers spanned the nineteenth and twentieth centuries, and who set themselves against "women's writing" altogether, get a chapter on their own. The 1850s were so momentous that they need two chapters. In my earlier book *A Literature of Their Own* (1977), a study of English women novelists in the nineteenth and twentieth centuries, I defined three phases in the development of women's writing that were akin to those of any other literary subculture. First, there is "a prolonged phase of imitation of the prevailing modes of the dominant tradition"; second, "there is a phase of protest" against these modes, and "advocacy" of independent rights and values; and third, a phase of self-discovery, a search for identity and a specific aesthetic. I called these phases in women's writing "feminine," "feminist," and "female." In the 1970s, I could only imagine a fourth stage, a "seamless participation in the literary mainstream."[10] By the end of the twentieth century, however, American women's literature had reached the fourth and final stage, which I would now call "free." American women writers in the twenty-first century can take on any subject they want, in any form they choose.

Although I am aware that literary judgments are subjective, and that they reflect critical tastes and temporal values rather than establish eternal and unchanging monuments of excellence, I still believe that such judgments are part of the ongoing arguments of a culture which need to be shared and made public. Harvard professor David Perkins, whose book *Is Literary History Possible?* (1992) forcefully raised questions about the genre, concluded that even if literary history is impossible, it has to be attempted, because "it has an indispensable role in our experience of literature and a broader social or cultural function as well."[11] I fully agree. I hope that this book will deepen our appreciation of these writers and affect our broader understanding of American history and culture. I hope as well that it will inspire and encourage others to read the poems, stories, novels, and plays of the women I've included, to discover great writers they may never have heard of, to reread familiar titles with a deeper comprehension, and to debate and even disagree with my choices. I am proud that this is the first literary history of American women writers, but I also hope it will not be the last.

A JURY OF HER PEERS

A New Literature Springs Up
in the New World

From the very beginning, women were creating the new words of the New World. The first women writers in America, Anne Bradstreet (1612–1672) and Mary Rowlandson (1637–1711), were born in England and endured the harrowing three-month voyage of storm, seasickness, and starvation across the North Atlantic. In Massachusetts, where they settled, they led lives of extraordinary danger and deprivation. Both married and had children; they thought of themselves primarily as good wives and mothers. Both made the glory of God their justification for writing, but they prefigured themes and concerns that would preoccupy American women writers for the next 150 years and more—Bradstreet, the poet, writing about the intimacies and agonies of domestic life, including pregnancy and maternity, the death of three of her grandchildren, and the destruction of her home by fire; and Rowlandson, writing a narrative of her captivity by Narragansett Indians, and pioneering the great American theme of interracial experience in the encounter with Native American culture.

Both Bradstreet and Rowlandson entered print shielded by the authorization, legitimization, and testimony of men. In Bradstreet's case, no fewer than eleven men wrote testimonials and poems praising her piety and industry, prefatory materials almost as long as the thirteen poems in the book. In his introductory letter, John Woodbridge, her brother-in-law, stood guarantee that Bradstreet herself had written the poems, that she had not initiated their publication, and that she had neglected no housekeeping chore in their making: "these Poems are the fruit but of some few houres, curtailed from her sleep and other refreshments." Rowlandson's narrative, too, came with "a preface to the reader" signed "Per Amicum" ("By a Friend"), probably the minister Increase Mather, which explained that although the work had been "penned by this Gentlewoman," she had written it as a "Memorandum of Gods dealing with her," and it was a "pious scope, which deserves both commendation and imitation." The author had not sought publication of her narrative out of vanity; rather,

> some Friends having obtained a sight of it, could not but be so much affected with the many passages of working providence discovered therein, as to judge it worthy of publick view, and altogether unmeet that such works of God should be hid from present and future Generation: and therefore though this Gentlewoman's modesty would not thrust it into the Press, yet her gratitude to God, made her not hardly perswadable to let it pass, that God might have his due glory, and others benefit by it as well as her selfe.

Having given a lengthy defense of the virtues of the book, the Friend concluded with the hope that "none will cast any reflection upon this Gentlewoman, on the score of this publication," and warned that any who did "may be reckoned with the nine Lepers," symbols of ingratitude. Apparently no one dared come forward to complain about Rowlandson after this endorsement.

We know that New England Puritans in the seventeenth century believed that men were intellectually superior to women, and that God had designed it so. They were notoriously unsympathetic to women who defied God's plan for the sexes by conspicuous learning or reading, and they could be hostile to women who went outside their sphere by preaching or writing. The most official expression of this hostility was the trial of Anne Hutchinson in 1637. Hutchinson belonged to a dissident sect, but she had also been leading her own discussion groups for women. Tried for "traducing the ministers" and for blasphemy while she was pregnant with her fifteenth child, Hutchinson was excommunicated and forced to leave the Massachusetts Bay Colony, with her husband and children. The entire Hutchinson family, with the exception of one daughter, were killed by Indians in 1643. In 1645, when Ann Yale Hopkins, the wife of Governor Edward Hopkins of Hartford, became insane, John Winthrop blamed her "giving herself wholly to reading and writing," rather than the hardships of colonial life, for her breakdown. "If she had attended to her household affairs, and such things as belong to women, and not gone out of her way and calling to meddle such things as are proper for men, whose minds are stronger . . . she had kept her wits."

Despite these instances, the shared hardships of life in the New World gave women an existential equality with men that allowed Bradstreet and Rowlandson self-expression. Both men and women shared cold and hunger, faced disease and death, and risked captivity and massacre. Almost two hundred members of the Massachusetts Bay Colony died during the first year. Women had to do the hard physical labor of cooking, baking, cleaning, dairying, spinning, weaving, sewing, washing, and ironing. They endured the dangers of childbirth in the wilderness, nursed babies, and often buried them. While in strict religious terms "goodwives" were not supposed to trespass on the masculine sphere of literary expression, in reality there was more flexibility and tolerance. As two of her modern editors observe, "Bradstreet was *not* censured, disciplined, or in any way ostracized for her art, thought, or personal assertiveness, so far as we know. Rather, she was praised and encouraged; and there are no indications that the males in her life treated her as 'property.' If anything, she was treated as at least an intellectual equal."[1]

A Poet Crowned with Parsley—Anne Bradstreet

Anne Bradstreet's *The Tenth Muse Lately Sprung Up in America* (1650) was the first book by a woman living in America, although it was actually published in London and entered in the Stationers' Register. Bradstreet wrote with both an awareness of her gender and a sense of rootedness in New England Puritan culture. Adrienne Rich has paid tribute to her achievement and summed up her inspiring example for future American women poets:

> Anne Bradstreet happened to be one of the first American women inhabiting a time and place in which heroism was a necessity of life, and men and women were fighting for survival both as individuals and as a community. To find room in that life for any mental activity . . . was an act of great self-assertion and vitality. To have written poems . . . while rearing eight children, lying frequently sick, keeping house at the edge of the wilderness, was to have managed a poet's range and extension within confines as severe as any American poet has confronted.[2]

But Bradstreet was much more than a heroic female survivor who courageously managed to compose poetry in her spare time. She was also a strong, original poet whose work can be read today with enjoyment and emotion, a woman who wrote great poems expressing time-less themes of love, loss, doubt, and faith. Despite her strict Puritan beliefs, she had wit and a sense of humor. And while she dutifully imi-tated the prevailing models of male poetic excellence, from Sir Philip Sidney to the French Protestant poet Guillaume Du Bartas (whose huge unfinished epic of the Creation was among the Puritans' most revered texts), she also explored some of the most central issues for the develop-ment of American women's writing—how to make domestic topics worthy of serious literature, and how to use strong and memorable lan-guage without ceasing to be womanly.

We don't know all the facts of Anne Bradstreet's life, but what we do know suggests that, growing up in England, she began to think of herself as a poet from an early age. While her brother went to Cambridge, she was tutored in Greek, Latin, French, and Hebrew by her father, Thomas Dudley, the steward to the Earl of Lincoln, and had access to the earl's large library. She had begun to compose her own poems by the time she was sixteen, when she married twenty-five-year-old Simon Bradstreet, a graduate of Emmanuel College, Cambridge, who had assisted her father in his stewardship. The marriage was a love match, and indeed Brad-street would dedicate to Simon one of the most beautiful poems a woman ever wrote about her husband.

In early April of 1630, the Bradstreets and the Dudleys were among the Puritan members of the New England Company who embarked on a three-month voyage to America on the *Arbella,* the flagship of a little fleet of four vessels. Another passenger, John Winthrop, who would become the first governor of the Massachusetts Bay Colony, preached a famous sermon to the pilgrims aboard, declaring that God was support-ing their expedition, and that their settlement would be like "a Citty upon a Hill," with the "eyes of all people" upon them. But when they arrived in Salem on June 12, 1630, they discovered that disease and starva-tion had decimated the small Bay Colony, and many among their own numbers died in the first weeks. The Salem settlers had been living in caves, huts, and wigwams, and had not even been able to plant crops. For the next few years the pioneers battled to survive, eating clams, mussels, nuts, and acorns; building shelters; and facing cold, hunger, and illness as well as anxiety and homesickness.

Both Bradstreet's father and her husband served as governors of the struggling colony. For the difficult first five years of their marriage, Anne was unable to have a child. In her journal she confessed: "It pleased God to keep me a long time without a child, which was a great grief to me, and cost me many prayers and tears before I obtain one, and after him gave me many more." She also became ill and was bedridden for several months in 1632 with fever and coughing. When she recovered, she wrote her first poem, "Upon a Fit of Sickness," thanking God for his mercy in sparing her life. And the following year, she gave birth to her first son, Samuel.

Anne Hutchinson came to New England in 1634, and Bradstreet witnessed the events of her rise and fall. But as Charlotte Gordon points out, "ironically, Mistress Hutchinson's downfall ushered in the most fertile decade of Anne Bradstreet's life—fertile in every sense of the word." Already the mother of a son and a daughter, Bradstreet gave birth to five more children during these years. From 1638 to 1648, she also "wrote more than six thousand lines of poetry, more than almost any other English writer on either side of the Atlantic composed in an entire lifetime. For most of this time, she was either pregnant, recovering from childbirth, or nursing an infant, establishing herself as a woman blessed by God, the highest commendation a New England Puritan mother could receive."[3]

The poems Bradstreet was writing were intellectual and scholarly, formally influenced by English and European masters. But she was aroused and provoked by the great political events taking place in England in the 1640s, particularly the English Civil War, which led to the execution of Charles I. Five thousand of the six thousand lines of poetry she composed during the decade came from her long poem in heroic couplets, "The Four Monarchies," in which she chronicled the pre-Christian empires of Assyria, Persia, Greece, and Rome, examining the legitimacy of kings and emperors. These were not the standard subjects of pious women's verse, and in a "Prologue" to her poems, Bradstreet protected herself from criticism by insisting that she was a modest woman who had no intention of competing with male epic poets:

> To sing of wars, of captains, and of kings,
> Of cities founded, commonwealths begun,
> For my mean pen are too superior things . . .
> Let poets and historians set these forth,
> My obscure lines shall not so dim their worth.

Like English women poets of her time, such as Anne Finch and Anne Killigrew, she emphasized her inferiority and temerity in writing at all, calling her Muse "foolish, broken, blemished." While men rightly contended for fame and precedence, Bradstreet flatteringly claimed, she was content with her humble domestic niche, and her poems would make those of her male contemporaries look even more impressive:

> *If e'er you deign these lowly lines your eyes,*
> *Give thyme or Parsley wreath, I ask no Bayes.*
> *This mean and unrefined ore of mine*
> *Will make your glist'ring gold but more to shine.*

Instead of striving for the bay or laurel wreath, she asked only for a wreath of parsley and thyme, kitchen herbs rather than Parnassian prizes. Bradstreet was the Poet Parsleyate, the woman poet whose domestic work enabled the leisured creativity of men; but her imagery of the humble kitchen of Parnassus would be echoed in many heartfelt cries by the American women writers who came after her.

The humility of these lines, however, was balanced by her request for men to give women poets the space and the chance they deserved:

> *Men have precedency and still excel,*
> *It is but vain unjustly to wage war;*
> *Men can do best, and Women know it well.*
> *Preeminence in all and each is yours;*
> *Yet grant some small acknowledgment of ours.*

In 1649, Bradstreet's brother-in-law, the Reverend John Woodbridge, who was in England acting as a clerical adviser to the Puritan army, arranged to have her poems published by a bookseller in Popes Head Alley, London, under the title *The Tenth Muse Lately Sprung Up in America, or Severall Poems, compiled with great variety of Wit and Learning, full of delight.* As the cover went on to explain, the book included "a complete discourse and description of the Four Elements, Constitutions, Ages of Man, Seasons of the Year" and "an Exact Epitome of the Four Monarchies . . . Also a Dialogue between Old England and New, concerning the late troubles, with divers other pleasant and serious Poems." In his prefatory verse, "To my Dear Sister, the Author of These Poems," he congratulated her on her achievements:

> *What you have done, the Sun shall witnesse bear,*
> *That for a womans Worke 'tis very rare;*

> *And if the Nine vouchsafe the Tenth a place,*
> *I think they rightly may yield you that grace.*

In England, *The Tenth Muse* was well received as evidence of the genius of the woman of the New World, and became one of the "most vendible," or best-selling, books of the period, at the top of the list with Shakespeare and Milton. In New England, it was widely read and esteemed.[4]

In the 1650s, Bradstreet was absorbed in personal and family matters—the birth of her eighth and last child, the death of her father, a lengthy illness. Instead of poems, "in much sickness and weakness" she wrote a spiritual autobiography in the form of a letter to her children, intended for them to have after her death. By 1657, however, she had recovered, and began to correct and revise her poems for a second volume, and to compose new ones with images drawn from her own experience. In June 1659, when only three of her children were left at home, the daughters having married, and the sons begun their careers, she wrote "In Reference to her Children," the first woman's poem about empty-nest syndrome:

> *I had eight birds hatcht in one nest,*
> *Four Cocks were there, and Hens the rest.*
> *I nurst them up with pain and care,*
> *No cost nor labour did I spare*
> *Till at the last they felt their wing,*
> *Mounted the Trees and learned to sing.*
> *Chief of the Brood then took his flight*
> *To Regions far and left me quite.*
> *My mournful chirps I after send*
> *Till he return, or I do end.*

When a fire destroyed the Bradstreet home in the summer of 1666, she was distraught, despite her best efforts to interpret the catastrophe as a divine warning against vanity and materialism. The poem she wrote, "Verses Upon the Burning of Our House," is a pious acceptance of God's will, but it also includes tenderly exact memories of the places

> *Where oft I sat and long did lie:*
> *Here stood that trunk and there that chest.*
> *There lay that store I counted best.*
> *My pleasant things in ashes lie,*
> *And them behold no more shall I.*

The finest of the poems Bradstreet wrote during this period was "To My Dear and Loving Husband":

> *If ever two were one, then surely we.*
> *If ever man were lov'd by wife, then thee.*
> *If ever wife was happy in a man,*
> *Compare with me, ye women, if you can.*
> *I prize thy love more than whole mines of gold*
> *Or all the riches that the East doth hold.*
> *My love is such that rivers cannot quench,*
> *Nor ought but love from thee give recompense.*
> *Thy love is such I can no way repay.*
> *The heavens reward thee manifold, I pray.*
> *Then while we live, in love let's so persevere*
> *That when we live no more, we may live ever.*

Although some American women writers over the centuries would be trapped in marriages to demanding, authoritarian husbands who insisted that their needs and wishes take precedence, the tradition began with Bradstreet's heartfelt love poem to a husband who was a true partner and who enabled her to fulfill her poetic gifts.

A Woman in Captivity—Mary Rowlandson

Mary Rowlandson was forced into writing by extreme and terrible circumstances—three months of captivity among the Narragansett Indians. If this dreadful event had not taken place, Rowlandson would never have written a word. Yet she was a born writer, observant, curious, graphic, concrete, able to notice subtle details despite her ordeal, and to treat her captors as individuals. Her memoir of her abduction, *A True History of the Captivity and Restoration of Mrs. Mary Rowlandson* (1682), was the first of the many Indian captivity narratives that fascinated American readers from the seventeenth to the nineteenth centuries.

We know even less about Rowlandson's early life than we do about Bradstreet's, but she was born in Somerset, England, one of nine children of Joan and John White. In 1638, her father emigrated to New England, and the family joined him there the following year. In 1656, at nineteen, she married Reverend Joseph Rowlandson of Lancaster, Massachusetts, a village with about fifty families, thirty miles west of Boston. A daughter, Mary, died at three years old; in 1676, they had three surviving children: Sarah, six; Mary, ten; and Joseph, fourteen.

Although she had some education, Rowlandson never planned or expected to be a writer; she was propelled into print by the traumatic events of King Philip's War, a major event in Puritan history. From June 1675 to August 1676, the Wampanoag chief Metacom, whom the English called King Philip, launched a series of raids against frontier settlements in western Massachusetts; other tribes, including the Narragansetts and the Nipmuck, joined in. On the tenth of February 1676, Narragansett warriors attacked Lancaster, burning the town and taking hostage twenty-four of the villagers, including Mary and her three children. Sarah Rowlandson was wounded in the raid and died nine days later in her mother's arms. The other two children were separated from her. Over the next eleven weeks, Mary was forced to travel with her captors, walking about 150 miles north into Vermont and New Hampshire and west to the Connecticut River. On May 2, 1676, Reverend Rowlandson was able to ransom his family for about twenty pounds' worth of goods.

Over the next year, Rowlandson wrote a memoir of her experience which was read and admired for its religious significance by a number of influential Puritan clergymen, including Increase Mather. Scholars believe that Mather, as well as Rowlandson's husband, may have made editorial additions to the text, since "several aspects of Rowlandson's story recall sermon stylistics and ministerial retellings of other captivities."5 First printed in Cambridge, Massachusetts, in 1682, it sold over a thousand copies, and was then published in England, where it also became a best seller, going through fifteen editions by 1800. Now seen as "an early American classic," it has been compared to *The Diary of a Young Girl* as a narrative that "transcends the historical and cultural circumstances that produced it and by combining stark details, honesty, and exquisite style, brings the experience of war and suffering to a personal and accessible level."6

Alongside the biblical quotations and moralizing in Rowlandson's book is a heartrending tale of survival, with all its immediacy and vigor of expression. Rowlandson had an innate sense of literary structure.

Because the Indians moved camp twenty times during her captivity, she divided her story into twenty chapters, which she calls "removes"; the term also suggests that, step by step, she was being separated from the life she knew and becoming immersed in the alien culture of the Narragansetts. Rowlandson's narration of each remove is as exciting and succinct as the most sensational adventure story, while her close familiarity with biblical rhythms and idioms gave her observations an epic rhetorical power. The narrative opens with a dramatic announcement: "On the tenth of February 1675 came the Indians with great numbers upon Lancaster."[7] Vividly describing the stages of the siege, Rowlandson also chose personal incidents that individualized it. Her older sister Hannah, seeing her son murdered and her friends massacred, cried out "Lord, let me die with them," and was instantly "Struck with a Bullet, and fell down dead over the Threshold." Mary herself went with her captors. As she reflected, the urge to survive was strong: "I had often before this said, that if the Indians should come, I should chuse rather to be killed by them than taken alive; but when it came to the trial my mind changed; their glittering Weapons so daunted my Spirit that I chose rather to go along with those (as I may say) ravenous Bears, than that moment to end my daies."

The historian Laurel Thatcher Ulrich was among those scholars in the 1970s and 1980s who charged that Rowlandson's narrative "is deeply and pervasively racist," because she viewed the Indians as barbarous savages and "was seemingly unaware of the suffering in the Indian camp."[8] I take a more moderate and less political view today. Rowlandson had seen twelve people close to her, including her sister and brother-in-law, murdered by the Indians, and her house burned to the ground; she had carried her wounded six-year-old daughter Sarah for nine days without food, had held the child when she died, and had been forced to leave her body behind. Not even an Anne Frank centuries later could have been so saintly as to have sympathized with the humanity and suffering of her captors, and Rowlandson had been steeped in a Puritan theology that made her see them as damned and diabolical heathens. Yet despite her fear of her captors, who drove her mercilessly on their trek, denied her food and shelter, laughed at her stumbling, and terrified her with their war whoops and constant threats of violence and death, Rowlandson did distinguish among them, describing their occasional acts of kindness and pity toward her, and her preservation from rape or sexual abuse; and noting their endurance, stoicism, and determination to survive the English rule. As Ulrich notes, Rowlandson wrote positively about Metacom, and also about her master among the Narragansetts, Quinnapin, "who comes across . . . as a dignified and rather distant male authority figure."⁹

Other Americanist scholars and critics have observed that Rowlandson's assumptions about the racial and cultural divide between herself and the Indians changed over time. Throughout her story of starvation, exposure, loss, and terror, Rowlandson also realized how extremity changed her personality. When her daughter Sarah died in her arms, she noted, "At another time I could not bear to be in the room where any dead person was, but now the case is changed; I must and could lye down by my dead Babe, side by side, all the night after." She also described how hunger and weakness made her able to eat food that previously would have disgusted her, including horse liver and bear meat: "The first week of my being among them I hardly eat any thing; the second week I found my stomach grow very faint for want of something; and yet 'twas very hard to get down their filthy trash; but the third week (though I could think how formerly my stomach would turn against this or that, and I could starve or die before I could eat such things, yet) they were pleasant and savoury to my taste." Indeed, Rowlandson provided a dramatic ethnographic description of the food that the Indians foraged when moving quickly in times of war:

> *Their chief and commonest food was Ground-nuts; they eat also Nuts, and Acorns, Hartychoaks, Lilly-roots, Ground-beans, and several other weeds and roots that I know not.*
>
> *They would pick up old bones, and cut them in pieces at the joynes, and if they were full of worms and maggots, they would scald them over the fire to make the vermin come out; and then boyle them, and drink up the Liquor, and then beat the great ends of these in a Morter, and so eat them. They would eat Horses' guts and ears, and all sorts of wild birds which they could catch: Also Bear, Venison, Beavers, Tortois, Frogs, Squirils, Dogs, Skunks, Rattle-snakes: yea, the very Barks of Trees.*

Rowlandson survived because she was able to use her skills in sewing and knitting to gain some advantages, trading them to get food and better treatment. Gradually, she gave up her passive dependence on the charity and chivalry of the Indians and her spiritual dependence on "Providence" to help her, and found ways to earn money and buy provisions. She also may have been prepared to survive captivity, Ulrich argues, because she understood "the nature of servility. Even though she hated and feared her captors, she knew how to please them. Growing up in a hierarchical society, she had learned what it meant to be an inferior."[10] Even if the habit of servility was the basis of Rowlandson's resourcefulness, her energetic narrative does not present her as a helpless victim, but as a woman of astonishing strength, intelligence, and determination to live.

We do not know how Rowlandson readjusted to life in Puritan New England after she was ransomed and the family was reunited. In the year after her safe return, while the family were living with friends, she suffered insomnia and other symptoms of post-traumatic stress; she endlessly relived her experience "in the night season," and reflected on the meaning of her trial and salvation: "The portion of some is to have their Affliction by drops, now one drop and then another; but the dregs of the Cup, the wine of astonishment, like a sweeping rain that leaveth no food, did the Lord prepare to be my portion." In 1678, her husband died suddenly, and the following year she married another community leader, Captain Samuel Talcott. He died in 1691, and Rowlandson lived as a widow until 1710. Her ordeal may have left her with more confidence to stand alone and less inclination to be servile. But she never published another word.

The Indian captivity narrative was the first American literary form dominated by women's experience. It described fear, powerlessness, and sexual threat; analyzed race and intermarriage; described women's abilities to survive and endure through stoicism and resourcefulness; and experimented with personal confession. But the captivity narratives, as Christopher Castiglia argues compellingly in his book *Bound and Determined* (1996), also "offered American women a female picaresque, an adventure story set . . . outside the home. In the American 'wilderness,' white women could demonstrate skills and attitudes of which their home cultures thought them incapable." They could indirectly critique their domestic situations as women at home, and "even in the most traditional narratives, women not only passively endure but discover active talents their home environments would never have brought to light, much less nurtured."[11] In their dramatization of the choices of resistance, assimilation into Native American culture, escape, or return with a new understanding of their own culture, the captivity narratives became the model for fiction by women about the confrontation between races and cultures in the New World.

2

Revolution: Women's Rights and Women's Writing

or the first half of the eighteenth century, American women published very little. Although women were writing letters, diaries, journals, and religious tracts, these historical documents were largely private; publication, when it occurred, took place in newspapers rather than books.

Letter and poetry columns in colonial newspapers, for example, often included women's "complaints" about courtship, marriage, or education, and men's responses. The *American Weekly Mercury* published a series of letters and poems about the sexual double standard between 1724 and 1731, which included the satiric poems of Elizabeth Magawley, who signed herself "Generosa." Such sentiments also appeared occasionally in Southern newspapers such as the *South Carolina Gazette.*[1] Jane Coleman Turell (1708–1735), the daughter of a Calvinist minister, published a few conventional religious poems before her early death. Sarah Kemble Knight's earthy travel diary, although written in 1704–5, was not published until 1825.

Of course, this period was a dry stretch for American male authorship, too. Sermons dominated the scanty field of publication, and among the writers who came out of the religious Great Awakening of the 1730s and 1740s, only Jonathan Edwards is remembered in literary history. From 1732 to 1758, Benjamin Franklin was editing *Poor Richard's Almanack*. But overall, during a great period of creativity, variety, innovation, and intellectual splendor for English and European literature, America was a barren outpost. In England, for example, the novel was flourishing in the hands of Defoe, Swift, Smollett, Richardson, and Henry Fielding, while Sarah Fielding, Henry's sister, was among the women who wrote popular novels of sensibility; women playwrights included Mary Delariviere Manley, Susanna Centlivre, and Eliza Haywood; Pope, Swift, Thomson, and Johnson were writing poems and essays that were widely read and privately imitated in the colonies. In contrast, no American play was produced until the 1760s, and during the Revolution the theaters were closed. And finally, before the Revolution there were no American novels.

By the second half of the eighteenth century, however, as women poets, playwrights, and novelists of distinction such as Fanny Burney and Ann Radcliffe came to prominence and achieved commercial success in England, American women, inspired by revolutionary fervor and dedicated to women's rights to life, liberty, and the pursuit of happiness, also turned to writing to accomplish their ends. The first steps toward this change were taken in education. In the 1760s, academies for girls began to be formed in New England, and by the end of the century major improvements had taken place.[2] After the Revolution there were major reforms in women's education, pushed by female patriots who argued that the Mothers of the New Republic also had to be educated as responsible citizens, and supported by a few eminent gentlemen who were impressed by this argument. The female seminaries of the postrevolutionary era often required that the student keep a journal which was both a private diary and a school exercise reviewed by teachers. These school exercises, as one headmaster noted, trained the students in "facility of expression."[3] There was a surge in women's writing in a wide range of forms, especially satire. Demands and protests from Revolutionary feminists often took a humorous form.[4] In the "Ladies [sic] Declaration of Independence" (1791), for example, women from Litchfield, Connecticut, closely parodied the language of the orginal Declaration of Independence to demand control of tea parties and social affairs. Behind the jokes, however, lay a serious message about women's exclusion from full citizenship.

In terms of artistic innovation, literary craft, critical reception, and influence on later generations, the outstanding women writers of this era were Mercy Otis Warren, Phillis Wheatley, Judith Sargent Murray, and Susanna Rowson, a groundbreaking quartet who followed Bradstreet and Rowlandson as the mothers of American literature. Warren was the first American woman playwright; Wheatley the first African-American woman poet; Murray the first feminist woman of letters; and Rowson the first American woman novelist. As professional writers, they overturned the constraints of the earlier Puritan and colonial generations of literary women, admitting their wish for attention, respect, publication, and even fame. They vigorously defended the moral worth of the novel and the theater against Puritan prejudice, and advocated a liberal education for women. It's no coincidence that Murray argued that girls should also be taught "to aspire," and to have the ambition to succeed with "avidity of application" and "intenseness of study."[5] Susanna Rowson ended her literary career as a headmistress in a young ladies' academy, for which she also wrote several textbooks. And in their letters and publications, all these women emphasized the importance of learning. While they were dependent on classical, European, and English models, and sometimes used neoclassical pseudonyms, they entered the public sphere as self-identified Americans and daughters of liberty. Their lives were venturesome and compelling, and their works are still readable and provocative today.

The Dramatist—Mercy Otis Warren

Mercy Otis Warren (1728–1814) quickly recognized that the American Revolution was an extraordinarily dramatic moment in history, and predicted that the people who played a role in it would create the literary future. In a letter to her best friend Abigail Adams on March 15, 1779, she wrote about the new nation in the metaphors of the stage: "America is a theatre just erected—the drama is here but begun, but while the actors of the old world have run through every species of pride, luxury, venality, and vice—their characters will become less interesting and the western wilds which for ages have been little known, may exhibit those striking traits of wisdom, and grandeur, and magnificence, which the Divine oeconomist may have reserved to crown the closing scene."[6] In her plays and her history of the Revolution, Warren would show the striking traits of the actors of the New World.

Born in Barnstable, Massachusetts, the third of thirteen children of a lawyer active in county government, Warren was educated by reading in her uncle's library, and sometimes sitting in while he tutored her brothers. She became an ardent admirer of Dryden, Pope, Shakespeare, Milton, Molière, and Catherine Macaulay, the celebrated republican author of the *History of England*. In 1754, she married High Sheriff James Warren, and in the 1770s their Plymouth household became a center of revolutionary meetings and debate. The Warrens had five sons, and sustained a happy marriage for fifty-four years.

In 1773, Catherine Macaulay and Warren began a correspondence that they maintained for almost two decades, an instance of the "epistolary networks" of women across the Atlantic, which offered not only satisfying feminine exchanges about personal life, but opportunities to test out their political ideas. "Be it known unto Britain," the American Hannah Winthrop wrote to Warren, "American daughters are politicians and patriots and will aid the good work with their efforts."7 In 1774, Warren wrote to Macaulay hoping that they would remain friends despite political conflicts between their countries, and declaring her disregard for "the opinion that women make but very indifferent politicians . . . When the observations are just and do honour to the heart and character, I think it is very immaterial whether they flow from a female lip in the soft whispers of the private friendship or whether thundered in the senate in the bolder language of the other sex."8 Even in the letters of personal friendship, eighteenth-century American women writers did not adopt colloquial styles; just picking up a pen made them conscious of striving for an effect very different from ordinary speech. Their letters were copied and read aloud to friends, and were written in the elegant neoclassical imagery of Augustan poetry rather than the American vernacular. When Abigail Adams ("Portia") tells her best friend Mercy Otis Warren ("Marcia") about the weather, she declares that "Ceres witherd Head reclines, Virtumnus is fled, and Pomona is scattering here and there the half Grown fruit e'er she too bids us adieu." In other words, summer is over.9 Still, in their letters and their literary writing, these women entered the public sphere, and entered it as self-identified Americans and daughters of liberty.

Warren published several plays—*The Adulateur* (1772), *The Defeat* (1773), and *The Group* (1775)—in the Boston newspapers under the signature "A Lady from Massachusetts." *The Group,* published in book form as well, satirized the Tory governing council that represented the British government in Boston. In her list of dramatis personae, Warren caricatured council members, citizens, and writers under such names as Hum Humbug, Sir Sparrow Spendall, Brigadier Hateall, and Scriblerius Fribble, and noted that they were attended by "a swarm of court sycophants, hungry harpies, and unprincipled danglers, collected from the neighboring villages, hovering over the stage in the form of locusts . . . the whole supported by a mighty army and navy from Blunderland, for the laudable purpose of enslaving its best friends." This blunt comic invective shows how forcefully Warren could express her political views in prose. Unfortunately, the rhetorical demands and neoclassical conventions of blank-verse drama defeated her natural gifts. Despite her grasp of the dramatic potential of the revolutionary moment, Warren was unable to express herself so vividly in iambic pentameter burdened with "thee" and "thou" and "ne'er" and "o'er." Some lines stand out, especially when she is depending on verbs; Beau Trumps, for example, a colonial who can't decide which side to support, says "I trimmed and pimped and veered, and wavering stood." Judith Sargent Murray praised Warren's "correct and elegant" dramas, and argued that they had "sufficient scenic merit and variety of situation" to warrant production; she even went so far as to hope that with proper encouragement, Warren and her American contemporaries would prove to be "Columbian Shakespeares."[10] The very "wealth of Warren's references" to "classical myth, British history, and world political figures," however, makes *The Group* difficult to read; to be understood today it needs copious annotation. Two later plays in prose, *The Blockheads* (1776) and *The Motley Assembly* (1779), and two blank-verse historical tragedies, *The Ladies of Castile* and *The Sack of Rome* had their admirers, but were never performed.[11]

After the colonists' victory in the Revolution, Warren was well connected to the government, and not shy about using her connections to promote her work. When she published *Poems, Dramatic and Miscellaneous* (1790), she shrewdly dedicated it to George Washington; she also sent copies to her other prominent male friends in the new federal government for blurbs. The president responded with the polite excuse that he hadn't had time to read it all, but "from the parts I have read . . . I am persuaded of its gracious and distinguished reception by the friends of virtue and science." Thomas Jefferson, the secretary of state, wrote that he could "foresee that it will soothe some of my moments of rest from drudgery." And the secretary of the treasury, Alexander Hamilton, chivalrously stretching the truth, wrote that "in the career of dramatic composition at least, female genius has outstripped the male."[12] By 1791, Warren had started writing her history of the American Revolution, which she published in three volumes in 1805 with the ambitious title *History of the Rise, Progress, and Termination of the American Revolution, Interspersed with Biographical, Political and Moral Observations.* She was a forceful and original, if idiosyncratic, historian, who unashamedly treated the British as villains and the rebel Americans as heroes. But to the victors belong the histories; Warren lived to be eighty-six, and enjoyed the fame of being among the first citizens to chronicle the birth of the nation.

The African-American Poet—Phillis Wheatley

The poet Phillis Wheatley (ca. 1753–1784) overcame immense racial, eco-nomic, and social obstacles to write, and her life was tragic and short. An African brought to America as a slave, who published accomplished neo-classical verse, she has been hailed by modern African-American critics as "the progenitor of the black literary tradition."[13] Wheatley occupied a symbolic role far beyond her work; her success proved that Africans were capable of learning and art, in an era when even Enlightenment philosophers like David Hume and Immanuel Kant, and learned men like Thomas Jefferson, assumed that they were an inferior race.

Born in Senegal, West Africa, the child arrived, frail and half naked, on a slave ship that docked in Boston Harbor on July 11, 1761. She was thought be about seven years old, because she was missing her two front teeth. She was bought by a prosperous tailor, John Wheatley, and named "Phillis" for the ship that brought her to America. The Wheatley family quickly recognized her exceptional intelligence and aptitude for learning. Susanna Wheatley and the family's teenage twins, Mary and Nathaniel, taught her English, Greek and Roman history, Latin, and English poetry. John Wheatley described her extraordinary intellectual progress:

> Without any assistance from School Education and by only what she was taught in the Family, she, in sixteen Months Time from her Arrival, attained the English Language, to which she was an utter Stranger before, to such a Degree, as to read any, most difficult Parts of the Sacred Writings to the great Astonishment of all who heard her.
>
> As to her Writing, her own Curiosity led her to it; and this she learnt in so short a time that in the Year 1765, she wrote a letter to the Reverend Mr. Occom, the Indian Minister, while in England.
>
> She has a great Inclination to learn the Latin tongue and has made some progress in it. This relation is given by her Master who bought her and with whom she now lives.[14]

By the age of thirteen, Phillis was writing poems herself. In 1770, her elegy on the sudden death of Reverend George Whitefield, an evangeli-cal English preacher who was lecturing in the United States, was pub-lished in New England and in London, to much excitement and acclaim.

According to Harvard professor Henry Louis Gates, Jr., she was "the Toni Morrison of her time."[15] Susanna Wheatley collected twenty-eight of Phillis's poems and tried to find subscribers in Boston to underwrite their publication as a book.

But the subscribers were not to be found. Bostonians were suspicious of the idea that an African slave had the capacity to create poetry. In a meeting convened at the Old Colony House in Boston, in October 1772, which Gates calls "the primal scene of African-American letters," Wheatley was cross-examined by eighteen prominent Massachusetts public figures, including John Hancock, Governor Thomas Hutchinson, seven ministers, and three poets, to determine whether she could indeed have written the poems published under her name.[16] Most of the interrogators had themselves been slaveholders, and of course none of them were women. In any case, Phillis Wheatley passed their oral examination, and the members of the tribunal signed and published an "attestation" to her achievement:

> We whose Names are under-written, do assure the World, that the Poems specified in the following Page, were (as we verily believe) written by Phillis, a young Negro girl, who was but a few years since, brought an uncultivated Barbarian from Africa, and has ever since been, and now is, under the Disadvantage of serving as a Slave in a Family in this Town. She has been examined by some of the best Judges, and is thought qualified to write them.

Even with this recommendation, American publishers refused to print the book. In 1773, Nathaniel Wheatley escorted Phillis to England, partly for her health, and partly to secure patronage and publication for the family's astonishing prodigy. There she was received by the Countess of Huntingdon and other notables; the Lord Mayor of London gave her a copy of Milton's poems; the Earl of Dartmouth gave her five guineas to buy the work of Pope; and Ben Franklin went to see her "and offer'd her any services I could do her." Wheatley's first book, *Poems on Various Subjects, Religious and Moral by Phillis Wheatley, Negro Servant to Mr. John Wheatley of Boston*, was published in London by Archibald Bell in 1773.

It was a momentous event, which initiated a long controversy about the quality and originality of Wheatley's art. Bell advertised the book as "one of the greatest instances of pure, unassisted genius that the world ever produced."[17] The *London Magazine* found this an overstatement, but admired the work nonetheless:

> *These poems display no astonishing power of genius; but when we consider them as the production of the young untutored African, who wrote them after six months* [sic] *of casual study of the English language and of writing, we cannot suppress our admiration of talents so vigorous and lively. We are the more surprised too, as we find her verses interspersed with the poetical names of the ancients, which she has in every instance used with propriety.*

A month after the book's publication, Phillis returned to Boston, and the Wheatley family freed her from slavery. When the war began in 1775, she dedicated a poem to General Washington: "Proceed, great chief, with virtue on thy side." As he had with Mercy Otis Warren, Washington wrote her back a polite form letter of thanks, but also invited her to visit him at his headquarters: "I shall be happy to see a person so favored by the Muses, and to whom Nature has been so liberal and beneficent in her dispensations." She did visit him in Cambridge, and he arranged to have her poem published in the *Virginia Gazette* in March 1776. By then Susanna Wheatley had died, and by 1778, John Wheatley died as well; the twins had grown up and moved away; and Phillis had to support herself. In 1778, she married a free black man, John Peters, with whom she had three children, all of whom died in infancy. He abandoned her when she gave birth to their third child. Not even a prodigy could support herself by poetry alone; during her marriage she worked as a seamstress, and published only two poems. She dedicated a second volume of poetry to Franklin, but it never attracted enough subscribers to be published, and the full manuscript has never been recovered. Peters may have sold it, since some poems have reappeared; in 1998, one of the poems from the book, "Ocean," came up for auction at Christie's and was bought by a collector for almost seventy thousand dollars. In her short lifetime, though, poor wages and her own ill health undermined Wheatley's efforts. She died, along with her baby, at the age of thirty in 1784.

Wheatley's literary reputation among African-Americans has veered from veneration to contempt, reaching its nadir in the 1960s during the black arts movement, which viewed her as a sellout, an inauthentic black woman with a white mind, who exemplified self-hatred and the servile mentality.[18] Her poems imitated eighteenth-century English models like Pope, rather than drawing on the black vernacular; most were freighted with references to classical mythology, or were elegies for friends and neighbors. Her early poem on slavery, "On Coming from Africa to America," although it is among her most direct poetic statements, and relatively skillful in its use of her preferred form of the heroic couplet, is also painfully abject, in modern terms, in its defense of slavery as a civilizing religious force.

> *'Twas mercy brought me from my* Pagan *land,*
> *Taught my benighted soul to understand*
> *That there's a God, that there's a* Saviour *too:*
> *Some view our sable race with scornful eye,*
> *"Their colour is a diabolic die."*
> *Remember,* Christians, Negroes, *black as* Cain,
> *May be refin'd and join th'angelic train.*

Gates calls this poem the "most reviled . . . in African-American literature," but he makes a moving plea for Wheatley to be liberated from racial tests and examinations, whether by white tribunals or black critics, and for everyone to read her work anew, "unblinkered by the anxieties of her time and ours . . . If Wheatley stood for anything, it was the creed that culture was, could be, the equal possession of all humanity."[19] In "Something like a Sonnet for Phillis Miracle Wheatley," the poet June Jordan (1936–2002) robustly defends Wheatley, concluding that despite her dutiful assimilation of deference, she remains a precursor of "the difficult miracle of Black poetry in America": "They dressed you in light but you dreamed / With the night."[20]

First Feminist—Judith Sargent Murray

America's first major feminist author, Judith Sargent Murray (1751–1820), experimented with drama, poetry, and fiction, and did her best work as an essayist and literary critic, championing equality for women and creative freedom for imaginative writers as well as political liberty for all Americans. Murray credited the Revolution with creating opportunities that American women had a civic obligation and moral responsibility to use. "I expect to see our young women forming a new era in female history," she wrote in 1798, and her own energy and ambition helped shape that era.[21]

Born in Gloucester, Massachusetts, Murray married a sea captain and trader, John Stevens, when she was eighteen. He died in the West Indies in 1786, and like many grieving women who could not accept the harsh Puritan doctrines of divine election, she broke with Calvinism and found comfort in the Universalist belief in general salvation. Two years later, she remarried, wedding a Universalist preacher, John Murray; he was supportive of her intelligence and her writing, but unable to earn enough money to keep the family comfortable. When their daughter Julia was born in 1791, Murray turned to writing as a source of income.

In 1790, under the pen name "Constantia," Murray published the sparkling essay "On the Equality of the Sexes," in which she wittily protested against the deliberate infantilization of women. With playful examples and forceful rhetoric, she challenged the idea of women's intellectual inferiority to men, blaming any differences on education and socialization. Weren't women acknowledged to have a "lively imagination," even if it was mainly employed in gossip? Didn't they equal men in memory, "since a loquacious old woman is as frequently met with as a communicative old man"? And if men had better judgment, they didn't start out that way; everyone would agree that a two-year-old girl was more sage than a two-year-old boy. The "contrary modes of education" were to blame for what happened in maturity, for "the one is taught to aspire and the other is early confined and limited." Murray was one of the first American women writers to complain about the monotony and lack of intellectual stimulation in housework; "I would calmly ask, is it reasonable, that a candidate for immortality, for the joys of heaven, an intelligent being . . . should be at present so degraded, as to be allowed no other ideas than those which are suggested by the mechanism of a pudding?" The education and recreation designed for girls could only "enervate the body and debilitate the mind."

Murray enthusiastically read Mary Wollstonecraft's *A Vindication of the Rights of Woman* when it appeared in 1792. For the next five years, Wollstonecraft was the most significant influence on American thinking about women's rights. The book had two American printings, and was available from 30 percent of American libraries.[22] In Philadelphia, Elizabeth Drinker noted in her diary that "in very many of her sentiments, she, as some of our friends say, *speaks my mind.*"[23] In New York, "A Young Lady of the City" spoke out vigorously in praise: "See Wollstonecraft, a friend, / Your injur'd rights defend, / Wisdom her steps attend."[24]

Encouraged by Wollstonecraft's feminist defense of women's rights to education and expression, Murray began to write a series of essays in the *Massachusetts Magazine* in 1792 under the male persona of "The

Gleaner," a Mr. Vigillius who depicted himself as "a plain man, who, after spending the day in making provision for my little family, sit myself comfortably down by a clean hearth and a good fire," with "a violent desire to become a writer."[25] The essays kept up the pretense of male authorship, and played with the fiction of readers' speculations. Was The Gleaner a bachelor living in Worcester, a graduate of Yale, or someone else altogether? Murray composed letters to The Gleaner from a variety of imagined readers, including men, whose names identify them as eighteenth-century types ruled by their humors—Charles Candour, George Seafort (a "tough old seaman"), Peter Laconic, Oliver Homestead, Richard Wary. She used these characters to emphasize the gender ambiguities of writing. On the page, the writer could be any sex, any age, any class; she was confident that no stylistic "effeminacy or tinsel glitter" would betray her gender. Her use of the male persona was an important step for American women writers in terms of skill and literary ambition, marking an assertion of the artist's imaginative claim to all experience.

Murray maintained an Enlightenment emphasis on equality between the sexes, in all realms including literature, and wanted to show that the merit of a work, rather than the identity or gender of the author, was the significant question. Returning to the theme of her early essays, she listed in *The Gleaner* ten categories in which women, "as far as relates to their understanding," were "*in every respect, equal to men*":

First, Alike capable of enduring hardships.
Secondly, Equally ingenious, and fruitful in resources.
Thirdly, Their fortitude and heroism cannot be surpassed.
Fourthly, They are equally brave.
Fifthly, They are as patriotic.
Sixthly, As influential.
Seventhly, As energetic and as eloquent.
Eighthly, As faithful, as persevering in their attachments.
Ninthly, As capable of supporting, with honour, the toils of government. And
Tenthly and Lastly, They are equally susceptible of every literary
  acquirement.[26]

Not a word about purity, maternal love, docility, timidity, or any of the other clichés about feminine nature that would dominate the next century.

Murray was also a friend and champion of the arts, especially fiction and plays. She vigorously defended the novel as proper reading matter for women (along with Mercy Otis Warren and Abigail Adams, she particularly liked *Clarissa*), and further defended the educational, moral, and intellectual advantages of storytelling itself. "Narrative," she wrote, "unencumbered with dry reflections, and adorned with all the flowers of fiction, possesses for the new-formed fancy a most fascinating charm; attention is arrested, every faculty of the soul is engaged, and the pages of the interesting and entertaining novelist are almost devoured." Captivated by novels, she argued, the young reader would move on to more serious intellectual subjects.[27] She was also an enthusiast of theater, and a staunch defender of its virtues. Like fiction, she believed, drama could be a powerful force for creating rational, educated, and engaged citizens. Involving herself in the campaign to establish a theater in Boston and rescind the prohibition of plays, she argued that the new nation needed its own dramatic literature, and it was important "to supply the American stage with American scenes."[28]

Murray tried to supply these American scenes herself in two comedies with patriotic plots, *The Medium, or Virtue Triumphant* (1795), which was the first play by any writer born in America to be produced in Boston after the theaters reopened in 1794, and also the first play by an American-born woman to be professionally staged; and *The Traveler Returned* (1796), which was also performed at the Federal Street Theatre. Both plays were presented anonymously, and indeed Bostonians speculated that they might be the work of her husband, John. Both included "remarkable female characters who initiate action, express and argue for philosophical principles, and form a self-sufficient community in which women of various ages support and protect one another."[29] The plays were included when she published *The Gleaner* in three volumes in 1798; the one hundred sections also included biography, history, moral essays, and literary criticism, and covered such subjects as women's rights, health, philanthropy, religion, and the celebration of Thanksgiving. In her preface to *The Gleaner,* writing as "Constantia," Murray boldly announced that she, for one, was not bound by traditional ideas of female modesty and self-deprecation, but wished for distinction, respect, and even fame: "I would descend with celebrity to posterity." In a final essay, "The Gleaner Unmasked," she explained to readers her motives for using a male persona—to get unbiased criticism, to establish herself as an independent writer unassisted by husband, father, or brother; and to confound the "indifference, not to say contempt, with which female productions are regarded." While her professionalism and disdain for special critical treatment would become the hallmarks of English women novelists when they chose to use male pseudonyms in the nineteenth century, in the United States, unfortunately, egalitarianism would be displaced by belief in a separate feminine sphere of imagination and obligation.

Murray also wrote a short novel, *The Story of Margaretta,* which was serialized in *The Gleaner.* Setting out her views on the proper education and training of girls, she told the story of Margaretta Melworth, an orphan who is raised by Mr. Vigillius and his wife, Mary. Mr. Vigillius is the narrator, but includes letters from Margaretta to give her point of view. Meticulously educated, according to her foster parents' high principles, in English, French, history, geography, astronomy, and philosophy, and accomplished in needlework, drawing, the minuet, and the pianoforte, Margaretta is nonetheless completely taken in by the romantic advances of a scoundrel, Sinisterus Courtland, whom she meets on a trip to visit Yale when she is sixteen. It's certainly disappointing that a heroine so well prepared intellectually should let herself be duped by a man named Sinisterus; but Margaretta realizes her mistake when she catches him plagiarizing his love poems to her, and ends up, after many trials, marrying a better man. Murray handles her didactic themes lightly, and, by having a male narrator, both emphasizes gender and tells the story of a father learning how to be an effective parent of a truly independent child. According to Sharon Harris, Murray "practiced what she preached," and allowed her own daughter to join her at the theater and to act herself, as well as teaching her about notable women in history.[30]

The Novelist—Susanna Rowson

Susanna Rowson (1762–1824) was the first American woman novelist to produce a best seller. Her fourth novel, *Charlotte Temple* (1794), was widely read well into the nineteenth century, and eventually went through two hundred editions. As late as 1870, Rowson's biographer Elias Nason wrote that *Charlotte Temple* "has stolen its way alike into the study of the divine and the workshop of the mechanic; into the parlor of the accomplished lady and into the bed-chamber of her waiting maid; into the log hut on the extreme border of modern civilization and into the forecastle of the whale ship on the lonely ocean." The novel outsold all its eighteenth-century rivals, reigning supreme until the era of Sir Walter Scott, and demonstrated, Nason concluded, that "the common mind of the common people is after all the true arbiter of the merit of works of genius."[31]

Prolific and versatile, Rowson wrote ten novels, two collections of fictional sketches, seven plays, two books of poetry, and six textbooks and books about education. Her career had three phases—actress/dramatist, novelist, and educator—and they were closely connected in her writing. She was born in Portsmouth, England, the daughter of William Haswell, a lieutenant in the Royal Navy; her mother died at her birth. When Haswell had to go to New England on naval business in 1763, Susanna was left behind with a nurse and relatives, and then sent to America to join him when she was five years old. The voyage was exceptionally stormy; the passengers encountered a hurricane, faced food rationing, and were greeted by sleet and ice when they reached Boston Harbor—experiences that she would later describe in her novel *Rebecca* (1792).

Meanwhile, Lieutenant Haswell had remarried an American woman and had two more children. The family lived for the next ten years in the village of Nantasket, on Boston's South Shore, and Susanna read the classics in her father's library. In 1775, in the heat of revolutionary fervor, he was imprisoned as an employee of the Crown, and thirteen-year-old Susanna became the family's caretaker and provider. After the war, Haswell was released on a prisoner exchange, and the family returned to London, where she continued to work and support them, going on the stage as an actress, dancer, and singer. She met William Rowson, an aspiring actor, trumpet player, and backstage handyman; they married in 1786, and stayed married for the rest of her life, although he was a drinker and né'er-do-well. Rowson had more independence with the title of wife than as a single woman trying to make her way in the world. She had also begun to write fiction.

In 1792, the Rowsons joined the London theatrical company of Thomas Wignell, who was recruiting actors for the postrevolutionary American stage. The following year, they emigrated to the New Theatre of Philadelphia, where Susanna flourished playing character roles in a company that included more celebrated actresses such as Mrs. Oldmixon and Eliza Kemble Whitlock. With this second emigration to America, Rowson's fortunes changed. She wrote three plays, and starred in a play of her own, *Slaves in Algiers: or, A Struggle for Freedom* (1794). Based partly on an episode from *Don Quixote* and partly on the piracy of American merchant ships by Algerian slave traders, the play was also a defense of women's rights. Its heroine, Fetnah, an unhappy wife in the Dey's harem, has been radicalized by Rebecca, an American female captive who teaches her that "woman was never formed to be the abject slave of man. Nature made us equal with them and gave us the power to render ourselves superior." Despite the crude stereotyping of Fetnah's father, a Jew who has converted to Islam, *Slaves in Algiers* is among the few comic plays in the period with real dramatic flair and convincing, natural dialogue. In an epilogue, a breathless Mrs. Rowson herself, "almost terrified to death," came out from behind the curtain to address her audience with self-deprecating wit: "Well, ladies, tell me: how d'ye like my play? / 'The creature has some sense,' methinks you say."

In 1794, *Charlotte Temple,* which had originally come out in England three years earlier, was published in a pirated edition in Philadelphia. In an era of long philosophical novels, *Charlotte Temple* was appealingly short, plot-driven, and intense. Young Charlotte is sent by her doting parents to the respectable boarding school of Madame Du Pont in Portsmouth, but there she falls under the malign guidance of the French teacher, Mademoiselle La Rue. Obviously Madame Du Pont has not checked deeply into her teachers" references, for La Rue is a French adventuress who eloped from her own convent, traveled to England, and "lived with several different men in open defiance of all moral and religious duties." She takes Charlotte out to meet dashing officers, especially the libertine Montraville, who promptly sets out to seduce her. Protesting that she will sacrifice her love for Montraville to duty toward her parents, the fourteen-year-old Charlotte is abducted, shrieking and fainting, by the wicked and determined Montraville and his accomplice La Rue. They take her by ship to America, where Montraville has been dispatched to fight in the Revolutionary War; intercept her letters to her parents; and set her up as his hapless mistress in an isolated little house near New York City. Montraville promises that he will marry her, but instead he falls in love with an even more beautiful, wealthy, and intelligent woman, Julia Franklin, and he abandons Charlotte. Pregnant, desperate, alone, she sets out for New York to find him, wanders half crazed in a blizzard, and gives birth to a daughter in an inn. After a heartrending reunion with her father, who has come to America to find her, she dies.

Rowson's lurid account of the evils facing young women was the book's biggest attraction, but she framed it in warnings against vice, materialism, and immorality. She echoed the feminist rhetoric of Mary Wollstonecraft in describing a marriage market of young girls "legally prostituted to old, decrepit men" that paralleled the illegal world of sex exploitation and prostitution. To make her sensational story of abduction, seduction, and betrayal acceptable to a genteel readership, Rowson invented an intimate, chatty, and maternal narrative persona who spoke directly to her audience, like the playwright peeking out from behind the curtain, in nine lengthy "authorial intrusions." In these passages, she created the illusion of a personal bond with her readers, anticipated their criticisms, defended the novel and women's writing as moral and educational genres, and underlined her intentions and values. Rowson's preface, for example, confided to "the young and thoughtless of the fair sex" that her "Tale of Truth" was designed to protect them from "the various and unexpected evils that attend" a girl's entrance into adult life. When she interrupted the flow of her narrative to speak to her reader, Rowson both reinforced the truth of the story and gave clues about her own personality. "Here let me stop to make one remark," she implores in chapter seven, "and trust me my very heart aches while I write it." These appeals to the heart, and the range of potential readers she singled out, from "sober matrons" to "men of philosophic temperament," increased identification with Charlotte Temple's many sufferings and travails. American readers were enthralled. Rowson's melodramatic tale was the biggest seller in the United States before the publication of *Uncle Tom's Cabin* in 1852. In the nineteenth century, readers made pilgrimages to Trinity Churchyard in New York, where they laid flowers and gifts at the grave of a woman named "Charlotte Temple" they firmly believed to be the real heroine.

The novel, Cathy Davidson suggests, could be read as "an allegory of changing political and social conditions in early America." The story of a young girl "misled by a conniving French schoolmistress, seduced by a British officer, and abandoned in a strange new country, an ocean away from beloved (but perhaps too paternalistic) parents" might have spoken to the secret hearts of Americans suffering "the almost inevitable separation anxieties that follow any declaration of independence."[32] But Rowson was discovering that the novel was a genre dealing with the personal rather than the political and thus uniquely suited to women's needs as writers, as well as to women readers, who found it a form of wish fulfillment and rebellion. Men, too, read *Charlotte Temple* with emotion;

Davidson found many copies with "touching inscriptions set down by male readers."[33] Although Rowson never received royalties from the American editions, this literary piracy brought her the profits of fame. A sequel, *Lucy Temple* (1828), published after Rowson's death and taking up the story of her daughter back in England, was also a best seller.

In 1797, however, Rowson gave up fiction for a distinguished third career as an educator and director of the Young Ladies' Academy in Boston, instructing her students in mathematics and science as well as more traditional female subjects. She wrote textbooks for them to use, including one on great women in history. Shortly before her death, she wrote in the preface to one textbook that she had "never promulgated a sentence that could militate against the best interests of religion, virtue, and morality . . . Soon will the gloom of night enshroud me, but to my latest hour I shall devote my leisure to the improvement or innocent amusement of youth."[34]

Her commercial success and absolute respectability enabled a new era of fiction by American women, including Hannah Webster Foster, Sally Sayward Barrell Keating Wood, Sukey Vickery, and Tabitha Tenney. Loudly asserting their modesty, gentility, and femininity, these novelists nonetheless overcame their reluctance to come before the public as authors. By the end of the eighteenth century, American daughters were reading so many novels that even women novelists expressed moral concern. Foster warned that "novels are the favourite, and most dangerous kind of reading now adopted by the generality of young ladies . . . They often pervert the judgment, mislead the affections, and blind the understanding."[35] But it was too late to turn back. Novels inspired young American ladies to become writers themselves, if only to correct the mistakes of others. By 1797, the editor of the *New York Magazine* proclaimed, "This is a novel-reading age."[36]

3

Their Native Land

n 1820, Sydney Smith, a literary critic for the *Edinburgh Review,* insultingly inquired, "In the four quarters of the globe, who reads an American book?" His witticism, however, appeared at exactly the time that James Feni-more Cooper and Washington Irving were launching their impressive international careers as "the American Scott" and "the American Lamb." By the 1820s, talented American women, too, were reading British fiction and aspiring to re-create such achievements on American soil. Sarah Josepha Hale (1788–1879), the editor of *Godey's Lady's Book,* recalled how she had read Ann Radcliffe's gothic classic *The Mysteries of Udolpho* (1794) and been inspired to write fiction herself: "The wish to promote the reputation of my own sex and to do something for my own country, was among the earliest mental emotions I can recollect."[1]

Other women of Hale's generation especially admired Scott's com-bination of fictional adventure with Scottish history, and wondered whether American history, too, could be the basis of exciting novels. As a young girl, Lydia Maria Child read *Waverly; or 'Tis Sixty Years Hence* (1814), Scott's tale of the Jacobite rebellion, and exclaimed, "Why cannot I write a novel?"[2] Her preface to *Hobomok* began with a quotation from Scott's most famous patriotic poem: "I never view the thriving villages of New England, which speak so forcibly to the heart, of happiness and prosperity, without feeling a glow of national pride, as I say, 'this is my own, my native land.'" Catharine Maria Sedgwick, who had especially loved Scott's novel *The Pirate,* wrote in the preface to *her* best-known novel, *Hope Leslie; or, Early Times in the Massachusetts* (1827), that "the ambition of the writer would be fully gratified if, by this work, any of our young countrymen should be stimulated to investigate the early his-tory of their native land."[3]

Motivated by a desire to celebrate their native land, and to contribute toward the creation of a distinctly American literature, three very gifted and very different women writers, Sedgwick, Child, and Caroline Kirkland, led the generation of the 1820s and 1830s. Sedgwick and Child set their fiction in New England; Kirkland wrote about backwoods Michigan, which was then the unsettled frontier or "the West." Products of postrevolutionary ideals of the intellectual equality of women, they were well educated, open-minded, advanced in their thinking about race and gender, and intellectually respected. Sedgwick, bold but ultimately conservative, was hailed by contemporaries as diverse as Cooper and William Cullen Bryant, while the American novelist Emma Embury declared, "She is one of our national glories—*our* Sedgwick."[4] The abolitionist leader William Lloyd Garrison called Child a political radical, "the first woman in the republic." Edgar Allan Poe admired all three writers, calling Child's work "an honor to our country and a signal triumph for our countrywomen," and praising the liberal essayist Caroline Kirkland for her "*truth* and novelty."[5] Together, they wrote novels, stories, children's books, cookbooks, and biographies; they edited magazines, worked for social reform, and fought for the end of slavery.

They received conflicting and ambiguous messages about femininity, intellect, and creativity, from both women and men. Women were certainly entering the publishing industry, as editors as well as writers. By the 1820s, they had begun to edit periodicals whose titles, including gender-marked terms like "Ladies," "Mother," and "Home," showed that they were addressed to a female audience. Patricia Oker has identified over six hundred American women who edited periodicals in the nineteenth century, a sign of their growing power even if they had to call themselves by the term "editress."[6] The publication of the first American annual anthology of poetry and fiction, *The Atlantic Souvenir,* in 1825, opened up more possibilities for women writers. Many annuals—*The Token, The Talisman, The Western Souvenir, The Literary Souvenir,* and *The Gift*—published exclusively American materials, and women wrote at least a third of their contents. The 1820s also saw the beginnings of a distinctly American children's literature, written mainly by women. Child began to edit the *Juvenile Miscellany* in 1824, and thought it was important to replace British content with "American scenes and American characters."[7] Although writing children's literature did not confer literary status, the market for such material was lucrative; as Child wrote frankly to her sister Mary, "children's books are more profitable than any others, and . . . I am American enough to prefer money to fame."[8]

But even such a prominent figure as Sarah Josepha Hale sent mixed messages to other aspiring literary women. In 1829, she declared that "the path of poetry, like every other path in life, is to the tread of woman, exceedingly circumscribed."[9] Yet in 1837, when she took over the merged editorship of the *Ladies' Magazine* and *Godey's Lady's Book,* she announced her wish "to encourage American authors, especially women, and to use the journal to speak to issues concerning women."[10] Her own anonymous fiction took much more conservative views. In *The Lectress* (1839), she told a warning tale of a speaker for women's rights who, despite impeccable motives, loses her husband and her health for her imprudence.

In 1834, Ann Stephens, a writer of short stories and the editor of the *Portland Magazine,* gracefully admitted that "the privilege of deep research is man's right; with it we have no wish to interfere. All we ask is permission to use the knowledge he has scattered over the enlightened world. But poetry, fiction, and the lighter branches of the sciences are woman's appropriate sphere, as much as the flower-garden, the drawing-room, and the nursery."[11] Of course, Stephens had managed to stake out poetry and fiction as well as a few scattered leftovers of masculine research for women. Five years later, in an essay on "Women of Genius" (1839), Stephens showed more pragmatically how even busy housewives and devoted mothers could juggle their domestic duties efficiently enough to allow time for literary production. "There are few American women," she wrote, "who, by a systematic arrangement of time, cannot command three or four hours out of every day, without encroaching upon her household duties . . . These hours devoted to authorship, at a moderate computation, would produce four duodecimo volumes a year."[12]

"Our Sedgwick"—Catharine Maria Sedgwick

Catharine Maria Sedgwick (1789–1867) never married and had no household duties to a husband or children. Furthermore, she had outstanding gifts as a writer: wit, intelligence, warmth, a sense of structure and coherence, an ear for believable dialogue, and an eye for accurate detail. She wrote six well-received novels and numerous short stories in the 1820s and 1830s, as well as children's books, tracts, and biographies; her work was translated into French, German, Italian, Swedish, Danish, and Dutch; and she corresponded with or met several of the leading European women writers of the period, including the Scandinavian novelist

Fredrika Bremer, the English essayist Harriet Martineau, and the Irish novelist Maria Edgeworth. Using the New England setting and American issues of race, ethnicity, and religion, Sedgwick created her own hybrid narrative forms. She also used the gothic tradition to imagine a fascinating series of madwomen whose rebellions and visions create a feminist subtext in otherwise decorous stories. She had a keen and daring sympathy for the outsider, whether the slave, the Native American, the religious dissenter, or even the criminal. Although Sedgwick did not sign her name to her books until the mid-1830s, everyone knew who she was, and in the period it was not unusual to publish anonymously or under a pseudonym. Sir Walter Scott, "The Great Unknown," whose Waverley novels were anonymous, was the most famous example, but Cooper and Hawthorne also veiled their names in their first books, and indeed between 1820 and 1840, more men than women were likely to do so.[13]

Sedgwick was born in Stockbridge, Massachusetts, a region known to its proud inhabitants as "the American Lake District" for its natural beauty and intellectual advantages. She had the warm support of her father, Theodore Sedgwick, one of the most influential Federalists of the early Republic. He was a lawyer and statesman who served in both the Massachusetts legislature and U.S. Senate; her four brothers— Theodore, Harry, Robert, and Charles—also believed in her talent and encouraged her to write. "My dear brother Theodore makes a most extravagant estimate of my powers," she noted modestly early on. "It is one thing to write a spurt of a letter, and another to write a book."[14] Because her mother, Pamela Dwight Sedgwick, became severely depressed when Catharine was two years old (Pamela had borne ten children, three of whom died in infancy), and because her father was away much of the year serving in Congress, Sedgwick was raised by a black woman, Elizabeth Freeman, whom she called Mumbet. Her love and respect for her nurse gave her a personal insight into the issues of slavery that would soon dominate the nation. In 1781, having read the Declaration of Independence, Mumbet asked Mr. Sedgwick, "Won't the law give me my freedom?" He represented her in a historic court case that brought an end to slavery in Massachusetts.

Sedgwick's first novel, *A New-England Tale, or Sketches of New-England Characters and Manners* (1822), was her effort, as she explained in her preface, "to add something to the scanty stock of native American literature." Dedicated to Maria Edgeworth "as a slight expression of the writer's sense of her eminent services in the great cause of human virtue and improvement," *A New-England Tale* seems structured more closely in imitation of Jane Austen.[15] The heroine Jane Elton is orphaned at twelve, and Sedgwick satirizes the debate between her three aunts about who will take her in. Mrs. Daggett is the pious hypocrite; she has no children herself but "no longer ago than that morning, Mr. D. and she had agreed to pay the expenses of one of the young Cherokees at the School at——." Mrs. Convers is the most frivolous and snobbish; she intends to spend all her money on clothes, and "the dancing-master, and the drawing-master, and the music-master" for her own daughters. She wants Jane to go out as a servant, but to change her name so as not to embarrass the family. Mrs. Wilson is the strict Calvinist who "would as soon . . . follow one of my children to the grave, as to see her in that broad road to destruction, which leads through a ball-room."

Mrs. Wilson takes Jane home, but she is soon exposed as a deluded mother of spoiled, worldly, and dishonest children. Her pampered daughter Elvira fantasizes that she is the heroine of a romantic novel: "I always fancy, when I read a novel, that I am the heroine, and the hero is one of my favourites, and then I realize it all, and it appears so natural." Elvira, dressed in a scarlet dress, with her hair "in imitation of some favourite heroine," in ringlets over her shoulders, defeats Jane in a school essay contest, but is then exposed as a plagiarist. She eventually elopes with a French confidence man. Mrs. Wilson's petted son, David, seduces and abandons a village girl, and then commits a robbery, is arrested, escapes, and goes to be a pirate. Mrs. Wilson washes her hands of him: "He has gone out from me, and he is not of me; his blood be upon his own head; I am clear of it . . . I have planted and I have watered and if it is the Lord's will to withhold the increase I must submit." She dies a painful lingering death, with Jane as her nurse. Jane, on the other hand, ends up happily married to a prosperous Quaker gentleman.

Sedgwick framed this satirical novel of manners with the story of a romantic and gothic madwoman, a character type who would show up in much of her subsequent fiction as a subversive emblem of the anger, emotion, and outrage that the genteel heroine must repress. Here called Crazy Bet, she appears first to chastise "the pride and hypocrisy and selfishness" of Jane's aunts. Sedgwick describes Bet as a village woman driven mad by love:

> Wherever there was an awakening, or a camp-meeting, crazy Bet was
> sure to be found; she was often seen by moonlight wandering in the

church-yard, plucking the nettles from the graves, and wreathing the monuments with ground-pine. She would watch for whole nights by the side of a grave in her native village, where twenty years before were deposited the remains of her lover, who was drowned on the day before they were to have been married.[16]

Partly based on Scott's Madge Wildfire, Crazy Bet is also an American variant of the standard Romantic madwoman, Crazy Jane, who appeared originally in 1793 in ballads by Matthew Lewis, and then had her "tragical history" told in early-nineteenth-century chapbooks, melodramas, and painting. Crazy Jane is always a woman whose lover has died or deserted her; she "would dress her head with willow straw and wild flowers, disposed in a fanciful style, and this seemed to be the only amusement that soothed her mind."[17] Sedgwick's Crazy Bet leads Jane to the cottage where David Wilson's abandoned lover and her child are being hidden. By this point, she is in full madwoman regalia: "She had taken off her old bonnet and tied it on a branch of the tree that shaded the grave, and twisted around her head a full leaved vine, by which she had confined bunches of wild flowers, that drooped around her pale brow and haggard face." The novel ends with Crazy Bet's death, which she calls her final struggle to be free. In Sedgwick's second novel, *Redwood* (1824), the Crazy Jane figure is a six-foot-tall Yankee Amazon, Aunt Deborah Lenox. One character calls her "a hideous monster—a giantess, I suspect a descendant of the New-England witches." Crazy Anny, a woman driven mad by the seduction and betrayal of her daughter by a British officer, appears in the revolutionary novel *The Linwoods* (1835), waving a pole "on which she had tied thirteen strips of cloth of every colour, and stuck them over with white paper stars."[18]

Hope Leslie (1827) was Sedgwick's most popular novel, and is the one most read today. Set in the seventeenth century, it opened with her trenchant authorial comments on the character of the Puritans and the Indian tribes they fought and displaced. Sedgwick always insisted that she respected the Pilgrim fathers despite their "bigotry," "superstition," and "intolerance."[19] She herself had converted from Calvinism to Unitarianism, but she carefully explained in her preface that "the first settlers of New England were not illiterate, but learned and industrious men. They seem to have understood the importance of their station. The Massachusetts colony, and some of the other establishments sparsely scattered on the coast, were illuminated spots, clear and bright lights, set on the borders of a dark and turbulent wilderness." Sedgwick was also sympathetic to the Native Americans, whom she describes in heroic terms as "the only race of men of whom it be said, that though conquered, they were never enslaved. They could not submit and live. When made captives, they courted death, and exulted in torture."[20]

Drawing on the overt and covert plots of the captivity narrative, Sedgwick invented an exciting plot based on the clash of these two obdurate cultures. In her novel, a young Englishwoman is kidnapped by her father's servants to prevent her from marrying; two Pequod children are captured and kept as servants by Puritans; and white women are abducted by the Pequods in revenge. Sedgwick insinuates that women are the victims of an exchange between men, and that captivity is part of the female condition. William Fletcher, a young Englishman, plans to elope to America with his cousin Alice, against her father's wishes; but at the last moment she is abducted by her father's servants and compelled to stay behind and marry another man, Charles Leslie. William emigrates to Springfield alone, and eventually marries the humble Martha, a devout Puritan, who bears his son Everell. After fourteen years, they learn that Alice Leslie, a widow, has died en route to the New World, and left William the guardian of her two daughters, whom he renames Faith and Hope. He keeps the older girl, Hope, with him in Boston, but sends Faith on ahead to join his family and their teenage Indian captive servants, the brother and sister Magawisca and Oneco, children of the Pequod chief Mononotto. When Mononotto leads a band of braves to rescue his children, Magawisca tries unsuccessfully to protect the Fletchers, but Mrs. Fletcher and her children are killed and Everell and Faith taken captive. In the Indian camp, Magawisca interposes her arm to prevent her father's hatchet from killing Everell. He escapes, but Faith stays behind. Loyal to her tribe, and generous to the white people who have befriended her, Magawisca, it has been noted, "embodies the noble Indian not in a warrior but in a woman."[21]

In the second half of the novel, a grown-up Hope falls in love with Everell, and they are united after many threats and mishaps. The mutilated Magawisca survives to lead Hope to her lost sister Faith, now completely assimilated to Indian ways and the loving wife of Oneco: "No speak Yengees," she tells the horrified Hope. No pleas or gifts will persuade Faith to return to her white family, and nothing can induce Magawisca to remain with Hope and Everell: "The Indian and the white man can no more mingle, and become one, than day and night." Despite its melodramatic aspects, Alexander Cowie, the exacting critic of the

American novel, concluded, "the whole story is given vraisemblance by the colloquial speech and natural action of Hope Leslie," whose "reactions to various situations in which her emotions are deeply involved are indicated with far more plausible psychology than had been evident in the heroines of Charles Brockden Brown or Cooper or any of the lesser novelists who had preceded her."[22] Contemporary reviewers of *Hope Leslie* not only praised its characters and style, but stressed its positive influence on American women readers. "A woman feels a laudable pride in the knowledge that a sister has distinguished herself in an intellectual career," the critic for the *North American Review* declared. ". . . It is a stimulus acting on the generous ambition of the whole sex; prompting all to an exertion of their highest faculties."[23]

Surprisingly, Sedgwick felt ambivalent about her literary success. By 1830, despite the well-received *Clarence, or, A Tale of Our Own Times* (1830), she was confiding to Lydia Maria Child that she was "not just now at all in love with novel-writing."[24] What was the source of her disaffection? By this time, Sedgwick knew she would never marry. Although she had enough money to lead an independent life, and enough loving relatives to provide her with familial support, she had experienced the pain of being "first to none," and the "unnatural state" of a "solitary condition." In 1830, she noted in her journal, she was still longing for "the independence and interests and power of communication of a home of my own," a household where she would not be "second best."[25]

In 1830, Sedgwick published a story in the *Atlantic Souvenir,* called "Cacoethes Scribendi"—the Roman satirist Juvenal's phrase for "the itch to write"—which dramatized her conflicts over professional authorship. In the "secluded and quiet village of H.," near the "literary emporium" of Boston, her narrator explains, all the young men leave as soon they are old enough to pursue adventure and profit, leaving a community of women and children behind. The girls of H. are astonished even to behold the few men who stray into their sanctuary. Moreover, H. is death-haunted, and particularly lethal for husbands, so that "every woman in H. was a widow or maiden." It is a locale in which women, like Sedgwick herself, do not have to worry about getting permission to write from men, and they are happy, busy, independent and untroubled about their futures.

One widow, Mrs. Courland, the mother of five lively boys and one teenage daughter, loves to read. When she discovers that a girlhood friend has published a piece in an annual, she suddenly *"felt a call* to become an author." Not only does Mrs. Courland begin to write short

stories, but at her urging, her three unmarried sisters immediately take
up their pens as well—Miss Anne writing a treatise on botany, Miss Ruth
on education, and Miss Sally on religious meditation. Soon the whole
family is scribbling away, except for the oldest daughter, Alice, who provides the subject matter for many of their stories. Alice refuses to be
either a literary heroine or an author, and thereby wins the love and
devotion of the only young and eligible man in the region, Ralph Hepburn. Hepburn does the writing for her, in the form of a note of proposal. "And when her mother and aunts saw her the happy mistress of
the Hepburn farm, and the happiest of wives, they relinquished, without
a sigh, the hope of ever seeing her an AUTHOR."[26]

Playful rather than didactic, the story endorsed the literary life as one
that allows feminine expression and economic freedom, but also hinted
that there is something dangerous and unnatural about women's literary
ambitions. Susan S. Williams has identified a group of nineteenth-century
American stories by women using the "cacoethes scribendi plot," and
taking various points of view about the legitimacy of women's writing.
In one version, female writers justify their itch by "turning from frivolous to useful subjects"; in another, they cure it by "giving up writing
altogether to take up the duties of being wives." By publishing her story
in a magazine, Sedgwick was both asserting her own legitimacy as a professional author and endorsing the priorities of marriage.[27]

Early in 1833, Sedgwick attempted to write about slavery, but she
could manage to complete only fifty pages. "I have abandoned my
book," she finally noted in her journal in April. "I am sick of it."[28] As she
told Lydia Maria Child, she became ambivalent about abolition, and
wondered about whether gradual education and vocational training of
slaves should be the preamble to full emancipation. "There is no sorrow
of humanity that I have so much at heart as the condition of the black
race," she wrote in 1834 to Child, who had requested a contribution for
her abolitionist gift book The Oasis; but "it does not appear to me that
immediate abolition is best for the slaves. God only knows what is best. It
is a dark and fearful subject." She offered to contribute something about
her views. On her side, however, Child had absolutely no patience
for what seemed like pious equivocation and helpless feminine dither-
ing. As she responded to Sedgwick: "I want none but unqualified Anti-
Slavery writers . . . On this subject I neither have, nor desire to have
moderation."[29]

By the mid-1830s, Sedgwick was backing away from any commitment
to writing as the center of her life:

*My author existence has always seemed something accidental, extrane-
ous, and independent of my inner self. My books have been a pleasant
occupation and excitement in my life. The notice, and friends, or
acquaintances, they have procured me, have relieved me from the danger of ennui and blue devils, that are most apt to infest a single person.
But they constitute no portion of my happiness—that is, such as I
derive from the dearest relations of life. When I feel that my writings
have made any one happier or better, I feel an emotion of gratitude to
Him who has made me the medium of a blessing to my fellow-creatures.
And I do feel that I am but the instrument.*[30]

Her self-image as a medium and an instrument, rather than an
autonomous creator, made writing more of a burden to her than a vocation and a pleasure, and that contradictory self-division may have prevented her from entirely fulfilling her promise. *The Linwoods, or, "Sixty
Years Since" in America* (1835) told the story of the Revolutionary War
from the perspective of two families who are deciding which side to
take. In a climactic encounter, one young man tells another: "You call
those poor fellows out there rebels, I patriots. You think they deserve to
be ground to the dust, I think they are infernally abused. You think
Washington is cold, selfish, calculating, ambitious; and I believe that he is
generous, disinterested, just . . . and humane." Although Sedgwick had
clearly not given up her wish to create the literature of her native land,
she did not feel confident about it. While her title alluded to Scott's
Waverly, she warned that its "title might be deemed ambitious; that it
might indicate an expectation that 'this sixty years since in America'
would take place with the 'sixty years since' of the great Master. I have
not yet forgotten the literature of my childhood—the fate of the ambitious frog. To those who know me, I need not plead 'not guilty' to a
charge of such insane vanity."[31]

Sedgwick wrote two more novels in the 1830s, *The Poor Rich Man and
the Rich Poor Man* (1836), and *Live and Let Live* (1837), and earned more
than sixty thousand dollars during the decade.[32] But after 1837, feeling
herself at a creative impasse, she gave up writing novels for the next
twenty years, and produced didactic and moralizing stories for children.
Her last novel, *Married or Single?* (1857), defended the unmarried woman,
but was a muted book that disappointed those hoping for more feminist
fire.

"The first woman in the republic"—Lydia Maria Child

Lydia Maria Francis Child (1802–1880) had started out wanting "to think and write, and be like" Catharine Maria Sedgwick, but as a fiery abolitionist she never forgave what she regarded as Sedgwick's cowardice.[33] When she read Sedgwick's *Memoirs* in the 1870s, she wrote to a friend, "She sincerely wished well to the negroes, but she could not bear to *contend* for them, or for anything else. She was afraid of the subject. She was very deficient in moral *courage* . . . During the Anti-Slavery battle, she cooled toward me. She was *afraid* of reformers."[34] Where Sedgwick was weak and tentative, Child was strong and sure; from the beginning of her literary career she not only wrote about racial intermarriage, but argued for it as the best way to benefit all groups.

Ironically, Child is most familiar to Americans for the holiday song beginning "Over the river and through the woods, / To grandfather's house we go." Of course, very few of those Americans who sing the song every Thanksgiving know the author's name, let alone that the iconic grandmother and her pumpkin pie don't appear until the final stanza. Child, however, was a prolific and important American writer, who pioneered, as her biographer Carolyn Karcher points out, "almost every department of nineteenth-century American letters: the historical novel, the short story, children's literature, the domestic advice book, women's history, antislavery fiction, and journalism. Not least among her accomplishments, she anticipated an acute need of our own time by publishing an anthology [*Looking Towards Sunset*, 1865] for the elderly, designed to promote positive images of old age. Her corpus amounts to forty-seven books and tracts (including four novels and three collections of short stories) with enough uncollected journalism and fiction to fill one or two more," plus a huge correspondence.[35]

How did such an eminent writer and intellectual enter literary history in such a humble way? Born to a working-class family in Medford, Massachusetts—her father was a baker—Child had little normal education, and her father actively disapproved her reading. Her brother Convers, though, was a precocious child who found patrons to send him to Harvard. He shared the wealth with her, passing on his old schoolbooks, directing her reading, and introducing her to his literary friends, including Emerson. Early on she was unafraid to challenge even the most elevated classics of the canon; *Paradise Lost,* she told her brother, was very grand, "but don't you think that Milton asserts the superiority of his own sex in rather too lordly a manner?"[36] Karcher believes that Child "appears never to have suffered from either the fear of unsexing herself or the paralyzing sense of inadequacy that inhibited so many other nineteenth-century women writers."[37] When Child was twelve, her mother died, and she was sent to Norridgewock, Maine, to live with her married sister. There she had many contacts with members of the Abenaki and Penobscot tribes who lived in the forests by the Kennebec River; she visited their wigwams. As a child, she saw a Penobscot woman who had borne a child and then walked four miles through the snow. She also met the Penobscot chief Captain Neptune.

Although Alexander Cowie in the 1950s would proclaim that when she wrote her first novel, *Hobomok*, in 1824, Child "knew little about the Indians or about life or about novel-writing," he was wrong on all counts.[38] As she recalled the genesis of her book, while visiting her brother at Harvard, where he had become a Unitarian clergyman, she read a review of *Yamoyden: A Tale of the War of King Philip in Six Cantos*, by James Wallis Eastburn and Robert Sands. The reviewer, John Gorham Palfrey, whom she had met through her brother, predicted that early New England history, especially the conflict between the Pilgrims and the Native Americans, was rich material for an authentic American novel. "Whoever in the country first attains the rank of a first rate writer of Fiction will lay his scene here. The wide field is ripe for the harvest, and scarce a sickle has yet touched it."[39] Child responded immediately:

> *I knew not what impelled me; I had never dreamed of such a thing as turning author; but I siezed [sic] a pen, and before the bell rang for afternoon meeting I had written the first chapter, exactly as it now stands. When I showed it to my brother, my young ambition was flattered by the exclamation, "But Maria, did you really write this? Do you mean what you say, that it is entirely your own?"*[40]

Unlike Sedgwick, Child wrote in a state of ecstatic imagination. In an essay on "The First and the Last Book" (1832), she unapologetically confessed:

> *One remembers writing his first book as he recollects the first time he saw the ocean. Like the unquiet sea, all the elements of our nature are then heaving and tumultuous. Restless, insatiable ambition is on us like*

a fiery charm. Everything partakes of the brightness and boundlessness of our own hopes . . . We then write because we cannot help it—the mind is a full fountain that will overflow—and if the waters sparkle as they fall, it is from their own impetuous abundance.

As Karcher points out, at the beginning of her career, Child had "so little consciousness of the limits imposed on women writers that she had essentially thought of herself as a man." The male pronouns, the metaphors of the overflowing fountain, the sense of "restless insatiable ambition" combine to "align her not with the typical female scribbler, who shrank from publicity and professed to write only when induced by divine fiat or desperate financial need, but with the male genius."[41] At the same time, Child also felt a deep identification with George Sand, whom she regarded as her twin sister and double: "I never read a book of hers without continually stumbling on things that seem to have been written by myself."[42]

Child's confidence in her own gifts was further demonstrated by her determination to get the novel published. She borrowed $495, probably from her father and brother, and had a thousand copies printed, to be retailed at seventy-five cents each. The *North American Review,* however, called *Hobomok*'s intermarriage plot "revolting," and Child was left with five hundred copies on her hands, owing $98. Learning that Harvard professor George Ticknor had praised the book, she wrote directly to him for help: "Your influence in the literary and fashionable world is very great, and a few words timely spoken by you would effect more than my utmost exertions. Your judgment would have much weight with those whose taste is law, and your notice would induce many to purchase, who would otherwise regard the subject with a very natural indifference."[43] Ticknor extended his patronage; he offered to help her pay the debt, persuaded Jared Sparks, the editor of the *North American Review,* to take a second look at the book, and invited Child to his prestigious Boston salon.

Nonetheless, Child signed her book only "By an American." She had been "gravely warned . . . that no woman could expect to be regarded as a *lady* after she had written a book."[44] *Hobomok* further removed itself from the taint of female authorship in a preface that attributes the composition of the novel to an unnamed young man, who declares to his friend Frederic: "Your friend P——'s remarks concerning our early history have half tempted me to write a New England novel." Frederic is skeptical; what kind of novel can compete with Scott and Cooper? "A novel! . . . when Waverly is galloping over hill and dale, faster and more successful than Alexander's conquering sword? Even American ground is occupied. 'The Spy' is lurking in every closet,—the mind is everywhere supplied with 'Pioneers' on the land, and is soon likely to be with 'Pilots' on the deep." But when he reads the document, which the young man has adapted from "an old worn-out manuscript," he is convinced: "Send it to the Printer."

Set in Salem, the novel proper anticipated *Hope Leslie* in dealing with Puritans and Indians. Child was much more critical of the Puritans, and much more idealistic about the Indians, than Sedgwick. The Puritans, she observed, "were struck off from a learned, opulent, and powerful nation, under circumstances which goaded and lacerated them almost to ferocity;—and it is no wonder that men who fled from oppression in their own country, to all the hardships of a remote and dreary province, should have exhibited a deep mixture of exclusive, bitter, and morose, passions."[45] In an anonymous book that was printed in 1829 but never circulated, she expanded her remarkably sophisticated analysis of Puritan psychology; she saw them as attempting to mitigate the repressed guilt they felt about mistreating the Native Americans with a punishing self-denial:

> However strong were their convictions of the justice of their cause, however plausible were their arguments in defence of their usurpations, they were unable to silence the voice of conscience; and they vainly attempted to escape from the remorse, which, with all its terrors, seizes on the hearts of the guilty, by redoubling their superstitious observances. They fasted and prayed, and the austerities they imposed on themselves and others destroyed in a great degree all social enjoyment; and, whilst they were systematically planning the destruction of the Indians, they were sharply engaged in discussing with each other points of faith altogether unimportant or incomprehensible.

Child grasped the sadomasochism of Calvinist doctrine, which cloaked its violence and contempt for human nature in divine sanction. She also formulated a more general psychic law—that people will struggle to justify their own crimes, and blame the victims. As she noted aphoristically, "people seldom forgive those whom they have wronged, and the first settlers appear to have fostered a moral aversion to the Indians, whom they had barbarously destroyed."[46]

Not even Hawthorne would achieve a deeper understanding, and in

Hobomok, Child anticipated Hawthorne in her use of real historical characters and her portrayal of Salem's obsession with savagery, the devil, and witchcraft as a dark reflection of itself. She treated her male Puritan characters, such as the Reverend Mr. Conant, as preachy and hypocritical patriarchs who drive their frustrated children to bizarre acts of rebellion. Conant's daughter Mary, in love with an Episcopalian man, Charles Brown, whom her father and the Puritan elders have rejected as a sinner, steals into the woods at the full moon, and practices witchcraft in order to see her future husband. She opens a vein in her arm, writes in blood with a feather on a white cloth, makes a circle on the ground with a stick, and walks around it three times chanting, "Whoe'er my bridegroom is to be, / Step in the circle after me."

It is poetic justice and retribution for Puritan repression that the man who steps out of the woods to confront her is their worst nightmare: a handsome young Indian, Hobomok. He speaks to Mary in the pidgin English that would mark the noble savage in American popular culture forever: "What for makes you afraid of Hobomok?" Of course, the occult prophecy of the ritual proves true. Mary is told that Charles Brown has perished on a voyage back to England, and, mad with despair, she asks Hobomok to marry her. Karcher suggests that Mary's two lovers, the Episcopalian and the Indian, stand for aspects of herself; the Episcopalian "with the rich cultural heritage [she] has been forced to leave behind in England," and the Indian with "the tantalizing wilderness she has been forbidden to explore," and the sexual freedom it symbolizes.[47] For some weeks after her forest wedding Mary is more or less in a coma, but then she recovers and decides to make the best of her decision. Her father has written to her in forgiveness, begging her "not to consider a marriage lawful, which had been performed in a moment of derangement," and telling her that she has been given a legacy by an English relative. Mary, however, "knew well she should only be considered an outcast among her brethren, and she could not persuade herself that her marriage vow to the Indian was any less sacred than any other voluntary promise." Meanwhile, she bears a son. Then Charles Brown suddenly reappears, and Hobomok generously gives up his claim to his wife and child and walks silently back into the forest. Their son, Charles Hobomok Conant, will be educated at Harvard and then in England, and eventually "his Indian appellation" will be "silently omitted." His racial assimilation and his father's disappearance were Child's uneasy resolution of the political problems of the novel.

Child hopefully dedicated her second novel, *The Rebels, or Boston Before the Revolution* (1825), to George Ticknor. Set on the eve of the Revolutionary War, like *The Linwoods,* it dramatized the choice of Tory loyalism or revolutionary patriotism. *The Rebels* was less favorably received than *Hobomok;* one glowing review was by David Lee Child, a young lawyer, radical, and journalist. Lydia married him in October 1828, and from then on she would be constrained by the need to earn money for them both— to pay his many debts and endless legal costs (he was such a reckless journalist that his nickname was David Libel Child)—and to redefine herself as a conventional woman writing out of economic necessity rather than artistic inspiration. At their lowest point, he served six months in jail on a libel conviction. While he supported her work, he was improvident and not very romantic. One New Year's, he gave her a gift of "a laurel wreath, the leaves of which were not very abundant."

Desperate, Child took in boarders to make extra money. She also published *The Frugal Housewife* (1829), "dedicated to those who are not ashamed of economy." In addition to providing recipes for liver and pig's head, Child advised women how to fix a frozen pump, make mattresses, and salvage spoiled foods. As Thomas Wentworth Higginson, one of the busiest mentors of nineteenth-century women writers, observed, "It seemed to be necessary for American women to work their passage into literature by first compiling a cookery book."[48] *The Frugal Housewife* was so direct and unprettified that some reviewers chastised Child for her indelicacy, and even Sedgwick wrote an obtuse, if well-intended note to her, hoping that she had not "forsaken the department for which the rich gifts of nature so eminently qualify you"—the novel.[49]

Novels, however, did not always sell, and Child did not write another until 1835. One of her finest stories, "The Church in the Wilderness" (1828), was historical fiction based on the true story of a massacre in Maine, in which a village of Abenaki Indians and their Jesuit priest were killed by English settlers. Here again she staged a conflict between two impossible choices, producing a story that dramatizes unbearably mixed loyalties and identities based on nationality, language, love, family, religion, and race. The plot turns on the mixed-race girl Saupoolah's decision to defy both her half-French, Abenaki-identified husband and the French priest, who speaks the Abenakis' language and had grown up in their midst. She warns an English friend that the Abenakis are planning to attack, although she knows that this may result in a preemptive counterattack, as it does. The Abenakis are destroyed, but they are not without blame; they were planning a race war against white people, including the priest's adopted son. Ultimately, the story creates a sense of both the arbitrariness and tragedy of early American history.

For the next several years, Child earned her claim to be the "first woman of the Republic" through her courageous activities on behalf of abolition and Native Americans. Her 1833 treatise, *An Appeal in Favor of That Class of Americans Called Africans,* aroused so much hostility with its uncompromising arguments for intermarriage that her children's magazine had to close. When she returned to fiction (a weak novel with a classical theme) in 1835, she was discouraged and deflated. Child would continue to play an important intellectual role in the women's movement and in antislavery causes, but after the 1820s, her creative zest diminished or was extinguished under the load of household duties and domestic obligations. A list she recorded in 1864 gives the key to the damming up of that once-overflowing fountain. Child reported her employments for the year:

> *Cooked 360 dinners.*
> *Cooked 362 breakfasts.*
> *Swept and dusted sitting-room & kitchen 350 times.*
> *Filled lamps 362 times.*
> *Swept and dusted chamber & stairs 40 times.*
> *Besides innumerable jobs too small to be mentioned . . .*[50]

Like many radicals, as Child grew older, she grew more conservative. She began to express doubts about the rapid acculturation of Native Americans, for whose rights she had once been an ardent advocate, and to take an interest in gradualism rather than full assimilation. "How ought we to view the peoples who are less advanced than ourselves?" she asked in *An Appeal for the Indians* (1868). "Simply as younger members of the same great human family, who need to be protected, instructed, and encouraged, till they are capable of appreciating and sharing all our advantages."[51] In 1870, she wrote to the great abolitionist Charles Sumner that her commitment to the Native American cause had been moral and intellectual, rather than emotional and spiritual:

> *I have no romantic feelings about the Indians. On the contrary, I have to struggle with considerable repugnance towards them; and something of the same feeling I have toward all fighters. War, even in its best*

*aspects, is a barbarism; and sooner or later, the world will outgrow it.
But though my efforts for the Indians are mere duty-work, I do it as
earnestly, as I should if they were a people more to my taste.*[52]

Repugnance, duty, earnestness—these are the sentiments of a Puritan. And it is ironic that Child, who started out as one of the most passionate, defiant, and iconoclastic writers of her generation, especially in her hatred of Calvinism, her resistance to patriarchal tyranny, and her opposition to American oppression of its "less advanced" peoples, should end by repeating the psychological patterns she had so brilliantly analyzed and condemned. Child's literary career was marked by debate and duality; in her fiction she structured plots around people with complex choices between two radically different ways of life, and excelled at representing exactly what was at stake in deciding rightly. But toward the end of her life, Child found herself "too old to write imaginative things." To the editor James Fields, she confided that "my Pegasus is somewhat stiff in the joints, from having had a heavy cart of stones to drag for many years."[53] A younger writer, Elizabeth Stuart Phelps, went to visit Child as an old woman, and described her living "in a quarter of Boston so unfashionable," in a room so colorless, "that I felt a certain awe upon me, as if I were visiting a martyr in prison."[54] As many other women writers would discover, inspiration did not keep and could not be postponed.

Funny, Free, and Flashy—Caroline Kirkland

Caroline M. Kirkland (1801–1864) was a comic writer with no political agenda, but she, too, came up against the limits of permitted female expression and encountered the obstacles facing talented women in the literary marketplace. Raised in New York, the oldest of eleven children, she was educated at a Quaker school run by an aunt, and mastered several foreign languages. In 1822, she met William Kirkland, the grandson of the founder of Hamilton College, and a tutor in languages at its campus in Clinton, New York, where she was teaching school. Although they did not marry until 1828, their union was a modern partnership in both family and work. They taught together at various schools and academies, and wrote and edited together as well; he shared child care, as her letters to him attest. Kirkland gave birth to seven children, but three died very young. In 1837, she and her husband bravely gave up their teaching jobs in Detroit, and set out to create a model frontier village of their own in Pinckney, Michigan, where they would spend the next six years.

For Kirkland, the realities and hardships of pioneer life were both a tremendous shock and also the stimulus for a literary career. "I little thought of becoming an author before I lived in the wilderness," she wrote to the editor John S. Hart. "There, the strange things I saw and heard every day prompted me to description, for they always presented themselves to me under a humorous aspect—Finding my letters amusing to my friends, I thought of 'more of the same sort' for a book."[55] She published *A New Home, Who'll Follow? Or, Glimpses of Western Life* (1839), her satiric observations of community building in the wilds, under the pen name "Mary Clavers." In her preface, "M.C." described her book as based on truth, but also embellished. She had intended to write "a veritable history, an unimpeachable transcript of reality," but she soon realized that throwing her satiric darts "in the teeth of one's everyday associates might diminish one's popularity." So she had fictionalized, added imaginary "glosses, and colourings, and lights, if not shadows," and used the English writer Mary Mitford's "charming sketches of village life" as models for her own "rude attempt."

Despite this caveat, Kirkland's rollicking tale, with its comic portraits of various uncouth neighbors, did make her very unpopular in rural Michigan. She wrote wicked and hilarious episodes about the cleaning lady Mrs. Jennings, who drank her strong green tea from the teapot spout and ate with her knife; the schoolmarm Cleory Jenkins, who smoked a pipe; the village gossip Mrs. Campaspe Nippers, who somehow knew everything going on in town; Mrs. Howard, the sponger who borrows the sifter, sugar, and tea, and once tried to borrow a neighbor's baby to draw off her milk when her own newborn couldn't nurse; and Miss Eloise Fidler, the sentimental village poetess. Kirkland herself was well aware that she was taking a risk; "you may say anything you like of the country or its inhabitants," she noted, "but beware how you raise a suspicion that you despise the homely habits of those about you. This is never forgiven." The most unforgivable part of the book may have been her account of the ne'er-do-well Newland family, who spent their money on whiskey and tawdry clothes, and lived in a "shanty, built against a sloping bank, with a fire-place dug in the hill-side and a hole pierced through the roof by way of chimney." The eldest Newland daughter, Amelia, appears in a silk dress and elaborate earrings. But a few months later, Mrs. Clavers is summoned to the shanty where Amelia has died, and sees the "swollen and discoloured" body of the dead girl, the victim, she hints, of a botched abortion: "but one fatal instance out of the many cases, wherein life was periled in the desperate effort to elude the 'slow unmoving finger' of public scorn."[56]

A New Home was well reviewed by American journals and praised by Poe, who wrote that it "wrought an undoubted sensation [because of its] truth and novelty." To Mrs. Kirkland, he maintained, "we were indebted for our acquaintance with the *home* and home-life of the backwoodsman."[57] But back in Michigan, folks were not so pleased. By disguising the town of Pinckney as "Montacute," and giving the inhabitants funny names, Kirkland had naïvely expected to get away with her mockery. Nevertheless, the citizens of Pinckney easily recognized themselves, and easily identified Kirkland as the author. They were outraged when they read what this neighbor thought of them and how she had betrayed their secrets. The Kirklands were threatened with lawsuits and worse.

In 1843, the Kirklands packed up and left Michigan for New York, where he edited the *New York Mirror* and she wrote for it, with the same high spirits but more caution and discretion. As she explained to Rufus Griswold, who wanted her to write for *Graham's Magazine,* "A lady always feels under a certain degree of restraint when she feels that the world is looking her in the face all the time—many a thought 'funny, free, and flashy' is checked through a feeling of diffidence or pride— I shall probably never write any thing as amusing as my first effort, because I accomplished that under the assured belief that the author would never be discovered."[58] Indeed, although she had a long professional career as a journalist and editor, Kirkland never again wrote with the same freedom or daring.

By the end of the 1830s, American books were being read everywhere, and the novels of Sedgwick, Child, and Kirkland had contributed to that change. Whether American literature had freed itself from English influence, and produced something unique, was still in question. Linguistic independence seemed far away when American English was still an "indebted language."[59] Literary independence was hard to imagine when American writers studied and used the traditional forms of poetry, drama, and fiction. Cultural independence was difficult to conceive in a raw new country still building its museums, libraries, and theaters. In the

1820s and 1830s, American writers had drawn on native history and native landscape. But writing American books, they understood, meant more than translating Scott into American terms, giving recipes for hasty pudding, or setting their stories in Puritan New England rather than Anglican Old England, or the backwoods instead of the Highlands.

Looking ahead, American women were thinking about a future in which they would play an equal part, but they were still inhibited by their internalized beliefs in woman's "natural" place. In 1836, Mary Griffith published a utopian narrative called "Three Hundred Years Hence," in which a man is frozen in an avalanche, cryogenically preserved, and reawakened in the year 2135 to find his native city of Philadelphia transformed by the emancipation of women. Not even a utopian feminist radical like Griffith, however, could imagine that three centuries would be long enough to bring about coeducation; when her hero visits Princeton, his alma mater, he finds the students growing their own vegetables and the faculty content to stay in one post forever, but there are no women among them. In their own careers, Sedgwick, Child, and Kirkland did not seem able to achieve the high goals they had set for themselves, but the next generation of American women writers were able to envision higher achievement because of their gallant example.

Finding a Form

he answer to the American quest for originality seemed to lie in the coming of the poet-hero, a genius who, through divine inspiration, would create immortal works, and an art commensurate with the vastness of the nation and the scope of its dreams. By the 1840s, American intellectuals were heralding the appearance of a great writer who would establish the nation among the classic literatures of the world. Nathaniel Hawthorne was among those who predicted the coming of "the Master genius, for whom our country is looking anxiously into the mist of time, as destined to fulfill the great mission of creating an American literature."[1]

Gender and Genius—Margaret Fuller

Could the "Master genius" be a woman? A fervent belief in female genius was an element in the movement for the emancipation of women that began in the 1840s. The leading American feminist intellectual of the era, Margaret Fuller (1810–1850), was also calling for American genius and American genres. In 1846, in a review for the *New York Tribune,* she compared American literature to the British tradition: "What suits Great Britain, with her insular position and consequent need to concentrate and intensify her life . . . does not suit a mixed race, continually enriched with new blood from other stocks the most unlike that of our first descent." America needed "a genius, wide and full as our rivers, flowery, luxuriant, and impassioned as our vast prairies, rooted in strength as the rocks on which the Puritan fathers landed." But Fuller was also thinking about the problem of gender. Just as American writers were indebted to the English language and the forms of English literature, women writers were indebted to masculine literature and its forms. Could they infuse these forms with new life? And how could gifted women transcend the problems of sexuality and powerlessness that contended with their desire for self-expression? "When woman has her fair chance," Fuller wrote, ". . . the poem of the hour will vie with that of the ages."[2] When, however, and under what circumstances would woman have a fair chance?

Fuller herself was an outstanding candidate for the position of American poet-hero and master genius. Brilliant, impassioned, courageous, she won a distinguished place as the only woman member of the Transcendentalist intelligentsia. Overcoming the limitations of her environment, upbringing, and gender to live a truly epic life, Fuller managed to be in all the right places, from high-minded New England, to brawling New York, to revolutionary Italy, at exactly the right times. Yet as a woman writer, Fuller could never feel comfortable in any literary genre. She identified this struggle with being a woman, rather than an American, writer: "One should be either private or public. I love best to be a woman; but womanhood is at present too straitly-bounded to give me scope. At hours, I live truly as a woman; at others, I should stifle; as, on the other hand, I should palsy when I would play the artist." If she followed her womanhood, her heart, she had to keep her feelings private. If she followed her intellect, her writing would seem stiff, artificial, and cold. As Fuller perceived it, the essential problem for women writers was finding, or inventing, a suitable form: not traditional poetry, not the romantic novel, not the philosophical essay, but some combination and transformation of them all. "For all the tides of life that flow within me, I am dumb and ineffectual when it comes to casting my thoughts into a form. No old one suits me. If I could invent one, it seems the pleasure of creation would make it possible for me to write."[3]

In her treatise on *Woman in the Nineteenth Century* (1845), Fuller found solace in a feminist version of the religious concept of the messiah, the female poet-redeemer of womanhood, the great American woman writer who would come to change all women's lives. "Will she not soon appear?" she asked. "The woman who shall claim their birthright for all women; who shall teach them what to claim and how to use what they obtain?"[4] She hoped that someday, through the example of this savior, or through finding a partner who could accept her fully for herself, the split in her psyche between the emotional but passive woman and the unfeeling but active man would be healed, and that "from the union of this tragic king and queen, shall be born a radiant sovereign self."[5] But as a writer, Fuller never achieved that sovereign self.

Some of the reasons came from her unusual childhood, and a rigorous education in reason, self-mastery, and self-restraint that resembled that of the British philosopher John Stuart Mill, who was a few years older. Like Mill, she had been early recognized as a child prodigy; when she turned six, her father, who had been impressed by reading Wollstonecraft's *Rights of Woman,* introduced her to his library, and taught her Latin and the stories of the great Roman heroes. But he also kept her from reading the novels, poems, plays, and etiquette handbooks deemed suitable for girls. When Fuller first discovered Shakespeare among her father's books at the age of eight, she was swept away: "The free flow of life, sudden and graceful dialogue, and forms, whether grotesque or fair, seen in the broad luster of his imagination, gave just what I wanted, and brought home the life I seemed born to live."[6] She braved her father's disapproval to read Shakespeare "at every hour at my command," but she came to associate the theater and the world of great poetry with a private feminine sensibility that had to be concealed behind closed curtains, "true life . . . veiled over by the thick curtain of available intellect."

Later she discovered the novels of Scott, Maria Edgeworth, and Catharine Sedgwick, and in 1835, while reading George Sand, considered writing fiction herself: "these books have made me for the first time think I might write into such shapes what I know of human nature." But the experiment was not a success. She was too proud to reveal her emotions in a tale of unrequited love, or limit herself intellectually to the world of relationships. As she finally decided, "I have always thought . . . that I would keep all that behind the curtain, that I would not write, like a woman, of love and hope and disappointment, but like a man, of the world of intellect and action."[7] Her only attempt at fiction was a short story, which has been lost.[8] Her poetry was skilled but unmemorable. Mill, whose schooling had a similarly relentless intellectual rigor, had a nervous breakdown at the age of twenty when he confronted his emotional and sexual repression; but Fuller had the additional burden of being a young woman who was not considered beautiful, and whose intelligence was an obstacle, if not a threat, to most men.

Fuller's intelligence was best expressed in discussion and teaching. In 1839, she led a series of influential seminars for women called "Conversations." She also tried to use journalism as a literary genre, editing the Transcendentalist journal *The Dial,* and then writing for Horace Greeley's *New York Tribune.* Her journalism included lengthy reviews of literature and art, as well as politics, travel, and social reform. She wrote in behalf of prisoners, prostitutes, Native Americans, slaves. In *Woman in the Nineteenth Century,* an expanded version of a group of essays she had written for *The Dial,* Fuller "proudly painted myself as Miranda," an intellectual woman based on Shakespeare's *The Tempest,* through whom she explored her own creative dilemma.[9] Her Miranda is the product of a demanding patriarchal education. "Her father was a man who cherished no sentimental reverence for Woman, but a firm belief in the equality of the sexes . . . From the time she could speak and go alone, he addressed her not as a plaything, but as a living mind . . . He called on her for clear judgment, for courage, for honor and fidelity." While Miranda grows up self-reliant and strong, she is disappointed in her lot, for she sees that men, despite their rhetorical esteem for feminine talent, regard her intellectual strengths as "unwomanly." She has to function in a world where the woman of genius is perceived as an anomaly, a hybrid, or a freak, a woman with a "masculine mind." Fuller's use of Miranda as a symbol of the loneliness of the American woman intellectual would resonate in the work of subsequent women writers from Harriet Beecher Stowe to Susan Sontag.

In Cambridge and New York, Fuller had suffered in thwarted romances with American men who admired her intellect but could not return her love. Meditating in her journal on the relationship between women and men, she was one of the first American women writers to use the imagery of bees and flowers to express the bitterness of sexual difference: "Woman is the flower, man the bee. She sighs out melodious fragrance, and invites the winged laborer. He drains her cup, and carries off the honey. She dies on the stalk; he returns to the hive, well fed, and praised as an active member of the community."[10] Fuller used her knowledge of botany to present this scenario; the female flower was passive and immobilized, so she had to attract men through the artifice of charm and perfume. But when the active, roaming male bee took up her invitation, and chose her from all the other flowers, he stole the very thing that kept her alive. Women had only one chance to attract love, and it was fatal; men were nourished and promoted in status on the basis of each woman they loved.

Fuller was determined to overcome the genteel feminine immobility that kept her from seeking love and praise, rather than waiting for it to come to her. In 1846, she left the United States for a long trip to Europe as a correspondent for the *New York Tribune.* It was her first trip abroad, and she found European culture more tolerant, nurturing, and sustaining than that of New England. She met her heroes—the revolutionary leader Giuseppe Mazzini; George Sand, who had dared to pursue both her literary and her sexual desires; and, most important, the Polish poet Adam Mickiewicz, who told her to live her life with the complete freedom, including sexual freedom, she had advocated in her writing. Living abroad, Fuller finally faced the obstacles to her creativity in personal, rather than national terms. It was unprecedented that an unmarried woman in her thirties, who had become the most notorious of the New England bluestockings, would enter upon an illicit affair with a younger, less educated, less cultured man. Yet in 1848, Fuller formed a secret liaison in Rome with a young Italian Catholic radical, Giovanni Angelo Ossoli; and she became pregnant with his child. That summer she lived in Rieti, a small town in the Abruzzi Mountains, seeking safety from the ongoing battles of the Italian Revolution. Fuller's moving letters from these months describe the revolution's collapse and her own emotional tumult as she accepted the tenderness, love, and devotion of a man her friends would have found her intellectual inferior.

In September 1848, Fuller gave birth to a son, Angelo Eugene Ossoli, and found herself unexpectedly and overwhelmingly changed by maternity. "I thought the mother's heart lived in me before," she wrote to her sister Ellen, "but it did not. I knew nothing about it." In her last dispatches to the *Tribune* from the Italian Revolution in 1849, when the brief Roman republic had fallen, her writing had gained a new directness, simplicity, eloquence, and power. Describing Rome after the French occupation, she could be writing timelessly about the carnage of any war: "A pair of skeleton legs protruded from a bank of one barricade; lower, a dog had scratched away [the] light covering of earth from the body of a man, and discovered it lying face upward all dressed; the dog stood gazing at it with an air of stupid amazement."[11] These dispatches were probably her greatest literary achievement.[12]

While Fuller was in Italy, awaiting her son's birth, American activists and reformers were meeting at Seneca Falls, New York, in July 1848, to call for women's political equality. In their manifesto, the "Declaration of Sentiments," written by Elizabeth Cady Stanton, they repeated the language of the Declaration of Independence in demanding an equal voice for women in government, law, education, in the professions, and in the church. The Declaration listed all the "injuries and usurpations" of women's civil and human rights, including the "different code of morals for men and women, by which moral delinquencies which exclude women from society, are not only tolerated but deemed of little account in man." Demanding women's admission "to all the rights and privileges which belong to them as citizens of the United States," the signers vowed to "use every instrumentality within our power to effect our object," despite "misconception, misrepresentation, and ridicule."

Two years later, in July 1850, Fuller made the courageous decision to return to the United States with Ossoli and their two-year-old son, to face whatever misrepresentation, scandal, or ridicule might await her, and to reclaim her role in American intellectual life and in the women's movement. Just off Fire Island in New York, their ship, the *Elizabeth*, encountered a severe hurricane, and was wrecked on a sandbar. Fuller was drowned, along with Ossoli and the baby; she was only forty years old. Just a few weeks after her death, in October 1850, at the first national Woman's Rights Convention in Worcester, Massachusetts, the delegates observed a minute of silence in her memory, and the president, Paulina Wright Davis, mourned Fuller's "guiding hand—her royal presence." Davis told the women that she had "hoped to confide the leadership of this movement" to Fuller, and had offered it to her by letter.[13]

Fuller had foreseen that she would never enter the promised land of American literature and female creative emancipation. In her essay "American Literature, Its Position in the Present Time, and Prospects for the Future" (1846), she had concluded that "though our name may not be written on the pillar of our country's fame, we can really do far more towards rearing it, than those who come at a later period and to a seemingly fairer task." It's tempting to speculate that had she survived, Fuller's new emotional and sexual freedom might have guided her to new forms and outlets of literary expression. If she had lived to read Charlotte Brontë's *Jane Eyre* or Emily Brontë's *Wuthering Heights,* which were published in 1847 while she was in Italy, she might have responded to their unconventional passion, and shattered the reserve that prevented her from expressing herself fully as a woman.

A Music of Their Own: Women Poets in the 1840s

If Margaret Fuller, with all her brilliance and daring, could not find a suitable literary form for her genius, the chances for other American women writers in the 1840s were even less promising. First of all, most of them were expected to write poetry, a form that seemed easy, ladylike, convenient, and publishable. The annuals, magazines, and newspapers offered a steady market for women's verse at a time before international copyright laws, when book publishers were struggling to survive against British competition. As Nina Baym points out, "poems were reprinted time and again in newspapers around the country; after appearing in books, favorite poems were extracted and gathered again in anthologies and yearbooks."[14]

Second, women's poetry was classified as sentimental, morbid, and weepy. As Paula Bennett, a specialist in nineteenth-century American women's poetry, wryly admits, "no group of writers in United States literary history has been subject to more denigration."[15] The British poet Felicia Hemans, who had achieved enormous reputation and commercial success in England, was the most influential model for American women poets, and "both Emma Embury and Lydia Sigourney were saddled with the title 'the American Hemans.' "[16] Poe wrote contemptuously: "Mrs. S. cannot conceal from her own discernment that she has acquired this title *solely by imitation.* The very phrase 'American Hemans' speaks loudly in accusation; and we are grieved that what by the overzealous has been intended as complimentary should fall with so ill-omened a sound into the ears of the judicious."[17] While W. M. Rossetti had damned Hemans with sexist praise by calling her "feminine in an intense degree," combining the "impulse of sentiment with the guiding power of morals or religion," her female contemporaries memorialized her as having "a music of thine own."[18]

Female poets often presented themselves as artless nightingales, whose music came straight from their hearts. Yet poetry is the least spontaneous of the genres; it is the art form that most demands imitation and study, the mastery of classical forms, literary conventions, and traditional meters. Poets have to demonstrate craft, to show that at the very least they can handle iambic pentameter and a few basic rhyme schemes. To be original as a poet is a more difficult task than to be original as a novelist; in nineteenth-century America, very few writers, male or female, were able to achieve such a breakthrough, and Dickinson and Whitman, to name the most famous, were uniquely independent figures who challenged tradition and had the determination and support to get away with it.

To be sure, in stylistic terms, American women's genteel lyrics in the 1840s were not very different from men's poetry, and we would have a hard time identifying the gender of the writer by looking at an individual poem. The 1840s, a critic in the *North American Review* conceded, were a decade of minor poets with "moderate skill in versification," a skill "poured into the minds of every schoolboy." The best-known male poets of the period, sometimes called "the Fireside Poets," or "the School-room Poets," were mild, scholarly men who practiced poetry as a side-line to their professions in the law, medicine, or the university. But not even Henry Wadsworth Longfellow, the most beloved and certainly the most popular of the Fireside Poets, let alone John Greenleaf Whit-tier, Oliver Wendell Holmes, and James Russell Lowell, appeals to modern tastes. "Even their framed, sepia-tinted likenesses," writes one Americanist critic, "that used to hang on schoolroom walls or over the mahogany bookcases of the genteelly elect, have faded from the com-mon memory, leaving behind only the superstitions of gray beards and dusty leather bindings."[19]

Like their male contemporaries, women poets liked "regular meters and conventionally poetic diction," and were obsessed "with death and moral platitudes."[20] Moreover, they faced constraints and social pres-sures about their subjects and styles which made them even dustier than men; as Sarah Josepha Hale wrote, the woman poet "may not revel in the luxuriance of fancies, images and thoughts, or indulge in the license of choosing themes at will, like the Lords of creation."[21] Many women's poems were self-conscious denials of literary ambition, complaints about the difficulties of writing poetry, and assertions of feminine mod-esty, like "Fanny Forrester" writing "Not a Poet" ("I'll never be a poet,/ My bounding heart to hush,/ And lay down at the altar,/ For sorrow's foot to crush"), or Lucretia Davidson's "Song" ("Fame is a bubble, daz-zling bright"). Even those women with something to say—political com-mitments, racial protests, luxuriant fancies—devoted their energies to new content rather than new forms.

So why pay attention to these poets, read them, or analyze their work? In many respects, they were more interesting, vigorous, and subversive than their male contemporaries; they had a lot more to hide and to hint. As Isobel Armstrong writes in her study of Victorian women poets, "the doubleness of women's poetry comes from its ostensible adoption of an affective mode, often simple, often pious, often conventional. But these conventions are subjected to investigation, questioned, or used for unex-pected purposes. The simpler the surface of the poem, the more likely it is that a second, and more difficult poem, will exist beneath it."[22]

Male poets and editors took an active role in mentoring, reviewing, anthologizing, and promoting women poets, and the literary canon has continued to reflect their sorting process rather than looking at the full range of women's poetry. It's hard to know how impartial they were about their protégées. Some Fireside Poets, especially Longfellow and Whittier, were known as warm supporters of aspiring and attractive young women poets. James Russell Lowell was a booster for his wife, Maria. "I will not compare her with any of our 'poetesses' because she is not comparable with them," he wrote in a letter.[23] Poe became romantically involved with a number of women poets in New York.[24] In England, the year 1848 saw respectful acknowledgment of *The Female Poets of Great Britain,* in an anthology edited by Frederic Rowton. Americans were not to be outdone. Three lengthy compilations—Caroline May's *The American Female Poets* (1848), Thomas Buchanan Read's *The Female Poets of America* (1849), and Rufus Griswold's *The Female Poets of America* (1849)—honored women's writing as a sign of American progress, if not superiority. In the preface to his anthology, Griswold claimed that "the proportion of female writers at this moment in America far exceeds that which the present or any other age in England exhibits." Hitting the same note, May wrote in her preface: "One of the most striking characteristics of the present age is the number of female writers . . . This is even more true of the United States, than of the old world; and poetry, which is the language of the affections, has been freely employed among us to express the emotions of woman's heart." American women's poetry, she proclaimed, "chiefly derived from the incidents and associations of everyday life" and the "quiet joys," "deep pure sympathies," and "secret sorrows" of home, formed a natural sphere for "woman, whose inspiration lies more in her heart than in her head."

May's, Read's, and Griswold's anthologies established the genteel lyric as the effortless and natural form of women's poetic essence. Their views of femininity, however, influenced their selections. Griswold observed: "The moral nature of women, in its finest and richest development, partakes of some of the qualities of genius; it assumes, at least, the similitude of that which in men is the characteristic or accompaniment of the highest grade of mental inspiration."[25] Unsurprisingly, he chose poems that were conventional in meter and artificial and flowery in diction. Their favorite forms were quatrains and couplets. Almost without exception, they employed a stilted rhetoric: "thee" and "thy"; "fain," "woe," "beauteous," "bootless," "perchance," and "tarry." Unskilled in fitting their thoughts to meter, they depended on "poetic" contractions like " 'twixt," "o'er," and "ne'er" to make their syllables fit their metrical patterns. In women's poetry, brooks are limpid, trees are lofty, a ship is a bark, a wave is a billow (and it is foaming), hair is tresses.

Elevating mythological applications abound; the sun is always "Phoe-
bus," poetic inspiration the "Aeolian harp." Griswold liked to hear that
women poets uttered verse spontaneously and did not revise, and they
told him as much. "We write with much facility, often producing two or
three poems in a day, and never elaborate," Alice Cary informed Griswold about herself and her sister.[26] While they read Wordsworth,
quoted him, visited him, parodied him, and even wrote sonnets to him,
the Griswold poets rarely adopted his theories of ordinary language or
thought of writing as women speaking to women. Their lack of confidence and their anxiety about self-promotion prevented them from writing with the great lyric poet's assertive "I." Caroline May even had
trouble extracting biographical information from her women poets: "no
woman of refinement, however worthy of distinction—and the most
worthy are always the most modest—likes to have the holy privacy of
their personal movements invaded. To say where they were born seems
quite enough while they are alive. Thus, several of our correspondents
declared their fancies to be their only facts; others that they had done
nothing all their lives; and some—with a modesty most extreme—that
they had not lived at all."

Modern feminist critics have expanded our knowledge of nineteenth-
century American women's poetry, and they rightly insist that antebellum women poets wrote in many different styles and modes. In the
mid-nineteenth century, women poets split between, on the one hand,
those who believed men and women were equal and entitled to the same
liberties in writing as in life—the Enlightenment feminists, inspired by
Wollstonecraft, who used eighteenth-century techniques of wit and
artful structure—and, on the other hand, those who saw women as different from men, more emotional, nurturing, sensitive, and pure, who
preferred inspiration to art—the sentimentalists.

The most interesting women poets swung between these extremes.
Frances Sargent Osgood (1811–1850), who had an unhappy marriage, a
flirtation with Poe, and an early death from tuberculosis, is often championed for her complexity of tone; she can be a tuneful singer, but she
has a darker side as well. In one oft-cited sentimental lyric, Osgood
insisted that women poets needed to conceal their deepest emotions,
and could not write spontaneously from the heart:

> *Ah! Woman still*
> *Must veil the shrine,*

Where feeling feeds the fire divine,
Not sing at will,
Untaught by art,
The music prison'd in her heart!

("Ah, Woman Still")

In other poems, Osgood was witty and cynical, like a nineteenth-century Dorothy Parker.[27] This bad Osgood could write flippantly to a man who rejected her:

"Forgive—forget! I own the wrong!"
You fondly sigh'd when last I met you;
The task is neither hard nor long—
I do forgive—I will forget you!

("Forgive and Forget")

Another provocative writer is Maria Gowen Brooks (1794–1845), who published two books of poems with religious and mystical themes, exploring strange feelings and behaviors. In 1834, Brooks published her long poem *Zophiel,* a tale of erotic obsession, and dedicated it to her mentor Robert Southey. Even though Brooks was touted by Southey, Griswold, and the other male literati whose favor she solicited, her book sold poorly and had no influence on other women poets.[28]

Elizabeth Oakes-Smith (1806–1893) became famous in 1842 for her long poem in seven parts, *The Sinless Child,* originally published in the *Southern Literary Messenger,* and much admired for its portrait of the innocent and angelic Eva, whose spiritual powers convert her lascivious suitor Albert Linne (a name all too obviously chosen to rhyme with "sin"). Eva fulfills her destiny by dying as she saves Albert's soul, and the character may have given her name to Stowe's Little Eva. Oakes-Smith herself, though, was unsatisfied with the form of the didactic long poem, and by the 1850s she had abandoned poetry and become a women's rights activist and feminist novelist.

A Woman of All Work—Lydia Huntley Sigourney

"If there is any kitchen in Parnassus," Lydia Huntley Sigourney (1791–1865) wrote in her autobiography, *Letters of Life,* "my Muse has surely officiated there as a woman of all work, and an aproned waiter."[29] Unlike Anne Bradstreet, who originated the kitchen metaphor of the Poet Parsleyate, Sigourney was not apologizing for her writing, but describing its range, variety, and quantity, and the astonishing demands made upon her as a woman of all literary work by her devoted readers and avid fans. During her long career, which peaked in the 1830s and 1840s, Sigourney was the most popular and prolific of the American women poets, producing more than sixty volumes of elegies, satires, epics, ballads, songs, and odes.[30]

Sigourney was another child prodigy. She began to speak very young, and "talked much and long" to her dolls, "reproving their faults, stimulating them to excellence, and enforcing a variety of moral obligations." Indeed, early in her childhood, Sigourney decided to try her hand at fiction: "A boldness of literary enterprise also came over me; and, though I had scarcely perused a novel except surreptitiously, I commenced to write one. It was in the epistolary style, and a part of the scene laid in Italy." She was only eight years old, and she never tried to write a novel again. Instead, for much of her life, she satisfied her didactic urges by teaching school. In *Letters to Young Ladies* (1833), she argued that "the natural vocation of females is to teach . . . It is true, that only a small proportion are engaged in the department of public and systemic instruction. Yet the hearing of recitations, and the routine of scholastic discipline, are but parts of education. It is in the domestic sphere, in her own native province, that woman is inevitably a teacher." In her autobiography, long after she had worked in a classroom, Sigourney described herself as "a schoolmistress and a literary woman." At the same time, she was attracted to the gothic and tragic fictional modes: "Whatever was plaintive I considered eloquent, and graduated my admiration of literature by its power to draw tears."[31]

While she had been a schoolmistress in her home state of Connecticut, Sigourney was driven to publish by the need to support herself, her three stepchildren, her aging parents, and her husband, Charles, after his business failed. Ironically, Charles Sigourney did not approve of women competing in the marketplace. In a letter he wrote her in 1827, he criticized his weary wife for having "an apparently unconquerable *passion* of displaying herself."[32] Fortunately for him and his daughters, she carried on writing. By 1840, Sarah Hale listed her as an editor of *Godey's Lady's Book,* and paid her five hundred dollars a year to contribute her poems, along with the right to use her name.

As a hardworking professional, Sigourney was often criticized for her relentless and unfeminine self-promotion. In August 1840, she sailed to Liverpool and toured England, where her books had sold well. British literary figures responded with dry politeness to her face, and often mockery behind her back. She called upon Wordsworth, who had invited her to tea at his home, Rydal Mount. On returning to Hartford, she sent him some verses honoring his birthday, which he mistook for an effusion from her teenage daughter. Nonetheless, Sigourney described their brief exchange as "epistolary intercourse and friendship." She could be shameless.[33] Jane Carlyle, one of the unhappiest wives and nastiest gossips among the English literary snobs, cattily described a visit in London from Sigourney:

> *We had all set in to be talkative and confidential—when this figure of an over-the-water-Poetess—beplastered with rouge and pomatum—bare-necked at an age which had left certainty far behind—with long ringlets that never grew where they hung—smelling marvelously of camphor or hartshorn and oil—all glistening in black satin as if she were an apothecary's puff for black sticking-plaster—and staring her eyes out, to give them animation—stalked in and by the very barber-block-ish look of her reduced us all to silence.*[34]

Throughout her lifetime Sigourney was searching for a literary form in which she might express her intelligence, wit, satiric eye, and strong political views. She could be surprisingly funny, tough-minded, and sarcastic. In her memoirs, she described dealing with the two thousand letters a year she received, many from strangers who demanded favors. A "gentleman in a distant State who was thinking of sending a daughter to some boarding-school" wanted an account "of the comparative reputation and terms of tuition and state of health of the female seminaries in this city." A servant-man wanted her to "write out all the answers" for his Sunday-school lessons, "to save his time." Relatives of a deceased man and his two children wanted epitaphs for all of them, with the stipulation that they must not exceed 250 words, since the tombstone was rather small. A gentleman from the South wanting to compile an anthology of "feminine Literature" requested "a list of all the female poets who have written in all languages, a statement of their births and deaths, with information on the best editions of their work and where they may be obtained." A man who found that punctuation gave him "a pain in the back of the neck" asked her to punctuate his thirty-page essay. An aspiring poet who wished to be anonymous wanted her to correct his poetry, submit it with enthusiastic recommendations to paying periodicals, and transmit the money to his post-office box.[35] Sigourney gets the credit for being the first nineteenth-century woman writer to publish a mini-genre in its own right—the comic list of solicitations.

In the preface to her *Select Poems* (1847), Sigourney emphasized the brevity of her poems and the rapidity of their composition, claims that were sure to please readers; but in fact she had also written several lengthy, carefully researched historical poems. Most of her writing focused on such topics as ancient and biblical history, Connecticut local history, the American Revolution, and the fate of the American Indians.[36] She was obsessed with the brutal treatment of Native Americans by the colonial settlers, the appropriation of Indian lands, and the destruction, rather than conversion and assimilation, of Indian culture. "Our injustice and hard-hearted policy with regard to the original owners of the soil," she wrote in her memoirs, "has ever seemed to me one of the greatest national sins."[37] She wrote about these concerns first in *Traits of the Aborigines of America* (1822), her longest poem, with four thousand lines in five cantos, plus annotations and footnotes. Through classical allusions, it tells the story of the extermination of Native American tribes who had welcomed the European settlers. Although Sigourney acknowledged that "the work was singularly unpopular, there existing in the community no reciprocity with the subject," she continued to write poems about unwanted and controversial subjects like the "Indian's Welcome to the Pilgrim Fathers" ("But who to yon proud mansions pil'd / With wealth of earth and sea, / Poor outcast from thy forest wild, / *Say, who shall welcome thee?*"), the Wyoming (Pennsylvania) Massacre of 1778, Pocahontas, and the removal of the Cherokee on the Trail of Tears.[38] In "Indian Names," she saluted the place-names, from Massachusetts to Kentucky, that enshrined the native tribes, and asked, in her epigraph, "How can the red man be forgotten, while so many of our states and territories, bays, lakes, and rivers, are indelibly stamped by names of their giving?" That is the question of a serious writer, someone who thinks through language. Longfellow's *Hiawatha* was surely indebted to her.

"Man—Woman" was another sophisticated poem, contrasting the masculine zest for wandering ("Man's home is everywhere") with the feminine attachment to the cherished places of childhood, courtship, marriage, and maternity. For Woman, Sigourney writes, the childhood home, "though ruinous and lone," is especially invested with feeling and remembered as an innocent prelapsarian paradise. Drawing upon the imagery of the bee and the flower which was so central to the sexual imagination of nineteenth-century American women writers, she described the home of girlhood as a place of unchallenged plentitude and romantic expectation,

> *Where every rose hath in its cup a bee,*
> *Making fresh honey of remembered things,*
> *Each rose without a thorn, each bee bereft of stings.*

Privately, Sigourney's life had many thorns, and her husband many stings. Unlike Margaret Fuller, who died in her prime, however, she lived into her seventy-fourth year. Professionally, she possessed great gifts, wrote prolifically, explored important themes, and dared to publicize herself. In her day she won wide respect and admiration, and left several works that deserve to be remembered. Yet she was a captive of the marketplace and her personal circumstances; she wrote to earn money and never broke free of conventional expectations to produce the work that might have identified her as a great writer.

The Stamp of Fashion—Anna Cora Mowatt

Anna Cora Ogden Mowatt (1819–1870), who was included in Griswold's anthology although she was not known primarily as a poet, was another candidate for fame and American female genius. Born in France to a New York merchant living abroad, she came to the United States with her family in 1825, and eloped with a young lawyer when she was fifteen. By 1841, her husband had moved from law to business, and lost all his property; he was also in poor health, and she launched her career as an elocutionist who gave public poetry readings to scandalously *mixed* audiences of men and women in Boston, Providence, and New York. In the winter of 1841–42, Mowatt further shocked and thrilled New Yorkers with her recitations of Shakespeare and Byron. Her friend Frances Osgood attended, and "defended" Mowatt in a poem that protested rather too much and summarized the criticism too explicitly, "To Anna Cora Mowatt, on hearing her read":

> *Ne'er heed them, Cora, dear,*
> *The carping few, who say*

Thou leavest woman's holier sphere
For light and vain display.

Mowatt's first professional play, *Fashion; or, Life in New York,* produced
at the Park Theatre in March 1845, was a smash hit. In her preface, she
said it was "intended as a good-natured satire upon some of the follies
incident to a new country, where foreign dress sometimes passes for
gold, where the vanities rather than the virtues of other lands are too
often imitated, and where the stamp of *fashion* gives currency even to
the coinage of vice." In a prologue, written by her friend Epes Sargent, a
"gentleman" enters reading a list of reviews of the play in a newspaper:
"What! From a woman's pen? It takes a man / To write a comedy—no
woman can." *Fashion* is set in the New York drawing room of the nouveau riche Tiffanys. Eager to shine in fashionable society, Mrs. Tiffany
has her black servant Zeke pretend to be a French footman, Adolph. She
has spent a full week studying "that invaluable work—'French without
a Master,' " and feels "quite at home in the court language of Europe,"
but she is embarrassed by her black valet: "To obtain a white American
for a domestic is almost impossible, and they call this a free country!"
Mrs. Tiffany fancies herself eternally youthful—"age is always out of
fashion"—and is an easy mark for a slick impostor who calls himself
"Colonel Jolimaitre," flatters the ladies, and insults the hearty American
Adam Trueman, a farmer from Catteraugus: "Pray, madame, is it one of
the aboriginal inhabitants of the soil?"

Most of the reviewers were ecstatic, seeing the play's cleverness as a
major step toward American cultural independence. Poe, reviewing
Fashion in *The Broadway Journal* after its opening night, was more skeptical, finding it unoriginal and too close to Sheridan's *The School for Scandal.* As in his comments about Sigourney, he was always on the lookout
for derivative women's writing. In the following week, however, Poe
went to see eight consecutive performances of *Fashion,* and published a
second review in which he grudgingly recanted: "We are not quite
sure, upon reflection, that her entire thesis is not an original one."[39] A
lively farce, with clever dialogue and a fast pace, *Fashion* is as relevant a
satire today as in 1845, and remains virtually the only nineteenth-century
American play that is still, if rarely, produced.[40]

Mowatt wrote other plays, and acted professionally in the United
States and Europe; she also tried her hand at a variety of literary genres—fictionalized autobiography, memoir, and a number of novels,

including *The Fortune Hunter* (1844) and *The Mute Singer* (1861), which anticipated George du Maurier's *Trilby* (1894) with its story of a singer suffering from hysterical loss of voice. With her play, she had better success in her search for an appropriate form than her female contemporaries. In her *Autobiography of an Actress* (1853), she set out her motives for writing for the stage:

> *I should never have adopted the stage as a matter of expediency alone, however great the temptation. What I did was not done lightly and irresponsibly. I reviewed my own past life, and saw, that, from earliest childhood my tastes, studies, pursuits had all combined to fit me for this end. I had exhibited a passion for dramatic performances when I was little more than an infant. I had played plays before I ever entered a theatre. I had written plays from the time that I first witnessed a performance. My love for the drama was genuine, for it was developed at a period when the theatre was an unknown place, and actors a species of mythical creatures.*[41]

Hawthorne, usually scornful of women writers, listed Mowatt's *Autobiography* among the most interesting American books of the 1850s.

The fashion for female poets in America certainly did not last long. Rereading Griswold's claims about the poetic population explosion forty years later, the poet and editor Helen Gray Cone was appalled:

> *"Awful moment in America!" one is led to exclaim by a survey of the poetic field. Alas, the verse of those "Tokens" and "Keepsakes" and "Forget-Me-Nots" and "Magnolias," and all the rest of the annuals, all glorious without in their red or white Turkey morocco and gilding! Alas, the flocks of quasi swan-singers! They have sailed away down the river of Time, chanting with a monotonous mournfulness. We need not speak of them at length. One of them early wrote about the Genius of Oblivion; most of them wrote for it.*[42]

Along with Mark Twain and other American wits, Cone caricatured the women writers of the 1840s as geniuses of oblivion, rather than geniuses of American originality. In the next decade, however, their struggles would form the solid groundwork for the first great era in American women's writing.

5

Masterpieces and Mass Markets

The Double Flowering
of American Literature

he 1850s were both a pivotal decade for American literature and a highly contested decade for American literary
historians. In 1940, the pioneering scholar Fred Lewis Pattee, a professor of American literature at Pennsylvania
State University, published a book called *The Feminine Fifties,* which
described the "period of the eighteen-fifties" as "a true unit, self-
contained, highly individual, and tremendously influential." It was a
flowering of American culture, and "it was mostly feminine." In 1850,
"feminine fiction began to appear in a flood, . . . and women and even
men were buying it in unheard of quantities." The flood of best sellers
written by women, Pattee maintained, was only one aspect of a decade
that also saw the California gold rush, religious emotionalism, and the
major work of Melville and Whitman; but these novels were essential to
our understanding of the nation and the times. The popular novel, he
contended, was "a mirror in which one may see the people who bought
it and may study the spirit of its age."[1]

The following year, another American literary historian, F. O. Matthiessen, who taught at Harvard, set out a different magisterial account
of the flowering of American literature. In *American Renaissance: Art and
Expression in the Age of Emerson and Whitman* (1941), Matthiessen defined
the first half of the 1850s as a period of American aesthetic glory,
America's "coming to its first maturity and affirming its rightful heritage
in the whole expanse of art and culture." These years were marked by
the literary masterpieces of five great men: Ralph Waldo Emerson's *Representative Men* (1850), Nathaniel Hawthorne's *The Scarlet Letter* (1850),
Herman Melville's *Moby-Dick* (1851), Henry David Thoreau's *Walden*
(1854), and Walt Whitman's *Leaves of Grass* (1855). "You might search all
the rest of American literature," he wrote, "without being able to collect

a group of books equal to these in imaginative vitality." Matthiessen was not particularly interested in asking "why this flowering came in just those years," but he did think that the common denominator of his literary group was "devotion to the possibilities of democracy."[2] He also believed that they shared obsessions with allegory and symbolism; patterns of influence by Elizabethan writers, especially Shakespeare; and the need to transform classical myths into American myths. Chief among those was a myth of the American hero, part of nature, rugged, intense. This American "Man in the Open Air" (a phrase he borrowed from Whitman and had considered as the title of the entire book) was big intellectually and physically.

Of course, Matthiessen acknowledged, there were American women turning out books in the 1850s as well; but they were not significant. They were writing for the marketplace. *Fern Leaves from Fanny's Portfolio* (1853) by "the sister of N.P. Willis" sold one hundred thousand copies in a year; the novels of Susan Warner, Maria Cummins, and Mrs. E.D.E.N. Southworth had a "triumphant vogue," while Thoreau, Hawthorne, and Melville "never came within miles of such figures." The "ceaseless flux" of best-selling women's writing in the 1850s offered "a fertile field for the sociologist and for the historian"; but women writers implicitly did not share the grand devotion to democracy, the mythic themes, and the sophisticated literary influences that made for greatness.[3]

The differences between Pattee and Matthiessen were not simply reducible to attitudes about gender; they also revealed conflicting attitudes toward democracy, art, and commerce. Does literary popularity preclude artistic greatness? And conversely, in a society that values democracy, is the literature of an elite automatically more worthy of serious study? If a writer is devoted to democracy, but unable to command the interest of many readers without intensive academic life-support, is he or she superior to a writer who is very widely read? Looking at the 1850s as a period of art and expression in the age of Julia Ward Howe and Harriet Beecher Stowe (to name two important women writers of the decade) rather than Emerson and Whitman, we can see patterns obscured by the extremes of Matthiessen's model of elite art and Pattee's model of commercial success. Indeed, in his important book *Beneath the American Renaissance* (1988), another literary historian, David S. Reynolds, called the 1850s a flowering of American *women's* writing, "the decade when American women's culture came of age: what might be regarded as the American Woman's Renaissance." In literary terms, it was "a decade of culturally influential and increasingly artistic women's literature." In political terms, the 1850s were "a decade of feminist agitation and organizing."[4] Hannah Gardner Creamer's *Delia's Doctors: or, A Glance Behind the Scenes* (1852) was the first novel to support women's suffrage, as well as women's right to train for any profession. "Women have the right to study everything for which they have the talent," one of her characters declares, "even magic, Chaldean, and Japanese." Another young girl tells her scandalized parents, "Ten years hence, I will do man's work . . . By-and-by, I will go through the country, lecturing on the rights of my sex. The women will have more power than the men. With equal privileges, they would raise far higher."[5]

The 1850s were also, however, a decade of open hostility toward women writers from their male competitors, but the tension was less envy of the writers and their gifts than contest for the readers and their interests. At mid-century, women were emerging as the majority of the readers of fiction—a fact of book marketing that one scholar believes may have been "the crucial fact about American literature in the 1850s."[6] Women readers were not always enthusiastic about man in the open air; they liked to read about woman indoors, in the home. For the first time, the American literary marketplace became a battlefield between women and men. To analyze the strategies, victories, and defeats on this literary battlefield, I begin this chapter by discussing poetry in the 1850s, the best-selling domestic novels of women in the home, and the large number of novels by American women influenced by Charlotte Brontë's *Jane Eyre*. In chapter six, I will turn to the novels of politics: the great subject of slavery, the fiction of Harriet Beecher Stowe and her Southern antagonists; and the first novels by African-American women. What I hope to accomplish for American women writers is akin to what literary historians have credited Matthiessen with doing for his five male master artists in 1941—"bringing these writers, some of them still on the fringes of discussion, to a central position . . . in American national history," and arguing that they "had created a literature for democracy."[7]

American Bards and American Poetesses

In understanding the difficulties facing women poets in the 1850s, it helps to look first at the career of one of the acknowledged male geniuses of the decade, Walt Whitman. What were Whitman's circumstances when he wrote *Leaves of Grass,* how did he get it published, and what were the responses of readers and critics? In the early 1850s, Whitman, who had been working as a journalist, made drastic changes in his life. He moved to Brooklyn, dressed like a workingman instead of a gentleman, and did construction work. In 1855, he was unmarried, unemployed, and living with his family. Whitman typeset ten pages of the first edition of *Leaves of Grass* in 1855 himself, at the printing shop of some Brooklyn friends, and had 200 out of 795 bound in green cloth. *Leaves of Grass* was anonymous, but Whitman used a steel engraving of himself in an open-necked shirt, bearded, casual, one hand in his pocket, the other on his hip, as the frontispiece. His initial efforts to find a bookstore to sell the book failed, but on July 4, Fowler and Wells, a firm that sold phrenological and health-fad books, agreed to take it on. According to Whitman, "I don't think one copy was sold . . . they had to be given away."[8] The few reviews were hostile, and reviewers were outraged by the book's "indecency"; but Whitman was unconcerned. Under cover of anonymity, he wrote several positive reviews of his book, calling himself "an American bard . . . one of the roughs," and had them bound into the second printing in 1856, along with more poems. In his greatest coup, he sent a copy of *Leaves of Grass* to Emerson, who responded with a famous letter of thanks and praise, which Whitman promptly published in a newspaper. Overall, he got his work published through confident initiative and tireless self-promotion, and if some reviewers found it scandalous, their views had no impact on his life. "I celebrate myself," the first poem famously began; and so he did.

Fanny Fern, one of the most popular woman writers of the 1850s, of whose career I shall say more further on, met Whitman through her husband James Parton, and was impressed by his deep voice, "muscular throat," and "fine, ample chest."[9] In May 1856, she wrote a rave review of *Leaves of Grass* for her journal the *Ledger,* praising its strength and honesty, and defending it against charges of coarseness. They became friends, and Whitman borrowed two hundred dollars from Parton, a debt he never repaid. The Partons turned the matter over to a bill collector and burned *Leaves of Grass* in their fireplace; Whitman retaliated by publishing a nasty editorial in the *Brooklyn Daily Times* in which he argued against education for girls: "The majority of people do not want their daughters to be trained to became authoresses and poets . . . One genuine woman is worth a dozen Fanny Ferns."[10]

The circumstances and opportunities of women poets in the 1850s could hardly have been more different from Whitman's. Their market was waning with the decline of the ladies' annuals. In 1853, *Putnam's* noticed that "it used to be the custom to issue when Christmas approached an almost endless variety of 'Gifts,' 'Remembrances,' 'Gems,' 'Tokens,' 'Wreathes,' 'Irises,' 'Albums,' &c, with very bad mezzotint engravings and worse letter-press . . . but that custom seems to be rapidly passing away."[11] Women were still likely to be publishing anonymously, although they were not printing and distributing their own books, let alone reviewing them. If they allowed any portraits of themselves, they would certainly not pose with open collars and hand on hip. They still veiled their egos as well, and would not have dared to celebrate themselves.

The closest women poets got to Whitman's license to use the American vernacular for describing everyday events and observations was to use a comic persona to lampoon the sentimental and melancholy effusions of their poetical sisters. Miriam Berry Whitcher (1811–1852) created the comic Yankee widow Priscilla Bedott, who composes occasional verses of up to forty-nine stanzas for her friends and neighbors. In "The Widow Essays Poetry," she writes an elegy for her late husband:

> If I was sick a single jot
> He called the doctor in—
> I set so much store by Deacon Bedott
> I never got married agin.[12]

Phoebe Cary (1824–1871), the sister of the poet and novelist Alice Cary, had her greatest success with *Poems and Parodies* (1854), which Paula Bennett describes as "half morbid sentimentality," half "stunning literary revenge."[13] A photograph of Cary shows her buttoned up, prim, and unsmiling, but in her clever parodies, she mocked the leading male poets of the age, including Wordsworth, Poe, William Cullen Bryant, and Longfellow:

> Tell me not, in idle jingle,
> Marriage is an empty dream,
> For the girl is dead that's single,
> And things are not what they seem.

Julia Ward Howe and *Passion-Flowers*

A woman poet who shared the ambition and attempted the honesty of Whitman in the 1850s would come up against impenetrable barriers. Julia Ward Howe (1819–1910) is mainly remembered today for writing "Battle Hymn of the Republic"; but she was also a poet with the daring and subversive intellect of an Emily Dickinson, the political and philosophical interests of an Elizabeth Barrett Browning, and the passionate emotions and gifts of a Sylvia Plath, who might have been an American female bard. Sadly, Howe's struggle against her husband and against American social convention stifled and effectively silenced her genius before it had the chance to develop fully.

Howe was born in New York with all the advantages of wealth, health, intelligence, and beauty, and her genius should have flowered without check. Under the guidance of her father, a wealthy banker (her mother died when she was five), she was educated at home in philosophy, science, mathematics, and languages, including Latin, Greek, French, and German. Even as a child, she had high literary ambitions, and "the vision of some great work or works which I myself should give the world. I would write the novel or play of the age."[14] Her Calvinist father disapproved, however, of ambition and artistic freedom for women, and kept her penned up and restricted like a princess in a fairy tale. As she recalled, "I seemed to myself like a young damsel of olden time, shut up within an enchanted castle. And I must say that my dear father, with all his noble generosity and overweening affection, sometimes appeared to me as my jailer."[15] He insisted that she should learn to bake, and she wrote to her aunt Annie about "the miseries of pie-making, of kneading up and rolling out the paste, of stewing, sweetening, and worse still tasting the gooseberries, of daubing oneself with butter, lard, and flour—hands, face, and clothes; of tearing the paste to pieces in trying to transfer it from board to dish! In two hours I made three pies and hope that I may never again have the same painful duty to perform."[16]

If Julia's father was her jailer, her older brother Sam Ward, Jr., was her liberator. He encouraged her to read in his personal library and brought her novels by Balzac and George Sand from his European travels. Sand was the most exciting of the European writers she encountered: "Was she not to all of us, in our early years," she later recalled, "a name of doubt, dread, and enchantment?"[17] By the age of twenty, Julia had already published magazine reviews of French and German poetry, and was hoping for a literary career.

On a trip to Boston with friends in 1841, she visited the New England Asylum for the Blind (later the Perkins Institution), and met Dr. Samuel Gridley Howe, the celebrated superintendent and pioneer in the medical treatment of the blind. Eighteen years her senior, a graduate of Brown and Harvard Medical School, Samuel Howe was a glamorous figure; like Byron, he had fought in the Greek war of independence against the Turks, for which the Greek government had given him the honorary title "Chevalier of the Order of St. Savior." His friends called him "Chev." The couple married in April 1843 and embarked on a yearlong honeymoon to Europe, which the groom also intended as a research trip and a tour of educational institutions abroad. Julia found herself relegated to the background while Chev was lionized. In her diary she noted that Maria Edgeworth "talked long, and with much animation, to my husband . . . Miss E. said to me what one says to little women in general."[18] (Edgeworth had also snubbed Mrs. Sigourney.)

When they returned from their honeymoon, the Howes moved into the bleak Institution, two miles away from the city. Trapped with a husband who was becoming another jailer, Julia lost confidence in her own literary ambitions; in January 1846, she wrote to her sister Louisa, "My voice is still frozen to silence, my poetry chained down by an icy band of indifference, I begin at last to believe that I am no poet, and never was one, save in my own imagination."[19] Nonetheless, she published nine poems in the conventional anthologies edited by Griswold and Read. "Woman" (in Griswold) began with a description of the ideal woman poet as "a vestal priestess," meek, calm, and indifferent to fame. Unfortunately, Howe wrote wittily in the final verse, she was not that kind of woman at all: "Alas, I wish that I were she."

Secretly, she had begun to write a novel about a hermaphrodite. Influenced partly by her reading of French novels about androgynous creatures, partly by a copy of the famous Greek statue "The Sleeping Hermaphrodite," which she had seen in the Villa Borghese in Rome, the novel follows the tragic experience of Laurence, born with both male and female sexual organs, but raised as a boy by his parents. Transparently a metaphor of her own feelings of androgyny, and an exploration of her husband's emotional unavailability, The Hermaphrodite was never completed.[20] Nevertheless, the manuscript is remarkably explicit about the plight of the lonely creature who belongs to neither sex.

The novel foreshadowed the mid-twentieth-century female gothic, and its obsession with freaks, monsters, and especially hermaphrodites as images of creative women's psyches, hinting that the great woman artist is a divided and emasculated man, a monster doomed to solitude and sorrow.

Chev, of course, knew nothing about the work in progress, and in 1850 the Howes went to Europe with two of their four children. Julia seized the opportunity to stay on and spend the winter in Rome with her daughters and her married sisters. Her time in Rome, free of Chev's surveillance, was ecstatic: she went to parties and operas, and attracted gossipy attention from men beguiled by her beauty and style. She also found "an exhilarating companion" in a young American tourist, Horace Binney Wallace, with whom she spent a great deal of time visiting monuments and discussing everything from philosophy to their similar traits as redheads. He treated her as an intellectual equal, and urged her to develop her literary genius.

Back in Boston, however, Howe heard in December 1852 that Wallace had committed suicide. She began to write a series of intimate poems about her spiritual and emotional history, as an outlet for her emotions, and decided not to tell her preoccupied husband about the contents of her book, especially because they were either directly or obliquely autobiographical. As she wrote to her sister Annie, "I have a great mind to keep the whole matter entirely from him, and not let him know anything until the volume comes out. Then he can do nothing to prevent its sale in its proper form."[21] Chev was too busy editing a newspaper, in addition to his medical work, to notice her writing, and he was as surprised as everyone else when *Passion-Flowers* appeared anonymously at the end of December 1853.

Reviewers guessed that the poet was a woman, but they were startled and impressed by the apparent autobiographical nature and intellectual range of the book. "The devil must be in the woman to publish them," Hawthorne wrote to their mutual publisher William Ticknor; the poems "seemed to let out a whole history of domestic unhappiness."[22] In the *New York Tribune,* George Ripley called *Passion-Flowers* "a product wrung with tears and prayer from the deepest soul of the writer . . . We should not have suspected these poems to be the production of a woman. They form an entirely unique class in the whole range of female literature."[23]

Literary insiders quickly identified Howe as the author, and initially she was not unhappy about being known; to her sister Annie she wrote, "the authorship is, of course, no secret now, and you had best talk openly of it, all of you, as it may help the sale of the book in N.Y."[24] Sales were good; *Passion-Flowers* quickly sold out its first edition, and was reprinted in February and again in March 1854. In male literary circles, though, there was gossip and shock. One poem that caused considerable specula-tion was "Mind Versus Mill-Stream," an allegory about a miller who sought a docile brook to grind his corn, and the "volatile rill he decides to tame." Howe made the moral of the story explicit in her final verses:

> If you would marry happily
> On the shady side of life,
> Choose out some quietly-disposed
> And placid tempered wife,
>
> To share the length of sober days,
> And dimly slumberous nights,
> But well beware those fitful souls
> Fate wings for wilder flights!
>
> For men will woo the tempest,
> And wed it, to their cost,
> Then swear they took it for summer dew,
> And ah! Their peace is lost.

In a disingenuous letter to Annie, Howe pretended that she had not realized how distressed Chev would be: "The Book, you see, was a blow to him, and some foolish and impertinent people have hinted to him that the Miller was meant for him—this has made him almost crazy."[25] By the second edition, she had changed the title of the poem to "The Mill-Stream" and taken out the verses on the moral.

Many other poems were just as frank and disturbing. The finest poem in the book, in my judgment, although it has been overlooked by other critics, was "The Heart's Astronomy," a sophisticated, outspoken, and memorable portrayal of the tensions between creativity and maternity. Beginning with an image of captivity, the narrator describes herself walking around her house while her three children watch her from the front window. She walks in desperation to escape, if only for a little while, from the confinement of domesticity. Using a metaphysical conceit, like Donne's compass in "A Valediction Forbidding Mourning," Howe compares her trudging to the fixed orbit of a star. From the children's point of view, the mother revolves around them, and although she sometimes disappears from view behind the house, they are confident she will come around again. Yet Howe suggests that she is not a steady maternal star, but a poetic comet, a creature with no fixed orbit, driven by inner compulsions, capable of suddenly shooting off into space:

> *They watched me as Astronomers*
> *Whose business lies in heaven afar,*
> *Await, beside the slanting glass,*
> *The reappearance of a star.*
>
> *Not so, not so, my pretty ones,*
> *Seek stars in yonder cloudless sky;*
> *But mark no steadfast path for me,*
> *A comet dire and strange am I.*
>
> . . . .
>
> *But Comets too have holy laws,*
> *Their fiery sinews to restrain,*
> *And from their outmost wanderings*
> *Are drawn to heaven's dear heart again.*
>
> *And ye, beloved ones, when ye know,*
> *What wild, erratic natures are,*
> *Pray that the laws of heavenly force,*
> *Would hold and guide the Mother star.*

"What a strange propensity it is in these scribbling women, to make a show of their hearts," Hawthorne wrote to Ticknor. ". . . However, I, for one, am much obliged to the lady, and esteem her beyond all comparison the first of American poetesses. What does her husband think of it?"[26] What *did* Chev think of it? He was enraged and distraught. For three months he refused to speak to Julia, and then demanded a divorce so that he could marry "some young girl who would love him supremely." He also threatened to take custody of the two older children unless she agreed to stop publishing such personal work. Howe gave in. "I thought it my real duty to give up every thing that was dear and sacred to me, rather than be forced to leave two of my children . . . I made the greatest sacrifice I can ever be called upon to make." By June 1854 she was pregnant again.

Despite their reconciliation, her husband remained emotionally and sexually distant: "Chev is cold and indifferent to me as man can be— I sometimes suspect him of having relations with other women and regret more bitterly than ever the sacrifice which entails upon me these moments of fatigue and suffering."[27] He punished her by selling their Boston house and moving the family back to the safety and isolation of the Institution, where she tried to find solace in reading, but frequently succumbed to fits of despair and nervous attacks: "loneliness, desolation, much fault finding, a cold house, no carriage, weary walks in and out of town, these things go far to counterbalance any pleasure that my Book has given me."[28] Like the Duke in Robert Browning's "My Last Duchess," Chev gave orders and all passion ceased. In the years that followed, he became a prominent abolitionist, and she continued to write and publish, but in a public political voice rather than as an artist.[29] In 1857, she published *Words for the Hour,* fifty-four poems on topical subjects including Florence Nightingale and slavery. The new book received respectful but muted reviews; critics found it deeply sad, suffused with an "unnamed and perhaps unnamable woe."[30]

In 1857, the publication of Elizabeth Barrett Browning's *Aurora Leigh,* a novel in verse about the coming-of-age of a woman poet, emboldened American women to believe that they, too, could create major poetry. Lydia Maria Child called Browning "A Milton among women!" The African-American writer Charlotte Forten Grimke noted a prayer for Browning in her journal: "may thy sublime and noble nature strengthen me for life's labor! I cannot but believe it will."[31] Emily Dickinson could recite *Aurora Leigh* from memory, had a portrait of Barrett Browning in her room, and wrote a number of poems about her. Dickinson, who did not attempt to publish her poems, was the first American woman poet to achieve greatness, to be a bard rather than a poetess. But if Julia Ward Howe had been able to develop freely, she, too, might have risen to greatness, not in the sunburned freewheeling style of Whitman nor in the metaphysical style of Dickinson, but on her own premises.

The *Atlantic Monthly*

At the same time that *Aurora Leigh* was published, the launch of the *Atlantic Monthly* in 1857 staked out, and attempted to police, the dividing line between high literary art and popular culture in the United States, the masterpiece and the mass market. In its first issue, editor James Russell Lowell had mocked didactic women's poetry: "Put all your beauty in your rhymes, / Your morals in your living." Women writers were not excluded from the *Atlantic;* indeed, they viewed publication in the magazine as the gold standard of aesthetic approval. But passionate, beautiful, daring work by women raised eyebrows, as *Passion-Flowers* had done. When Harriet Prescott Spofford (1835–1921) submitted her first story, "In a Cellar," to the *Atlantic* in 1859, her friend Thomas Higginson had to vouch for its authenticity: "I had to be called in to satisfy them that a demure little Yankee girl could have written it," he recalled. With its debonair male narrator, Parisian setting, and complicated mystery plot, the story dazzled readers.[32] A native of Maine, who had been raised in the Massachusetts town of Newburyport, Spofford published her best-known story, "Circumstance," in the *Atlantic* the following year. Based on an incident that had happened to her grandmother, it is a gothic allegory with a surprise ending, which uses the Puritan setting as a sophisticated commentary on the contradictions of women's writing, and on predestination and emancipation. "Circumstance" begins with the unnamed heroine returning from the bedside of a sick neighbor, walking alone through the snow reddened by sunset, into the woods above her log-cabin home. In the twilight, she has a vision of a ghastly winding-sheet, held aloft by four hands, and a voice sighing "The Lord have mercy on all the people!" Alarmed by this apparition, she is hurrying home to her husband and infant son when she is seized and dragged up into a tree by a mountain lion (she calls it a panther), "that wild beast—the most savage and serpentine and subtle and fearless of our latitudes—known by hunters as the Indian Devil."

With the term "serpentine," Spofford introduces the theme of Eve's temptation by the serpent in the Garden of Eden. Here the temptations are not intellectual, but sexual, spiritual, and creative. The beast slashes and gnaws at her, pins her down and threatens her with mutilation, penetration, and death. Her life depends on her ability to soothe, hypnotize, and distract him, like a big cat, which she does by singing throughout the

night—first lullabies, then reels, jigs, national anthems, country airs, ballads, and finally hymns and psalms. At dawn, as her voice is giving out,
her husband comes with the baby to rescue her, and kills the beast with
a single shot. As they return home through the snow, the wife suddenly
notices a footprint; from the top of the hill, they see that their little
encampment has been destroyed during the night by Indian marauders.
"The log-house, the barns, the neighbouring farms, the fences, are all
blotted out and mingled in one smoking ruin. Desolation and death
were indeed there, and beneficence and life in the forest. Tomahawk and
scalping-knife descending, during that night, had left behind them only
this work of their accomplished hatred and one subtle foot-print in the
snow." The apparition has foretold this destruction, and the Indian Devil
of the forest has been a providential savior. Spofford ends with Milton's
line from *Paradise Lost:* "The world was all before them, where to
choose." This Puritan Adam and Eve have lost their paradise, but have
been given another kind of free will and choice.[33]

Emily Dickinson was impressed and frightened by Spofford's work;
she wrote to Higginson that "I read . . . 'Circumstance' but it followed
me in the Dark—so I avoided her—." She told her sister-in-law Susan
that the story was "the only thing that I ever saw in my life that I did not
think I could have written myself."[34] Not everyone, however, admired
"Circumstance." Hawthorne's wife, Sophia Peabody Hawthorne, for
example, found it too sensual and explicitly physical, as she wrote to
Annie Fields, "I wish she would spare the *Atlantic* her crudeness and her
bald passion."[35]

The *Atlantic,* New England, and the Concord coterie of high-minded
intellectuals would continue to dominate American letters for a long
while. As one Southern woman aspirant joked, "A stranger . . . after
strolling half a day through [Concord's] quiet streets, seized the first living creature he met—a small boy, of course—and said, 'Look here,
sonny, what do you people do here in Concord?' and the youngster, in the
fine shrill voice of youth, replied, 'We writes for the *Atlantic Monthly*!' "[36]

The Domestic Novel in the 1850s

The flowering of women's writing in the 1850s took place as the nation
was developing a mass market for fiction. Americans acknowledged the
novel as the dominant literary genre in the United States as well as the

most effective vehicle for persuasion and the influence of public opinion. "Do you wish to instruct, to convince, to please? Write a novel! Have you a system of religion or politics or manners of social life to inculcate?" *Putnam's* exhorted its readers. "Write a novel! . . . Would you lay bare the secret workings of your own heart, or have you a friend to whom you would render that office? Write a novel! . . . And lastly, not least, but loftiest . . . would you make money? Write a novel!"[37] Women novelists could write novels, inventing stories or disguising the secret wishes of their own hearts; they had more freedom and opportunity than women poets. "If woman's place was in the home," according to Michael Davitt Bell, "the home—the domestic life of women—was the great subject of these writers . . . For them, the home was, by definition, the world."[38] They could also make a lot of money. Susan Warner's *The Wide, Wide World* (1851) sold a million copies worldwide; a run-of-the-mill domestic novel like Maria Cummins's *The Lamplighter* (1854) sold 70,000 copies its first year. As women's fiction became more and more commercially popular, male editors and writers protested more vigorously against a female invasion of the literary marketplace.

Hawthorne was the angriest and most resentful of these competitors. From his consular post in Liverpool in January 1855, he complained to his publisher William Ticknor that he was thinking about giving up fiction in the light of Cummins's fortune: "America is now wholly given over to a d——d mob of scribbling women, and I should have no chance of success while the public taste is occupied with their trash—and should be ashamed of myself if I did succeed. What is the mystery of these innumerable editions of *The Lamplighter* and other books neither better nor worse?" Hawthorne's panic about female market dominance was probably influenced by similar complaints of male critics in England at the same time. In reality, however, men were still the majority of American novelists, and Hawthorne was also outsold by a mob of scribbling men, including "Ik Marvel" and George Lippard.[39] But he was more frustrated by female competitors, and by women editors like Grace Greenwood of *The Little Pilgrim* magazine. "I am getting sick of Grace," he told Ticknor in January 1854. "Her 'Little Pilgrim' is a humbug and she herself is—but there is no need of telling you. I wish her well, and mean to write an article for her by and by. But ink-stained women are, without a single exception, detestable."[40]

Like their male contemporaries, however, American women writers turned to the novel in the 1850s to instruct and persuade, to bring political ideas to life, to investigate the human psyche. In fact, their poetry and fiction was extremely varied in its subjects and techniques, covering, as Nina Baym has pointed out, "social, religious, and political issues including abolitionism, states' rights, baptism by complete immersion, temperance, the annexation of Texas, Manifest Destiny, insanity, divorce, relations with the indigenous population, immigration, Mormonism, Catholicism, party politics, and virtually every other current topic both local and national."[41] The decade saw the emergence of the African-American woman writer, and the vogue of gothic sensationalism and historical fiction. But the dominant genre of women's writing was the domestic novel.

Rowing Against Wind and Tide

Domestic fiction has been the most controversial genre in the literary history of American women's writing, an easy target for mockery and an embarrassment to feminist critics who wish to change the canon. First of all, how to answer charges that the female best sellers of the 1850s, with their suffering orphans, weeping maidens, pious mothers, blind or lame minor characters, and happy endings, are vulgar and "sentimental"? Judith Fetterley, making a strong offense the best defense, argues that "sentimental" is in fact a code word for "female subject and woman's point of view and particularly for the expression of women's feelings."[42] Joanne Dobson also stands up for sentiment, defining an "aesthetics of sentimental literature . . . premised on an emotional and philosophical ethos that celebrates human connection, both personal and communal, and acknowledges the shared devastation of affectional loss."[43] Nina Baym, in her groundbreaking study *Woman's Fiction* (1978), avoids the term "sentimental" altogether. Instead, she argues, these novels told "the story of a young girl who is deprived of the supports she had rightly or wrongly depended on to sustain her throughout life and is faced with the necessity of winning her own way in life." Because she is forced to make her own way, the heroine develops a new confidence, independence, and "conviction of her own worth . . . and inevitably, the change in herself has changed the world's attitude towards her, so that much that was formerly denied now comes to her unsought." Women could change others by changing themselves, and "the phrase 'woman's sphere is in the home' could appear to mean 'woman's sphere is to reform the world.' "[44]

Another influential feminist critic, Jane Tompkins, defends domestic fiction by stressing its cultural power. She argues that "the popular domestic novel of the nineteenth century represents a monumental effort to reorganize culture from the woman's point of view . . . remarkable for its intellectual complexity, ambition, and resourcefulness," and suggests that criticism should address the "cultural work" done by such novels rather than their aesthetic value.[45] Unfortunately, the feminist critical effort to defend domestic fiction in the 1970s collided with the politicized agendas of American studies in the 1990s, when the domestic novel came under renewed attack—not as aesthetically unsatisfying, but as imperialist, racist, masochistic, materialist, or exploitative of the disabled.[46]

We have to acknowledge that domestic life, the everyday life of the home, had to be a central concern for women writers. While English women novelists, even those as poor as the Brontës, had servants, American women were expected to clean, cook, and sew; even in the South, white women in slaveholding families were trained in domestic arts. In Northern census records, the occupation of Emily Dickinson as well as Rebecca Harding Davis is listed as "keeping house." In 1850, Dickinson wrote half jokingly to a friend that there were "so *many* wants—and me so *very* handy—and my time of so *little* account—and my writing so *very* needless," that she felt guilty for even writing a letter.[47] The popular American fabric crafts of piecing, patching, and quilting were identified with women's culture, and the quilting bee became a metaphor for bonds between women and female creativity. Piecing, stitching together small bits of cloth to make a design, was a tradition with multiracial and multiregional aesthetic vitality, but also "an art of making do and eking out . . . It reflects the fragmentation of women's time."[48] Women's texts often used the economy and artistry of piecing to signify a woman's language, as when a writer in the *Lowell Offering* (1845) called her patchwork quilt "a bound volume of hieroglyphics."

At the same time, many American women writers grew up feeling an aversion to sewing, which they saw as a wearisome and pointless discipline that took away time from reading and writing. As a girl Elizabeth Stoddard despised sewing: "reading has been laid up against me as a persistent fault, which was not profitable; I should peruse moral and pious works, or take up sewing—that interminable thing, 'white seam,' which filled the leisure moments of the right-minded." After she married, she told her husband Richard, "I am never going to do any more housework if I can help it. I am an AUTHOR."[49] In *Rena; or, the Snow-Bird* (1852) by Caroline Lee Hentz, the heroine, Rena, is a tomboy, who says, "I don't want to learn how to knit and sew. I don't want to be a little woman. I never will be one." The heroine of Fanny Fern's autobiographical novel, *Ruth Hall* (1855), is also unwilling to become a little woman rather than a literary woman: "For the common female employments and recreations, she had an unqualified disgust. Satin patchwork, the manufacture of German worsted animals, bead-netting, crochet-stitching, long conversations with milliners, dress-makers, and modistes, long forenoons spent in shopping, or leaving bits of paste-board, party-giving, party-going, prinking and coquetting, all these were her aversion."

Like it or not, married women had to cope with the responsibilities of housework and make it fit in with their writing. In a letter to her sister-in-law Sarah in 1850, Harriet Beecher Stowe described a typical day in her life: "Since I began this note I have been called off at least a dozen times—once for the fish-man, to buy a codfish—once to see a man who had brought me some baskets of apples—once to see a book man . . . then to nurse the baby—then into the kitchen to make a chowder for dinner and now I am at it again for nothing but deadly determination enables me to ever write—it is rowing against wind and tide."[50] The 1850s saw the beginning of a kind of self-help literature for women writers telling them how to handle their housework efficiently. But some women could not cope. Annie Fields was distressed to hear from her friend Celia Thaxter that "she thought she should never write any more for she had no servant now-a-days and did all the work of her house, that she could not afford to do otherwise! I could not help thinking what a mighty shame it was for this woman with a husband in the prime of life with three sons to be obliged to work for them in this manner."[51]

The Itch to Write

Surprisingly, however, the figure of the literary woman, her happiness, sorrow, duties, and dreams, appeared in a variety of forms in women's writing of the 1850s, suggesting that novelists, too, were asking questions about the conflicts between domesticity and creativity. "No happy woman ever writes," Fanny Fern declared in her best seller *Ruth Hall,* although her own success story belied the claim. Grace Greenwood (Sara Jane Clarke Lippincott, 1823–1904) wrote optimistic short stories about the relationship of genius and love in a woman's life. In "Elinor

Vernon," included in *Greenwood Leaves* (1850), she described a woman poet who resembles Julia Ward Howe, "the reigning queen of song, the fashion and the passion in the literary world." Elinor falls in love with a man who demands that she give up writing, and suppress "the volume which you have in publication." She proudly refuses his proposal. In the sequel, "Amy Macdonald," however, she has married a man who supports her literary ambition, and "occupies an enviable position in the world of letters."[52]

Other women wrote self-punishing and self-contradictory fiction, in the model of Sedgwick's "Cacoethes Scribendi," about the pressures of ambition. Elizabeth Stuart Phelps (1815–1852) grew up in Andover, Massachusetts, the daughter of a professor of theology at Andover Theological Seminary. As a young woman, she began to publish articles in religious magazines under the pseudonym (and anagram) "H. Trusta." In 1842, she married Austin Phelps, a student at her father's seminary, and they moved to Boston, where they lived for six happy years. Her husband described her pleasure in using city life as material for realistic fiction: "She would go out of her way to walk in the thoroughfare, where she could see life in its greatest variety."[53] Then, in 1848, Austin Phelps gave up his pulpit and joined the faculty at Andover Seminary, immersing Elizabeth again in the rigidity of both religion and provincial campus life. Despite her chronic depression, she managed to combine the life of a novelist and breadwinner with her heavy obligations as mother and faculty wife.

In her first adult novel, *The Sunny Side; or, The Country Minister's Wife* (1851), Phelps wrote about the struggles of a young married clerical couple trying to make ends meet on a very limited income. Its sequel, *A Peep at Number Five* (1852), tells a similar story from the perspective of a city parish. Lucy Holbrook and her minister husband settle at the Downs Street Church in an unfashionable section of the city, and while he has to face the realities of overwork, clerical competition, and the need to network, she is overwhelmed by the many demands on a minister's wife. When she hears the other ministers' wives talking about the amazing Mrs. D., who called on each parishioner three times a year and had six children, she expresses a wish to meet this paragon. "She is dead," they reply.

In her short story "The Angel Over the Right Shoulder," published in a Christmas annual in 1852, Phelps described the creative woman's struggle to balance both sides of her temperament and desires. Mrs. James has two children, but she also wants to study and write. In a dream, she sees two angels, one who records her good domestic deeds and the other her neglectfulness of daily tasks. In the end, the angel over the right shoulder outweighs the angel of selfish creativity. This was the compromise that many gifted women writers of the 1850s felt called upon to accept. Although Mrs. James finds contentment in her compromise, Phelps was not so fortunate. She died at age thirty-seven. "Her last book and her last baby came together," wrote her daughter, "and killed her." As her daughter explained, Phelps had "lived one of those rich and piteous lives such as only gifted women know; torn by the civil war of the dual nature which can be given to women only."[54]

Jane Eyre Mania

The image of the woman writer was transformed by Charlotte Brontë's *Jane Eyre* (1847; first American edition 1848). Brontë's novel was avidly read by American women of all ages and classes, and created what Elizabeth Stoddard called "a *Jane Eyre* mania."[55] Mill girls read it in Lowell, Massachusetts; Fred Pattee's mother, who had been one, told him "how 'Jane Erie,' as her companions pronounced it, ran through the mill-girl community like an epidemic. Before she died, aged eighty-eight, she had reread it five times."[56] When Elizabeth Gaskell's biography of Brontë came out in 1857, American women took heart from the novelist's tragic history. Brontë's American "Eyresses," as the critic John Seelye calls them, were as much inspired by her life as by her work.[57] The black diarist Charlotte Forten Grimke commented, "What a noble life was hers. Poverty, illness, many other difficulties which should have seemed insurmountable to a less courageous spirit were nobly overcome by one, who was yet as gentle and loving as she was firm. Such a life inspires me with faith and hope and courage . . ."[58] A number of aspiring women writers, who felt excluded from professional literary schools and publishing circles but had sisters who also wanted to write, identified with the Brontë sisters and their special literary community of the home. The Warner sisters of New York, the Cary sisters of Cincinnati, the Alcott sisters of Concord, could see themselves reflected in the Brontë sisters of Haworth. In her diary, Louisa May Alcott vowed, "I may not be a C.B., but I shall do something yet."[59] Novelists translated the plots and themes of *Jane Eyre* into American contexts, and used the genius of

Brontë to defend women's domestic liberation; short-story writers cited Charlotte Brontë's example for their bookish, introspective, rebellious, and haunted heroines; and Emily Dickinson wrote two verse-elegies about Brontë's death.

Madwomen in the American Attic

In the 1850s, the madwoman appeared in the American novel as a metaphorical double for the heroine and the author. While Catharine Maria Sedgwick's Crazy Bet had introduced the idea of the American Romantic madwoman in the 1820s, the mid-century novelists imagined a figure much more like Bertha Mason, Rochester's first wife and the madwoman in the attic in *Jane Eyre,* who expresses the suppressed sexuality, rage, imagination, and violence underneath Jane's subdued feminine exterior.[60] The American madwoman was deranged by household drudgery, resistant to compulsory domesticity, and, often, drawn to literary and artistic careers. In *Woman in America* (1850), Maria McIntosh described the pressures on the overburdened housewife and mother: "Work—work—work, till heart and hand fail, till the cloud gather on her once sunny brow, and her cheeks grow pale, and friendly consumption come to give her rest from her labors in the grave, or the throbbing brain and over-anxious heart overpower the reason, and a lunatic asylum receive one more miserable inmate."[61]

Women novelists used subplots of the incarcerated madwoman to express subversive rebellion against domestic oppression. In 1849, when she was sixteen, Lillie Devereux Blake (1833–1913) had written a declaration called "I Live to Redress the Wrongs of My Sex," which vowed that "Women have been from time immemorial duped and deceived by men . . . I will live but to redress these terrible wrongs!" Her first novel, *Southwold* (1859), tells the gothic tale of the brilliant femme fatale, Medora Fielding, who is driven to murder, insanity, and finally suicide as she tries to manipulate her fate. Blake's jagged and melodramatic narrative includes passages of dialogue as if in a play.[62] Alice Cary (1820–1871), Phoebe's sister, was best known for her poetry and short stories, but in the 1850s she, too, published Brontëish novels of women's madness and discontent, particularly *Hagar: A Story of Today* (1852). Innocent Elsie, a nineteenth-century Hester Prynne, is seduced by the minister Nattie Warburton. He deceives and rejects her, and, taking the symbolic name

Hagar, she sets out to find him in New York, giving birth to a child who dies. In repentance, she spends the rest of her life alone and grieving. The critics were shocked, and even the feminist paper *The Una* thought the novel "had no aim or purpose but to give utterance to sickly, morbid fancies."[63] Cary's three collections of short stories in the 1850s, set in the Midwestern village of Clovernook, were also very dark; in the first volume, six stories are about death. Many of her heroines are women who faced the problems of self-realization in a repressive environment; as Cary noted of her own melancholy childhood, "We hungered and thirsted for knowledge; but there were not a dozen books on our family shelf, not a library within our reach."[64]

The American Brontës

The themes of the rebellious girl, the madwoman, and the writer came together in many mid-century novels by American Brontës. Laura Curtis Bullard's *Christine; or, Woman's Trials and Triumphs* (1856) has been called "the *Jane Eyre* of women's rights fiction."[65] Bullard (1831–1912) grew up in a family of abolitionists in Maine, and in the 1850s moved to New York where she edited her own monthly newspaper, *The Ladies Visitor and Drawing Room Companion,* in which she often published her own short fiction. Her first novel, *Now-a-Days* (1854), was a love story set in the logging camps and rural villages of Maine. *Christine,* however, "not only endorsed every demand of the suffrage movement but also possessed the dramatic intensity and stylistic tautness of classic women's fiction."[66] Christine Elliot, one of many Christ figures in mid-nineteenth-century women's fiction, is an intelligent, dreamy, bookish girl growing up on a farm, where her mother calls her "shiftless" and she laments the monotony of her life: "Here I must stay and drag out my life. Get up in the morning, scrub, wash dishes, churn, and do all sorts of drudgery, till night comes, and sleep only to go over the same thing the next day. Oh, it is not living." She dreams of being rich, and having "a splendid house, where I would have all the great people, the writers, and all sorts of talented persons come; and I would help the poor authors, who struggle on and die sometimes in the midst of their struggles."[67]

Like Jane Eyre's, Christine's prayers for a larger life are ambivalently answered when she is sent away to a fashionable boarding school run by her cold aunt Julia. Here she meets three women who will become her lifelong friends. Helen Harper is a devout and dutiful girl like Helen Burns in *Jane Eyre,* whose school composition is "a weird-like tale, . . . simple in its style and touching in its narration of the struggles of an earnest but weak spirit." Helen eventually marries a poor artist for love, and is content. Annie Murray, who is rich and spoiled, torments Christine at school. She is severely punished; she marries an abusive man for money, runs away from him with her daughter Rosa, tries to work as a seamstress, becomes the mistress of a former suitor, and dies of consumption, leaving Rosa to the care of Christine. Mrs. Warner, Christine's ideal, is a feminist who believes that "if girls could only be brought up like boys, with the idea that, when at a suitable age, it was their duty to earn their living, how much more self-respect they would feel." She holds out hope for progress: "all reform movements are slow in their beginnings. They are like the avalanche, which creeps on so gently at first, that its onward course is almost imperceptible, but gathering strength and velocity as it proceeds, it rushes on, bearing before it all that men have deemed most stable and immovable." At a school reception, Christine also meets and becomes engaged to the eligible Philip Armstrong, but soon she overhears a seamstress, Grace, reproaching Philip for seducing her. Christine breaks off her engagement with him, and Philip angrily rejects Grace, who drowns herself.

Left alone in the world, Christine decides to become a women's rights speaker. "She would enter upon this great work, and she thanked God for giving her so noble a task, one that would require all her powers—all her soul." In a final Brontëish twist, her father and her aunt Julia, feeling disgraced by her actions, conspire to have her committed to a lunatic asylum, where she stays imprisoned under a false name for almost a year. At last, the reformed and contrite Philip and Mrs. Warner get her out. She marries Philip, and they establish a home for single women, both "the poor and friendless" and the professionals—"engaged in every trade that was open to women . . . students of law, theology, and medicine."

Southern domestic novelists were ambivalent or even hypocritical about their commitment to a literary career for women; emotionally attracted to the passion of the Brontës and the pleasures of financial independence, they nonetheless constructed plots that seemed to negate and punish their autobiographical intellectual heroines. Similarly, they were divided in their treatment of slavery. Seeming to support slavery as a benign patriarchal institution, they were sensitive to both abolitionist arguments and feminist rhetoric that compared women and slaves.

Often they presented their narratives of female ambition as allegories of radical North and traditional South.

Mary Virginia Hawes Terhune (1830–1922) grew up in Richmond, Virginia, the privileged daughter of Samuel Hawes, a Whig slave owner and politician. As a girl, she had a governess, a tutor, and access to her father's large library, where she read Dickens, Scott, and the novels of Charlotte Brontë, for whom she had "since my early girlhood, nourished admiration that ripened into reverence, as I read with avidity every page and line relating to the marvelous sisters. I had conned her books until I knew them, from cover to cover. Her dramatis personae were friends more familiar to the dreaming girl than our next-door neighbors."[68] In her teens, Terhune published stories and essays under various pseudonyms, such as "Mary Vale" and "Robert Remer"; she chose her final nom de plume, "Marion Harland," in her early twenties, and maintained it all her life; she even published her autobiography in 1910 under the name, explaining that she had a "hazy idea of, in some degree, preserving my identity to myself."[69] In her conduct of her professional life, she was canny and discreet.

In 1853, Terhune showed her brother and sister the first draft of a novel she had written called "Alone." They encouraged her to rewrite it, and when a local bookstore refused to print it, her father subsidized the publication in "bindings of dark-blue and purple, and crimson, and leaf-brown."[70] Her ambition, she declared, was "to relieve literary domesticity from the odium that rests upon it."[71] *Alone* is a Southern version of *Jane Eyre*. It begins with the heroine, Ida Ross, at her mother's funeral on the idyllic Sunnybank plantation. The orphaned Ida follows the trajectory of Jane Eyre, first by going to stay in the family of her father's friend Mr. Reid in Richmond, where she is bullied and snubbed by his daughter Josephine, and second, by studying at a fashionable school, where she tries to develop her gifts as a writer but is falsely accused of plagiarism. At seventeen, Ida faces the dilemma of the brilliant female artist: "I have intellect—genius—so says the world." But "I have no home—no friends—I am cut off from my species."[72]

She denounces her guardian Mr. Reid much as Jane Eyre denounces her aunt Mrs. Reid: "I despise you and I owe you nothing." (Eventually, as in Brontë's novel, Ida has the satisfaction of caring for her guardian as he is dying.) In Richmond, where she is teaching school, Ida falls in love with the young minister Morton Lacey, but he becomes engaged to someone else. Brokenhearted, she returns to Sunnybank, where she is comforted, spiritually healed, and converted to Christianity by a pious

slave, Uncle Will. All alone, she devotes herself to restoring the plantation, building a chapel and school, and doing good works for her slaves.
Morton Lacey learns his lesson, too; he returns to marry her and they
settle at the plantation. While her father had been opposed to slavery,
Terhune became its apologist. In *Alone,* she editorializes: "The slave lies
down at night, every want supplied, his family as well cared for as himself, not a thought of tomorrow! He is secure of a home and mainte-
nance, without disturbing himself as to the manner in which it is to be
obtained. Can the same be said of the menial classes in any other country under the sun?"[73] The language here seems to reflect her compromise about women, independence, and marriage as well; women were
supported and protected, even if their literary dreams were curtailed.

"In unconscious imitation of Charlotte Brontë, who began *Jane Eyre*
while *The Professor* was 'plodding his weary round from publisher to publisher,' " Terhune recalled, "I had begun another book by the time *Alone*
was turned over to the tender mercies of Mr. Morris's 'reader.' " While
working on *The Hidden Path* (1855), she had dreamed of carrying a wail-
ing baby—in this case, her manuscript—and thought of Jane Eyre's similar dream when she flees Rochester and Thornfield.[74] Terhune's dream,
however, suggests that she was burdened with the internal conflict
between her creativity and her need to believe in traditional gender
roles, issues that emerged in *The Hidden Path.* Her closely doubled and
almost identically named heroines, the cousins Bella and Isabel, represent two stages of the female literary self; Bella is a teacher who yearns
to be a novelist, while Isabel (her Northern cousin) is a successful writer
who has chosen her vocation over marriage. Bella gives up her work in
order to win love, but her brother Maurice, a graduate student at Princeton, consoles her that "the time is certainly coming when the glittering
diadem of the authoress will not blind men to the loving eyes beneath it;
when, through the sacerdotal robe in which your worshippers have
arrayed you, shall be perceptible the rise and fall . . . of the woman's
heart."

In 1856, Hawes's life dramatically changed when she married a Northern Presbyterian minister, Edward Payson Terhune, and moved to
Newark, New Jersey. She wrote her most tormented domestic novel,
Moss-side (1857), about her anxieties of relocation to the North and her
anguish about the propriety of her writing. The heroine, Grace Leigh,
leaves her Virginia plantation and goes to New York for the wedding of
her school friend Louise Wynne. There she feels like a country mouse;
Louise's costly mansion is magnificently furnished, and her friends are

witty and sophisticated. Back in Virginia, Grace is ashamed of her simple environment, and neglects her domestic duties. A romance goes wrong, and she falls into a deep depression. When Grace's doctor prescribes a trip to New York to restore her health and spirits, she is eager to renew her friendship with Louise, who has become a noted writer on women's rights. And when she reads Louise's book, significantly titled "Woman The Slave," she is initially dazzled. Woman, Louise argues, is actually the superior being; she "should be enthroned, no lower than the angels, while he who ruled her . . . should be well-pleased to occupy a subordinate place, and adore as queen and priestess the radiant Immaculate." But Grace's eyes are finally opened to the loveless masquerade of Louise's marriage and the pernicious effects of her message, and she sees the light: "Had I read fewer books; had introspection been less of a study with me; had I looked more into the hearts and lives of others . . . the duration of my delusion would have been shortened."[75] Returning to Moss-side, she resumes her domestic responsibilities, accepts her femininity and its satisfactions, marries happily, and thinks of writing a rebuttal to Louise's book: "Women! Sisters! In piling the blazing beacons that signal your resistance to thralldom old as earth and time—take heed lest you trample out the fires upon your own hearthstones."[76] The plantation—Sunnybank or Moss-side—was the sanctuary of traditional domestic womanhood, and yet the ancient thralldom was all too real.

By the 1870s, Terhune was the mother of six children, and she had moved from fiction to domestic advice, publishing her last novel in 1873. Using her pseudonym "Marion Harland," she became one of the most prolific and acclaimed writers of books on housekeeping, cooking, etiquette, child care, hygiene, and menopause, educating her thousands of readers on everything from cleaning catfish to growing old gracefully. When she died, her obituary in *The New York Times* called her a "homemaking genius."[77] But even behind her mask of happy housekeeper, Terhune retained some of her Brontëish spirit to the end. In 1899, she proposed an article to an editor on domestic monotony as a cause of female madness. "It will be a plea,' she explained, "for the class who make up three fourths of the women lunatics in N.E. insane asylums— the women whose intellects and finer tastes never have a chance."[78] Toward the end of her career, Terhune made two pilgrimages to Haworth, and wrote a biography of Charlotte Brontë. The glittering diadem of the novelist was still part of her dreams.

Doing God's Work—Augusta Jane Evans

Terhune met another Southern novelist, Augusta Jane Evans (1835–1909), in the New York office of their mutual publisher J. C. Derby in 1859, and they liked each other right away. Terhune found Evans "quietly refined in manner and speech"; Evans found Terhune "a genial, impulsive, noble-souled, warm-hearted Southern woman, par excellence."[79] Both revered Charlotte Brontë. Evans, however, came to writing from a much less stable background than Terhune. In the 1840s, her father went bankrupt, and moved his wife and five children from Georgia to the West to find new opportunities. Until 1849, they lived in San Antonio, where she saw gold rush fever and the fight over the annexation of Texas. Evans's first novel, *Inez, A Tale of the Alamo* (1855), written when she was fifteen, was largely an attack on Mexican Catholicism, and came out of her own adolescent religious crisis. When the family moved on to Mobile, Alabama, Evans became a devout Methodist, moralist, self-taught intellectual, and fierce partisan of the Deep South. Although she rarely depicted slaves or discussed slavery in her novels, she was one of the most fervent propagandists of the plantation tradition and Confederate cause.

As she assured a friend, writing could be a noble activity for unmarried women: "Though our Sisterhood work in dark lonely corners, we have joys and encouragements peculiar to the vocation . . . literary women as a class are not as happy, as women who have Husbands and Children to engage their attention and monopolize their affections; yet . . . they experience a deep peace and satisfaction, and are crowned with a glory such as marriage never gave." Furthermore, writing was not just a means of gratifying female ambition or avoiding melancholy, but a means to "the nobler aim of doing *God's work.*"[80] Attracted to philosophy, theology, and classical literature, Evans justified her intellectual appetites as another form of divine self-sacrifice. "If I have given much time and attention to the abstruse speculation of metaphysicians," she explained, "it was because . . . I strove to combat their arguments for love of my countrymen and women."[81] Making many heroines of her fiction women of genius, Evans argued "for the centrality of female artists" both to the high culture of the South and to the creation of a national literature.[82]

Evans's second novel, *Beulah* (1859), was both the most *Jane Eyre*-ish book of the decade and the most original.[83] She intended the novel as a "fictional confession" of her own religious doubts, designed to "help others to avoid the thorny path I have trod ere I was convinced of the fallibility of Human Reason."[84] The story begins in a Southern orphan asylum, where twelve-year-old Beulah Benton, clever but plain and pale, must endure a separation from her pretty six-year-old sister, Lilly, who is adopted by the rich Grayson family and taken away from her care. Beulah is sent out to work as a nursemaid for another family, and barred from visiting her sister. When Lilly dies of scarlet fever, Beulah pronounces a curse on Mrs. Grayson: "May you live to have your heart trampled and crushed, even as you have trampled mine!" She is rescued from brain fever by a doctor, Guy Hartwell, who adopts her and sends her to school.

Beulah grows up lonely, learned, and proud. "I live in a different world," she tells a schoolmate. "Books are to me what family, and friends, and society, are to other people." She also rejects conventional notions of feminine beauty and dependence. In a prizewinning essay titled "Female Heroism," she argues that "the female intellect was capable of the most exalted attainments," concluding with a call to her fellow students "to prove themselves truly women of America—ornaments of the social circle, angel guardians of the sacred hearthstone, ministering spirits where suffering and want demanded succor . . . qualified to assist in a council of statesmen." Although she has trained to be a music teacher, Beulah sets out to support herself by writing, under the pseudonym "Delta." When she takes her work to an editor, she is shocked to discover that he will offer no payment for publication. She coolly rebukes him: "I happen to know that the Northern magazines are not composed of gratuitous contributions, and it is no mystery why Southern authors are driven to Northern publishers. Southern periodicals are mediums only for those of elegant leisure, who can afford to write without remuneration. With the same subscription price, you cannot pay for your articles. It is no marvel that we have no Southern literature." Suitably chastised, he promises to pay her for her work.

Before long, her book *The Inner Life,* in which she defends the spiritual importance of art and intellectual culture, becomes a great success, and fame goes to her head. "She no longer wrote incognito; by accident she was discovered as the authoress of several articles commented upon by other journals, and more than once her humble home had been visited by some of the leading literati of the place. Her successful career thus far inflamed the ambition which formed so powerful an element in her mental organization, and a longing desire for Fame took possession of her soul." Soon she is writing an article "designed to prove that a woman's happiness was not necessarily dependent on marriage. That a single life might be more useful, more tranquil, more unselfish. Beulah had painted her heroine in glowing tints, and triumphantly proved her theory correct, while to female influence she awarded a sphere (exclusive of rostrums and all political influence) wide as the universe and high as heaven."[85] Evans and her heroines always expressed themselves in this ostentatiously intellectual and alarmingly pedantic way.

After many years of theological discussions, visits to Lilly's grave, and accounts of other people's marriages, however, Beulah (who has become stately and beautiful) marries her guardian Guy Hartwell, and gives up writing, or at least her literary ambition, for domestic happiness. "Reader," Evans tells us in the famous style of Charlotte Brontë, "marriage is not the end of life; it is but the beginning of a new course of duties; but I cannot now follow Beulah. Henceforth, her history is bound up with another's." *Beulah* was glowingly reviewed as a work of Southern literary genius.

The Wide, Wide World

Although Susan Warner (1819–1885) began writing her best seller *The Wide, Wide World* (1851) before the publication of *Jane Eyre*, her sister Anna (1827–1915) compared herself and Susan to the Brontë sisters at Haworth parsonage, living their "strange, exceptional life."[86] The Warner sisters had been raised in affluence and privilege, the pampered daughters of a New York lawyer; they had pretty clothes, music lessons, French lessons, and trips to the opera, concerts, and art galleries. Then their father lost his fortune in the financial panic of 1837, and had to retrench. The townhouse on St. Marks Place was sold, and the family moved to Constitution Island, across from West Point. As Anna wrote, the teenage sisters moved from "crimson cushions and tall mirrors . . . greenhouse, carriage, and a corps of servants" to a cold and isolated farmhouse. They did their own housework, and, unable to afford fashionable clothes and bonnets, they could no longer go into society or into the city. Joining the Presbyterian Church and becoming devout Christians helped them spiritually but not economically. In 1848, their financial situation became even more desperate; to pay off the mortgage, they sold most of their furniture, their books, even the piano. In the winter, the unheated farmhouse was below freezing. Writing a novel was Susan's last-ditch effort to save them from penury. Anna recalled that "it was written in closest reliance upon God: for thoughts, for power, and for words . . . In that sense, the book was written upon her knees."[87] At first Susan could not find a publisher, but the mother of the editor George Putnam picked it up in his office, read it, and insisted that her son bring it out.

Published under the pseudonym "Elizabeth Wetherell," *The Wide, Wide World* was the most celebrated domestic novel of the 1850s, going through thirteen editions in two years, selling over a million copies and probably causing much grinding of teeth among male novelists. Anna Warner's novel *Dollars and Cents* (1852), published under the pseudonym "Amy Lothrop," also sold well. Like Susan, Anna continued to turn out fiction until her death; the sisters went on to write twenty-one books separately and together, although every penny went to pay their father's enormous and ever-mounting debts from bad investments and foolish lawsuits. In 1860, Anna wrote the words for "Jesus Loves Me"; set to music the following year, it became one of the most popular American hymns, but hymn writing was not a good way to make money.

Despite its title, *The Wide, Wide World* actually portrayed the narrow and claustrophobic world of an intelligent child, Ellen Montgomery. When her beloved mother develops a fatal illness, and her parents go off for an extended therapeutic European holiday, eight-year-old Ellen is sent to live on a New England farm with her aunt, the harsh and punningly named Miss Fortune. Despite her loneliness and culture shock, Ellen copes well with her new environment; she learns to clean, to study, to read her Bible, and to care for the neighbors Alice and John Humphreys, who become surrogate parents. Warner followed the pattern of *Jane Eyre* in having Ellen torn between her attachments to a woman and a man, who represent work and independence versus love and submission.

Just as she is feeling happy in her new home, however, Ellen's parents die at sea, and she is shipped off again to her mother's family in Scotland, the Lindsays. They are affectionate and generous, but they are also snobbish anti-American aristocrats who expect her to take on their values and customs. Among other indignities, they force her to drink wine, take away her books, and forbid her to correspond with her American friends, all the while professing the most complete love for her. "I wonder how many times one must be adopted," Ellen thinks. She is well aware that they wield "the hand of power" over her: "they would do with her and make of her precisely what they pleased, without the smallest regard to her fancy."

Every reader has remarked upon the amount of weeping in *The Wide, Wide World;* Fred Pattee counted "245 tear-flows in the 574 pages."[88] In fact, there is almost as much kissing, fondling, palpating, stroking, hair smoothing, hugging, and embracing imposed on Ellen by her pseudo-relatives of both sexes and all ages. Yet along with her weepiness and Lolita-like appeal, Ellen is tough and curious; she becomes a studious young woman, who resents being infantilized: "I wonder why everybody calls me 'little;' I don't think I am very little." Finally, she is rescued from the Lindsays by John Humphreys, who takes her back to the United States, marries her, and gives her everything Susan Warner could imagine in the way of comfort and security.

Following in Ellen Montgomery's path, many heroines of domestic fiction found their rewards in submission and sacrifice. Maria Susanna Cummins (1827–1866), among many others, retold the story in her best sellers *The Lamplighter* (1854) and *Mabel Vaughan* (1857). Even Jo March has a good cry over it in Louisa May Alcott's *Little Women;* Helen Hunt Jackson compared it to some of her friends: "I do not admire them, I would not be like them, I could delight others by a detail of their character—but I do love dearly to be with them."[89]

Ellen Montgomery longs to run away from her aunt, but she learns to be patient and endure, leading one critic to conclude that "a girl cannot run away in the world of nineteenth-century women's fiction, any more than the Warner sisters in real life could have run away from Constitution Island. Women writers of that era, unlike their male counterparts, could not walk out the door and become Mississippi riverboat captains, go off on whaling voyages, or build themselves cabins in the woods."[90] Yet in Southern domestic fiction, girls and women do run away, set off on riverboats, build cabins in the woods, and otherwise rebel against their captivity. Perhaps because they grew up in a culture where tales of runaway slaves were heard every day, Southern domestic novelists were more drawn to fantasies of escape.

For example, in Caroline Lee Hentz's *Linda; or, The Young Pilot of the Belle Creole,* published the year before *The Wide, Wide World,* Linda Watson, the high-spirited young heiress of a great Louisiana plantation, is devastated when her mother dies, and her father remarries a mercenary widow with a self-willed son. Like Jane Eyre suffering the blows of her brutish cousin John Reed, little Linda is whipped by her stepmother and forced to sit for hours sewing, while her passive father wonders why she is "drawing her needle through and through the everlasting patchwork, with a look of sad endurance." The stepmother even tries to have Linda's beloved black nurse, Aunt Judy, sold at auction, but Linda persuades a kindly neighbor to buy the devoted slave. When her stepmother pressures her to marry her stepbrother and consolidate the family fortune, Linda runs away again and goes to live in the woods with a noble Indian, Tuscarora, and his wife.

A New England native who never owned slaves, Caroline Lee had started writing as a child. In 1824, she married Nicholas Marcellus Hentz, a French émigré who had studied medicine and entomology, and they moved to Chapel Hill, North Carolina, where he was a professor of modern languages at the university. Nicholas Hentz, however, suffered from depression, and had trouble keeping a job. With their three children, the couple began an unhappy twenty-year period during which they moved frequently, and both taught at various schools in Kentucky, Ohio, Alabama, and Georgia. By 1850, Nicholas Hentz had become a withdrawn invalid, and Caroline took over as the family breadwinner.

By the mid-1850s, like most white Southerners, she had embraced the argument that slavery was a positive good. Hentz's own experience, however, made her an advocate of independent girls and women; she alternated between novels defending slavery, and novels about rebellious young women with artistic ambitions. In her last book, *Ernest Linwood; or, The Inner Life of the Author* (1856), Hentz wrote in the first person and drew on her own life and marriage. Her narrator, Gabriella Lynn, is a precocious poet: "I had lisped in rhyme—I had improvised in rhyme— I had dreamed in poetry when the moon and stars were looking down on me with benignant luster—I had thought poetry at the sunset hour, amid twilight shadows and midnight darkness. I had scribbled it at early morn in my own little room . . . but no human being, save my mother, knew of the young dream-girl's poetic raptures." Gabriella wants to become a teacher, but her mother dies in an epidemic and she is adopted by the wealthy Mrs. Linwood. Despite Mrs. Linwood's warnings of hereditary insanity in the family, Gabriella marries her son Ernest. Apparently based on Hentz's husband, Nicholas, he is paranoid, agoraphobic, and severely depressed, keeping Gabriella captive in their home until he has a breakdown and shoots her in a fit of madness. But Gabriella has discovered that her beloved mother was also a secret novelist; she has left a story called "The Mother's History," a novel within the novel, which suggests that rebellion as well as literary genius is passed on in the female line.[91]

Mrs. E.D.E.N. Southworth (Emma Dorothy Eliza Nevitte Southworth, 1819–1899) was the most prolific and popular of the Southern women novelists of the 1850s; between 1849 and 1860 she published an astonishing eighteen novels, and during her lifetime, she probably wrote more than fifty. Southworth, who was born in Washington, D.C., recalled in 1854, "I was a child of sorrow from the very first year of my life. Thin and dark, I had no beauty except a pair of large, wild eyes . . . [but when a year old] I was struck with an inflammation of the eyes that ended in total, though happily temporary, blindness." Her adored father died when she was three years old; her stepfather, a schoolmaster, educated her in his academy. She married at twenty-one, but in 1844, she was deserted by her husband, Frederick Southworth, who went off to Brazil and left her pregnant and destitute, with a small child. "In those sad days," she wrote to her daughter, "I used to go to the post office in hopes of getting a letter from Brazil and . . . come home crushed and disappointed."[92] Although she tried teaching in the Washington public schools, her salary was not enough to support her family, and by 1845, she was ill and desperate, and frantically writing short pieces for newspapers in Baltimore and Washington.

With her first novel, *Retribution* (1849), Southworth turned the tide: "Friends crowded around me—offers for contributions poured upon me. And I, who six months before had been poor, ill, forsaken, slandered, killed by sorrow, privation, toil, . . . found myself born as it were into a new life; found independence, sympathy, friendship, and honour, and an occupation in which I could delight." *Retribution* was a gothic story of two friends, one rich and one poor, who sequentially marry the same wealthy domineering man. The first wife, Hester, is killed by his coldness; the second, Juliet, punishes him by eloping with another man. In the conclusion, the chastened husband returns to Hester's vast Southern estate for a reunion with their daughter, and, according to Hester's dying wish, frees all their slaves. Although the novel is only tangentially about slavery, its title and themes suggested, as Lyde Cullen Sizer points out, "the eventual response of God (and, one imagines, the slaves themselves) to the domestic evil that the institution of slavery encouraged."[93]

Southworth's taste for strong and eccentric heroines was demonstrated in her semiautobiographical novel *The Deserted Wife* (1855). The heroine Hagar Churchill defies her sadistic husband in the ringing tones of Jane Eyre confronting Rochester: "I have a will! And tastes, and habits, and propensities! And loves and hates! Yes, and conscience! That all go to make up the sum total of a separate individuality—a distinct life! For which I alone am accountable, and only to God!" Meanwhile, Fanny, the betrayed mad wife of another male protagonist, appears to his fiancée like Bertha Mason, "with streaming yellow hair and emaciated, claw-like fingers," to declare, "Do not marry him!"[94] "Hagar" was the standard American name for the heroine as an outcast or fallen woman betrayed by men. H. Marion Stephens's melodramatic *Hagar the Martyr; or, Passion and Reality* (1855) sympathetically portrayed the fate of a passionate Southern woman who is seduced and blackmailed into a false marriage by a man who convinces her that she is the daughter of a slave. Stephens's Hagar gets away, and redeems herself by becoming a celebrated writer, and is reborn into Boston society.

In 1856, Southworth was offered an exclusive contract for her work by Robert Bonner, the enterprising editor of the *New York Ledger*. "My own belief," he told her, "is that there is no female author either on this or the other side of the Atlantic, who can write so excellent a story."[95] His faith was repaid by Southworth's sensational best seller *The Hidden Hand* (1859). Capitola, an adventurous street waif who earns her living disguised as a newsboy, has a birthmark of a little crimson hand in her palm. When Cap discovers her lost mother in a lunatic asylum, the reader is suddenly propelled into the gothic settings of Hawthorne's stories and Dickens's *A Tale of Two Cities*. Like Hawthorne's "The Birthmark," in which the tiny red hand on the heroine's cheek is the symbol of female sexuality and the brand or "mark" of the woman's fate to give birth, *The Hidden Hand* traces Cap's fate to her mother and her female destiny. As in Dickens's story of aristocratic sexual corruption, the mother was a victim of kidnapping, rape, and abuse that drove her mad. The midwife who attended Cap's birth tells her, "I saw a young creature tossing about on the bed, flinging her fair and beautiful arms about, and tearing wildly at the fine lace that trimmed her night-dress. But . . . that wasn't what almost made me faint—it was that her right hand was sewed up in black crape, and her whole face and head completely covered with black crape, drawn down and fastened securely around her throat, leaving only a small slit at the lips and nose, to breathe through."

All of these novelists would continue to write throughout the decade of the Civil War, which forced them to confront their deepest and most sacred beliefs. Southern women writers idealized the order and harmony of their way of life, and defended slavery as a benevolent and even divinely ordained system, related to a larger system of dominance and subordination which defined women's roles as well; of course, they also benefited from slavery.[96] While they opposed "women's rights," which they even denounced as ungodly, Southern women writers still faced internal conflicts over women's role that shaped their plots and voices. As professional writers, working to earn money, these novelists were living in ways very unlike those they championed for their readers.

"Ruthless Hall"—Fanny Fern

"I am sick, in an age which produced a Brontë," wrote "Fanny Fern" (Sarah Payson Willis, 1811–1872), ". . . of the prate of men who assert that every woman should be a perfect housekeeper."[97] Fern was a subversive journalist and novelist who had no patience with organized religion, middle-class piety, or romantic ideas of marriage. Her father, a deacon in Edward Beecher's Park Street Church, had been called "Brimstone Corner" for his fierce sermons. Her brother was Nathaniel P. Willis, a celebrity poet, editor, and New York man-about-town. Fern married three times. Her first husband, "Handsome Charlie" Eldredge, died of typhoid fever in 1845 and left her with two children; neither her father nor her father-in-law would help her support them. In desperation she made a marriage of convenience to a rich widower, Samuel P. Farrington, whom she divorced in 1853. When she began to write journalism, Nathaniel Willis was almost comically cruel and unsympathetic: "You overstrain the pathetic and your humor runs into dreadful vulgarity sometimes," he wrote to her. "I am sorry that any editor knows that a sister of mine wrote some of these which you sent me."[98] When she started to have some success elsewhere, he spitefully ordered James Parton, the editor of his magazine, the *New York Home Journal,* not to reprint her work. But, in a wonderful drama of wish-fulfilling revenge, Parton resigned in protest, and married Fern in July 1856.

Fern claimed to have chosen her woodsy pseudonym because it recalled her mother's garden: "When a child and walking with my mother in the country, she always used to pluck a leaf of it . . . That gloomy morning when I almost despaired of earning bread for my children, I had been thinking of her, and wishing that she were living, that I might lay my head upon her bosom and tell her all my sorrows; and then, memory carried me back . . . to those childish days when I ran before her in the woods, to pluck the sweet fern she loved; and then I said to myself, my name shall be 'Fanny Fern.' "[99] The hyperfeminine name set an American fashion for alliterative floral pseudonyms; Elizabeth Stoddard recommended "the pugilism of Fanny Fern, the pathetics of Minnie Myrtle, or the abandon of Cassie Cauliflower," and Gail Hamilton mocked the school of Maggie Marigold, Kittie Katnip, Delia Daisy, Fanny Foxglove, and Harriet Honeysuckle.[100]

Ruth Hall, based on the melodramatic details of the author's own life and influenced by *Jane Eyre,* electrified readers in 1855; Grace Greenwood called it "Ruthless Hall."[101] The first half of the novel is all about women's wrongs from parents, brother, in-laws, employers, and society, beginning with the death of the heroine's beloved young husband; her mistreatment by her brother and her in-laws; her struggle to survive economically; and her battles to maintain custody of her daughters. The second half is about women's rights and writings, as Ruth Hall becomes an author under the pen name "Floy," gains financial independence, and establishes her own household. In her book about the writer as heroine in American women's fiction, Linda Huf suggests that Ruth's husband "had to die that she might live as an artist." It was common in "the nineteenth-century woman's artist novel" for the "heroine's lifework" to be sanctioned "by the sudden death or disappearance of a father, lover, or husband."[102] Fern not only used the vigor of her writing in an exposé of women's wrongs, but by exposing the cruelty and hypocrisy surrounding the aspiring author, demonstrated for the first time that writing well could be the best revenge. Elizabeth Cady Stanton was among the readers who cheered to see tyranny revealed. *Ruth Hall,* she asserted, was "as much a slave narrative as Frederick Douglass's."[103]

In several respects, *Ruth Hall* showed the influence of *Jane Eyre.* Both novels begin with a female figure sitting at a window, show the heroine encountering cruelty and insensitivity, and watching her women friends endure even more extreme neglect.[104] In the subplot of Ruth's incarcerated friend Mary Leon, Fern provides a "madwoman" story to intensify the potential tragedy of Ruth's situation and the wrongs done to other docile and dependent women. During the prosperous days of her early marriage, Ruth befriends the beautiful Mrs. Leon at a beach resort. Mary Leon, who has married a fussy, rigid man for his money, is prone to debilitating attacks of migraine, and comes to a tragic end; her husband leaves her in a lunatic asylum "for her health," while he travels in Europe, and she breaks down, refuses to eat, and dies, leaving Ruth a pathetic note: "I am not crazy, Ruth, no, no—but I shall be; the air of this place stifles me; I grow weaker—weaker." Mary Leon's fate shows the fatal weakening of women who are totally dependent on male economic and emotional support.

The most important part of the novel is Fern's autobiographical account of her own development as a writer. Waking at dawn in her garret as the newspaper is being delivered, Ruth has an epiphany: "Write for the papers, why not?" When she first sends her work to her brother Hyacinth Ellet, he returns a cruel and arrogant note of rejection, but his arrogance liberates her to feel anger and determine to succeed. Persisting in writing and marketing her work, she gets her articles accepted for publication in *The Standard,* and they are an immediate hit; soon she is bargaining for her work with John Walter, the editor of the *Household Messenger,* who treats her like a genius. Fame, fortune, and revenge on all who have wronged her follow in quick succession. She even begins to receive a hilarious assortment of begging letters from men who want her to marry them, sign their manuscripts, get their work published, and fund their businesses.

Breezy and modern, *Ruth Hall* is composed of ninety short chapters, some just scraps of overheard conversation, some incorporating letters and newspaper snippets. In her preface to the reader, Fern declared her preference for informality and brevity: "I am aware that it is entirely at variance with all rules for novel-writing. There is no intricate plot; there are no startling developments, no hair-breadth escapes. I have compressed into one volume what I might have expanded into two or three." Dickens was a major influence on her satirical style; Ruth is surrounded by Dickensian characters, including the maternity nurse, Mrs. Jiff, the school examiners Squizzle and Fizzle, the tradesmen Tiffkins and Flake, the insane hospital matron Mrs. Bunce, and the Micawberesque Skiddys. Even Hawthorne was amused and impressed. "The woman writes as if the Devil was in her," he wrote admiringly, "and that is the only condition under which a woman ever writes anything worth reading. Generally women write like emasculated men, and are only to be distinguished from male authors by greater feebleness and folly; but when they throw off the restraints of decency and come before the public stark naked . . . then their books are sure to possess character and value."[105]

In a pioneering and revolutionary article on Fern and American women's writing—the first serious critical examination of domestic fiction in the 1850s—the critic Ann Douglas concluded that although *Ruth Hall* was Fern's "finest and most central work," she continued throughout her life to express "not only the financial but also the emotional needs and frustrations that drove her and her sisters to the pen."[106] In her journalism, she championed women writers, and mocked the stuffiness, prejudice, and envy of those who belittled them. In 1857, Fern came forward to testify to the American woman of genius as epitomized by Harriet Beecher Stowe: "I thank the gods that [she] has had the courage to assert herself—to be what nature intended her to be—a genius—even at the risk of being called unfeminine, eccentric, and unwomanly . . . I am glad that a new order of women is arising . . . who are evidently sufficient unto themselves, both as it regards love and bread and butter."[107] *Ruth Hall* was not a masterpiece, and Fanny Fern was not a literary genius; but her professionalism, feminism, and staunchly democratic values cleared the path for Stowe and the new order of women to come.

6

Slavery, Race, and Women's Writing

rom Harriet Beecher Stowe's *Uncle Tom's Cabin* (1852), the most widely read American novel of the century, to the Southern "anti-Tom" novels that tried to refute Stowe's picture of plantation life, to the emergence of memoirs, stories, and novels by African-American women, questions of slavery and abolitionism dominated women's writing in the 1850s. The debate over domestic fiction versus high culture was being carried on in the midst of heated and violent confrontations between proslavery and antislavery groups. From the Fugitive Slave Act of September 1850, which required all U.S. citizens to assist in recovering escaped slaves and returning them to their owners, to John Brown's raid on the government arsenal at Harpers Ferry in 1859, American writers argued over the great national questions of racism and freedom, and connected American literature with worldwide struggles for self-determination. At the same time, these subjects allowed women writers to transcend many of the taboos on subject matter and expression.

The Great American Novel: *Uncle Tom's Cabin*

The commercial success of *Uncle Tom's Cabin* surpassed even the domestic best sellers of the 1850s. It appeared as a book in two volumes in March 1852, and sold 305,000 copies the first year in the United States, and two million around the world. By the end of the decade, it had been translated into eighteen languages. *Uncle Tom's Cabin* was also the first of the great global best sellers that changed the marketing and influence of fiction. In a prophetic review, Charles Frederick Briggs, the editor of *Putnam's,* predicted that the popularity of the novel was the "commencement of a miraculous Era in the literary world. Hereafter, the book which does not circulate to the extent of a million copies will be regarded as a failure."[1]

The international critical acclaim for *Uncle Tom's Cabin* was extraordinary as well. In France it was reviewed by George Sand as a work of genius and created a "Tom *manie*," even greater than the *Jane Eyre* mania in the United States; in Russia, it was read by Tolstoy, Turgenev, and Pushkin; in England, Stowe's novel was hailed as a masterpiece. Her fiction played a major role in the shift from American dependence on British and European literary models to acknowledgment of distinctively American subjects and forms. By the end of the century, many American critics acknowledged that Stowe was a major writer, and that *Uncle Tom's Cabin* was a "great work of imaginative fiction."[2] In 1890, Helen Gray Cone credited Stowe's triumph with the coming-of-age of all American women writers: "In face of the fact that the one American book which had stormed Europe was the work of a woman, the old tone of patronage became ridiculous, the old sense of ordained and inevitable weakness on the part of the 'female writer' became obsolete. Women henceforth, whatever their personal feelings in regard to the much-discussed book, were enabled, consciously or unconsciously, to hold the pen more firmly, to move it more freely."[3]

In the twentieth century, however, *Uncle Tom's Cabin* was attacked by African-American critics for its stereotyped and even racist picture of blacks; Uncle Tom, according to Harvard professor Henry Louis Gates, Jr., became "the most reviled figure in American literary history."[4] James Baldwin famously wrote in "Everybody's Protest Novel" (1949) that "*Uncle Tom's Cabin* is a very bad novel, having in its self-righteous, virtuous sentimentality, much in common with *Little Women*. Sentimentality, the ostentatious parading of excessive and spurious emotion, is the mask of dishonesty, the inability to feel . . . and it is always, therefore, the signal of secret and violent inhumanity, the mask of cruelty." While Baldwin may not have read *Little Women,* the two most popular nineteenth-century novels by American women were frequently linked. At the same time, Stowe was categorized as a melodramatic and old-fashioned novelist, and excluded from the canon by Matthiessen and other white critics. By 1948, when Baldwin wrote his damning essay, *Uncle Tom's Cabin* was actually out of print.

Despite these attacks, *Uncle Tom's Cabin* is an American masterpiece, and Harriet Beecher Stowe is a great writer, a daring and forceful architect of narrative, a gifted painter of character, and a sophisticated manager of symbolism, irony, and allegory. The critical neglect of *Uncle Tom's Cabin* has less to do with its alleged literary flaws, its racial politics, or even its enormous and suspect popularity, than with its awkward placement in the middle of a period where the American literary canon was perceived as exceptionally narrow, strong, and male. Moreover, Stowe published nine more novels. Her achievements and her wide influence make her the most important figure in the history of American women's writing.

A Literary Woman—Harriet Beecher Stowe

By the time Stowe came to write *Uncle Tom's Cabin*, she knew from personal experience about the difficulties of marriage, the challenges of maternity, and the problems of writing on the great issues of the day. In a letter she wrote to the abolitionist Eliza Cabot Follen in 1852, Stowe described herself and the beginning of her career with the self-deprecating humor, vivacity, and pathos that both endeared her to readers and led critics to underestimate her abilities:

> To begin, then, I am a little bit of a woman,—somewhat more than forty, about as thin and dry as a pinch of snuff—never very much to look at in my best days and looking like a used up article now.
>
> I was married when I was twenty-five years old to a man rich in Greek and Hebrew and Latin and Arabic, and, alas, rich in nothing else . . . But then I was abundantly furnished with wealth of another sort. I had two little curly headed twin daughters to begin with and my stock in this line has gradually increased until I have been the mother of seven children, the most beautiful and most loved of whom lies buried near my Cincinnati residence. It was at his dying bed and at his grave that I learned what a poor slave mother may feel when her child is torn away from her . . .
>
> During these long years of struggling with poverty and sickness and a hot debilitating climate my children grew up around me. The nursery and the kitchen were my principal fields of labor. Then one of my friends pitying my toils copied and sent a number of little sketches from my pen to certain liberally paying "Annuals" with my name. With the first money that I earned in this way I bought a feather bed! For as I

had married into poverty and without a dowry, and as my husband
had only a large library of books, and a great deal of learning—the bed
and pillows was thought on the whole the most profitable investment.
After that I thought that I had discovered the "Philosopher's Stone,"
and when a new carpet, or a new mattress, was going to be needed . . .
then I used to say to my faithful friend and factotum Anna who shared
all my joys and sorrows "now if you will keep the babies and attend to
all the things in the house for one day I'll write a piece, and then we
shall be out of the scrape." And so I became an authoress.[5]

In Cincinnati, in 1836, Harriet Elizabeth Beecher had married Calvin
Stowe, a widowed teacher nine years her senior, who had been a classmate of Hawthorne at Bowdoin College in Maine. The marriage was
stormy and shaky; Calvin was supportive of her writing, sexually faithful, and intellectually devoted, but he was also sexually demanding and
financially useless. By 1838, Harriet began to augment their meager
income by writing sketches for the *Western Monthly Magazine, Godey's
Lady's Book,* and the *New-York Evangelist.* At that point, she made the decision to hire some household help, so that she had "about three hours per
day in writing . . . I have determined not to be a mere domestic slave . . .
I mean to have money enough to have my house kept in the best manner
and yet to have time for reflection and that preparation for the education
of my children which every mother needs."[6]

They moved to Portland, Maine, where Calvin worked as a librarian
at Bowdoin, and Harriet continued to write and to have children. When
Harper Brothers approached her in April 1842 about bringing out a volume of short stories, she traveled to Boston to negotiate a contract, and
Calvin encouraged her decision to become a professional writer: "You
must be a *literary woman.* It is so written in the book of fate. Make all
your calculations accordingly, get a good stock of health, brush up your
mind, drop the E out of your name, which only encumbers it and stops
the flow and euphony, and write yourself only and always, Harriet
Beecher Stowe, which is a name euphonous [*sic*], flowing, and full of
meaning; and my word for it, your husband will lift up his head in the
gate and your children will rise up and call you blessed."[7] She stayed in
Boston through the summer, and upon returning, insisted on a room of
her own: "If I am to write, I must have a room to myself, which shall be
my room."[8]

Stowe always thought of writing, maternity, and domesticity as related activities. "Creating a story," she wrote, "is like bearing a child and it leaves me in a state as weak and helpless as when my baby was born."[9] Writing also had parallels to other forms of female creativity. Like piecing a quilt, assembling a novel required the stitching together of many short pieces and scenes; the overall design of *Uncle Tom's Cabin*, with its alternating focus on the black and white characters in their settings, was akin to the Log Cabin quilt, with its contrasting triangles of dark and light materials. Serializing the novel, as Dickens did, emphasized the parts that made up the great design. Stowe had been impressed with the essays on slavery Grace Greenwood had been publishing in the *National Era,* and decided to serialize her story there; Greenwood edited the first drafts. To Gamaliel Bailey at the *Era,* Stowe emphasized her visual imagination; her technique would be "that of a painter" and "there is no arguing with *pictures.*"[10]

So much attention over the decades has been devoted to the political content of *Uncle Tom's Cabin* that its literary qualities have been overlooked. Yet Stowe went far beyond any other American woman novelist of the period in her range and defiance of conventional expectations. She handled a huge cast of characters, black and white, young and old, from different regions of the country, and moved easily from humor to horror to tragedy. She could be subtle as well as didactic. Edmund Wilson was one of the first modern critics to recognize Stowe's distinction. In *Patriotic Gore* (1962), he noted the novel's "eruptive force," the irresistible vitality of its characters, the evidence of "a critical mind . . . at work, which has the complex situation in a very firm grip, and which, no matter how vehement the characters become, is controlling and coordinating their interrelations."[11] Ellen Moers, a pioneer of feminist criticism, described *Uncle Tom's Cabin* as an epic novel with a complex structure. Writing in 1976, she explained that a modern understanding of Stowe's art depended also on a modern appreciation of Dickens: "It is today easier than it was in the 1850s to make high claims for *Uncle Tom's Cabin* as a work of literature, because we read Dickens better than his contemporaries did, because we can see in *Bleak House* as in Stowe's novel (they were published almost simultaneously) an organizing principle which makes sense out of a vast social panorama, and patterns underlying the apparent slapdash hazards of serial publication . . . Stowe uses the swelling waters of the Mississippi as vantage points—for *Uncle Tom's Cabin* is a novel of continental destiny as well as slavery."[12]

Openly appealing to her readers to condemn slavery, Stowe quietly staked her claim to a literature unchecked by female limitations. The opening chapter, ironically titled "In Which the Reader is Introduced to a Man of Humanity," is a dialogue between two men, the weak but respectable Kentucky plantation owner Shelby and the Dickensian scoundrel of a slave trader, Haley, the self-described "man of humanity." In this scene of tension, suspense, excitement, indignation, satire, and black humor, they strike the bargain to sell Shelby's loyal slave Tom, and the serving girl Eliza's little son Harry. Traditionally, women writers had shied away from showing men talking without the presence of women. Stowe indirectly declares her right to go where women were not allowed, and to present business conversations women were not supposed to hear. In its way, this opening scene is as important for the authority of American women's writing as the famous episode that follows early in the novel—Eliza and Harry's escape across the frozen Ohio.

A "Dragon-Like Book": Anti-Tom Novels in the South

Uncle Tom's Cabin inspired outrage in the proslavery South, and its political message far dominated its literary merits. Some parents forbade their children to read it; "it was not allowed to be even spoken of in our house!" Grace King of New Orleans remembered. *Uncle Tom's Cabin* was a monster to scare children with, a "hideous, black, dragon-like book that hovered on the horizon of every Southern child."[13] Southern women writers responded with pious self-justification and angry self-defense. Between 1852 and 1860, they published nine "anti-Tom" novels, which feature loyal and contented slaves, benevolent plantation owners, pious death scenes of devoted and beloved mammies, dire warnings of the pitfalls of freedom, and an emphasis on the rewards to be found in heavenly mansions where master and slave shall be equal.[14] Their emphatic Christianity is actually indoctrination in white supremacy, and behind their glorification of the saintly and powerful planter's wife is a recurring fear of slave insurrections.

Mary Eastman's *Aunt Phillis's Cabin* (1852) was the first and the most popular of the anti-Tom novels, selling eighteen thousand copies in a few weeks. In contrast to Stowe's betrayed and martyred Uncle Tom, Eastman's Aunt Phillis is a loyal and beloved mammy whose death occasions demonstrations of white tenderness and praise. The planter's son extols her to his Northern college friends: "We have a servant woman named Phillis; her price is far above rubies. Her industry, her honesty, her attachment to our family, exceeds every thing. I wish Abolitionists would imitate one of her virtues—humility . . . She is a slave here, but she is destined to be a saint hereafter."

Caroline Hentz also joined the anti-Tom bandwagon. In *The Planter's Northern Bride* (1854), she tried to imitate Stowe's rhetorical style, but with a corresponding passion for the divine rights of white supremacy. "There will be no Cabin in it, most assuredly," she promised her publisher; "—the public have had cabins enough for one century."[15] Hentz's preface contended with Stowe for veracity by citing her personal experience of plantations in North Carolina, Alabama, Georgia, and Florida, and claiming real people as the sources for her characters. She called upon "noble, liberal minds" in the North to "appreciate and do justice to our motives," and declared that "the negroes of the South are the happiest *labouring class* on the face of the globe," that fugitive slaves have been "disaffected by the influence of others"; and that during her long residence in the South she and her family "never *witnessed* one scene of cruelty or oppression."

The planter of her title, Russell Moreland, is traveling in the North when he meets Eulalia Hastings, the beautiful daughter of a rabidly abolitionist professor. Professor Hastings views slavery as a satanic institution; he tells Moreland that "as long as you allow the existence of slavery, you are living in sin and iniquity . . . you are violating the laws of God and man, and incurring the vengeance of heaven and the retribution of eternity." When Moreland proposes marriage to Eulalia, Professor Hastings regards it as a fate worse than death: "I would rather see a daughter of mine laid in the deepest grave of New England than married to a Southern planter."[16]

Eulalia, however, has already fallen in love with Moreland; she goes into a decline, and eventually her father relents and she becomes the planter's bride. Moreland is a staunch believer in the divine mission of wealthy Southerners to lift the slaves out of their ignorance and barbarity, to care for them as children. He contrasts indigent Northern workers with slaves who are cared for unto death, have job security, so to speak, and lifelong health insurance—"it is true the nominal bondage of the slave was wanting, but there was the bondage of poverty." Eulalia's raptures about her husband's benevolence are punctuated with Hentz's lengthy sermons about the affection the slaves feel for their owners: "The admiration, love, and devotion which the negro feels for the children of a beloved master, is one of the strongest, most unselfish passions the human heart is capable of cherishing." Hentz tells a cautionary tale about Chrissy, a slave who is persuaded to escape through the Underground Railroad by a pair of Quaker troublemakers; she deeply regrets her decision, but when she tries to return to the old plantation, her kind master has died and the plantation is deserted. Another evil abolitionist, Brainard, attempts to incite a rebellion among Moreland's slaves. The effort fails, but Brainard vows to continue his incendiary activities: "I will go back to the North, deliver such lectures on the South as will curdle the blood with horror . . . The more horrors I manufacture, the more ecstasy they will feel!"

Despite these tales of outside agitators, and the mutual devotion of slaves and their masters, the anti-Tom novels had to confront the grim reality, more and more documented, of the mounting anger of the slave population, and the fear and powerlessness of the planter class in the face of potential black insurrection. The brides of the planters were writing in their diaries about the truth of sexual exploitation on the plantation and the rumors of interracial slaughter in various Southern cities.

Bleeding Kansas and Bleeding Sumner

Stowe was moved to open political intervention in 1854, when the Kansas-Nebraska Act, authored by Senators Douglas of Illinois and Butler of South Carolina, allowed settlers of new states to vote on whether they preferred to be slave-owning or free. In "An Appeal to the Women of the Free States of America, on the Present Crisis in Our Country," she called on women to educate themselves on the issues and do whatever they could to influence the voting. But the antagonism between the two sides was becoming increasing violent. On May 22, 1856, Senator Charles Sumner of Massachusetts, who had denounced the act in the Senate and mocked its authors, was attacked and beaten unconscious with a cane by South Carolina congressman Preston Brooks. Sumner spent three years recuperating from the attack.

Outraged Northerners regarded Sumner as a martyr. William Cullen Bryant, in the *New York Evening Post,* asked whether Northerners were also "slaves for life, a target for their brutal blows, when we do not comport ourselves to please them?" Lydia Maria Child was so agitated that she had an attack of "painful suffocations of the heart, alternating with painful throbbings of the brain." She wrote to Sumner, offering to rush to his side in Washington and nurse him. "To have labored so long against slavery, and yet to see it always triumphant! The outrage upon Charles Sumner made me literally ill."[17] By contrast, Southerners made Congressman Brooks a hero. The *Richmond Enquirer*, like other Southern newspapers, praised Brooks and proclaimed that "these vulgar abolitionists in the Senate . . . must be lashed into submission."

During the same short period in 1856, proslavery men in Lawrence, Kansas, destroyed abolitionist presses and torched other property. In retaliation, the religious fanatic and terrorist John Brown and his sons massacred five proslavery male settlers with broadswords in an attack on Pottawatomie Creek. Brown believed that the way to end slavery was to foment slave uprisings and carry out guerrilla warfare. After the raid, he escaped, and traveled through New England raising funds for his campaign.

Dred and Dread

"Under the impulse of our stormy times, as the blood and insults of Sumner and the sack of Lawrence burn within us," Stowe had begun to write a new novel.[18] Black readers of *Uncle Tom's Cabin* had objected to her support for Liberian colonization rather than full citizenship for the slaves, and she had been rethinking and changing her position. More aesthetically adventurous and politically radical than *Uncle Tom's Cabin*, but also more disturbing, *Dred* (1856) refuses the comforting moral certainties of *Uncle Tom's Cabin*, and legitimates black insurrection. In her preface, Stowe explained her reasons for returning again to the subject of slavery. She put aesthetic motives first: "From a merely artistic point of view, there is no ground, ancient or modern, whose vivid lights, gloomy shadows, and grotesque groupings, afford to the novelist so wide a scope for the exercise of his powers." Political and philosophical motives were second: "God, in his providence, is now asking the American people, Is the system of slavery, as set forth in the American slave code, *right*? Is it so desirable, that you will directly establish it over broad regions, where till now, you have solemnly forbidden it to enter?"

Dred contains two interrelated stories. The dominant narrative is a masterful realistic picture of life among the elite and the lowly on a plantation in North Carolina, owned by a young belle, Nina Gordon; the second narrative, contained within the first, is a surreal, mythic picture of a colony of fugitives and runaways, black and white, in the Great Dismal Swamp, led by the outlaw slave Dred. Stowe expertly deployed a large cast of characters, from slaves to poor whites, from Southern belles to drunken harridans, from plantation owners to black revolutionaries, and set out their ideas, viewpoints, prejudices, and evidence on both sides of the argument. In chapter twenty-one, "The Desert," she addressed the relative nature of truth and the importance of point of view:

> One might almost imagine that there were no such thing as absolute truth, since a change of situation or temperament is capable of changing the whole force of an argument. We have been accustomed, even those of us who feel most, to look on the arguments for and against the system of slavery with the eyes of those who are at ease. We do not even know how fair is freedom, for we were always free. We shall never have all the materials for absolute truth on this subject, till we take into account, with our own views and reasonings, the views and reasonings of those who have bowed down to the yoke and felt the iron enter into their souls.

In contrast to the passive, loving Uncle Tom, Dred is violent and vengeful. He makes his first shocking appearance almost two hundred pages into the novel, when he arises in the moonlight in the forest to confront Harry Gordon, a slave who supervises the Gordon plantation but knows secretly that he is Nina's mulatto half brother. In the biblical rhetoric of a prophet, Dred challenges him: "How long wilt thou cast in thy lot with the oppressors of Israel?" In Stowe's description, Dred is part Spartacus and part Hawkeye. "He was a tall black man, of magnificent stature and proportions. His skin was intensely black and polished like marble. A loose shirt of red flannel, which opened very wide at the breast, gave a display of a neck and chest of herculean strength. The sleeves of the shirt, rolled up nearly to the shoulders, showed the muscles of a gladiator."[19] He is armed like a hunter with a bowie knife, hatchet, and rifle, but also garbed like an "old warrior prophet" with a scarlet turban, and burning eyes "that betokened habitual excitement to the verge of insanity."

Dred is also a magical and symbolic figure—the horror on the other side of slavery, lurking in the swamps of the Southern unconscious. Stowe acknowledged as much in a letter to the Duchess of Argyll in 1856:

"After all, my book may have a significance in its title Dread and the tragedy of that dismal swamp of slavery may be a world's wonder."[20] As a young girl, Stowe avidly read a tattered copy of *The Tempest* that she found in her grandmother's attic, and the figures of Shakespeare's play powerfully shaped her imagination. In 1852, she had written the first half of *The Pearl of Orr's Island* (1862), a semiautobiographical novel about a Miranda-like New England girl. In *Dred*, she drew on *The Tempest* again in one of the earliest American uses of Caliban as a figure for the rebel slave. Convinced that he has inherited the magical powers of an African sorcerer, that he possesses second sight and can tell the future, Dred experiences moments of religious ecstasy that relate the swamp to Prospero's magic island. In chapter nineteen, Stowe gives a detailed naturalistic description of the swamp's geography and wildlife, but it is also, she writes, a mythic region "of hopeless disorder, where the abundant growth and vegetation of nature, sucking up its forces from the human soil, seems to rejoice in a savage exuberance, and bid defiance to all human efforts either to penetrate or subdue." Populated by alligators and rattlesnakes, dense with "climbing vines and parasitic plants," its wild and vast solitudes are the breeding place of conspiracy, madness, and hallucination. Like slavery, like the evil entwined with good in the human soul, the swamp is a heart of darkness. More Melvillean than "sentimental," *Dred* shows Stowe's art at its most intense.

In creating Dred, Stowe turned the South's rhetoric against itself, making him both an evangelical preacher and a devotee of the sacred texts of American history. In Dred's mind, the Bible and the Declaration of Independence are both texts that legitimize and even demand revolutionary violence against the white oppressor. He uses the rhetoric of the prayer meeting and the courts, but from a perspective that makes it a weapon against slave owners and their families. Just as the authors of the "Declaration of Sentiments" in 1848 had interpreted the language of the Declaration of Independence in relation to men and women, Stowe adapted it to the situation of slaves and slave owners. Ironically, she pointed out, the Southern slave states themselves had taught their slaves the philosophy of revolution, by publicly broadcasting the "principles of universal equality"; indeed, "the slave has heard, amid shouts, on the Fourth of July, that his masters held the truth to be self-evident, that all men were born equal, and had an *inalienable right* to life, liberty, and the pursuit of happiness." Even more shockingly, she demonstrated that the Bible was the most incendiary text of all—"a book that has always been

prolific of insurrectionary movements, under all systems of despotism."
Even for illiterate slaves, "its language and sentiment" have filled their
imaginations with all the "passionate energy" of the "prophets against
oppression and injustice." When Harry Gordon at last runs away to join
Dred in the swamp, he explains his decision in a letter to a white friend in
the terms of these two texts: "if it were proper for your fathers to fight
and shed blood for the oppression that came upon them why isn't it right
for us?"

Stowe was not able to pursue the terrible logic of her scenario to its
bloody end. We expect a violent insurrection, but instead we get Dred's
death, and a happy ending, that most cherished convention of the domestic novel. The outcasts in the swamp escape by boat to New York, along
with Harry and some white children in the keeping of a resilient black
caretaker, Uncle Tiff. Like Margaret Fuller, or characters in *The Tempest*,
they are shipwrecked just offshore; but they are all miraculously saved.
While Stowe never explicitly repudiates Dred's call for a holy war, she
does not depict one. Instead she sends her good characters to Canada,
where they establish an enlightened, almost utopian, interracial colony.
In Joan Hedrick's view, "neither evolutionary reform nor slave rebellion
appeared a feasible solution to Stowe, and the failure of her plot reflected
a failure of her political imagination."[21]

Dred was not a publishing phenomenon like *Uncle Tom's Cabin*, but it
was a best seller and a critical success. Reviewing the novel anonymously
in the *Westminster Review* in October 1856, Marian Evans—not yet the
novelist "George Eliot"—called it "a novel inspired by a rare genius—
rare both in intensity and in range of power." Comparing Stowe's management of character to Scott's, she placed the author of *Uncle Tom's
Cabin* and *Dred* in the "highest rank of novelists who can give us a
national life in all its phases—popular and aristocratic, humorous and
tragic, political and religious."[22]

The Minister's Wooing

Stowe's third novel of the 1850s, *The Minister's Wooing* (1859), departed
from the questions of slavery and took up New England Calvinism and
its harsh responses to death and grieving. Set in Newport, Rhode Island,
at the end of the eighteenth century, the novel presents a powerful critique of Calvinist orthodoxy, rooted in terms of sexual difference:

"Where theorists and philosophers tread with sublime assurance, woman often follows with bleeding footsteps;—women are always turning from the abstract to the individual, and feeling where the philosopher only thinks," Stowe's narrator writes in chapter two. The bereaved women in the novel get scant solace from the preaching doctrinal clergy, but the black cook Candace consoles them with her passionate account of a loving and forgiving Christ.

Stowe also gave a vivid and often very funny portrait of women's domestic life. The omniscient, unnamed narrator of the novel, who occasionally mentions in chapter one that she has discovered the story in old letters, indicates her immersion in mid-nineteenth-century American women's culture by the patchwork metaphors she uses for the writing process. "When one has a story to tell, one is always puzzled which end of it to begin with. You have a whole corps of people to introduce that you know, and your reader doesn't; and one thing so presupposes another, that whichever way you turn your patchwork, the figures still seem ill-arranged." One major scene of the novel takes place in chapter thirty at a quilting bee, an activity compared to the aims of the realist novelist in dealing with quotidian detail: "Those pretty bits, which, little in themselves, were destined, by gradual unions and accretions, to bring about at last substantial beauty, warmth, and comfort,—emblems thus of that household life which is to be brought to stability and beauty by reverent economy in husbanding, and tact in arranging the little morsels of daily existence." The quilting party is not only the basis of sisterly bonding but also political organization: "One might have learned in that instructive assembly how best to keep moths out of blankets . . . how to bring up babies by hand . . . and how to put down the democratic party."

The Minister's Wooing is Stowe's most self-reflective book in terms of women's artistic experiences and traditions. The village dressmaker, Miss Prissy Diamond, is another writer-surrogate who revels in the challenges of design, including "turning, twisting, piecing, contriving," and in the communication of gossip and stories. As the narrator observes in Miss Prissy's defense, anyone in a small town immune to such curiosity is "a cold, fat oyster, to whom the mud-tide of propriety is the whole of existence." The novel also connects to the British reform tradition of Gaskell and Eliot. The romantic heroine, Mary Scudder, is an ardent young woman, a New England village St. Teresa who prefigures George Eliot's Dorothea Brooke: "The elixir of the spirit that sparkled within her was of that quality of which the souls of poets and artists are made;

but the keen New England air crystallizes emotions and ideas, and re-
stricts many a poetic soul to the necessity of expressing itself only in practical living."

Indeed, many of the narrator's comments in *The Minister's Wooing*
resemble the voice George Eliot was beginning to make her own in
Adam Bede. Stowe's narrator is a wise, compassionate, realistic observer
of everyday life and its tragedies. "So we go,—" she writes at the end of
chapter four, "so little knowing what we touch and what touches us as
we talk! We drop out a common piece of news,—'Mr. So-and-so is
dead,—Miss Such-a-one is married—such a ship has sailed,'—and so, on
our right or our left, some heart has sunk under the news silently,—gone
down in the great ocean of Fate, without even a bubble rising to tell its
drowning pang. And this—God help us!—is what we call living!"23
Although they never met, Stowe and Eliot corresponded and exchanged
ideas about the art of fiction. "Did you ever think of the rhythmical
power of prose," Stowe confided to Eliot, "how every writer when they
get warm fall into a certain swing and rhythm peculiar to themselves the
words all having their place and sentences their cadences."24 In the midst
of social protest and national crisis, Stowe was also leading the way
toward considerations of style in fiction that most critics assume to have
developed much later.

A White Dred—John Brown and Harpers Ferry

In October 1859, another great and divisive political event further exacerbated the antagonism between North and South. Funded by a group
known as the Secret Six, which included Thomas Higginson and Samuel
Gridley Howe, John Brown led twenty-one men on a raid on the government armory at Harpers Ferry in Virginia, with the plan of stealing guns
and creating an armed uprising among slaves. Although Brown's men
took the undefended armory without difficulty, they were quickly block-
aded within by local farmers and militiamen; by the morning of October 18, the building was surrounded by a company of U.S. Marines
commanded by Jeb Stuart and Robert E. Lee. Brown was given the
chance to surrender but he refused, and the Marines stormed the building, wounding him and taking him prisoner. In November, he was tried,
convicted, and sentenced to death by hanging.

While Southerners saw Brown as a deranged and dangerous terrorist, many Northern abolitionists viewed him as a heroic martyr. Because her husband was one of the Secret Six, Julia Ward Howe was closely involved in the turmoil; she was seven months pregnant with her sixth child when Chev fled to Canada to avoid prosecution, returning after Brown's execution. She admired Brown's courage: "The attempt I must judge insane but the spirit heroic."[25] Thoreau spoke out for Brown at a public meeting in Concord; Emerson declared that John Brown "will make the gallows glorious as the Cross." Lydia Maria Child was obsessed by the case; she wrote to the condemned man and conducted a passionate correspondence about slavery and violence with Governor Henry Alexander Wise of Virginia.

On December 2, the day of his public execution, Brown handed his final message to a prison guard: "I, John Brown, am now quite certain that the crimes of this guilty land will never be purged away but with blood. I had, as I now think, vainly flattered myself that without very much bloodshed it might be done." The drama of Brown's self-sacrifice fueled both the religious fervor of the North and the militarism of the South.[26] To black intellectuals, antislavery lecturers, and teachers, Brown was a Christlike figure. Frances Watkins Harper (1825–1911) wrote to Brown in prison, stayed with his wife for two weeks before his execution, and made him the subject of her early forays into fiction. Harper was a free black woman raised in Baltimore by an aunt and an evangelistic Methodist uncle who directed a well-known school, the William Watkins Academy for Negro Youth. She had studied there until the age of thirteen, and began early to write poems and essays. After 1850, however, her life in Baltimore was threatened by the hostile environment of the Fugitive Slave Act, and she left to become a teacher, first in Ohio and then in Philadelphia, where she began to publish in the abolitionist press. Three of her poems were written in response to *Uncle Tom's Cabin,* and "To Mrs. Harriet Beecher Stowe" thanked the author herself:

> *For the sisters of our race*
> *Thou'st nobly done thy part*
> *Thou hast won thyself a place*
> *In every human heart.*[27]

Harper was drawn to the themes of division and alternative choices in the lives of black women. Her short story "The Two Offers," in *The Anglo-African* (1859), the first by an African-American writer, contrasted the decisions of two cousins, Laura and Janette, about whether to marry simply for the sake of avoiding spinsterhood, or to dedicate themselves to a higher purpose. In her best-known work, *Iola Leroy* (1890), she would return to the problem of love and work for black women in white society. But her story "The Triumph of Freedom: A Dream" (1860) was a passionate and graphic allegory of the defeat of the "blood-stained goddess" Slavery, using some of the language from her letter to Brown in November 1859. Brown, "an aged man" of "solemn radiance," is condemned to death by the goddess and her minions, but "from the prison came forth a cry of victory; from the gallows a shout of triumph . . . His blood was a new baptism of Liberty."[28]

Black Writers and the Development of Women's Fiction

Frances Harper was only one among the African-American women who began to publish in the late 1850s. Stowe's influence and John Brown's death were stimulants to the emergence of a literature by black women that drew upon the conventions of the slave narrative, but also upon sentimental, domestic, feminist, and gothic fiction. What is most important is that in the 1850s black women writers, both former slaves and freewomen, began for the first time to speak in their own voices about slavery and race in a way that even a deeply sympathetic white writer like Stowe could not equal. Moreover, they began to write about their lives as women and Americans.

Some of these books and stories were published at the time and widely discussed; some were published but ignored; some were never published and were only discovered in the late twentieth century. Virtually all of them have raised problems of authorial identification.[29] Were they written by ex-slaves, free black women, white women, or white men, and were the authors even Americans? Critics have also found it difficult to categorize them in terms of genre: Are they thinly disguised autobiography, partly fictionalized memoirs, or completely fictional novels? Are they combinations of the domestic novel and the slave narrative, or are they entirely new forms? As scholars have discovered more about the lives and circumstances of African-American women in the nineteenth century, many of the mysteries behind these works have been solved, and we can be hopeful that those remaining will be deciphered as well. What we do know about their composition suggests that they were very closely interwoven into the fabric of American women's writing in the 1850s in terms of their literary influences, networks of production, narrative concerns, and even publishing communities. As a group, they raise important questions for women writers at mid-century about the treatment of female sexuality, the racism of the North, and the possibilities through writing for self-disguise, impersonation, and adaptation of classic texts.

INCIDENTS IN THE LIFE OF A SLAVE GIRL—HARRIET JACOBS

Incidents in the Life of a Slave Girl, Written by Herself was published in Boston in 1861, attributed to the narrator "Linda Brent," and "edited" by Lydia Maria Child. In a preface, Linda Brent insisted that her sensational story was true: "Reader, be assured this narrative is no fiction. I am aware that some of my adventures may seem incredible; but they are, nevertheless, strictly true." Brent explained that she had been "born and reared in Slavery" and "remained in a Slave State twenty-seven years." In the North, she had worked to support her children, but she had been moved to write in order to "arouse the women of the North to a realizing sense of the condition of two millions of women at the South, still in bondage, suffering what I suffered." Child attested to the authenticity of the work: "The author of the following autobiography is personally known to me, and her conversation and manners inspire me with confidence." Although she had "revised the manuscript," she promised that she had changed very little of Linda Brent's text: "with trifling exceptions, both the ideas and the language are her own."

Child was a celebrated abolitionist writer at this time; her brilliantly polemical correspondence with Governor Wise and Margaretta Mason, the wife of the Virginia senator who had fathered the Fugitive Slave Act, had been published by the Anti-Slavery Society. Her fame and Harriet Jacobs's obscurity and disguise under a pseudonym affected the history of the book. For over a century, scholars of African-American literature questioned its genuineness as the composition of a black woman, and as a truthful autobiography. They agreed that Lydia Maria Child was the real author, and that the book was "too melodramatic" and sentimental to be a credible slave narrative.[30] Of course, these conclusions were based on comparison with male models. Not until 1971, when American women's writing was being rediscovered by feminist critics, did Jean Fagan Yellin set out to solve the mystery. She quickly located letters at the University of Rochester from Jacobs to a Quaker abolitionist, Amy

Post, which proved conclusively that Jacobs had written the book. Then she spent fifteen years tracing the details of Jacobs's life, to show that the book was based on facts.[31]

Yellin's research established that Harriet Jacobs had been born a slave near Edenton, North Carolina, about 1815. An orphan, she was taught to read and write, but then sold at fifteen to a married man who demanded that she become his mistress. She chose instead to give herself sexually to an unmarried white lawyer in the town, to whom she bore two children. When her owner's sexual demands became threatening, she ran away, and hid for seven years in the crawl space of the attic of her grandmother, a freed slave, who also took in her children. In 1842, she escaped to the North, reconnected with her children, and worked as a nursemaid in New York for the family of Nathaniel Willis, the brother of Fanny Fern. For a year she lived in Rochester, New York, with her brother John, a fugitive slave who had become a leader in the abolitionist movement. Back in New York City in 1850, she and her children were formally bought and manumitted by the Willises, who continued to employ her to care for their children; and, with the encouragement of Quaker friends in Rochester, she began to think about writing her memoir as a way of awakening public opinion. As she would write in her preface, "I want to add my testimony to that of abler pens to convince the people of the Free States what slavery really is."

Initially Jacobs hoped that Harriet Beecher Stowe would write the book from her dictation. In 1853, when she heard that Stowe was going to England, she asked Mrs. Willis to write to Stowe proposing that she take Jacobs's daughter Louisa on the trip as "a very good representative of a Southern Slave." Stowe's response doubly offended Jacobs; she declined to escort Louisa, and asked to use Jacobs's narrative in her own compilation of documents, *Key to Uncle Tom's Cabin.* As Joan Hedrick comments, "Wedded to the notion that she 'spoke for the oppressed, who cannot speak for themselves,' [Stowe] tried in this instance to appropriate the story of a former slave who could—and eventually did—speak for herself."[32]

Jacobs began to prepare herself to tackle the memoir by writing letters and short pieces for the newspapers, and also sought help with the mechanics of her writing from Amy Post and Louisa, who had been trained as a teacher. In 1860, with a completed manuscript, she approached Child with a request for an introduction to help the book's publication, and Child spent a month in the summer of 1860 working on it. She recommended that Jacobs cut superfluous words; put descriptions of the worst abuses into one chapter, "Neighboring Planters"; expand the discussion of the Nat Turner rebellion; and cut the final chapter on John Brown. "It does not come naturally to your story and the M.S. is already too long," she explained to Jacobs. Overall, Child found the manuscript "wonderfully good, for one whose opportunities for education have been so limited. The events are interesting and well told." Her suggestions were intended to clarify the chronology and render the "story much more clear and entertaining."[33] With her assistance, Jacobs found a publisher in the fall of 1860, but in its own day, the book received scant attention; probably tensions about the imminent war were a distraction.

Incidents is a first-person narrative that closely followed the real history of Jacobs's life. It ended with an allusion to the conventions of romantic fiction, especially *Jane Eyre,* but with a twist. "Reader," Jacobs wrote, "my story ends with freedom, not in the usual way, with marriage." Its greatest importance for American women's writing was its relatively candid treatment of female sexuality. In five chapters, Jacobs openly discussed the sexual vulnerability of female slaves to their owners, and her own decision to become the mistress of "Mr. Sands," another white man in the community. "It seems less degrading," she wrote, "to give one's self, than to submit to compulsion. There is something akin to freedom in having a lover who has no control over you, except that which he gains by kindness and attachment." Although she then repressed details of her liaison, sexual and emotional, with Sands, in these guarded admissions of her consent to the relationship, Jacobs opened the door for other women to speak about their sexual choices.

OUR NIG—HARRIET WILSON

Like *Life of a Slave Girl,* Harriet E. Wilson's *Our Nig; or, Sketches from the Life of a Free Black, in a Two-Story White House* (1859) went unreviewed at its original publication, and had virtually disappeared in the twentieth century, when it was believed to be a novel rather than an autobiography. Henry Louis Gates, Jr., who edited a republication of the book in 1981, introduced it as a black sentimental novel, which used the conventions of the "woman's novel" and the slave narrative to create a new genre of black women's fiction. In her preface, Wilson offered the standard apology for publication: "Deserted by kindred, disabled by failing health, I am forced to some experiment. My humble position and frank confession of errors will, I hope, shield me from severe criticism." In appendices to the book, three people, signing themselves "Allida," "Margaretta Thorn," and "C.D.W." testified to the authenticity of the story.

Gates nonetheless found it difficult to believe that Wilson's story was entirely autobiographical, because it was so different from other stories by black writers in its setting and unhappy ending. The book is narrated in the third person, and describes the mistreatment and eventual rebellion of Frado, a mulatto girl indentured to the Bellmont family, who treat her cruelly. Frado is the child of an alcoholic white mother and a black free man, and her narrative ends when she marries a professed fugitive slave who turns out to be a fraud and leaves her with a son. Gates praised the work as "a 'missing link'. . . between the sustained and well-developed tradition of black autobiography, and the slow emergence of a distinctive black voice in fiction."[34] In its second incarnation as fiction, *Our Nig* was warmly received as part of the "black women's literary revival" of the 1980s, and became "an important text in American, women's, and African American letters."[35] Alice Walker, herself a leading figure in the revival, hailed it as highly significant: "It is as if we've just discovered Phillis Wheatley—or Langston Hughes."[36]

In 1993, Barbara A. White discovered evidence that *Our Nig* was a fictionalized true story, and, most shockingly, that the white New England family who treated Wilson so harshly were prominent abolitionists. Indeed, Wilson's wish to expose the hypocrisy of these antislavery activists was a more important motive for her book than she acknowledged.[37] Subsequent research has filled in the details about Harriet Wilson's life and identified the originals of the characters and events in the book.[38] Wilson's multiple stories, of racism, intermarriage, and female hardship, opposed the lingering romanticism of even Stowe's writing about black women, especially in her mixture of religious piety and blunt language, including the use of the terms "nigger" and "nig."

THE BONDWOMAN'S NARRATIVE—"BLACK HOUSE"

The third of the books about black women written in the 1850s is the most controversial and the most astonishing. Purchased in manuscript form at an auction in 2001 by Henry Louis Gates, Jr., and first published in 2002, *The Bondwoman's Narrative* by "Hannah Crafts" was presented with much fanfare as the autobiographical narrative of a fugitive woman slave, and hailed as "a wonderful, really spectacular discovery," and "a milestone in African American and women's studies." The manuscript was authenticated as dating from the period 1853 to 1861. However, its authorship is still unresolved, and in the short time since its discovery, many questions have been raised about the identity, gender, and even nationality, of "Hannah Crafts."

Bondwoman is a work of high imagination and literary sophistication, gothic rather than sentimental, and packed with original inventions. Although it begins like other slave narratives with an apologetic preface, it is a stunning advance in literary techniques for the period, making use of sophisticated, even postmodern, experiments in narrative adaptation. First of all, the plot is only incidentally about slavery. The opening part of the novel, told by Hannah, is about her adolescent years at the "ancient mansion of Lindendale," the ancestral home of the De Vincents in Virginia, which is haunted by the ghost of a slave gibbeted on a linden tree. Before dying, she has cursed the house and the line of the Vincents, warning that when sickness, misfortune, or death is approaching, the linden tree will creak and moan. Indeed, much creaking is to come in this gothic plot. A new bride arrives at Lindendale, and Hannah becomes her personal maid. But a sinister slave trader, Mr. Trappe, blackmails Mrs. Vincent with the information that her mother was actually a slave from Georgia. Hannah and Mrs. Vincent run away together, but are eventually captured, and Mrs. Vincent bursts a blood vessel and dies. We later learn that the linden tree has been cut down and the curse is ended.

The second half of the novel focuses on Hannah herself; she moves from one owner to another without suffering any serious hardship, and then is placed with the Wheeler family in Washington, D.C. Mrs. Wheeler is cruel but also comical; in one chapter, she manages to turn her face black with a cosmetic ointment, and the family return in humiliation to their plantation in North Carolina. She becomes convinced that Hannah has been gossiping about her with the other slaves, and orders the refined young woman to leave the house, work in the fields, and marry Bill, one of the black field laborers whom Hannah regards as "vile, foul, filthy" and brutalized. Disguised as a man, Hannah immediately runs away to Virginia and takes refuge with the kindly white couple who had taught her to read as a child. With their help, she escapes to New Jersey, is reunited with her mother, and marries a freeman who is a Methodist preacher.

Crafts's diction is formal and decorous. The black characters are always called "Negroes," the slave trader Trappe calls Mrs. Vincent "madam." Hannah herself is educated, pious, ladylike, and disdainful of the ordinary run of slaves who speak in dialect, while she speaks an elegant English; when she mingles with them, she complains of their "highly improper and indecent language." Overall, *Bondwoman* sounds more like a British novel about a servant girl than an American novel about slavery. On the eve of its publication, moreover, *Bondwoman* was discovered by a Princeton graduate student, Hollis Robbins, to contain heavy borrowings and careful rewritings of passages from Dickens's *Bleak House* (1853), an influence so pervasive, detailed, exact, and deliberate that one critic has called the novel *Black House*.[39] Crafts closely based Hannah's first-person narrative on Esther Summerson; modeled one of the slave owners, Mrs. Cosgrove, on Lady Dedlock; took the slave tracker Mr. Trappe from Mr. Tulkinghorn; and combined and reworked fragments of description separated by up to thirty chapters in Dickens's novel. In short, *Bondwoman* was not just a hybrid, but an intermarried text, as Robbins suggests when she asks how we should read the novel: Is it "a British text, a Black text, a Bleak text, or an amalgamation thereof?"[40]

Americanist scholars outside the United States have been much more skeptical about the provenance and authorship of *The Bondwoman's Narrative* than American literary critics and historians. They have pointed out that the book has cliff-hangers approximately every two chapters, suggesting that it might have been designed for and perhaps published as a magazine serial. They have noted many elements in the novel that point to Hannah's being a servant rather than slave, and perhaps a British or Irish one. They have also seen parallels to books by white abolitionists that masqueraded as slave narratives. "Why has nobody suggested the author might be white?" two British scholars have inquired. "It is as if, in contemporary America, sensitized to any form of racial slur, this was literally unthinkable, comparable to the doubts poured upon nineteenth-century slave narratives by Southern pro-slavers."[41]

In the United States, to be sure, scholars have made intellectual, professional, political, and commercial investments in rediscovering early work by black women writers. Such texts are valuable and rare. Hannah Crafts's identity ought to be pursued and established, not only because she may have been an ex-slave, or a free black woman—although either discovery would be momentous—but also because her craft adds immeasurably to the American literary canon.

7

The Civil War

Two Armies

he Civil War began with shots fired by Southern troops at Fort Sumter, South Carolina, on April 12, 1861, and ended with Lee's surrender at Appomattox, Virginia, on April 9, 1865, but its literary reverberations are still heard today, and women's role in that literature is still being underestimated. As Henry Timrod, the "laureate of the Confederacy," wrote in "Two Armies," the War Between the States was fought on Southern ground by men and women with very different roles and expectations:

> Two armies stand enrolled beneath
> The banner with the starry wreath;
> One, facing battle, blight and blast,
> Through twice a hundred fields has passed . . .
>
> The other, with a narrower scope,
> Yet led by not less grand a hope,
> Hath won, perhaps, as proud a place,
> And wears its fame with meeker grace.

In the North, another writer saluted the "feeling and heroism" of Northern woman, who cheered the trains with their "freight of living valor," and then stood alone with "a tired child asleep upon her shoulder." When the war was over, the writer predicted, "the page shall reflect the working of that woman's face," even though her name would be "concealed with moss upon her forgotten head-stone." Women's sublime stoicism would inspire the American literature of the future, but "men of talent" would write it.[1]

American literary historians have traditionally maintained that the

Civil War years themselves did not produce a literary masterpiece.[2] Although it was a modern war that presaged the conditions of World War I—a technological war, fought mainly by the young, with a terrible death toll (360,000 in the North, 260,000 in the South), and the first documented cases of post-traumatic stress syndrome—the Civil War did not produce a generation of trench poets. Walt Whitman served as a nurse, but no important male writers were directly involved in combat. Some were too old; others left the country; still others paid poorer men to take up their commissions; and Henry James was judged unfit for service because of an "obscure hurt." By the end of the war, Hawthorne and Thoreau were dead, Melville had turned to writing poetry, Emerson was silent, and Mark Twain was in the West.

Moreover, the publishing industry underwent profound change. In the North, many writers and publishers initially thought that the war would mean a depression in the book industry.[3] By the summer of 1861, the Boston publishers Ticknor and Fields had drastically cut back their list of new books. "Nothing alive but the military," Longfellow lamented. "Bookselling dead." Hawthorne predicted that "the book-trade, and everything connected with it, is bound to fall below zero, before this war, and the subsequent embarrassments, come to an end."[4] Book reviewers, too, saw the audience for fiction disappearing: "It certainly requires considerable stoicism," wrote the literary editor of *The New York Times* in 1862, "to sit down to a tale of imaginary woes and sorrows while one great wail is going up from the sick and wounded in the swamps and trenches before Richmond."[5] Some established writers who could adapt to the new circumstances shifted to military subjects; others put their careers on hold; still others were forced to enter the popular literary market for the first time, providing humor, romance, and children's literature for the illustrated weeklies.

The war changed people's reading habits on both sides of the Mason-Dixon line. First, newspapers and bulletin boards outside newspaper offices took priority over books, and almost-hourly news bulletins became part of people's daily routine. In South Carolina, Mary Chesnut wrote, "we haunt the bulletin board"; in Boston, Oliver Wendell Holmes described the urgency of getting the news: "if we must go out at unusual hours to get it, we shall go, in spite of after-dinner nap or evening somnolence."[6] Second, readers' appetites for serious literature declined and their appetite for escapist fiction, military treatises, and biographies increased. In the South, which had very little independent publishing of its own, William Gilmore Simms said that "people here breathe nothing but war, and read none but military books now."[7]

Even Harriet Beecher Stowe, "the little woman who wrote the book that started this great war," as President Lincoln called her, wrote very little directly about it. In April 1861, she was working on two novels: *The Pearl of Orr's Island,* which was being serialized in the *Independent,* and *Agnes of Sorrento,* a novel about the Italian Renaissance, which was set to appear in *Cornhill,* the English journal that had also purchased George Eliot's Italian novel, *Romola.* While she remained engaged in abolitionist protest, visiting President Lincoln in Washington and celebrating the ex-slave orator Sojourner Truth as the "Libyan Sibyl," Stowe's distress over her son Fred, wounded at Gettysburg, may have kept her from writing directly about combat.[8] Harriet Jacobs went to Washington to nurse black troops.

Yet many American women did write during the 1860s, and indeed the Civil War created a crisis in gender, turning the world upside down for the sexes as well as for the races. Even before the fighting broke out, women writers (for example, Elizabeth Stuart Phelps) had used "civil war" as "a metaphor to express internal rebellions, conflicts, and fractures."[9] Mary Terhune had lamented that although men fought their battles openly and with companions, "Woman finds her warfare within."[10] In the 1860s, women writers on both sides of the conflict explored the political and the psychological effects of the war, focusing on themes of sacrifice, power, independence, and attraction to the forbidden and illicit. For them, the war marked a shift from sentimentalism to realism and often a shift from the domestic topics of poetry and fiction to a more wide-ranging analysis of society, gender, and public issues.

Initially, women made use of the masculine literary rhetoric of the war, which was heightened and heroic. In 1861, the New York poet and editor Edmund C. Stedman wrote to his mother that while he had always had contempt for politics, he now felt that "the Homeric grandeur of the contest surrounds and elevates us all."[11] Women writers in both the North and the South also imagined epic roles for women, looking to classical, biblical, and fictional legends of female sacrifice and valor. "We are leading the lives which women have led since Troy fell," wrote a woman from Louisiana.[12] Southern newspapers editorialized about women's ennobling contributions, called for self-denial, sacrifice, and service, those triple pillars of the feminine ideal. Poets and song-writers, male and female, urged women to encourage their menfolk to enlist. In "A Loyal Woman's No," Lucy Larcom tauntingly declared her refusal to marry a man who does not fight for the Union:

> *Not yours,—because you are not man enough*
> *To grasp your country's measure of a man.*
> *If such as you, when Freedom's ways are rough,*
> *Cannot walk in them, learn that women can!*

Meanwhile, in a popular song in Georgia, a belle insists that she will only marry a man who is

> *A veteran from the wars,*
> *One who has fought for "Southern Rights"*
> *Beneath the Bars and Stars.*[13]

Warfare redistributed some of men's traditional power to women, and brought women's conflicts over their roles to the surface, as conventional rules of feminine decorum were suspended, and women on the home front took over many of the jobs men left behind them, or became teachers and military nurses. Southern women were called upon to play a significant role in the war effort, including taking over the management of their households, farms, and plantations.

Few women were satisfied with such symbolic roles. Four hundred women actually disguised themselves as men and enlisted in the Union or Confederate armies. The great majority who stayed behind were frustrated by their uselessness and inactivity. Many women poets lamented their impotence in the struggle. In "The Will for the Deed," Caroline A. Mason wrote,

> *No sword have I, no battle-blade,*
> *Nor shining spear; how shall I aid*
> *My Country in her great Crusade?*[14]

And a Southern woman, Julia LeGrand, felt "like a pent-up volcano. I wish I had a field for my energies." In both North and South, they began to protest, at least privately, against the feminine constraints that kept them paralyzed. "How I wish I was a man!" wrote Emma Walton in New Orleans.[15] In Massachusetts at the same time, Louisa May Alcott declared, "I long to be a man; but as I can't fight, I will content myself with working for those who can."[16]

Mrs. Southworth supported the Union and thought "it was a great pity that an army of women had not been added to our army in the war." Annie Fields thought Southworth was being ridiculous: " 'But what department would you assign to them?' somebody asked. 'Oh, the cavalry *of course,* they should have worn a uniform of orange and black bloomer dresses which would have produced a fine effect.'—As some one said it would have been frightful enough to have driven the rebs into the Mexican Gulf for very horror."[17] In Southworth's Civil War novel *How He Won Her* (1866), the Yankee heroine, Britomarte, disguises herself as a soldier and follows her lover Justin into twenty battles, while the Southern heroine Elfie makes a less successful effort to enlist.[18] In Augusta Jane Evans's *Macaria,* a young Southern woman runs the naval blockade in order to smuggle dispatches to the Confederate army in Alabama.

Battle Hymns and Anthems

Writing rather than fighting was an honorable outlet for loyalist women. The war years saw an outpouring of poetry; indeed, so many people in the Confederacy wrote terrible patriotic verse that the beleaguered *Southern Illustrated News* had to call a halt to the flood of submissions from the "rebel muse."[19] Southerners were looking for inspiring new national anthems, which, Henry Timrod believed, "must run glibly on the tongue," contain a sentiment appealing to "some favorite pride, prejudice, or passion of the people," and be "married to an effective but not complicated air."[20] But no anthem captured the public imagination.

In the North, however, Julia Ward Howe's "Battle Hymn of the Republic" combined mood, timing, and a stirring and familiar tune to speak eloquently for the Union cause. Howe, too, had felt frustrated by her inability to contribute to the war effort. In November 1861, she and her husband were invited to Washington to advise the Sanitary Commission, which was setting up military hospitals. Howe recalled her

> *feeling of discouragement . . . I thought of the women of my acquaintance whose sons or husbands were fighting our great battle; the women themselves serving in the hospitals, or busying themselves with the work of the Sanitary Commission . . . I could not leave my nursery to follow the march of our armies, neither had I the practical deftness which the preparing and packing of sanitary stores demanded. Some-*

thing seemed to say to me, "You would be glad to serve, but you cannot help anyone; you have nothing to give, and there is nothing for you to do."[21]

Howe made the pen her sword, blade, and spear. On November 18, the Howes visited a Union army camp across the Potomac, which came under a surprise Southern attack. As they were slowly returning to the city on the road jammed with soldiers, they joined in the troops' singing of the popular ballad "John Brown's body lies a-moldering in the grave; His soul is marching on." Their friend the minister James Freeman Clarke suggested that Howe should set better words to the melody. She woke up in her Washington hotel at dawn the next morning with the poem clearly in her mind, and wrote it down in the dark, so as not to disturb the baby:

> *Having thought out all the stanzas, I said to myself, "I must get up and write these verses down, lest I fall asleep again and forget them." So, with a sudden effort, I sprang out of bed, and found in the dimness an old stump of a pen . . . I scrawled the verses almost without looking at the paper. I had learned to do this when, on previous occasions, attacks of versification had visited me during the night, and I feared to have recourse to a light lest I should wake the baby, who slept near me. I was always obliged to decipher my scrawl before another night should intervene, as it was only legible while the matter was fresh in my mind. At this time, having completed the writing, I returned to bed and fell asleep, saying to myself, "I like this better than most things I have written."*[22]

The bellicose hymn, with its appeal to a God of wrath who has "loosed the fateful lightning/of His terrible swift sword," was also an expression of the rage Howe had stifled in her marriage, and the rapidity of its composition came partly from her long-repressed and unused anger. Published anonymously in the *Atlantic Monthly* in February 1862, the "Battle Hymn," with its biblical imagery from the books of Isaiah and Revelation, spoke directly to the religious fervor of the Union's apocalyptic mission. To the armies of the North, the Civil War was indeed a holy war, and Howe's anthem captured its spirit, preaching vengeance and divine retribution.

Before the War—Rebecca Harding Davis

Almost up to the last minute, many writers did not expect that the North and South would actually come to armed combat. Having grown up in West Virginia, which was then still part of Virginia, Rebecca Harding Davis (1831–1910) remembered "the uncomprehending horror of the bulk of the American people" after the attack on Fort Sumter. "Politicians or far-sighted leaders on both sides knew what was coming . . . But to the easy-going millions, busied with their farms or shops, the onrushing disaster was as inexplicable as an earthquake."[23] Over her fifty-year career, Davis would publish twelve novels, and hundreds of stories and essays, many about the Civil War, slavery, and race.[24] But her first, best, and best-known story, "Life in the Iron Mills," which appeared in the *Atlantic Monthly* in April 1861, just as the war began, was about Welsh miners and the sufferings of the laboring poor.

One reason for the story's impact is that Davis, like "Hannah Crafts," chose Dickens's *Bleak House* for her model. She imitated Dickens's techniques and even borrowed some of his language in describing the symbolic slums, fog, and mud of an industrial city: "The idiosyncrasy of this town is smoke. It rolls sullenly in slow folds from the great chimneys of the iron-foundries, and settles down in black, slimy pools on the muddy streets. Smoke on the wharves, smoke on the dingy boats, on the yellow river—clinging in a coat of greasy soot to the house-front, the two faded poplars, the faces of the passers-by." As Dickens demanded that his educated readers attend to the tragedies of the poor, the homeless, and the orphaned masses of the London slums, Davis's narrator calls for the reader's attention: "Stop a moment. I am going to be honest. This is what I want you to do. I want you to hide your disgust, take no heed to your clean clothes, and come right down with me,—here, into the thickest of the fog and mud and foul effluvia. I want you to hear this story." In her descriptions of the dark and swarming basements where ragged workers huddle, Davis takes her readers down into the depths of urban life, echoing Dickens's descriptions of the London slum Tom-all-Alone's.

The narrator tells a tale of thirty years earlier, one of the myriads of forgotten stories of the furnace hands, which she chooses because it has some "secret underlying sympathy" with the "impure fog" and "thwarted sunshine," and because her house used to be the lodging place of the Wolfe family, Cornish miners who had become ironworkers in the mills. Hugh Wolfe was a young furnace worker with artistic dreams. From the korl, or refuse of the iron-smelting process, he sculpted a rough figure of a woman: "There was not one line of beauty or grace in it: a nude woman's form, muscular, grown coarse with labor, the powerful limbs instinct with some one poignant longing." The longing, Wolfe stumblingly explains to the professional men who come to visit the mill, is hunger for "summat to make her live." At the end of the story, we learn that the narrator has the statue in her study, as an emblem of that spiritual starvation. Wolfe's destiny is to be a Christ figure of the slums, falsely arrested and imprisoned for theft, and a martyr whose suicide represents the callous destruction of the human spirit by industrialization, but also its hopes for redemption.

Davis was determined to write about the lives of men as well as women, and to write from a masculine point of view. For some of her contemporaries, this androgynous capacity was an asset; Elizabeth Stuart Phelps wrote that "her intensity was essentially feminine, but her grip was like that of a masculine hand."[25] Modern feminist critics, however, have seen her decision to make the frustrated artist a man as a withdrawal from what Judith Fetterley calls the "ratification of women as serious subjects." In Fetterley's view, some of Davis's "stylistic difficulties" in the story, "the occasionally heavy, even clumsy quality of her prose, the sense it conveys of repression more than expression, derive from a discomfort with her subject matter, a conviction that the lives of men, even working-class men, do not constitute an appropriate subject for a woman writer."[26] Such socially sanctioned discomfort, I would argue, was one of the obstacles confronting women writers who wanted access to all human experience. Davis was among the women writers of the 1860s who broke out of the confines and constraints of the female perspective, and dared to take on a masculine persona.

In many respects, Davis would have been the ideal author of a distinguished Civil War novel.[27] She had the requisite familiarity with both North and South, the appreciation of language and prophecy, the dual perspective of an insider and an outsider, the willingness to deal with both masculine and feminine experience. But some unknown combination of events prevented her from applying these tough insights in her fiction of the 1860s. Her stories from the decade—fourteen for the *Atlantic* alone—touched on the war but were tepid and conventional. Scholars have speculated that Davis may have compromised her literary vision because she was pressured by her editors to create happy endings, constrained by her marriage, and exhausted and inhibited by her responsibilities as a mother. In 1863, she had married Lemuel Clarke Davis, a young abolitionist lawyer, and moved to Philadelphia, where they lived with his sister and her family. Just before the marriage she had written to Annie Fields that she planned to keep on writing: "I must have leave to say my word in the *Atlantic* as before, when the Spirit moves me. It is necessary for me to write—well or ill—you know every animal has speech and that is mine."[28] Soon after her marriage she suffered a serious depression for which she was treated by the neurologist Silas Weir Mitchell with the "rest cure" he had developed for traumatized and hysterical Civil War soldiers. He forbade "the least reading or writing for fear of bringing back the trouble in my head."[29] In April 1864, she gave birth to the first of her three children, Richard Harding Davis.

Davis's "Civil War novel," *Waiting for the Verdict* (1867), was intended to confront Northern prejudices about intermarriage, but it is laden with mixed messages about three couples whose lives are connected. One hero, John Broderip, is a light-skinned mulatto who is raised by a Philadelphia Quaker and becomes a noted surgeon. When the war begins, he tells his fiancée Margaret Conrad the truth about his parentage, and she, viscerally repelled by the idea of black blood, marries another man, while Broderip goes off to war and dies a martyr's death at Andersonville. Davis has her black characters insist that they have no interest in "mixin' de blood," and covertly reinforces the sense that intermarriage was a crime against nature. Charlotte Forten Grimke wrote very critically of the novel in a letter to the *National Anti-Slavery Standard,* pointing out Davis's obsessive interest in "blood" and bloodlines, whether dogs, horses, or men.[30] Henry James was even more harsh. In *The Nation,* he ridiculed the book: "She drenches the whole field beforehand with a flood of lachrymose sentimentalism, and riots in the murky vapors which rise in consequence of the act."[31] Stowe wrote supportively to Davis: "*The Nation* has no sympathy with any deep and high moral movement—no pity for human infirmity."[32] Ultimately, however, the verdict is in that Davis could not sustain the prophetic power of her early work.

Louisa May Alcott's Civil War

In 1862, Rebecca Harding visited Boston to meet her editor, James Fields, and his wife, Annie, with whom she had begun what was to be a long friendship. She liked the city, but had little sympathy with the war fever of the "Atlantic coterie," who spoke of the war with "the same strained note of high exaltation." She was particularly annoyed by Bronson Alcott and his high-minded bloviating about patriotic battle. An eccentric visionary, Bronson was known for his innocence and improvidence even among the unworldly Transcendentalists, and had taught his four daughters to believe in his sacred trinity of vegetarianism, abolitionism, and the martyrdom of John Brown. Brown's widow and her daughters had been the honored guests of the Alcott family in Concord, and the Alcotts cheered the advent of war with romantic fervor. But in Davis's view, Bronson knew absolutely nothing about the reality of war. She had

> *just come up from the border where I had seen the actual war; the filthy spewings of it; the political jobbery in Union and Confederate camps; the malignant personal hatreds wearing patriotic masks, and glutted by burning homes and outraged women; the chances in it, well improved on both sides, for brutish men to grow more brutish, and for honorable gentlemen to degenerate into thieves and sots. War may be an armed angel with a mission, but she has the personal habits of the slums.*

She also took note of Louisa May Alcott, "a tall thin young woman" in a shabby red merino dress, "standing in a corner . . . [with] that watchful, defiant air with which the woman whose youth is slipping away is apt to face the world which has offered no place to her." Alcott had returned home to get her only good dress, and had traveled all day to prepare for the party: "These people may say pleasant things to you, but not one of them would have gone to Concord and back to see you, as I did to-day. I went for this gown. It's the only decent one I have. I'm very poor."[33] On her side, Alcott took note of Rebecca Harding: "A handsome, fresh, quiet woman, who says she never had any troubles, though she writes about woes. I told her I had had lots of troubles; so I write jolly tales; and we wondered why we each did so."[34]

Louisa May Alcott (1832–1888) was just about to join the war effort. She had grown up as the Alcott family's surrogate son, and had gone through many difficult years, faced with the family's poverty, the destruction of her own hopes for education and independence, the marriage of one sister and the death of another. The Civil War came as a thrilling liberation. "I've often longed to see a war, and now I have my wish," she wrote. On her thirtieth birthday, Alcott enlisted as an army nurse: "I set forth . . . feeling as if I was the son of the house going to war."[35] On December 11, 1862, she traveled to Washington, D.C., where she served at the Union Hotel Hospital, a ramshackle remodeled tavern that lacked the modern medical facilities she had expected.

Alcott's letters about her nursing experience were first printed in *The Boston Commonwealth* beginning in May 1863. As a Dickens enthusiast, she used a comic female persona, "Tribulation Periwinkle," to tell the story of the war in a colloquial American voice that mediated the gory and shocking details of an army hospital ward. It was a name and a voice that deliberately mocked her own self-importance and dedication; but Tribulation's journey from Dickensian comic spinster into serious and eloquent witness makes *Hospital Sketches* not just a war narrative but the story of a woman's passage from innocence to maturity. She sets out as "Topsy-turvy Trib," confidently mustering up her belongings to enlist. With each day, though, she is drawn deeper into the maelstrom of the war, and forced to cope with it emotionally and verbally. Arriving at the hospital, she must immediately face forty ambulances bearing the "ragged, gaunt, and pale" wounded from Fredericksburg, "some on stretchers, some in men's arms, some feebly staggering along propped on rude crutches." At first she does not have the language to describe her feelings about the contact with men's naked and wounded bodies, and with their pain and death; indeed, she becomes virtually speechless when she is told to wash them: "to scrub some dozen lords of creation at a moment's notice was really—really—"[36]

As she finds or rather creates her voice, Trib becomes an angry and articulate narrator, disillusioned by her experience and shocked by the contrast between the fabled and the real war. As in other situations when she was faced with strong and potentially sexual feelings for men, Alcott compensated by defining her emotions as maternal, and describing the soldiers as "big babies," "boys," or "sleepy children." The relationship between the powerful female nurse and the wounded male soldier becomes a metaphor for the American woman writer's ethical relationship to the country in wartime.[37] She judges the politics and the conduct of the war even if she cannot fight it. Alcott is at her best when she can vent her outrage at the mismanagement of the hospital, and her indignation at the callousness and indifference of the male surgeons. She is also sharply critical of the "spiritual paralysis" of the hospital chaplain, whose "dry explanations and literal applications" of Scripture brought no comfort to the dying men.

After only six weeks in Washington, however, Alcott contracted typhoid fever and was brought back to Concord by her father, to convalesce. She was treated with calomel, a compound containing mercury, which caused her to lose her hair; it was an emblematic castration analogous to the amputations she had witnessed at the hospital.[38] In August 1863, James Redpath published the letters as a book called *Hospital Sketches,* and Alcott added "A Postscript" that defended the "tone of levity in some portions of the Sketches," explaining that "it is a part of my religion to look well after the cheerfulnesses of life, and let the dismals shift for themselves." *Hospital Sketches* ends with a much more subdued spirit than its jaunty and patriotic beginning, but Trib's commitment to abolition is unchanged; she vows to serve next in a hospital for the "colored regiments" who are "proving their right to the admiration and kind offices of their white relations, who owe them so much."

While she was still at the Union Hotel Hospital, Alcott had won one hundred dollars, in a contest sponsored by the flamboyant New York weekly *Frank Leslie's Illustrated Newspaper,* for her sensational short story "Pauline's Passion and Punishment."[39] During her convalescence from typhoid, Alcott began to write more sensational stories and serials under the pseudonym "A. M. Barnard" for Leslie's periodicals, and for James Elliott's *The Flag of Our Union.* Dealing with masquerade, mesmerism, rebellion, desire, anger, revenge, and incest, these thrillers allowed her to express the volcanic side of her personality, and to release repressed emotions. "I think my natural inclination is for the lurid style," she told a friend. "I indulge in gorgeous fantasies and wish that I dared inscribe them upon my pages and set them before the public."[40] Alcott scholars are still unearthing her pseudonymous stories and thrillers in obscure nineteenth-century magazines.[41]

In one of her best tales, "Behind a Mask; or, a Woman's Power" (1866), set in England, an actress and adventuress, Jean Muir, masquerades as a girlish governess in order to gain fortune and social position by marrying a rich old man. For Alcott, the story, influenced by British women's sensation novels of the 1860s such as *Lady Audley's Secret,* used the performance of little womanhood to dramatize her double life as dutiful housebound daughter and rebellious literary son. "I'll not fail again," Jean declares of her plot, "if there is power in a woman's wit and will!"[42] She disguises herself to look much younger than she is, makes up a story of her unhappy childhood, and arrives at the estate, where all feel pity "at the sight of the pale-faced girl in her plain black dress, with no ornament but a silver cross at her throat. Small, thin, and colorless she was, with yellow hair, gray eyes, and sharply cut, irregular, but very arresting features." That evening, when she retires to her room, Jean strips off her disguise: "She unbound and removed the long abundant braids from her head, wiped the pink from her face, took out several pearly teeth, and slipping off her dress appeared herself indeed, a haggard, worn, moody woman of thirty at least."

The Woman of Thirty

It may sound funny to twenty-first-century readers that a thirty-year-old would be haggard and worn; yet such unmaskings of the woman of thirty, no longer an innocent girl but laboring to maintain the perfect façade of girlishness, would return in many books by American women from Constance Fenimore Woolson to Edith Wharton, though with shades of meaning specific to each literary era. These novels take thirty as the age of female maturation—the point at which girlhood irrevocably passes into womanhood. They ask what can happen to an American girl when she grows up. Does she have a future, especially if she is unmarried? Is her narrative life over, or is she capable of generating new plots? While for men and fictional heroes, the age of thirty was a beginning, for women and heroines it was traditionally an end. As Elizabeth Oakes-Smith, the poet-novelist who became a women's rights lecturer, sadly observed in her diary in 1861, "How few women have any history after the age of thirty!"[43]

After her nursing experience, Alcott also thought of extending her history by going to Port Royal on the Sea Islands of South Carolina to teach contrabands, the slaves who had escaped to Union forces and established a community there. In "My Contraband; or, The Brothers," a story published in the *Atlantic Monthly* in 1867, she wrote about Nurse Dane, who is assigned to care for a wounded white Confederate officer, and given the help of a mulatto contraband named Robert, who is the officer's half brother. Racial and class conflict between the two brothers constitutes the main plot of the story, although it also has a sexual subtext; Nurse Dane, too, is a contraband figure who is struggling against her illicit desire for the mixed-race hero. He is a divided soul; one side of his face is extraordinarily handsome, with "Saxon features, Spanish complexion darkened by exposure, color in lips and cheek, waving hair, and an eye full of . . . passionate melancholy." The other side is horribly scarred, with a wound across the forehead and cheek "held together with strips of . . . transparent plaster . . . Part of his black hair had been shorn away, and one eye was nearly closed." Like the nation, his body is split in two.[44] Dane stops Robert from killing the white half brother who has stolen and caused the death of his enslaved wife. In the end, Robert enlists in the Fifty-fourth Massachusetts regiment of black soldiers and kills his half brother in honorable battle at Fort Wagner. Another story Alcott wrote in 1867, "M. L.," is about the love between a rich white woman and a handsome octoroon musician, who marry and make an idyllic world elsewhere in a bohemian society that rewards genius and is indifferent to race. Like all of Alcott's Civil War stories, this one is "violently partisan." All white Southerners are evil; all Northerners are good.[45]

At this stage of her career, Alcott's ambitions were set high and she planned to write serious literary fiction for adults using the sensation earnings as a cushion. She worked on a long exciting novel about a young woman who makes a pact with the devil in order to escape her boring and confined life.[46] Then in 1868, the publisher Thomas Niles invited her to write a book for girls, and she published the first part of *Little Women*. The March family is living through the war years, but Mr. March has gone off to serve the Union army as a clergyman, leaving his wife and four daughters to fend for themselves. The military parts of the story are marginalized and negated; even when Mr. March is wounded, the letter telling the family comes from "Blank Hospital."[47] Alcott suppressed her own anger and ambition to write this enormously influential and popular domestic novel about four sisters, based on her own family.

In the second volume, Jo March becomes a writer of sensation stories for the "Weekly Volcano." Her model is the prolific and successful Mrs. S.L.A.N.G. Northbury—obviously based on Mrs. E.D.E.N. Southworth—and Alcott moralizes about what was her own recent and satisfying experience:

> *Jo soon found that her innocent experience had given her but few glimpses of the tragic world which underlies society; so, regarding it in a business light, she set about supplying her deficiencies with characteristic energy. Eager to find material for stories, and bent on making them original in plot, if not masterly in execution, she searched newspapers for accidents, incidents, and crimes; she excited the suspicions of public*

librarians, by asking for works on poisons; she studied faces in the street,—and characters good, bad, and indifferent, all about her . . . she . . . introduced herself to folly, sin, and misery, as well as her limited opportunities allowed. She thought she was prospering finely; but, unconsciously, she was beginning to desecrate some of the womanliest attributes of a woman's character.

In short, Jo is becoming a professional writer of genre fiction, and using the techniques all serious writers use to understand human experience; but even for a little woman who would be womanly, such secondhand efforts are risky and taboo, while the firsthand "limited experience" available to her as a woman excludes her from attempting more than domestic subjects. Jo's uneasiness is reinforced by the reaction of her fatherly suitor, Professor Bhaer, who tells her that he does not like to see "good young girls" reading such stories, much less writing them, and makes her feel as if "the words 'Weekly Volcano' were printed in large type on her forehead." In Bhaer's eyes, she is almost as sinful as Hester Prynne; and instead of trying to expand her limited experience or challenging society's restrictions on good girls, Jo burns her manuscripts. By the novel's end, she has given up, or at least postponed, her dream of becoming a great author in exchange for marriage and motherhood, and regards the life she had once desired as "selfish, lonely, and cold."

The battle between selfless femininity and artistic creativity in *Little Women* is the reason many feminist critics have called it the story of Alcott's personal Civil War.[48] Even in *Little Women,* she came up against New England propriety. Her admiration for Dickens and her fondness for the American idiom gave her a taste for the rowdy vernacular and the distinctive accents of American girls. Her publishers disagreed. After *Little Women* became a best seller, they revised it to change her vigorous slang, colloquialism, and regional expressions to a more refined, ladylike prose. Jo calls her father "papa" rather than "pa," says "work" instead of "grub," and "notions" instead of "quinydingles."

With *Little Women,* the United States finally had a novel that rivaled *Jane Eyre* for the affection of women readers in England and all over the world. *Uncle Tom's Cabin* inspired awe, but Jo March was loved, and she influenced female intellectuals and artists everywhere; Gertrude Stein and Simone de Beauvoir would cite her example decades after. A woman's novel did not have to be the highest art to have this impact; it only needed to have unforgettable characters and genuine situations.[49]

The Work of Sacrifice—Augusta Jane Evans

When her home state of Alabama seceded from the Union in January 1861, Augusta Jane Evans had been thrilled: "let the star of the Empire blaze along the way to freedom; let us conquer or perish together; delay is ruinous, suicidal; the time has come!"[50] She broke off her engagement to a Northern editor, James Reed Spaulding, over political differences, and denounced her former friend Mary Terhune's apostasy: "It was with painful emotions of mingled shame and indignation that I learned that 'Marion Harland,' the boast and ornament of Virginia literature, had deserted the cause of her native state, of the bleeding South, who had felt so proud of her genius," she wrote to a friend.[51] In 1862, the same year that Alcott volunteered as a nurse in Washington, Evans went as an army nurse to "Camp Beulah" in Alabama, named for the heroine of her 1859 best seller. "For two months past," she wrote, "I have been constantly engaged in nursing sick soldiers, keeping sleepless vigil by day and night, and this morning sitting beside one whose life has hung upon a slender thread for many days." Evans, a passionate defender of the Confederacy, had no zest for writing fiction: "While a nation's history is daily being written, page by page, in characters of blood, one has little thought for the dusty records of the dim bygone."

By 1864, however, Evans's itch to write had irresistibly returned. Her novel *Macaria; or, Altars of Sacrifice,* was a huge best seller during the war. It was dedicated to "the Army of the Southern Confederacy, who have delivered the South from despotism, and who have won for generations yet unborn the precious guerdon of constitutional republican liberty . . . by one who, although debarred from the dangers and deathless glory of the 'tented field,' would fain offer a woman's inadequate tribute to the noble patriotism and sublime self-abnegation of her dear and devoted countrymen." By the end of the century, this dedication had been removed from Northern reprints along with most of her most vitriolic anti-Northern declarations.

Evans wrote to sanctify the emotional and sexual sacrifice of Confederate women. *Macaria,* titled for the Greek mythological heroine who sacrificed herself to the gods to save Athens, is the story of two talented Southern cousins who represent two sides of herself, the beautiful heiress Irene Huntingdon, and the orphaned and passionate Electra Grey. Irene has an "intellect of the masculine order, acute and logical, rather deficient in the imaginative faculties, but keenly analytical," and devotes herself to science, especially astronomy. When the war breaks out, Irene cannot bear having to stay home, "useless and inactive"; but ironically, war brings her liberation from feminine subservience even as she masks her freedom in the rhetoric of service. After the war, Irene dedicates herself not only to spinsterhood but also to the professional task of "building up a noble school of Southern Art," devoted to training women in design, drawing, and engraving.

Electra is less of a scholar, but she dreams of becoming a great painter, and looks to "a glorious sisterhood of artists" leading her on. Her refusal of her cousin Russell's invitation to live as his dependent in Washington—she plans instead to earn her living and study painting in Europe—is a powerful declaration of female artistic ambition, and economic and emotional independence:

> I, too, want to earn a noble reputation, which will survive long after I have been gathered to my fathers; I want to accomplish some work, looking upon which, my fellow creatures will proclaim: "That woman has not lived in vain; the world is better and happier because she came and labored in it." I want my name carved . . . upon the living, throbbing heart of my age! . . . Upon the threshold of my career, facing the loneliness of coming years, I resign that hope with which, like golden thread, most women embroider their future. I dedicate myself, my life, unreservedly, to Art.

The war changes her plans. Like Irene, Electra believes that "the women of the South must exercise an important influence in determining our national destiny . . . It is not my privilege to enter the army, and wield a sword or musket; but I am going into true womanly work—into the crowded hospitals, to watch faithfully over sick and wounded." By the novel's end, Electra is planning a painting called "The Modern Macaria," as "the first offering of Southern Art." A vast mural of the anticipated Confederate victory, the painting juxtaposes two symbolic female figures, Independence, holding the Confederate banner of the cross, and Peace, in a battlefield of dying men and grieving women. Electra will be the head teacher at Irene's School of Design for Women, and together they will serve their society, creating the independent Southern art Evans had hoped to see. To be sure, as Irene tells Electra, they will be lonely; but they will also be triumphant: "our future holds much that is bright."

Sitting It Out—Stoddard and Dickinson

Elizabeth Barstow Stoddard (1823–1902) and Emily Dickinson (1830–1886) lived through the Civil War but did not write about it. Stoddard moved from poetry to fiction during the 1860s, and published three novels between 1862 and 1867, none of which deal with the Civil War; they were reprinted in 1887–88 to greater critical appreciation, but soon disappeared again from literary history. Of Dickinson's more than 1,800 poems, 917 were written between 1861 and 1865, with a peak of 295 in 1863, although only a few referred directly to contemporary events. After the war, nonetheless, her productivity declined; she never wrote more than forty-eight poems in a single year and usually considerably fewer. Moreover, she published only ten of her poems, anonymously and reluctantly, during her lifetime. From 1860 onward she was a recluse closed up in her father's house in Amherst, Massachusetts, sharing her poems with a few friends and relatives, but refusing to have them in print. Helen Hunt Jackson was among the friends who had pleaded with Dickinson to publish. "It is a cruel wrong to your 'day & generation' that you will not give them light. I do not think we have a right to withhold from the world a word or a thought any more than a deed, which might help a single soul."[52] But not even Jackson's entreaties could persuade Dickinson to publish her work. After her death in 1886, her sister discovered 833 poems sewn into tiny booklets. Not until 1890 were Dickinson's poems printed for a public readership, and not until 1955 were they presented in an accurate and definitive edition.

Writers like Stoddard and Dickinson pose a challenge to the literary historian because they disturb the periodization and categories of history; they do not fit neatly into literary generations, political contexts, or social categories. Like most women writers, they were not affiliated with "schools" or movements. Although Dickinson is now accepted as a major American writer, and Stoddard is still dubbed a "perpetual misfit," critics of the two writers have used many of the same terms in discussing them; as one notes, "there is an indirection to [Stoddard's fiction] . . . that has reminded many readers of Emily Dickinson's poetry and confused them accordingly."[53] Stoddard's modern editors, Lawrence Buell and Sandra Zagarell, have stressed her biographical similarities of "attitude, upbringing, and milieu" to Dickinson, and emphasized her use of a severely limited narrative mode, with "minimal narrative clues . . . minimal transitions, and dramatic, linguistic, and aphoristic impact."[54] Her writing, they and other defenders claim, was, like Dickinson's, ahead of its time—jagged, harsh, abrupt, stark, innovative—and her critical neglect was the product of her "disturbing of neat boundaries."[55] Variously labeled as "a domestic novelist, an antisentimentalist, a local-color precursor of realism, a Brontë-inspired gothicist, a provincial gothicist, and a proto-modernist, she seems to have fallen between the critical cracks" of genre.[56] Similarly, Dickinson's first editors regularized the meter and syntax of her poems in order to make them more conventional; even so, some critics complained about her harshness, unusual rhymes, or grammatical innovations.

THE STODDARDESS

Elizabeth Barstow Stoddard was born on Buzzards Bay in Mattapoisett, Massachusetts, the daughter of a shipbuilder. Her family did not support her writing at all; her father loaned her first novel to a friend and forgot about it for twenty years. To her closest friend she wrote in 1852, "What is there for such women as you and me are? I have decided that an irresistible will compels me to some destiny, but vaguely shaped much less desired."[57] That December, she married the New York poet and editor Richard Stoddard, a member of the New York "Drawing-Room Poets" along with Edmund Stedman, Bayard Taylor, and George Henry Boker.[58] Although she admired this literary fraternity, she could also recognize its ridiculously insular and self-promoting aspects. On a typical evening, she noted:

> *A finds B writing a poem. A insists on B's reading it. B reads and A says "glorious." Then A takes a manuscript from his pocket, which B insists shall be read. A reads and B says "glorious." A asks if B has seen his last squib in Young America. B asks if A has seen his last review of that book by Muggins. Each man puts his feet on the sofa . . . and then Tennyson, Browning, Longfellow, and their faults are discussed.*[59]

Presumably Stoddard herself was in the kitchen making the refreshments.

In his dated aestheticism and self-importance, her husband was a poor model for her development; she, too, strove to be an "Arcadian," and, like an apprentice, submitted her poems to his rigorous critique. "Stoddard is a severe master and I get so discouraged that I *cry* dreadfully," she confessed.[60] On the other hand, he believed in her talents as a poet, and insisted that his friends do the same. Taylor affectionately called her "The Stoddardess (a wild female specimen of the poetic animal)."[61] If she sometimes felt patronized by the men, she also felt herself to be aiming higher than other American women writers. As she observed, they had produced no masterpiece either, whether "metaphysical tale, novel, or poem . . . We have no Elizabeth Browning, Brontë, George Sand, or Miss [Fredrika] Bremer."[62]

Two of Stoddard's poems in 1860 deal with the problems facing the woman poet in the contexts of both male and female culture. In "The Poet's Secret," she described her sense of baffled blindness about the sources of poetic inspiration and creative confidence:

> In vain I watch the day and night,
> In vain the world through space may roll;
> I never see the mystic light,
> Which fills the poet's happy soul.

In "Before the Mirror," she used the tale of the Lady of Shalott to express her sense of entrapment in old forms and old myths:

> Now, like the Lady of Shalott
> I dwell within an empty room,
> And through the day and through the night,
> I sit before an ancient loom.
> . . . .
> And as my web grows darker too,
> Accursed seems this empty room;
> I know I must forever weave
> These phantoms by this hateful loom.

If we take Stoddard's images of the empty room and the ancient loom to suggest her sense of frustration and limitation within the sterile confines of traditional women's poetry, we can read this poem as a farewell to poetic expression. Her problems, though, were not only with poetic conventions. By 1859, she had started to write short stories, and she continued to publish in *Harper's*, the *Atlantic Monthly*, *The Aldine*, the *Independent*, *Hearth and Home*, and *Aldington's Journal*. These stories reveal her serious difficulties with plotting and dialogue. In "My Own Story," for example, she frequently backtracks to explain something the reader should have known from the beginning, and it is hard to figure out who is speaking.

Stoddard completed her first novel, *The Morgesons,* in 1860–61, before the war broke out, and her interest in the war was personal rather than political, according to her biographer James Matlack: "Once the war began, her major concern lay with relatives and friends who were in the armed forces, not with the moral or political principles at stake."[63] For the Drawing-Room Poets in general, the war was a distraction. Richard Stoddard complained that the war spoiled the sales of an anthology of "amatory verse" he and Bayard Taylor edited.[64] "These war times are hard on authors," Taylor whined.[65] Elizabeth Stoddard displayed huge insensitivity and narcissism when she told Edmund Stedman, who had been a war correspondent and seen the reality, that the failure of *"The Morgesons* was my Bull Run."[66] After her book's publication, Stoddard suffered from "nervous prostration," and spent several weeks in bed. To Stedman she wrote, with typical self-centeredness, "the horrors of the war affect me deeply, when will it be over? As for my book, did you *like* it?"[67]

He tried to like it, and her husband hounded all their friends for good reviews, none of which she found good enough to satisfy her need for approval. Any criticism infuriated Stoddard, although she admitted to Stedman that "my radical defect in form is hard to struggle with."[68] *The Morgesons* is a brusque semiautobiographical novel told in the first person about the childhood and young womanhood of the significantly named Cassandra Morgeson, a truth teller whose prophecies are not believed. She is intelligent, passionate, skeptical, and rebellious; before her marriage to a reformed rake, she comes close to having an affair with a married man and flirts with several other men. Cassandra, however, is not a woman of genius, and has no intellectual or literary ambitions; Stoddard lovingly traces her subjectivity, but her romantic adventures do not have much point. Stoddard published two more novels in the 1860s, *Two Men* (1865) and *Temple House* (1867), which were poorly received. She took their failure badly to heart, and did not attempt to publish a novel again.

Stoddard desperately wished to be recognized and rewarded as an important writer, a serious artist who could be part of American high literary culture. As she wrote to a friend, she wanted to be "compared . . . with Shakespeare, Milton, Dante & Co."[69] These lofty ambitions were far beyond her abilities. Although she had moments of debilitating self-doubt, Stoddard generally believed she was an unappreciated female genius. When her books were badly received, she blamed the stupidity and malice of the critics, the wearying demands of domesticity, competition and discouragement from her husband, her lack of education and training, her persistent poor health, the obligations of caring for her son—everything but her own limitations. In "Collected by a Valetudinarian" (1870), she used the example of Charlotte Brontë to lament the tragic fate of women of genius: "What a mockery the life of genius is!" This story imagines the dead woman poet rightly estimated and remembered by her women friends; in her fiction at least, Stoddard created a sympathetic jury of her peers.

The Americanist literary scholar Lawrence Buell attributes Stoddard's obscurity to her "cerebral, elliptical narrative style . . . her transitional position between romance and realism, and . . . the coincidence of her most ambitious—but ostensibly 'apolitical'—novels with the Civil War." He believes that she will someday be recognized as an important writer: "As with Dickinson, so too it will eventually be with Elizabeth Stoddard."[70] I disagree. Stoddard's linguistic innovations are more self-indulgent than illuminating, and she had many serious flaws as an artist, especially her weak sense of construction and plot. Above all, her indifference to the great public issues of her time and her inability to identify with, let alone sympathize with, the suffering of others doomed her to insignificance.

A CAMPAIGN OF THE INTERIOR—EMILY DICKINSON

Tellingly, Elizabeth Stoddard did not admire Emily Dickinson's poetry when she finally read it in the 1890s. "I see very little in her favor," she confided to one woman friend; "she is confused, broken, a kaleidoscope without any color."[71] In 1892, she condemned Dickinson even more sharply and blindly: "An eccentric arrangement of words—or ebullition of feeling do not constitute poetry."[72] Emily Dickinson was indeed the most eccentric, but also innovative, daring, and determined woman artist of the nineteenth century; she exploded all the conventions by which nineteenth-century poetry was written.

Many critics have attempted to normalize, categorize, or historicize Dickinson as representative of her time, or as the epitome of traditional New England Puritanism. She has been called "the ghost that haunts American literature," and a gothic American "woman in white," suggesting that she was somehow the shadow and specter of a self-publicizing age.[73] Feminist critics have argued that she was the most highly developed representative of nineteenth-century women's writing, pointing out that she used many of the most popular feminine literary images, such as the pent-up volcano, the spider-artist who spins her solitary web, and the housewife stitching and piecing her verbal quilt.

In my view, to compare any other American poet of the period to Dickinson, even to see her as the subversive antithesis or evolutionary end of nineteenth-century sentimental poetry, is to understate her exceptional originality and uniqueness. Along with Walt Whitman, she reinvented American poetry. Her poems are unmistakable, while the verses of virtually all of her female contemporaries are interchangeable. Although she used the template of English common meter, she constantly ruptured its forms. Like many nineteenth-century women poets, Dickinson indeed drew upon a repertoire of domestic and natural imagery—houses, kitchens, sewing, stitching—as well as gothic images of volcanoes, earthquakes, ghosts, haunted houses, cemeteries, and death. In her hands, all these images explode in erotic and unexpected directions. For example, Dickinson employs the bee and flower imagery common to other nineteenth-century American women writers. She mentions a long list of flowers native to New England, including the rose, violet, crocus, clover, daisy, foxglove, gentian, geranium, columbine, daffodil, carnation, dandelion, iris, aster, anemone, harebell, lily, buttercup, water lily, jessamine, cowslip, and primrose.[74] Bees appear 125 times in her poems.[75] But while other women poets used the female flower and the male bee as the symbolic dyad of female sexual passivity and male sexual mobility, Dickinson's flowers are independent and self-fertilizing, calmly accepting or rejecting the advances of the intrusive, rapacious, or "fainting Bee" (205) eagerly humming around the blossom.[76] While "The Rose received his visit / With frank tranquility" (1139), Dickinson also instructs the Flower annoyed by the Bee "that seeketh his felicity / Too often at her door" to have her Footman say she is "not at home" (235). At times, Dickinson wished "just to be a Bee" and "visit only where I like / And No one visit me" (1056).

Similarly, Dickinson's treatment, or avoidance, of the Civil War is unique. To be sure, she was aware of the war, mentioned it more than once in her letters, and even alluded to it in one or two occasional poems. Her poetic mentor, the clergyman and man of letters Thomas Wentworth Higginson, was a passionate abolitionist who had befriended John Brown, helped him raise money, and continued to support him after his arrest at Harpers Ferry. During the war, Higginson commanded the first black regiment, the First South Carolina Volunteers, and Dickinson wrote to him in fear that he had been wounded. Higginson, who also befriended Harriet Spofford, Charlotte Forten Grimke, Emma Lazarus, and many other women writers, was fully aware of the pressures facing women who spoke on public issues.

Yet while other American writers took fervent political sides on the war, Dickinson spent the years meditating on death and loss. Her poems ask how it feels to die, how it feels to grieve, whether spiritual immortality can coexist with earthly decay; and she asks these questions with an urgency and immediacy that transcend the philosophical and theological jargon of her day. As Wendy Martin observes, "In order to achieve psychological and artistic autonomy, she had to undergo a 'civil war' of the self against the very authorities—religious, familial, literary—she sometimes sought to follow."[77] Daniel Aaron, in his study of the Civil War in American literature, has a brief appendix about Dickinson. As he explains it, "isolation did not signify indifference. The War inflamed her imagination, illuminated old enigmas, touched her deeper sympathies. Since the national conflict coincided with her private anguish, martial analogies and imagery naturally entered into her depictions of the wars of the Heart and Mind."[78] There is no patriotic gore in Dickinson's poems, and they are certainly not consoling. Her civil war, as she said in one poem, was "a campaign of the interior."[79]

How did an Emily Dickinson appear in the mid-nineteenth century in Amherst, Massachusetts? In many respects, she was the kind of enigmatic and anomalous American genius the Transcendentalists had called for. We can't explain her in terms of literary influence, historical stimuli, intellectual environment, or poetic ambition. Dickinson came from a prominent family, and had relatives and friends who wrote, but she paid no attention to their example or suggestions. She was staunchly independent and stayed away from the movements of her day, including abolitionism, religion, temperance, and women's rights, and mocked a woman (possibly Elizabeth Stuart Phelps) who wrote to her, "requesting me to aid the world by my chirrup more . . . I replied declining."[80] She idolized the work of Elizabeth Barrett Browning, Charlotte Brontë, and George Eliot, but did not imitate it. For every great poem she wrote, Dickinson wrote ten that were imperfect or flawed; like all great artists, she left sketches, drafts, fragments, and experiments.

In Dickinson's prosperous family the men were lawyers and politicians and the women were devoted housekeepers and devout Christians. She was good at domestic tasks, which took up a great deal of her time; but she was also daring and courageous in her defense of her art and her solitude. Starting in adolescence, she refused any formal profession of Christian faith. By the 1860s, when she was in her thirties, she had stopped even going to church. Becoming a recluse who did not leave the house and spent much of her time in her own room may have helped her avoid domestic and religious obligations. Biographers have speculated that she was agoraphobic, sexually repressed, or even mentally disturbed. Wendy Martin takes a more pragmatic view of Dickinson's behavior, arguing that she "was a dedicated and disciplined poet whose relative isolation was a self-imposed strategy that gave her time and space in which to write . . . To protect herself from more conventional opinions, she largely divorced herself from her social context and created a very private life that suited her artistic needs."[81]

Dickinson's exceptional and iconic status as *the* great nineteenth-century American woman poet also stands in the way of dispassionate critical response. Feminist critics can feel intellectually pressured to find her representative; rivalrous male poets can experience her seclusion, white dresses, and virginity as metaphors for muselike seduction. Critics and readers of other nationalities may have an advantage in reading Dickinson freshly. The British critic John Carey, for example, compares some of Dickinson's language to the strategic "nonsense" of Victorian sexual outsiders such as Lewis Carroll and Edward Lear, a "criticism of language"; and suggests that "women poets, who have had to re-make male language for their own use, have found nonsense especially serviceable."[82]

After the War: The Lost Cause of the South

Women on both sides of the conflict were embittered by their experience of war, and disillusioned by its romantic rhetoric. As with Dickinson, their Civil War was finally a campaign of the interior. The female "pen and ink warriors" of the Confederacy began with heroic ideals and confidence in the battle.[83] Often, however, the ideology of sacrifice came to seem to them like a sham, and anger toward their own culture followed the failed promises of the Confederacy. Sarah Piatt (1836–1919), a poet from Kentucky, and a daughter of slaveholders, rejected the nostalgic Southern myth of the Lost Cause, and wrote bitterly of the waste of life, talent, and ambition for the combatants and the women who mourned them. In "Army of Occupation," written for the 1866 dedication of Arlington Cemetery on the site of Robert E. Lee's estate, she blamed Lee's recklessness for the carnage, and suggested that he haunted the graves of the two thousand dead at Arlington, and was haunted himself by their memory. Piatt never recovered from the embittering trauma of the war; in 1910, she wrote a sardonic hymn for "A New Thanksgiving":

> For war, plague, pestilence, flood, famine, fire,
> For Christ discrowned, for false gods set on high;
> For fools, whose hands must have their hearts' desire,
> We thank Thee![84]

In the immediate aftermath of the war, Augusta Jane Evans was planning a major undertaking: a history of the Confederacy, which she hoped would be "the great end of all my labors in the realm of letters." Two years later, though, she abandoned her plan in deference to a man, Alexander Hamilton Stephens, the former vice president of the Confederacy, who was planning his own history. "I humbly put my fingers on the throat of my ambitious daring design of becoming the Confederate Xenophon, and strangled it," she confided to her friend General Beauregard. "Abler hands snatched it from my weak womanly fingers and waved me to humbler paths of labor."[85] Stephens published a dry constitutional overview of the Civil War in 1868–70; Evans's book would surely have been more comprehensive and reflective.

The war made the search for new fictional forms even more urgent for Southern women. The Southern domestic novel, Elizabeth Moss argues, "provided an inadequate explanation of the recent past," and could no longer "sustain the narrative demands" that were being made on it.[86] The "war story" of self-abnegation imposed on Southern women at the beginning of the conflict, according to Drew Gilpin Faust, "had been internally flawed and contradictory . . . it was an ideology designed to silence, rather than address, the fundamental interests of women in preservation of self and family."[87]

Evans's postwar novel, St. Elmo (1866), was about a female genius, Edna Earl, whose suitor, St. Elmo, was both a glamorous roué, like

Byron or Mr. Rochester, and a pedant. Evans sees him without irony or humor. As a young orphaned girl, Edna first meets the dashing St. Elmo when she is out walking and he gallops up savagely beside her to recover his dropped copy of Dante. She wants to be educated, too, and when—amazing coincidence!—she is adopted by St. Elmo's mother, the wealthy Mrs. Murray, she studies Latin, Greek, Hebrew, and Chaldee: "I should not think I was well or thoroughly educated if I could not understand Greek and Latin; and beside [*sic*], I want to read what Solon, and Pericles, Demosthenes wrote in their own language."

Framed by Victorian statements of proper womanhood from Ruskin's "Of Queens' Gardens," and Tennyson's *The Princess*, *St. Elmo* is freighted with sermons against intellectual women. Her teacher, the Reverend Mr. Hammond, denounces women writers:

> *The history of literary females is not calculated to allay the apprehension that oppresses me, as I watch you just setting out on a career so fraught with trials of which you have never dreamed. As a class they are martyrs, uncrowned and uncanonized, jeered at by the masses, sincerely pitied by a few earnest souls, and wept over by the relatives who really love them. Thousands of women have toiled over books that proved millstones and drowned them in the sea of letters. How many of the hundreds of female writers scattered through the world in this century, will be remembered six months after the coffin closes over their weary, haggard faces? You may answer, "They made their bread." Ah, child! It would have been sweeter if earned at the wash-tub, or in the dairy, or by their needles . . . If you succeed after years of labor and anxiety and harassing fears, you will become a target for envy and malice, and possibly, for slander. Your own sex will be jealous of your eminence, considering your superiority an insult to their mediocrity; and mine will either ridicule or barely tolerate you; for men detest female competitors in the Olympian game of literature.*

In debate with Mrs. Murray, Hammond nonetheless defends learned women: "Remember, my dear, that where one woman is considered a blue-stocking and tiresomely learned, twenty are more tiresome still because they know nothing." He instructs Edna "to circumnavigate the world of *belles-lettres*, in search of new hemispheres of thought."

Meanwhile, in a Bluebeard-like plot twist, St. Elmo goes off on an expedition to exotic lands, entrusting Edna with the key to a marble temple in his sitting room, and ordering her not to "open the tomb or temple unless I fail to return at the close of four years." To his bitter disappointment, when he returns five years later, even more cynical and cruel, she has not used the key. No fairy-tale heroine, Edna is much more interested in her own writing than in his secrets. "The daring scheme of authorship had seized upon Edna's mind with a tenacity that conquered and expelled all other purposes." She is writing "a vindication of the unity of all mythologies," and she is writing it in the form of a novel. (George Eliot's *Middlemarch,* in which the pedant Casaubon is writing a similar treatise, would appear six years later.) Edna publishes her book, and achieves fame and respect. At last the repentant St. Elmo returns, having found religion and become a minister, to claim her as his bride and to rescue her from what he considers the unwomanly burdens of fame, wealth, and "literary bondage"—"There shall be no more books written! No more study, no more toil, no more anxiety, no more heartaches! And that dear public you love so well must even help itself and whistle for a new pet."[88]

St. Elmo was read by a million people in its first four months on the market; but true to her values, upon its publication Evans married Colonel Lorenzo Madison Wilson, the wealthy sixty-year-old owner of an Alabama plantation.[89] For the rest of her life she followed humbler paths, giving parties, cultivating her garden, and singing in the church choir.

While Evans was traumatized by the South's defeat, Mary Terhune was even more troubled by her position as a Southerner in the North, who had lost family members on both sides, and who lamented the senseless carnage. In 1861, her publishers Derby and Jackson had gone bankrupt; her Southern readers were alienated by her marriage to a Northerner, while her Northern readers were skeptical about her loyalties. Who would be her audience after the war? *Sunnybank* (1866) picked up the story of Ida Ross from *Alone,* following her family through the war years. Terhune invented a theory that Virginia had been forced by the more fanatical Southern states to throw in its lot with the Confederacy, despite its own better wishes. *Sunnybank* gives a graphic picture of the wartime deprivations on the plantation, and ends with a marriage of reconciliation between Ida's daughter Elinor Lacy and a Northerner, Harry Wilton, tacitly acknowledging Terhune's own choices and the dominance of the North.

From Edna to Ida to Elsie

Some Northern women writers tried romanticizing and eroticizing the pleasures of female submission, and linking it to nostalgia for the defeated Old South. Martha Finley (1828–1909), who built her lucrative career on the romance of the South, was the descendant of a long line of Yankee Presbyterians—her grandfather had been an officer in the Revolutionary Army, and her great-uncle was the first president of Princeton Theological Seminary. Finley was an impoverished teacher in Philadelphia who had attempted to support herself in the late 1850s by writing more than twenty Sunday-school stories with such titles as *Lame Letty* and *Little Joe Carter the Cripple*. During the Civil War, she worked out a better literary formula—the trials of Elsie Dinsmore, a beautiful, motherless, and devout child heiress in the Old South, whose sense of piety brings her into conflict with the worldly demands of her formidable father, Horace. With her devoted mammy, Aunt Chloe, to support her in her martyrdom, Elsie played out an unyielding rebellion against patriarchy in the name of Jesus, allowing readers to enjoy a sinless and vicarious rebellion of their own, and a good deal of masochistic pleasure in her suffering and triumph. Starting in 1867, with Elsie at eight years old, the series was hugely popular, and eventually went to twenty-eight volumes, taking its heroine through the Civil War, marriage, motherhood, and even grandmotherhood. Finley earned a quarter of a million dollars during her long lifetime.[90]

Elsie's Womanhood (1875), the fourth novel in the series, is prefaced by Finley's defense of her material, and her apology for taking up the controversies of the war even a decade after its conclusion. "Dates compelled the bringing in of the late war, and it has been the earnest desire and effort of the author to so treat the subject as to wound the feelings of none; to be as impartial as if writing history." She contrives the plot so as to have Elsie, her father and his family, her husband, Edward Travilla, and their young children, spend the entire war in Naples. But before they depart, Finley shows Elsie as the tenderhearted, benevolent, but complacent absentee owner of her mother's Louisiana plantation, Viamede, with "between two and three hundred Negroes." When she comes of age, Elsie learns from her father that her beloved mammy, Chloe, once had a husband, who was "sold away from her," and children, who died. On the journey to Bayou Teche to see the plantation, Chloe happens to meet her former husband, whom Elsie immediately buys for five hundred dollars. As they arrive, the plantation overseer, Spriggs, is in the midst of whipping a woman slave who is stripped to the waist; Elsie stops the proceedings and orders the whipping post chopped into kindling, telling Spriggs that in the future, he is to substitute locking up the recalcitrant slaves for a few days on bread and water.

Elsie welcomes news of Lincoln's Emancipation Proclamation when it arrives in Europe, but Aunt Chloe is devastated: " 'Dis chile don't want no freedom,' sobbed the poor old creature at length . . . 'your ole mammy don't want no freedom. She can't go for to leave you, Miss Elsie, her bressed darlin' chile.' " Elsie assures her that she can stay on in the family as a paid servant forever. When the war is over, the Dinsmores and Travillas return to the South, and sadly behold the destruction of their plantations, but with a prayer "that their dear native land never again be visited with that fearful scourge of civil war." Although its explicit political sympathies are always with the Union, rather than either the abolitionists or the rebels (one chapter describes the atrocities at Andersonville prison), *Elsie's Womanhood* fascinated Northern readers with its images of chivalrous Southern gentlemen dying for a lost cause, devoted slaves, and the vanished and ruined fairy-tale world of the plantation.

After the War: The Consolations of the North

If Southern women writers like Evans and Terhune were questioning the value of their literary bondage after the war, Northern women were even more urgently looking to writing as self-expression, vocation, and political engagement. The journalist Gail Hamilton (Mary Abigail Dodge; 1833–1896), who had contributed to the antislavery paper *National Era,* was living in Washington during the war years. In *Country Living and Country Thinking* (1862), Hamilton recommended authorship to her women readers as the "great safety-valve of society." Even women who felt no call to create could learn to write. "Girls, do not be deceived," Hamilton insisted:

> Write. Write poetry,—write in rhyme,—if it is only "One, two, Buckle my shoe, Three, four, Open the door." Form the habit. It is often convenient. It is a refuge from ennui. It may do good. Any one of you who refrains from writing for fear of ridicule, is a coward. Don't be a coward. There is not much to a woman at best. She is not expected to have

physical courage; but if she has not moral, pray, what has she? The more a man tells you not to write, the more do you write . . . If your heart is stirred within you to write, write! If you can find an editor or publisher who is willing to print for you, print!

The brutal lessons of the war only heightened women's need to tell their stories as truthfully as they could. One Northern woman writer recalled in 1864 how we had "entered gaily on our great contest." But when we "saw our brave boys, whom we had sent out with huzzas, coming back to us with the blood and grime of battle upon them, maimed, ghastly, dying, dead, we knew that we, whom God had hitherto so blessed that we were compelled to look into the annals of other nations for misery and strife, had now commenced a record of our own. Henceforth, there was for us a new literature, new grooves of thought, new interests."[91]

In the aftermath of the war, Fanny Fern urged all American women to write this new literature:

Look around and see innumerable women, to whose barren and love-less lives this would be improvement and solace, and I say to them, write! . . . write! It will be a safe outlet for thoughts and feelings that maybe the nearest friend you have has never dreamed had place in your heart and brain . . . it is not safe for the women of 1867 to shut down so much that cries out for sympathy and expression, because life is such a maelstrom of business or folly or both, that those to whom they have bound themselves, body and soul, recognize only the needs of the former . . . One of these days, when that diary is found, when the hand that penned it shall be dust, with what amazement and remorse will many a husband, or father, exclaim, I never knew my wife, or my child, until this moment.[92]

Spiritualism—Elizabeth Stuart Phelps

One woman who heeded the call was Elizabeth Stuart Phelps (1844–1911), who wrote in many genres but achieved her first great success writing consolation literature for the survivors of the war. Born Mary Gray Phelps, the daughter of the popular 1850s novelist Elizabeth Stuart Phelps, who died when she was eight years old, she took her mother's name. Her father, Austin Phelps, was a professor at Andover Theological

Seminary, and she had grown up in the company of Stowe and other New England luminaries. Like many New England women writers, she rebelled against Calvinist orthodoxy. In her first published story, "A Sacrifice Consumed," Phelps emphasized the losses of women during the war. Ruth is a lonely, desperate, and helpless seamstress who "thought every one would always think I was old and homely; and I thought the room would always be lonely and dark, and I'd never have anyone to love me." A good man named John Rogers unexpectedly proposes to her, but then he enlists and soon after Ruth is told of his death by a stranger: "Gone; he got shot at Antietam on Wednesday, just two weeks ago, poor fellow!"[93]

Like Julia Ward Howe, Phelps felt frustrated by her inability to act during the war, and she was obsessed with the suffering of women. "I wished to say something that would comfort some few . . . of the women whose misery crowded the land. The smoke of their torment ascended, and the sky was blackened by it. I do not think I thought so much about the suffering of men—the fathers, the brothers, the sons— bereft; but the women,—the helpless, outnumbering, unconsulted women; they whom war trampled down, without a choice or a protest; the patient, limited, domestic women, who thought little, but loved much, and, loving, had lost all,—to them I would have spoken."[94] New England Calvinism, with its dogmas of predestination and damnation, had no consolation to offer afflicted women: "Creeds and commentaries and sermons were made by men . . . They were clangs of rusty iron, eating into raw hearts."[95]

Phelps spent two years writing and revising a book in the unheated attic space in her father's house, which was her only room of her own. In *The Gates Ajar* (1868), she told the story of one afflicted woman, twenty-four-year-old Mary Cabot, whose brother Royal has been killed in the war. Mary is visited by unfeeling neighbors, the preachy pastor Mr. Bland, and the unimaginative Deacon Quirk.[96] They present New England Calvinist theology like "a great black gate" that bars out hope.

At last she is visited by her aunt Winifred from Kansas, a prematurely gray young widow with her three-year-old daughter Faith, who reopens the gates of heaven by combining maternal sympathy with a reassuring view of a cheerful, homelike heaven where the dead do what they enjoy most while awaiting reunion with those they love—play the piano, wear their favorite clothes instead of long white robes, and, if they are Union soldiers, meet President Lincoln. Mary is consoled by her aunt's vision of a happy afterlife, and poor Reverend Bland is punished by having his wife killed in a fire, after which he burns his sermon, and becomes a more compassionate man and a better minister. *The Gates Ajar* sold more than eighty thousand copies in the United States, and Phelps followed it up with two more books about heaven and theology, *Beyond the Gates* (1883) and *The Gates Between* (1887). She even got her own sunny room to write in. She had, however, confronted her father in public about theology, and the book began a family battle that would last for many years. Her father, Austin Phelps, would argue against women's suffrage after the war, maintaining that women were intellectually inferior to men.

Phelps was also influenced by the social realism of Rebecca Harding Davis. In October 1868, she published a short story, "The Tenth of January," that recalled "Life in the Iron Mills," but centered on the tragedy of women rather than men. For New Englanders in the 1860s, the tenth of January was a date as iconic as the eleventh of September today. Seeing the title, contemporary readers of Phelps's story would have shuddered in knowledge of what was coming. On January 10, 1860, the Pemberton cotton mill in Lawrence, Massachusetts, collapsed on the 750 workers inside, burying 88 of them alive in the wreckage; a rescuer dropped a lantern and ignited a fire in which they perished. Phelps had been fifteen when the fire took place, three and a half miles from her home in Andover. Before the disaster, Lawrence was only a place she and her girl-friends went to get ice cream at a hotel. When the fire started, Phelps could see the red glare even from Andover. Her brother was sent to Lawrence to see what was happening, but she was not allowed to go. Instead she listened

> to the whispers that told us how the mill-girls, caught in the ruins beyond hope of escape, began to sing . . . their young souls took courage from the familiar sound of one another's voices. They sang the hymns and songs which they had learned in the schools and churches. No classical strains, no "music for music's sake," ascended from that furnace; no ditty of love or frolic; but the plain religious outcries of the people: "Heaven is my home," "Jesus, lover of my soul," and "Shall we gather at the river?" Voice after voice dropped. The fire raced on. A few brave girls sang still,—Shall we gather at the river, . . . There to walk and worship ever?[97]

Thomas Higginson was among the readers who sent her a letter of congratulations for the story, and its pioneering techniques of realism and reportage. It is also a fable of heroic suffering and religious consolation.

The Literary Legacy of the Civil War

As early as 1867, William Dean Howells was lamenting that the war "had laid upon our literature a charge under which it has hitherto staggered very lamely." In his prophetic critical masterpiece *Patriotic Gore* (1962), Edmund Wilson adopted a radically unromantic view of the war and its literature. Taking his title from "Maryland, My Maryland," one of the anthems of the South, and his epigraph from John Brown—"without the shedding of blood there is no remission of sins"—Wilson declared that all war was a primitive drive for power and aggrandizement, cloaked in religious zeal, a "rabble-rousing moral issue," and "warlike cant." He included the Civil War in this terrible history of bloodshed, foreseeing that America would never escape from its rhetoric; "whenever we engage in a war, or move in on some other country, it is always to liberate somebody."[98]

No writer of the nineteenth century, male or female, could have been this subversive and disillusioned in their assessment of the war. Women were nevertheless undoubtedly radicalized by the 1860s. They won the public battles to create and determine their forms of publication, but they often lost their private battles of duty, love, and vocation. Neither the enormous success of "Battle Hymn of the Republic" nor peace and national reconciliation brought a truce in the Howe marriage. In 1865, Howe wrote in her journal, "I have been married twenty-two years today. In the course of this time I have never known my husband to approve any act of mine which I myself valued. Books—poems—essays—everything has been contemptible or contraband in his eyes, because it was not *his* way of doing things."[99] Howe also suffered the death of her little son during these years. By 1870, she had become a feminist and a pacifist. In her "Appeal to Womanhood Throughout the World," Howe called on women to end war:

> *Arise, all women who have hearts, whether your baptism be that of water or of tears! Say firmly:* "We will not have great questions decided by irrelevant agencies. Our husbands shall not come to us, reeking with carnage, for caresses and applause. Our sons shall not be taken from us to unlearn all that we have been able to teach them of charity, mercy, and patience."[100]

Women may not have written a masterpiece during the Civil War, but their experience of the war would have effects far beyond the decade of combat. In volume two of their *History of Woman Suffrage* (1882), Elizabeth Cady Stanton, Susan B. Anthony, and Matilda Joslyn-Gage declared that the war transformed the "social and political condition" of American women: "It created a revolution in woman herself, as important in its results as the changed condition of the former slaves."[101]

8

The Coming Woman

he heroine of women's writing in the 1870s was "the coming woman," the emancipated woman of the future. She had been introduced satirically in *The Spirit of Seventy-six; or, The Coming Woman,* a private theatrical performed in suburban Boston in 1866, a "utopian centennial play" anticipating the centenary of the American Revolution. In the standard utopian plot, Tom Carberry returns to Boston after ten years in China and discovers women have been enfranchised and have turned the world topsy-turvy. Meeting a young lady, Victorine, he is shocked to learn that women no longer read novels about "Woman in her degraded state," which have been burned, and they misremember Tennyson's well-known song as "Come into the garden, George."[1] Perhaps Alcott heard about the performance; in *An Old-Fashioned Girl* (1870), Becky, who shares a studio with another woman artist, sculpts the "coming woman"—"strong-minded, strong-hearted, strong-souled, and strong-bodied; that is why I made her larger than the miserable, pinched-up woman of our day," she explains. "Strength and beauty must go together. Don't you think these broad shoulders can bear burdens without breaking down, these hands work well, these eyes see clearly, and these lips do something besides simper and gossip?"

In a significant essay in 1871, Elizabeth Stuart Phelps described the obsolescence of the old vision of feminine dependence and the dawn of a better vision of what woman might become. The traditional woman did not want a public voice or political role; she was fulfilled by her home and children; she merged her identity with that of her husband. But she had become "an enormous dummy," a scarecrow to frighten the timid. Only when women were "admitted to their rightful share in the administration of government; when, from the ballot to the highest executive honors, they shall be permitted fairly to represent, in their own characters, the interests of their sex; when every department of politics, art, literature, trade is thrown open, absolutely, without reservation, to the exercise of their energies," could the true woman arise.[2]

Suspended for the duration of the war, the women's suffrage movement came roaring back to life in the 1870s. Radical abolitionists had promised that after the emancipation of the slave would come the emancipation of woman. That would not be the case. The Fourteenth Amendment to the Constitution, ratified in 1868, specified that voting rights applied only to males; the Fifteenth Amendment, adopted in 1870, enfranchised black but not women voters. Men who had once supported women's suffrage declared that this was "the Negro's hour," and that "women would have to wait." Many women did not want to wait patiently for their hour to come round. In politics, the flamboyant Victoria Woodhull, along with her sister Tennessee Claflin, was challenging traditional views of female chastity, and campaigning for both women's suffrage and free love. Running for the presidency in 1872, she also proclaimed her symbolic kinship with Queen Victoria, and predicted "a new security of peace, if a twin sisterhood of Victorias were to preside over the two nations."[3]

In literature, many women writers turned their energy from antislavery to women's rights, and found hope and purpose in this new allegiance. Julia Ward Howe had a conversion to feminist activism. "During the first two thirds of my life," Howe recalled, "I looked to the masculine idea of character as the only true one. I sought its inspiration, and referred my merits and demerits to its judicial verdict . . . The new domain now made clear to me was that of true womanhood—woman no longer in her ancillary relation to her opposite, man, but in her direct relation to the divine plan and purpose, as a free agent, fully sharing with man every human right and every human responsibility. This discovery was like the addition of a new continent to the map of the world, or of a new testament to the old ordinances."[4]

Harriet Beecher Stowe had been privately converted to "the Women's Rights Church" by reading John Stuart Mill's *The Subjection of Women,* and in one of her pieces for *Chimney-Corners* she announced, "this question of Woman and her Sphere is now, perhaps, the greatest of the age. We have put Slavery under foot, and with the downfall of Slavery the only obstacle to the success of our great democratic experiment is overthrown, and there seems no limit to the splendid possibilities which may open before the human race."[5] In her affectionate letters to George Eliot, Stowe declared her new commitment: "We are busy now in the next great emancipation, that of woman—This session I trust Connecticut will repeal *the whole of the old unjust English marriage property laws as regards woman* and *set her free* and then I shall be willing to claim Connecticut as my mother . . . The day of woman's co-equal reign however is coming and *you* dear tho you little think it are helping to bring it in. *Merely by being what you are!"*[6]

Women's fiction in the 1870s was a series of female Declarations of Independence. In Stowe's novel *My Wife and I* (1871), Ida van Arsdel chose to study medicine rather than marry, however strongly her family might object: "I have made my declaration of independence, and planted my guns, and got ready for war." In *The Battle of the Books* (1870), Gail Hamilton denounced the machinations of her publishers, Ticknor and Fields, with another version of the familiar preamble: "When in the course of human events it becomes necessary for an author to dissolve the bonds which have connected him with his publishers, a decent respect for the opinions of mankind requires that he should declare the causes which impel him to the separation."[7] Hamilton was a feisty advocate of women's rights: "I belong to the women's rights women. I belong to all—to those who suffer, and those who, however clumsily, are trying to mitigate suffering. The brawniest Amazon that ever stalked over the pavement, the vilest harlot that ever crouched in the cellars beneath it—I belong to them all."[8] Alice Cary published a novel called *The Born Thrall* in the suffrage newspaper *The Revolution,* which one reviewer praised as being to the cause of women "what *Uncle Tom's Cabin* was to the anti-slavery movement."[9] And Elizabeth Stuart Phelps wrote to Whittier in October 1871, asking him to write a poem on the future of women: "I am, as perhaps you may suppose, almost *invested* in the 'Woman Cause.' It grows upon my conscience, as well as my enthusiasm, every day. It seems to me to be the first work God has to be done just now."[10]

In *My Opinions and Betsey Bobbet's* (1873), the comic writer Marietta Holley created Samantha Allen, the wife of the widower Josiah Allen, whose musings on the Woman Question summarized and affectionately mocked the surplus political energies of women in the 1870s:

> *In the first days of our married life, I strained nearly every nerve to help my companion Josiah along and take care of his children by his former consort, the subject of black African slavery also wearin' on me and a*

mortgage of 200 and 50 dollars on the farm. But as we prospered and the mortgage was cleared and the children were all off to school the black African also bein' liberated about the same time of the mortgage, then my mind bein' free from these cares—the great subject of Wimmen's Rites kept a-goarin' me, and a voice kept a-sayin' inside of me, "Josiah Allen's Wife, write a book givin' your views on the great subject of Wimmen's Rites."[11]

Through the figure of Betsey Bobbet, a skinny, man-crazy spinster with thinning hair and a big nose, Holley also parodied the antebellum sentimentalists: "I have seen a good many that had it bad, but of the sentimental creeters I ever did see, Betsey Bobbet is the sentimentalist, you couldn't squeeze a laugh out of her with a cheeze press." She also comically suggested that the pleasures of matrimony could be overrated. The doleful Betsey finally marries old Simon Slimpsey, a widower with seven children, and changes her tune, hymning her lost maidenhood and longing to be set free:

> *The calm and peace of single life;*
> *Oh strangely sweet this lot doth seem,*
> *A female widder is my theme.*

The calm of single life had a new appeal to women in the 1870s. Susan B. Anthony called the decade "an epoch of single women." The "Boston marriage," as long-term intimate friendships and domestic partnerships between two women were called, became a trademark of the postwar era. Whatever their personal lifestyles, many women writers speculated on the conflicts between artistic and biological creativity. Motherhood, which had been seen as the motivating force of American women's writing before the war, came under question. Did maternal fulfillment mean giving up artistic ambition, and did artistic success demand the sacrifice of maternal drives? Were men antagonistic to women's success, and were women disadvantaged by their sex?

Lillie Devereux Blake created an adult female cross-dresser in *Fettered for Life* (1874), which David S. Reynolds has called "the most comprehensive women's rights novel of the nineteenth century."[12] The novel follows the interwoven destinies of three women—Laura Stanley, who comes to New York to seek her fortune and become an artist; Flora Livingstone, who publishes poetry to keep her sanity in a wretched mercenary marriage; and the investigative journalist "Frank Heywood," who we finally discover is a woman. By using three heroines, Blake established a model for other women writers of the 1870s seeking to explore a range of female options and roles. Laura Stanley encounters prejudice and discrimination: "my whole life long," she laments, "I have been reproached on account of my sex, as if it were a crime for which I was personally responsible." Even when she applies for a job as a clerk in an office, she is rejected, "not because I am stupid or incompetent, not because I have not good references, but because I am a woman!" Frank (whose real name we are never told) has seen that "women are shut out from every means of earning a living that is really remunerative," and resolves "to carve out for myself a place in the world as a man, and let death alone reveal my secret and prove what a woman can do." Flora's husband, like Samuel Gridley Howe, forbids her "ever again to print anything." He burns the manuscript of her poems, and she kills herself.[13] All three women have been fettered by gender in their lives, but only two manage to break their chains and escape.

The Work of Writing

By the early 1870s, Alcott, too, had announced her alliance with the American Woman Suffrage Association. Alcott had long pondered the issues of women's creativity, independence, and domesticity, and had decided that marriage and writing were incompatible. "I'd rather be a free spinster and paddle my own canoe," she had concluded, and she often felt that she was driven by ambitions her society coded as masculine. "I am more than half-persuaded that I am a man's soul, put by some freak of nature into a woman's body," she confided to a friend.[14] As a young writer, Alcott had dared to dream of fame; she dedicated her first book of short stories, *Flower Fables,* to her mother as "the first fruits of my genius." But as she became more experienced, she recanted that claim; she wrote to her publisher Thomas Niles in 1864 that "people mustn't talk about 'genius'—for I drove that idea away years ago and dont want it back again. The inspiration of necessity is all I've had, and it is a safer help than any other." Safer, perhaps, because closer to the ideal of female self-lessness. Melville could brag that men as good as Shakespeare were born every day in the United States; but only in dreams and Faustian fantasy could Alcott imagine Shakespeare's American sisters. At one point, she thought of writing a novel called "Genius," but it would have been about her father, not herself. Indeed, "genius" came to seem like the tawdry, masculine, self-aggrandizing opposite of "work," and work was what Alcott valued the most. "Work and wait," she lectured herself.[15]

Work (1872), the most feminist of her novels, alluded to the Victorian credo theorized by Thomas Carlyle, and adopted by Alcott as self-help for anxiety, frustration, and despair. "Work is and always has been my salvation," she wrote in 1872, "and I thank the Lord for inventing it." The novel's frontispiece was a morning glory erect and in full bloom being fertilized by a large and energetic bee—the female flower as powerful as the male bee that services it. Alcott also used the novel to revise her own domestic fiction. Like *Little Women*, *Work* is a female bildungsroman based on *Pilgrim's Progress*, with the heroine Christie Devon (the female version of Bunyan's Christian) setting out to find her own Celestial City of self-fulfillment. Christie is a woman of the future, who makes her own way in the world, plays an Amazon onstage, and ends up in a feminist commune.

Christie declares her independence when she turns twenty-one: "Being of age, I'm going to take care of myself and not be a burden any longer."[16] She leaves home and tries her hand at all the kinds of respectable jobs available to American women in the nineteenth century, jobs that had been explored by earlier writers of women's fiction, and that Alcott knew at first hand: domestic servant, actress, governess, companion, and seamstress. Less respectable jobs are hinted in the portrayal of Rachel, a "fallen woman" Christie meets in a milliner's sweatshop, and with whom she almost forms a Boston marriage. Alcott also portrays the manual labor of a washerwoman, Cynthy Wilkins, and a courageous ex-slave, Hepsy. Ironically, authorship, the kind of work Alcott knew best, is omitted, although it is constantly implied.

In the second half of the novel, Christie has a breakdown, and recuperates by retreating into the soothing domestic realm. When the war breaks out, she is working in a nursery alongside a gentle, feminine man named David. His greenhouse is a space of veiled, almost maternal, sensuality: "the damp, sweet air made summer there . . . Strange vines and flowers hung overhead; banks of azaleas, ruddy, white, and purple, bloomed in one place; roses turned their lovely faces to the sun; . . .dusky passion-flowers and gay nasturtiums climbing to the roof." But David himself is timid and asexual, although courageous and patriotic. He enlists; and Christie decides to enlist as a nurse along with him. "I've always wanted to live in stirring times," she tells him, "to have a part in great deeds, to sacrifice and suffer something for a principle or a person; and now I have my wish . . . it's a grand time to live, a splendid chance to do and suffer; and I want to be in it heart and soul, and earn a little of the glory or the martyrdom that will come in the end." They get married wearing their uniforms, and Alcott gives Christie many of her own wartime experiences. After two years, David is wounded and conveniently dies, leaving Christie with a baby daughter she names Pansy. True to the imagery of bees and flowers, David seems to have existed mainly to fertilize the ambitious female flower.

The novel ends with Christie "at forty"—becoming a women's rights speaker and leader, and presiding over a meeting of "a loving league of sisters, old and young, black and white, rich and poor, each ready to do her part to hasten the coming of the happy end." David's "faded cap and sheathed sword hanging on the wall" behind them is the impotent remnant of New England martial masculinity. With David gone, Christie has the credibility of the widow without the burden of the wife. While some critics have complained about the novel's structural coherence, seeing the second half as a retreat to sentimental domestic resolutions, I think that Alcott intends us to see that marriage is another form of work for women, another stage in Christie's pilgrimage. Alcott underlined this point in her dedication "To my mother, whose life has been a long labor of love."

The contrast between Christie's feisty independence and the vacillation of heroines in British novels shows how much more radical American thinking on the Woman Question was by this time. Christie admires Jane Eyre, but "can never forgive her for marrying that man." George Eliot's Dorothea in *Middlemarch* (1871), a touchstone for American women novelists of the decade, agonizes over her vocation for eight hundred pages without reaching a decision; in contrast, Christie regards the cause of women as her calling, and her choices reflect Alcott's strong sense of American self-determination. When his daughter became famous, Bronson lectured about her at suffrage conferences, with the theme of "what an American girl can do." Louisa May, however, never resolved her ambivalence about love versus duty. In other works of the 1870s, she continued to explore women's communities, and to ponder the question of whether women could combine artistic ambition with wifely, sisterly, and daughterly service.

Little Men (1871), which continued the story of the March family, gave

Jo a school to run with her husband, and showed how girls should be educated alongside boys. *Eight Cousins* (1875) and *Rose in Bloom* (1876) called for dress reform, physical education for girls, and serious work for women. In the latter book, the heroine Rose demands an identity beyond marriage for all women: "We've got minds and souls as well as hearts; ambition and talent as well as beauty and accomplishments; and we want to live and learn as well as love and be loved. I'm sick of being told that is all a woman is fit for! I won't have anything to do with love until I prove that I am something beside a housekeeper and a baby-tender!" Alcott also felt, however, that she had pandered to public demand and financial need by writing moralistic children's books. In her subsequent writing, she investigated the tension between the domestic angel in the house and female artistic ambition, and the Faust theme became increasingly compelling to her imagination. In 1877, in *A Modern Mephistopheles,* published in the anonymous No-Name series, she wrote about a young writer who bargains with the devil in order to become a great poet.

Alcott had made her own Faustian bargain for success. Yet in her fiction she continued to ask whether women could make other choices. *Diana and Persis,* a novel she began in 1879, used her sister May's life to ask whether female genius is compatible with marriage and maternity. Beginning in 1873, Alcott had subsidized May's art training in Europe, where she shared lodgings with other aspiring women painters and worked at the Académie Julian. In her letters home, May extolled the more relaxed and supportive domestic lifestyle of European women. "Here it is possible for a woman to pursue art with sufficient diligence to achieve success, and at the same time be faithful to her domestic duties."[17] In 1877, she married a much younger Swiss clerk, Ernest Nierecker, and set out to experiment with having it all. "We mean to live our own life free from conventionalities," she wrote Louisa.

In the novel, two friends are separated when Persis goes to Europe to study painting, and Diana stays behind to sculpt. As her name suggests, Diana is a vestal virgin of art, whose work is chilly and formal; Persis is an ardent Shelleyan figure, who falls in love with a musician, and attempts to combine art with marriage and maternity. Diana goes to visit them and to see for herself whether it is possible to combine love and art. She is left hopeful but undecided; after the visit, however, she goes on to Rome, where she meets a famous sculptor and falls in love. That his motherless little son is named Nino, like Margaret Fuller's child, suggests how powerfully Fuller's choice to seek fulfillment in her Italian exile had inspired Alcott to hope that female genius would blossom in marriage. The figure of Diana, though, also resembles Harriet Hosmer, the most iconoclastic American woman sculptor of the century, who lived in a well-known colony in Rome and had decided not to marry in order to dedicate herself to art: "I am the only faithful worshipper of Celibacy," she wrote, "and her service becomes more fascinating the longer I remain in it. Even if so inclined, an artist has no business to marry . . . for a woman, on whom matrimonial duties and cares weigh more heavily, it is a moral wrong, I think, for she must neglect her profession or her family."[18] May Alcott Nierecker's experiment was brief; she died in childbirth within a year of her marriage. With the agreement of the Nmiereckers, Alcott adopted the little girl, Lulu; but she was unable to finish the novel. Neither celibacy nor maternity seemed like an appropriate ending. Alcott's final book in the March trilogy, *Jo's Boys* (1886), gave Jo March Bhaer her own commercial success and a happy family as well.

American Eliots

By 1870, George Eliot had replaced Charlotte Brontë as the most admired and influential British woman novelist in the United States, and Eliot's intellectualism and literary ambition had replaced the passionate spontaneity and gothic plots of the Brontës as a model for American women writers. *Middlemarch,* her novel about the ardent intellectual Dorothea Brooke, who can only realize her ambitions vicariously through consecutive marriages to the dried-up pedant Casaubon and the handsome young politician Will Ladislaw, became the iconic text of the postbellum period. Harriet Beecher Stowe was reading it avidly in 1872, and seeing in it a fable of the exceptional woman in an ordinary community: "How like yourself is that Dorothea—You are preparing a way for a tragedy I see—your spider webs are well attached and the web will be strong—It is *you* in this I care for—more than the story—and it is very much of you that I feel in it." She was sure that Casaubon, who sounded so much like Calvin Stowe, was also a portrait of Eliot's partner, George Henry Lewes:

> My darling I confess to being very much amused & sympathetic with
> Dorothea's trials with a literary husband. Of course I see that he was a

stick & all that but the wifely feeling of Dorothea is exactly what you & I and all of us who make real marriages marry with and then these husbands! Now, don't show this to Mr Lewes but I know by my own experience with my Rabbi that you learned how to write some of these things by experience. Dont these men go on forever getting ready to begin—absorbing learning like sponges—planning sublime literary enterprises which never have a now to them? Years ago my husband made all the researches for writing a life of Martin Luther. He imported tons of books—he read he lectured he fired me into a flame of eagerness he prepared and prepared and prepared but his ideal grew and he never came to the time of completion—and now alas—never will. Still he goes on reading studying investigating subject after subject apparently for no object but to entertain me and when I try to make him write the books he ought to he is never ready—and I believe I sometimes make myself a sort of trouble some outside conscience to him by trying to push him up to do what he has been so long getting ready to do—So you see I sympathise with poor Dorothea but then her husband is too much of a stick!—Yet I understand too that girls often make a false marriage and plight their faith to an unreal shadow who they suppose inhabits a certain body—I am intensely curious to know what is to become of her.[19]

Eliot hastened to reply that Lewes was an exemplary partner, and nothing like Casaubon at all. But Stowe, with her spontaneity and warmth, comes off very well in this exchange—what other woman novelist would have dared to call the reserved Eliot "my darling"? And her ideas about character and structure in fiction were intelligent and incisive despite the informality of her prose. In September 1876, the Stowes were reading *Daniel Deronda* together. "We, my husband & I, have strictly confined ourselves to the *serial* form, taking it in our monthly installments & meditating there on—as if it were a passage of scripture." She preferred the tragedy of the heroine Gwendolyn to the didactic sections about Mirah, Deronda, and Judaism:

But after all I confess that my hearts blood vibrates more towards Gwendolin than Mirah & that I feel a more living interest in her feelings, struggles and sorrows than those of Mirah—The two characters of Gwendolin and Grandcourt are I think the artistic gems. Grandcourt as doing the work of the villain in the play without any of the burnt cork of a stage villain—I cant imagine any character more utterly worthless and disagreeable, yet invested throughout with such an air of worldly respectability and probability. There is great reticence in his wickedness. Not a monster by any means, Making suitable and even generous provision for the woman he is tired of—and treating the woman he marries with every external form of consideration & only occasionally swearing at her in the strictest privacy. The point in the courtship where he ejaculates "damn her!" under his breath is a comment on such marriages worth pages of disquisition and the beauty of it is—that you have no moral reflection. The grim distinctness with which you set forth "marriage a la mode" with the rector pointing out to the young girl the duty of securing a brilliant match and comforting himself with the reflection that she cannot know anything about previous irregularities—is a stroke of satire on English good society which I suppose they hardly appreciate—but I do—[20]

A NEW ENGLAND *MIDDLEMARCH: THE STORY OF AVIS*

In their high ideals and thwarted aspirations, the American disciples of *Middlemarch* were more like Dorothea Brooke than George Eliot. Aiming for immortality, they fell short of their dreams; they did not write the great American novel, fully analyze a woman's character, or tell the story of a woman artist's development. Instead, like their British sisters, they told the stories of women who lived in obscurity, but who might have been great artists under better circumstances. If these women's lives remained hidden and their graves unvisited, they were nonetheless worthy models for the Coming Woman Writer.

In November 1872, Elizabeth Stuart Phelps nervously delivered a series of lectures on Eliot at Boston University, from which hundreds of people had to be turned away.[21] Phelps especially admired *Middlemarch* and had begun to think of writing an American version. As she wrote to Eliot in February 1873,

You have written the novel of the century—but that is one matter; you have almost analyzed a woman—and that is quite another! I say "almost" because I believe it remains for you to finish what you have begun and that Middlemarch itself is the hint and proposition for the study of another problem with a great solution. One of our leading theologians said to me "Dorothea should never have married." So faintly can theology comprehend her! Rather should she never accept wifehood

as a métier. The woman's personal identity is a vast undiscovered coun-
try with which society has yet to acquaint itself, and by which it is yet
to be revolutionized. I cannot tell you how earnestly I feel that it will
require a great novel to proclaim the royal lineage of the Coming
Woman to the average mind, or what a positive personal longing it has
become to me that you should write it—if no other reason to prevent
my writing a small one![22]

Phelps's novel of the Coming Woman was *The Story of Avis* (1877),
which tries to set Eliot's story of female identity in the vast undiscovered
country of the United States. She portrays three generations of women:
Avis's mother, a gifted but thwarted actress; Avis herself, a trained and
dedicated painter; and her daughter Waitstill, who may be the woman of
the future. Avis is the daughter of Hegel Dobell, a professor of ethics
and intellectual philosophy at Harmouth College in New England.
Brought up and "matronized" by her aunt Chloe, Avis must learn sewing
and cooking, which she detests. "I hate to make my bed, and I hate, hate
to sew chemises, and I hate, hate, *hate* to go cooking round the kitchen."
At sixteen, she reads Elizabeth Barrett Browning's *Aurora Leigh,* and
decides to be an artist. Her father tells her she makes "pretty little
copies," and "must be satisfied." But Avis insists on being trained in Florence. She goes abroad at twenty, and spends five years studying; Phelps
wanted to emphasize the difficulty and responsibility of art.

Avis intends to remain single. "My ideals of art," she observes, "are
those with which marriage is perfectly incompatible. Success—for a
woman—means absolute surrender, in whatever direction. Whether she
paints a picture, or loves a man, there is no division of labor possible in
her economy. To the attainment of any end worth living for, a symmetrical sacrifice of her nature is compulsory upon her." She tells Philip
Ostrander, a young lecturer who courts her, that "marriage is a profession to a woman. And I have my work; I have my work." Indeed, Avis
believes that trying to be an artist and a wife "is like civil war." At this
point in the novel, Phelps introduces the Civil War as a reality as well
as a metaphor. Philip enlists in the summer of 1862, "the summer of
battles—Fair Oaks, The Seven Days, Cedar Mountain, Bull Run, Harpers
Ferry, Antietam." Meanwhile, in her bedroom in the college town, Avis
hears boys singing the "Battle Hymn of the Republic," and wonders
whether war and the military spirit are "what the work of women
lacked?—high stimulant, rough virtues, strong vices, all the great peril

and power of exuberant exposed life?" The "Battle Hymn," however, *was* women's work. Avis has an epiphany that offers the hope of equaling Howe's achievement in her own painting, which will be about women's suffering:

> *Instantly the room seemed to become full of women. Cleopatra was there, and Godiva, Aphrodite and St. Elizabeth, Ariadne and Esther, Helen and Jeanne d'Arc, and the Magdalene, Sappho and Cornelia . . . these moved on solemnly and gave way to a silent army of the unknown. They swept before her in file, in procession, in groups. They blushed at altars; they knelt in convents; they leered in the streets; they sung to their babes; they stooped and stitched in black attics; they trembled beneath summer moons; they starved in cellars; they fell by the blow of a man's hand; they sold their souls for bread; they dashed their lives out in swift streams; they wrung their hands in prayer . . . The mystery of womanhood stood before her, and said "Speak for me!"*

Phelps develops several myths and metaphors for her woman artist, including the caged bird; but the most important is that of the Sphinx, the subject of Avis's major painting. While for male artists of the period, the Sphinx is a mute monster, for Phelps she stands for the enigmatic nature of female genius.

Philip is wounded in the war, and out of pity Avis agrees to marry him, although before the wedding she tries to tear off "the ring that fettered her finger." Too late; Philip is an unfaithful husband and an undisciplined scholar who does not even get tenure: "He has shirked the drudgery of the class-room," her father sorrowfully tells her. Motherhood drains her energy; their son Van cries all the time, and "she felt half-ashamed of herself for being the mother of so cross a child." Domestic duties soak up all her time: "It was impossible to express, without giving them both useless pain, her inherent, ineradicable, and sickening recoil from the details of household care." Avis has another child, a daughter to whom she gives the old-fashioned Puritan name Waitstill, but things get worse and worse. Van dies; Philip soon follows, although Avis tries taking him to Florida to recover. Avis loses her gift for painting, and must teach art in order to support herself and her little daughter, to whom she wistfully reads the story of the Holy Grail. As Phelps concludes:

> *We have been told that it takes three generations to make a gentleman: we may believe that it will take as much, or more, to make A WOMAN. A*

being of radiant physique; the heiress of ancestral health on the mater-
nal side; a creature forever more of nerve than of muscle, and therefore
trained to the energy of the muscle and the repose of the nerve; physi-
cally educated by mothers of her own fibre, and by physicians of her
own sex,—such a woman alone is fitted to acquire the drilled brain, the
claimed imagination, and sustained aim, which constitute intellectual
command.[23]

Some reviewers compared *Avis* to *Middlemarch*. *The Nation* wrote that "Miss Phelps has shown herself an apt pupil of George Eliot . . . The influence of the greater novelist is to be seen on every page so that it may be fair to wonder if this novel would have been written if *Middlemarch* had not appeared." In a letter to Eliot, Phelps belittled her own novel, and blamed the exigencies of financial need for too soon exhausting her intellectual energies: "I do not hope much for it now; I am physically too far spent even to do what is a bitter comfort to hope I might have done, if the success of 'The Gates Ajar' had not driven a *very* young woman who wanted money, into rapid and unstudious work before the evil days came when work must be quietly put out of the imagination like other forms of suicide."[24]

A SOUTHERN *MIDDLEMARCH: LIKE UNTO LIKE*

During Reconstruction, the clash between old ideals and new aspirations, the Lost Cause and the woman's cause, inspired Southern women's interest in Eliot's realism and broad social understanding. "The old life of the South has passed away," says a character in Sherwood Bonner's *Like unto Like* (1878). "It only remains for the genius of a George Eliot to grasp these old materials, and from their wreck build a memorial of its glory in a Southern 'Middlemarch.' "[25]

Bonner saw herself as well situated to take up the challenge. Born Katherine Bonner Sherwood in 1849, in Holly Springs, Mississippi, she had been a dreamy, literary girl, and the Civil War had interrupted her life when Union soldiers closed down the female seminary she was attending.[26] When the war was over, she longed for romance, adventure, and escape, and found it only in books; in her diary she wrote of Charlotte Brontë's *Villette,* "Oh! The inexpressible pathos of the book! How exactly it suits the wild spirit that, weary of its useless rebellings against fate, rests at last in the calm of despair."[27] Like Alcott, Bonner wrote gothic stories for the local newspapers, but saw her best chance for escape in marrying Edwin McDowell, who had been educated in England. Her expectations for the marriage, however, were disappointed when McDowell could not establish a career either in the South or in Texas, where he had moved his wife and infant daughter in 1872.

Bonner wanted to leave their baby, Lilian, with her family and attend Vassar College, but her relatives were adamantly opposed to such a radical change. Instead, she went to Boston to attend a free school, and find work as a writer. There she quickly made influential friends, among them the aging poet Longfellow, the temperance lecturer Dio Lewis, and the radical journalist James Redpath. The publisher of Alcott's *Hospital Sketches,* Redpath was a glamorous figure who was well known as a militant abolitionist and as the biographer of John Brown. Born in Scotland, he had emigrated to the United States at the age of seventeen; by age nineteen, he had so impressed Horace Greeley with his writing gifts that he was made an editor at the *New York Tribune.* In the 1850s, Redpath traveled through the South, interviewing slaves, and publishing his impassioned accounts of their suffering and hardship. In 1856, he went to Kansas, where he reported on the violence between free-state and proslavery forces; fatefully, he found John Brown hiding after the massacre at Pottawatomie, and celebrated him as a "warrior-saint." After Harpers Ferry, Redpath defended Brown in the press; he even owned a piece of the scaffold on which Brown was hanged, which he had labeled "A Bit of the True Cross." Despite their political differences, Redpath, like the elderly Longfellow, was charmed by and enamored of the charismatic Kate McDowell.

By 1874, she was supporting herself as a journalist and correspondent of the *Memphis Avalanche,* under the name "Sherwood Bonner." As a Southerner reporting on her experiences in the North, she reversed the usual mode of postbellum travel literature. In particular, she satirized Boston and the Concord intelligentsia, including Alcott, whose comments on Southern women ("dressed up dolls") infuriated her. In May 1875, Bonner published "The Radical Club," an anonymous satire of Bronson Alcott, Ednah Dow Cheney ("a magnus corpus, with a figure like a porpus"), and Elizabeth Peabody ("the Kindergarten mother") in the *Boston Times.* Her mischievous mockery of the "Orphic utterances" of Emerson alienated William Dean Howells, and she would never be published in the *Atlantic Monthly.*[28]

In 1877, Bonner attempted a reconciliation with her husband, and began an autobiographical novel called "The Prodigal Daughter." The manuscript has disappeared, but instead she wrote *Like unto Like,* the story of a North-South romance during Reconstruction. It was a "romance of reunion," as such narratives were called, and it turned her personal story into one with social breadth and meaning. Dedicated to Longfellow, *Like unto Like* is set in the fictional town of Yariba, Alabama, and begins in the summer of 1875 as three unmarried girls, Betty Page, Mary Barton, and the heroine, Emma Blythe Herndon, are awaiting the arrival of Union soldiers in their town. The situation suggests Jane Austen, and indeed Emma's name is a strong reminder; but soon we learn that she is called Blythe rather than Emma, and that she is no Austen maiden but an American girl who makes her own "declaration of independence": "I would marry any man I loved—be he Jew, Roman Catholic, Yankee, or Fiji Islander." Blythe also admires Margaret Fuller: "I read something the other day . . . that a Boston woman said—Fuller, I think, was her name—yes, Margaret Fuller: 'to give her hand with dignity, woman must be able to stand alone.' " Like Eliot's Dorothea, she is an ardent young woman who wishes she could "find out the meaning and the use of my life."

Blythe's values are soon tested. Unlike Betty (one of the first characters in American women's literature to worry about her weight and wear black because it makes her look thin), she is not a belle or coquette. She is a daring spirit who has read *Tom Jones,* defended abolitionism, and questioned religion. But the Yankee she falls in love with, Roger Ellis, is twenty years older and much more advanced in his opinions and behaviors. Based on James Redpath, he is a staunch abolitionist, to whom John Brown is a martyr, the Civil War a battle between civilization and barbarism, and Reconstruction too kind: "The North was too mild . . . It should have treated the South as it would the shark or the tiger. It should have . . . razed every house, burned every blade of grass, drowned opposition in blood . . . The whole Southern country should have been reduced to a territorial condition—a ward of the nation, to be recognized when education and thrift had made it worthy of admission into a nation of freemen." He is in Alabama to investigate "outrages," or atrocities and acts of violence against freedmen, and becomes what the Southerners regard as an outside agitator, who travels around speaking to black audiences.

Ellis adopts a bright black child known locally as "Civil Rights Bill," and educates him; but Blythe, although she disapproves of slavery, is not ready for equality and cannot bring herself to eat at the same table with the boy. Ellis also tells her about his past affair with an unhappily married woman, and his sympathy for an unhappily married man the folks of Yariba regard as a scoundrel; even Blythe is shocked by his easy acceptance of divorce. At the Mardi Gras carnival in New Orleans, they clash, and Blythe decides to break their engagement: "There can be no harmony in our lives. You may be right, but you are at the end of things, I at the beginning. If ever I come to where you are, it must be by my own slow steps." Blythe's refusal is a symbol of the position of the white Southern intelligentsia in 1875—ready to change, but unable to accept an imposed and rapid transformation.

Politically, Bonner's sympathies lie with Ellis, who has the most persuasive and prophetic arguments about race, while Blythe is still locked into her prejudices. Personally, though, he is no Mr. Knightly, but a domineering man who shares some of Casaubon's rigidity and pedantry. Bonner suggests that marriage to this powerful man would imprison Blythe in a subordinate role, and limit her free development. Their arguments are not just about the future of the Confederacy but also about "the politics of gender."[29] Although *Like unto Like* has nothing of the ambition and depth of *Middlemarch*, Bonner sets the love story within the context of the wider community, and her black characters, especially Civil Rights Bill, are not the sentimentalized devoted servants of much Reconstruction fiction. Her treatment of the problems facing the North and South as they attempt to forge a united country is serious and critical, something like Forster's view of Anglo-Indian relations in *A Passage to India*. Reunion, however romantic to imagine, cannot happen in postwar Alabama. Like must cleave unto like. Moreover, Blythe needs her freedom in order to grow. As Bonner concludes, "the story of her life is not yet told."

Reviews of *Like unto Like* were generally positive, and many compared Bonner to George Eliot. Bonner continued to aspire to writing serious fiction; she told the editor of *Harper's Monthly* that "in ten years I shall be an artist." But she did not have ten years. Having divorced her husband, and recovered custody of her daughter, Bonner wrote commercial short stories to support them. In July 1883, she died of breast cancer in Mississippi.

In her compassionate epitaph for Dorothea in the great concluding paragraphs of *Middlemarch*, Eliot may also have written the epitaph of the American women writers of her generation, whose lives were not fully told and who did not fully realize their gifts, but nonetheless made a difference in literary history:

Certainly those determining aspects of her life were not ideally beautiful. They were the mixed result of young and noble impulse struggling amidst the conditions of an imperfect social state, in which great feelings will often take the aspect of error, and great faith the aspect of illusion . . . Her full nature . . . spent itself in channels which had no great name on the earth. But the effect of her being on those around her was incalculably diffusive; for the growing good of the world is dependent on unhistoric acts; and that things are not so ill with you and me as they might have been, is half owing to the number who lived faithfully a hidden life, and rest in unvisited tombs.

9

American Sibyls

hen George Eliot died in December 1880, American women writers felt both saddened that a great era had passed and relieved that so formidable a literary rival was gone. At the start of Constance Fenimore Woolson's career in 1882, a reviewer praised her by saying that "a fragment, and not an inferior fragment, of the mantle of George Eliot had fallen on her shoulders." Such compliments were kindly meant, but Woolson may not have been so grateful to inherit Eliot's cast-off clothes. Earlier she had dutifully composed a sonnet "To George Eliot" (1876) in which she praised the novelist as a colossus who inspired lesser women to write, but also as a "grand, unapproachable" mountain.[1] After Eliot's death, when she read the first biography of the great author, Woolson noted with some asperity that she had been pampered and sheltered compared to her American sisters: "she had one of the easiest, most indulged and 'petted' lives that I have ever known or heard of." In London, Henry James's sister, Alice, ranted in her diary that Eliot "makes upon me the impression, morally and physically, of mildew or some morbid growth—a fungus of a pendulous shape, or as of something damp to the touch."[2]

This was extreme, but women writers did experience Eliot's death as the exorcism of an oppressive ghost. The unapproachable terrain of the female genius had long loomed before them; now they tried, with considerable success, to claim the heights for themselves and their country. They began to take themselves seriously as artists and sibyls, and to relocate their shrines to native soil. In Greek and Roman mythology, the sibyls were women who delivered their prophecies at holy sites and oracles. In a return to classical mythology as well as religious spiritualism after the Civil War, Americans closely studied the Greek goddesses; as

Thomas Higginson perceived, "their genealogies have been ransacked, as if they lived in Boston or Philadelphia."[3] During a period when the great male author was revered as a "master" (Longfellow's work, wrote Sarah Orne Jewett, "stands like a great cathedral in which the world may worship"), and high culture enthroned the classic and the canonical, women writers embraced the image of the sibyl. The figure of the great woman writer as wise mother, high priestess, and oracle has endured until the twenty-first century.[4]

Harriet Beecher Stowe had introduced the idea of the American prophetess when she called the ex-slave Sojourner Truth, who had traveled the country speaking for both women's rights and abolition, "The Libyan Sibyl." Stowe stressed Sojourner Truth's charismatic and prophetic gifts: "I do not recollect ever to have been conversant with any one who had more of that silent and subtle power which we call personal presence than this woman." In 1861, on a visit to Rome, Stowe described her to the American sculptor William Wetmore Story: "The history of Sojourner Truth worked in his mind and led him into the deeper recesses of the African nature—those unexplored depths of being and feeling, mighty and dark as the gigantic depths of tropical forests, mysterious as the hidden rivers and mines of that burning continent whose life-history is yet to be."[5] Story was inspired to create a marble statue, *The Libyan Sibyl,* a mysterious, brooding, and infinitely wise woman in full maturity, which is now on display at the Smithsonian American Art Museum.[6]

Sibyl Judaica—Emma Lazarus

Memorializing the death of the poet Emma Lazarus (1849–1887), the editor Charles DeKay called her the "Sibyl Judaica," a prophetess who had come to scourge anti-Semitism as Sojourner Truth had scourged racism. Lazarus would have welcomed the image; she taught her generation not only that Jews would become part of American culture but also that they would change its soul.[7] A fourth-generation descendant of a prosperous New York Sephardic family, Lazarus was a precocious child who began to write in her teens. Her proud father had her first book, *Poems and Translations Written Between the Ages of Fourteen and Sixteen,* privately printed in 1866.

In 1868, the firm of Hurd and Houghton republished the book, and Lazarus boldly sent a signed copy to Emerson, whom she had met at a party. They began an intense correspondence, with the sixty-five-year-old sage flirtatiously offering to be her "professor," and the eighteen-year-old Emma seeking his recommendations and mentorship. Unfortunately, Lazarus overestimated his chivalrous appreciation of her poetry as real sponsorship, while Emerson underestimated her increasingly aggressive demands for literary recognition. She dedicated her second book, *Admetus and Other Poems* (1871), to him; but in 1874, when Emerson brought out his poetry anthology, *Parnassus,* Lazarus was shocked to find that her work was not included. She rashly wrote him a long and indignant letter demanding an explanation: "I cannot resist the impulse of expressing to you my extreme disappointment at finding you have so far modified the enthusiastic estimate you held of my literary labors as to refuse me a place . . . I can only consider this omission a public retraction of all the flattering opinions & letters you have sent me, and I cannot to any degree reconcile it with your numerous expressions of extravagant admiration."[8] Emerson did not reply to the letter; he may have been embarrassed by the way Lazarus confronted him, fearful of her further demands, or simply falling victim to the Alzheimer's that shadowed his last years. She paid him a visit before his death, at which his daughters stood guard to ward off her more zealous efforts at intimacy.

Undaunted, Lazarus befriended Thomas Higginson at her family's summer home in Newport, and joined the Town and Country Club, which he had founded along with Julia Ward Howe. She became close to the artist Helena de Kay Gilder and her husband, *Century* editor Richard Gilder, and in 1877, she also met Edmund Stedman. Despite her outward success, good connections, and confident self-promotion, Lazarus presented herself as one who wrestled inwardly with the self-doubt of the conventional woman poet. In "Echoes," a sonnet written in October 1880, she described herself as "late-born and woman-souled," unable to claim "the might / Of manly, modern passion" or twang "the full-stringed lyre through all its scope," and "one in love with solitude and song." She confided these "feelings of despondency as to her poetic work" to Stedman, and he responded by advising her to write about her Jewish heritage: "It suddenly occurred to me to ask her why she had been so indifferent to a vantage-ground which she, a Jewess of the purest stock, held above any other writer . . . She said that, although proud of her blood and lineage, the Hebrew ideals did not appeal to her; but I replied that I envied her the inspiration she might derive from them."[9] In a debate with Stedman over the future of poetry in America, Lazarus had declared her belief that "wherever there is humanity, there is the theme for a great poem." But she had not yet discovered her own theme.

However, she had begun to write poems about European anti-Semitism, and in the 1880s she also began to study Hebrew, to discuss "the Jewish Question" in the *American Hebrew* and elsewhere, to advocate Zionism, and to become an eloquent champion of the persecuted immigrants escaping the ghettos of Eastern Europe for America's golden promise. These commitments gave her something besides feminine inhibition to write about, and liberated her as an American poet. "The Jewish Question which I plunged into so wrecklessly [*sic*] and impulsively last spring," she wrote to Hawthorne's daughter Rose in 1882, "has gradually absorbed more and more of my mind and heart—It opens up such enormous vistas in the Past and Future, and is so palpitating alive at the moment . . . that it has about driven out of my thought all other subjects." Meeting her that summer in Newport, William James described her to his wife as confident and energetic, "a poetess, a magaziness, and a Jewess, Miss Emma Lazarus," who "brandished the Jewish flag, phylactery, golden calf, or whatever the standard of the Nation might be."[10]

In 1883, the novelist Constance Cary Harrison asked Lazarus to write a poem for a fund-raising exhibition, with the purpose of buying a pedestal for the statue of "Liberty Enlightening the World." "I begged Miss Lazarus to give us some verses appropriate for the occasion," Harrison recalled. "She was at first inclined to rebel against writing anything 'to order,' as it were . . . 'Think of that Goddess standing on her pedestal down yonder in the bay, and holding her torch out to those Russian refugees of yours you are so fond of visiting on Ward's Island,' I suggested. The shaft sped home—her dark eyes deepened—her cheek flushed—the time for merriment was passed—she said not a word more, then."[11]

Lazarus had only seen the statue in photographs, but in her sonnet "The New Colossus," she contrasted the ancient Colossus of Rhodes, a giant masculine emblem of imperial conquest, with the "mighty woman with a torch," a maternal, welcoming, figure, the "Mother of Exiles" who symbolized America. In the sonnet's sestet, Lazarus imagined the statue's silent message:

> *"Keep, ancient lands, your storied pomp!" cries she*
> *With silent lips. "Give me your tired, your poor,*
> *Your huddled masses yearning to breathe free,*

The wretched refuse of your teeming shore.
Send these, the homeless, tempest-tost to me,
I lift my lamp beside the golden door!"

Writing about the sibyl of Liberty unlocked Lazarus's deepest feelings about her own identity as a woman, a Jew, and an American, and connected a monument with an idea. As James Russell Lowell told her, "Your sonnet gives its subject a *raison d'être* which it wanted before quite as much as it wanted a pedestal."[12] Nevertheless, when President Cleveland dedicated the Statue of Liberty in 1886, "The New Colossus" was not read. Lazarus died of Hodgkin's disease the following year, her work forgotten. Although "The New Colossus" was engraved on the pedestal of the statue in 1903, her legacy, as Esther Schor notes, had still been whittled down to "a single sonnet."[13] She left behind translations, poems about Judaism, and poems about womanhood, especially "Assurance," an undated, unpublished sonnet about a lesbian dream-vision. To quote Schor's eloquent memorial:

> [H]owever colossal the legacy of her sonnet, the legacy of Emma Lazarus exceeds it . . . In her brief thirty-eight years, she did what no woman of her day did, what no Jew of her day did. She lived the double life of American Jewry without apology. She emboldened American Jews to be proud of their doubleness, to learn and cherish their heritage, to claim a future as a nation . . . And she was not afraid to face herself: . . . her own erotic desires; her own vaulting, later chastened, ambition.[14]

Women's Regionality

Images of prophetic American womanhood also shaped the literary genres of local color and regionalism.[15] Through short stories as well as novels, women wrote about the declining villages as shrines to the past and oracular sites ruled by aging spinsters and wise matriarchs, sibylline heroines and far-sighted storytellers. In an eloquent essay published in 1972, at the beginning of the academic revival of interest in American women's writing, and indeed in the first issue of the journal *Women's Studies*, Ann Douglas Wood described regional and local color fiction as a dramatic departure from the women's fiction that dominated the 1850s.

These authors "wanted recognition as writers because they were, more or less, artists," in an age "which favored the short story and saw its development as a serious art form." They were "stranded in the nearly manless backwater of northern New England and the rural South," and fascinated by the figure of the "old woman . . . who is barren and child-less, even if she once bore children; she is alone, superannuated, almost deformed," but strangely powerful—almost a witch.[16]

Regional fiction has been one of the most controversial topics of American literary history, a sign that it is extremely interesting, rich, var-ied, and shaped by a multiplicity of social, economic, racial, and aes-thetic forces as well as geographic ones. American men, including Bret Harte, Hamlin Garland, and Charles Chesnutt, made their literary repu-tations in these genres as well as women; indeed, there was so much demand for fiction about remote or rustic places, manners, and dialects, that regionalism actually became the entrée or route to a literary career for many writers, including women, who were outsiders themselves: it offered "an extension of the literary franchise."[17] In New England espe-cially, it "favored women writers," Josephine Donovan suggests, "for, like the domestic novel, it allowed them to describe their own bailiwicks, realms that they knew intimately. It did not requite heroic experiences on an epic scale that they themselves could never have had."[18] On the other hand, regionalism could also be seen as an inherently minor liter-ary genre, closely linked to the short story and the novella, evading the manifest destiny of the great American novel, and thus suitable for the lesser ambitions of women.[19] As Cheryl Torsney has ruefully observed, in much American literary criticism, "if the novel is a Moby Dick in a tur-bid sea of symbol, the local color story is a five-cent goldfish in a tank at Woolworth's."[20]

Critics disagree about whether regional fiction was primarily a woman's genre, the chosen "site for the articulation of a feminist analy-sis of the situation of women."[21] A less political approach is to describe this writing as the psychological fiction of "women's regionality." Women writers used geography as a way to talk about gender: "under cover of regionalism . . . these women writers explored the territory of women's lives. Their essential agenda . . . was to map the geography of their gender. They were regionalists—but not solely in the ways critics have conventionally thought. The geography of America formed an important part of their work, but essentially they charted the regions of women's lives, regions both without and within the self."[22] Women's regionality was as much psychological, spiritual, and metaphorical as sociological and geographic. The best of the stories have the power of legend as well as the grit of realism, dealing with the tragic lives of women subject to the power of abusive, alcoholic, tyrannical fathers and husbands. For these qualities, regional and local-color fiction became the first women's genres to be subjected to strongly opposed interpretations and evaluations. "From the distance of a decade," two specialists in American women's regionalism have noted, "we can more readily acknowledge that recovery work has its dangers, one of which is a representation of earlier writers geared to contemporary tastes . . . This dilemma might translate, on the one hand, into a taste for grim, psychologically realistic stories of women and hardship amenable to modernist-inflected criticism, or, on the other hand, into a desire for representations of utopian female communities that invite empowering feminist readings."[23] Women regionalists have suited these contemporary tastes and shifting political agendas, and been taken up by various critical schools; but they also were the first group of American women writers to take themselves seriously as artists, and to locate themselves in an American female literary genealogy as well as in a European tradition of high art. It is the period when "a publishing American woman author first claims the duty (hence the right) to take her art seriously," and "to define her proper self as the maker of her art," writes the literary historian Richard Brodhead. It is a moment "of immense historical resonance."[24]

New England Sibyls

ROSE TERRY COOKE

Although regional fiction covered all of the United States, it was strongly associated with New England. Born in Hartford to an old New England family, Rose Terry Cooke (1827–1892) spent most of her life in Connecticut. She also set her fiction there, in imaginary towns and districts called Cranberry and Bassett, which suggest Elizabeth Gaskell's Cranford and Anthony Trollope's Barsetshire. A precocious child who could read at three, Cooke was educated at Catherine Beecher's school in Hartford, and was a longtime friend of Harriet Beecher Stowe. After her father suffered "reverses" in her teens, she supported herself by teaching and writing poems and stories that described the tragic lives of rural New England women. As Cooke asked, given "the daily dullness of work, the brutality, stupidness, small craft, and boorish tyranny of husbands, to whom they are tied beyond escape, what wonder is it that a third of all the female lunatics in asylums are farmers' wives?"[25] When she was forty-six, Cooke recklessly married a much younger widower, Rollin H. Cooke, and he quickly squandered her money. No surprise that many of her best stories, published in the 1880s, warned other women not to risk their emotions or their savings with charming but deceitful men.

One such story was "Odd Miss Todd." Raised by her eccentric father in almost total isolation, Miny (Hermione) Todd educates herself, and when she moves into town after his death, she is an eccentric freethinker with no regard for social amenities. She then falls in love with a handsome and sympathetic younger man, tries to change, but is rejected. Embittered and confirmed in her "oddness"—Cooke uses the word, like George Gissing in *The Odd Women* (1893) to mean both unconventional and unmatched or single—she becomes a strong feminist, leaves her money to found a women's college, and defies community decorum by insisting on being buried in her nightgown. From the point of view of feminist critics, odd Miss Todd "does not see herself as odd but rather finds odd those behaviors others label normal."[26]

SARAH ORNE JEWETT

While odd Miss Todd had some oracular qualities, Mrs. Almira Todd, the "learned herbalist" who presides over Sarah Orne Jewett's *The Country of the Pointed Firs* (1896), was clearly the American priestess of an alternative religion. In her kitchen, standing "in the center of a braided rug," Mrs. Todd's "height and massiveness . . . gave her the look of a huge sibyl, while the strange fragrance of the mysterious herb blew in from the little garden." Set in Dunnet Landing, an imaginary maritime village in eastern Maine, the first-person narrative describes the responses of an unnamed woman writer to her summers in the seaside village ruled over by Mrs. Todd, who is its historian and storyteller as well as its physician and mythic matriarch.[27]

Sarah Orne Jewett (1849–1909) was also a central and sibylline figure in American women's literary history. She had been strongly influenced by Stowe's *The Pearl of Orr's Island* (1862); in her preface to the 1893 edition of the short stories she collected as *Deephaven,* Jewett credited Stowe as her major influence: "Mrs. Stowe had written of those who dwelt along the wooded seacoast and by the decaying, shipless harbors of Maine. The first chapters of *The Pearl of Orr's Island* gave the younger author of *Deephaven* to see with new eyes, and to follow eagerly the old shore paths from one gray, weather-beaten house to another where Genius pointed her the way." At the same time, Jewett allied herself to Flaubert in her commitment to the art of fiction, and the need to put it first. She repudiated the priority of selflessness over art that had been a given for Stowe's generation. Six years later, after Stowe's death, Jewett made important distinctions about why she had gone beyond Stowe's example. In a letter to Annie Fields, she talked about rereading *The Pearl of Orr's Island* and noticing its structural incoherence, which she attributed to the obligations and interruptions of Stowe's domestic life. "You must throw everything and everybody aside at times, but a woman made like Mrs. Stowe cannot bring herself to the cold selfishness of the moment for one's work's sake, and the recompense for her loss is a divine touch here and there in an incomplete piece of work."28

Sarah Orne Jewett grew up in South Berwick, Maine, one of three daughters of a doctor who took her with him on his country rounds, as well as giving her access to his library, where she read Austen and Flaubert. She started to write as a young woman, but her first serious publication was a story, "The Shore House," in the *Atlantic* in 1873. The editor William Dean Howells accepted it and befriended her, as did the publisher Horace Scudder, who wanted her to write a novel. But, she wrote to him, that was out of the question. "In the first place, I have no dramatic talent. The story would have no plot, I should have to fill it out with descriptions of character and meditations. It seems to me I can furnish the theater, and show you the actors, and the scenery, and the audience, but there never is any play!" Brodhead sees this choice as part of Jewett's perennial self-miniaturization; in her own day, Jewett was often patronized as the epitome of the little woman writer, someone whom Henry James praised for her "beautiful little quantum of achievement," writing what Howells called her "perfect little stories."29 She may have colluded in projecting this image of the minor artist.

In the late 1870s, Jewett was revising a group of her stories and sketches for the book that became *Deephaven* (1877). Anticipating her later work, *Deephaven* centers on two friends, Helen Denis and Kate Lancaster, who spend a summer in the quiet seacoast town, and return home to Boston changed by their sojourn.30 Even at this early stage, Jewett's writing was small in scope but large in meaning and resonance. In one of the chapters, "The Circus at Denby," Helen and Kate take an

excursion to see a traveling circus, accompanied by their wise Deephaven Demeter, Mrs. Kew. It is a disappointing outing; Denby is an
"uninteresting town which had grown up around some mills." The circus animals "looked tired and as if they had been on the road for a good
many years." The elephant is especially "shabby" and "dejected"; the
clown seems "tired" and hopeless; the advertised huge snake is actually
long dead and buried. The trip is redeemed, however, when they stop at
the sideshow tents to view the "largest woman ever seen in America—
the great Kentucky giantess!" At first the giantess, too, seems much thinner than her picture and rather depressed; but then Mrs. Kew recognizes
her as a former neighbor, Marilly, whose father died of drink and left her
destitute. She was rescued when the circus master took her on to replace
his old fat lady, who had "begun to fall away considr'ble." Marilly finds a
home in the circus, but "it's a pretty hard business," and although she is
billed as six hundred pounds, she weighs barely four hundred, and
admits she does "lose heart sometimes."[31] The story is both Jewett's
ironic satire of the slender hopes of even the largest women in America
and the beginning of a tradition of writing about freakish doubles in
American women's fiction. The circus is not a carnivalesque, topsy-
turvy world of hedonistic celebration, but the remnants of a lost age of
magic and transformation.

By 1882, Jewett's father had died, and she became closer to Annie
Fields, who was mourning the death of her husband. In May 1882, they
traveled together to Europe, visiting Ireland, England, Norway, Bel-
gium, Italy, France, and Switzerland; and upon their return in the fall,
Jewett collected her clothes from the family home and moved into the
Fields's house at 148 Charles Street in Boston. Their relationship was one
of the most celebrated and accepted of the Boston marriages. Dr. Nan
Prince, the heroine of Jewett's *A Country Doctor* (1884), is a dedicated professional who does not wish to marry. "If I have good reasons against all
that," Nan asks, "would you have me bury the talent God had given me,
and choke down the wish that makes itself a prayer every morning that I
may do this work lovingly and well?" She briefly becomes infatuated
with an eligible young man, George Gerry, and her ambitions temporarily fade; but she then finds out there is insanity on her mother's side of
the family, and has an excuse to break off the match. No fairy-tale
princess, Jewett's Dr. Prince takes a male role. "I know that all the
world's sympathy and all tradition fight on his side," she concludes, "but
I can look forward and see something a thousand times better than being
his wife." She returns to her village, Oldfields, to practice medicine.

"A White Heron" (1886), one of Jewett's most-anthologized stories, is also a parable about a girl's refusal to enter the heterosexual and urban worlds, a fairy tale about a New England princess who refuses to be rescued from her isolation by the handsome prince. Nine-year-old Sylvia lives in the forest with her grandmother, who chose to raise her out of all her siblings and took her away from a noisy and crowded manufacturing town. She has become a woodland native herself, climbing the tall oaks, and learning the ways of its birds and animals. Into her rural sanctuary comes a tall young man, an ornithologist who "knows all about birds"; as he tells her, "they're stuffed and preserved, dozens and dozens of them, and I have shot or snared every one myself." He asks Sylvia to show him the nest of the white heron, and promises to pay her ten dollars, but she keeps silent: "She cannot tell the heron's secret and give its life away." As various critics have pointed out, Sylvia is a kind of white heroine, a rare, pure, and reclusive creature who resists and evades the predations of the modern world.[32]

The Country of the Pointed Firs (1896) first appeared in serial form in the *Atlantic,* and then was published as a book. In twenty-one chapters, it follows a young woman writer, rich enough to spend some of her summers in France or London, during her visit to the tiny Maine maritime village of Dunnet Landing, where she lodges with the widowed herbalist, Almira Todd. Through the course of a summer, she accompanies Mrs. Todd to visit her even more oracular mother, Mrs. Blackett, who lives on Green Island with her silent, aged, and almost autistic son, William; to Shell-heap Island, where a jilted woman, Joanna Todd, exiled herself in bitterness and rage; and to a festive reunion of the Bowdens, the largest family group of the island. Led in a procession to their picnic by an old shoemaker whose face, like those of the other islanders, suggests his descent from the Huguenots, the Bowdens end their feast by eating a gingerbread model of their ancestral home and an apple pie decorated with pastry letters and words. In addition, the narrator gets to know the secrets and the stories of Dunnet's eccentric inhabitants. Mrs. Todd confesses that she has never stopped loving her first suitor, whose mother had opposed the match "because he come of a high family, an' my lot was plain an' hard-workin'. I ain't seen him for some years; he's forgot our youthful feelin's, I expect, but a woman's heart is different; them feelin's come back when you think you've done with 'em, as sure as the spring comes with the year."

Jewett is cautious and even self-contradictory in introducing the narrator. First we learn of her from a distance, as a stranger and a "lover of

Dunnet Landing," and her views are stated in passive impersonal con-
structions ("the discovery was soon made"). Then Jewett switches to the
second person ("even when you were half-awake in the morning"), and
finally begins to talk about "my landlady" and to note that "I felt the July
days fly fast." The narrator rents the local schoolhouse as a studio, but
we are told nothing about what she is writing. And when she departs at
the end, it is as if she has never been there; "my room looked empty as it
had the day I came. I and all my belongings had died out of it . . . So we
die before our own eyes; so we see some chapters of our lives come to
their natural end." Has anything happened to her during this chapter of
her life? Is the point of the pointed firs that the narrator has overcome
her own isolation and will be a better writer? Who knows? Willa Cather,
who was Jewett's most important disciple, thought the design of the
novel was its own meaning: "The design is the story and the story is the
design."[33]

Prefeminist readings of *The Country of the Pointed Firs* found the book
charming but slight, striking "a mingled tone of respect and deprecia-
tion," even diminution.[34] Critics suggested that Jewett had problems
with the construction of plot, and certainly the book seemed formless
and shapeless. She herself had added two more chapters to the serial
when it was published in book form; and in 1910, when Houghton Mifflin reissued it in a seven-volume edition of Jewett's complete works,
they picked up two later stories, in which the elderly William marries a
woman he has been courting for forty years, and inserted them before
Jewett's final chapter. They added another story, "The Queen's Twin," in
1919, thereby destroying the chronological unity of the original work. In
1925, when Willa Cather edited Jewett's stories, she deliberately set out
to "increase Jewett's size, literally and figuratively." She demanded that
Houghton Mifflin print in a larger format than Jewett's previous books,
and in her famous introduction to the edition, she "addressed her real
aim—increasing Jewett's literary stature," and called *The Country of the
Pointed Firs* "a masterpiece," to be ranked with *The Scarlet Letter* and
Huckleberry Finn.[35] Even Cather, however, pulled back from this assertion
in the 1930s; and by 1959, a sympathetic critic, Warner Berthoff, saw "distorted, repressed, unfulfilled, or transformed sexuality" in the women of
Dunnet Landing (the same could be said about the men), viewing their
lives as making a virtue of necessity.[36] As Michael Davitt Bell concluded a
century after its publication, *The Country of the Pointed Firs* had secured
Jewett a place in the literary canon, but one that was "very small."[37]

Feminist critics had to confront these issues of narrative form, significance, and scale when they set out in the 1970s to enlarge Jewett's historical place. The leading revisionist was Elizabeth Ammons, who analyzed the matrifocal form of *The Country of the Pointed Firs,* calling it an "archetypal myth of primal, omnipotent female love." Ammons made a strong case for reading Jewett's novel as a female narrative structure emerging from the feminist contexts of the late nineteenth century, and with correspondences to women's sexuality. *The Country of the Pointed Firs,* she argued, was not constructed as a sequential, accelerating narrative leading to a climax, but rather as a radial, concentric "pattern of development and experience based on retaining and maintaining relationships of connectedness . . . rather than being linear, the shape of this pattern is nuclear," organized like "a web." Its most charged experience, the trip to Green Island, occurs in the middle of the book, not at the end. It is a "sacred female space," signifying the imaginative position of the woman artist.[38] In the same spirit, Marjorie Pryse identified Mrs. Todd as the "guide, herbalist, and priestess" who helps the narrator "go directly to the source of all vision and inspiration."[39]

This ecstatic phase of Jewett's recovery soon subsided; indeed, no other American woman writer has had such a dizzy ride on the roller coaster of critical politics. By the 1990s, in a startling volte-face, Jewett had become the nineteenth-century American woman writer most often excoriated and banished by feminist critics for her endorsement of bourgeois values and her political thought crimes. Amy Kaplan accused her of tacitly supporting American imperialism and "literary tourism," and depicted Dunnet Landing as an enclave battening on the spoils of whalers' conquests.[40] Susan Gillman described the family reunion feast of the Bowden clan on the island as a display of white supremacy akin to the Ku Klux Klan. Even Elizabeth Ammons retracted her earlier judgment. She called Mrs. Todd racist and ethnocentric, noticed the "traces of empire" scattered through Dunnet Landing, souvenirs and tea caddies the mariners have brought back from the West Indies and Tobago, and she interpreted the "military and religious rhetoric" in the Bowden reunion as "the subtle but clear proto-fascist implications of all those white people marching around in military formation ritualistically affirming their racial purity, global dominance, and white ethnic superiority and solidarity."[41] Obviously, Jewett's work had not changed; but a new jury had been summoned to look at the evidence.

"Proto-fascist" seems way over the top to me, and I would certainly vote to acquit Jewett on those charges. Moreover, I would prefer to see criticism based on aesthetic principles rather than such time-bound reflections of political sensitivities. In my view, the limitations of *The Country of the Pointed Firs* come from Jewett's problems with the frame narrative, a very popular form of late-nineteenth-century storytelling used by Henry James, among many others. We need to know why particular narrators tell particular stories. What does the story mean to them, and for them? Does it tell us something about their own psyche? One linear, sentimental way to end the book might be for Mrs. Todd to be reunited with her lost love. A more sophisticated frame closure would be for the narrator to work through her own emotional experience by proxy. Neither happens; we just move on.

Nevertheless, I think it's a good sign that Jewett's work is now the subject of feminist contention and dispute, however accusatory. Jewett set the model, Richard Brodhead concludes, "for women's high-artistry literary identity in America." She "aligned women's writing with high-cultural aspiration, with antifamilial careerism and profound artistic seriousness . . . and with regional subject matter and its richnesses and its self-enclosures."[42] In a famous letter to Cather toward the end of her career, Jewett advised the younger writer to stay away from "those who admire and wonder at everything one does."[43] She deserves the respect of serious judgment.

MARY WILKINS FREEMAN

The work of Mary E. Wilkins Freeman (1852–1930) has escaped some of the invigorating, if overstated, rereading that Jewett has received, although they used similar regional sources and many similar themes. Freeman's life had parallels to Cooke's and Jewett's. Born Mary E. Wilkins, she spent her childhood in Randolph, Massachusetts, and Brattleboro, Vermont.[44] A good student, she attended Mount Holyoke Female Seminary, but lasted there only a year. As she described it, "I was very young . . . and went home at the end of the year a nervous wreck"; regimentation and lack of privacy made her miserable.[45] By 1883, her parents and sister were dead, and she moved back to Randolph to live with her childhood friend Mary Wales in a "Boston marriage" that lasted almost twenty years, at almost exactly the same time that Jewett lived with Annie Fields. Mary Wilkins had a room of her own, a secluded writing space at the Wales farm. The friends quarreled, however, and in 1902, Mary Wilkins married a doctor and moved with him to New Jersey. Publishing as "Mary E. Wilkins" before her marriage, she is now known as "Freeman," although Dr. Freeman was an alcoholic who was eventually institutionalized, and the couple legally separated.

Freeman's long and prolific career extended from the 1870s to 1918, and she published seven novels as well as almost 250 short stories; but she did her best writing in the 1880s, producing 52 short stories that were collected as *A Humble Romance and Other Stories* (1887) and *A New England Nun and Other Stories* (1891). The stories dramatize women's ambiguous choices. Have they opted for autonomy or against maturity? For independence or for isolation? Early-twentieth-century critics of Freeman saw her as grim and eccentric. As one wrote in 1922, "Her characters mostly are unmarried women . . . With such material there are infinite possibilities for depressed realism."[46] Later feminist criticism saw her as the high priestess of a dying women's culture. In her fiction, "a way of life—the woman-centered, matriarchal world of the Victorians—is in its last throes . . . The mothers are taking a last stand, going down to apparently inevitable defeat. The hopelessness of their prospect drives many of them to a kind of obsessive protectiveness of their daughters; at times their behavior becomes almost perversely destructive."[47] In a story she never finished, Freeman described one such woman's frank pleasure in her vocation: "I am a graft on the tree of human womanhood. I am a hybrid. Sometimes I think I am a monster, and the worst of it is, I certainly take pleasure in it."[48]

Freeman wrote so much and in so many different modes that it is risky to characterize her overall, but her best-known short stories explore women's negative or destructive power. "A New England Nun" begins with an elegiac announcement: "It was late in the afternoon and the light was waning." It is late in the afternoon of life for Louisa Ellis, who has been engaged for fourteen years to Joe Dagget, while he has been off trying to make his fortune in Australia. The feminine rituals of Louisa's life have become obsessive; when she sews a seam, she often rips it out for the pleasure of sewing it again. She prepares her dainty vegetarian meals with as much stately formality "as if she had been a veritable guest to herself." Even her dog, Caesar, is kept on a vegetarian diet; once he bit a neighbor, and ever since has been chained while Louisa "fed him an ascetic fare of corn-mush and cakes, and never fired his dangerous temper with the heating and sanguinary diet of flesh and bones."

Freeman carefully develops the parallels between Louisa's sexuality and her habits, clothes, and surroundings:

> *She gloated gently over her orderly bureau-drawers with their exqui-*
> *sitely folded contents redolent of lavender and sweet clover and very*

purity. Could she be sure of the endurance of even this? She had visions, so startling that she half repudiated them as indelicate, of coarse masculine belongings strewn about in an endless litter of dust and disorder arising necessarily from a coarse masculine presence in the midst of all this delicate harmony.

Like a member of a ritualistic tribe, Louisa customarily shields her lower body behind three aprons, an outer one of green gingham, a "shorter one of pink and white print," and beneath them all, the white linen apron with cambric edging that is her most intimate apparel. Every detail of her household can be read as the externalization of her anxieties about contact with men. The books on her table are arranged with the "square red autograph album" on the bottom and a "Young Lady's Gift Book" on top. When Joe awkwardly starts "fingering them," and puts the heavy red one on top, Louisa is upset and puts them back: "I always keep them that way," she murmurs. She does not want a man tracking dust onto her rug, but neither she nor he knows how to get out of their engagement with honor. When Louisa overhears Joe confess his love to a younger woman, Lily Dyer, she is flooded with relief. She tactfully sets him free, and repossesses her kingdom: "If she had sold her birthright she did not know it, that taste of the pottage was so delicious . . . serenity and placid narrowness had become to her as the birthright itself . . . and her heart went up in thankfulness." In the last lines of the story, Freeman invokes the bee and flower imagery of so much American women's writing. Louisa's summer is over; she has given up her woman's right to give birth; like an "uncloistered nun," she "prayerfully" closes her door on "the sounds of the busy harvest of men and birds and bees; there were halloos, metallic clatterings, sweet calls, long hummings."[49]

A late story, "Old Woman Magoun," was Freeman's most sinister and gothic rendition of this female withdrawal. Fourteen-year-old Lily Barry has been kept childish by her grandmother, who dresses her hair in curls and lets her play with a rag doll, to protect her against the loutish neighborhood men, who "air a passel of hogs." The most hoggish of all, Nelson Barry, "was the fairly dangerous degenerate" who had married and deserted Lily's mother. Like Little Red Riding Hood, Lily goes to the store and attracts Nelson's attention; he immediately gambles and loses her to another man in a card game. In desperation, Old Woman Magoun tries to have Lily adopted by a lawyer's wife; and when this fails, leads her to a berry patch and lets her eat deadly nightshade. Lily's slow death is a flashback to the female heaven of *The Gates Ajar*, surely a fantasy that Freeman had rejected. "You will come to a gate with all the colors of the rainbow," her grandmother tells her, and find "a little white room," where her mother has been waiting for her. Why does Old Woman Magoun kill Lily instead of Nelson? The murderous anger of the story is directed at the awakening of Lily's adolescent desire; sooner or later a man will come along to take advantage of her. Freeman even hints that Old Woman Magoun poisoned Lily's mother in the same way. Her many ghost stories explored similar themes of female entrapment and self-immolation.

In a little-known story, "Noblesse" (1909), Freeman wrote from the point of view of a circus fat lady in a freak story like Jewett's "The Circus in Denby." "Margaret Lee," she begins, "encountered in her late middle age the rather singular strait of being entirely alone in the world. She was unmarried, and as far as relatives were concerned, she had none except those connected with her by ties not of blood, but by marriage. Margaret had not married when her flesh had been comparative; later, when it had become superlative, she had no opportunities to marry. Life would have been hard enough for Margaret under any circumstances, but it was especially hard, living, as she did, with her father's stepdaughter and that daughter's husband." The family hires her out to a traveling circus for the sideshow.

> *Daily her absurd unwieldiness was exhibited to crowds screaming with laughter. Even her faith wavered. It seemed to her that there was nothing for evermore beyond those staring, jeering faces of silly mirth and delight at sight of her, seated in two chairs, clad in a pink spangled dress, her vast shoulders bare and sparkling with a tawdry necklace, her great, bare arms covered with brass bracelets, her hands incased in short, white kid gloves, over the fingers of which she wore a number of rings—stage properties. Margaret became a horror to herself. At times it seemed to her that she was in the way of fairly losing her own identity.*

As Freeman herself confided to Fred Lewis Pattee, what she really wanted was not realism, however depressed, but "more symbolism, more mysticism." Because of her need to "consider selling qualities," she was only sporadically able to pursue these literary interests.[50] Nonetheless, Freeman was an important American writer. At her best, as Josephine Donovan claims, "Her stories have an aesthetic purity that gives them great power."[51] Her classic tales look ahead to Sherwood Anderson, Willa Cather, and other American modernists.

Southern Sibyl—Mary Noailles Murfree

Few American women followed George Eliot's example by using male pseudonyms, but in 1878, Mary Noailles Murfree (1850–1922) began publishing stories about Tennessee mountain folk in the *Atlantic* under the pseudonym "Charles Egbert Craddock." She was not revealed to be a woman until 1885, to the shock of the editor and his readers. By then she was publishing widely in many magazines. Sarah Orne Jewett was among Murfree's admirers, and regarded her as a serious artist; in 1890, she wrote to Annie Fields, "I do so like Craddock, who takes time, and is lost to sight, to memory . . . and writes a good big Harper's story."[52] Murfree was born near Murfreesboro, Tennessee; although an early childhood illness left her permanently lame, she was educated at the Nashville Female Academy and went to finishing school in Philadelphia. Murfree learned about what she called the "primitive customs, dialect, and peculiar view of life" of the Tennessee mountaineers during summer vacations with her family.[53]

Murfree's father was a lawyer who had instructed her in the law at home, and many of her stories have legal plots. "The 'Harnt' Who Walks Chilhowee" (1883) combined the ghost story and romance with an examination of the conflict between law and womanly sympathy, as "Jury of Her Peers" would do in the twentieth century. At first the story seems to center on the humorously handled love triangle of young Clarsie Giles, her poor suitor Tom Pratt, and the prosperous elderly widower Simon Burney. Clarsie is a warmhearted sympathetic creature who loves animals so much that "them pigs most climb the fence when she shows her face at the door." Simon is among her admirers, although his values are very different, and he is neither a philanthropist nor a supporter of women's rights. " 'It 'pears toler'ble comical ter me,' said Simon Burney, with a sudden perception of a curious fact which has proved a marvel to wiser men, 'that no matter how good a woman is, she ain't got no respect fur the laws of the country, an' don't sot no store by jestice.' " When Clarsie encounters Reuben Crabb, a "stunted, one-armed little critter" who has been falsely accused of murdering the town bully and is hiding in the woods, stealing food and pretending to be a ghost, she insists on feeding him rather than taking the two-hundred-dollar reward.

"I can't gin my consent ter starvin' of folks even ef they air a-hidin' an' a-runnin' from jestice." Surprisingly, Clarsie's view persuades Simon, who helps Reuben clear his name. Through the partnership of an outcast and a woman, the reader discovers a new understanding of "jestice." Of all the regionalist writers, Murfree wrote the most extreme dialect; Fetterley and Pryse say "it sounds like a foreign language"; but this difference may have helped her narrative role as a mediator and wise judge.[54]

California Sibyl—Helen Hunt Jackson

After Helen Fiske Hunt Jackson's death in 1885, so many pilgrims came to visit her grave that her husband had it moved to a private cemetery.[55] Jackson's novel *Ramona* (1884) was one of the most popular and influential books of the decade. When it was published, Jackson was fifty-four years old, a good age for an American sibyl; but she had already undergone a long literary apprenticeship. Born in 1830, she grew up in Amherst, Massachusetts, both a neighbor and a friend of Emily Dickinson; her father, Nathan Welby Fiske, was an orthodox Calvinist minister who had become professor of Latin and Greek at Amherst College. Another New England patriarch like Alcott, Beecher, or Phelps, he was known at Amherst as erudite but humorless and narrow, and for most of Helen's childhood he was writing a vast "Manual of Classical Literature" that her mother regarded as a "sister wife." To please him, Helen studied Latin, German, and philosophy, but at the age of eleven she petitioned him for respite in a verse letter:

> I'm tired to death of Latin,
> As you no doubt do know.
> I get on slow with practising,
> Alas! Alas! How slow!
> I think it is but fair,
> That I should have some rest,
> And 'tis my fervent prayer
> That you may think it best.

Her mother encouraged her imaginative reading and writing, and was creative and funny herself. On a trip away, she wrote to little Helen that a neighbor had asked her if Professor Fiske believed clams could be mesmerized; "I did not know what *he* thought," she replied, "but *my* opinion was they *could* be, because clams didn't *know enough* to resist the mesmeric influence."[56] With her mother's guidance, Helen read Austen, Charlotte Brontë, Elizabeth Gaskell, and Susan Warner, and told a friend she was "book-mad" and "word-crazy." Both parents died while she was still in her teens; and although she began her studies at Ipswich Female Seminary, Helen lost her appetite for learning, left the seminary, and soon married an army officer, Edward Hunt, in 1852. Although the marriage was happy, it was marked by tragedy: the couple lost a baby, then Edward died in an accident in 1863, and their nine-year-old son died in 1865.

Devastated, Helen moved to Newport, Rhode Island, the following year in hopes of remaking her life. There, a few years ahead of Emma Lazarus, she met Thomas Higginson, who encouraged her to write and publish her poems, which she signed "Marah," and then "H.H." They were collected as *Verses* (1870). Although the poems were conventional examples of nineteenth-century feminine verse, Emerson reprinted five of them in his 1874 anthology *Parnassus*, much to the annoyance of Lazarus. The competition between women poets and their designated male mentors and patrons was fierce if covert. Higginson also reintroduced Helen to Emily Dickinson, with whom she pleaded to publish her poems. Dickinson refused, but found that Helen's support gave, "as no other person ever did, a sense that her poems were of great importance."[57]

Many readers believed that the central character in Helen's first novel, *Mercy Philbrick's Choice* (1876), was based on Dickinson. Mercy is a young widow who always wears white, and writes strange, brilliant poetry. She is admired by her landlord, a New England eccentric who has given up his personal life to care for his mother, but they drift apart, unable to compromise. Thomas Niles called this gloomy book "The Great American Novelette," and published it anonymously in his No-Name series. Using the pseudonym "Saxe Holm," Helen also published a number of formulaic short stories in the magazines; she was always in need of money.

Her motives and her life changed in May 1872, however, when she traveled to California for her health, and began to think about the meaning of American fiction and her contribution to it. In a review of John De Forest, she wrote that there could be "a good novel which is truly American." It would be "strongly sectional, in geography of plot and in tone of coloring . . . There are as yet many Americas."[58] The following year, seeking further health cures in Colorado Springs, Helen began to discover some of these Americas for herself. She met William Sharpless Jackson, a banker and railroad magnate, and married him, moving to Colorado and becoming fascinated by the West and its history.

On a trip back to Boston, Jackson attended a lecture by Chief Standing Bear of the Ponca tribe, who was on a tour to draw attention to the Ponca's removal from Nebraska, and became a passionate advocate, activist, and campaigner for Indian rights. "I cannot think of anything else from night to morning and from morning to night," she wrote to Higginson in 1880.[59] She did extensive research for *A Century of Dishonor* (1881), a summary of American dealings with seven Indian tribes, the Ponca, Cherokee, Delaware, Cheyenne, Nez Perce, Sioux, and Winnebago. Of course, such diatribes might impress politicians, but would not win readers. In May 1883, she wrote to Thomas Bailey Aldrich, the editor of the *Atlantic,* "If I could write a story that would do for the Indian a thousandth part of what *Uncle Tom's Cabin* did for the Negro, I would be thankful for the rest of my life." As she confided to Aldrich, the novel was already in her mind: "My story is all planned: in fact it is so thought out it is practically half written. It is chiefly Indian—but the scene is in Southern California and the Mexican life will enter it largely. I hope it will be a telling book—and will reach people who would not read my *Century of Dishonor.*"[60]

Jackson wrote *Ramona* (1884) in three months in a hotel in Berkeley, on a desk facing an unframed photo of "two heads, a man's and a woman's, set in a nimbus of cloud, with a strange beautiful regard and meaning in their eyes. They were exactly her idea of what Ramona and Alessandro looked like."[61] The novel was very different from her conventional verses and her cheery stories, a dark story of a tragic love between Ramona, a half-Indian, half-Scottish orphan girl raised on a Southern California ranch, and her Indian lover, Alessandro. For the first time, Jackson "had no qualms about calling herself an 'artist.' "[62]

She began to write a novel about women's right to divorce, called *Zeph,* but she did not have long to enjoy the popular and critical success of *Ramona.* Her health was deteriorating, and she wrote a pathetic letter to her husband, telling him to remarry and to name a daughter for her after her death. (He did; in fact, he had seven children.) Jackson's memorial service was a great public event; Ina Coolbrith read a poem:

> *For her the clamorous today*
> *The dreadful yesterday became.*[63]

Ramona never had a dreadful yesterday. It has never been out of print, and it inspired a theatrical pageant that is still an annual event attracting thousands of spectators. It has also been acknowledged as a landmark in the special literary history of Southern California,

> *the founding work in a powerful local dystopian tradition. With Ramona and Alessandro, who wander through Southern California as through a nightmare world, isolated, dispossessed of their rightful connection to the land, and longing to be consoled for the ruin of their dreams, Jackson created the first figures in the long line of disappointed, deracinated heroes who populate the later Southern California fiction of writers as diverse as Nathanael West, Evelyn Waugh, Thomas Pynchon, and Joan Didion.*[64]

In 1887, the Cuban poet and patriot José Martí translated *Ramona* into Spanish, and many Mexican and Mexican-American artists did versions of it in movies. In its "opposition to American imperialism" and "hope for a more equitable, multicultural America," it influenced Jackson's Latino contemporaries.[65] One of these contemporaries was Maria Amparo Ruiz de Burton (1832–1895), a native of a prominent Baja Californian family who married an American army officer. Ruiz de Burton was widowed in 1869 and left to support their two children. Her first novel, with the Trollopian title *Who Would Have Thought It?* (1872), published anonymously, was a wicked satire of Northern abolitionists. Her second novel, *The Squatter and the Don* (1885), was set in California but written from the point of view of Mexican-Americans who were still excluded from power. It used the Romeo-Juliet plot to explore the injustices of those Californian aristocrats of Spanish descent with landed property and those Mexican newcomers forced to "squat" or occupy government land.

Miss Grief—Constance Fenimore Woolson

Born in New Hampshire, a great-niece of James Fenimore Cooper, Constance Fenimore Woolson (1840–1894) had lived a nomadic life in the Midwest, New York, Florida, and Italy, although she described herself as "very strongly 'New Hampshire' in all my ways."[66] Most of Woolson's early stories were set "in the American equivalents of desert islands:

Mackinac Island in Lake Michigan, a mining camp on an island in Lake Superior, a solitary house on a salt marsh on Lake Huron, a cotton plantation abandoned after Sherman's march, a Southern cemetery for Union soldiers. Many of these stories focus on people who are geographically, socially, and emotionally stranded . . . The isolated settings also function as a metaphor for women's various forms of exile—from themselves, from their society, from their art—and for Woolson's sense of herself as a homeless outcast."[67]

Although she had little respect for Southern literary taste, and thought the novels of Augusta Jane Evans were a mass of "words, words, words," Woolson also felt that she had been permanently changed by the Civil War.[68] "The war," she wrote to Edmund Stedman, "was the heart and spirit of my life, and everything has seemed tame to me since."[69] Some of her finest stories, such as "Rodham the Keeper," which portrayed the Yankee keeper of the Union Cemetery at Andersonville, Georgia, were about the melancholy state of the South in the years just after the war, told from a Northern point of view. In 1876, in fact, the editor Joseph W. Harper told Woolson to stop writing about the Civil War.

Nonetheless, she continued to write about the war more obliquely. *For the Major* (1883) is set in May 1868, three years after Major Scarborough Carroll, his wife, Marion, and his son, Scar, have settled in the town of Far Edgerley, an imaginary Southern enclave in the "Chillawassee Mountains." The Major is a Civil War veteran and Confederate "prince" from the Sea Islands who "gave his sword to his state, and served with great gallantry." As a neighbor confides, he was wounded twice, and "when our Sacred Cause was lost, with the small remains of his small fortune, he purchased this old place called The Farms, and . . . has come to pass the remainder of his days in . . . the Past—the only country left open to him, as indeed to many of us." Like the ladies of Elizabeth Gaskell's *Cranford,* the citizens of Far Edgerley live in a fantasy of past refinements and gentility.

When the Major's daughter, Sara, comes home to see her father and stepmother, she is astounded by Mrs. Carroll's beauty and youthfulness. She was "very small and slight. Her muslin gown, whose simply gathered waist was belted by a ribbon sash, had a youthful, almost childlike aspect, yet at the same time a pretty quaintness of its own, like that of an old-fashioned miniature. The effect of this young-old attire was increased by the arrangement of the hair. It was golden hair, even and fine, and it hung in curls all round her head—long curls that fell below the waist." Overall, she resembles "the pictures in the old 'Annuals' and 'Keepsakes' "—an obsolete form of genteel and ladylike women's writing.[70]

With her blue eyes, lavender frills and ribbons, and girlish complexion, Mrs. Carroll sounds like Jean Muir in Alcott's *Behind a Mask* or a murderess out of the late Victorian sensation novels of Mary Elizabeth Braddon; but her disguise is benign. The Major has dementia, what we would now call Alzheimer's disease; she is playing a role in order to make him happy, and also to help him keep up a façade of health, elegance, and charm for the town. When the Major becomes seriously ill, and can no longer see her, Mrs. Carroll stops disguising her age. "Her veil of golden hair, no longer curled, was put plainly back, and fastened in a close knot behind; her eyes . . . looked tired and sunken and dim, with crow's-feet at their corners; all her lovely bloom was gone, and the whole of her little faded face was a net-work of minute wrinkles." As she confesses to her stepdaughter, it has been a long masquerade; she is forty-eight years old, had been married before to a man who deserted her and took their son, and had lost her daughter. In the course of the novel, she learns that the husband was not dead when she married the Major, and goes through another ceremony at the Major's deathbed in order to legitimize their son.

Behind this romantic story, there is another plot, that of the South in its cultural Alzheimer's. As Carolyn Hall argues, "*For the Major* reads as an allegory of the United States after the Civil War when it allowed reconciliation and so-called redemption to supplant and suppress legacies of war and Reconstruction through a national tendency towards repression; Woolson here imitates and thus quietly indicts this national pattern." While Mrs. Carroll's "efforts to spare the Major's feelings suggest love and devotion, the behavior simultaneously bespeaks a desire to maintain a life that is no longer true, a desire the entire town shares and that causes the rest of its residents, too, to take pains to maintain a fictional vision of their lives."[71] They collude in polite fictions that mask their poverty, their defeat, and their guilt, and play a collective game of selective memory and denial. They, too, are keepers of a flame.

Suffering from increasing deafness, a malady that tormented her as it would Ellen Glasgow in the next generation, and from chronic depression, Woolson attributed her problems to the conflicts of her gender and her vocation. "Why do literary women break down so?" she asked Stedman. "It almost seems as though only the unhappy women took to writing."[72] When her mother died in 1879, she went to Europe, and made the sorrows of women artists the subject of her short fiction.

Woolson's "Miss Grief," published in *Lippincott's* in May 1880, created a memorable and mythic figure of the woman writer. The story is constructed as a frame narrative, told to us by a fashionable young male writer, who begins with the words "a conceited fool." Only a year before, in Rome, he had not thought of himself that way, only as "passably good-looking," with money, fashionable friends, good clothes, and the beginnings of a literary career. Then he was visited by a gaunt, pale, "shabby, unattractive, and more than middle-aged" woman called "Miss Grief," who asks him to read the manuscript of her unpublished drama called "Armor." When he sits down to read it, he discovers that her name is actually "Aaronna Crief," and that, to his amazement, the drama is "inspired," a work of "earnestness, passion, and power." At his invitation, she brings him all her manuscripts, and persuades him to help her find a publisher. He is overwhelmed by the task and by the oddity and genius of her poems and stories: "Such a fantastic collection of words, lines, and epithets I had never before seen, or even in dreams imagined. In truth, they were like the work of dreams; they were *Kubla Khan*, only more so. Here and there was radiance like the flash of a diamond." But all the texts were "marred by some fault or lack which seemed wilful perversity, like the work of an evil sprite." When publishers reject the works, he tries to edit and correct them, but discovers that they cannot be changed without destroying their singularity. "I amended, altered, left out, put in, pieced, condensed, lengthened," but finally he admits that "either my own powers were not equal to the task, or else her perversities were as essential a part of the work as her inspirations, and not to be separated from it."

When she is on her deathbed, he is summoned to her side by an aunt, and tells her that "Armor" will be published. She dies content. He returns to his pleasant life, but with a much fuller understanding of his own creative limitations and his extraordinary good luck. He has learned that he is a conceited fool. As Cheryl Torsney explains, through her choice of a name for "Miss Grief," Woolson connects her to "the Israelites' high priest Aaron." Aaronna "becomes the high priest of art, the voice of oppression, carrying out, despite her gender, the duties and responsibilities of the chief celebrant of the artistic faith." Although in her lifetime she will be misunderstood and rejected, she "is a type of Messiah, a harbinger of an era yet to come, when powerful women will direct their own creative destinies."[73]

"Miss Grief" was the first of three remarkable stories Woolson wrote during the 1880s about a woman artist with genius confronting the chilling world of "male-sanctified artistic taste," male conceit, and female surrender. Critics have frequently noted that the men in the stories who act as judges resemble Henry James. As the greatest "master" in an era that revered the master, James played a significant role for American women writers. He had reviewed books, unfavorably, by Alcott, Rebecca Harding Davis, and Helen Hunt Jackson, whose first novel he called a "pale, unlighted representative of a dry and bloodless population, and a style of manners farther removed from the spectacular than a cranberry-bog from a vineyard."[74] Even the feisty Elizabeth Stuart Phelps had felt pushed aside by James; Howells asked her to shorten one of her pieces in the *Atlantic* to make more room for James's story, and she refused: "The very fact that there is so much of Mr. James makes it more important to me that my story should have its fair artistic effect."[75]

When she wrote "Miss Grief," however, Woolson had not actually met Henry James, although she may have "harbored some resentment towards" him, and thought Howells favored him over other contributors, especially if they were women.[76] When Woolson and James met in Florence, they quickly became friends, and even shared a house together for a few months in 1886–87. James called her "The Litteratrice," but he turned to her for serious discussions of fictional form.[77]

From the start, she was candid with him about his treatment of women in fiction and in publishing, and her own diffidence in attempting to equal his range. "How did you ever dare write a portrait of a lady?" she wrote to him in February 1882. "Fancy any woman's attempting a portrait of a gentleman! Wouldn't there be a storm of ridicule! . . . For my own part, in my small writings, I never put down what men are thinking but confine myself simply to what they do and say. For, long experience has taught me that whatever I suppose them to be thinking at any especial time, that is sure to be exactly what they are *not* thinking." The same year she chided him for his literary arrogance: "You do not want to know the little literary women. Only the great ones—like George Eliot."[78]

In "The Street of the Hyacinth," another Jamesian figure in Rome, an art dealer, looks at the paintings of a vivacious young American woman, and concludes "they were all extremely and essentially bad." He atones by falling in love with her and eventually marrying her, but her artistic dreams are ruined. In "At the Château of Corinne" (1887), the critic John Ford intimidates an American woman poet, Katharine Winthrop, by mocking the château's original inhabitant, Madame de Staël: "A woman of genius! And what is the very term but a stigma? No woman is so proclaimed by the great brazen tongue of the Public unless she has thrown away her birthright of womanly seclusion for the miserable mess of pottage called 'fame.' " His comments on Katharine's poems are just as harsh: "We do not expect great poems from women any more than we expect great pictures; we do not expect strong logic any more than we expect brawny muscle. A woman's poetry is subjective." Not surprisingly, the most unforgivable aspects of her poems are their daring and boldness, "for a woman should not dare in that way. Thinking to soar, she invariably descends."

Reviewing Woolson in 1887, Henry James gave a gentlemanly nod to the achievement of American women writers. We need no longer question "their admission into the world of literature; they are there in force; they have been admitted with all the honours on a perfectly equal footing." He went on to sprinkle faint praise on Woolson's novel *East Angels* as a "performance which does Miss Woolson the highest honour, and if her talent is capable, in another novel, of making an advance equal to that represented by this work in relation to its predecessors, she will have made a substantial contribution to our new literature of fiction."[79]

In 1894, Woolson killed herself, a suicide that some have interpreted as an act of unrequited love. Shortly before her death, however, she had expressed her hopes as an artist, wishing to "turn into a peak when I die, to be a beautiful purple mountain, which would please the tired, sad eyes of thousands of human beings for ages."[80] Woolson did not want to be a grand, unapproachable alp, like George Eliot, or a distant and mysterious peak like James, but a comforting, perhaps American, mountain, a sibyl of nature that would bring solace and peace.

The Coming American Novelist

Writers at the end of the century disagreed about the importance of regionalism and local color, and about the virtues of what we now call "multiculturalism" versus the allure of a grand unified narrative of American character, a Great American Novel. One anonymous critic in the *Nation* complained in 1892 that "instead of a national novel, we now have a rapidly accumulating series of regional novels," but in the same year, the novelist Edward Eggleston argued that "the 'great American novel' . . . is appearing in sections."[81] Of course, the choices were not limited to these oppositions. Regional fiction and the short story flourished alongside novels as they continue to do today. If women in the 1880s specialized in shorter genres, they had not abandoned the novel, and they envisioned an American literature more inclusive of women's perspectives and more willing to grant legitimacy to women's narratives as part of the great American story.

Already looking to the next century, more utopian thinkers were beginning to speculate on the future of women's writing and literary genius. In 1886, "A Lady from Philadelphia" had predicted in *Lippincott's Monthly Magazine* that the "Coming American Novelist" would be an African-American woman: "It was a woman who, taking the wrongs of the African as her theme, wrote the novel that awakened the world to their reality, and why should not the coming novelist be a woman as well as an African?" In Edward Bellamy's *Looking Backward* (1888), young Julian West falls asleep in Boston on May 30, 1887, and magically wakes up in the year 2000. The twentieth century, he discovers, has been "an era of unexampled intellectual splendor," and he stays up all night reading one of its literary masterpieces, *Penthisilea*. The author is a man, but the title refers to the queen of the Amazons, suggesting that prophetic and powerful women will occupy a central place in the fiction of the future.

10

New Women

he decade of the 1890s ushered in the era of the New Woman. Christened in the pages of the *North American Review* in 1894, the New Women rejected conventional female roles, redefined female sexuality, and asserted their rights to higher education and the professions. The feminist historian Carroll Smith-Rosenberg has described American New Women as "single, highly educated, economically autonomous," usually "children of small-town America," products of the new women's colleges, drawn to urban centers and work in settlement houses, in rebellion against their mothers and marriage.[1] Another aspect of New Womanhood was social nonconformity. In American cities, especially in New York, bohemian New Women, including art students, editors, actresses, and journalists, "could be seen on the streets, walking alone, or on the omnibuses . . . marked by a graceful, athletic bearing and the lack of a wedding ring." They no longer saw themselves as "friendless, forlorn, and sexually vulnerable," like the Hagar figures in nineteenth-century women's fiction, but rather as daring modern heroines in search of "feminine self-realization."[2]

New Womanhood had its political base in women's activism, and the 1890s were a decade of American feminist organizing. The National American Woman Suffrage Association, with Elizabeth Cady Stanton as its first president, called for "equal pay for equal work." Black women were also in the vanguard of political change. The National League of Colored Women (1893), the National Association of Colored Women (1896), and the National Association of Colored Women's Clubs (1896) brought black women into the public sphere, while black intellectuals including Ida B. Wells, Mary Church Terrell, and Anna Julia Cooper spoke out against lynching and racism. The suffrage movement in the

1890s, however, pursued votes for women rather than racial equality and, to gain support, colluded in racist moves to disenfranchise black voters through devices like the poll tax. Black women therefore organized their own suffrage associations, while New Negro Women emphasized racial equality.[3] In 1893, the Women's Building at the Chicago World's Fair celebrated women's artistic and technological achievements, but African-American women were not represented; Ida Wells protested against the discrimination in a pamphlet, *The Reason Why the Colored American Is Not in the World's Columbian Exposition*.

New Women's attitudes toward the sexual double standard and female sexuality were also revolutionary. While most American New Women believed that men should be as sexually chaste as women, they also saw women's relative passionlessness as constructed rather than natural. In 1883, Elizabeth Cady Stanton had written in her diary that "a healthy woman has as much passion as a man."[4] Readers and reviewers were shocked by Kate Chopin's stories about female sexuality and her emphasis on women's coming to self-awareness through physical awareness—swimming, caresses, hunger, even the pain of childbirth. In New Women's utopian fiction, radical writers imagined female sexual emancipation, single motherhood, and even brothels where women could pay for the sexual services of handsome young men.

Gender and Genre

The label of "New Woman" was applied to the fiction of the 1890s as well as to its authors. Ann Heilmann, a leading historian and theorist of New Women's writing, describes it as experimental in its challenge to realism, "moving into allegorical, utopian . . . sensational, mythical, even dream-like sequences of writing." The work of New Women "exploded narrative conventions by . . . mixing incongruous elements, fragmenting narratives, . . . and introducing shifting points of view as well as stream-of-consciousness techniques." But it also "retained its links with realism in that it always located the conditions of women's oppression in contemporary social reality."[5]

American New Women writers were thinking about transformations of traditional genres that would best express and convey their messages. Poetry was lowest on the scale. In the United States, contemporary poetry declined in quantity, quality, and popularity, although Emily Dickinson's poems, published for the first time in 1890, went into several editions and caused a literary sensation. In 1898, the *Saturday Evening Post* suggested that the "taste for poetry is becoming a lost accomplishment" and declared that poetry had reached its twilight.[6] New Women poets sought to make their way in the marketplace with their frankness and passion. Louise Imogen Guiney (1861–1920) rewrote mythology and history to find relevant female heroines. In "Tarpeia," she dramatized the paradox of a woman condemned by her society for the mercenary values it has encouraged in her, through the story of the Roman woman who betrayed her city to the Sabines in exchange for gold bracelets, and then was crushed under the invaders' shields. Ella Wheeler Wilcox (1850–1919) had emerged as a spokeswoman for female sexuality in 1883, with her *Poems of Passion;* she followed it up with *Poems of Pleasure* (1888) and *Three Women* (1897), a long narrative poem in which one of the women, Ruth, decides to become a doctor because she sees the hypocrisy of men's lip service to domesticity:

> *Well, I'm done with the role of housewife. I see*
> *There is nothing in being domestic. The part*
> *Is unpicturesque, and at war with all art.*
> *The senile old Century leers with dim eyes*
> *At our sex, and demands that we shock or surprise*
> *His thin blood into motion.*

New Women Onstage

The American theater was still not a major venue for innovative writing, but with the plays of Ibsen, Strindberg, Wilde, and Shaw making the theater a showcase for new ideas abroad, some New Women writers took an interest in the possibilities of the stage; the young Willa Cather, for example, began her career as a theater critic. The most remarkable woman playwright, actress, and producer of the decade, Elizabeth Robins (1862–1952), was an American, but she went to England in search of a serious theatrical career. Born in Lexington, Kentucky, Robins had become an actress in the 1880s with the Boston Theatre Company, and married a fellow actor. In 1887, when she "refused to be a full-time wife," he put on a full suit of stage armor, went out at midnight, and jumped into the Charles River.[7] Robins did not remarry. After her husband's death, she moved to London, and began a second career as translator, writer, actress, and producer. She learned Norwegian in order to translate Ibsen and produced and starred in the first English production of *Hedda Gabler.*

Robins saw the London theater as a potentially revolutionary site for women. In her unpublished novel *The Coming Woman, or a Leading Lady,* she described the "Theatre of the Future," which would be free of sex and class discrimination, and include a school of dramatic arts, a library, and a meeting ground for critical and literary debate.[8] Along with another American actress, Marion Lea, she tried to win support for her ideas from powerful men in the theater world, including Oscar Wilde. But Wilde's disgrace in 1895 led to a reactionary period of theatrical conservatism and caution, and other men, such as Henry James, seemed horrified at the idea that a woman should attempt to write a play. In 1900, the great impresario Beerbohm Tree told Robins that he had "never . . . read a good play from a woman's hand."[9] Despairing of fighting the forces ranked against her, Robins turned to campaigning for women's suffrage.

New Women, New Words: The Short Story

American women writers believed that the short story was the most authentic and open-ended American genre at the turn of the century, and that they were hastening its development. In 1892, the *Atlantic Monthly* declared that "American writers . . . have taken the short story as their province . . . There is no sign that the art is anywhere so rich, so varied, or so fresh as it is with us . . . It appears to have become in truth, the national mode of utterance in the things of the imagination, and, taking its own wherever it finds it, the short story has become more and more vicariously expressive."[10] New magazines like *McClure's, Munsey's,* and *The Saturday Evening Post* provided an expanded market for writers of short fiction. Moreover, short stories seemed attuned to the pace and intensity of modern life. In contrast to their 1870s adulation of Eliot, and their attraction to the epic form of the novel, women writers in the 1890s were striving for brevity and concentration. Bliss Perry pointed out that "the reaction against the *Atlantic Monthly* three-volume novel," with its moral certainties and family audience, and especially against the realism of its greatest practitioner, George Eliot, had "been caused by the universal passion for the short story." Americans were busy people, with less and less time to read, and higher standards for what they did read. Writers of short fiction did not have three volumes in which to waffle around or shift their point of view. While "George Eliot pictures Dorothea in *Middlemarch* now in this position now in that," Perry observed, the short-story writer "has but one chance."[11] Women writers found the short story, with its focus on a single narrative voice, an appropriate form for the exploration of female psychology. Looking at the great European short-story writers in *The Writing of Fiction* (1924), Edith Wharton admired their penetration: "instead of a loose web spread out over the surface of life," their fiction was "a shaft driven straight into the heart of experience."

Art for Truth's Sake

The male aesthetes and decadent artists of the art nouveau movement, featured in such little magazines as *The Yellow Book* in England and *Vogue* in the United States, also symbolized the 1890s, with its credo of "art for art's sake." American women writers, however, deplored the frivolity, amorality, and misogyny of aestheticism. In an essay on "Art for Truth's Sake," Elizabeth Stuart Phelps recorded her belief that "the province of the artist is to portray life as it is, and life *is* moral responsibility."[12] Charlotte Perkins Gilman, who had been trained in design, questioned the sinuous deceiving curves of the art nouveau movement versus the straight honest lines of California arts and crafts, and criticized the narcissism of the aesthetic school. She insisted that it was "a pretty poor thing to write . . . without a purpose."[13] New Women writers on both sides of the Atlantic often deplored the frivolity and loose morals of the aesthetes, especially Oscar Wilde. Willa Cather ridiculed and mocked him in some of her early newspaper reviews. In 1894, she described aestheticism as a result of "the artificial way in which men and women are living . . . Every century or so society decides to improve on nature. It becomes very superior and refined indeed, until right through its surface there breaks some ghastly eruption that makes it hide its face in shame."[14]

Even sexually unconventional New Women were shocked by Wilde's *The Picture of Dorian Gray* (1891). "Vile and revolting and not interesting in any way," Robins confided to her diary; "—Oh Mr. Wilde! Mr. Wilde!"

Another American New Woman, M. Carey Thomas, herself a lesbian and the president of Bryn Mawr College, initially followed Wilde's trial closely and sympathetically. "I have hopes he will get off," she wrote to a friend. But by 1898, Wilde's post-prison behavior in Paris led her to change her mind. "I fear we must give up his defense," she wrote, and when she actually saw him a few weeks later, she found him looking "inconceivably vile," with the "most cruel face that I have ever seen."[15] Gertrude Atherton had been eager to meet Wilde at a London party, but decided not to go when she saw his photograph: "the most lascivious coarse repulsive mouth I had ever seen . . . I should feel as if I were under the sea pursued by some bloated monster of the deep."[16] Nevertheless, Wilde's allegorical genres, and his themes of the repressed and secret self, the mask, and the costly pursuit of pleasure, influenced American women's short stories from Gilman's "The Yellow Wall-paper" to Cather's "Paul's Case."

The Black Woman's Era

American New Women writers had to deal with internal differences of race, region, national origin, and religion that were absent or obscured in England, and most white writers of the decade, however advanced on feminist issues, were regressive in their attitudes toward immigration, other racial groups, and religious minorities. At the same time, the years from 1890 to 1910 were labeled "The Black Woman's Era" because of the visibility of significant black women writers. "It seems almost as if the inspiration of the times had created a new race of colored women," wrote Pauline Hopkins, "a new tide set in, new forces called into play a new era in the world's history, and through all this the moral and social regeneration of a race."[17] In the early part of the decade, Frances Harper, a novelist from an older generation, published *Iola Leroy* (1892), which looked back to the black experience of the Civil War. Iola has been raised as a carefree heiress, who even defends slavery; but as she is gaily chatting about the pleasures of a season in New Orleans and "the sunny South," slave traders are watching her and estimating that she would "bring $2000 any day in the New Orleans market." Her racial identity as a mulatto is revealed to her when her plantation-owner father dies suddenly, and his family is sold into slavery. As Iola later tells a white doctor she meets while nursing Civil War soldiers, she was indeed "sold from

State to State as an item of merchandise," sexually abased and abused. But her terrible experience has been an awakening to her mission in life—the betterment and uplift of black people in the South. As she concludes, "I might have led a life of careless ease and pleasure. But now my life has a much grander significance . . . Fearful as the awakening was, it was better than to have slept through life."[18]

Harper's melodramatic theme of the agonized but necessary awakening would reverberate in women's writing of the 1890s; but a younger New Woman writer, Pauline Hopkins (1859–1930), revised popular mainstream fictional genres by both men and women to raise radical questions about black female identity. Raised in Boston, Hopkins started to write fiction in 1899, and became the most prolific black woman writer of the period, publishing four novels and many short stories, and serving for four years as the editor of the *Colored American Magazine*. *Contending Forces* (1900), her best-known novel, was explicitly reformist in its intentions. In her preface, Hopkins declared that "fiction is of great value to any people as a preserver of manners and customs—religious, political, and social. It is a record of growth and development from generation to generation. *No one will do this for us; we must ourselves develop the men and women who will faithfully portray the inmost thoughts and feelings of the Negro with all the fire and romance which lie dormant in our history,* and, as yet, unrecognized by writers of the Anglo-Saxon race."[19]

Contending Forces, like *Iola Leroy,* was primarily melodrama, making use of "noble heroes, and virtuous heroines, melodramatic situations, unsavory villains, exotic locations, highly emotional scenes, amazing coincidences," as well as titillating and sadistic scenes of whipping.[20] Almost all her "white" characters turn out to have black blood in their past in some complex history unraveled through flashbacks or long-lost letters. Hopkins also made use of the familiar domestic imagery of the quilting bee. In a chapter called "The Sewing-Circle," young black women come together under the direction of Mrs. Willis, the widow of a prominent black legislator and the descendant of an old Boston family, who earns her living as a lecturer on "the advancement of the colored woman." One woman in the sewing circle, the beautiful Sappho Clark, is hiding a secret history of racial sexual abuse; her name associates her with the female poetic tradition and the failed artist heroine. In the historical mode of Stowe, Hopkins also based two of her characters on W. E. B. DuBois and Booker T. Washington. In her second novel, Hopkins wrote about a black fallen-woman figure in *Hagar's Daughter: A Story of Southern Caste Prejudice* (1901).

In *Of One Blood; or the Hidden Self* (1902–3), however, Hopkins daringly reimagined the white male quest romances of the 1880s and 1890s from a black female perspective. These hugely popular imperialist adventure stories, including Kipling's "The Man Who Would Be King," H. Rider Haggard's *She* and *King Solomon's Mines*, Stevenson's *Treasure Island*, Stoker's *Dracula*, and even Conrad's *Heart of Darkness*, represented a yearning for escape from a confining society, rigidly structured in terms of gender, class, and race, to a mythologized place elsewhere where white men could be freed from the constraints of Victorian morality and class roles in the anarchic space of the "primitive." Quest narratives involved a penetration into the imagined center of an exotic civilization. For fin de siècle writers, this space was usually Africa, the "dark continent," or a mysterious district of the Orient, a region of sexual and racial difference. In the caves, jungles, mountains, islands, or deserts of this other place, individual men, or groups of men, explored their secret and inner selves, both their sexuality and their psychology. Freed from the pressures of genteel Victorian society, and the needs to marry, reproduce, and succeed, the men encountered their inner dark continents, entering symbolic sexual landscapes at whose heart was often a dangerous and seductive native woman. Structurally, male quest romances were usually presented as frame narratives, with one man telling the story about another, and thus revealing something about himself.[21]

Hopkins's hero is Reuel Briggs, a brilliant Harvard medical student who not only passes for white but completely denies his black ancestry. Described as a mixture of romantic hero, genius, and athlete, Briggs reads texts about modern psychology and the hidden, occult self testifying to the "undiscovered country within ourselves—the hidden self lying quiescent in every human soul."[22] Like Stevenson's Dr. Jekyll, he leads an outwardly unblemished life, "free from the vices which beset most young men of his age and profession, his daily life . . . a white, unsullied page." But his Hyde is the black ancestry he is concealing and despising. In his quest, Reuel must find the undiscovered Africa within himself.

The first step toward self-acceptance is through love. Reuel goes to a concert of the Fisk Jubilee Singers, where he is smitten with the great black soprano Dianthe Lusk. "Not in any way the preconceived idea of a Negro," Dianthe is fair-skinned, with chestnut hair, and a voice "that passed all conceptions, all comparisons, all dreams." She enraptures her audience with her singing of "Let My People Go." Reuel marries Dianthe, but then he is desperate for money and agrees to go away for two years as the doctor on an expedition to find an ancient Ethiopian city and the treasure "which the shifting sands of the Sahara have buried for centuries." Along with a rich playboy, Charlie Vance, and an anthropologist, Professor Stone, Reuel sets off for Africa. If the men can find the city, Meroe, they will prove that the "Negro . . . [is] the most ancient source of all that you value in modern life, even antedating Egypt." When they find it, Telassar, the secret capital of Meroe, is both a utopian city of civilized architectural splendor and the cradle of learning. It has eighty pyramids, adorned with murals; magnificent statues, great temples, and gorgeous sepulchres of their kings and queens, especially the curvy Queen Candace ("corpulency [is] a mark of beauty in Eastern women"). Reuel is crowned as Ergamenes, the lost king of Telassar. Like Dianthe, Telassar is very different from preconceived European ideas of Central Africa; it is blossoming and dramatic, not "the howling wildernesses or an uninhabitable country."

In a melodramatic subplot, Dianthe is wooed by Reuel's best friend, and both die, leaving Reuel free to return to the Hidden City, where he marries Queen Candace and is reunited with the blood heritage of Africa. Elizabeth Ammons concludes that in *Of One Blood,* Hopkins "pushed narrative form fully over into the mode of allegorical vision, prophecy, and dream projection that African-American fiction, and particularly fiction by women—Toni Morrison, Rosa Guy, Gloria Naylor— would brilliantly mine later in the twentieth century."[23] But Hopkins more immediately pioneered and prefigured the genre of feminist quest romance, which Charlotte Perkins Gilman would take up a decade later. In her own time, however, she was too subversive. Shortly after the serial publication of her book, supporters of Booker T. Washington bought the *Colored American Magazine* and moved its office to New York. Hopkins was fired from her position. Officially, the magazine announced, "On account of ill-health, Miss Pauline Hopkins has found it necessary to sever her relations with this Magazine and has returned to her home in Boston." Unofficially, W. E. B. DuBois commented, "it was suggested to [her] that her attitude was not conciliatory enough."[24] Hopkins returned to her job as a stenographer at MIT; she edited a journal called *New Era* in 1916, but it lasted only two issues. Even in the heyday of the Harlem Renaissance, she was overlooked and ignored. In August 1930, she died in a fire that also destroyed any work in progress.

New Women, New Worlds: Feminist Utopias

Literature at the ends of centuries tends to have special preoccupations with the past and future. It can be pessimistic, looking despairingly to the end, or utopian, dreaming of a new beginning. Between 1886 and 1896, over one hundred utopian novels were published in the United States, many by and about women, and often dealing with sex roles, sexual arrangements, and reproduction.[25] As the critic Susan Gubar has observed, "If a woman is dispossessed, a nobody, in the somewhere of patriarchy, it may be that she can only become somebody in the nowhere of utopia."[26] If women's dreams of sexual and intellectual freedom could not be realized in the real world, they could at least be imagined in utopian fiction. Hoping for a brighter future, some Darwinian feminist intellectuals prophesied that in the next century men and women would evolve beyond the animal demands of the body. In *Hiero-Salem* (1889), Eveleen Mason envisioned a new "civilization for the coming generation" in a utopian community in the Midwest. The "conglomerate household" of the future would be egalitarian and free of racial, religious, regional, class, and sexual prejudice:

> *You see, we have now Tama and 'Dolph, the colored people, who are warm-hearted Methodists; and we have now, with us, Mrs. Mancredo's old coachman and his family, Sullivan, who is a Fenian and a drinker of intoxicants; a Chinese laundry-man and a Japanese gardener, one a Confucian and the other a Hindoo; and we have Mrs. Mancredo, Baptist and Yankee, late from Boston; and Mrs. Aubrey, Romanist and Southerner, half-French and wholly unreconstructed. Besides these, there are the Othniels, brother and two married sisters, young, proud-spirited Hebrews . . . [and] Bertha Gemacht . . . a goddess-like-natured girl, but who, born under the difficulties of illegitimacy, has passed on to a child she was duped into bearing the same difficulties mid which she herself was born.*[27]

Mason's understanding of comparative religion might have been sketchy and her notions of the communitarians stereotyped, but her underlying idea of a multicultural and pluralistic American society was ahead of its time. Kate Douglas Wiggin, who sought refuge from her husband in the Women's Community House of the Shaker settlement in Alfred,

Maine, also wrote a utopian novel, *Susanna and Sue* (1909), based on her experience.[28]

The most startling of the feminist utopias dealt with female sexuality. One utopian novelist, Lois Waisbrooker (1826–1909), has been called "the strongest personality among American feminists." Waisbrooker was an autodidact who wrote of her harsh childhood, "my early advantages were few. I did not come of a literary stock of ancestry. My parents worked hard for daily bread, had but little education, and less time to use it." Her mother died at thirty-six, and Waisbrooker worked as a domestic servant: "I have worked in people's kitchens year in and year out when I never knew what it was to be rested."[29] After the Civil War, she began teaching black children in country schools, and lecturing on women's rights, free love, and spiritualism. She also became an anarchist, publishing in anarchist journals like *Lucifer*. In 1901, Waisbrooker joined the utopian community "Home," for anarchists, vegetarians, and nudists, in Puget Sound. Waisbrooker was sixty-seven when she published *A Sex Revolution* (1893). In it, a Civil War widow, Margaret Mulgrove, falls asleep reading George Noyes Miller's well-known pacifist tract, *The Strike of a Sex* (1891), in which the entire female population of a futuristic American town called Hustleberg goes on sexual strike, demanding that the men practice birth control. Mulgrove dreams of a future society in which women are fully equal with men, and demanding peace and sexual rights.

In the same year, two married women from Cedar Rapids, Iowa, Alice Ilgenfritz Jones (1846–1905) and Ella Merchant (1857–1916), collaborated on *Unveiling a Parallel: A Romance*, a utopian novel in which women have exactly the same rights to sexual experimentation, initiative, and prostitution as men. On a visit to Mars, the novel's male narrator finds a sexually egalitarian society where women have access to brothels and drugs and are free to embrace single motherhood. He pays a visit to Cupid's Gardens, a luxurious brothel for women, where "lounging about on the lawn" are "several handsome young men." The fate of a professional lover on Mars is not a happy one. Some young men are seduced into the brothel when they are fresh and innocent; others are driven by "reverses and disaster" or a "cheerless home environment" into a life of degradation. The most enticing aspect of life on Mars is women's freedom to initiate romantic relationships and even to propose marriage, although marriage is looked upon as merely a necessary social convention.[30]

Feminist Nightmares—Charlotte Perkins Gilman

Charlotte Perkins Gilman (1860–1935), the leading American feminist theoretician and New Woman writer to come out of the 1890s, also experimented with utopian writing, and with the idea that writing itself could be a separate country for women. Her father, Frederick Beecher Perkins, was related to the great Beecher family, but he abandoned his wife and children a year after Charlotte was born in Hartford, Connecticut, and the couple were divorced in 1873. Through the rest of her life, Charlotte's father was absent as a source of love and support. As she wrote in her autobiography, *The Living of Charlotte Perkins Gilman* (1935), "The word 'Father,' in the sense of love, care, one to go to when in trouble, means nothing to me, save indeed in advice about books and the care of them—which seems more the librarian than the father." In fact, her father was a professional librarian who eventually became head of the San Francisco Public Library, and despite his remoteness, she maintained an irregular correspondence with him and consulted him about her reading. Thus, like many of her precursors, she was educated in her father's library.

Charlotte's mother, Mary Westcott Perkins, raised her son and daughter in Providence, Rhode Island, living with various relatives and struggling to support the family. Because she had been so betrayed and hurt herself, she tried to train Charlotte to do without affection: "She would not let me caress her, and would not caress me, unless I was asleep," Gilman sadly recalled. Her mother also tried, unsuccessfully, to curb her imagination and ambition; she was forbidden to read novels, write poetry, or go to the theater. Nevertheless, at eighteen, Charlotte went to study art at the Rhode Island School of Design, and was soon able to support herself as a commercial artist.

In her girlhood years, her most intense relationship was with a girlfriend, Martha Luther, and when Martha married, she was heartbroken and resolved always to live alone and independent: "I am fonder of freedom than anything else . . . I like to have my own unaided will in all my surroundings—in dress, diet, hours, behaviors, speech, and thought." Yet soon after, she met and married a young painter, Charles Walter Stetson. Their daughter Katherine was born in 1885, and Charlotte suffered a severe bout of postpartum depression. At first, she tried going away to visit a friend, Grace Channing, in California, but the symptoms came back when she returned home.

Dr. Silas Weir Mitchell (1829–1914), who had treated Rebecca Harding Davis in the 1860s, was the leading American specialist on female depression and neurasthenia, and had developed a famous "rest cure" for its treatment. Believing that neurasthenic New Women were suffering from a deep resistance to the female role, he attempted to induce a therapeutic state of dependence, weight gain, and inertia. He removed the exhausted and often anorexic patient from the family setting to a clinic, where she was confined to bed for several weeks, forbidden to do any intellectual work, and treated with a rich diet, massage, and electric stimulation. As Mitchell understood, the boredom and isolation of the treatment was "rather a bitter medicine" that made many women "glad enough to accept the order to rise and go about when the doctor issues a mandate." For depressed, anxious, and exhausted men, however, he recommended the "West cure"—a vacation on the frontier, or in the country, with physical labor and wholesome outdoor living replacing their stressful urban lives and repetitive jobs.[31]

Gilman turned to Weir Mitchell in desperation, writing a letter about her family genealogy and her emotional torment after her daughter's birth: "This agony of mind set in with the child's coming. I nursed her in slow tears. All that summer I did nothing but cry, save for times when the pain was unbearable and I grew almost hysterical, almost imbecile at times."[32] In the spring of 1887, Gilman went to Weir Mitchell's clinic in Philadelphia for a last-chance rest cure. Ordered to "live as domestic a life as possible" and "have your child with you all the time," and never "to touch pen, brush, or pencil as long as you live," Gilman had a complete breakdown. She saved herself by determining on a separation from her husband: "It seemed plain that if I went crazy it would do my husband no good and be a deadly injury to my child." In October 1888, she decided that what she really needed was the "West cure." Moving to Pasadena, California, with her little daughter, Gilman lectured, tutored, acted in community theater, and wrote stories, poems, articles, and satirical pieces.

As Gilman's biographer Mary A. Hill points out, "California in the early 1890s was an ideal training ground for rebels. It was a vital center of contemporary protest thought, a relatively supportive community for radicals and nonconformists, an engaging political environment in which Charlotte could broaden and intensify her sense of alliance with nationally based currents of reform."[33] Gilman realized that the change of environment and lifestyle was a rebirth: "With Pasadena begins my professional 'living.' Before that, there was no assurance of serious work." She reveled in "the vivid beauty of the land, its tumultuous growth of flowers and fruit, the shining glory of the days and nights, [which] gave me happiness and health."34

On a June day in Pasadena, with the "thermometer at one hundred and three," Gilman wrote her most important short story, "The Yellow Wall-paper."35 Told in a series of brief paragraphs of one or two sentences, "The Yellow Wall-paper" is a first-person narrative, a secret journal covering three months from approximately June 1 to the end of August. Its author is an unnamed woman who has been taken by her physician-husband, John, to a secluded house in the country, a "colonial mansion, a hereditary estate," in order to cure a nervous illness, a "slight hysterical tendency," she has developed after the birth of a son. The house is isolated, three miles from the nearest village. On its extensive grounds there are high hedges and locked gates, and inside the house, at the top, a large room with barred windows, rings on the walls, and an iron bed nailed down to the floor, which is "gouged and splintered," while the room's yellow wallpaper has been ripped and torn. This is the bedroom the narrator and her husband share at night, although she is alone in it during the long summer days when she secretly writes in her diary.

The realistic subtext of the story is that she is suffering a postpartum depression so severe that her husband and relatives are afraid she may harm herself or the baby or both. The remote house sounds like an abandoned private mental hospital, where the barred windows and nailed-down bed are signs of former patients who have been incarcerated. Like the "dead paper" of her journal, to which she confides her thoughts, the narrator also projects her suicidal feelings and violent obsessions onto the art nouveau wallpaper, which has a maddening pattern, a "florid arabesque." "It is dull enough to confuse the eye in following, pronounced enough to constantly irritate and provoke study, and when you follow the lame uncertain curves for a little distance they suddenly commit suicide—plunge off at outrageous angles, destroy themselves in unheard of contradictions." The pattern of the wallpaper takes on elements of a human face, which reminds her of a strangled baby: "there is a recurrent spot where the pattern lolls like a broken neck and two bulbous eyes stare at you upside down."

The color of the wallpaper also begins to prey upon her mind: "The color is repellent, almost revolting: a smoldering unclean yellow, strangely faded by the slow-turning sunlight. It is dull yet lurid orange in some places, a sickly sulphur tint in others." Later the narrator has olfactory hallucinations about the paper as well: "There is something else about that paper—the smell! . . . It creeps all over the house." She even thinks of burning down the house to destroy the "yellow smell." Although never stated directly, the odor suggests urine and soiled diapers.

In contrast to the disgusting paper inside the room is the "delicious" garden she can see from her window, a garden that suggests another traditional imagery of femininity and the maternal body much celebrated by American women writers, full of "mysterious deepshaded arbors, . . . riotous old-fashioned flowers, and bushes and gnarly trees." Soon she sees another woman—her double—trapped behind the paper and trying to get through, "but nobody could get through that pattern—it strangles so"; she also sees women creeping around in the garden, perhaps the ghosts of former mental patients. By the end, the narrator is completely mad, and contemplating murder and suicide. When her husband breaks into the room where she has locked herself, she has ripped off all the paper, and is creeping around the walls. "I've got out in spite of you," she tells him triumphantly, and he faints in shock. Gilman constructed an impossible narrative, for the narrator is apparently still writing in her diary in the present tense while she is mad. She expresses her anger toward men and medicine in self-destructive illness.

Gilman, however, did not destroy herself but used her writing to fight back against confinement. She sent the story to the *Atlantic Monthly,* but it was rejected by the editor Horace Elisha Scudder. She then sent it to a literary agent, Henry Austin. Austin told her he had got it published and then absconded with her forty-dollar fee, but probably William Dean Howells intervened to get it published in the *New England Magazine* in 1892. There it was well received; Henry B. Blackwell wrote: "Nothing more graphic and suggestive has ever been written to show why so many women go crazy, especially farmers' wives, who live lonely, monotonous lives."[36] Gilman said that she had also sent the story to Weir Mitchell, who never acknowledged it, but that she had been told by friends "that the great specialist . . . had altered his treatment of neurasthenia."[37] There is, alas, no evidence of this. He continued to use the rest cure for other women, including Edith Wharton, and in 1908, he was still defending it before the American Neurological Association. The rest cure became the subject of other feminist fiction at the turn of the century, but from a romantic or comic point of view. Elizabeth Robins wrote a novel in 1905, *A Dark Lantern,* which featured a seductive Byronic doctor who awakens his patient's sexuality; it was made into a movie in 1920. Ruth McEnery Stuart, who had consulted Mitchell on behalf of her son, and had enjoyed her own cures for being "nerve-tired" at the Jackson Health Resort in New York, published *The Cocoon: A Rest-Cure Comedy* (1915), in which a rebellious patient, sent for treatment because she cannot have children, sneaks away from the sanitarium for a treat like a mischievous girl at boarding school.[38]

Charlotte divorced Charles Walter Stetson in 1894, and they formed a new arrangement that scandalized their friends: he married Grace Channing, and nine-year-old Katherine was sent to live with her father and stepmother. For several years, Charlotte also had a passionate friendship with a woman journalist, Adeline Knapp. But in 1900 she was happily remarried to her cousin George Houghton Gilman, by whose name she was known thereafter. In a rapid series of books and articles, Gilman outlined her Darwinian agenda of sexual evolution and equality. Some of her most progressive ideas were about the differences between masculine and feminine literature. Men, she wrote, have written about adventure, hunting, war, crime, and punishment. But New Women's literature promised something different, with the familiar male bee of nineteenth-century American women's writing reduced to the level of a drone, and the queen bee and her servants, the feminist symbols of the twentieth century, taking over their power:

> If the beehive produced literature, the bee's fiction would be rich and broad, full of the complex tasks of comb-building and filling, the care and feeding of the young, the guardian-service of the queen; and far beyond that it would spread to the blue glory of the summer sky, the fresh winds, the endless beauty and sweetness of a thousand flowers. It would treat of the vast fecundity of motherhood, the educative and selective processes of the group-mothers, and the passion of loyalty, of social service, which holds the hive together.
>
> But if the drones wrote fiction, it would have no subject matter save the feasting, of many, and the nuptial flight, of one.[39]

Daughter of the Vine—Gertrude Atherton

In April 1891, Gilman read "The Yellow Wall-paper" to a friend in California, and recorded in her diary, "she likes it." The friend was Gertrude Atherton (1857–1948), a widowed young novelist who soon left the country and went to seek her literary fortune in London. Her real feelings about "The Yellow Wall-paper" were quite different from the impression she gave Gilman. In her autobiography, *Adventures of a Novelist,* she describes hosting an unnamed visitor—"the most able and intellectual woman in California" and "an EMINENT FEMINIST"—at a soiree at her San Francisco home. The guest announced that she "had written a wonderful ghost story," and would read it aloud. Sitting in the dark, by the light of a single candle, she read and read and read. "That was probably the worst story ever written," Atherton opined, "ghost or otherwise. It went on and on and on. In the author's nasal monotonous voice. An atmosphere of depression settled over the room. Sighs. Rustlings. Every one, I knew, cursing me in his or her heart."[40] She assured Gilman, however, that she had been vastly impressed. As Atherton's biographer writes, "Although she wrote one frankly suffragist novel, another in which women stage a revolution against men, and many others with spirited, bright, and assertive heroines, Atherton was the kind of feminist who complains about how ugly most other feminists are."[41]

Gertrude Atherton was a clever and energetic Californian who spent a number of years in London and, like Bret Harte and other expatriates, figured out how to market the exoticism of the West to the British. She was also the first of the popular women writers to trade heavily on her glamorous looks, her artificially maintained blond hair, and her devotion to makeovers and medical rejuvenation treatments about which she wrote the best seller *Black Oxen.* But Atherton was also an ambitious novelist, who had read *Jane Eyre* six times, as well as Shakespeare, Byron, Dickens, and Henry James. One of her early novels, *Patience Sparhawk and Her Times* (1897), was published in London in the feminist avant-garde series "Keynotes," by John Lane. Dedicated to Paul Bourget, "who alone, of all foreigners, has detected, in its full significance, that the motive power, the coloring force, the ultimate religion of that strange composite known as 'The American,' is Individual Will," it tells the story of little Patience, the daughter of Madge Sparhawk, the alcoholic town slut of Monterey, California. Patience is the smartest girl in her class, avidly reading Scott, Thackeray, Dickens, the Brontës, and Boccaccio; but when she discovers her mother in bed with the farmhand, Patience declares she will henceforth read only "what is dry." Madge dies in a fire, and Patience goes to New York, where she is taken in and adopted by two sisters active in the temperance movement. She marries her romantic and decadent idol, Beverly Peele, and goes to work for a newspaper. She is then accused of murdering Peele when he has actually taken an overdose of morphine. Patience is convicted and sent to die in the electric chair, but she is saved at the last minute by a New Man who gets her pardoned. To research the novel, Atherton attended a murder trial in New York, and sat in the electric chair at Sing Sing prison.

This was lurid stuff even for John Lane, and Atherton found herself lionized and notorious in London. She had written a letter to the *Daily News* describing the natural affinities of American women and English men; American New Women were "alive to their finger-tips; they have cast off the yoke of conventionality, cut-and-dried religion and all the old forms and traditions," and were perfect Darwinian partners for English men, "the most dominant, perfectly balanced . . . and highly developed . . . the world has ever known."[42] In *American Wives and English Husbands* (1898) she told the story of a free-spirited California girl, Lee Tarleton, who marries Cecil Maundrell, the heir to the Earl of Barnstable. At first, Lee sacrifices herself entirely to help Cecil further his career in Parliament. Soon, however, she rebels against her subordination, and asks to return to California for a year. At the end of the novel, she changes her mind and accepts her role and her love for England. British critics admired the novel for its undogmatic portrayal of an independent American woman, but Henry James, of course, thought it was superficial.[43] Like every other American woman writer abroad, Atherton had met James in London. "I abominate the woman," he wrote to his secretary when Atherton requested advice about hotels in Paris.[44]

A few years later, she went to stay in Haworth and wrote the novel *A Daughter of the Vine* (1899), about another dashing California girl, Nina Rudolph, whose terrible secret is the alcoholism she has inherited from her dissolute mother. Nina marries an Englishman, hoping to escape to a more literary environment. "So far," she opines, "California has evolved no literature . . . When it does, I don't doubt it will be a literature of light and charm and comedy—and pleasurable pathos. Writing will continue to go to the dreary moorlands, the dun-colored skies of England for tragedy settings, and for the atmosphere of tradition and history. It will be hard for any writer who has traveled over the wonderful mountains and valleys of California . . . to imagine tragedy in a land of such exultant beauty . . . Fancy Emily Brontë writing 'Wuthering Heights' in California." Nina's fate nevertheless overtakes her; she cannot escape the fruit of the California vine. At the end of the century, Atherton, too, returned to California, where she became well known for her "California Series" of novels and stories about the West.

New Women and New Orleans

For most of the nineteenth century, Boston and New York had been the centers of the literary elite. After the Civil War, however, New Orleans began to emerge not only as the literary center of the New South, with its own "New Orleans School" of writers, but also as the headquarters of the New Woman. Louisiana had long been mythologized as an American utopian space reflecting a universal North/South fantasy: "Catholicism and warm weather come to represent a blurred sensuality."[45] New Orleans, with its sophisticated Creole culture, its European lifestyle, its hurricanes, floods, and fevers, its reputation for the hedonistic, sensual, and volatile, was a feminine city, the "exotic remote site of the female libido."[46] In the 1880s and 1890s, the number of women writing fiction in Louisiana steadily increased. The New Orleans *Daily Picayune* was the first major American newspaper edited by a woman, Eliza J. Nicholson, and from 1895, it published the first women's-advice column, by "Dorothy Dix" (Elizabeth Gilmer, 1861–1951). New Orleans women writers were also viewed as exotic blossoms, flowers of freedom; Ruth McEnery Stuart compared herself to the orchid, which "answers to no one for where, when, or how it chooses to throw out a petal, nor for the color, shape, or contortions of the same. Its leaves are its own. It is the orchid's affair . . . There is an idea afloat that the Ladye Orchid abounds especially among literary women."[47]

In 1884, Julia Ward Howe had visited New Orleans with her daughter Maud to preside over the Women's Department of the Cotton Centennial Exhibition; she also launched a literary discussion group called the Pan-Gnostics.[48] At the time, New Orleans men regarded even literary clubs as a dangerous deviation from Southern ladyhood; as Mrs. J. C. Croly noted, "a 'club' was a plunge [into the outside world] which carried with it only the idea of something dreadful to their minds, and particularly to the minds of the men of their families."[49] But under Howe's influence, some New Orleans women began to experiment with writing fiction and essays. Maud Howe herself wrote *Atalanta in the South: A Romance* (1886), a feminist novel that condemned "the neglect and maltreatment of both women and blacks, urging greater independence and self-reliance on the former," and better education and opportunities for the latter.[50] Following the example of the Howes, New Orleans women set up their own literary salons and book clubs. Sophie Newcomb College for Women was founded in 1888.

About half the population of New Orleans was black, but almost all the women writers were white, daughters and wives of planters and professionals, educated in their fathers' libraries or in convents and boarding schools, and holding orthodox Southern views about race.[51] The first women's suffrage association in New Orleans, the Portia Club, was formed in 1892, but Southern suffragists were motivated as much by racial bigotry as by the prospect of female emancipation, and hoped to install educational and property requirements for voting that would disenfranchise African-Americans. Three groups dominated the population—the French-speaking Creoles, rich white descendants of the early French and Spanish settlers; the Acadians or Cajuns, who had emigrated from Canada in the eighteenth century and settled in the bayous; and the African-Americans, mainly former slaves. New Orleans had been one of the most liberal parts of the country with regard to racial mixing before the war, but during Reconstruction, attitudes had hardened, and white supremacist organizations were rampant.

Among the central images of femininity for New Orleans women writers in the 1890s were the convent and the brothel. Louisiana was a predominantly Catholic state; unlike the New England nuns of Freeman and Jewett, the convent girls and nuns of Kate Chopin, Grace King, and other writers were taken from life. Chopin, according to Helen Taylor, "saw the convent both as a site of emotional intensity and also as a kind of death—certainly a retreat from adult sexual life."[52] At the other extreme, women were aware of the infamous red-light districts of New Orleans; Storyville was a licensed area of prostitution in the late 1890s, but long before, white men had taken mixed-race women as mistresses, as Sherwood Bonner had suggested in her chapters on the quadroon ball in *Like unto Like*. Mardi Gras, with its carnivalesque mixture of entertainment and subversion, was a New Orleans tradition that suited fin de siècle themes of boundary violation, racial and sexual masquerade, and metamorphosis. Women also drew on the archetypal images of the river, the bayou, and, especially, the Gulf of Mexico, which came to symbolize the gulf between men and women in the 1890s, and the oceanic nature of women and death.

A SOUTHERN WOMAN OF LETTERS—GRACE KING

Grace King (1852–1932) was born in New Orleans, and remained all her life a partisan of the Lost Cause, and an angry opponent of those Southern writers, like George Washington Cable, who would apologize for the South, or even worse, support black emancipation. Like Augusta

Evans, she believed that the South could rise again as a cultural force: "The South must write itself to the front of the nation—its old place," she wrote fervently to a friend.[53] Despite this aspiration, in her fiction she used metaphors and themes of mixed race to explore her own conflicts about wanting to be a serious artist while maintaining the propriety, modesty, and frivolity of the ideal Southern lady.

When King was nine years old, New Orleans fell to federal troops, and her mother fled the occupied city with her children to hide at the L'Embarrass plantation. King wrote about the siege in *Memories of a Southern Woman of Letters:* "I recall standing one evening at the side window of Grandmother's room looking at surging flames rising higher and higher through black smoke . . . The city shook with explosions. I knew, but only vaguely, that the city was being prepared for surrender to the 'enemy' . . . [W]ill they kill us all when they take the city, I wondered . . . recalling pictures of captured cities in the Bible."[54] With two black maids, the Kings "drove through dark and ugly streets to the levee and stopped at a landing where a steamboat was moored, with steam up. The river was black, and we children were frightened. We clung to the carriage, and had to be lifted out bodily by 'hands' from the boat, who carried us up the gang-plank and the steep steps to the deck and deposited us in a large cabin."[55] This nightmare voyage of invasion and flight would inspire some of King's most haunting stories.

When the Kings returned after the war, they had lost all their property. Grace was educated in a French Creole school in New Orleans, and determined to be a writer; but after her father died in 1881, she had to postpone her plans. Yet the family continued to entertain intellectual, literary, and society figures. King joined the Pan-Gnostic Club, became its secretary, and read an essay called "The Heroines of Novels," which credited Charlotte Brontë and George Eliot with creating believable women who spoke for themselves.[56] In addition, she attended six meetings that focused on women and women's rights; on her first trip north, to Hartford in 1887, she met Isabella Beecher Hooker, Stowe's sister and a staunch feminist, "who," she wrote to a friend, "talked to me about 'Woman's Rights' and converted me to her point of view."[57]

During this period she also met the influential editor of *The Century,* Richard Watson Gilder, who encouraged her to write. Her first story, "Monsieur Motte," was rejected when she submitted it anonymously to *Scribner's,* but it was taken up by the novelist and editor Charles Dudley Warner, who helped her get it published anonymously in the *New*

Princeton Review. In 1888, with three sequels, it appeared as a novel. As King later recalled, "A first novel, you know, is a first revelation of one's self . . . It writes itself. Criticism is useless upon it, because one can write a first novel only once. Never again will you be so possessed by your characters."[58]

"Monsieur Motte" is named for a character who does not exist—the alleged rich uncle of an orphaned convent girl, Marie Modeste Motte. Approaching her graduation from the school, Marie is eager to meet her guardian, about whom she has been told for years by Marcelite, a quadroon hairdresser who acts as a go-between. But when the ceremony takes place, the uncle does not appear, and two days later, everyone learns from the distraught and disheveled Marcelite that it has all been a charade. She was a slave in the family of the parents, who died during the Civil War, and has been laboring to raise the child in luxury. The headmistress, the school lawyer, and Marie herself believe at first that Marcelite is actually Marie's mother, and for a brief moment, the girl declares her wish to live with her true parent. But this potential awakening turns out to be a mistake; Marcelite has documents to prove the girl is white, the headmistress and lawyer adopt her, and she is reassimilated into the racial and class system. King told Warner that to her the story represented the "holy passion of the Negro Women for white children," and the honor of Southern women that they should be so served and loved by slaves.[59]

In her later story "The Little Convent Girl," collected in *Balcony Stories* (1893), King revisited the plot of the girl who is unaware of her true family background. The "little convent girl" is actually eighteen; she is traveling alone by steamboat from Cincinnati to New Orleans because her father has died, and for the first time in twelve years she is meeting her mother, with whom he had had some "disagreement." Never named, the girl is as helpless as a doll, veiled and tightly groomed in her starched black mourning clothes. The river journey is both a shock and a thrill for her; she is horrified by the swearing of the crew, which they stop for her sake; and exhilarated by the brief glimpse of freedom, sexuality, and temptation the river offers, including the black roustabouts stripped to their waists on the docks, and the kindly pilot's talk of the river itself. "It was his opinion that there was as great a river as the Mississippi flowing directly under it—an underself of a river, as much a counterpart of the other as the second story of a house is of the first." This whirlpool of a subterranean river symbolizes the "underself" of the girl, who has repressed her entire identity in the model of the convent, of goodness and littleness and feminine decorum. When the boat arrives in New Orleans, the mother who comes to meet her is black. But while for Marie the revelation of the black "mother" is quickly overcome, for the little convent girl it is a death sentence. When the boat returns to dock at New Orleans, the mother brings her mute and depressed daughter on board to revisit the captain, with an unstated hope that he will adopt her. But he does not understand, or respond, and the girl jumps overboard, perhaps, as the narrator says, "to the underground river, to that vast, hidden, dark Mississippi that flows beneath the one we see."

We could argue that the story simply illustrates King's racism—black parentage is such a curse that the tragic mulatto must die. Yet King's language is so eloquent and haunting, her vision of the river voyage so evocative of the traumatic trip she had taken as a child, that a deeper reading seems called for. Anne Goodwyn Jones argues very persuasively that the story is an allegory of "the Southern woman writer in a man's world." The little convent girl is silent throughout; she hears the "fortissimo" language of the men, but can never speak in a meaningful female voice. The black mother has more freedom of speech and action, but the little convent girl cannot allow herself to speak her "mother's tongue." Yet in her suicide, she "accepts the hidden values of that deeper Mississippi," of the alienated and passionate underself.[60]

King's own career suggests that she could not resolve the dilemma of white Southern ladyhood and dark literary ambition. After *Balcony Stories,* King did not publish any books of fiction for twenty-three years. Instead, she wrote biographies and histories, returning to fiction with *The Pleasant Ways of St. Medard* (1916) and finally her posthumous autobiography, *Memories of a Southern Woman of Letters* (1932). Until the end of her life, she could not untangle the mixed threads of her identity as Southerner, woman, and writer. Despite her attachment to the Old South and its customs, King's anger about the oppression of Southern women, white as well as black, found full expression only in her private journals, where she noted "subjects for a Southern novel" she could never write: "the public chivalrous talk and bearing of the men; their utter contempt of the claims of women in private." Was slavery "accountable for the degraded position of women in the South?" she mused. "For degraded they are, beyond belief, beyond imagination."[61]

A CREOLE FLAUBERT—KATE CHOPIN

Kate O'Flaherty Chopin (1851–1904) first visited New Orleans as a girl of eighteen, a graduate of a St. Louis convent school. On this auspicious visit, she smoked her first cigarette, that essential accessory of New Womanly style. In 1870, after her marriage to Oscar Chopin, a Creole cotton broker, she moved to New Orleans, and lived there for eight years. Despite giving birth to six children, Chopin found ways to satisfy her curiosity about the city and defied convention by walking unaccompanied through its districts and markets. When her husband died, she turned to writing as a means of support. During the 1890s, Chopin published a novel, *At Fault* (1890), and two books of short stories about the French Creoles of New Orleans, *Bayou Folk* (1894) and *A Night in Acadie* (1897). Although her Creole stories were sometimes described as "local color," Chopin herself found the genre too artless: "special problems, social environments, local color, and the rest of it," she wrote in a review of Hamlin Garland, could not guarantee "the survival of a writer who employed them."[62] She resented being compared to Grace King, and unlike Jewett, Freeman, or Woolson, did not employ an old woman as a narrator.[63] Her heroines were young, passionate, thwarted, and searching. Moreover, she did not admire the didacticism of the English New Women novelists such as Sarah Grand. The eleventh commandment, she noted, is "Thou shalt not preach."[64] She did not join the women's suffrage movement or form close female friendships as an adult.

The Awakening (1899) drew upon, but went far beyond, the themes and structures of women's writing at the end of the century. Chopin's heroine Edna Pontellier shares her name with Augusta Evans's Edna Earle in *St. Elmo,* but she is very different from the heroines of domestic fiction. She has neither mother nor daughter, and even refuses to attend her sister's wedding. Where Louisa May Alcott, in her novel *Work,* had taken her heroine, Christie, on a pilgrimage through various forms of work available to a woman of her time, Chopin takes Edna on a passionate journey through forms of love, which begins with her childhood attraction to a cavalry officer in Kentucky, and then goes through the stages of an adolescent crush on a famous tragedian, a rebellious marriage to an older Catholic man of whom her family disapproves, a homoerotic fascination with a Creole friend, an unconsummated dalliance with a younger man, and an affair with a roué that makes her aware of her own sexuality: his kiss "was a flaming torch that kindled desire." No frail anorexic, Edna is a robust woman whose sensual appetites include voluptuous midnight swims, erotic fragrances, and stroking drowsy cats, as well as a healthy relish for food and alcohol. Compared to the agonizing experiences that shock Iola Leroy out of her cocooned sleep into racial and social awareness, Edna's awakening is personal, metaphysical, and narcissistic. She is blind to the real oppression of the black women who serve her, but keenly alert to the "vague anguish" of the "soul's slavery." Such an epiphany, Chopin observes, "is necessarily vague, tangled, chaotic, and exceedingly disturbing." When she attends her friend Adele's childbirth, she is struck by the pitiless biological destiny of women, and understands romantic love as "a decoy to secure mothers for the race." Nonetheless, like Iola, Edna does not regret having seen the truth. "The years that are gone seem like dreams—if one might go on sleeping and dreaming—but to wake up and find—oh! well! Perhaps it is better to wake up after all, even to suffer, rather than remain a dupe to illusions all one's life."

Edna would like to become an artist, but she lacks both the talent and the discipline. She would like to share a grand passion, but she realizes that her limited society offers infatuation, notoriety, or conformity. As she swims out alone purposely to her death, Edna's last thoughts recycle images of the feminine illusions of her childhood. She "heard her father's voice and her sister Margaret's. She heard the barking of an old dog that was chained to the sycamore tree. The spurs of the cavalry officer clanged as he walked across the porch. There was the hum of bees and the musky odors of pinks filled the air." The images of the booted cavalry officer, the sound of bees and the erotic fragrance of the pinks, lure women into a long slumber, but even in drowning Edna cannot escape their seductiveness. To ignore their claim, Chopin suggests, is also to cut oneself off from the "humming" life of creation and art.[65]

Formally, *The Awakening* was equally original, with thirty-nine numbered sections instead of titled chapters, ranging in length from a single paragraph to a sustained scene, unified by the repetition of key motifs and images: music, the sea, swimming, shadows, eating, sleeping, and birth. Reviews of *The Awakening* were generally harsh; the *St. Louis Daily Globe-Democrat* called it "a morbid book." The most important review, for its intelligence and connection to an ongoing genealogy of American women's writing, if not its empathy, was Willa Cather's "A Creole Bovary" in the *Pittsburgh Leader*. Cather praised Chopin's "light, flexible, subtle" literary style, but deplored her "trite and sordid theme." Most of her critique, condemning Edna as a woman who asks too much of love and expects it "to fill and gratify every need of life," missed the ironic distance of Chopin's narrative, and the complexity of her portrayal of Edna.[66]

In reaction to such obtuse reviews, and to the book's subsequent disappearance from libraries and bookstores, Chopin lost confidence in her writing. In 1892, she had published "At the 'Cadian Ball," in which the sultry Calixta flirts with the dashing French planter Alcée, but loses him to his cousin, while she marries the good-hearted but dull Bobinôt. While *The Awakening* was in press, she wrote a sequel, "The Storm," which picks up the story five years later. Alcée and Calixta meet again during a tropical storm, away from both their spouses, and go to bed together in an ecstatic sexual consummation. The results of this occasion are not tragic, or even damaging to the marriages of the protagonists; each party feels pleasure and renewed happiness. As Chopin wrote, "So the storm passed and every one was happy." Nonetheless, she never even tried to publish the story.

The Awakening was the first novel by an American woman that was completely successful in aesthetic terms, but it was read by very few of Chopin's contemporaries, and even fewer of the writers in the next generations, until its critical revival in the 1960s. American women's writing as a whole suffered when Chopin's revolutionary work was taken out of circulation. As her first biographer and champion, Per Seyersted, observed, "though she was so much of an innovator in American literature she was virtually unknown by those who were now to shape it . . . and she had no influence on them."[67] It would be many more decades before American women writers would even attempt to write so profoundly about female sexuality.

CARNIVAL—ALICE DUNBAR-NELSON

Born in New Orleans, Alice Dunbar-Nelson (1875–1935) came from European, African, and Indian ancestry, and identified herself as Creole. Dunbar-Nelson often felt lost between white and black culture; though she was an activist in the antilynching movement and in crusades for the improvement of African-American education, she occasionally passed for white to evade the limits of segregation. The most formally educated of the New Orleans women writers, she had attended Straight University in New Orleans, as well as studied education and psychology at Cornell, Columbia, and the University of Pennsylvania. In the 1890s, she taught school in New Orleans, and published only two books, *Violets and*

Other Tales (1895) and *The Goodness of St. Rocque and Other Stories* (1899), set in the French Quarter.[68]

Dunbar-Nelson's first husband, the poet Paul Dunbar, whom she married in 1898, had encouraged her to use New Orleans for her material. "Its very atmosphere must teem with stories and its streets and by-ways must be redolent of dramatic incident that lingers as a sort of perfume from a fragrant past. No wonder you have Grace King and Geo. W. Cable, no wonder you will have Alice R. M.," he wrote her in 1896, in the correspondence that became their courtship.[69] But Dunbar-Nelson wished neither to emulate a white Grace King nor to use her writing solely for racial uplift. In her first letter to Paul Dunbar, she had noted that "when I start a story I always think of my folk characters as simple human beings, not as types of a race or an idea."[70] She resisted writing black dialect as well, and chose Creoles, upper-class whites, and sometimes Irish immigrants as her subjects. These choices, as Elizabeth Ammons points out, were "so politically radical in 1899 as to be virtually suicidal." Despite her contention that as a black woman she should be free to write about anything she pleased and "to cross both the color and the gender line," her decision cut her off from her black identity and found no support from white publishers.[71]

Like Kate Chopin, Dunbar-Nelson stopped publishing fiction after the 1890s. She had begun two other collections of short stories, but was discouraged from completing them. She proposed to Bliss Perry at the *Atlantic* that she expand her fine short story about passing, "The Stones of the Village," into a novel, but he told her that there was no market for fiction about the color line. Three of her subsequent novels were rejected by publishers because they had flaws of plot, action, and climax, but we can also speculate that her suspended identity made it more difficult for her to find the new plots and endings she required.[72] "Nowhere else in the period," Ammons concludes, "does the promise of a young writer's career get extinguished so prematurely."[73]

Both Chopin and Dunbar-Nelson were caught between their culture's views of proper women's writing and their own ambitions to write a fully emancipated fiction. Chopin broke away from the conventions of literary domesticity and yearned to write fiction about men and women that went beyond female plots and feminine endings. Dunbar-Nelson was ahead of her time in aspiring to transcend race and take on the full range of New Orleans society. Both were silenced.

Sweeping Cobwebs

At the end of the century, women writers produced a number of feminist allegories, fairy tales, and anti-utopian fables that acknowledged the bitter disappointments of personal life and literary ambition. These fables, which the authors often called "dreams" to tame their disturbing content, were darker than the short stories and novels of the decade, involving cross-dressing, gender confusion, and anger toward men. Although her marriages had been happy ones, Helen Hunt Jackson told a different story in her last published work, "The Prince's Little Sweetheart" (1885). The story begins like "Cinderella"; an innocent girl marries a prince and becomes a pampered princess in the royal palace. The next day, though, she discovers a crowd of young women sweeping up spiders in the corridors of the palace. They explain that they are all former sweethearts of the prince.

> *"Is it only for one day, then?" she asks in terror.*
> *"Only for one day," they all replied.*
> *"And always after that do you have to kill spiders?" she cried.*
> *"Yes, that or nothing," they said.*[74]

Jackson claimed that the story was only a transcription of a bad dream; but it speaks of disillusion, exhaustion, and the end of romance.[75] Girls may be seduced by fairy tales and promises of luxury and adoration; but in the end, marriage is about killing spiders every day of your life.

Mary Wilkins Freeman's book of fairy tales, *The Pot of Gold* (1892), is rarely discussed even by Freeman specialists; hiding subversive material in the category of children's literature was one way to escape censure. In "The Patchwork School," Freeman describes a "reform School . . . of a very peculiar kind." Naughty, complaining, or dishonest children are caught by special police, who send them away to an institution where they are forced to do patchwork all day—sentenced to the tedious and repetitious labor that so many American women and girls had endured. "Every day bales of calico were left at the door of the Patchwork School, and it all had to be cut up in little bits and sewed together again." One child so condemned is a boy named Julia; he has been raised by four grandmothers, whose dropped knitting and lost spectacles he must constantly recover. Every Christmas they give him eight pairs of blue yarn stockings and nothing else. When he is sent to the Patchwork School for grumbling, however, he is rescued by the Chinese ambassador, who hears his story and fills his Christmas stockings with presents, including Chinese tops. Is Julia a boy or a girl or both or neither? In the future, Freeman hints, androgynous children will be rescued from their social incarceration in sex roles, and set free to enter the topsy-turvy world of self-definition.

One of Dunbar-Nelson's stories of St. Rocque, "A Carnival Jangle," tells the tale of a young woman who dresses up as a white male troubadour and accompanies a seductive young man dressed as Mephisto to the Mardi Gras, where all racial and sexual identities are in flux:

> The streets are a crush of jesters and maskers, Jim Crows and clowns. Ballet girls and Mephistos, Indians and monkeys; of wild and sudden flashes of music, of glittering pageants and comic ones, of befeathered and belled horses, a dream of colour and melody and fantasy gone wild in an effervescent bubble of beauty that shifts and changes and passes kaleidoscope-like before the bewildered eye.

In an abrupt and macabre ending, the girl is killed in a street fight; to cross-dress, or aspire to male art, is to sell one's soul to the devil; and to cross the color line, Dunbar-Nelson hints, is fatal for a woman. Elizabeth Ammons suggests that the Dionysian masquerade of Carnival is Dunbar-Nelson's central metaphor, "a kaleidoscope of human emotions, experiences, stations of life, rituals, belief systems, and sexual and national identities."[76] It is a trope well suited to Dunbar-Nelson's own complex identity as black, female, and bisexual, a writer who created white characters of varied ethnicity as well as black characters from various classes and backgrounds.

Kate Chopin, too, wrote a number of cynical allegories in the 1890s. In "The Story of an Hour" (1894), published in *Vogue*, a woman hears that her husband has been killed, and, after the first shock, realizes that she feels liberated. The story ends with a twist: he comes home and she dies of "heart trouble"—disappointment that she is still a wife. In "An Egyptian Cigarette," also published in *Vogue*, in 1900, the heroine has an erotic fantasy, brought on by smoking a yellow opium cigarette, in which she is passionately attracted to a cruel and dashing sheik.

Edith Wharton's "The Valley of Childish Things" (1896) is a parable of a little girl who wants to leave the valley where children play "all manner of delightful games," and to "see something of the world about which the lesson-books had taught her." She escapes, and after a hard journey, which leaves her face "beaten by the weather," gets to the city, where she works and grows to become a woman. With this knowledge and maturity, she decides to return to the valley, but when she returns she discovers that "her former companions, instead of growing into men and women, had all remained little children . . . playing the same old games." There is only one adult man in the valley, but he is captivated by "a dear little girl with blue eyes and a coral necklace," who is too young to talk. And when "she who had grown to be a woman laid her hand on the man's shoulder, and asked him if he did not want to set to work with her building bridges, draining swamps, and cutting roads through the jungle," he refuses, adding "in the kindest possible way, 'Really, my dear, you ought to have taken better care of your complexion.' "[77] Wharton's biographer Hermione Lee says that the story is a satire of "American infantilism," and indeed "The Valley of Childish Things" seems to be one of Wharton's disparaging judgments of her countrymen and -women.[78] She wrote it in the 1890s, though, before she had become an expatriate herself, and the unkind remark about the woman's complexion suggests rather that Wharton had in mind the infantile relation of the sexes, and male preference for a pretty plaything rather than an equal partner.

In 1895, twenty-two-year-old Ellen Glasgow published her first short story, "A Woman of Tomorrow." Set in the bleak fields of Virginia, fertile before the Civil War but now running wild in goldenrod, sassafras, broomsedge, brush, and sour blackberries, the story has the landscape she would make her trademark in *Barren Ground* and other novels of the 1920s and 1930s. But its heroine, Patricia Yorke, is a New Woman, a lawyer and a feminist idealist who links her aspirations to the visions of the coming new century. Although she is briefly tempted to give up her career to follow her lover, she renounces him: "You may not understand, for the women of to-day are different from the women you know—the women you have read of. In the nineteenth century a woman would have stayed; in the twentieth she must go."[79] Unlike the grim heroines of Glasgow's mature work, Patricia sacrifices the man and saves herself from a life of poverty, grinding labor, and premature age. With the shining eyes of New Woman's vision, Glasgow imagined her ending up a decade later on the Supreme Court, a position American women did not actually attain until 1981.

. . .

Overall, however, while male artists in the fin de siècle feared an apocalypse and the destruction of the existing culture, including literature,
women writers had less to lose in the disappearance of old cultural
forms, and much to hope for in the transformation of gender and genre.
Despite the bitterness of their parables, their critique of marriage, and
their truncated careers, American women writers of the 1890s demanded
recognition as artists, and invented new forms rather than adapting old
ones for their self-expression. Indeed, describing the literary scene dominated by the self-important old men of the new American Academy,
Glasgow called them "elderly, but . . . not yet mature," unable to face
reality as her generation of women could.[80] In her 1890 essay on
"Women in Literature," Helen Gray Cone foresaw a "golden morrow"
of great American women's fiction.[81]

11

The Golden Morrow .

The first years of the twentieth century seemed like the promised golden dawn of American women's writing. Women playwrights, especially Susan Glaspell, changed the form, structure, language, and focus of the theater. Women editors, including Harriet Monroe at *Poetry,* Inez Haynes Irwin at *The Masses,* and Lola Ridge at *Broom,* created an accessible market for a generation of serious women poets; at the opposite extreme, women writers created a lively, adventurous literature for adolescent girls. In Paris, the expatriate Gertrude Stein expressed the ideas of Cubism and Post-Impressionism in a modernist experimental prose that baffled most readers but impressed other artists and mesmerized twentieth-century scholars. At the same time, a group of talented black writers and artists, children of Reconstruction, claimed their place in American and race literature, testifying to an era of "New Negro" women's art. First-generation Americans, the daughters of immigrants from Eastern Europe, Asia, and Mexico, participated in the redefinition of American culture and identity.

To many participant-observers, the years 1912 and 1913 signaled the end of genteel Victorianism and the beginning of modernism. According to Floyd Dell, 1912 "was really an extraordinary year, in America as well as Europe. It was the year of intense woman-suffragist activity. In the arts, it marked a new era. Color was everywhere—even in neckties. In Chicago, Harriet Monroe founded *Poetry* . . . The Irish Players came to America. It was then that plans were made for the Post-Impressionist Show which revolutionized American ideas of art . . . One could go on with the sense of a New Spirit come suddenly to birth in America."[1] The New Spirit extended to human relationships as well. According to the *salonnière* Mabel Dodge Luhan, "It seems as though everywhere, in that year of 1913, barriers went down and people reached each other who had not been in touch before; there were all sorts of new ways to communicate as well as new communications. The new spirit was abroad and swept us all together."[2]

The prewar years were a period of exhilarating female solidarity, in the suffrage movement, in feminist clubs and professional communities, in literary and artistic schools, and in Greenwich Village bohemia, and this communal spirit was later manifested even in war work. The new term "feminism" replaced the "Woman Question" to suggest a quest for intellectual, political, sexual self-determination, as well as for the vote, and active feminists joined the New Women. In 1912, the minister Marie Jenney Howe created the feminist society Heterodoxy to help women in New York pioneer this new consciousness. Heterodoxy flourished until 1920, with many women writers among its charter members. As Inez Haynes Irwin recalled, Heterodoxy was a utopian sorority, in which the members "talked about everything. Heterodoxy members were . . . democrats, republicans, Prohibitionists, socialists, anarchists, liberals, and radicals of all opinions . . . The rosta [sic] included many publicists, newspaper-women, war correspondents, radio commentators. There were dramatists, novelists, and poets; painters and musicians. Our occupations and preoccupations ranged the world."[3] Members thought of themselves as an avant-garde tribe; they invited Margaret Sanger to address them on birth control, included lesbian couples in their club, and satirized their own sexual experiments in a mock anthropological study, "Marriage Customs and Taboo Among the Early Heterodites." Indeed, Heterodoxy reflected the rise of the social sciences as careers for New Women; anthropologists and sociologists including Elsie Clews Parsons, Ruth Benedict, and Margaret Mead used scientific methods and fieldwork to explore the idea of women's culture, while they themselves escaped small towns and narrow domestic arrangements to explore the world.

The intellectual agenda of feminism demanded a redefinition of literary traditions and history as well. There were new biographies of Margaret Fuller, studies of the fictional representations of women, and the embryonic signs of a feminist literary criticism.[4] Beatrice Hale emphasized the historical importance of *Jane Eyre* for American women writers: "Without half the charm of Jane Austen [Brontë] accomplished what that sprightly damsel never even attempted . . . the creation of a heroine whose salient characteristic was neither beauty nor virtue but sheer force of character."[5] In the collective spirit of the age, Elizabeth

Robins called for women writers to support each other; both George Eliot and Margaret Fuller, she argued, "failed to further the cause they advocated because they tried to do alone what can only be accomplished if women writers work together."[6]

Women who wanted to work together, including feminists, socialists, suffragists, bohemians, and pacifists, left their small towns and Midwestern villages, and congregated in New York, especially in Greenwich Village. Randolph Bourne aptly described the Village bohemians of the period to a friend thinking of moving there:

> They are all social workers, or magazine writers in a small way. They are decidedly emancipated and advanced, and so thoroughly healthy and zestful, or at least so it seems to my unsophisticated masculine sense. They shock you constantly . . . They have an amazing combination of wisdom and youthfulness, of humor and ability, and innocence and self-reliance, which absolutely belies everything you will read in the story-books or any other description of womankind. They are, of course, all self-supporting and independent; and they enjoy the adventure of life.[7]

In Mary Johnston's novel *Hagar* (1913), Hagar Ashendyne is a born feminist; even as a child she asks her aunt, "Why is it that women don't have any money?"[8] Johnston (1870–1936) was a founder of the Equal Suffrage League of Virginia, and *Hagar* is set in the contemporary South. As a teenager, Hagar begins to write and publish, and, like Johnston, becomes a socialist and suffragist. As soon as possible, she goes to New York, and although she is surprised that the golden city of her dreams actually has sweatshops, slums, alcoholics, and abused children, she foresees a procession of women, "each of them carrying a blossoming bough," who will create the new society: "To write—to write—to produce, to lead forth, to give birth, to push out and farther on forever, to make a beautiful thing."[9]

Would women have the leisure to make beautiful things? Despite the technological advances of the automobile, the airplane, the telephone, and even the clothing industry, most women were still imprisoned by domestic drudgery. With the twentieth century came an effort to redefine housework as "home-making," and to professionalize what Henrietta Rodman, a leader of the radical Greenwich Village Feminist Alliance, called the "four primitive home industries"—child care, cooking, housework, and laundry. Alongside the development of home economics in universities, feminist theorists such as Charlotte Perkins Gilman in her book *The Home* (1903) called for fundamental changes in domestic life. In 1915, Rodman incorporated many of Gilman's ideas in her proposal of a new kind of urban housing for professional women, and an architect even drew up plans for a model apartment building in Washington Square that would utilize the latest technology and include space for a communal kitchen and day nursery. Professional cooks and teachers, hired by the families in the building, would take over the tasks of food preparation and child care.

But the building was never constructed, for not all women writers wanted to work together or march in Johnston's procession. The new century also gave birth to women who did not want to create the new society, or to join in solidarity with other feminists, but rather to stand alone and aloof and above. When Francis Whiting Halsey compiled a book of interviews called *Women Authors of Our Day in Their Homes* (1903), Edith Wharton declined to be included, and Gertrude Atherton insisted, "But I have no home."[10] Few women writers could be so airy and dismissive. For some, nevertheless, their changed psychology took the form of a superb egoism and unshakable belief in their own genius, which marked a welcome change from the low confidence and self-effacement of earlier periods. If they were wealthy enough, they could employ servants to free themselves from domestic chores, or live as expatriates in a more congenial environment in Europe. For others, the new consciousness brought a powerful sense of alienation from domestic life and its obligations.

Woman Alone—Mary Austin

In the anonymous memoir she wrote for a symposium in *The Nation* in 1925–26, Mary Hunter Austin (1868–1934) called her story "Woman Alone," and she always saw herself as an outsider. One critic described her as "a maverick in the literary world of the early twentieth century, who formed no major enduring literary or professional connections"; she knew many feminist activists, but said that she was bored by the suffrage campaign.[11] Austin insisted that "home" should not be "the place of the apotheosis of its male members," but as a woman alone she never managed to make a home for herself.[12]

Her childhood had much to do with this self-construction. Born in Illinois when her mother, who had lost two infants, was burdened with care of a sickly one-year-old son, Austin recalled that given "my own position in the family as an unwanted, a personally resented child . . . I had made myself believe that being liked was not important. I had, at least, learned to do without it." From childhood, when she felt like the "unwished-for ugly duckling," she found comfort in reading and claimed "always to have known that I would write." But the family wanted her to marry. "Being plain and a little 'queer,' it was hoped rather than expected that I would marry." At that point in her life, she also liked "domestic life and [had] a genuine flair for cooking. And I wanted children profoundly."

After graduating from Blackburn College, Mary traveled by train with her family to homestead in Southern California. In 1891, she married an engineer and would-be viticulturist, Stafford Wallace Austin; but he was constantly in debt and she had to work as a boardinghouse cook to support them throughout her pregnancy. Their daughter Ruth was born mentally handicapped. "My first baby came in the second year and left me a tortured wreck," she wrote in "Woman Alone." "I know now that I did not have proper medical treatment, but at the time nothing much was thought of such things. My memory of the first seven or eight years of marriage is like some poor martyr's memory of the wheel and the rack, all the best things of marriage obscured by a fog of drudgery impossible to be met and by recurrent physical anguish."[13] Later, Austin would realize that she had had the bad luck to be born into a nineteenth-century generation burdened by sexual ignorance, prudery, and inhibition.

> In those late nineteenth-century decades all the disabilities of excessive child-bearing were charged to the horrid appetites of the husband. Not only did the current phases of birth-control and contraceptives not come into use until the women of the pioneer suffrage generations were past being interested in them, but nobody, positively nobody, had yet suggested that women are passionately endowed even as men are; not good women! That sexual desire was something to which God in his inscrutable wisdom had sacrificed all women, was so certainly believed by my mother's generation that it was never even successfully camouflaged by preachers and teachers with blague about the sanctity of motherhood. But my generation still lacked even a vocabulary by which measures of escape could be intelligently discussed.[14]

Her husband's vineyard failed, and they moved to San Francisco, and then to Lone Pine in Inyo County near Death Valley. The marriage failed as well. But as she came to realize in "Woman Alone," "this tragic end of my most feminine adventure brought the fulfillment of my creative desire, which had begun to be an added torment by repression. Caring for a hopelessly invalid child is an expensive business. I had to write to make money." Luckily, Austin soon met Ina Coolbrith, and with her help, she published her first story in the *Overland Monthly*.

In 1907, Austin left her husband and moved to Carmel, where she joined the writers' colony that included Jack London and Ambrose Bierce. Years later it also included the photographer Ansel Adams, who took a number of portraits of her frowning in priestesslike robes and with knee-length hair. Austin based some of her early fiction on her unhappy marriage and often returned to its disappointing lessons in short stories throughout her career. Her autobiographical story "Frustrate" (1912) was about an ordinary woman's longing for self-fulfillment with her obtuse husband. When it was published in *The Century*, the editor deleted the paragraph in which the narrator describes her plain looks: "I couldn't bear," he said, "to have a woman with such beautiful thoughts, looking like that."

Austin's first important novel, *A Woman of Genius* (1912), was also autobiographical.[15] The narrator Olivia Lattimore wants to escape her small Midwestern town, and insists that she be given her legacy from her father's will; but female sexual ignorance is an even bigger problem for women, especially women of genius, than financial dependency. "You must imagine for yourself from what you know of nice girls thirty years ago," Olivia writes, "how inarticulate the whole business was; the most I can do is to have you understand my desperate need to know, to interpose between marriage and maternity never so slight an interval in which to collect myself and leave off shrinking." She asks her mother for advice about birth control, but is told, "I'm sorry, daughter. I can't help you. I don't know . . . I never knew myself."

Within two years of her marriage to Tommy, a good-hearted shopkeeper in Higglestown, Olivia loses two infants. "Does anybody remember," she asks the reader, "what the woman's world was like in small towns before the days of women's clubs? Boring and horrible . . . it was the world of all the care and expectancy of children overshadowed by the recurrent monthly dread." She takes up part-time acting in St. Louis, and is encouraged to believe that she is a great actress and "a woman of genius." Back home, Tommy gets into a fight defending her honor and conveniently dies of a stroke, setting her free to pursue her gift. By the end of the novel, Olivia is reconciled to sacrificing love and family for a career, and has made a marriage of convenience to a playwright with whom she can share her work.

In 1914, Stafford Austin finally agreed to a divorce, and Austin placed Ruth in an institution, where she died four years later. "Released thus to the larger life which opened to me with literary success," she wrote in "Woman Alone," "I found plenty of reasons for being a feminist in the injustices and impositions endured by women under the general idea of their inferiority to men." Partly in response to these impositions and stereotypes, Austin took on the role of drifter, vagabond, adventurer, and loner in an American Western culture generally dominated by men. Novels such as Owen Wister's *The Virginian* (1902), Jack London's *The Call of the Wild* (1903), and Zane Grey's *Riders of the Purple Sage* (1912) had popularized the figure of the taciturn outdoorsman. Austin cultivated her own semimystic attachment to nature and especially the desert. In her autobiography *Earth Horizon,* she explained that early in her life "it was clear that I would write imaginatively, not only of people, but of the scene, the totality which is called Nature. And that I would give myself intransigently to the quality of experience called Folk, and to the frame of behavior known as Mystical."

In the 1890s, she had begun to write stories set in the Mojave Desert, which she called the "land of little rain" and the "country of lost borders." She also studied Native American art and culture, from which, she claimed, she had learned her principles of design and form. The central story of *The Land of Little Rain* (1903) is "The Basket-Maker," about the blind Indian basket-maker Seyavi, whose art epitomizes the organic creation Austin admired in Paiute culture: "every Indian woman is an artist,—sees, feels, creates, but does not philosophize about her processes." Austin dedicated the book to Eve Lummis, the wife of Charles Lummis, editor of the magazine *Land of Sunshine:* "To Eve: 'The Comfortress of Unsuccess.' " But soon success began to arrive. She was able to travel to New York and the Southwest, and her play *The Arrow-Maker,* about an Indian woman shaman, was produced Off-Broadway in 1911.

The Country of Lost Borders (1909), Austin's most sophisticated collection of stories, emphasized both landscape and the vulnerability of women, especially Indian women on the racial borders of California who were seduced and abandoned by white men. The desert itself is passionate and patient, like a woman, she suggests in the first story, "The Land," "deep-breasted, broad in the hips, tawny, with tawny hair, great masses of it lying smooth along her perfect curves, full-lipped like a sphinx, but not heavy-lidded like one." Several of the stories are set in a desolate mining town she called "Maverick," with its "stark houses," "rubbishy streets," and "days all of one pattern." Sardonically, she contrasted it to the elegant London district of Mayfair, symbolizing everything polished and refined that the maverick country could not support. In "A Case of Conscience," an English miner takes up with a Shoshone woman, and they have a daughter. He decides to take the baby back to England with him, leaving the mother behind. But the child wails and refuses to eat, and eventually he congratulates himself for his wisdom in allowing the mother, who has been trailing them, to take her back. In "A Woman of the Eighteen-Mile," an Indian woman loves, nurses, and saves from death a mining engineer, who then goes back to his oblivious wife and family.

The final story in the book is "The Walking Woman," Austin's manifesto of female independence, equality, and sorrow. Like many turn-of-the-century stories, it is a frame narrative, with an unnamed first-person narrator, a woman, as the reader gradually realizes, asking questions about her own life through her fascination with a legendary character of the Southwest known as "the Walking Woman":

> The cow-boys call her Mrs. Walker but nobody knows her name. She told one of the women at Temblor that her first name is Jenny, but she answers to Mrs. Walker. She is not very tall, but her hair is thick and grayish and it is impossible to tell how old she is. She has a black bag which she carries over her shoulder on a stick. The men say she does not allow any liberties. They say she has just as good sense as anybody except that she is a little bit crazy.

Many rumors circulate about the Walking Woman. "Mother says she looks like a woman who has had a child"; is she a fallen woman, an outcast? Is she crazy or normal, handicapped or strong, mannish or comely? But according to the narrator, when they meet one day at Warm Springs, none of these terms fit: "At the time I knew her, though she wore short hair and a man's boots, and had a fine down all over her face from exposure to the weather, she was perfectly sweet and sane." Despite all these external signs of masculinity, the Walking Woman is womanly within, but bereaved and proudly alone. As she confides to the narrator, she has been the lover of a shepherd, Filon Geraud, and worked with him in a storm to save his lambs. This was a partnership of equals: "I worked with a man, without excusing, without any burden on me of looking or seeming. Not fiddling or fumbling as women work, and hoping it will all turn out for the best." They have a baby, but the baby dies, and she becomes a solitary wanderer. As she concludes her story, she has had two of the important things in a woman's life, "to work together" and "to love together," but she has lost the joy of motherhood. The price of her refusal to own or be owned is that she must walk alone for the rest of her life, but Austin's language in the story's last lines emphasizes her purity and her moral balance: "There in the bare, red sand the track of her two feet bore evenly and white." In this fine story, Austin conveyed what she later said were "the things I had long missed from American life . . . tenderness, the strength of tenderness, compassion."[16]

Sherwood Anderson wrote admiringly to Austin in 1923 that "what Twain and Harte missed you have found and set down with such fine understanding. The books have been a real joy to me."[17] But the 1920s were not happy years for Austin as a woman alone. After her death, her friend Elizabeth Shepley Sergeant eulogized Austin's "essentially lonely life": despite her sympathy with feminist principles and her belief that "women more than men carry the creative fire, she actually preferred the society of men, and depended on men for her deepest companionship."[18]

Women in Charge: *Herland*

In the early 1900s, Charlotte Perkins Gilman found publishers less receptive to her books, and decided to edit and publish her own magazine which would allow her "to preach." From 1909 to 1916, she single-handedly wrote the entire contents of the monthly *The Forerunner*: short stories, utopian novels, poems, and essays. In one utopian novel, *Moving the Mountain* (1911), Gilman borrowed the plot device of Rip Van Winkle to offer a vision of the United States in the 1940s. John Robertson wakes up as a young man in a feminist and socialist society, which is run by practical women who have set up communal kitchens and expert child care and eliminated crime and disease, partly through eugenic methods.

Gilman's best utopian novel, *Herland* (1915), followed Pauline Hopkins in reimagining the male quest romance. Three American men on a scientific expedition—Vandyck Jennings, a sociologist and the narrator;

Terry O. Nicholson, a millionaire entrepreneur and playboy; and Jeff Margrave, an idealistic and romantic doctor—hear tales of a "strange and terrible Woman Land in the high distance," and decide to find it. Terry thinks he will take power and "get myself elected King in no time," like Kipling's "Man Who Would Be King"; Jeff, who "idealized women in the best Southern style," expects to worship goddesses; and Van holds "a middle ground, highly scientific, of course, and used to argue learnedly about the physiological limitations of the sex." The trio hire a biplane, and land in a mountainous but highly cultivated country, which, in accordance with the male quest romance convention, is symbolically like a female body, but in this case a virginal one with pink walls and white houses, all kept "in perfect cleanness." When they are surrounded by calm, curious women, the men attempt to overpower them physically, but they are quickly immobilized and drugged.

Gradually, the men learn that their Herland captors have a country with a population of three million women, an autonomous land originating in volcanic explosions that cut it off from the rest of the world, followed by a war in which all the men were killed. The country was repopulated by girls who intensely wished to become mothers—and developed parthenogenetic means of reproduction. At the age of twenty-five, the five finest women spontaneously give birth to five daughters. Because they are women, Herlanders are maternal, sisterly, cooperative, reasonable, and nurturant. Because there are no men, their society is not aggressive and is without nationalistic feeling, competitive sport, or, indeed, sexuality. The state religion is based on nature, vegetation, and plenitude, and the country is one vast garden: "Here was Mother Earth, bearing fruit."

At first the male invaders mock the new country as "Ladyland," "Woman Country," or "Feminisia" (we never find out what the women themselves call it) and apply both idealistic and hostile stereotypes of femininity to what they see. Jeff imagines a female society as very much like women's domestic and sentimental fiction. "He thought that country—if there was one—was just blossoming with roses and babies and canaries and tidies, and all that sort of thing." Terry envisions having a harem, "Girls and Girls and Girls." Van is more cautious. "You'll find it's built on a sort of matriarchal principle, that's all. The men have a separate cult of their own, less socially developed than the women, and make them an annual visit—a sort of wedding call." Each falls in love with a Herland woman, and they set about to understand the society and adapt to it. Among the more controversial elements of *Herland* is Gilman's insistence that their evolution depends on their acceptance of diminished and controlled sexual desire. For men to do well in Herland, they must learn to redirect their erotic feelings toward worship of women rather than domination, to "loving up," as Gilman puts it.[19]

The Genius of Them All—Gertrude Stein

Gertrude Stein (1874–1946) solved the problems of creativity versus domesticity and leisure versus drudgery by taking a wife who did all the work. As Janet Malcolm writes in *Two Lives,* her wickedly debunking book on Stein and Alice B. Toklas, "the division of household labor between the two women, with one doing everything and the other nothing, was another precondition for the flowering of Stein's genius. 'It takes a lot of time to be a genius, you have to sit around so much doing nothing, really doing nothing,' Stein cheerfully reported in *Everybody's Autobiography.*"[20] Stein was so sure she was a genius that she convinced everyone around her, and persuaded them to manage all the annoying details and chores of her everyday life. *The Mother of Us All,* the title of the opera she wrote about Susan B. Anthony, was also her own persona, and she never flagged in her faith that she was the source of artistic inspiration for a generation of lesser beings.

The youngest of five children in a wealthy Jewish family, Stein was born in Allegheny, Pennsylvania, but after her mother died in 1888 and her father died in 1891, she was raised by an aunt in Baltimore along with her brother Leo. She studied modern psychology and philosophy at Radcliffe with George Santayana and William James, went on to Johns Hopkins Medical School, but dropped out and joined Leo in Paris in 1903. There they became collectors of Post-Impressionist and Cubist art by Matisse, Cézanne, Picasso, and other important painters; and there, in 1907, she also met the woman who would be her life partner, typist, and housekeeper, Alice B. Toklas.

Stein began the stories that make up *Three Lives* (1909) while reading Flaubert's *Trois Contes* and looking at the paintings of Cézanne; the stories combine accounts of simple domestic lives with the Cubist form of multiple perspectives. Guy Reynolds sees *Three Lives* as "a novel about housekeeping. Two of its protagonists are servants. The action of the book consists of the quotidian lives of these women, their

routines, friendships, partnerships; the writing is defiantly unmelodra-
matic, and the conventional features of plot (choice, chance, event) are
eschewed . . . Stein, along with Gilman, Chopin and Alice James, marked
the end of the Victorian ideology of domesticity simply by acknowledging its underside, by bringing the home, housework, and the routines of
married life into the purview of fiction."[21]

One of the stories in *Three Lives*, "Melanctha," told the life of a poor
black woman. Carl Van Vechten, who would become the main white
patron of the Harlem Renaissance, congratulated Stein on producing
the "first American story in which the negro . . . is regarded . . . not as an
object for condescending compassion or derision."[22] Richard Wright
claimed to have read "Melanctha" to a group of black stockyard workers
who "slapped their thighs, howled, laughed, stomped"; he, too, felt that
the story "was the first long serious treatment of Negro life in the United
States," much more authentic than the work of Zora Neale Hurston.[23]
Janet Malcolm, however, reveals that "Melanctha," which "by today's
less innocent standard of what is advanced, can only be called patronizing and uncomprehending," was not based on "Stein's experience of
black life in America," but was a disguised version of "a romance between
herself and a woman named May Bookstaver," and the dialogue of
Melanctha and her lover Jeff is "a new version of the talk between the
white women lovers" in a novel Stein wrote the same year but never
tried to publish.[24]

As a wealthy *salonnière*, Stein did not need to earn a living from her
poems, plays, and prose portraits, which she had privately published
through the mid-1920s. In 1925, her thousand-page tome, *The Making of
Americans*, was published by a small press, and Toklas, too, started a publishing house called Plain Edition devoted to Stein's work. To many in the
avant-garde, she was the very essence of modernism, writing in a combination of babble, nonsense, "chanting, automatic writing, Cubist painting, and atonal music" that Sandra Gilbert has wittily called "Steinese."[25]
Mabel Dodge Luhan claimed that "Gertrude Stein is doing with words
what Picasso is doing with paint." Stein herself compared her method of
verbal repetition and minute variations to the film frame: "in a cinema
picture no two pictures are exactly alike each one is just that much different from the one before."[26] Although even her mentor William James
confessed to Stein that he had been unable to finish the book, carrying a
copy of *Three Lives* in the 1920s in Greenwich Village was a signal of progressive ideals and avant-garde tastes.

Two Gertrudes

In the 1920s, Stein formed a strange and almost farcical friendship with Gertrude Atherton. The two Gertrudes could hardly have been more different. Stein was a massive, crop-haired, mannish lesbian; Atherton kept up her hyperfeminine blond coiffures, designer gowns, and elaborate makeup through her eighties. They also detested each other's writing. Stein found Atherton's popular novels pathetically old-fashioned; Atherton regarded Stein's prose as a "clever hoax."[27] But when they met in Paris in 1925, they liked each other. "A less affected, nicer woman you couldn't ask to meet," Atherton confided to a friend. When she published *The Autobiography of Alice B. Toklas* (1933), Stein had her first popular success. She decided that it was time to return to the United States and meet her audience, and undertook a lengthy tour, which included a meeting with Eleanor Roosevelt at the White House. She asked Atherton to handle her schedule in the Bay Area. Atherton was privately annoyed at being thus exploited.

> *I am very subtly having Gertrude Stein landed on my back. She won't have an agent so wouldn't I speak to clubs, colleges, etc.? She is not on the make but wants enough to pay her expenses out here. The University of California won't have her at any price, and Stanford is a little more interested, but I have called up the presidents of the two principal women's clubs here and across the Bay and asked them to interest other clubs to make a good sized purse. I'll see that PEN gives the Ariel dinner in her honor, and of course I'll have to give her a tea or something. I like her personally, and although her stuff is tripe I am glad to do anything for her, but she comes at an inconvenient time.[28]*

Stein and Toklas enjoyed their visit so much they could hardly tear themselves away, but the experience left Atherton exhausted and cynical: "I thought Mary Austin was about as conceited and swollen in the head as a writer could be, but Gertrude Stein goes her one better."[29]

Although she is widely acknowledged to be unreadable, incomprehensible, self-indulgent, and excruciatingly boring, in the twentieth century Stein always had a cult of devotees. Some were academics tantalized by her difficulty and obscurity, who hoped to decipher her. Some were feminist critics who saw her as a major innovator of a woman's language, and who quoted from her long chant "Patriarchal Poetry" (1927): "Patriarchal poetry makes it as usual / Patriarchal poetry one two three / Patriarchal poetry accountability" and so on for forty pages, which they regard as "a treatise on male-dominated Western literature."[30] Some were lesbian readers who credited her with bringing love between women into modern literature. Some were playful writers and poets who recommended Stein because nobody had a clue what her work meant and she was thus a wild card completely outside of "dogma, protocol, and usefulness."[31] But as more information about Stein's ongoing battles with Toklas, the casualness of her texts and methods of composition, and the unsavory details of the couple's survival in Vichy France as the pet Jews of a Nazi collaborator comes to light, through Janet Malcolm and other scholars, the harder it will be for Stein's supporters to defend an investment of time in her work. Stein seems more and more like the Empress Who Had No Clothes—a shocking sight to behold in every respect.

Imagiste—H.D.

Even in her seventies, Hilda Doolittle (1886–1961), known as "H.D.," impressed those who met her with her grave Hellenic beauty. The British novelist Bryher, her longtime lesbian partner, said that she had "a face that came directly from a Greek statue, and, almost to the end, the body of an athlete."[32] Her appearance, as well as her poems, cast her as the muse of modernism, a role she had to fight against throughout her life. Although she was only two years younger than the poet Sara Teasdale, H.D. lived a much more twentieth-century life. She was among the gifted group of women who attended Bryn Mawr College at the turn of the century, along with Gertrude Stein's first beloved, May Bookstaver, Marianne Moore, and Martha Gellhorn. Even while seeking her own distinct and feminine voice, she formed intense relationships with several modernist male iconoclasts including Ezra Pound, D. H. Lawrence, and Freud.

It would have been easy for H.D. to play the part of the exquisite dryad, unattainable nymph, and enigmatic muse, which men bestowed upon her. In a famous anecdote, Ezra Pound christened her and created her persona in the tearoom of the British Museum in August 1912: " 'But Dryad, this is poetry.' He slashed with a pencil. 'Cut this out, shorten this line . . . I'll send it to Harriet Monroe of *Poetry*'. . . and he scrawled 'H.D.

Imagiste' at the bottom of the page."³³ She liked the pen name, as her biographer Susan Stanford Friedman points out—inhabited it, performed it, identified with it, signed her personal letters with it, used it on her bookplates and stationery. She liked its anonymity, its genderlessness, having "an authorial identity beyond masculine and feminine," and a literary persona that was not exactly her real self.³⁴

She soon rebelled against Pound's overbearing guidance and sexual infidelity, however, and in 1913 she married Richard Aldington, a poet, translator, and editor she had met through Pound. Under Aldington's influence, she began to construct her own poetic universe and to seek her own muses in Greek mythology and matriarchal legends. At the same time, her work was taken up by Amy Lowell, who publicized it in three Imagist anthologies she edited for American audiences. From 1911 on, H.D. remained in Europe as an expatriate, except for a brief return to the United States in 1960. Her life was thrown into disarray by the First World War, in which Aldington was posted to the French front and her brother was killed. Both she and Aldington had affairs, and H.D. became pregnant, gave birth to her daughter Perdita, but then suffered an emotional collapse. Winifred Ellerman, an independently wealthy writer and admirer who called herself Bryher, rescued her in this crisis, and they remained intimate friends and partners thereafter. Despite this partnership, H.D.'s creative inspiration underwent a decline between the two world wars, at least in her own view; it was one of her motives for consulting Freud in 1933.

Her Imagist poems, which she herself called the work of "the early H.D.," had short lines, strong natural imagery, and classical themes, but also subtexts about male dominance and female victimization. In "Orchard" (1913), she described the blossoms and fruit of the pear tree, a figure for female sexuality, and the rapacious "honey-seeking" male bees who "thundered their song," while the female poet asks for less "loveliness" and more of the "unbeautiful." "Eurydice" (1917) speaks for the anger of the woman condemned to remain in Hades because of the arrogance of Orpheus.

After World War II, however, H.D. turned to a longer, epic mode of poetry, in *Trilogy* (1944–46) and *Helen in Egypt* (1961). These poems denounce the brutality and stupidity of violence and war, which are presented as masculine vices and contrasted with women's roles. The poems defend women who have been vilified and even blamed for men's follies, like Mary Magdalene and Helen of Troy. Many academic scholars and critics regard the late poems as her best work, and they contain brilliant passages; but their length has been a deterrent to readers, and H.D.'s restraint and precision seemed out of date in the postwar years. For most readers, H.D. remains the poet of a few outstanding anthology pieces from the early years of her career.

Amygiste—Amy Lowell

Although she was a popular Boston debutante from an old New England family, expected to marry and live the life of a proper Boston matron, Amy Lowell (1874–1925) had to confront some disadvantages: she was creative, intellectual, and fat. In 1902, at a performance by Eleanora Duse, Lowell first realized that she had a poetic vocation. Ten years later she published her first book of poems, *A Dome of Many-Colored Glass,* and met her life partner, Ada Dwyer Russell. While Sara Teasdale seemed too feminine and ethereal to be taken seriously as a poet, and H.D. was too beautiful and graceful, Lowell was too big and awkward. Pound called her the "Hippopoetess," and labeled her poetry "Amygism." She tried unsuccessfully to become more nymphlike on a diet of tomatoes and asparagus. But she had money of her own, and was able to live more or less as she pleased—large, flamboyant, smoking cigarillos; and with her administrative ability, she took over the promotion of Imagism in the United States. Eliot called her the "demon saleswoman of poetry."[35]

An admirer of Charlotte Brontë and a biographer of Keats, Lowell was sure that the years before the war were "the beginning of a great poetic renaissance."[36] Including Frost and Sandburg as well as H.D., the poetic upheaval of 1912–13, she believed, was based on the determination "to voice America" and "drop the perpetual imitation of England." Rejecting love poems in favor of daily life, a wide and sparkling canvas, the new voice was, "whether written by men or women . . . in essence masculine, virile, very much alive. Where the nineties had warbled, it shouted."[37]

Lowell's contemporary reputation mainly rests on her rediscovery as a lesbian poet, but she was also an antiwar poet of some distinction. "It is impossible for any one writing to-day not to be affected by the war," she wrote in *Tendencies in Modern American Poetry* (1917). "It has overwhelmed like a tidal wave. It is the equinoctial storm which bounds a period." In her preface to *Men, Women, and Ghosts* (1916), she acknowledged that some of the poems were "obliquely" touching on "the great war raging in Europe." Her most-anthologized poem from that book, "Patterns," is a dramatic monologue influenced by Robert Browning. An eighteenth-century English society woman, dressed in elaborate brocades and with powdered hair, is walking in her formal garden when she learns that her betrothed, Lord Hartwell, has been killed fighting with the Duke of Flanders. Locked into the rigidity of her class and age, she nonetheless foresees a lifetime of confinement in the patterns of gentility,

> *For the man who should loose me is dead*
> . . . .
> *In a pattern called a war.*
> *Christ! What are patterns for?*

With its obvious allusions to Flanders Fields, this was an antiwar poem that mixed female protest with political protest.[38] Lowell also published a sequence of poems against "this most unholy of wars," including "The Bombardment," which imagines the allied attack from the point of view of French villagers.

Women on the Borderlines: The Promised Land

Immigrant women writers played an important role in recording and shaping the experience of transformation in the first decades of the twentieth century. In their stories, they asked what it meant "to be a wife, mother, or daughter in a new world where individual self-realization . . . clashed with Old World traditions of family responsibility and family loyalty." Writing on the borders between the Old World and the New World, in a variety of forms, including memoirs, novels, stories, and plays, they helped mothers and daughters "make sense of the world and their place in it."[39] Born in Russia, Mary Antin (1881–1949) emigrated to the United States in 1894, and settled in Chelsea, a poor urban area near Boston rapidly becoming the first stop for Yiddish-speaking Jewish immigrants from Eastern Europe. Over the course of the century, as they became Americanized, they would move on, first to the working-class tenements of Dorchester and Roxbury, and then to the prosperous suburbs of Brookline and Newton. Antin was a gifted child, who had published her first little book, *From Plotzk to Boston*, in 1899, attracting the admiration and attention of Josephine Lazarus, Emma's sister. She dreamed of the day when she would find her name close to Louisa May Alcott's in a dictionary of American writers. By the beginning of the century, she was publishing in such strongholds of New England tradition as the *Atlantic Monthly*. The old-guard Boston firm Houghton Mifflin published her twenty-chapter memoir, *The Promised Land* (1912), with the Statue of Liberty on the cover and a golden torch on the spine.[40]

In *The Promised Land*, Antin both told the story of her life from the patriotic point of view of one who had succeeded and pioneered many of the literary strategies that would become standard for immigrant writing: the emphasis on the sensuality of memory, for fragrances and tastes; the use of biblical language to narrate the exodus to the United States; the changes in language and vocabulary. Although she was among the earliest of these immigrant autobiographers, Antin was also among the most sophisticated in her understanding of the conventions of life writing. Addressing the assumed gentile reader as "my American friend," she casts herself as a self-consciously fictionalizing first-person narrator. Antin had even considered calling herself "Esther Altmann" in the text, a female opposite of Henry James's paradigmatic American hero Christopher Newman.[41] The book sold over eighty-five thousand copies, and gave Antin a career as a lecturer and essayist specializing in immigration and civic responsibilities. But it also created a backlash against a Jewish immigrant woman who dared to claim the Puritans as her forefathers, too, and who compared Ellis Island to Plymouth Rock: "Every ship that brings your people from Russia and other countries where they are mistreated is a *Mayflower*."[42]

For Antin, America never quite fulfilled its promises. In 1901, she married Amadeus Grabau, a German-American Lutheran professor who taught science at Columbia, but their happy partnership was torpedoed by World War I, when he took a public position on neutrality that was seen as pro-German. He lost his job at Columbia, left the marriage, and moved to Peking to direct a geological laboratory. By the mid-1920s, Antin had become disillusioned by American isolationism and anti-immigrant sentiment, and in the last twenty-three years of her life she fell almost silent as a writer. In her last published essay, in 1941, she reflected profoundly on her broken ties to European Jews, and the impossibility of reclaiming an old identity:

> *Today I feel myself pulled by the old forgotten ties, through the violent projection of an immensely magnified Jewish problem. It is one thing to go your separate way, leaving your friends and comrades behind in*

peace and prosperity; it is another thing to fail to remember them when the world is casting them out . . . I can no more return to the Jewish fold than I can return to my mother's womb; neither can I in decency continue to enjoy my accidental personal immunity from the penalties of being a Jew in a time of virulent anti-Semitism. The least I can do, in my need to share the sufferings of my people, is to declare that I am as one of them.

Uprooted—Zitkala-Ša

Photographed by Gertrude Käsebier in 1898 wearing a filmy white dress and holding a violin, Gertrude Simmons Bonnin (1876–1938), who wrote under her Dakota Sioux name, Zitkala-Ša (which means "red bird"), could have easily passed or been mistaken for a genteel young lady with a privileged upbringing. The child of a Sioux mother and white father (she also had a white stepfather from whom she took the name Simmons), she had grown up on the Pine Ridge reservation in South Dakota, but left home to go to a mission school in Wabash, Indiana, attended Earlham College in Indiana, and then studied the violin at the Boston Conservatory of Music.[43] Käsebier, who specialized in photographing Native Americans, emphasized her subject's multiple identities in a series of beautiful portraits now in the collection of the Smithsonian Institution. In one photograph, Zitkala-Ša is in full Sioux dress; in another she wears a white gown but hugs an Indian basket to her chest. Her long dark hair hangs loose, Indian style, or is pulled back with a ribbon or a snood. Delicate, strong, glamorous, Zitkala-Ša was featured on *Harper's Bazaar*'s list of "Persons Who Interest Us" in 1900, when she performed in Paris.

Her memoirs, "Impressions of an Indian Childhood" and "The School Days of an Indian Girl," published in the *Atlantic Monthly* in January and February 1900, tell the story of her schooling and her half-voluntary, half-coerced entrance into American culture, drawing on the conventions of women's fiction back to *Jane Eyre,* and reshaping them for the story of border crossing and ethnic assimilation. As a little girl, she clings to her mother, listens to the old women's stories and legends, learns the maternal and tribal skill of beadwork, as Puritan girls learned patchwork. "Close beside my mother I sat on a rug, with a scrap of buckskin in one hand and an awl in the other. This was the beginning of my practical observational lessons in the art of beadwork." Beadwork, like patchwork, allows leeway in the choice of colors and patterns, but imposes restrictions on structure and composition: "My original designs were not always symmetrical nor sufficiently characteristic, two faults with which my mother had little patience."

School in what she calls "the land of red apples" offers the opportunities of mastering English, discovering Christianity, reading, and winning her first academic prize, but it is also submission to the "iron routine" of a "civilizing machine," which begins with the cutting of her long hair. Zitkala-Ša did not write about her subsequent training as a classical musician, which must have been another iron routine, but she lamented her spiritual alienation from the world of her mother: "In the process of my education I had lost all consciousness of the nature world about me . . . For the white man's papers [the Bible] I had given up my faith in the Great Spirit. For these same papers I had forgotten the healing in trees and brooks. On account of my mother's simple view of life, and my lack of any, I gave her up, also. I made no friends among the race of people I loathed. Like a slender tree, I had been uprooted from my mother, nature, and God."[44] The red apples for which she has traded her tribal identity are like the apples that tempted Eve, and she feels that she has betrayed her past.

In the opening years of the twentieth century, Zitkala-Ša edited Sioux legends in a book for children, *Old Indian Legends* (1901), and published short stories in magazines. "A Warrior's Daughter" (1902) has an eight-year-old trickster-superwoman as heroine; Tusee daringly rescues her lover from an enemy Indian camp.[45] But Zitkala-Ša's journey left her a woman alone, and her literary career was brief. Unable to find a voice to speak from both inside and outside her culture, she gave up writing for teaching and advocacy.[46] In 1902, she married Raymond Bonnin, a Sioux working for the Bureau of Indian Affairs, and moved to the Uintah and Oiuray Reservation in Utah. In 1918–19, she edited the *American Indian Magazine,* and rewrote "America the Beautiful" as "The Red Man's America":

> *Land where our fathers died,*
> *Whose offspring are denied*
> *The Franchise given wide,*
> *Hark, while I sing!*

Creating Hybridity—Sui Sin Far

Edith Maud Eaton (1865–1914), who wrote about Chinese-American immigrants under the name "Sui Sin Far," had an even more complicated transition. The oldest daughter of fourteen children of a Chinese mother and a British father, she grew up in England, Canada, Jamaica, and the United States. "I have no nationality and am not anxious to claim any," she wrote in her autobiographical essay, "Leaves from the Mental Portfolio of an Eurasian." "Individuality is more than nationality."[47] Like Zitkala-Ša, she felt alienated from both sides of her parentage. "I do not confide in my father and mother. They would not understand. I am different to both of them—a stranger, tho their own child."[48] But working in Seattle as a journalist, she was encouraged by Charles Lummis at the *Land of Sunshine* magazine to write about the Eurasian experience in the United States. Thirty-seven of her stories about cultural misunderstanding, narrated through a Chinese-American woman she called "Mrs. Spring Fragrance," were published as a book in 1912. In one story, Mrs. Spring Fragrance announces her own intention to become a writer: "I desire to write an immortal book . . . My first subject will be 'The Inferior Woman of America.' "

Eaton's sister Winifred wrote several novels under the pen name "Onoto Watanna," presenting herself as Japanese-American. As Werner Sollers points out, "At first glance one sister would seem to be 'authentic' and the other 'fake,' yet both had to work at imagining and sustaining the divergent Asian images they wished to project."[49]

Women Together: The Theater

Women writers in New York came together around the suffrage movement, bohemia, and the theater. In the 1890s, the European realist theater of Ibsen and Strindberg had been a strong influence on American New Women, especially Elizabeth Robins. In 1903, the American actress Minnie Maddern Fiske starred in Ibsen's *Hedda Gabler* in Manhattan, a production sometimes called "the beginning of twentieth-century theatre in the United States."[50] Robins's British suffrage play, *Votes for Women,* was performed in New York in 1909, and encouraged American suffrage plays, which showed that women could provide a special audience for theater, as well as writers and actresses. Rachel Crothers (1878–1958), who wrote more than thirty plays, and also acted and directed, introduced feminist themes of marriage, the sexual double standard, and the woman artist into commercial theater.[51] Crothers's mother had been a doctor, and many of her plays featured women of genius, usually artists, trying to fulfill their gifts in the face of discrimination and domestic pressure. "Frank Ware," the heroine of *A Man's World* (1910), is a celebrated novelist who has passed as a man, until a critic exposes her masterpiece *The Beaten Path* as a woman's work. In *He and She* (1911), in which Crothers starred, the married sculptors Ann and Tom Herford compete for a commission, and she wins, but gives up her career to raise their troubled teenager.

Susan Glaspell

Susan Glaspell (1876–1948), who came of age at the beginning of the twentieth century, moved out of Davenport, Iowa, to become one of the key players in American theatrical history. Davenport was also the home of Floyd Dell, who described it as an anomalous mixture of populist radicalism and conventional moralism. It was "largely German and Jewish, with an 1848 European revolutionary foundation, and a liberal and socialist superstructure," with the "bravado of an old Mississippi river-port, and the liberal 'cosmopolitan' atmosphere of a place that is in touch with European influences . . . It had an intelligentsia, who knew books and ideas. It even had some live authors."[52] Glaspell met some of them, not only Dell but also his friend the socialist visionary George Cram Cook (nicknamed "Jig"), the Harvard-educated son of a rich local family. Like Bronson Alcott, Cook was a brilliant but impractical sage, a Midwestern Transcendentalist, who had been radicalized by reading Thoreau. Twice married, and the father of two, he had attempted to make a living by vegetable farming rather than writing. When Glaspell met him, she was thirty-three, a graduate of Drake University in Des Moines, and a reporter for the *Des Moines Daily News*. She tried to escape the entanglement with Cook by moving away, first to Chicago, and then even to Paris, but the relationship continued. After a miscarriage in 1911, she accepted their destiny together, although her obsession with the themes of infidelity, adultery, divorce, scandal, and childlessness marked much of her literary work. Meanwhile, she wrote short stories for the magazines, and published two novels, *The Glory of the Conquered* (1909) and *The Visioning* (1911). *Lifted Masks* (1912), her only book of short stories, was set in a fictionalized Davenport; its image of people concealing their feelings behind masks anticipated Sherwood Anderson.

When his divorce at last came through in the spring of 1913, Cook and Glaspell married and moved to Greenwich Village, where they connected to other radicals and writers; in the summers they lived in the fishing village of Provincetown, at the tip of Cape Cod, which had become an artists' colony.[53] As she reminisced,

> We were supposed to be a sort of "special" group—radical, wild, Bohemians, we have been called. But it seems to me we were a particularly simple people, who sought to arrange life for the thing we wanted to do, needing each other as protection against complexities, yet living as we did because of an instinct for the old, old things, to have a garden, and neighbors, to keep up the fire and let the cat in at night. None of us had much money, these were small houses we lived in; they had been fishermen's before they were ours. Most of us were from families who had other ideas—who wanted to make money, played bridge, voted the republican ticket, went to church, thinking one should be like every one else. And so, drawn together by the thing we really were, we were as a new family: we lent each other money, worried through illnesses, ate together when a cook had left, talked about our work. Each could be himself, that was perhaps the real thing we did for one another.[54]

Glaspell's third novel, *Fidelity* (1915), written soon after her marriage, reflects her thinking about the repressive morality of the Midwest but also the impulsive antimorality of the avant-garde. In it, Glaspell told the story of Ruth Holland, who falls in love with a married man, Stuart Williams, and elopes with him to Colorado because his wife will not give him a divorce. Twelve years later, Ruth returns to her hometown of Freeport when her father dies, and asks herself whether her sacrifice of respectability, her family's shame, her lover's exile, have been justified. Is fidelity to the ideals of romantic love worth sacrificing the possibilities of individuality and freedom? Having inherited some money from her father, finally able to marry her lover when his wife agrees to divorce him, she has to decide whether to legitimize her girlhood rebellion or to seize the chance at mature freedom. *Fidelity* has been called as important as any novel "by Kate Chopin, Charlotte Perkins Gilman, Edith Wharton, or Willa Cather."[55] This claim is hard to defend, however; despite its audacious themes, the novel does not, in my view, measure up to the works of these other writers. Glaspell spends too much time on the melodramatic and dated attitudes of the Freeporters, and not enough on Ruth's self-examination. For most of the novel, she seems to go along with the notion of the great romantic passion that justifies and indeed demands resistance to convention, whereas Ruth's affair with Stuart seems much more the result of mutual boredom and opportunity. Edith Wharton would have made an ironic short story out of the same material.

Glaspell had never written a play, but Jig Cook brought her into the theatrical community of New York, and insisted that she write for the stage.[56] Together they read Strindberg and Ibsen, and discussed Synge and the Irish playwrights of the Abbey Theatre, who had astonished audiences in tours of New York and Chicago. In 1914, Cook and Glaspell founded the Provincetown Players, announcing in their manifesto their desire "to establish a stage where playwrights of sincere, poetic, literary, and dramatic purpose could see their plays in action and superintend their production without submitting to the commercial manager's interpretation of public taste." This first Off-Broadway theater, with a New York base on MacDougal Street, quickly attracted the talent of Eugene O'Neill, and suddenly European expressionism and realism had found voices in the United States.

Glaspell wrote ten plays for the company between 1914 and 1921. According to her biographer Linda Ben-Zvi, "nothing in a Glaspell play is linear. Plots do not have clearly defined beginnings, middles, and ends; they self-consciously move out from some familiar pattern, calling attention as they go to the fact that the expected convention will be violated, the anticipated order will be sundered."[57] Women characters who would have been marginal in mainstream drama became central in Glaspell's writing. *Suppressed Desires: A Freudian Comedy,* written with Jig Cook, parodied the Greenwich Village craze for psychoanalysis. "What am I to do with my suppressed desire?" Mabel asks, and Stephen answers, "Mabel, just keep right on suppressing it!"

In the summer of 1916, Glaspell, Cook, and O'Neill were in Provincetown for their second season. They had staged O'Neill's *Bound East for Cardiff,* and Cook urged Glaspell to write a short play for their third bill. "So I went out on the wharf, sat alone on one of our wooden benches without a back, and looked a long time at that little stage. After a time the stage became a kitchen—a kitchen there all by itself . . . Then the door at the back opened, and people all bundled up came in—two or three men [and] two women who hung back." *Trifles* opened in Provincetown on August 8, 1916, with Glaspell and Cook playing the leads, and its kitchen set suggesting Strindberg's *Miss Julie.* In March 1917, Glaspell published it in *Everyweek* magazine as the short story "A Jury of Her Peers." The dialogue in her early plays won the acclaim of reviewers like Edwin Bjorkman in *The Freeman,* who compared her favorably to Synge: "Her farmers do not talk like Aran Islanders. If they did, Miss Glaspell's credit would be less than it is. The tongue of Ireland breeds poetry naturally and almost mechanically. It has to be wrung by hard labor and unusual vision out of the thrifty soil of the Middle West."[58]

Glaspell's interest in women's culture and language shaped several of her other plays. Influenced by Ibsen and Strindberg, *The Verge* (1921) is set in a greenhouse in the snow, frost on its windows, where the horticulturist Claire Archer is trying to breed an exotic plant, the Breath of Life, which will assume new forms of life and vitality. Glaspell's experiments with expressionist form and the female psyche are provocative, but by this point, O'Neill had already gone far beyond her, in stunning plays like *The Dreamy Kid* (1918) and especially *The Emperor Jones* (1920), which dealt with racism, the American legacy of slavery, and the black unconscious. O'Neill had a clarity of thought and exposition Glaspell never mastered, and a sense of theatrical spectacle she could not begin to equal. After 1924, she wrote only one more play, *Alison's House,* which won a Pulitzer Prize in 1931; inspired by the life of Emily Dickinson, it was well made, but "a diminuendo, conventionalized version of the great plays of her middle years."[59]

Meanwhile, Jig Cook decided that even the Provincetown Players had become too commercialized for a philosopher-idealist of his pure gifts, and Glaspell went with him to Greece in 1922, where he died two years later and was buried at Delphi. She eulogized him and explored his legacy in *The Road to the Temple* (1927). Despite his affectations, Cook was a real partner who supported Glaspell's literary development. Her subsequent alliance with an abusive, much younger man, Norman Matson, was disastrous; he finally left her to have a child with another woman. After Glaspell's death in 1948, her reputation plummeted; up until the 1970s only one book and a single article had appeared on her work.

Popular Fiction and Girls' Literature

At the start of the twentieth century, several women writers built iconic novels for the children's market around spunky girls—orphaned, or fatherless, or on bad terms with their mothers—who find ways to resolve the conflicts between their ambitions and affections and their obligations as daughters. Kate Douglas Wiggin (1856–1923) was a pioneer in the development of kindergarten education in the United States, but also a novelist. Her *Rebecca of Sunnybrook Farm* (1903) was one of the first twentieth-century books for adolescent girls to promote assertiveness and independence. One of the seven children of the dead Lorenzo de Medici Randall, ten-year-old Rebecca Randall is sent to Maine to live with her Yankee spinster aunts, Miranda and Jane, and get educated so she can help her mother pay off the mortgage on Sunnybrook Farm. With her ambition, her storytelling ability, her misfit status, and her deep and self-sacrificial sense of responsibility to her family, Rebecca is definitely a descendant of Jo March. She writes poetry, daydreams, spoils her clothes, and lets flies into the immaculate house, but, of course, she gradually wins over her aunts. Wiggin updated the familiar triangle of *The Wide, Wide World* by having Rebecca torn between male and female figures. On one side is a rich and glamorous neighbor, Adam Ladd (she calls him "Mr. Aladdin"), who buys her gifts and comes up with ways to give her money without her knowing it. On the other side is her high school English teacher, Miss Maxwell, who encourages her to train as a teacher. They fight over Rebecca's future, Miss Maxwell arguing that she was made to write and Adam arguing that she was made for love. Wiggin avoids making a choice by the Victorian expedient of giving Rebecca financial independence through a legacy. Her aunts leave her the family estate:

> It was home; her roof, her garden, her green acres, her dear trees; it was shelter for the little family at Sunnybrook . . . And she? Her own future was close-folded still; folded and hidden in beautiful mists; but she leaned her head against the sun-warmed door, and closing her eyes, whispered . . . "God bless aunt Miranda! God bless the brick house that was; God bless the brick house that is to be."

Geneva Stratton-Porter (1863–1924) was the youngest of twelve children of farmers in Indiana. She married in 1886, and had one child, but retained her mobility to pursue her interests in the environment, fiction, and the new movie industry, changing her first name to "Gene" and hyphenating her maiden and married names in the androgynous modern style. Her most popular books were her girls' stories, *Freckles* (1904) and *A Girl of the Limberlost* (1909). Stratton-Porter used the Limberlost Swamp in Indiana as both a naturalistic setting and a lurid gothic space of nightmares, sexuality, sadism, voyeurism, and madness, like the Great Dismal Swamp in Stowe's *Dred* or Austin's *Country of Lost Borders*. Elnora Comstock, the girl thereof, is a budding naturalist who earns her way through high school by selling butterflies. Her father drowned in the swamp as she was being born, and her widowed mother haunts the place, conversing with her dead husband's spirit. As a child, Elnora is alone in the house when a lustful man, who seems to be a threatening avatar of her dead father, climbs on the roof to watch her as she prepares for bed, then writes her a warning letter telling her that if she values her safety she shouldn't go into the swamp alone or something might "git her." But with maturity, Elnora leaves these gothic shadows and swamps behind. She becomes engaged to a rich young lawyer who will take her away to live the high life in Chicago, where she will give up her ambition to make a career as a naturalist but will resist becoming a social butterfly.

Jean Webster's *Daddy-Long-Legs* (1912) was an epistolary novel about the new generation of female college students. Strongly influenced by *Jane Eyre* and *Little Women,* Webster (1876–1916) told the story of an orphan girl, Judy Abbott, who wants to be a writer, and who must discard both the patriarchal models of her education and the sensational stories of her imagination if she is to find her own voice. Judy is secretly sent to Vassar by a rich philanthropist who later falls in love with her. *Daddy-Long-Legs* was an overwhelming success both in the United States and abroad in translation. As one critic has argued, it is "the ideal love story" of a feminist: "a girl is brought by a distinguished man to absolute independence and is then in a position to have an equal relationship with him."[60] In 1914, Webster turned the novel into a stage play that had an extensive run at New York's Gaiety Theatre.

Webster was not an orphan. Her father had been Mark Twain's publisher, and she entered Vassar College with the class of 1901, rooming with the poet Adelaide Crapsey (with whom she carried the socialist banner in a campus parade). After graduation, she energetically pursued a literary career, publishing stories, articles, and novels for adolescent girls. She traveled in Europe, then settled in Greenwich Village, serving on committees for prison reform and marching in the Women's

Suffrage May Day parade. In the summer of 1908, she fell in love with a married man, Glenn Ford McKinney, an 1891 graduate of Princeton. They embarked on a long-term, largely epistolary affair, which *Daddy-Long-Legs,* dedicated "To You," seemed to celebrate. In July 1913, she wrote to him: "Our salvation is work and work and *more* work. Fortunately we both have some ready to our hands. Set to work with all promptitude and cheerfulness at your farm and accomplish as much as possible against the time when I can look at it with you."[61] Alcott could not have put the case for work and duty better.

In June 1915, McKinney's wife divorced him on the grounds of desertion. Although divorce was no scandal in Greenwich Village, Webster chose to keep her wedding modest and small. For a year they lived in Manhattan, and at his farm in Dutchess County, New York, where they raised ducks and pheasants. Tragically, this idyll did not last long. Webster died from complications of childbirth less than a year after her marriage, only a few hours after the birth of her daughter, Jean Webster McKinney, who survived. Webster's obituary and the birth announcement for her daughter appeared side by side in the newspaper.

In 1913, Eleanor H. Porter (1868–1920) captured the girls' reading market with the much more saccharine *Pollyanna* (1913).[62] Pollyanna Whittier, the orphan child of a poor missionary who has been living out West on the charity of the Ladies' Aid, goes to Vermont to live with her wealthy aunt Miss Polly Harrington. Pollyanna annoys her aunt by being untidy, but she also exudes gladness at all times, makes friends with the servants, and brightens up the life of the rich recluse John Pendleton. She teaches everyone she meets the "glad game," which is to find whatever there is to be glad about in any situation. Despite her commitment to the power of positive thinking, Pollyanna is sorely tried when she is hit by a car and presumed to be paralyzed for life. But Miss Polly, inspired by her niece's courage, nurses her back to health, and even reconciles with her own long-lost fiancé. Perhaps the most influential of the girls' books, *Pollyanna* inspired countless "Glad Clubs" formed by both children and adults, including prisoners, and the name has become emblematic of an American message of mindless optimism.

The Great War

Optimism was sorely needed by the time the United States entered the First World War in 1917. The suffrage movement split over the war, but most suffrage leaders endorsed President Woodrow Wilson's decision to enter. Nearly a million women took up war work on the home front, and thirty thousand served as nurses in the Army, Navy, Marines, and Coast Guard. Other American women writers were helping the war effort in France between 1916 and 1918. Responses to women's literary, patriotic, philanthropic, and military efforts during the war were mixed at best. Women got the vote, but for the golden morrow to dawn, great writers had to appear. Edith Wharton and Willa Cather, the most important American women writers of the first half of the twentieth century, deserve a chapter of their own.

12

Against Women's Writing:
Wharton and Cather

merican women's writing had first been feminine, obeying national expectations about womanly submission and domestic obligation; from the 1890s, it had taken a feminist position on women's rights and literary daring. But Edith Wharton (1862–1937) and Willa Cather (1873–1947) refused to be defined as women at all. Wharton and Cather never met, never wrote about each other, and would have disliked being linked together. Socially they could not have been more different. Wharton was the daughter of New York high society, Cather the prairie dweller; Wharton was the product of tutors and governesses, Cather the classicist and university graduate; Wharton was photographed in Parisian fashions, Cather in her famous middy blouse. Cather wrote about the plains of Nebraska; Wharton mocked the raw lifestyles of the American Midwest, and said about the Paris flood of 1910, "if only it could have happened in Omaha!"[1] But both were determined to transcend the stereotypes and expectations of women's writing. Both admired but did not want to be linked with George Eliot, found their own literary influences in European writers and artists, and shared an intense aesthetic admiration for Henry James,[2] whose shadow both had to escape in order to find a personal voice. Unlike other prolific women writers of their generation, they openly criticized the tradition of American women's literature, disliked the "feminine" sensibility, and wrote often from the viewpoint of men.

I might have chosen to devote a separate chapter to Wharton and Cather simply on the basis of their literary achievement and their historical range. They were great novelists whose careers spanned a long period from the 1890s to the 1940s; both won the Pulitzer Prize in the 1920s, although neither won a Nobel. Starting out as short-story writers, and unsure of their abilities to construct novel-size narratives, they conscientiously developed their art to its fullest range and grandeur. Wharton published more: twenty-two novels and novellas, plus collections of short stories, poems, essays, travel writing, literary criticism, and a memoir. Cather published fourteen novels, in addition to stories. By far the more private of the two, she left instructions for her letters to remain unpublished. But these two women need a separate chapter not only because they were giants of their age, but also because of their commitment to an art beyond the limitation of gender. For any literary subculture, I would argue, aesthetic maturity requires a rejection of special categories, and an insistence on access to any subject, any character, and any style. Paradoxically, American women's writing could not fully mature until there were women writing against it.

Edith Wharton: Writing like a Man

Edith Wharton regarded herself as a man's woman, and attributed her sophistication to the advantages of moving in a European male society: "it is because American women are each other's only audience, and each other's only companions," she wrote, "that they seem, compared to women who play an intellectual and social role in the lives of men, like children in a baby school."[3] But she realized that at best she combined a masculine and intellectual approach to fiction with a feminine attention to detail and feeling: "I conceive my subjects like a man—that is, rather more architecturally and dramatically than most women—and then execute them like a woman; or rather I sacrifice to my desire for construction and breadth, the small incidental effects that women have always excelled in, the episodical characterization, I mean . . . This is the reason I have always obscurely felt that I didn't know how to write a novel . . . [which is] such a sharp contrast to the sense of authority with which I take hold of a short story."[4] When she started out as a writer, she worried whether she had "constructive power" enough to achieve more than "isolated character studies, or the stringing together of picturesque episodes."[5] Although most of her fiction would be about women, Wharton needed to maintain her aesthetic distance and control, a problem she solved in part by writing from an imagined male perspective.

Wharton rejected not only the category of "woman writer," but also that of "American writer." From the time she was ten years old, she recalled, she had felt like "an exile in America"; she spent the last twenty-six years of her life as an expatriate in France.⁶ In her work and life, Wharton repudiated the customs of her country, including the slangy sounds of her mother tongue. "My first weeks in America are always miserable," she wrote to her friend Sally Norton upon one return from France in 1903. ". . . All of which outburst is due to my first sight of American streets, my first hearing of American voices, and the wild, disheveled backwoods look of everything when one first comes home!"⁷ The following year, her alienation had increased: "A whole nation developing without the sense of beauty, and eating bananas for breakfast." It was virtually impossible for Wharton to find anything beautiful that came from the United States, and she had little but scorn for the possibilities of an American popular culture or national art. Although she traveled extensively in England, France, Italy, Germany, and North Africa, Wharton saw little of the United States beyond New England and New York. For much of her career, she mocked American ways from abroad, while Willa Cather was exploring the dreams and tragedies of the inhabitants of those backwoods towns. But in her later work, she returned with a new insight to American streets and voices, and defended the democratic society and the free-spirited American women she had scorned.

Born to an upper-class family in New York, Edith Newbold Jones was expected to be beautiful, elegant, and well dressed, certainly not to think of herself as intelligent, creative, or sexual. Of her childhood, she recalled the "almost pagan worship of physical beauty," and the emphasis on feminine appearance. Fastidious about grammar, her mother, the stately New York matron Lucretia Rhinelander Jones, forbade her to read the popular children's literature of her day; by the time she was allowed to read *Little Women* and *Little Men,* she was sufficiently brainwashed to be "exasperated by the laxities of the great Louisa."⁸ Her mother also held up successful women writers as the worst examples of vulgarity. "I cannot hope to render the tone," she noted in her memoir *A Backward Glance,* "in which my mother pronounced the name of such unfortunates, or, on the other hand, that of Mrs. Beecher Stowe, who was so 'common,' yet so successful."

Wharton first attempted writing when she was eleven years old. Her fledgling novel began: "Oh, how do you do, Mrs. Brown? . . . If only I had known you were going to call I should have tidied up the drawing room." When she offered it to her mother, the response was chilly and withering: "Drawing rooms are always tidy." All the seeds of Wharton's work and psyche are contained therein—her fascination with the ethnography of upper-class societies from Old New York to the Parisian *faubourg*, and her obsession with interior décor and its suggestive symbolism of the pristine female body. Like Margaret Fuller and many other women writers, Wharton identified writing and the imagination with a lush maternal garden, and reading and the intellect with an immense paternal library. Her father let her read in "the kingdom of [his] library," where she devoured Swift, Sterne, Defoe, Scott, Shakespeare, Milton, the French and English poets, and the great historians. But Wharton called her writing "The Secret Garden," suggesting both the overgrown sanctuary in Frances Hodgson Burnett's popular children's book, and the erotic temptations of creativity and fantasy. From childhood, Wharton was possessed with what she called "the ecstasy of making-up," almost a form of illicit sexual indulgence: "The call came regularly and imperiously and . . . I would struggle against it conscientiously."[9]

Paraded on the New York marriage market, she married Harvard graduate Edward Wharton in 1885. Although the couple were not intellectually or sexually compatible, Teddy's love of travel and his comfortable income made her life a pleasant and even adventurous one; he spent a year's income taking her on a sea tour of the Mediterranean. Photographs of Wharton at this period show her elaborately dressed, and accompanied by one of the many small dogs, Pomeranians and Pekingese, which became substitute children for the couple. Toward the end of the marriage, the dogs in the photographs sit snarling on her lap, shoulders, and arms, totemic bodyguards of her erogenous zones.

So far, nothing unusual for a girl of her class, although she had formed the habit of serious reading, and her strenuous intellectual self-formation included Darwin, Spencer, Nietzsche, Huxley, Frazer, and Veblen. But Wharton was already beginning to break free. The twelve years between her marriage and her first book, *The Decoration of Houses* (1897), cowritten with Ogden Codman, were spent growing into her vocation as a writer. A long apprenticeship, perhaps, but Cather, with fewer encumbrances, spent a decade trying out her craft; women writers often took longer than men to launch themselves with confidence as authors. For many of those years, Wharton had attacks of asthma, or nausea, or neurasthenia, or depression. Her biographers have usually explained these illnesses as psychosomatic symptoms of her unhappiness in the marriage. R. W. B. Lewis was the first to suggest that she had a neurasthenic breakdown at the end of the 1890s, and underwent a rest cure in Philadelphia with Silas Weir Mitchell. Hermione Lee casts doubt on this theory, not only because Mitchell was away during the four months Wharton was in Philadelphia, but also because she was "leading a complicated, active, energetic life, all through the period in which she was *also* unwell, unhappy, and depressed."[10] She may have been an outpatient at Mitchell's clinic, having a modified version of the cure, but she was stronger and more resilient than most rest-cure patients.

In any case, with the publication of her first book of short stories, *The Greater Inclination* (1899), she began to think of herself as an artist. She described this moment in her life as a coming-of-age, a breakthrough to a new professional identity:

> At last I had groped my way through to my vocation, and thereafter I never questioned that story-telling was my job . . . I felt like some homeless waif who, after trying for years to take out naturalization papers, and being rejected by every country, has finally acquired a nationality. The Land of Letters was henceforth to be my country, and I gloried in my new citizenship. The publishing of The Greater Inclination broke the chains which had held me so long in a kind of torpor. For nearly twelve years I had tried to adjust myself to the life I had led since my marriage; but now I was overmastered by the longing to meet people who shared my interests.[11]

Some of the stories nonetheless mocked the self-aggrandizing American female literary tradition; "The Muse's Tragedy" (1899) had a minor character she called "the Female Milton of America." In a later story, "The Touchstone" (1900), the male narrator Glennard recalls meeting the great novelist, Margaret Aubyn, when she was young: "the poor woman of genius, with her long pale face and short-sighted eyes, softened a little by the grace of youth and inexperience, but so incapable even then of any hold upon the pulses." In Glennard's judgment, "genius is of small use to a woman who does not know how to do her hair." He has love letters from her but "he had never thought of the letters objectively, as the production of a distinguished woman, had never measured the literary significance of oppressive prodigality."

With her first novel, *The House of Mirth* (1905), Wharton signaled her rebirth as a citizen of the Land of Letters. Writing the novel as a serial for *Scribner's Magazine,* with an agreement to complete it in five months, she had to abandon the "distractions of a busy and sociable life, full of friends and travel and gardening" for the "discipline of the daily task." The necessity for "systematic daily effort" also gave her for the first time the sense of "mastery over my tools." As she wrote in *A Backward Glance,* she changed from a "drifting amateur into a professional," and "gained what I most lacked—self-confidence."[12]

Among the issues *The House of Mirth* raises is the question of women's writing, in terms of both female creativity and the relation to a female tradition. Wharton explored the changing worlds of women and the equally limiting worlds of men, and located herself in relation to both male and female fin de siècle literary traditions. With stark fatalism, rather than the optimism of women's fiction, she took her heroine Lily Bart from the heights to defeat and death; her relentless fall suggests the motto of Hardy's *Tess of the D'Urbervilles:* "The woman pays." In deciding that the Perfect Lady who cannot be touched must give way to the modern woman who will work and love, Wharton announced her own belief in a Darwinian survival of the fittest.

At the critical age of twenty-nine, on the marriage market for eleven years, Lily still thinks of herself as an exquisite aesthetic object who will be purchased by a rich husband; but as she sees decorative girlhood slipping into impoverished womanhood, the very heart of "dinginess," she awakens to her own uselessness and marginality. Lily was "the American heroine as a woman of thirty" for the beginning of the twentieth century, but Wharton's view of her was as bleak as Kate Chopin's view of Edna Pontellier. Wharton was a Darwinian, but like her contemporary Sigmund Freud, she was pessimistic about the possibilities of growth and survival for the woman, especially the American woman, after the age of thirty. In his essay on "Femininity," Freud wrote that "a woman of thirty often frightens us by her psychical rigidity and unchangeability. Her libido has taken up fixed positions and seems incapable of exchanging them for others."[13]

Wharton's understanding of Lily's psychological complexity, and her sympathetic but clear insistence that Lily is accountable for her life, makes *The House of Mirth* a tragedy, much more profound than the sentimental story of a victim. Wharton was never a feminist; as the critic Elizabeth Ammons concludes, while "she agreed that the position of women in American society was the crucial issue of the new century," she did not "believe that change was occurring. In her opinion the American woman was far from being a new or whole human being."[14] Wharton had come to the understanding that, while upper-class society either in Old New York or Europe was "too shallow to add anything to the most searching gaze," a "frivolous society can assume dramatic significance . . . through what its frivolity destroys: a woman's life."

Lily Bart's plight as a perennial and useless adornment of the New York marriage market is akin to Wharton's dilemma as the elegant scribe of upper-class New York society, the novelist of manners and décor who combined writing fiction with hostessing, an elaborate form of female masquerade. It's appropriate that Lily's most triumphant moment occurs when she dresses up as "Mrs. Lloyd," a painting by Sir Joshua Reynolds, at a society party. Her ambivalent suitor, Lawrence Selden, believes he sees the authentic Lily, with a "streak of sylvan freedom," in her "dryad-like" performance, but Wharton insists that he sees only the Lily of his own fantasies, the woman he would like her to be. We are reminded that Ezra Pound, at about this time, was imposing the title of "dryad" on the equally plastic H.D.

Yet readers often overlook Wharton's development of a full cast of male characters in *The House of Mirth,* whose dilemmas parallel those of the women. Her critique of the marriage system extends to the loneliness, dehumanization, and anxiety of men. Selden is typical of the bachelor figure in Wharton's fiction between 1905 and 1920, cautious about commitment, fond of luxury and status, rebellious but weak; Edmund Wilson described this figure as "a man set apart from his neighbors by education, intellect, and feeling, but lacking the force or courage either to impose himself or get away."[15] Lily's father, an "effaced and silent," "neutral-tinted" figure in the prehistory of the novel, is an exhausted witness to the economic stresses his society places on men. Mr. Bart, who resembles Melville's enigmatic Bartleby, does not so much die as get discarded; to his wife, when he has lost his money, "he had become extinct," and she sits by his deathbed "with the provisional air of a traveler who waits for a belated train to start." Wharton also writes sympathetically of the businessmen Lily attempts to exploit—the shy millionaire Percy Gryce, the beefy and bullying Gus Trenor, and the Jewish financier Simon Rosedale, who is the butt of her anti-Semitism, but also the only man in the novel who likes children.[16] For Wharton they are never merely foils or caricatures, but products of their own crisis of gender.

With *The House of Mirth,* Wharton made tough choices about her nar-

rative, choices that reflected her transition to professionalism, crafts-
manship, and control. Through Lily Bart, she was judging and rejecting
the infantile aspects of her own self, the parts that lacked confidence as a
working writer, longed for the sanctuary of the lady's world, and feared
the sexual consequences of creating rather than becoming art. The
death of the Perfect Lady was also the death of the Lady Novelist. As
Lily, unable to evolve, gave way, Wharton survived to become one of
the founders of a twentieth-century American literary history of female
mastery and growth.

Two years later, at the age of forty-six, Wharton had an ecstatic sexual
affair in Paris with the bisexual American journalist Morton Fullerton. "I
have drunk the wine of life at last," she wrote in her diary. "I have known
the thing best worth knowing, I have been warmed through and through
never to grow quite cold again until the end . . ."[17] The affair would not
last; but in 1911, she separated from Teddy (they were divorced in 1913),
and sold their country home, The Mount, in the Berkshire Hills of Massachusetts. In her summers there, Wharton had "become very familiar
with the aspect, the dialect, and the general mental attitude" of the village residents.[18] She was dismissive of the "New England of fiction," a
landscape of "vague botanical and dialectical" realism, which enumer-
ated the local flora of "sweet-fern, asters, and mountain-laurel," and
attempted a "conscientious reproduction of the vernacular" while senti-
mentalizing the harshness of village life. Jewett and Freeman, she charged
(unfairly—she could not have read many of their stories), saw rural
New England through "rose-colored spectacles."[19] But to Wharton,
this region, "with its lonely lives in half-deserted . . . villages, before the
coming of the motor and the telephone," became for her imagination what Flintcomb Ash was to Hardy or the Yorkshire moors to the
Brontës, a primal landscape that exposed the harsh face of human existence. The "snowbound villages of Western Massachusetts were still
grim places, morally and physically: insanity, incest, and slow mental
and moral starvation were hidden away behind the paintless wooden
house-fronts of the long village street, or in the isolated farm-houses on
the neighbouring hills." Indeed, she noted, "Emily Brontë would have
found as savage tragedies in our remoter valleys as in her Yorkshire
moors."[20]

In *Ethan Frome* (1911), she took on what she saw as soft New England regionalism from a hard and unsparing point of view. Generations of Americans have studied *Ethan Frome* in high school, recommended less, I suspect, for its artistic brilliance than for its brevity and absence of explicit sexual references. Ironically, however, this classic example of American female gothic is a twisted tale of sexual hysteria and thwarted adultery, perhaps the darkest novel Wharton ever wrote. Moreover, despite its apparent stylistic simplicity, *Ethan Frome* is a complex frame narrative, the construction of which gave Wharton the satisfaction of an "artisan's full control of his implements."

Rather than telling the story through a sibylline woman narrator, or sitting the protagonist down "before a village gossip who would have poured out the whole affair . . . in a breath," Wharton chose to invent a reserved male storyteller who is the "sympathizing intermediary" between the New England characters and the reader. Like Lockwood in *Wuthering Heights,* whose interest in the tale he relates reveals himself as well, the narrator of *Ethan Frome* is also telling his own story. He is an unnamed engineer who visits the town of Starkfield twenty-four years after the tragic events of the novel have taken place. Piecing together the story bit by bit from various sources, he also gives his own version of the past, marked by silences, hints, and ellipses that invite the reader to fill in the blanks.[21] In 1922, in her only introduction to any of her novels, Wharton explained that while each Starkfield witness "contributes to the narrative just so much as he or she is capable of understanding . . . only the narrator of the tale has scope enough to see it all, to resolve it back into simplicity, and to put it in its rightful place among his larger categories."

Wharton drew attention to this formal structure in the first lines of the novel: "I had the story, bit by bit, from various people, and, as generally happens in such cases, each time it was different." In the introductory section, the narrator meets the lame, scarred, ruined Ethan, and goes with him to his isolated farmhouse in a snowstorm. As they enter, he hears "a woman's voice droning querulously." The main section of the novel is a long flashback, the narrator's reconstruction of the events leading to Ethan's smashup. Trapped in a miserable and childless marriage to Zeena, who has false teeth and thin hair at thirty-five, the awkward and inarticulate Ethan has become a resentful caretaker. Zeena is a career hysteric who fills the empty spaces in her life, possibly in her body, with "doctoring" and imaginary ailments; she has sent away for an "electric battery of which she had never been able to learn the use"—

a patent remedy advertised for gynecological problems and "female complaints"—and reads about "Kidney Troubles and Their Cure." In the 1936 stage version of *Ethan Frome,* which Wharton approved, the battery is an Energex Vibrator, sold by Sears Roebuck for $22.95.[22] When Zeena's pretty young cousin Mattie Silver arrives to help out in the house, Ethan falls in love and begins to daydream about running away with her. Zeena develops ominous "complications"; she is in many respects the most interesting character of the trio, but Wharton is determined to stay outside her. As a neighbor makes explicit in the end, "nobody knows Zeena's thoughts." While the novel accentuates themes of sterility and barrenness, Ellen Glasgow, rather than Wharton, would explore these images from a woman's point of view in the 1920s.

Instead, Wharton hints at Ethan's repressed murderous rage, in his fantasies of Zeena being killed by "tramps." But while Susan Glaspell, in "A Jury of Her Peers," turned the drama of marital loneliness, confinement, and childlessness into a parable of crime and justice, Wharton aimed for even darker psychological and symbolic punishments. Ethan and Mattie make a suicide pact that they will go out in the snow and crash the sled into a huge tree. But both survive, physically maimed and emotionally destroyed. In the closing frame, the narrator reveals that the "querulous voice" belonged to Mattie, crippled for life, and being cared for until eternity by Zeena in their claustrophobic three-person hell. When *Ethan Frome* was serialized in *Scribner's* in the summer of 1911, reviewers praised it for having "the inevitability of a great Greek tragedy." It was not a popular success.

In her most satiric novel, *The Custom of the Country* (1913), Wharton compared the social rise of two ruthless Americans from Apex, Kansas, Undine Spragg and Elmer Moffatt. Undine is the opposite of the refined and scrupulous Lily Bart, and has no ladylike instincts at all. With her significant initials—U.S.—she reflects Wharton's sardonic view of an acquisitive but ignorant American culture. Undine uses her looks and her father's money to launch herself in New York society and then climb to the top of European aristocracy. A fashion plate with magnificent reddish-gold hair, she spends most of her time "in the scientific cultivation of her beauty" and in patronizing dressmakers, milliners, society artists, and jewelers. Unlike the helpless Lily, Undine is a social climber and seductress, magnificently equipped to survive and dominate in her society.

Her partner in these adventures is the entrepreneur Elmer Moffatt.

Wharton is fascinated by Moffatt's art of the business deal, and appreciates its heroic qualities; she calls him "Homeric" and compares him to Othello, and although these references are perhaps more mock-epic than genuine, they nonetheless imply respect. Moffatt, too, turns up first in Apex, Kansas, behind the counter at Luckabuck's Dollar Shoe Store, then at the office of the coal merchants, then at the Apex Water Works. Soon he becomes "a leading figure in the youthful world of Apex," and despite some scandals, he is clearly a man of destiny. He and Undine elope, but the marriage is quickly annulled, and she is hustled off to New York by her anxious parents.

"Great men," Elmer notes in a Balzacian aside, "always gravitate to the metropolis," so despite being red-faced, balding, and swaggering, he makes it to New York, and somehow makes a fortune.

> It was said that he had bought a house in Seventy-second Street, then that he meant to build near the Park; one or two people . . . had been to his flat in the Pactolus, to see his Chinese porcelains and Persian rugs; now and then he had a few important men to dine at a Fifth Avenue restaurant; his name began to appear in philanthropic reports and on municipal committees (there were even rumors of his having been put up at a well-known club).

Undine is clever and ruthless, but cleverness and ruthlessness alone do not make the epic figure of the American tycoon. We can see some of her limitations by comparing her to the heroine with whom she has most frequently been linked, Thackeray's Becky Sharp. Undine has many of Becky's worst qualities, but she lacks Becky's spirit, irreverence, and humor. She is never forced to confront real hardship or to fight for her survival. She is always a comic character whose many marriages, her "experiments in happiness," allow Wharton to analyze the class systems and social stratospheres of America and France. Her second husband, Ralph Marvell, seems to speak for Wharton when he reflects that Undine's mind "was as destitute of beauty and mystery as the prairie schoolhouse in which she had been educated; and her ideals seemed . . . as pathetic as the ornaments made of corks and cigar-bands with which her infant hands had been taught to adorn it." At the end of the novel, Wharton writes that Undine "had everything she wanted, but she still felt, at times, that there might be other things she might want if she knew about them." Undine's desires are a mixture of opportunity, exposure, and imitation.

In contrast, Wharton gives Moffatt many qualities Undine lacks. In addition to intelligence and daring, he has a genuine disdain for religious piety and social cant. He sees that the New Yorkers are also pretentious and self-congratulatory in their tastes; and he is tolerant of but basically bored by Undine's social ambitions. He cares about children, and he has an aesthetic sense that is more than restlessness, brute acquisitiveness, or greed. When she takes him around Paris to buy collectibles, Undine is aware that he has a sensual as well as a financial response to art. When he and Undine—the epic hero and the femme fatale—get back together, European high culture is doomed to go under.

There is obviously much of Wharton's own anti-American prejudice in one aristocrat's accusations of American barbarism: "You come from hotels as big as towns, and from towns as flimsy as paper, where the streets haven't had time to be named, and the buildings are demolished before they're dry, and the people are as proud of changing as we are of holding to what we have." The critical vote on this novel has always been divided, with some finding it Wharton's masterpiece and others deploring its cold and brittle surface.

Early in 1914, Wharton had begun to write a big novel called "Literature," which she imagined as "a full and leisurely chronicle of a young man's life from his childhood to his end."[23] Although the main character was a man, the novel would be autobiographical; he would be a writer, who goes from "abortive attempts at play-writing," to "opposition from jealous critics," one of them Jewish, to "writers' block, the aftermath of success, posthumous glory."[24] When the war broke out that summer, Wharton was in Paris, where she quickly became active in war work. By December, she told Scribner's, who were patiently waiting for the book, that she had put it aside; the suffering of the war and her charities had temporarily displaced writing fiction. She helped French refugees, especially women and children, and also published two books about French culture collected from articles she had published in American magazines, *Fighting France* (1918) and *French Ways and Their Meaning* (1919).

Working with refugees gave her some sympathy for feminism. In 1915, in a eulogy for her friend Jean du Breuil de Saint-Germain, she admitted that

> *he made me see that the only thing that matters, in the feminist movement, is the fate of . . . those poor hard-working women who accept their long misery with an animal fatalism because they do not know*

they have a right to a more humane existence. In short, one would be
very tempted to say that women who argue the right to vote could very
well do without it, but it is necessary for those women, so much more
numerous, who do not even know what it is, or why others are demand-
ing it in their name.[25]

Summer (1917), the novel she published at the end of the war, returned
to the New England setting to tell the story of one such young woman,
Charity Royall, the adopted daughter of the widowed town lawyer in
North Dormer, Massachusetts. Charity works in the town's one-room
"Honorius Hatchard Memorial Library," where the books are covered in
cobwebs and dust, *Uncle Tom's Cabin* is the only novel anyone wants to
borrow, and a disintegrated copy of *The Lamplighter* is a bobbin for her
lacework. Looming over Charity are the specters of female decline into
animality—her real mother, an alcoholic who lives in a feral community
on the Mountain, and Julia Hawes, who got pregnant, had an abortion in
nearby Nettleton, and became a prostitute. The abortionist's brick
house, on the corner of Wing Street and Lake Avenue, with its big black
sign reading "Dr. Merkle: Private Consultations at all hours, Lady atten-
dants," is the opposite and yet the twin of the library, a female destina-
tion of last resort. When Charity discovers that she is pregnant and that
her upper-class lover has abandoned her, she makes the trip to that house
and meets Dr. Merkle, "a plump woman with small bright eyes, an
immense mass of black hair coming down on her forehead, and unnatu-
rally white and even teeth" who "smelt of musk and carbolic acid."
(Hermione Lee thinks she is meant to be Jewish.)[26] Although Charity
decides against the abortion, she is cheated and blackmailed by Dr.
Merkle, and survives only because she is rescued by the fatherly Lawyer
Royall, who marries and protects her. Although Wharton could feel
compassion for powerless women, she did not believe in feminism or sisterhood as a panacea.

In *The Age of Innocence* (1920), the novel that won her a Pulitzer Prize,
Wharton told the story of a male writer manqué, Newland Archer, who
longs, but does not dare, to escape from his dull tribal clan in Old New
York.

[Archer] knew that there were societies where painters and poets and
novelists and men of science, and even great actors, were as sought after
as Dukes; he had often pictured to himself what it would have been like

*to live in the intimacy of drawing-rooms dominated by that talk of
Mérimée, . . . of Thackeray, Browning, or William Morris. But such
things were inconceivable in New York, and unsettling to think of.*

One of his cousins, Medora Manson, has tried to start "a 'literary
salon;' but it had soon died out owing to the reluctance of the literary to
frequent it." Her home is the closest thing he has seen to a bohemian
enclave, and it is populated by weird men like Dr. Agathon Carver, the
founder of the Valley of Love Community in Newport, and Professor
Emerson Sillerton, who gives parties for "long-haired men and short-
haired women," and takes his bride on their honeymoon to "explore
tombs in Yucatan instead of going to Paris or Italy."

Newland's virginal society bride, May, stimulates his feelings of "pos-
sessorship." He would never dream of taking her to Yucatan, but he
looks forward to reading *Faust* with her by the Italian lakes, "somewhat
hazily confusing the scene of his projected honeymoon with the masterpieces of literature which it would be his manly privilege to reveal to his
bride." His manly but very literary regret is that sexually he can't offer
her "a blank page" in exchange for her "unblemished one." When Newland meets his distant cousin Ellen Olenska, who has returned to New
York after a disastrous marriage to an abusive Polish count, he is immediately smitten by seeing the books scattered about her untidy drawing
room—Bourget, Huysmans, the Goncourt brothers. When she asks him
if the arts have a milieu in New York, he replies, "they're more like a very
thinly settled outskirt."

He dreams of a world with Ellen where she cannot be his wife but will
be more than his mistress: "Where we shall be simply two human beings
who love each other." But, she replies, "Oh my dear—where is that
country? Have you ever been there? I know so many who've tried to find
it; and believe me, they all got out by mistake at wayside stations at
places like Boulogne, or Pisa, or Monte Carlo—and it wasn't at all different from the old world they'd left, but only rather smaller and dingier
and more promiscuous." Interestingly, Wharton puts her commentary
on Archer's failed nineteenth-century marriage into the mouths of his
grown children many years later. "You and mother never did ask each
other anything, did you? And you never told each other anything . . . A
deaf-and-dumb asylum, in fact." It sounds like the marriage of Julia and
Samuel Howe, and their incarceration in the Perkins School. No one else
at the time, with the possible exception of F. Scott Fitzgerald, was writ-

ing with such insight about sexuality, marriage, and the conflicting dreams of women and men.

Willa Cather—"Women are so horribly subjective"

When she was starting out as a book reviewer and journalist in the 1890s, Willa Cather (1873–1947) emphatically declared her low opinion of women writers, especially women novelists:

> I have not much faith in women in fiction. They have a sort of sex consciousness that is abominable. They are so limited to one string and they lie so about that. They are so few, the ones who really did anything worth while; there were the great Georges, George Eliot and George Sand, and they were anything but women, and there was Miss Brontë who kept her sentimentality under control, and there was Jane Austen who certainly had more common sense than any of them and was in some respects the greatest of them all. Women are so horribly subjective and they have such scorn for the healthy commonplace. When a woman writes a story of adventure, a stout sea tale, a manly battle yarn, anything without wine, women, and love, then I will begin to hope for something great from them, not before.[27]

Cather never tried to write a sea tale, but early on, she had formed a "dedication to classical, heroic forms of narrative with hard clear lines, strong stories, and epic simplicity." When she became a novelist herself, she tried to create "an American writing which can be at once heroic and female."[28]

From childhood, Cather boldly resisted the cultural trappings and the intellectual limitations of being a girl. She was born in Virginia, the eldest child of seven, but in 1883, the family moved to the vast exposed plains of Red Cloud, Nebraska, in search of purer air, better soil, and more opportunity. It was a real culture shock for the ten-year-old girl. Suddenly she was transported from the lush "woods and hills and meadows" of her Virginia childhood to "a country as bare as piece of sheet iron."[29] But there were compensations. She was free to read whatever she wanted in her parents' large library—Dickens, Poe, Hawthorne, and especially boys' adventure romances by Stevenson, Kipling, and Twain. She immersed herself in classical literature, especially Virgil. By 1888, she had cut her long hair, dressed as a boy, and started to call herself William Cather. Sometimes she added "M.D." or "Jr." to the name. One old man in Nebraska called her "that morpheedite."[30]

She was determined to go to the University of Nebraska in Lincoln, where she was immediately encouraged in her writing by members of the English department, and mentored by professional journalists at the *Nebraska State Journal.* At the age when Wharton was still planning her wardrobe for New York society balls, Cather was already a working journalist and critic. She also made many accomplished women friends in Lincoln, including Dorothy Canfield, whose father was the university chancellor, and Louise Pound. Both Cather's daring, in her disguise as the short-haired, suspender-wearing "Billy," and the tolerance and respect of her classmates, were extraordinary. Harper Lee probably had a rougher time socially at college in Alabama half a century later.

By the 1890s, Cather was bluntly questioning women's ability to create art, and rejecting the demeaning category of lady writer she dubbed the "authorine."[31] "Sometimes I wonder why God ever trusts talent in the hands of women," she wrote in 1895; "they usually make such an infernal mess out of it."[32] In addition to Austen, the Brontës, and George Eliot, she liked the poetry of Christina Rossetti, and used a passage from "Goblin Market" as the epigraph to her book *The Troll Garden.* In the 1920s, she wrote an appreciative essay on Katherine Mansfield. But for American women writers, she had scant respect. She was unimpressed by the philosophical pretensions of Margaret Fuller and the biblical scholarship of Elizabeth Cady Stanton. Like Wharton, she rejected the artistic claims of Harriet Beecher Stowe: "the mind that can follow a 'mission' is not an artistic one. For this reason, *Uncle Tom's Cabin* will never have a place in the highest ranks of literature."[33] She was bored by *The Awakening.* To lavish art on a simple love story, she believed, was a waste of talent. Edna, the Bovary-like heroine, was an example of that class of female romanticizers who "expect the passion of love to fill and gratify every need of life, whereas nature intended that it should meet one of many demands."[34] Surprisingly, she never mentioned, and perhaps never read, Emily Dickinson.

After her graduation in 1895, Cather first returned to Red Cloud, where she began to call herself "Willa Sibert Cather" and to dateline her letters ironically from "Siberia." Soon she was able to escape, first to Pittsburgh, where she spent ten years as a journalist and editor, and then to New York, where she joined the staff of *McClure's Magazine*. The short fiction she was writing and publishing during these years was very much under the influence of Henry James—she admitted that she "laboriously strove" to imitate him—and in some degree indebted to Wharton, although she confided in a letter that she found them both artificial.[35]

Several of the seven short stories in her first book, *The Troll Garden* (1905), were in the Jamesian high-society style. But in the last two she began to develop one of her central and permanent themes—the desperate escape from the ugly and raw provinces to the city of light and culture. "A Wagner Matinee" is narrated by Clark, a young man who has fled his Nebraska village for the splendors of Boston. His aunt Georgiana, a former music teacher, is coming to visit Boston on legal business, and he plans to show her the city. Although she is shabby and dazed by a "dullness of thirty years," he takes her to a matinee of the Boston Symphony. There she is transfixed, transported, by the music, especially the Venusberg theme from *Tannhäuser*. At the end of the concert, in tears, Aunt Georgiana says, "I don't want to go, Clark, I don't want to go!" He understands. "For her, just outside the door of the concert hall lay the black pond with the cattle-tracked bluffs; the tall, unpainted house, with weather-curled boards, naked as a tower; the crook-backed ash seedlings where the dishcloths hung to dry; the gaunt, molting turkeys picking up refuse about the kitchen door." It is Cather's vision of the wasteland, the nightmare landscape of failed quest, like Robert Browning's poem "Childe Roland to the Dark Tower Came."

The adolescent protagonist of "Paul's Case: A Study in Temperament," like Cather herself, is also ravished by music and theater.[36] Working as an usher at Pittsburgh's Carnegie Hall, he "felt a sudden zest of life; the lights danced before his eyes and the concert hall blazed into unimaginable splendour." A dandy, a compulsive liar, sensitive, theatrical, tense, Paul seems to the twenty-first-century reader a case study of a provincial homosexual boy trapped in a bourgeois world of "Sabbath-school picnics, petty economies, wholesome advice as to how to succeed in life, and the inescapable odours of cooking," a story told many times over by gay writers who escaped. He could be Andy Warhol, born in Pittsburgh later in the century. Even in 1961, Katherine Anne Porter called it "the most contemporary" of Cather's stories.[37] But in 1905,

Paul's case was more enigmatic; Cather explains that for his teachers, family, and employers, "the real cause of the trouble . . . lay in a sort of hysterically defiant manner of the boy's; in the contempt which they all knew he felt for them, and which he seemingly made not the least effort to conceal."

Expelled from high school, Paul steals some money from the office where he works, and runs away to New York to spend it all in one glorious fling. This is a plot that Mary Wilkins Freeman and other women regionalists had used—the small-town drudge who goes to the city for a binge and returns satisfied and redomesticated. But Paul is beyond the mild heroines of New England regionalism, and before the fabulous urban flowering of a Warhol. He is not an artist himself, but someone who lives in the glittering make-believe of art. When he runs out of money, he has only one choice. As he throws himself theatrically in front of a train, he regrets only what "he had left undone. There flashed through his brain, clearer than ever before, the blue of Adriatic water, the yellow of Algerian sands."

Cather would go on to leave nothing undone, and would write great novels, but she would never write more brilliantly than in this story, where character, setting, and a vision of human existence come together. Meanwhile, she was living with Isabelle McClung and had met the woman who would be her lifelong companion, Edith Lewis. While in Boston on assignment for *McClure's Magazine,* she also met Sarah Orne Jewett, who became her great literary mentor. Jewett's letter to Cather in 1908, passing on the professional torch and counseling her to give up journalism and devote herself full-time to her writing, is one of the classics of American literary history:

> If you don't keep and guard and mature your force, and above all, have time and quiet to perfect your work, you will be writing things not much better than you did five years ago . . . You need to dream your dreams and go on to new and more shining ideals. . . Your vivid, exciting companionship in the office must not be your audience, you must find your own quiet centre of life and write from that to the world that holds offices, all society, all Bohemia, the city, the country—in short, you must write to the human heart, the great consciousness that all humanity goes to make up . . . To work in silence and with all one's heart, that is the writer's lot; he is the only artist who must be solitary and yet needs the widest outlook on the world.[38]

In the fall of 1911, Cather took a leave of absence from *McClure's*. The following spring, she made a momentous journey to the Southwest. The landscape and mythology of Arizona and New Mexico, especially the vanished civilizations of the Pueblo cliff dwellers, made the Southwest equivalent in her imagination to Gilman's Herland—a utopian space of freedom, imagination, and enchantment. Lee observes that "just at the point when her new life as a writer was about to begin," she had found "a landscape that needed a new writing."[39] Not everything about the trip was female in its imagery; Cather was also charmed and attracted by the Mexican guide, Julio. But out of this phase of her life came the pastoral novels about heroic women pioneers that feminist critics have set high in her oeuvre, and, more generally, a reinvention of the American women's novel as a work of art that was not political, romantic, or didactic.

O Pioneers! (1913), set on the plains of Nebraska, was the first novel to draw on Cather's experience of the large landscape over which the heroic woman presides. Cather dedicated the book to Jewett. "I tried to tell the story of the people as truthfully and simply as if I were telling it to her by word of mouth," she said.[40] But she also took her epic title from Whitman; her sources, like her themes and style, were androgynous. At the center of the novel is the Amazonian immigrant Alexandra Bergson. In a key passage, Cather described Alexandra's mind as "a white book with clear writing about weather and history and growing things . . . She had never been in love, she had never indulged in sentimental reveries. Even as a girl she had looked upon men as workfellows." Lee comments on some of the implications of this image—virginity, "the white space of the land," "the white pages on which Cather is writing a hitherto unwritten woman's pioneer novel," its simplicity of form.[41] Alexandra is a majestic heroine, but also rather onedimensional and dull in her attachment to the land and her oracular utterances about its endurance.

The Song of the Lark (1915), the next novel in this series, had some formal problems. She cut the manuscript by almost 25 percent when she published it as a book, and cut another tenth of the novel for the Autograph Edition of her works in 1937; but she was still dissatisfied, believing, rightly, that she should have minimized the end of the book, which dwells on the opera singer Thea Kronberg's triumphs on the stage. Although critics have praised its originality as "the first completely serious . . . portrait-of-the-artist-as-a-young-woman," Cather was working alongside Mary Austin and others writing about the woman of genius.[42] Thea was based on the Wagnerian soprano Olive Fremstad, whom Cather had interviewed for *McClure's,* a "Nordic superwoman" who also became her friend.[43] In her preface to the 1937 edition, Cather noted that she wanted to title it "Artist's Youth," making the idea of the artist as a young woman explicit, but her publisher discouraged her. She also compared the story to Oscar Wilde's *Dorian Gray,* although she had been scathing about Wilde the man in the 1890s. "The life of nearly every artist who succeeds in the true sense (succeeds in delivering himself completely to his art)," she wrote, "is more or less like Wilde's story . . . as she is more and more released into the dramatic and musical possibilities of her profession, as her artistic life grows fuller and richer, it becomes more interesting to her than her own life . . . The interesting and important fact [is that] in an artist of the type I chose, personal life becomes paler as the imaginative life becomes richer."

The Song of the Lark follows Thea's artistic formation in overlong, loving detail, and obviously Cather was talking about her own growth as a writer as well. But the part of the novel that has been most discussed is "Part IV: The Ancient People," when Thea, exhausted by performing, goes to stay at a ranch in Panther Canyon, Arizona, which belongs to the father of her suitor Fred. Cather's description of this place has become legendary in feminist criticism.

> *Panther Canyon was like a thousand others—one of those abrupt fissures with which the earth in the Southwest is riddled; so abrupt that you might walk over the edge of any one of them on a dark night and never know what had happened to you. This canyon headed on the Ottenburg ranch, about a mile from the ranch house, and it was accessible only at its head. The canyon walls, for the first two hundred feet below the surface, were perpendicular cliffs, striped with even-running strata of rock. From there on to the bottom the sides were less abrupt, were shelving, and lightly fringed with piñons and dwarf cedars. The effect was that of a gentler canyon within a wilder one. The dead city lay at the point where the perpendicular outer wall ceased and the V-shaped inner gorge began.*

In her pioneering study *Literary Women* (1976), Ellen Moers was the first critic to draw attention to Cather's sexual iconography, and to identify this landscape, with its walls, cliffs, clefts, and V-shaped inner gorge, as one of female solitude and ecstatic self-discovery. Elizabeth Ammons calls it "female and erotic, even before [Thea] in a ritual of ecstatic purification, stands naked in a pool of water at the canyon's base . . . and feels the presence of the Indian women potters who came before her."[44] Thea has an intense epiphany about art, the body, music, and form: "What was any art but an effort to make a sheath, a mould in which to imprison for a moment the shining, elusive element which is life itself—life hurrying past us and running away, too strong to stop, too sweet to lose?"

But while Thea apprehends the purpose of art, and Cather expresses that apprehension in a sexualized language, she also emphasizes that it is an *effort,* and that if Thea wants to achieve it, she must take control of her life, make a break with her past, go to Germany to study and grow. In the last paragraph of Thea's story, Cather summarizes it as an "account of how a Moonstone girl found her way out of a vague, easy-going world into a life of disciplined endeavor." That message of effort and discipline is more important, and more androgynous, than the primordial female imagery.

The third novel in Cather's pastoral trilogy, *My Ántonia* (1918), displayed the extraordinary narrative mastery she had achieved, and it is unexpectedly funny, feminist, and violent. One man kills his family; another shoots himself in the head with a rifle; a despairing tramp jumps into a harvester. Cather tells all this in a deadpan style: "the machine ain't never worked right since," a character says. In the introductory section of the novel, an unnamed woman writer meets an old friend, Jim Burden, on a train in the Midwest, and they reminisce about a Bohemian girl, Ántonia Shimerda, they both knew as children in Black Hawk, Nebraska: "more than any other person we remembered, this girl seemed to mean to us the country, the conditions, the whole adventure of our childhood." Some months afterward, Burden comes to the writer's apartment with a lengthy manuscript he has written about the girl, which he has called "My Ántonia." The book we are reading is his story. Thus what we learn about "Tony," the immigrant girl he grew up with, taught to speak English, loved, left behind, and reencountered as an adult, we learn through a man's eyes.

Some critics find Jim's narrative rambling and incoherent, "a collection of sketches, remembered vignettes and repeated stories that are loosely tied together."[45] But the apparent leisure and understated technique allowed Cather to contrast Jim's life with Ántonia's. He is an orphan, sent to Nebraska to live with his grandparents; she survives her father's suicide. He studies Latin and Greek, goes to the university in Lincoln, and is especially moved by Virgil's wish to "bring the Muse into my country," a great ambition that Cather had taken as her own credo. He manages to get to Harvard to study Virgil, and then to Harvard Law School, and makes a splendid but unhappy marriage with Genevieve Whitney, a New Woman of independent fortune, who "gave one of her town-houses for a Suffrage headquarters, produced one of her own plays at the Princess Theatre, was arrested for picketing during a garment-makers' strike," a description that cannot have endeared Cather to her more heterodox Village readers at the time. Cather goes on to accuse her of hypocrisy and superficiality: "she finds it worth while to play the patroness to a group of young poets and painters of advanced ideas and mediocre ability."

Tony, however, goes away to marry Larry Donovan, "a passenger con-ductor who was a kind of professional ladies' man," and he gets her pregnant and runs off without marrying her. She comes back in dis-grace, but makes the best of her lot, and eventually marries a local man, has "ten or eleven" children; becomes weather-beaten, toothless, and grizzled, and can be seen as either an earth mother or what one critic derides as "an ambulatory womb."[46] Despite these handicaps, she remains "a rich mine of life" for Jim, a person who has somehow lived more deeply and truly than he has succeeded in doing. She becomes an allegorical figure, a sibyl, who leaves "images in the mind that did not fade."

More realistically, Cather also develops some astonishing possibilities for women in two other characters, Tiny Soderball and Lena Lingard, who are among the Norwegian hired girls whom Jim gets to know as a teenager in Black Hawk. Pretty and flirtatious, they have no intention to marry. "Men are all right for friends," Lena tells Jim, "but as soon as you marry them, they turn into cranky old fathers, even the wild ones. They begin to tell you what's sensible and what's foolish, and want you to stick at home all the time. I prefer to be foolish when I feel like, and be accountable to nobody." When she is harassed by a married man, she says cheerfully, "I can't order him off. It ain't my prairie." She becomes a dressmaker, so gifted she is almost an artist. Tiny Soderball has the most amazing trajectory. A kittenish flirt in short skirts and striped stockings who tempts the upright Black Hawk boys, she is no little woman, despite her name. She takes off for Seattle to run a lodging house, and then joins the gold rush in the Yukon, where she makes a fortune as a hotel-keeper, miner, and investor. When she settles down in San Francisco, she invites Lena to join her, and they look out for each other. Cather was certainly not writing a feminist utopia; Tiny has lost three toes to frostbite, and has become "thin" and "hard-faced." Nonetheless, it's as if Cather has retold a Jack London story with women, and found a way to describe adventure without too much "feminine" subjectivity.

In her greatest novel, *The Professor's House* (1925), Cather tells about the midlife crisis of a male academic. Like George Eliot's Casaubon, Godfrey St. Peter is completely burned out although he is only fifty-two. He is a historian whose lifework, an eight-volume study of the *Spanish Adventurers in North America,* has won him acclaim, even the Oxford prize for history. But the meaning seems to have gone out of his life and his teaching; at the novel's conclusion, he is resigning himself to spending the remainder of his days without feeling. "Theoretically he knew that life is possible, may even be pleasant, without joy, without passionate griefs. But it had never occurred to him that he might have to live like that."

Rather than a vision of a female life force like Ántonia, the contrasting vision at the center of St. Peter's life is another trip to the Southwest. "Tom Outland's Story" is the manuscript of his most brilliant student, an inventor who discovered the magnificent ruins of an ancient culture in the "Blue Mesa," but died young without managing to persuade the Smithsonian to preserve its archaeological treasures. St. Peter has been a lucky and a prosperous man, but he has never had the almost religious experience of pure discovery without profit, self-interest, or compromise. Tom Outland had "escaped all that. He had made something new in the world—and the rewards, the meaningless conventional gestures, he had left to others."

Could Cather live up to this stern credo? Could Wharton? In the 1920s, they were established, famous, and prolific. Wharton, still living in Paris, was examining the relationships of parents and children in American settings, productive in *The Mother's Recompense* (1925), *Twilight Sleep* (1927), *The Children* (1928), and *Hudson River Bracketed* (1929). These novels, Hermione Lee argues, also "emerged out of an abiding fascination with the stuff of modern America" and were "filled with detail about the very culture from which she felt herself so alienated."[47] In *The Mother's Recompense,* Kate Clephane, returning to New York from Paris, even finds poetry in the Brooklyn Bridge. James was dead, but Wharton had some contacts with the younger generation of American writers; Sinclair Lewis dedicated *Babbitt* to her, and Scott Fitzgerald was so flatteringly nervous about meeting her that he had to get roaring drunk. Women writers of the 1920s from Jessie Fauset to Zona Gale were inspired by her ambition and achievement. Gale wrote to her that "you have been to me cloud and fire. Not only in your own, but in that you were taking us all, writers and readers, with you to new places. Because of you we could not stay where we were."[48] Wharton enjoyed thinking that the gold digger Lorelei Lee, in Anita Loos's *Gentlemen Prefer Blondes* (1925), had been influenced by Undine Spragg; as she wrote to a friend, "I am now reading the great American novel (at last!) and I want to know if there are—or will be—others and if you know the young woman [who wrote it] who must be a genius."[49] If she had lived to read *Gone with the Wind*, she would surely have recognized another Undine in Scarlett O'Hara.

Cather, too, had a period of intense creativity and acclaim in the 1920s. She published five books in addition to *The Professor's House: Youth and the Bright Medusa* (1920), *One of Ours* (1922), *A Lost Lady* (1923), *My Mortal Enemy* (1926), and *Death Comes for the Archbishop* (1927). She scooped up literary prizes and honorary degrees, acquired an agent, talked to Hollywood producers, and was generally one of "America's best-loved writers."[50] But neither Wharton nor Cather was in step with the 1920s—a haughty dowager and a Midwestern spinster in the middle of the Jazz Age, they were seen by younger writers as too old, too rich, and too traditional to flap or roar; and they were even more out of place and time in the Depression. Wharton had lived abroad so long that she was out of touch with American events; Cather actually lived in Greenwich Village, but she was no Village radical. Fanny Hurst said that Cather's apartment on Bank Street was "no more a part of Fitzgerald's twenties than of Mars."[51] To Katherine Anne Porter, Cather seemed as sexless and wholesome as "the president of the Girl Scouts."

Although her essay "The Novel Démeublé" (1922), which called for an unfurnishing and stripping down of the overstuffed house of fictional realism, and her appreciative essay on Katherine Mansfield's art of suggestion, implication, and unnamed feelings could have allied her with the modernists, Cather's dismissal of Freud, Marx, and the modern city tied her to the past. *One of Ours* sold very well and won the Pulitzer Prize, but infuriated male writers who regarded it as feminine in the worst sense, anachronistically patriotic, secondhand, and simplistic. In 1923, Hemingway wrote to Edmund Wilson:

> Look at One of Ours. *Prize, big sale, people taking it seriously. You were in the war weren't you? Wasn't that last scene in the lines wonderful? Do you know where it came from? The battle scene in Birth of a Nation. I identified episode after episode. Catherized. Poor woman she had to get her war experience somewhere.*[52]

By then, both Wharton and Cather were seeing their precarious places in the American literary canon come unstuck as they were attacked for snobbery, conservatism, and irrelevance by scornful Marxist critics. Cather's collection of essays, *Not Under Forty* (1936), which emphasized the effects of the generation gap, and declared that "the world broke in two in 1922 or thereabouts," further reinforced the critical sense of her obsolescence as an artist. Wharton's stately and reticent autobiography, *A Backward Glance* (1934), convinced readers that she, too, was yesterday's woman. But both novelists seemed revitalized in their final books. Wharton came full circle in her unfinished novel, *The Buccaneers* (1938), set in England in the 1870s at about the same time as *The House of Mirth*. Following the lives of rich American girls going to England to trade their money for a title, she came to the defense of the democratic American woman she had always despised, and found much to admire in the courage, curiosity, and intelligence of American girls who brought a "blast of outer air" to "a sleeping world."[53] Cather's last book, *Sapphira and the Slave Girl* (1940), still her least well-known, was set before the Civil War and retells a story of escape not unlike those she had disdained as melodramatic in Harriet Beecher Stowe.

Wharton and Cather would not have wanted to see themselves as part of women's literary history, but in the 1920s, American women writers were demoted and denigrated by a nation taking pride in its military victory. In the years following the armistice, women writers were gradually but systematically eliminated from the canon of American literature as it was anthologized, studied, and taught. The four-volume *Cambridge History of American Literature* (1917–21), the first national literary history of the twentieth century, made its viewpoint explicit in its statement of purpose: "Acquaintance with the record of these two centuries should enlarge the spirit of American literary criticism and render it more energetic and masculine." With the founding in 1921 of the American literature section of the Modern Language Association, and the establish-ment of American literature as an academic field, most women scholars were excluded from leadership, as many women writers were edged out of history.[54] Women writers in the 1920s were reading Wharton and Cather, but they were still far from harvesting the literary seeds the two writers had planted. Women had won the vote; now they had to figure out what equality and emancipation might mean.

13

You Might as Well Live

lthough American women got the vote in 1920, the decade that followed was not as triumphant as the suffragists had expected. The 1920s were feminism's awkward age. The political coalitions of the suffrage campaign had dissolved into warring factions; the unified women's vote did not materialize, and many female activists were repelled by the roar of party politics. Finally, the "feminist–new style," the good sport and good pal heralded by twenties women and welcomed by twenties men, wanted to have it all, "marriage and children as well as a career," but these hopes were premature. Men's role in the family was largely unchanged and unexamined, and women were still expected to bear most of the responsibility for child care and homemaking.[1] Ex-feminists, disillusioned and exhausted, published their complaints and confessions in the magazines. Others exploited their allotted roles as dumb blonde, gold digger, baby vamp, or flapper princess.

For the feminist literary avant-garde of the 1920s, the novelist Josephine Herbst recalled, "freedom to write was synonymous with freedom to love."[2] But for these women, love was never free. In "Résumé," published in *Enough Rope* (1926) and dedicated to Elinor Wylie, Dorothy Parker jauntily mocked her own and her generation's sense of despair. Even suicide was too complicated and too painful a solution to their impasse:

> *Guns aren't lawful;*
> *Nooses give;*
> *Gas smells awful;*
> *You might as well live.*

Barren Ground—Ellen Glasgow

Thus while American men in the 1920s wrote about postwar impotence and spiritual sterility through such images as Eliot's Waste Land and Fitzgerald's Valley of Ashes, American women in the 1920s wrote about disillusion, desolation, and childlessness in images of weeds and parched fields. In her preface to *Barren Ground* (1925), Ellen Glasgow (1874–1945) wrote: "Not only is this the kind of novel I like to read and had always wished to write, but it became for me, while I was working upon it, almost a vehicle of liberation. After years of tragedy and the sense of defeat that tragedy breeds in the mind, I had won my way to the other side of the wilderness, and had discovered, with astonishment, that I was another and a very different person." *Barren Ground* is about a woman winning her way through loneliness and hardship to rebirth and serenity, symbolized in the novel by three sections titled Broomsedge, Pine, and Life-Everlasting, for the hardy scrub plants that could survive and endure in even the most burnt-out soil. Glasgow tells the story of Dorinda Oakley, who refuses to be a tragic victim when the doctor she adores, Jason Greylock, gets her pregnant and jilts her to marry the rich Geneva Ellgood. Dorinda flees to New York, and loses the baby when she is hit by a car. She supports herself by working as a children's nurse in a rich family, and for a long time believes she is "dried up to the core," like the landscape of her rural beginnings. But she returns home, brings the dry farmland back to life, and marries a decent man. *Barren Ground* ends in a grim revenge fantasy; Geneva kills herself, and Dorinda takes Jason into her home to care for him as he dies. It's as if *Ethan Frome* had been rewritten from the viewpoint of a triumphant Zeena.

Glasgow wrote that "Dorinda, although she had been close to me for ten years before I began her story, is universal. She exists wherever a human being has learned to live without joy." Living without joy had become Glasgow's motto. Mourning the deaths of her lover, her mother, and a beloved sister; trying to accept the deafness that made her feel isolated and awkward; horrified by the war; and, on a more professional note, disappointed by her failure to compete with Wharton and Cather, she found some delayed gratification when *Barren Ground* sold over a thousand copies a week. Moreover, as a Southern lady who associated high art with men, she "denied, buried, hid, or projected and transferred her true feelings as a woman," which included rage at men.

True, Wharton and Cather had also struggled with their ingrained tendency to link art with men, but as Linda Wagner observes, Glasgow took "twenty years to be comfortable writing about a female protagonist."[3] Furthermore, she viewed the contemporary literary scene as sterile and inhospitable to her stately and traditional fiction. When Gertrude Stein toured the United States in the 1930s, Glasgow agreed to host a dinner for her in Richmond. Stein enjoyed herself in the city and at the party; Glasgow recorded her private view that Stein was an "overgrown child" and a "freak writer," but that even if Americans could not "read a line of her writing," they loved a sideshow and were "always willing to pay for the pleasure of being fooled."[4] This analysis of Stein's success may owe more to Glasgow's resentment at being overshadowed than to her critical acuity, but her assessment of her own standing was accurate. Despite producing twenty novels in a career spanning more than four decades, capped by a Pulitzer Prize for fiction in 1942, Glasgow could not build on the "feminist" breakthrough of *Barren Ground*.

Weeds—Edith Summers Kelley

Glasgow was one of a number of American women writing about barren ground and hard times in the 1920s. Elizabeth Madox Roberts (1881–1941) attracted critical attention with her first novel, *The Time of Man* (1926), about the illiterate daughter of a Kentucky migrant farmer. In another first novel, *Weeds* (1923), Edith Summers Kelley (1884–1956) suggested that poor farm women are hardy and tough, but survive only by giving up all that is beautiful, idealistic, tender, and meaningful in life. Although she was born in Canada, Kelley spent most of her life in the United States. In Greenwich Village, after she graduated from the University of Toronto, Kelley shared a flat with an actress and an art student, and met Upton Sinclair, who hired her as his secretary at his experimental commune Helicon Hall. There she met Sinclair Lewis, to whom she was engaged in 1906–7; but in 1908, she married Lewis's roommate, the poet-novelist Allan Updegraff. She taught night school, supported his artistic efforts, and raised their two children. When they finally divorced, she entered a common-law marriage with a young artist, Fred Kelley, which lasted fifty years. They had another child together, and turned to migrant farming and chicken ranching to support their family, moving around from New Jersey to Kentucky to California.

Weeds told the story of a bright farm woman, Judy Pippinger, over-whelmed by hardship, childbearing, and the monotony of rural life. Judy "had always disliked the insides of houses. The gloom of little-windowed rooms, the dead chill or the heavy heat as the fire smoul-dered, or blazed, the prim, set look of tables and cupboards that stood always in the same places engaged in the never-ending occupation of col-lecting dust both above and beneath; these things stifled and depressed her." The house mirrors the female body, its demands, its seasons, its needs to be cleaned and kept up, its heat and its cold. Pregnant after a brief affair, Judy desperately tries several means of abortion; knitting needle, galloping on horseback, drinking "pennyroyal and tansy and other noxious herbs." She loses the baby, but survives.

The unrelenting darkness of the novel, which had mixed reviews but no commercial success, is captured in the narrator's declaration that the idea of the goodness and simplicity of country folk is a "misleading fal-lacy. No decadent court riddled with lust of power, greed, vice, and intrigue, and falling to pieces of its own rottenness, ever moved under a thicker atmosphere" than that of her country characters. Kelley tried to finish a second novel, *The Devil's Hand,* about farmers in the Imperial Val-ley. Unpublished during her lifetime, it was preserved by her son Patrick Kelley and was finally printed in 1974.

Women Poets of the 1920s: Sappho's Sisters

Floyd Dell called the period from 1900 to 1916 "the lyric years," after the poetry annual that was among its most prestigious publications—Edna St. Vincent Millay published her first poem, "Renascence," in *The Lyric Year* in 1912—but lyric poetry was becoming old-fashioned by 1920. Male modernist poets spurned the Romantics for tougher and more intellec-tual poetic models like the metaphysical Donne and the impressionist Jules Laforgue. But American women poets, apart from Stein and H.D., were still influenced by, even addicted to, the traditions of English Romanticism, the sonnet, and the lyric. Elinor Wylie was preoccupied by Shelley, Amy Lowell devoted to Keats.[5] Genevieve Taggard had two kittens named Sheats and Kelley.

Women poets also looked to Sappho, the Greek lyricist whose work survived only in fragments, for a literary matrilineage. Louise Bogan sometimes signed herself "Louise Sappho Bogan."[6] One man-about-the-

Village called Millay the "modern Sappho," and both Millay and Teasdale wrote poems about her.[7] They also read Emily Dickinson, Elizabeth Barrett Browning, and Christina Rossetti. Yet none of these precursors seemed wholly satisfying. Lowell thought about writing a biography of Emily Dickinson, but Dickinson was a problematic precursor for women poets in the 1920s; although she was admired, she was seen as spinsterly, sexless, insufficiently engaged with passion.

In "The Sisters" (1925), Amy Lowell summed up this postwar sense of marginality and oddness: "Taking us by and large, we're a queer lot / We women who write poetry."

Considering Sappho's "leaping fire," and Barrett Browning's "stiff conventions," Lowell concluded that neither in their personal lives nor their careers did they offer a model for her:

> Goodbye, my sisters, all of you are great,
> And all of you are marvellously strange,
> And none of you has any word for me.

LYRIST—SARA TEASDALE

Sara Teasdale (1884–1933), who was older than most of the women poets of the 1920s, published her first book of poems, nine sonnets addressed to the actress Duse, in 1907, but she remained popular through the decade. Born in St. Louis to a wealthy family, Teasdale believed in the romantic feminine myth of love as woman's whole existence, and she could never allow herself to acknowledge a primary commitment to art, or sisterhood with other women artists. As she wrote to an admirer, "I don't *want* to be a literary woman." Indeed, she wanted to be a muse for men rather than a maker of poems: "Art can never mean to a woman what it does to a man. Love means that."[8] This conflict between her role as a poetess or "songstress," and her ambitions as an artist, created psychic problems for Teasdale; in 1908, she had a rest cure. Afterward, she expressed her conviction that "a woman ought not to write. Somehow it is indelicate and unbecoming. She ought to imitate the female birds, who are silent—or, if she sings, no one ought to hear her music until she is dead."[9]

Teasdale's many suitors adored her but sent double messages about her art. Vachel Lindsay urged her to write but as a mother: "The woman heart of America must needs sing itself . . . You ought to make yourself the little mother of the whole United States and especially the Middle

West."[10] Before their marriage in 1914, Teasdale's businessman husband
Ernst Filsinger wrote that "ever since I knew her she has put the duties of
true womanhood (motherhood and wifehood) above *any* art and would,
I believe, rather be the fond mother of a child than the author of the
most glorious poem in the language."[11] Teasdale worried that marriage
might make her so happy that she would lose her poetic drive, but in
fact she had married for security and convenience, and soon became
depressed and ill. In 1917, she had an abortion, unable to imagine maternity and poetic creativity as anything but antagonistic.

Gradually Teasdale retreated into isolation and psychosomatic illness,
as her poetry focused on themes of frustration and suffering. Having
made friends with Amy Lowell and Harriet Monroe, she contemplated
the new movements of modernism, free verse, and Imagism, and read
Eliot, Stevens, Joyce, and Pound, but she was uninterested in their experimentation. Yeats and Frost were much more appealing; she met Yeats in
1920 and always regarded him as the finest poet of the century. In the
1920s, she read and very much admired Virginia Woolf, whose literary
voice combined the lyric and feminine with modernist forms. She
formed a relationship with a younger woman, Margaret Conklin, and
divorced her husband in 1929. But changing her life did not renew her
art, and in 1933, she took a fatal overdose of sleeping pills.[12]

EGOISTE—ELINOR WYLIE

One strategy for women lyric poets of the 1920s was to attempt to reconcile femininity and art in celebrating the miniature and the decorative.
Elinor Wylie (1885–1928) specialized in images of whiteness, crystal, ice,
glass, silver, and jewels. In books such as *Nets to Catch the Wind* (1921), and
poems like "Silver Filigree," and in her essay "Jewelled Bindings" (1923),
Wylie gave her view of the lyric poem as a "small jeweled receptacle,"
associating the poetic stanza with the female body and, as Freud would
have interpreted the image, with female sexuality. "I love words opales-
cent, cool, and pearly," she wrote in the sonnet "Pretty Words." She
became famous for her silver gowns, which reminded Van Wyck Brooks
of "some creature living in an iridescent shell."[13]

This self-image, of course, also worked against her, since it connected
her to the tradition of miniature and minor women poets. In reality,
Wylie was a tough competitor and self-promoter ("unflinchingly ego-
iste," in Henry Canby's view), whose scandalous life, including adultery,
divorce, and desertion of her son, did not mesh well with her carefully

promoted public image, or the preciosity of her work.[14] Virginia Woolf
was deeply disappointed when she met Wylie in England in 1926: "I
expected a ravishing and diaphanous dragonfly . . . a siren, a green and
sweet-voiced nymph—that was what I expected, and came a tiptoe into
the room to find—a solid hunk; a hatchet-minded, cadaverous, acid
voiced, bareboned, spavined, patriotic, nasal, thick legged American. All
evening she proclaimed unimpeachable truths; and discussed our sales;
hers are 3 times better than mine, naturally."[15] Thomas Wolfe, who met
Wylie at a studio party in New York the following year, thought she was
"a horrible woman," although she "is all the go nowadays."[16]

Wylie published four books of poetry and four novels between 1921
and 1929. The poems—*Nets to Catch the Wind* (1921), *Black Armour* (1923),
Trivial Breath (1928), and *Angels and Earthly Creatures* (1929)—were more
medieval than modernist in their style, featuring what one critic called
"defenses in the form of wit, masks, and surfaces," techniques highly
valued by writers of the 1920s.[17] The sonnet sequence "Wild Peaches"
was a fantasy of escaping with a lover to a paradisal village on the Eastern Shore of Maryland where "the winter will be short, the summer
long." But Wylie, the descendant of New England Calvinists, prefers the
"look, austere, immaculate" of "bare hills, cold silver on a sky of slate."
Despite her lush surroundings, Wylie's narrator is discontented:

> *Down to the Puritan marrow of my bones,*
> *There's something in this richness that I hate.*

The poem is about Wylie's bleak internal landscape, and her attraction to brief moments of ecstasy and long periods of gloomy paralysis,
"sleepy winter, like the sleep of death." In this attraction to intensity
and surfaces, she was an aesthete, and her second marriage, to the
poet William Rose Benét, allowed her to indulge that side of her
talent. Her most interesting poems were the blunter ones that explored
her masochism, fear of aging, and horror of dependence. In "False
Prophet," the forty-year-old narrator tries to persuade herself that she
is too old to be attracted to a beautiful young man, who might have
been her son, but self-deceivingly declares that "he cannot hurt me
now." A sardonic self-portrait, "Portrait in Black Paint, With a Very Sparing Use of Whitewash" (which was published in *The New Yorker* in
1927, but not reprinted until after her death) mocked Wylie's fascination with stark contrast and turned her "tongue's sharp side" against

her own narcissism, romantic nostalgia, vanity, and selfishness: "She gives you friendship; but it's such a bother / You'd fancy influenza from another."

Originally intended to be anonymous, the poem was signed "E.W." and created quite a stir. Wylie wrote to Burton Rascoe, who guessed her identity, that "so many people are telling me that Bunny [Edmund Wilson] wrote the piece that I believe even Edith Wharton may be held responsible in some quarters."[18] In another uncollected *New Yorker* poem, "Anti-Feminist Song, for My Sister" (1929), Wylie wrote cynically about the pleasures of feminine romantic suffering: "It's more fun to be the victims / Than the bloody conquerors."[19]

FEMINIST—EDNA ST. VINCENT MILLAY

Edna St. Vincent Millay and Elinor Wylie were friends, but Millay forthrightly identified herself as a feminist from an early age, and consistently acted in solidarity with other women poets who might have been her rivals. In one famous incident in March 1927, Wylie and Millay were invited to be the honored guests at the Authors' Breakfast of the League of American Pen Women in Washington. At the last minute, Wylie was notified by one of the hostesses that she was unwelcome; the ladies of the LAPW had objected to Wylie's scandalous divorce. Millay immediately withdrew her own acceptance, declaring that "it is not in the power of an organization which has insulted Elinor Wylie to honor me."[20] For Wylie, however, the friendship always had a poisoned stream of rivalry. In 1925, she had stormed out of a room when someone called Millay the "greatest woman poet." "Everyone knows *I* am!" she angrily told her hostess.[21]

Few American readers would have agreed. Edna St. Vincent Millay (1892–1950) was widely regarded as "the Miss America of 1920," and remains the most gifted, hardworking, and important woman poet of the period, truly the "American Poetess Laureate."[22] Millay came from a Camden, Maine, family much like Louisa May Alcott's—an absent, improvident father; an industrious, beloved Marmee-like mother, Cora, who also wrote poetry, and had a rough edge and a bohemian streak; and two sisters, Norma and Kathleen. Edna, called "Vincent" by her sisters, was boyish, beautiful, and bisexual.

Millay was precocious in writing, sex, drinking, drugs, and politics. In her diary in 1912, she wrote about being trapped in the drudgery of a small-town life and also trapped by her sexuality: "I do not think there is a woman in whom the roots of passion shoot deeper than in me."[23] That year, her poem "Renascence" was published to wide acclaim, and various female mentors helped her prepare for admission to Vassar. Going to Vassar at the age of twenty-one was one of the few actions Millay ever took late. On the campus she was a star, seductress, and heartbreaker, whose bisexuality was well known; in the Village after graduation, she was a femme fatale who made conquests everywhere she went, and threw herself without reserve into risky relationships with men. Edmund Wilson and John Peale Bishop were among the hordes who "fell irretrievably in love with her," as Wilson recalled.[24] By 1920, Millay had her first abortion. By January 1921, when she left for Europe as a correspondent for *Vanity Fair*, she was already a celebrated poet.

The poems that made her famous offered a self-portrait of bohemian daring, sexual bravado, and defiance, even embrace, of emotional risk and social consequences, tempered by a vulnerability and tenderness that seemed to speak for women's silenced emotions and longings. Millay's poems showed women readers not how they felt, but how they wanted to feel—not the mysteries of female nature but its modern aspirations. In melancholy, world-weary sonnets like "What Lips My Lips Have Kissed," as well as her famous epigrams, "First Fig" and "Second Fig," Millay invented the image of the modern woman who is as open to sexual experiment and variety as a man, and as emotionally uninvolved, and yet saddened by the passage of time and the departure of unnamed young lovers.[25] This sonnet, memorized by thousands of women, was probably responsible for more seductions than bathtub gin.

Sandra Gilbert makes the persuasive case that Millay created the role of "Edna St. Vincent Millay," dressed for it, performed it, and finally was suffocated by it. Millay was "masquerading as a femme fatale," Gilbert argues, "in order to expose the artifice and absurdity of romance"; in her prose, written under the pseudonym "Nancy Boyd," she even made fun of her image as "Edna St. Vincent Millay," ethereal but steely girl poet.[26] Certainly Millay was in control of her image and chose her costumes, poses, and publicity to promote it. But were the poems also a pose? Was her melancholy another masquerade? She was skilled in a wide variety of verse forms, but was most celebrated and remembered for her sonnets. According to Gilbert, the sonnet (scorned by male modernists) "became a kind of archaic costume in which the rebellious poet sometimes seriously, sometimes parodically adorned herself to call attention to the antiquated garb of femininity."[27] But another critic of Millay, Deborah Fried, argues that her love sonnets were "an apt form in which to scrutinize the inherited stances of men toward women and poets toward their muses."[28] In the 1920s, Millay was also the heroine of the traditionalists, a poet who could do battle with modernism, and whose "work could serve as a rallying-point for the rejection of free verse, imagism, and Prufrockian envy."[29]

SOCIALIST—GENEVIEVE TAGGARD

When she first went to New York in the 1920s, Genevieve Taggard (1894–1948) idolized Millay from afar: "She's the only girl that's at all like us," she told a friend.[30] The most politically engaged of the women poets of the 1920s, Taggard was born on an apple farm in Waitsburg, Washington, and grew up in Hawaii, where her missionary parents built and ran a large multicultural school. She loved the easygoing Hawaiian society, "our garden of Eden, our newfoundland," with its mixture of "the Portuguese, the Filipinos, the Puerto Ricans, the Japanese, the Chinese, the Hawaiian Chinese and the hapa haoles."[31] When her father's health failed, the Taggards returned with difficulty to Waitsburg, which she found desolate. "I gave up the hope of finding girls for friends who were like Jo and Polly in Louisa May Alcott's books." Her classmates teased her about her clothes and her accent, and "whispered that [she] had lived in a grass hut with cannibals."[32] Taggard found the narrowness and prejudice of Waitsburg an instruction in what to "work against and what to work for."[33] In 1914, a scholarship allowed her to enroll at the University of California at Berkeley, where her mother ran a student boardinghouse to help pay her expenses, and she also received a small salary for editing the college literary magazine. It took her five years to graduate, and by then she thought of herself as a socialist.

She moved to Greenwich Village, and began to publish her poetry and enter enthusiastically into political life. Yet as much as she admired Millay's glamorous bohemianism, Taggard was a sexual conservative. Her first book, *For Eager Lovers* (1922), contained poems about love, courtship, and pregnancy. In her sonnet "Everyday Alchemy" she praised women who selflessly put men ahead of themselves: "Men go to women mutely for their peace; / And they, who lack it most, create it." Despite her socialist sympathies, moreover, in the 1920s Taggard insisted that dogma did not make good poetry. In her introduction to *May-Days* (1925), an anthology of poems from *The Masses,* she declared that "the artist's concern is not to persuade or educate, but to overpoweringly express."[34]

In 1921, she married another radical writer, Robert Wolf. Initially, the couple played at idyllic partnership.[35] But the idyll ended when Taggard became pregnant; the birth of daughter Marcia in December 1921 decimated the illusions of equality in the marriage. Wolf was writing a novel, and demanded that Taggard take full responsibility for child care while he devoted himself to art. They moved back to California, and Taggard took a teaching job at Mills College while Wolf moved into a cabin at Bolinas by himself. Meanwhile, Taggard discovered she was pregnant once again, and had an abortion in San Francisco.

The realities of marriage to a demanding and selfish man destroyed her illusions of romance, and the drudgery of housekeeping and motherhood changed her view of herself as a free woman. As she confessed to her close friend Josephine Herbst, "when you struggle for weeks with stoves and mud and diapers and canned food, and hardly have time to wash your face, your attitude to Robert as an artist, your attitude to yourself as an artist, changes. You have a wooden determination to be one, and an iron determination to make it possible for Bob, but all that grimness is a joke in the face of endless attempts to be practical."[36] In an anonymous autobiographical essay for *The Nation* in 1926, Taggard defended her choice to marry a demanding left-wing artist:

> *I think I have not been as wasted as my mother was—or as wasteful. I have made worse mistakes, which might have been more fatal than hers and yet have not been, at least for me. My chief improvement on her past was the man I chose to marry. I did not want a one-way street of a marriage, like hers. I married a poet and novelist, gifted and difficult, who refused defeat as often as I did. Hard as it is to live with an equal, it is at least not degrading. We have starved, too; struggled as hard as ever my folks did. But the struggle has not been empty; I have no grudges . . . Seven years with a real person is better than her thirty with a helpless, newspaper-reading gentleman.*[37]

But seven years with Robert Wolf took their toll, as I shall discuss in the next chapter.

PESSIMIST—DOROTHY PARKER

Dorothy Parker (1893–1967) was another admirer of Millay. "Like everybody else," she confessed to an interviewer, "I was following in the exquisite footsteps of Miss Millay, unhappily in my own horrible sneakers."[38] During the 1920s, she recalled, "we were all being dashing and gallant, declaring that we weren't virgins, whether we were or not."[39] (Parker was not.) She, too, became an iconic figure for other clever women: "All I wanted in the world," wrote Nora Ephron in 1976, "was to come to New York and be Dorothy Parker."[40] Behind the glamorous façade, though, Parker lived a tragic life.

Born in New Jersey to a Jewish father and raised by a Catholic step-mother, she regarded herself as a mongrel; "Mongrel" was to be the title of her often mentioned but never written autobiography. When her father died in 1913, she got a job at *Vogue* and then at *Vanity Fair*, and became a member of the notorious Algonquin Round Table of journalists and wits. In 1920, she and Robert Benchley were fired from *Vanity Fair*, and set up their own office as writers. But she had begun drinking hard and loving recklessly, and that year she had an abortion and made a failed attempt at suicide.

In her writing, Parker became famous for her wry joky tone about women living without joy or hope. Her semiautobiographical story "Big Blonde" won the O. Henry Prize in 1929. Hazel Morse, a dress model, a "good sport," gets divorced, starts to drink, and drifts from man to man. As in "Résumé," Parker captures Hazel's suicidal depression: "But how would you do it? It made her sick to think of jumping from heights. She could not stand a gun . . . There was no gas in her flat . . . a cut with razor blade, and there you'd be. But it would hurt, hurt like hell." She takes sleeping pills, but is mercilessly "rescued." At the end, praying to stay drunk, "there passed before her a slow, slow pageant of days spent lying in her flat, of evenings at Jimmy's being a good sport . . . she saw a long parade of weary horses and shivering beggars and all beaten, driven, stumbling things."[41]

In the 1930s, Parker went to Hollywood, where she had a period of fame and wealth, but her alcoholism and a wretched marriage contributed to severe writing blocks. She went to France to work on a novel, to be called "The Events Leading Up to the Tragedy"; but she never completed it. Her prayer at the time—"Dear God, please make me stop writing like a woman. For Jesus Christ's sake, amen."—may have had something to do with her inability to finish the book.[42] Parker's political activism has received much less attention than her lifestyle and personal misfortunes. She joined the Communist Party and was eventually blacklisted in Hollywood. In her will, however, she remained loyal to her beliefs in American equality, leaving her estate to Martin Luther King, Jr., and the NAACP.

CRITIC—LOUISE BOGAN

"Isn't it wonderful how the lady poets are coming along?" Millay exclaimed to Edmund Wilson with feminist delight after being "quite thrilled" with the work of Louise Bogan (1897–1970).[43] Bogan, however, chose to distance herself from the female tradition in poetry and what she saw as its intellectual slenderness and emotional excess. She refused to edit an anthology of women's poetry because "the thought of corresponding with a lot of female songbirds made me ill. It is hard enough to bear with my own lyric side."[44] In a review of Millay, she noted that "women who have produced an impressively bulky body of work are few." By her twenty-seventh birthday she was lamenting that she had not produced "fat works ranged on shelves," and confessed that she longed to write "fat words in fat poems." But she seemed able only to produce spare, chiseled, anorexic verse, poetry that made her feel barren and unfulfilled.[45]

An admirer of Auden and Yeats, Bogan was the purest intellectual of the women poets of her generation, a subtle, witty, piercingly honest poet who should be more widely known and read, and a brilliant essayist, literary critic, and letter writer. In the 1920s, Bogan wrote many reviews, mainly of women writers, in *The New Republic.* From 1931 until 1969, she was the poetry editor of *The New Yorker.* She also mentored a number of younger writers, including Theodore Roethke and William Maxwell, and taught at various universities, including New York University and the University of Washington. At the same time, she was a harsh and unforgiving critic of her own work, and as she grew older found it harder and harder to write poems. "Has there ever *been* an old lady poet?" she sadly inquired.[46] When the years of beauty, youth, libido, maternity were past, what was left to say?

Born in Maine, Bogan grew up in various mill towns in the Northeast, moving often with her parents and brother. Her early education at Boston Girls' Latin School, which she attended with the help of a benefactor, gave her a rigorous academic foundation; after her first year at Boston University in 1915–16, she was offered a scholarship to Radcliffe. Instead, she eloped with a German immigrant, Curt Alexander, who was serving in the U.S. Army, and she followed him to the Canal Zone, where their daughter, Maidie, was born in 1917. The couple separated soon after, and when Alexander died of pneumonia in 1920, Bogan received a small pension, which enabled her to move to Vienna for three years with her child, and begin to write. She returned to New York in 1923, and soon met other writers in the city's thriving literary community: William Carlos Williams, Marianne Moore, and, most important, Edmund Wilson, who became her early mentor. Wilson, already a writer and critic of reputation, urged her to write book reviews for periodicals, and this eventually became a steady source of income.

The 1920s and 1930s were Bogan's most productive poetic years; she published three volumes of poems, *Body of This Death* (1923), *Dark Summer* (1929), and *The Sleeping Fury* (1937), as well as a number of short stories. Nevertheless, she struggled with her self-doubt and self-hatred; her poem "Women" ascribed what she felt was her own timidity to women generally: "Women have no wilderness in them, / They are provident instead."

During these years, she also suffered two periods of writing block, depression, and psychiatric hospitalization, brought on in part by her paranoid fears of sexual betrayal. She wrote some of her finest poems about these episodes, but had to disguise them as private postscripts to letters or alleged "parodies"; their content was too bitter, intimate, and dark, their language too free and direct, for either the aesthetic twenties or the leftist thirties. During her first hospitalization in 1931, she wrote about the Neurological Institute in New York, where she had psychiatric and occupational therapy:

> *O, I shall mend! Even now I grow quite well,*
> *Knitting round wash-cloths on the paths of hell.*

In the 1960s, these subjects and tones would find their audience in the work of Robert Lowell, Anne Sexton, and Sylvia Plath. In the 1930s, Bogan resisted the pressures to conform to the proletarian mode of writing; she detested joiners. In her final book of poems, she published a defiant credo about poetic immortality, a defense of the mad and bad against the phony and genteel:

> *Come, drunks and drug-takers; come perverts unnerved!*
> *Receive the laurel, given, though late, on merit; to whom and*
> *wherever deserved.*

> *Parochial punks, trimmers, nice people, joiners true-blue,*
> *Get the hell out of the way of the laurel. It is deathless*
> *And it isn't for you.*[47]

Modernism and Feminism

The relationship between feminism and modernism had been antagonistic at the turn of the century, with feminism linked to Victorian aesthetic practices and modernism committed to the overthrow of all conventions and repressions. In recent cultural and critical studies, the connection between the two continues to be viewed as hostile. On one hand, Ann Douglas leads a contingent arguing that modernism was an admirable rebellion against everything American feminist reformers stood for—sentimentality, piety, racism, sexual repression, cliché. On the other hand, Sandra Gilbert and Susan Gubar maintain that modernism was a male war against women's rising power, fueled by misogyny, anxiety, and emotional repression.[48] A small number of women writers, like the poet Mina Loy (1882–1966), proclaimed themselves modernist revolutionaries in art; in her "Feminist Manifesto" (1914), inspired by the Italian Futurists, Loy called upon women to discard their illusions, abandon their old-fashioned morality, and embrace "Absolute Demolition" as their artistic credo: "there is no half-measure, no scratching on the surface of the rubbish heap of tradition."[49] But, like Gertrude Stein, Loy was an expatriate whose program had little impact on American women's writing. A much more typical attitude toward avant-garde experiment was expressed by the poet Lola Ridge (1873–1941), an immigrant anarchist who wrote passionately about radical politics, yet resigned from her position on the magazine *Broom* when the editor decided to publish Gertrude Stein. Stein's poetry, Ridge declared, "has only an occasional gleam . . . In a few years her work will be on the rubbish heap with the rest of the literary tinsel that has fluttered its little day."[50]

In the United States, bohemia and the culture of free love provided a middle ground of adventurous thinking, aesthetic tastes, and modern living, where heterodox women and modernist men could meet. As the journalist Dorothy Dunbar Bromley envisioned the "feminist—new style" in 1927, "she aspires to understand the meaning of the twentieth century as she sees it expressed in the skyscrapers, the rapid pace of city life, the expressionist drama, the abstract conception of art, the new music; the Joycean novel. She is acutely conscious that she is being carried along in the current of these sweeping forces, that she and her sex are in the vanguard of change."[51]

In 1927, however, a series of cultural, political, and legal events also made many women writers wonder if they were in the vanguard or simply swept away in the flood. On April 10, 1927, George Antheil's "Ballet Mécanique," which used the noise of real machines along with music and dance to represent modern life, had its New York premiere at Carnegie Hall. "Ten grand pianos stood in a great horseshoe led by one mechanical piano. Two great tables held mechanical devices to imitate factory whistles, roaring elevated trains, canning machinery . . . There were two airplane propellers, four bass drums, and eight xylophones."[52] Among the writers at the performance were Nella Larsen and Josephine Herbst, who described how "the sound stunned the senses . . . Titters broke out, followed by indignant hisses from the faithful. The performance closed to thunderous applause, boos, catcalls." No further production was attempted for sixty years. For Herbst, the cacophony seemed "no more than a hallelujah to the very forces I feared."[53] What did this worship of the machine mean for women? Was the experimental high art of modernism a celebration from which they would be excluded?

Sacco's Sisters

Five months after the Antheil premiere, on August 23, 1927, the anarchist immigrants Nicola Sacco and Bartolomeo Vanzetti were executed in Massachusetts. Herbst, along with Millay, Dorothy Parker, and Katherine Anne Porter, had participated in protests outside the prison where the men were being held after their conviction in July 1921 for the murder of two payroll guards in a robbery. "If these men are executed, justice is dead in Massachusetts," Millay declared. Outraged by the case, writers and artists were arrested in demonstrations that proved futile in stopping the execution, and Sacco and Vanzetti became the subjects of hundreds of American essays, songs, paintings, plays, and poems. Herbst placed their deaths alongside the Antheil concert as signaling the end of the twenties: "All I knew was that a conclusive event had happened. What it meant I couldn't have defined. Looking back . . . I might add explanations that would signify. But I don't want to do that. I want to try to keep it the way it was back there, on the early morning of August 23, 1927 . . . a kind of shuddering premonition of a world to come. But what it was to be we could never have foreseen."[54] As the trial and execution of John Brown in the nineteenth century had inspired women writers in the North, many women writers lost their faith in the promises of American democracy, believing that Sacco and Vanzetti were innocent martyrs, sacrificed to the anti-immigrant feeling and fear of radicals, the Red Scare, that swept the United States after the Bolshevik Revolution and that lingered through the twenties.[55]

Expressionism and Feminism

Expressionist theater and film in the 1920s made use of the techniques of avant-garde performance to represent modern urbanism and mechanization. In New York, plays by European forerunners of expressionism including Strindberg and Wedekind were produced alongside American plays by Eugene O'Neill and Elmer Rice. In these plays, "visual and emotional qualities often featured in elements of distortion, exaggeration, or suggestive symbolism, frequently achieving a dream-like or nightmarish quality to the action," and used sound effects, short cinematic scenes, and abstract characters. Sophie Treadwell (1885–1970), the most innovative and productive woman playwright of the decade, brought these techniques together in her astonishing play *Machinal* (1928), which also tried to create "a decidedly feminist aesthetic in the theatre."[56]

Treadwell was not at the Antheil premiere. In April and May, she was attending another emblematic cultural event of 1927, the trial of a Long Island housewife, Ruth Snyder, and her lover Judd Gray, for the murder of Snyder's husband. Snyder and Gray were convicted, and electrocuted at Sing Sing on January 12, 1928; it was the first execution of a woman in the twentieth century, and the case made headlines everywhere, especially since Snyder and her nine-year-old daughter had been beaten and abused by the murder victim. Treadwell had covered other murder trials of women as a reporter for newspapers in California and New York. In one article, she described the accused woman facing a juggernaut "coming towards her, silent, powerful, implacable," an account that her biographer Jerry Dickey interprets as suggesting "the crushing weight of an entire society whose masculine laws and orientations stifle the voices and emotional needs of women."[57]

In *Machinal,* Treadwell made the murderess Everywoman, driven to her fate by the combination of oppressive and destructive forces in her world. The heroine is called Young Woman, and signified "an ordinary young woman, any woman." Other characters are called Mother, Husband, or Doctor. *Machinal* was written in nine scenes representing "the different phases of life that the woman comes in contact with, and in none of which she finds any place, any peace": "To Business," set in a jangling office; "At Home," where she is bullied by her mother; "Honey-moon"; "Maternal"; "Prohibited," set in a speakeasy, where she meets a sexy adventurer (played by Clark Gable in the premiere); "Intimate"; "Domestic"; "The Law"; and "A Machine," in which she is being pre-pared to go to the electric chair. In her stage directions, Treadwell stressed the contrast between the feminine and the mechanical. "The woman is essentially soft, tender, and the life around her is essentially hard, mechanized. Business, home, marriage, having a child, seeking pleasure—all are difficult for her—mechanical, nerve-nagging." Tread-well also emphasized the "use of many different sounds chosen primar-ily for their inherent emotional effects (steel riveting, a priest chanting, a Negro singing, jazz band, etc.) but contributing also to the creation of a background, an atmosphere," and preventing the peace and harmony the Young Woman craves. Other sound effects in the play came from telegraph instruments, an airplane engine, office machines, and an elec-tric piano.

Machinal was enthusiastically received by the New York critics; *The New York Times* wrote that "in a hundred years it should still be vital and vivid."[58] Yet while they praised the play's fusion of expressionism and realism, critics did not respond to its feminism. Treadwell tried writing in other theatrical modes without much success, and her career stalled in the 1930s. Dickey concludes that "her themes, while never totally aban-doning her inquiries into gender inequities, lack the depth and insight of her earlier dramas."[59] A Russian friend, Alexander Koiransky, warned that she was too radical in both her politics and her experimentalism for the commercial theater: "Sometimes I think that there is in you a definite perversity," he wrote to her, "with which you insist upon bringing into your plays things and situations which make them unacceptable to the bosses of Broadway."[60]

Treadwell's own life had been adventurous and unsettled. She and her mother were abandoned by her Mexican-European father; she worked her way through Berkeley, did some acting, became a secretary-typist for the great Polish actress Helena Modjeska, and then, with her sports-writer husband, William O. McGeehan, moved to New York, where she became involved in suffrage activism. As a journalist, Treadwell was fear-less, traveling to Mexico to interview Pancho Villa; but she also suffered from episodes of anorexia so severe that she had to be hospitalized.

There were no children in the marriage; in 1949, when she was a widow and sixty-four years old, Treadwell adopted a German baby boy, and raised him, but at her death in Arizona in 1970, she left her entire estate to the Roman Catholic Diocese of Tucson. She had given up as a writer as well as a mother. The year before her death she wrote to her friend Gerald Brenan: "Why did I quit? Because I had nothing to say? No. I am bursting with things I long to say. Because of weariness? No. I am just quivering with energy (mental energy) . . . No. The reason was because I suddenly realized the devastating truth that I wasn't a good writer."[61] But Treadwell was rediscovered along with other American women writers in the recovery movement of the 1970s and 1980s, and *Machinal* has had numerous important revivals in the 1990s, beginning with the New York Shakespeare Festival in 1990 and the Royal National Theatre in London in 1993, with Fiona Shaw. In 2005, the Arena Stage theater in Washington, D.C., premiered her play *Intimations for Saxophone.*

Other American women playwrights managed to achieve commercial and critical success, and to come through with their literary confidence intact. Zoë Akins (1886–1958) had a long career as a playwright and screenwriter. Her Broadway hit, *Daddy's Gone A-Hunting* (1923), showed the effects of free love and broken families on women and children. Although the play was moralistic and melodramatic, it had an open ending, in which the heroine wonders what she will do next. Akins moved to Hollywood in 1928 and became a well-known screenwriter for such directors as Dorothy Arzner and George Cukor. Zona Gale (1874–1938), who became the first woman to win a Pulitzer Prize for drama in 1921, also experimented with open endings. She had attended the University of Wisconsin, worked as a reporter for the *New York Evening World,* joined Heterodoxy, and published several novels about Midwestern village life. In 1904, she moved back to Portage, Wisconsin, where she married, adopted a child, and remained until her death.[62] Gale was a central figure in mentoring and bringing together women writers of different races, ethnicities, and agendas. She came forward to write the introduction to Charlotte Perkins Gilman's autobiography, got it published, and made sure Gilman's family received royalties.

Gale's prizewinning play, *Miss Lulu Bett,* had first been a novel. Influenced both by Ibsen's *A Doll's House* and by American local-color fiction, the play dramatized the self-emancipation of Lulu, the unmarried maid-of-all-work living in her brother-in-law's house, who pathetically insists that she is "single from choice." In the novel, Lulu has a chance to escape through a risky marriage, but instead she goes off on her own like Nora: "I'm going I don't know where—to work at I don't know what. But I'm going from choice!"[63] In the 1920 stage version, this "open ending" was so controversial that Gale changed it, and had Lulu marry after all.[64] She defended her decision in a newspaper correspondence: "Why at this moment is the unmarried ending the artistic ending? . . . Why in *Miss Lulu Bett* is Lulu less artistic in marriage at the final curtain than in going off to work for herself?. . . Why is marriage inartistic? Thirty years ago the woman's declaration of independence would have been propaganda, fifty years from now it will be a common-place, to thousands of us it is a common-place now. Art is longer than this."[65] Nonetheless, the *New Republic* congratulated her on doing "what perhaps only a *feminist,* and certainly what an *artist* can do. She has shown, in perfect American terms, the serious comedy of emancipation."[66]

Women Novelists of the 1920s

THE HOME-MAKER—DOROTHY CANFIELD FISHER

The twentieth-century project to redefine housework as homemaking, and to emphasize technology, training, and professionalism, continued in the 1920s, and became part of the American "comedy of emancipation." The Institute for the Co-ordination of Women's Interests at Smith College attempted to find ways for women to share and streamline domestic chores. Yet even this program perpetuated the assumption that women had full responsibility for housework and child care. In "Why Women Fail" (1931), Lorine Pruette remarked sardonically that upon marrying, "men appear to lose a large part of their capacity as adults; they can no longer feed themselves, house themselves, look after their health, or attend to their social responsibilities . . . most of them upon marriage lose the capacity even of writing to their own mother."

Dorothy Canfield Fisher (1879–1958) tackled this paradox head-on in her novel *The Home-Maker* (1924), which imagined a realist, rather than a utopian, role reversal in the family. *The Home-Maker* was Fisher's finest novel, and the only one in which her interest in Freudian psychoanalysis, feminism, and the Montessori method of child-rearing united in a memorable whole. Although the content of the novel was contemporary and detailed, Fisher's narrative method was influenced by modernist fiction; she told the story from a different point of view in each chapter, getting into the minds of each member of the family, including the children. She had experimented with the technique in an earlier novel, *The Brimming Cup* (1921): "Each chapter is meant to be a revelation of what lies under the surface of that particular character. I have tried to make a glass door through which the reader looks into the heart and mind of another . . . so that, once for all, he knows what sort of human being is there."[67]

The Home-Maker is the story of the Knapp family—Evangeline, Lester, and their three children Helen, Henry, and Stephen—whose lives are being destroyed by the pressures of proper male and female behavior. Lester, by nature a poet and intellectual, detests his job as department store manager, feels like a slave to the clock, and misses spending time with his children. The energetic Evangeline has become a neurotic and hysterical housewife, endlessly cleaning, suffering from eczema, and scolding the children into fits of vomiting, rage, and terror. "What was her life? A hateful round of housework, which, hurry as she might, was never done. How she *loathed* housework! The sight of a dishpan full of dishes made her feel like screaming. And what else did she have? Loneliness; never-ending monotony; blank gray days, one after another full of drudgery."

When Lester is fired from his job, he attempts suicide so that the family can have his life insurance, but his leap from an icy roof leaves him alive and paralyzed. Fisher traces with restraint the unexpectedly positive effects of this accident on their lives. Evangeline takes over her husband's job at the department store, and flourishes as a sales executive. From his wheelchair, Lester takes over the housekeeping, and slowly gets to know his children; they all bloom in the new atmosphere of relaxation and fulfillment. Inevitably, the idyll faces a crisis when both partners separately realize that Lester's paralysis is psychological rather than organic. If he is "cured," they must return to the soul-destroying roles of their former life; neither has the independence of mind to challenge conventions. In the end, the Knapps are rescued from their agony by a wise family doctor, who gives his judgment: "It would be very dangerous for Mr. Knapp ever to use his legs." One critic, Dorothy Goldman, notes that "a conspiracy of lies between husband, wife, and doctor preserves the happiness of the family but at the cost of self-respect and personal integrity."[68] Within the realistic frame of the novel, however, this is the only possible ending, and a metaphor for Fisher's grim belief that one partner in a marriage had to be crippled if the partnership was to work.

Named after Dorothea Brooke in Eliot's *Middlemarch*, Dorothy Canfield Fisher was the author of ten novels, more than a hundred short stories, several books for children, and many articles.[69] She grew up in an academic and artistic family. Her mother was an artist who took her on tours to Paris and Madrid; her father, James Hulme Canfield, became chancellor at the University of Nebraska in Lincoln when she was twelve. Later she confided to Pearl Buck that "the particular shadow which darkened my adolescent years was a complete lack of harmony between my father and mother."[70] At Nebraska, she came to know Willa Cather, her brother's classmate, who remained a lifelong friend. In 1893–94, they collaborated on a ghost story about a football game.[71] When her father became the chief librarian at Columbia University, Canfield moved there and earned a Ph.D. in French. Instead of teaching, she began to write short stories that she signed "Stanley Crenshawe." But in 1907, she married M. John Fisher, a former captain of the Columbia football team, and they settled in Arlington, Vermont. Dorothy Fisher saw the small town as the site of Ibsenesque and Chekhovian tragedy, as well as New England regionalism, and began a series of stories about "Hillsboro' people" based on the Vermont villagers. In 1912, with profits from her first novel, *The Squirrel Cage,* she took a trip to Rome and was won over by the Montessori system of early childhood education. It became the basis for two more novels, *The Bent Twig* (1915), a sentimental story of a girl's coming-of-age, and a popular children's book, *Understood Betsy* (1917).

During the war, John Fisher volunteered to serve in the American Ambulance Hospital at Neuilly, and Dorothy decided to accompany him to Paris with their two children. While working for the Red Cross, she sent back articles about French life to American magazines. Collected as *Home Fires in France* (1918), the book went through six printings, and was praised by Yale professor William Lyon Phelps: "I have read many books from Europe during the great war," he wrote to her, "but nothing so good as yours."[72] After the war, however, when they returned to Vermont, John could not find employment, and she became the family breadwinner. The adjustment was not easy; he had a number of illnesses and accidents, ran unsuccessfully for the state legislature, and had to watch his best friend, Alfred Harcourt, establish a profitable New York publishing company while he was a Vermont househusband. If John Fisher was the model for Lester Knapp, the Fishers never admitted it. But *The Home-Maker* was almost the only novel of the period to tackle the psychology and the stigma of role reversal, and the extremes by which it had to be justified.

SWEATSHOP CINDERELLA—ANZIA YEZIERSKA

In 1931, Anzia Yezierska (1881–1970) arrived at Fisher's door in Vermont, "weeping and distraught, to try to live here—and I think to get some new materials to write about." Fisher helped her to rent a farmhouse, furnish it, and get food in. Not surprisingly, Yezierska was no more at home in Vermont than in other places she had fled. She loudly lamented that "the ghetto was with me wherever I went." Fisher saw that "her efforts to get in touch with the Vermonters of Arlington, their efforts to understand her enough to help her—all proved futile. The enormous psychological differences between them were impassable." Fisher advised Yezierska to tone down the sexual details about Vermont in her book *All I Could Never Be* (1932), to which she responded that "a Russian Jewess could never achieve the heroic power of restraint of an Emily Dickinson."[73]

Yezierska's family had emigrated from Ukraine to the Lower East Side in the 1890s, and she had displayed heroic power in fighting her way out of patriarchy and poverty to become acclaimed as a novelist of the immigrant experience. Yezierska's own daughter, however, was the first to acknowledge that she had embellished and exaggerated a life story that was already vivid and dramatic. Truly needy as a girl, she became a lifelong, relentless, and shameless user of people, a schnorrer and a leech. She attached herself sequentially to a number of powerful American women writers, always presenting herself as a grateful and adoring disciple, while she was milking them for blurbs, boosts, and patronage. To Mary Austin she wrote, "The longing for friendship—for the stimulus of intellectual association which I had to choke in me—you have roused in me again. I walked away from you weeping. It was the first time an American woman spread for me a table in the wilderness and filled my cup with all she . . . had." To Amy Lowell, she wrote begging for friendship and "an interpretive review . . . for the Times." (Lowell sent regrets through her secretary.)[74] To Zona Gale, she expressed undying gratitude for being "the rock of refuge in the wilderness to whom the lost one [*sic*] from all the corners of the earth crowd for shelter."[75] In 1930, Gale arranged for her to have a fellowship at the University of Wisconsin; overwhelmed, she wrote, "Zona—dearest friend—this moment—I feel closer to you than to any human being I have ever known." Wisconsin, though, was not a place where Yezierska could be happy; she quarreled with Gale, had a breakdown and was hospitalized, and after that, made her way to Vermont. Overall, Yezierska was not an easy person to get along with, either for other writers or for her patient editors. Her own story was nonetheless remarkable, and her fiction uneven but gripping.

The youngest of thirteen children, she left home at seventeen, worked in sweatshops and laundries, and in 1901 won a scholarship to the Domestic Science Department of Columbia Teachers College, itself a product of the homemaking reform movement. Ironically for Yezierska, who grew up eating coarse Russian black bread, spicy herring, and sour pickles, Domestic Science specialized in the most flavorless, inauthentic WASP cuisine imaginable. It trained students in "scientific cookery" that would "transubstantiate food . . . blanket it with whipped cream and candied violets. Containing and controlling food, draining it of taste and texture, packaging it, . . . decorating it—these were some of the culinary themes of the domestic science movement."[76] The most important ingredient of the program was "white sauce"—a metaphor for assimilation into white Protestant America.

After her graduation, she had two brief marriages to Jewish men, and gave birth to her daughter Louise, but like Gilman, she was unable to endure the intimacy of marriage, and left the child with her second husband while she began to write. At the age of thirty-five, she returned to study at Columbia Teachers College, and began an affair with the sixty-year-old married educational theorist John Dewey. He gave her her first typewriter.[77] Dewey, himself repressed, cerebral, and very Protestant, was exhilarated by his encounter with a sensual younger woman, and wrote his own secret love poems about their affair. Yezierska, however, "put her emotional life—in particular, her love for Dewey—at the center of her work." He wrote about "Generations of stifled words reaching out / Through you"; she wrote "I am a Russian Jewess, a flame—a longing! I am the ache of unvoiced dreams, the clamor of suppressed desires."[78]

Dewey broke off the affair in 1918, when he traveled to China, but Yezierska revisited the plot of a passionate immigrant girl falling in love with a reserved academic throughout her entire career.[79] Several of the short stories in her first book, *Hungry Hearts* (1920), were variants on this theme. In "Wings," John Barnes, writing a thesis on "Educational Problems of the Russian Jews," meets Shenah Pessah, who is reading Olive Schreiner's *Dreams* (1890). Her own dream is to be worthy of him: "You got to work not with the strength of one body and one brain, but with the strength of a millions bodies and million brains. By day and night, you got to push, push yourself up till you get to him and can look him in his face eye to eye." In "The Miracle," Sara Reisel's English teacher tells her, "You are the promise of the centuries to come. You are the heart, the creative pulse of America to be," and begs her to "free me from the bondage of age-long repressions . . . lift me out of the dead grooves of sterile intellectuality. Without you I am the dry dust of hopes unrealized." Yezierska also drew on her romance with Dewey in her first novel, *Salome of the Tenements* (1923), the fictionalized story of Rose Pastor (1879–1933), another Russian immigrant, socialist, and writer-activist, who in 1905 married the Ivy League and Social Register millionaire James Graham Phelps Stokes (1872–1960). Yezierska believed her friend's fairy-tale wedding united two worlds and signaled a new era; but the novel portrays a failed romance between the immigrant Sonya Vrunsky and the aristocrat John Manning, foreshadowing the Stokeses' very public divorce in 1925. In *Arrogant Beggar* (1927), the characters are called Adele Lindner and Arthur Hellman; in *All I Could Never Be,* they are called Fanya Ivanova and Henry Scott, but they are always the same flaming radical immigrant and cool WASP intellectual.

In 1927, Yezierska forced a final meeting with Dewey, by then a widower, at his office; but he arrived late, took a phone call, and gave her time to see that the pages of his copy of *Hungry Hearts* were uncut. That year, in "Wild Winter Love" (1927), Yezierska told the story of Ruth Raefsky, who desperately wants to be a writer but is misunderstood by her husband. "Wild Winter Love" reflected both Yezierska's creative talent and her enthrallment to a narrowing vision of personal and aesthetic liberation. "This is a story with an unhappy ending," it begins. "And I too have become Americanized enough to be terrified of unhappy endings." Like the title, this phrasing echoes Fitzgerald in *The Great Gatsby,* a story of fatal American dreams and fantasies of self-creation, but told through a woman. Ruth is consumed by her need to write, and after she publishes her book, *Out of the Ghetto,* and is hailed as the "New Voice of the East Side," she believes she can fulfill herself in a "wild winter love" for a gentile lawyer. To Ruth, this is more than a love affair; it is a mystical union of opposites and enemies, an American transcendence of prejudice and bigotry through love that will release her imagination from its bonds. "These centuries of antagonism between his race and mine," she tells the narrator, "have burst out in us into this transcendent love." Ruth leaves her husband and children, but the lawyer abandons her to return to his milieu, and she kills herself by jumping off a bridge, leaping "into the gulf that she could not bridge."

So, too, Yezierska alternated between her desperation to escape Jewish culture and the Lower East Side, and her comprehension that these were the true sources of her writing. *Hungry Hearts* changed her fortunes. Samuel Goldwyn bought it for the movies and brought her to Hollywood to work on the script. The tabloids and magazines publicized her as the "Sweatshop Cinderella" who had gone from rags to riches. She used some of her money to travel abroad, visiting London and Paris, where she met Gertrude Stein, "a very nice big cow." But she also realized, as she wrote in "This Is What $10,000 Did to Me," that "you can't be an immigrant twice."[80] Throughout the 1930s, she had trouble getting published, and worked for the WPA Federal Writers' Project. In 1950, W. H. Auden wrote an introduction to her last book, *Red Ribbon on a White Horse,* although she insisted that he make so many revisions that she finally alienated him as well.

As with so many American women writers, Yezierska's work fell into oblivion, although her novel *Bread Givers* (1925), based on her own family, was among those rediscovered and reprinted during the feminist recovery movement of the 1970s. Why did she fall out of favor with readers? One critic argues that her decline was the product of her own narrow obsession, "America's response to a writer whose sole subject was the immigrant and whose single theme was the immigrant's passionate desire to find her place in the New World."[81] Another blames American anti-Semitism, which increased during the Depression. "Like a shooting star, Yezierska's public life was brilliant and brief."[82] Yezierska's problems were only partly about her society, and much more about her internal divisions, her wish for independence and her exploitation of victimhood, her anger at the environment of wealth, privilege, and class status that oppressed all immigrants, and her unexamined fatal attraction to its white-sauced splendor. Indeed, Yezierska was exploring the "passing" plot that also troubled, haunted, and compelled black women writers in Harlem in the 1920s, writers she never met.

Women Novelists in the Harlem Renaissance

The masquerades of Millay's poetry and persona, and the fantasy union of different classes and religions that obsessed Yezierska, also showed up in the fiction of two important novelists of the Harlem Renaissance, Jessie Fauset and Nella Larsen, caught up in what Cheryl Wall calls the "self-destructive masquerade of passing."[83] Both novelists included minor characters who were Jewish, suggesting that they understood the parallels in immigrant culture. Both came from unusual backgrounds. Jessie Redmon Fauset (1882–1961) was born in Philadelphia, the daughter of an African Methodist Episcopal minister. She applied to Bryn Mawr, and would have attended at the same time as H.D. and Marianne Moore if she had been accepted, but racial discrimination kept her out. Instead she graduated Phi Beta Kappa from Cornell in 1905, received an M.A. in French from the University of Pennsylvania, and studied at the Sorbonne. From 1919 to 1926, Fauset was the literary editor of the NAACP journal *The Crisis*.

A Harlem modernist and intellectual, Fauset had an education that set her apart from the black mainstream, while her race separated her from white women writers of the period. She served as the hostess or *salonnière* for the black intelligentsia; Langston Hughes described her parties, in which literary conversation took place in French. But her male guests also mocked her novels as "vapidly genteel lace-curtain romances."[84] Claude McKay, who wrote *Home to Harlem* (1928), one of the sensational best sellers about the Harlem cabaret world, called her books "fastidious and precious," although he praised her for being "as prim and dainty as a primrose."

To be sure, "dainty" was one of Fauset's favorite words, implying an immaculate and pristine feminine sexuality. Nonetheless, in her novels she often referred parenthetically to the covert labors of skin care, dressmaking, laundry, and especially hairdressing necessary to maintain the polished appearance of fashionable beauty she admired in black women. Although Fauset touched boldly on some of the sexual topics that engaged women in the 1920s, her discomfort with the work of staying dainty kept her from writing with the passion of Yezierska, Millay, or Larsen.

Fauset's four novels examined sophisticated black women like herself, who struggle with their identities and the destiny of their "blood." They often include stories of passing. Unlike Kate Chopin or Grace King, however, who dramatized the tragic possibility of a light-skinned mother bearing a black child, or that child's discovery of her racial lineage, Fauset was more concerned with issues of ethics, guilt, betrayal, and snobbery. Her first novel, *There Is Confusion* (1924), was rejected by several publishers because it contained "no description of Harlem dives, no race riot, no picturesque abject poverty." As she protested, many publishers were only interested in black primitivism and exoticism, "and if an author presents a variant they fear that the public either won't believe in it or won't stand for it." Her portraits of affluent and fashionable black life had no ready-made audience; "white readers," her publishers complained, "just don't expect Negroes to be like this."[85]

Plum Bun: A Novel Without a Moral (1929) contrasted two sisters, the light-skinned Angela, who passes as white, and the dark-skinned Virginia; each represents a side of Fauset's identity. Through Ginny, she satirized the intellectual world of the Harlem Renaissance and its male idols. Through the gifted artist Angela, she showed the subversion of female talent by myths of romance, domesticity, and racial conformity. Fauset took her provocative title from the nursery rhyme that also forms the sections of the book:

> *To market, to market,*
> *To buy a plum bun,*
> *Home again, home again,*
> *Market is done.*

Originally she had more bluntly called the novel "The Market," referring to the marriage market and the sex market as well as the art market. The subtitle, "A Novel Without a Moral," is equally daring. Angela's passing is an act that requires her to deny and betray her own sister, lie to all her friends, and act in bad faith with regard to urban prejudice and snobbery. In Fauset's romantic comedy, though, she is not severely punished, but rather rewarded with a fairy-tale happy ending—love, marriage, and art. Fauset takes up large questions of social responsibility among a privileged generation of black Americans, but ultimately treats it inconsequentially.

Fauset was one of the first women novelists to make use of the movies as emblems of the American dream. Newly arrived in New York, Angela spends most of her time at the movies, "studying the screen with a strained and ardent intensity," following the adventures of "these shadowy heroes and heroines." Here she begins to dream that the fantasy life of Hollywood could be a life of her own. Like Virginia Woolf in *Mrs. Dalloway* (1925), Fauset also used cinematic techniques in her fiction, adopting the sweeping perspective of the camera to represent life in Manhattan and Harlem.

One of the themes of her "passing" plot is the conflict between femininity and creativity. Like Phelps's protagonist in *The Story of Avis*, Angela aspires to create a great painting about the streets of Harlem and the souls of its people, but this ambition is in direct conflict with her belief, learned from her mother, that a woman's highest ambition is devotion to her husband and family. Fauset also conducts a sustained critique of the Harlem Renaissance itself, its pretensions, bohemian lifestyle, and aesthetic strictures. Angela attends a lecture by the great black seer Van Meier, a fictional version of W. E. B. DuBois, who preaches to an audience of "the most advanced coloured Americans" urging "the deliberate introduction of beauty and pleasure into the difficult life of the American Negro." She is also troubled by the example of her friend Rachel Salter, an aspiring Jewish art student who speaks easily of "psychiatry, housing problems, Zionism, child welfare," but whose Orthodox parents object to her marriage to a Catholic, and who is horrified by the idea of racial intermarriage.

In her third novel, *The Chinaberry Tree, A Novel of American Life* (1931), Fauset wrote about middle-class black people in Red Hook, New Jersey, for whom race is a given and to whom prejudice is distant and remote.[86] A woman from this community, Sarah Strange, has had an affair with a white man, Colonel Halloway (another echo of Woolf's Richard Dalloway), who loved and supported her and her daughter Laurentine, but could not defy prejudice to marry her. The Strange legacy of "bad blood" haunts Red Hook as if it were a gothic Southern town out of Tennessee Williams, and while Laurentine and her cousin Melissa try to escape their fate by staying dainty and sitting under the chinaberry tree, the Fates pursue them, especially Melissa, who nearly marries her half brother Mallory. In this novel Fauset uneasily melded Greek myth with the light tone of Scott Fitzgerald describing his Southern belles. Again, she could not quite rise to the heights of her subject matter, and resolved difficult problems with melodrama and romantic comedy. Zona Gale wrote the introduction to *The Chinaberry Tree*. The characters, Fauset explained to her, "don't begin to measure up to the capable and efficient colored women you've been meeting at conventions." And therefore no one wanted to publish the book: "The joke of it is that the people in my story . . . are just decent ambitious folks with sensibilities. Yes—their like is unknown." Gale picked up on this in her introduction, writing that these characters, "quite unconnected with white folk . . . carry on their lives as . . . if there were no white people in America save those who serve them in shops and traffic."[87]

Among the reasons for Fauset's decline and her unpopularity with the Harlem literati were her friendships with white women writers and her general sympathy for feminist concerns, at a time when neither were acceptable among the Harlem group. In 1925, after a trip to Algiers, Fauset told a terrible story about the Arab women of the Kasbah, sitting on the floor in a dark room, hidden from the eyes of men, "their backs . . . against the wall . . . their hands in their laps. They sit thus, listless, doing nothing, absolutely nothing; life slips by."[88] Read today, these observations testify to Fauset's range and her ability to think beyond the immediate issues of race. But in the 1920s, the Harlem Renaissance had more urgent priorities. Once hailed as the most productive novelist of the Harlem Renaissance, Cheryl Wall concludes, Fauset became "the least respected."[89]

Nella Larsen

Nella Larsen (1891–1964) has been called "the mystery woman of the Harlem Renaissance," and her life is one of the most complex and enigmatic in the history of American women writers.[90] Larsen's mother was a Danish immigrant, her father a black seaman from the Dutch West Indies, and her racial identification has divided and troubled critics. Was she a tragic mulatto, between two races? Was she mistakenly cut off from her black sisters and brothers in embracing the interracial bohemian life of Harlem and Greenwich Village? Was her fascination with racial passing only a mask for her deeper anxieties about heterosexual passing? Or was she a pioneer who crossed and recrossed the color line, and transcended racial identity when this was still an avant-garde choice in the United States, where it remains controversial? And finally, how do all these questions impinge on her writing?

The most complete answers to the puzzles of Larsen's biography have been supplied by George Hutchinson, in his groundbreaking book *In Search of Nella Larsen,* which produced new evidence about her life and new readings of her work.[91] Hutchinson takes issue both with traditional critics who ignored or denigrated Larsen's writing and with feminist critics who rediscovered her in the 1970s, but reinterpreted her writing to conform with contemporary models of black sisterhood, racial identity, and female sexuality, and forced her into a matrilineal line of descent from black foremothers. In Hutchinson's view, Larsen was critically and socially damned by having the "wrong mother." If she had been the child of a black mother and a white father, like Grace King's little convent girl, she would have found a secure culture and identity. But her love for her mother, who is an enemy, a member of the ruling elite, put her at odds with her "rightful" community—that is, the black community—while her efforts to be part of white European culture or bohemia were doomed by racism. "By the time Larsen's life came to seem worth investigating in depth," Hutchinson charges, "much of what she had said about herself—much, in fact, that she had experienced— seemed out of place. Feminist critics tended to explain it with compassionate condescension for a lost sister who was to be forgiven for her statements and embraced by the racial family she always needed."[92]

Born in Chicago, Larsen took a long childhood trip to Copenhagen with her mother and stepsister Annie. When she turned sixteen, however, her white stepfather insisted that she be educated away from their Chicago home, at all-black Fisk University in Nashville. Fisk, the home of the celebrated Jubilee Singers, was devoted to "the elevation and advancement of the race" and especially the "intelligence, frugality, virtue, and noble aspirations of its women."[93] Although she found comfort in the secluded and sheltered black environment, and took advantage of the courses, Larsen was frustrated by the strict rules for girls, especially involving dress. She was expelled after only a year.

At this point, she decided to return to Copenhagen. Although she always described her period in Denmark in job and fellowship applications, biographers before Hutchinson were unable to confirm her travel, and even suggested that she had fantasized it. But we now know that she lived in Askov, Jutland, from 1909 to 1910, returned home for a visit, and then went back to Copenhagen until 1912, auditing courses at the university. Many details in the plot of her first novel, *Quicksand* (1928), were drawn from this experience.

The Scandinavian trips, along with a later residence in Spain and France, connected Larsen to other American expatriates, New Women, and bohemians. She became devoted to Ibsen and also to fin de siècle French literature, aestheticism, and decadence. Yet Larsen did not start out as an artist herself; indeed, throughout her life she vacillated between the pleasures of writing and the duties of more socially useful careers. She trained first as a nurse in New York, and spent a year from 1915 to 1916 at the John A. Andrews Memorial Hospital at Tuskegee Institute in Alabama. Like Fisk, Tuskegee had been established on the principles of racial uplift advanced by its founder, Booker T. Washington, and Larsen was not temperamentally disposed to be redeemed and rescued. "Uplift" is always a term of scorn in her novels. Women were to be trained for service and decorum. Again, Larsen rebelled, and was dismissed after a year. After three years nursing in New York at Lincoln Hospital, where nurses were desperately needed because of the war and influenza epidemic, she met her future husband, Dr. Elmer Imes, the second black Ph.D. in physics in the United States. The descendant of a prominent black Southern family with connections to Fisk, Imes was Larsen's intellectual equal and supporter, her introduction to the black elite. Their marriage and move to Harlem in 1921 seemed to augur perfect happiness.

Larsen sent Gertrude Stein a copy of her first novel, *Quicksand,* with a note praising "Melanctha" as a "truly great story" and wondering "just why you and not one of us should so accurately have caught the spirit of this race of mine."[94] An epigraph from Langston Hughes's "Cross" signals Larsen's theme of the mixed-race woman who has no stable identity. The novel's heroine, Helga Crane, is the daughter of a Danish mother and a black father who abandoned the family. Her mother remarried a white man unkind to Helga, and then died; her maternal uncle Peter is the only member of the family to whom she can turn for financial help. Helga starts out as a very young instructor at Naxos, the proper, highly regimented Southern college for Negro uplift, but walks out in the middle of a term. She gets to Harlem as the companion of Anne Grey, a wealthy black society woman, but tires of Anne's obsession with race and the "constant prattling of the incongruities, the injustices, the stupidities, the viciousness of white people." She goes to visit her relatives in Copenhagen, where she is feted, pampered, and courted by artists and intellectuals, but she longs to be among black people. Returning to Harlem, she is almost drawn into an affair with Anne's husband, and begins to hate herself. Whenever she decides to leave a place, she expects people to plead with her to stay.

Indeed, Helga is happy nowhere, self-centered everywhere, immature, impulsive, and restless. While the novel is usually read as a tragedy of racial displacement, Helga is difficult to like, and Larsen seems to be satirizing and criticizing her throughout for her serial convictions "that she had, as she put it, 'found herself.' " An aesthete, Orientalist, and avid consumer of luxury goods, Helga is happiest when she is admiring her own elegant feet in their exquisite shoes, shopping for exotic clothes, and staying in other people's expensive houses. Although she mocks Anne's campaigns for racial equality, she is acutely aware of skin color; Larsen makes this racial awareness aesthetic by using an enormous variety of terms to describe it—saffron, ebony, lemon, bronze, mahogany, copper, taupe. Helga's emotions are easily triggered by sentimental associations; she decides to leave Copenhagen after hearing Dvořák's New World Symphony and getting teary-eyed over black spirituals.

Larsen several times calls Helga "hysterical," and there is definitely an element of hysterical sexual repression in her behavior, especially in the conclusion to the book. Anxious about her mother's example, repeatedly warned by friends and relatives to keep above scandal, pursued by men toward whom she feels no attraction, Helga is tormented by spasms of feeling she does not understand. Back in Harlem after her sojourn abroad, she is kissed by Anne's husband and feels sexual desire for the first time: "a long-hidden half-understood desire welled up in her with the suddenness of a dream." That night she has "riotous and colorful dreams"; afterward she wanders the Harlem streets, increasingly panicked and desperate; and ends up in a storefront church where an evangelical service is going on. Listening to the congregation singing and chanting, she is overcome: "She felt an echo of the weird orgy resound in her own heart; she felt herself possessed by the same madness; she too felt a brutal desire to shout and sling herself about."

Caught up in the mass hysteria of the revival meeting, believing herself "saved," Helga impulsively marries the preacher, Reverend Mr. Pleasant Green, and goes to live with him in his home parish in Alabama. He is fat, dirty, and ignorant, but perhaps because he is so utterly outside the cultivated world she has known, she is able to release her sexuality in his embrace: "Emotional, palpitating, amorous, all that was living in her sprang like rank weeds at the tingling thought of night, with a vitality so strong that it devoured all shoots of reason." But even this release is quickly over. Worn out by childbirth and poverty, Helga comes to her senses and thinks once more of running away when her fourth baby dies; but in the novel's chilling last line, "hardly had she left her bed and become able to walk again without pain . . . when she began to have her fifth child." Once she steps into the quicksand of desire, she cannot pull herself out.

As Cheryl Wall points out, in Larsen's second novel, *Passing* (1929), "passing," like "quicksand," is "a metaphor of death and desperation, and it is similarly supported by images of asphyxiation, suffocation, and claustrophobia."95 Two childhood friends, Irene Redfield and Clare Kendry, meet again as married women in Chicago. Clare is wed to a rich and racist businessman, has sent her only child to boarding school in Europe, and is passing as a white society lady. Irene is happily married to a prosperous black doctor, and has two sons. Nevertheless, for mysterious reasons, Irene is discontented, filled with vague longings, envious of the confident and exquisite Clare but also contemptuous of her, and tormented by the notion that Clare is after her husband. Throughout the novel, Larsen hints that "race" may actually be a false category and a construct, and that people may need to define their own identities. Gossiping with her friends, Irene hears about Claude Jones, a black boy from their old neighborhood, who has converted to Judaism, "won't eat ham and goes to the synagogue on Saturday . . . he's really too funny for words." "He might possibly be sincere in changing his religion," Irene objects. But this is a subversive idea in the novel's strict binary arithmetic. One must choose to be either an individual, and damned, or part of a community, and stifled—"a person or the race." For Larsen, either choice led to guilt and punishment: Clare dies, but Irene has a psychic collapse.

In 1930, Larsen's marriage broke up when she discovered that her husband was having an affair with a white woman, as if the plot of *Passing* had come true. Having received a Guggenheim Fellowship for creative writing, the first African-American woman to do so, she spent several months in Spain and France, where she worked on a new novel about "the different effects of Europe and the United States on the intellectual and physical freedom of the Negro." This book, "Fall Fever," was never published and even the manuscript has disappeared. In 1930, in fact, Larsen's literary career came to an abrupt end when she was accused of plagiarizing a short story, "Sanctuary" (published in January in *Forum*), from one by the English writer Sheila Kaye-Smith, but transposing the story to the South with black characters. The editors of *Forum* supported her, calling the close similarity of the stories in theme and language an "extraordinary coincidence," and Larsen denied the charges; but all of her biographers concede that, for whatever reasons, she had decided to commit "literary suicide."96 Wall offers the most insightful account of the scandal as the acting out or surfacing of Larsen's questioning of the meaning of racial difference and racial artistic tradition: "Examining the intersection of race, class, and gender was a perilous business . . . Ambiguity may be a mark of complexity and sophistication in modern literature, but a black writer whose political commitment is not patently clear is suspected of ideological confusion at best, evasion and cowardice at worst. Nella Larsen has been charged with all of these."[97]

After her divorce in 1933, Larsen never published anything again, and she gradually disappeared from the literary scene, working as a nursing supervisor under the name of "Mrs. Nella L. Imes." When her body was discovered in her apartment in March 1964, she had been dead for several days. As with so many other American women writers of the 1920s, what had seemed like fertile soil for a rich artistic career ended in barren ground.

By the end of the decade, psychologists and sociologists had begun to ask what was happening to modern women, and why they were "failing" in combining marriage, motherhood, and work. Elizabeth Ammons attributes the failures to the absence of feminism:

> No one factor accounts for the relative decline in literary production by women after the 1920s, with women writers as a group not emerging in force again until the late 1960s and early 1970s. Certainly a major contributing factor, however, was the subsidence in widespread women's movements following the First World War and the accompanying resurgence in conservative ideologies about women. One thing that the vitality and brilliance of women's literary production at the turn of the century seems to illustrate is the crucial connection between political agitation and empowerment and art.[98]

But Lorine Pruette, a psychologist who wrote an autobiographical essay called "The Evolution of Disenchantment" for a symposium in *The Nation* in 1926–27 about the problems of feminism, felt otherwise. "I have at a comparatively early age," she wrote, "lost all my motivating faiths, faith in the righteous cause of women, faith in the recreating powers of science, faith in the ennobling possibilities of education . . . I have become that futile creature, a writer . . . If I were building a Utopia . . . I would leave principles out . . . even feminism; in place of principles I would give us all a magnificent and flaming audacity."[99] Without the flaming audacity of the 1920s, the political agitation of the 1930s, which enlisted women but did not take their problems seriously, neither empowered women writers, nor reseeded the ground.

14

The Great Depression

fter the stock market crash in October 1929, American publishing crashed as well. Between 1929 and 1933, the industry's earnings dropped 50 percent, while the number of books published fell by 20 percent.[1] Despite the shrinkage, the 1930s began with some cause for optimism about the standing of women writers. Emily Dickinson's centenary in 1930 was the occasion for accolades, celebrations, and new biographies that hailed her as a major American poet. Susan Glaspell's play *Alison's House,* inspired by Dickinson's life, won the Pulitzer Prize in 1931, and the same year Willa Cather received an honorary degree from Princeton—the first woman to be so recognized—and was profiled in *The New Yorker* by Louise Bogan as an "American classic."[2] In the midst of the Depression, some writers enjoyed enormous celebrity and commercial success. Two colossal best sellers, Pearl Buck's *The Good Earth* (1931) and Margaret Mitchell's *Gone with the Wind* (1936), bracketed the decade; Buck was also the first American woman to win the Nobel Prize in Literature in 1938. Lillian Hellman's *The Children's Hour* (1934) and *The Little Foxes* (1939) were Broadway hits, along with Clare Boothe Luce's satiric comedy *The Women* (1936), which ran for two years and became a popular movie.

Yet these gains were too often illusory, with both literary prizes and commercial rewards for the few only increasing male critical contempt for women's writing in general. In his condescending essay, "When Ladies Write Plays," Joseph Mersand called women playwrights hacks who accurately recorded the "fleeting words of everyday life," but "rarely hit the high note of great drama."[3] Women novelists also came under attack, especially from left-wing men. Reviewing novels by Cather, Wharton, and Glasgow in 1932, the Marxist critic Granville Hicks dismissed them as "the victims of timidity" who "lacked the courage to strike out into the world of strife . . . [E]ven their failures are minor failures."[4] Nathanael West was alluding to Cather in *Miss Lonelyhearts* (1933), when a group of male reporters make brutal fun of American women writers as sexually repressed or abnormal: "Mary Roberts Wilcox, Ella Wheeler Catheter . . . what they all needed was a good rape." Among the women of the Harlem Renaissance, Jessie Fauset published her last novel in 1933, and spent the rest of her life as a teacher. Nella Larsen disappeared from the literary scene. "It was unheard of for a young black girl to aspire to be a writer," Margaret Walker recalled.[5] Critics also derided women's best sellers of the 1930s as evidence of an innate female talent for a debased commercial fiction that could never compete with serious art. Malcolm Cowley attacked *Gone with the Wind* as a silly love story pandering to the ignorant woman reader; Bernard De Voto linked it with a feminized mass culture, the product of "slick writers of the highest bracket (. . . practically all women)" who fed a lowbrow audience the junk it demanded.[6] Reminiscent of the attacks on "scribbling women" of the 1850s, the backlash against women writers' ability to attract great numbers of readers would be repeated with increasing intensity throughout the twentieth century. It is a serious disadvantage to be a lady author, Cather conceded, and anyone who thinks otherwise is just foolish.[7]

American literary historians concede that overall, the 1930s were not "a period of remarkable poetic activity."[8] But the worst casualties of the decade were the women poets; the number of books of poetry by women declined by two thirds, and during the Depression, most of the little magazines edited by women, which had shaped careers in the twenties, folded.[9] Women poets faced stresses from all sides, but particularly from modernists and Marxists. Modernists regarded women as muses who could inspire major poems but lacked the genius and the detachment to create them. Eliot, Pound, and their disciples advocated a severe, intellectual, impersonal, and experimental poetry that transcended personal experience and emotion—precisely the modes in which women poets had been encouraged to specialize. Marxist writers demanded a poetry of the people that emphasized the working class. In "Poem Out of Early Childhood" (1935), Muriel Rukeyser declared the new affiliation and poetic allegiance of her generation: "Not Sappho, Sacco/ Rebellion pioneered among our lives." But not all women poets could be as inspired by Sacco as they had been by Sappho. In 1933, convinced that her lyrics had become unfashionable, and unable to develop a new poetic style, Sara Teasdale took her own life.[10] Millay tried to incorporate political concerns into her writing in the 1930s, but critics and readers were fixated by her image as the romantic lyric poet, and when the audience that wanted her to remain a romantic icon abandoned her, Millay suffered a series of breakdowns. In a review of Millay called "The Poet as Woman" (1936), John Crowe Ransom sweepingly excluded all women from poetic distinction: "A woman lives for love . . . safer as a biological organism, she remains fixed in her famous attitudes, and is indifferent to intellectuality."[11]

Writing Red: Women of the Left

The term "Red Decade" has become synonymous with the 1930s as a period of American attraction to socialism, Marxism, and Communism. Women writers in this radical tradition were not necessarily Communist Party members; according to the editors of the anthology *Writing Red*, many were writers who "contributed to and were themselves moved by the intellectual, literary, and political energy of the left during that turbulent decade."[12] Nonetheless, the Left was a male preserve; there were only six women among the sixty-one editors and writers on the masthead of the *New Masses*, and women were often assigned topics the men regarded as frivolous and lightweight, like book reviewing or theater. Women writers also found themselves marginalized by party lines and slogans that insistently valued male experience and perspectives. The ideal Marxist-American writer was a hairy-chested tough guy, as the critic Mike Gold proclaimed: "A wild youth of about twenty-two, the son of working-class parents, who himself works in the lumber camps, coal mines, and steel mills, harvest fields and mountain camps, of America."[13] Of course, few of the pale urban intellectuals of the left-wing journals were lumberjacks either, but this macho ideal condemned women's writing to inferior status. Gold's prescriptions for the "androcentric left" (as Constance Coiner dubs it) also extended to critics, who had to be giants, soldiers, poets rather than pedants, and above all, manly. As homophobic as he was misogynist, Gold attacked his liberal male rivals as effeminate pansies who bled "violet ink."[14] Interestingly, American women writers in the thirties did not attempt to disguise their gender with male pseudonyms or attempt to pass as men; their political loyalties made them accept their second-class position, and although many were bisexual, they could not be mocked as unwomanly.

In a manifesto in the *New Masses* in 1930, Gold announced the laws of proletarian realism that the good Marxist writer should obey. "Proletarian realism deals with the real conflicts of men and women who work for a living," he proclaimed. "It has nothing to do with the sickly mental states of the idle Bohemians, their subtleties, their sentimentalities, their fine-spun affairs."[15] In *The Radical Novel in the United States* (1956), Walter Rideout identified the four basic plots of the proletarian realist novel as the strike, the conversion to Communism, the episodic wanderings of the hero in America, and the tale of the capitalist family in decline. Women, too, wrote proletarian fiction, including Mary Heaton Vorse's *Strike!* (1930), Myra Page's *Gathering Storm* (1932), Clara Weatherwax's *Marching! Marching!* (1935), and Beatrice Bisno's *Tomorrow's Bread* (1938), which fit these categories, often adding sexual conflicts to class conflicts, and creating novels of "sex and strikes."[16]

Women on the left were also drawn to journalism and reportage, a genre of personal witness to injustice. While a nineteenth-century woman writer like Elizabeth Stuart Phelps had to watch the smoke of a factory fire from the safety of her home miles away, Meridel Le Sueur and Tillie Olsen covered strikes and demonstrations, Josephine Herbst went to Spain to cover the Spanish Civil War as a journalist, and Lillian Hellman worked with Ernest Hemingway on the documentary *The Spanish Earth*. Martha Gellhorn (1908–1998) dropped out of Bryn Mawr in her junior year to become a journalist. By the thirties, already a veteran of a several love affairs and two abortions, she had talked her way into covering the Spanish Civil War, where she met Hemingway; he wrote about her as the tough writer Dorothy Bridges in the play *The Fifth Column,* the survivor of "men, affairs, abortions, and ambitions."[17] They married in Cuba in 1940, but Gellhorn's ambitions were always too strong for Hemingway to accept, and pulled the marriage apart in a few years.

Yet radical women writers were still expected to be more decorous in their use of language, especially sexual language. They felt much less confident than Hemingway, who emerged in the thirties as the alpha-male American writer. As Herbst noted ruefully, he "wanted to be *the* war writer of his age, and he knew it and went toward it."[18] When she wrote forcefully about her generation, a male reviewer commented that "Miss Herbst yields nothing to Hemingway . . . scatologically."[19] And when Meridel Le Sueur submitted her short story "Annunciation" to

Scribner's, the editor asked her to write more like Hemingway. Although Le Sueur protested that "fishin', fightin' and fuckin' were not my major experiences," the story was rejected.[20]

Abortions and Ambitions

The major experiences of women, even radical women like Le Sueur, tended to include menstruation, loss of virginity, pregnancy, childbirth, and abortion. All of these subjects occurred in women's literature of the thirties, along with lesbianism. Abortion had been discussed obliquely before, as an issue of sexual power games in women's writing of the 1920s; in Treadwell's *Machinal,* for example, there is a scene in which a nameless man is persuading his girlfriend to have an unnamed operation. Hemingway had described a very similar argument between a man and a woman about abortion in his short story "Hills Like White Elephants," published in his collection *Men Without Women* (1927). In the 1930s, women wrote much more openly about abortion, sexual politics, and literary creativity.

In fact, because of the rising demand to control childbirth during hard times, the thirties were a decade in which "abortion was not extraordinary, but ordinary." As Leslie Reagan's thorough study shows, American women of all races and social backgrounds, married and unmarried, "turned to abortion in greater numbers during the Depression."[21] In big cities, rich women were quietly referred by their physicians to other doctors who performed relatively safe abortions in a clinical setting with anesthesia, at prices ranging from fifty to two hundred dollars— a great deal of money in the 1930s.[22] Others found out about abortionists through a network of friends. Some attempted abortion at home with coat hangers, lye, and knitting needles.

An illegal abortion, whatever its form, was a risky undertaking that many women writers personally experienced as a traumatic rite of passage. Women wrote about abortion as the product of masculine coercion, something violent that was done to women, like rape, rather than an expression of their individual desires or personal wishes. They also saw it as a stark symbol of the antitheses of maternity and creativity, one of the most blatant examples of the divisions and doubleness of their lives. While they dutifully published reportage for the Communist press, they recorded very different experiences and attitudes in their journals and letters to other women. In their daily routines and self-presentations, they often felt masked and secretive, not only as political radicals, but also as women who, for a number of reasons, lied about their age; pretended to admire and respect lovers or husbands they were writing about as bullies, sponges, and sloths; and often concealed feelings of love and desire for other women. In the prefeminist era of the 1930s, they were encouraged to read about the "Woman Question" but not to talk to each other about the conditions of their lives. Secretly, radical women writers were influenced by the techniques of female modernists, especially Virginia Woolf and Katherine Mansfield, as well as male radical writers like John Dos Passos. These techniques, including imagery, multiple points of view, and stream of consciousness, were hard to assimilate into the naturalist prose of the proletarian narrative. Women novelists wrote, too, about the special situation of the leftist feminist intellectual, whose political and sexual awakenings often occurred at the same time, but quickly came into conflict. While the tensions in their personal lives led to divorce and breakdowns, the divisions in their writing selves produced writing blocks, silences, and many unfinished or unpublished books.

CAMOUFLAGE—MERIDEL LE SUEUR

For a committed woman of the Left, like Meridel Le Sueur (1900–1996), the Red Decade promised to be "a good time to be a woman writer, or any kind of writer."[23] But Le Sueur also confessed that she had survived the decade "by camouflage."[24] She was brought up in Iowa to be a political radical; her mother was a suffragist, women's rights lecturer, writer, and teacher, who left her first husband to marry the socialist editor of a newspaper called *The Iconoclast*. Through her mother and stepfather, Meridel met the heroes of the Left, from Emma Goldman to Woody Guthrie. She joined the Communist Party in 1924, wrote for the *Daily Worker*, and was arrested for protesting against the execution of Sacco and Vanzetti. The single mother of two beloved daughters, she began living with a Party comrade, the artist Bob Brown, in 1930. Publicly, Le Sueur always praised Brown; he "honored my creativeness," she told Constance Coiner, and she was proud of having chosen a "creative man who wasn't going to support [me] . . . I had no security from him . . . not in the sense of bourgeois living, I mean, who needs that?" In her private journals, however, entries about Brown's drinking, violence, and destructiveness tell a different story, and she admitted that he did not like her writing.[25]

In her fiction, Le Sueur returned obsessively to themes of pregnancy, abortion, and enforced sterilization, both realistic motifs and metaphors for her own restricted and divided creativity. Her first short story, "Persephone" (1927), was a haunting allegory about a young girl's abduction from her mother. "Annunciation" (1935), dedicated to her daughter Rachel, described a pregnant young woman filled with joy, whose husband, Karl (an unemployed worker whose name suggests Marxist ideology), wants her to abort the child: "Get rid of it. That's what everybody does nowadays. This isn't the time to have a child. Everything is rotten. We must change it." The woman looks for comfort to the flowering pear tree outside her window, a symbol of fertility and feminine creativity: "If the pears were still hanging upon it each would be alone and separate with a kind of bloom upon it. Such a bloom is upon me at this moment." She, too, feels like a pear, "secret within the curling leaves, just as the pear would be hanging on its tree . . . Perhaps after this child is born, then everything will harden and become small and mean again as it was before." When even her neighbors describe her pregnancy as bad luck, the heroine turns to the mysterious pear tree for hope; it "stands motionless, its leaves curled in the dark, its radiating body falling darkly, like a stream far below into the earth."

Although she romanticizes and idealizes maternity and female nurturance, "Annunciation" is Le Sueur's most effective piece of fiction. It is also clearly influenced by Katherine Mansfield's short story "Bliss" (1920), in which the heroine, in her first blooming of womanhood and sexual desire at age thirty, identifies her emotions with the "tall, slender pear tree in fullest, richest bloom" in her garden. Mansfield, though, was not on the approved list for left-wing writers; Genevieve Taggard mocked her writing as "neat little feminine cajolery . . . helpless, forlorn, honest, childlike, lost."[26] Already in the 1930s, Le Sueur's explorations of women's awakening were condemned by leftist critics, and she herself admitted that the Communist Party tried to "beat the lyrical and emotional out of women."[27]

Le Sueur's novel *The Girl* describes a community of women helping each other to survive the Depression. The unnamed heroine, the girl, is an oppressed Everywoman of the working class, a waitress who finds strength to resist masculine control through solidarity with other working women, including a prostitute and a gang moll. When her lover tries to make her have an abortion, she refuses, unlike one friend who has had thirteen abortions, and another who has died as a result of one. Instead of ending with a triumphant strike, the novel ends with a women's mass demonstration for maternal health care.[28] Too feminist and expressionist for its time and place, *The Girl* was rejected by publishers in the thirties, and it did not appear until the recovery movement of the 1970s, when Le Sueur was hailed as the "socialist tribal mother" of the New Left.[29] True, she had been blacklisted in the 1940s and 1950s, and restricted to publishing in Party journals; finally she was reduced to running a boardinghouse. Yet she was a more complex figure than this agitprop caricature. She was also, as she said, silenced and "almost blacklisted by the Left" for her emotional writing.[30] Constance Coiner compares Le Sueur to Rebecca Harding Davis as a woman writer who used "the working class . . . to protest her own oppression"; like Davis, Le Sueur's "strong sense of justice and collective responsibility" was a motive for "adopting the working class as her literary milieu," but political pressures also prevented her from "writing for publication about her own fear, anger, doubt, defeat." Toward the end of her life, Le Sueur declared that her own story remained untold: "I don't know how to write about women. I feel I have to learn to write a final book about myself as a woman."[31] Although she lived into her nineties, she did not live long enough to write that book.

FEMINIST INTELLECTUAL—TESS SLESINGER

Tess Slesinger (1905–1945) was much more urban, sophisticated, and intellectual than Le Sueur. The daughter of a cultivated and secular Jewish family in New York, she was educated at the progressive Ethical Culture School, and studied writing at Swarthmore and the Columbia School of Journalism. In 1928, she married Herbert Solow, an "intellectual man-about-town," according to Elizabeth Hardwick, and an assistant editor of the *Menorah Journal*.[32] The marriage ended in divorce in 1932, and Slesinger used her disillusion and the whole cultural spectrum of the thirties for her brilliant satiric novel, *The Unpossessed* (1934).

Hardwick discusses *The Unpossessed* as a roman à clef about the Jewish Marxists who founded the *Menorah Journal*—"a disorderly, self-appointed group: intellectuals critical of society's arrangements and very critical of each other"; parlor radicals and pinkos.[33] Primarily, though, *The Unpossessed* is a novel about the feminist intellectual. Slesinger uses two heroines to express the divided woman of the 1930s, torn between radical politics and personal emancipation, a woman based closely on herself. One heroine, Margaret Flinders, is a New York working woman married to a Marxist writer, while the other, Elizabeth Leonard, is a boyish expatriate art student who has bohemian love affairs, reads *Ulysses,* and tells herself that she is free. Elizabeth has her awakening when she realizes that she "lived in a frame of men's reactions, building herself over from one man to the next; her character seemed compounded by what various men had told her she was." Like Edna Pontellier and Lily Bart, Margaret is a woman of twenty-nine, facing deadlines of maturity, sexuality, and independence. "One grew older," she reflects. "Twenty-nine! What was the deadline for babies?" When she gets pregnant, however, her husband Miles persuades her to have an abortion because he fears that parenthood would make them soft and bourgeois. The death of their child signals not only the death of their marriage, but the infantilism and sterility of the men in their political movement, which has no room for the adult responsibilities of family and parenthood. Slesinger ends with a despairing image of Margaret's barrenness and sexlessness: "She had stripped and revealed herself not as a woman at all, but as a creature who would not be a woman and could not be a man."

Like Le Sueur, Slesinger was drawn to modernist experimentation, and especially the narrative techniques of Mansfield and Woolf. Her narrative style in *The Unpossessed* clearly borrowed from Woolf's *Mrs. Dalloway,* especially in part three, called "The Party." The "Hunger March Party," an event with champagne and fancy food to which all the characters are invited, is both an ironic piece of social observation and a very funny lampoon of the Left, exposing the members of this "party" as driven by vanity, political trendiness, and competition. As their leader, Professor Bruno Leonard, drunkenly reminds them, they think they are sponsoring intellectual revolution, but they are actually sponsoring "sublimation, constipation, procrastination, masturbation, prevarication, adumbration, equivocation, . . . anything that's phony or a fake."

Slesinger's message that personal relationships on the Left needed to be revolutionized as much as political ones went unheeded by her male contemporaries. In the *Partisan Review,* Philip Rahv complained that *The Unpossessed* lacked "a disciplined orientation for radicalized intellectuals," and Joseph Freeman in the *Daily Worker* called it "bourgeois and reactionary." Sidney Hook insisted that Slesinger was a "political innocent" whose novel had no "coherent presentation of a political idea in it."[34] In short, they could not understand sexual politics as a legitimate subject of analysis for a woman intellectual. Slesinger left the Village and went to Hollywood, where she happily remarried, had two children, and wrote the screenplays of *The Good Earth, A Tree Grows in Brooklyn,* and director Dorothy Arzner's feminist *Dance, Girl, Dance*. She also became an organizer of the Screen Writers Guild.[35] When she died of cancer at the age of thirty-nine, Slesinger was working on a novel about the film industry, including the creation of stars, the contradictions of Hollywood excess and political activism, and the costs for the employees of the Dream Factory.

SILENCES—TILLIE OLSEN

Tillie Lerner Olsen (1912–2007) grew up in a socialist family of Russian immigrants in Omaha, Nebraska. She attended an elementary school that was almost all black, and lived in a mixed neighborhood of Croatians and Czechs. Her father became the state secretary of the Socialist Party, and their house was a place where traveling radicals and organizers would often stay. As a girl she read Rebecca Harding Davis, Willa Cather, and Katherine Mansfield, and later she memorized poems by Sara Teasdale and Edna St. Vincent Millay. She also was familiar with the stories of Mary Wilkins Freeman, Gail Hamilton, and many other nineteenth-century writers.

Olsen always emphasized the pleasures of sexuality for the working class, but it had its risks and dangers for women. "I grew up at a time when birth control was still very little known, and very hard indeed to come by. There was a kind of prayer, I guess, that women had for their daughters, even if they never put it into words: Please don't let my daughter know that she is a sexual human being with sexual desires, because all it will do will be to get her into a mess where she marries too early and has more kids than she can handle."[36]

When she joined the Young Communist League in 1931 as an idealistic young woman, Olsen was assigned to carry out political tasks in the Midwest, including writing skits and plays for the Party. At the same time she also was being educated and introduced to a broad and cosmopolitan range of reading: "In the movement people were reading like mad," she recalled, ". . . we were reading all the black writers, books like Arna Bontemps's *Black Thunder;* Langston Hughes. We read Ting Ling, we read Lu Hsun, we read the literature of protest that was beginning to be written in English out of South Africa . . . The thirties was a rich, international period . . . And from whatever country or color this was considered to be part of our literature."[37]

Olsen contracted pleurisy, and while recovering began to write her novel *Yonnondio*. Then, at nineteen, she became pregnant and bore a daughter, Karla. The writing had to stop. In April 1934, when she was twenty-one, Olsen did publish a short story, "The Iron Throat," in the *Partisan Review*, which attracted notice as "a work of early genius."[38] When publishers tried to track down the gifted young writer, they came up short—she was in jail for demonstrating at a waterfront strike. Eventually Random House found her and signed her to a contract for her unfinished novel, offering her a monthly stipend in return for completing a chapter every month. Olsen sent her two-year-old daughter to live with her parents and moved to Los Angeles to write. She felt out of place and homesick, however, and in 1936, she gave up the contract and moved back to San Francisco to care for Karla.

That year was a turning point in Olsen's career. She began to live with Jack Olsen, another member of the Young Communist League, who had been arrested with her in 1934; they had three more daughters and stayed together for the rest of their lives, marrying in 1944. Although she loved her children and thought motherhood deepened her imagination, Olsen also worried about having the money to support a family; she had several abortions, and took a series of low-paying jobs—waitressing, laundry work, clerical work—while her children were growing up. She also became active in union organizing. As she understood, "it was not a time that my writing self could be first."[39]

Olsen left the Communist Party in 1948, troubled by "its callous treatment of people," among other reasons.[40] When she won a Wallace Stegner Fellowship at Stanford University in 1955, she was able to devote herself to her writing for the first time in twenty years, and *Tell Me a Riddle* (1961), a collection of four short stories she developed while at Stanford, won her national acclaim. The title story, the uncompromising and unsentimentalized "Tell Me a Riddle," described a Russian Jewish grandmother's bitter death. Olsen had vowed in 1938 "to write the history of that whole generation of exiled revolutionaries . . . the mothers of six and seven . . . the housewives whose Zetkin and Curie and Brontë hearts went into kitchen and laundries and the patching of old socks; and those who did not speak the language of their children, who had no bridge . . . to make themselves understood."[41] She began that history in her fiction, but never completed it. Although she was awarded a steady series of fellowships and teaching appointments at universities and colleges, Olsen was unable to recover the momentum of her youthful energy as a writer. In her book *Silences* (1978), she lamented the interruptions of women's writing by family responsibilities, motherhood, and work:

"Among these, the mute inglorious Miltons: those whose waking hours are all struggle for existence; the barely educated; the illiterate; women. Their silence the silence of centuries as to how life was, is, for most of humanity."

Olsen's novel, *Yonnondio: From the Thirties,* was never completed, but was published as a fragment in 1974. In it, she traces the odyssey of the Holbrook family from mining in Wyoming to a slaughterhouse in Nebraska, concentrating on the relationship between the mother, Anna, and the daughter, Mazie. Constance Coiner explains that Olsen had originally intended the novel to be "a portrait of a radical artist as a young woman," with Mazie becoming a writer, and Anna, the oppressed working-class woman of the past, dying in a self-inflicted abortion.[42] The published work, however, represented a compromise between Olsen's lyrical view of a young woman's coming-of-age and her more didactic narrative interludes about class and poverty.

Despite the gaps in her career, Olsen was a beloved, even revered and sacrosanct, figure among feminist critics, for whom she became an iconic figure of women's silencing by the patriarchy. In my view, however, she was silenced as much by her activity in a repressive political movement as by her domestic life.[43] In a controversial book about writers who stop writing, published two years before Olsen's death, Myles Weber argued that she never strayed from her "author legend . . . as the representative silenced female author," a legend that became a self-fulfilling prophecy. The adulation and adoration Olsen received in this persona, he harshly charged, may ultimately have prevented her from seizing the opportunities to write when they came to her.[44] In any case, by the 1960s and 1970s, when she became recognized and rewarded, she no longer had the confidence and determination to make the most of her many chances to become a writer. Her postcards and letters to feminist friends, in a microscopic handwriting very similar in appearance to the miniaturized juvenile writings of the Brontë sisters, were symptomatic self-portraits of her diminished writing self.

A WIDER CONSCIOUSNESS—TAGGARD, HERBST, PORTER

Genevieve Taggard, Josephine Herbst, and Katherine Anne Porter were a trio of friends who shared their most intimate experiences of love, politics, and writing. At the same time, their rivalries and betrayals demolish any sentimental mythology of literary sisterhood. Their lives dramatize the ways in which women's allegiances to each other in the

1930s were stretched and torn by their political commitments, literary ambitions, and personal demons; the arcs of their literary careers are examples of the different ways women writers negotiated the conflicts between art and politics.

Taggard's life was changing in the thirties, and she rejected any connection with the female lyric tradition she had embraced in the 1920s. Her husband Robert Wolf, whose bohemian lifestyle and political commitments had seemed so romantic to her in the 1920s, became ever more competitive, unsupportive, and harassing. Taggard was rescued from the marriage only by his mental collapse and institutionalization in 1934. After receiving a divorce, she married Kenneth Durant, a journalist who represented the Soviet news agency TASS in the United States. They visited Soviet Russia together on a sort of busman's honeymoon in 1936, and upon her return, in an interview with the *Daily Worker*, Taggard repudiated her earlier feminine lyrics: "I really hadn't as yet found a way of writing. Most of the poems in my first few books were about love and marriage and having children."[45] She also began to write more insistently on social and political issues. "I have refused to write out of a decorative impulse," she explained in the introduction to her *Collected Poems, 1918–1938*, "because I conceive it to be the dead end of much feminine talent. A kind of literary needlework. I think the later poems and some of the early ones hold a wider consciousness than that colored by the feminine half of the race. I hope they are not written by a poetess, but by a poet. I think, I hope, I have written poetry that relates to general experience and the realities of the time."

Calling Western Union (1936), her book of Depression poems, was well received by left-wing critics when it came out, and has been singled out by feminist critics as the best example of her efforts to merge women's concerns with working-class politics. Nancy Berke, for example, points out that Taggard links "bread lines, picket lines and party lines" with class lines and "lines of poetry," and gives working-class women a voice.[46] Some of the poems in *Calling Western Union*, such as "Up State—Depression Summer" (1936), are indeed moving dramatic monologues of rural hardship, reminiscent of Edgar Lee Masters's *Spoon River Anthology* (1915), which Taggard had long admired. In my view, however, many other poems sound strained, politically correct, and painfully self-abasing. "A Middle-Aged, Middle-Class Woman at Midnight" mocks her own anxious class position, as does "Interior," a poem about a woman of leisure who hates "her life and . . . tiresome friends," and stares blankly in the mirror while "all around you gathers the rage / Of cheated people." In "To My Mother," she called her work of writing "nervous," "unsteady," "nothing well-done," in contrast to her mother's bustle of housework and "habit of rising early." In "Chant for the Great Negro Poet of America Not Yet Born" (1941), she looked to the coming of "our poet," the "poet of all rising people," but imagined this savior as a man, and black. In her quest for a wider political consciousness, Taggard stifled the ardent feminine voice that had made her poetry alive.

A WOMAN AND A MENSCH—JOSEPHINE HERBST

"I was never a little lady—and I never wanted to be," wrote Josephine Herbst (1892–1969), Taggard's closest friend and confidante in the 1920s. "Wanted to be a woman and a mensch in Rosa Luxembourg's terms."[47] Growing up in Sioux City, Iowa, Herbst was a bookish tomboy; when she began to menstruate at age eleven, she was shocked and distressed by the change. Menstruation was a rite of passage from the physical and psychological freedom of girlhood into the constraints of womanhood. For Herbst, it was also an initiation into a secret female society. She recalled that her mother "had taken me to a room apart and, closing the door, spoken tenderly of the mysteries of the womb." These euphemisms gave her no clue about the realities of sex or reproduction. "I was boiling with questions to which I could not, for the life of me, give tongue. I stalked away from her, rigid with self-important dignity, seething with wonderment, dread, anticipation of I hardly knew what." In the public library she found some explanations, albeit veiled in poetic language; and she realized that she shared this mystery, this birthmark, with the women she most admired, women of intellect and imagination. "I was amazed to discover myself part of a vast company, exclusively female, who were regularly reminded in language of the blood of what they were. Not only my mother, my sisters, my teachers, but the Brontë girls, George Sand!"[48]

When her father's business failed, Herbst had to drop out of the University of Iowa and move home to work as an elementary school teacher. Frustrated by her entrapment as a dutiful daughter, she wrote to a friend, "I fairly writhe to think of how fine it would have been if I had been a boy . . . As it is I'm a girl with the ambitions and aspirations of a boy."[49] When she finally saved enough money to enroll at Berkeley in 1917, Herbst lied about her age, subtracting five years so that her college classmates would see her as their contemporary. She wrote poems about free love for the college literary magazine, and was seduced by the vision of egalitarian partnerships of New Women and New Men.

The slogans of love and revolution, however, proved as deceptive for Herbst as they had been for Taggard. After graduation, she moved to New York, joined a circle of radical writers, and had an affair with the playwright Maxwell Anderson, then a young journalist and a married man with children. When she became pregnant, Anderson insisted that she have an abortion in New York because he could not afford to support another child. She kept the incident a secret from her family, and when her younger sister Helen, married, still living in Sioux City, and trying along with her husband to save money, became pregnant in the fall of 1920, Herbst, posing as a liberated New Woman, blithely advised her to have an abortion. She attributed her own experience to Taggard: "Genevieve got over it in no time . . . do try to find a doctor and let me hear from you."

Helen did manage to find a doctor, but conditions in Sioux City were not as advanced as in New York, and she died from the operation. Herbst was overcome with guilt—"It's my little sister. I did it," she told Taggard.[50] After the funeral, with the family pretending Helen had died of appendicitis, Herbst had a breakdown and spent two weeks in a sanitarium. Afterward she had to deal with the news of Anderson's wife's pregnancy: "It is so unfair. That's *my* baby," she wrote to Taggard. "I wanted my baby so much and only gave it up because he had so many burdens all ready [*sic*]. But it would have made such a difference in my life . . . But he was so quick to advise *me* to get rid of it."[51]

When she had recovered, Herbst set out alone to live in Berlin, and wrote about the affair in an autobiographical novel called "Unmarried." According to Herbst's biographer, Elinor Langer, "Unmarried" follows her experience precisely: "An unmarried woman falls in love with a married man, becomes pregnant, and has an abortion, and her sister also has an abortion, and her sister dies." Herbst told Taggard that simply writing the novel had been therapeutic; in any case, she never tried to publish it.[52] Langer describes "Unmarried" as incoherent and weak in characterization, but also far ahead of its time, "like the notes of a consciousness-raising group from the feminist revival of a half-century later." In Berlin, Herbst met the left-wing writer John Herrmann. They married in 1926, and while they were enjoying their bohemian lives in Greenwich Village, she became close to Katherine Anne Porter, who replaced Taggard as her most intimate woman friend. Herrmann was a member of the Communist Party, and Herbst was drawn in, although she never actually joined. As she wrote to Porter in 1931, the Marxist "gents," like their bourgeois brothers, did not want women closely involved in their "revolutionary conversations," and in her view "they would probably not rise very high."[53]

Herbst's major writing during the 1930s was a trilogy of novels based on her family's history from the Civil War through the 1930s—*Pity Is Not Enough* (1933), *The Executioner Waits* (1934), and *Rope of Gold* (1939)—which used the devices of documentary realism pioneered by John Dos Passos in *U.S.A.* Tracing several generations of the Trexler and Wendel families, Herbst had to compress the individual characters into a complex panorama of social detail. Victoria Wendel, her alter ego, appears in interchapters of the main narrative, reflecting on her mother's stories as she rediscovers the family's documents. *Rope of Gold* covers the years from 1934 to 1937, and crowds in portraits of the two families plus workers, farmers, and businessmen. One critic found it emotionally compelling in its tragic sweep: "Everywhere in the book people suddenly realize that something has gone terribly wrong . . . The very texture of life seems to be disintegrating."[54] On the other hand, Herbst had difficulties connecting Victoria's inner life with her survey of American capitalism in crisis. Although reviewers commented on her "fierce masculine virility that does not falter at the language of the beer joint and the lavatory," the language of the novels is subdued and oblique about female sexuality.[55]

At the same time, during the thirties, Herbst was confronting her bisexuality, which emerged when she had a passionate love affair with the painter Marion Greenwood. She separated from Herrmann, who found another lover. In her biography, Elinor Langer juxtaposes excerpts from Herbst's notes from Havana on the Cuban situation in 1934, with her abject, pleading letters to Herrmann ("if you will just send your name, John, that will mean that you love me still"), and concludes that she seemed "to divide herself in two."[56]

Herbst and Herrmann divorced; she had some brief affairs with other women, tried to work on her fiction, but in the spring of 1937, went to Madrid to write about the Spanish Civil War. She was also beginning to have some doubts about the Communists, who did not seem responsive to the humanitarian concerns of the Spanish people, and she was disturbed by the Moscow trials. Porter, then living in New Orleans, was her closest confidante. "I would give years of my life for a little literary talk again, with some feeling for it . . . At the present moment, politics has ceased to illuminate."[57] The friendship, however, was undermined by Porter's resentments and homophobia. After Pearl Harbor, Herbst badly needed a steady income, and got a job in Washington on the German desk at the office of the Coordinator of Information. Suddenly, on May 21, 1942, she was seized by security guards and ushered out of the building. She was never to know the source of the charges against her, or to be able to defend herself. Only after Langer's biography of Herbst appeared in 1984 was it revealed that Porter had told the FBI in Reno, where she was getting her fourth divorce, that Herbst was a Communist agent. Porter never told anyone what she had done, and her "friendship" with Herbst went on for many years. It finally ended in 1947, when Porter published a malicious essay on Gertrude Stein, charging that Stein was "on the whole a bore and a little bit of a fraud." Herbst was outraged by the article, which she saw as an attack on modernism in general; she published a letter in the *Partisan Review* defending Stein, and she and Porter went their separate ways.[58]

The break had many ironies; Porter was actually much more attuned to and influenced by high modernism than Herbst. In the late 1950s, however, Herbst began to think about writing both more honestly and more artfully about her generation of women. Reading Doris Lessing's *The Golden Notebook* in the summer of 1962 was a revelation to her. "It's a very bold book—really good . . . It's so jolting and provocative and I don't know anyone who has written so openly and frankly about women—she really puts it on the line," she wrote to the poet Jean Garrigue.[59] She courageously determined to learn from Lessing's example, and to achieve the historical detachment and artistic distance necessary for writing a great book about the 1920s and 1930s. But it was too late. When she died in 1969, the unfinished manuscript was discovered in a box under her bed. Published posthumously in 1991 as *The Starched Blue Sky of Spain*, the memoir contains Herbst's most evocative and luminous writing.

A VERY GRAND DAME—KATHERINE ANNE PORTER

Obviously Katherine Anne Porter (1890–1980) was a formidable figure, as devious as she was gifted.[60] Since her death, several biographers have attempted to sort out the details of her confusing and astonishing life, and to judge her standing as a twentieth-century writer. Porter was a fabulist who constantly embellished her life, a political chameleon who changed her politics as often as she changed her wardrobe, an angry closet feminist who insisted that she was above all delightfully "feminine," and a restrained modernist writer who vacillated between admiration for the giants of the century, and a perverse wish to attack them.

Born in a log cabin in Texas, and raised in real poverty, Porter was sexually and culturally adventurous and eager to reinvent herself. She got out of Texas in her teens, participated in the bohemian life of Greenwich Village in the 1920s, lived in Mexico and Berlin in the years between the wars, married four times, and was in Washington during and after World War II. Porter mythologized her own life story, portraying herself variously as the descendant of Southern aristocrats, the sexual prey and victim of various unscrupulous men, the romantic heroine of impossible loves, the hard-boiled dame who could drink men under the table, and the grande dame who wore pearls and emeralds, posed in elaborate gowns, and made theatrical appearances to read her work or accept honorary degrees. Her hair had turned prematurely white after a bout with tuberculosis; she bleached it blond, and perfectly suited the era's ideas of Jean Harlow–ish female glamour. She managed to captivate men throughout her life, and to have tempestuous love affairs with younger men well into her seventies.

At the same time, Porter was absolutely dedicated to her art, and to the highest standards of style and form. At the crucial age of twenty-nine, she vowed to her sister that she would become as fine a writer as anyone in America.[61] In her series of short stories about a girl she called Miranda Gay, Porter joined a tradition of women writers, including Fuller, Stowe, and Alcott, who used *The Tempest* to signify American women's creative isolation in the New World.[62] She had been obsessed with Shakespeare since early childhood, but had thought of the name Miranda, "my alter-ego name,"[63] not only in terms of Shakespeare's motherless heroine, but also in its Spanish sense, "the seeing one."[64] Miranda Gay is the female witness, the one whose gaze transforms the world. The first group of these stories, which she called the "Miranda cycle," appeared in *Flowering Judas and Other Stories* in 1935, and they deal with female initiation into the adult world of sexuality, knowledge, and death. "The Grave" is a female equivalent or parallel to Hemingway's "Indian Camp" and Faulkner's "The Bear"—a coming-of-age through blood. Nine-year-old Miranda is exploring the family cemetery, a "neglected garden of tangled rose bushes," with her twelve-year-old brother Paul. She is dreamily thinking about growing up, putting on the organdy dresses and violet-scented talcum powder of the Southern belle. But Paul, already a hunter, shoots a pregnant rabbit, and eviscerates it: "He . . . pulled the bag open, and there lay a bundle of tiny rabbits, each wrapped in a thin scarlet veil . . . there they were, dark grey, their sleek wet down lying in minute even ripples . . . their unbelievably small delicate ears folded close, their little blind faces almost featureless." As she sees the blood running over the dead babies, Miranda begins to "tremble without knowing why." She has discovered that for women, birth comes at the risk of death. And unlike Hemingway's Nick, sure that he will never die, and comforted by his father, Porter's Miranda is alone, without female reassurance. In "Old Mortality," in *Pale Horse, Pale Rider* (1939), Porter evoked the myths and realities of the Gay family history, with its fearless and romantic female figures, and Miranda's responses to it. And in *The Leaning Tower and Other Stories* (1944), she described Miranda as a child at the circus where a dwarf with "not-human golden eyes" gestures at her "imitating her own face."

Porter was a brilliant short-story writer, but she had always found the construction of the narrative difficult and uncongenial, and took every opportunity to avoid writing—teaching, traveling, lecturing, socializing, drinking. After the war, however, she succumbed to the temptation of writing a big novel on a big historical and allegorical theme—*Ship of Fools,* based on a trip to Berlin she had taken on a German ship in 1931. She wanted it to show the world the savagery of the German people. As the years went by, however, the size of the project, the huge cast of characters, her perfectionism, and her changing viewpoints, overwhelmed her. Responding to an interviewer, she blamed her slowness on being a woman "brought up with the . . . curious idea of feminine availability in all spiritual ways and in giving service to anyone who demands it. And I suppose that's why it has taken me twenty years to write this novel; it's been interrupted by just anyone who could jimmy his way into my life."[65] Her evasions, downright lies, and endless self-interruptions and diversions during the decades she worked on the novel sound very much like the strategies Ralph Ellison employed in his long and ultimately futile effort to produce a novel to follow the triumph of *Invisible Man* (1952). Like Ellison, too, Porter used the work-in-progress as an excuse to refuse to help other writers, to be ungenerous and uncharitable in numerous ways, and to let vanity and the need for reassurance and praise distract her from her task.[66]

Her patient and perceptive editor Seymour Lawrence managed to cajole, bribe, and flatter Porter into finishing the book. When *Ship of Fools* at last appeared in 1962, it became a best seller and a Hollywood movie, and made her a great deal of money. At the same time there were also numerous critical dissenters who pointed out that the novel was misanthropic and anti-Semitic. It also appeared too belatedly to have the historical impact she had desired. Janis Stout, Porter's most judicious biographer-critic, makes a convincing case that *Ship of Fools* did not work as an allegory of the journey because it was more about departure than arrival, and that the classic literary journey of self-discovery and dynamic transformation became a static middle passage in Porter's hands. Stout sees this failure as linked to the female literary tradition; "leaving the house, setting one's face toward unfamiliar and even undetermined territories, has been the crucial act as women writers have rejected their known social roles and set out to find or to create new 'places' that have not traditionally existed for them . . . The course of the voyage itself, not to speak of the moment of arrival, is often . . . uncreated, unprojected."[67]

Stout also gives the most eloquent and balanced critical summary of Porter's achievement, concluding that she will survive as a writer because of her masterly short stories. "If importance as a writer were proportionate to volume of output, she would have to be considered a minor figure. If sheer intellectual or philosophical depth were the sole criterion, she could by no means be compared to a Herman Melville, a T. S. Eliot, a Toni Morrison, a Thomas Pynchon . . . What gives Porter's stories their literary significance is that they represent a convergence of two great forces: consummate artistry and significant response to deeply human concerns."[68]

Expatriates and Cult Writers

While the male exiles of the 1920s were returning to the United States, the most avant-garde women writers were leaving for European cities, where they felt they could escape from politics, and explore the private and secret night-worlds of the female psyche. One such writer was Djuna Barnes (1892–1982). Escaping to the Village at seventeen from an eccentric polygamous household, she worked as a journalist in New York covering circuses and vaudeville, and came to see the modern city as a surreal, carnivalesque habitation for the alienated and perverse. When she moved to Paris in the 1920s to write for *McCall's* magazine, Barnes fell in love with the alcoholic American artist Thelma Wood, whom she pursued for nine years. In *Ladies Almanack* (1928), she wrote about Parisian lesbian circles; in her cult novel *Nightwood* (1936) she fictionalized her romance with Wood in the lesbian lovers Robin Vote and Nora Flood, and portrayed a Viennese and Parisian decadent underworld of outcasts and grotesques. Barnes's critical admirers included James Joyce and T. S. Eliot: the latter wrote the introduction to the American edition of *Nightwood,* praising its "brilliance of wit and characterization, and a quality of horror and doom very nearly related to that of Elizabethan tragedy." Feminist enthusiasts suggest that the novel sympathetically "foreshadows . . . the spectre of Fascism casting a long shadow over its landscape."[69] Her detractors, however, point out that "the politics of female modernism, like the politics of male modernism, could encompass a disturbing fusion of formalist experiment and crude cultural stereotyping."[70] Barnes never misses a chance to generalize about the nature of "the Jew," who "seems to be everywhere from nowhere."

Anaïs Nin (1903–1977) was among Barnes's admirers, and wrote her a fan letter about "the great, deep beauty" of *Nightwood* and its authentic woman's voice.[71] She named the heroine of her own collection of stories, *Winter of Artifice* (1939), "Djuna"; perhaps their strange first names signaled a kind of female twinship for her. In the 1920s and 1930s, she moved restlessly back and forth between New York and Paris with her prosperous and patient husband, whose income also allowed her to maintain her many lovers, including Henry Miller. Nin's publications during these years included erotica and fiction, but she became best known after 1966 for her diaries, in which she recorded her views on female creativity and sexuality. Nin became an iconic figure of emancipated womanhood for some feminists, a role she wholeheartedly embraced and tirelessly promoted; she also attracted amused criticism from those in the women's movement who saw her as exhibitionistic and vain.

STAYING FREE—ZORA NEALE HURSTON

Zora Neale Hurston (1891–1960), one of the most gifted women writers of the 1930s, was exceptional in her determination to stay free of all ideologies, parties, and narratives of victimization. "I do not belong to the sobbing school of Negrohood," she declared in "How It Feels to Be Colored Me." She also refused to limit herself to the female territory of the "woman writer." "What I wanted was to tell a story about a man," she wrote; ". . . my interest lies in what makes a man or a woman do such-and-so, regardless of his color." Finally, Hurston was unswayed by left-wing arguments about her proper politics or suitable style. She saw social realism as the path of "least resistance and least originality" for the modern black writer.[72] Somehow she managed to keep her aesthetic identity free of the pressure from white scholars and writers to intellectualize, eroticize, or sensationalize black experience, and the pressure of the black literary left to limit herself to social protest and racial uplift. Hurston's resolve to avoid fashionable issues of racial tension, feminist oppression, or class struggle set her apart from and antagonized many of her contemporaries, but gave her writing integrity, individuality, and originality. In a decade of women marching to the tune of a party or a grievance, she danced to her own song.

Hurston's resistance to being a "Race Woman," or a proletarian writer, did not mean that she was indifferent to race or working people. Raised in the all-black community of Eatonville, Florida, where her father was the mayor, she had the direct experience of rural Southern culture that writers like Nella Larsen and Jessie Fauset lacked. After her mother's death, her stepmother sent her away to school, but Hurston rebelled, and struck out on her own for ten hard years. In 1917, she decided to take advantage of a Maryland Code that gave free schooling to "all colored youths between six and twenty years of age." Although she was already twenty-six, Hurston claimed to be ten years younger, and enrolled in an evening high-school program run by Morgan College (now Morgan State University) in Baltimore. "Becoming sixteen again," according to her biographer Valerie Boyd, marked "the moment she was reborn, by her own imaginative labor, as the woman she was to become."[73] Giving birth to herself, Hurston remained outside families and movements throughout her career.

After high school Hurston moved to Howard University to study English literature. She was also writing fiction. When her short story "Drenched in Light" was published in the arts journal *Opportunity* in December 1924, Hurston decided to move to Harlem in order to market her writing and earn money to complete her education. With her flamboyant style, wicked wit, and easy charm, she rapidly became a star of the community. In 1925, *Opportunity* offered cash prizes for the best submissions, and Hurston entered a short story, "Spunk," and two plays in the competition. Although she only won second prize in each category, her talent and personality made an indelible impression on the white philanthropists gathered for the occasion. Among them, Annie Nathan Meyer arranged for her to be admitted to Barnard College, where she was the only black student. In her second year at Barnard, Hurston began her study with Franz Boas, a legendary scholar who had founded the first department of anthropology at Columbia University. Trained as a cultural anthropologist, Hurston went on to do fieldwork in the black South, Jamaica, the Bahamas, and Haiti, with the eyes of an observer and the methods of a social scientist rather than an artist.

Hurston's task was to collect, analyze, and dissect, rather than reenact and perform, the tall tales of her childhood and the folklore of black culture, a professional conflict exacerbated by her financial subsidies from a wealthy white patron, Mrs. Osgood Mason. Mrs. Mason, whom she called "Godmother," also supported Langston Hughes, and was devoted to what she saw as the primitive energies of African-American art. Another white friend and mentor was the wealthy Jewish-American novelist Fannie Hurst (1889–1968), who hired Hurston as a secretary in 1925. Although Hurst was an enthusiastic mentor of her fiction, and wrote an introduction to *Jonah's Gourd Vine* (1934), Hurston was wary of becoming "Hurstized," a disciple or imitator in any way.[74] When Hurst's novel about racial passing, *Imitation of Life* (1933), became a hit movie, Harlem intellectuals like Sterling Brown denounced it as a repugnant exploitation of stereotypes of "the contented Mammy and the tragic mulatto." Hurston, however, adroitly stayed out of the controversy.

Although the books she published in the 1930s—*Mules and Men* (1935), *Their Eyes Were Watching God* (1937), and *Moses, Man of the Mountain* (1939)—were characterized by what she called "a Negro way of saying," a subtle, pungent, and stylized language that took its force from the black vernacular, Hurston would not limit herself to "the Race Problem." "I was and am thoroughly sick of the subject," she wrote.[75] Her best-known and most fully achieved book, *Their Eyes Were Watching God*, is a modernist novel that alternates between the sophisticated linguistic range of the omniscient narrator, and the dialect and folk idiom of the black characters, and incorporates surreal elements into its realism. Hurston was not afraid to make female sexuality a central theme in her fiction, and she, too, had read Katherine Mansfield. As a girl, her heroine Janie Crawford has her sexual awakening watching the pear tree being fertilized by bees: "She saw a dust-bearing bee sink into the sanctum of a bloom; the thousand sister-calyxes arch to meet the love-embrace and the ecstatic shiver of the tree from root to tiniest branch creaming in every blossom and frothing with delight. So this was marriage!" "The image is remarkably sexually explicit for a woman novelist of Hurston's time," Cheryl Wall comments; but it also echoes Mansfield's story "Bliss."[76]

In contrast to the American novels that ended women's lives on the brink of thirty, Hurston shows Janie Crawford with three husbands, representing three stages of her development. Married first at sixteen to Logan Killicks, an older man for whom she feels no desire, who would turn her into a drudge and a mule, she bolts. Her second marriage at twenty-four to the domineering and possessive Joe Starks becomes a power struggle that ends with her silencing and subordination. But after Starks's death, when she is forty, she chooses a younger man, Tea Cake, a partner who includes her in his work and his play and insists that she "partakes wid everything." Tea Cake teaches her to fish and to shoot; he cooks for her and encourages her to tell stories alongside the men. Yet at the end of the novel, Tea Cake is bitten by a rabid dog, and Janie is forced to shoot him. Hurston dramatizes issues of race, community, and justice in Janie's trial for the killing. Ironically, the white jury votes to acquit her, while the black people in the courtroom, her peers, harshly condemn her. "They were all against her, she could see. So many were there against her that a light slap from each one of them would have beat her to death." Janie's trial could be a metaphor for Hurston's aesthetic trial, for it reveals similar complexities and ironies.

Black male critics of the 1930s did not like *Their Eyes Were Watching God*. They accused Hurston of pandering to a white audience and attacked her use of dialect humor as a "minstrel technique." Richard Wright charged that Hurston "seems to have no desire whatever to move in the direction of serious fiction." Moreover, "the sensory sweep of her novel carries no theme, no message, no thought. In the main, her novel is not addressed to the Negro, but to the white audience whose chauvinistic tastes she knows how to satisfy."[77] Unintimidated, Hurston did not back down. In 1943, she gave an interview to the *New York World-Telegram* asserting: "I don't see life through the eyes of a Negro, but those of a person."[78] She went on to publish a novel about poor white characters in Florida, *Seraph on the Suwanee* (1948). Most of her black critics saw it as the final sellout, but some reviewers commended it for her astonishing ability to write about all "the sexes, the professions, and the races."[79] During the last years of her life, out of favor with publishers and the public, Hurston moved from job to menial job; when she died in 1960, she was working as a maid and living in a welfare home. Her grave was unmarked.

"WHAT BECOMES A LEGEND MOST"—LILLIAN HELLMAN

In the 1930s, many literary talents that might have been directed toward the live stage were instead turning toward the motion picture industry, where the challenges were even greater, but the financial rewards commensurate with the risks. Several women novelists, including Hurston, Le Sueur, Porter, Parker, and Slesinger, went to Hollywood at some point in the thirties to have a try at screenwriting. Twenty-nine movies were made from Fannie Hurst's novels and stories, and she wrote several screenplays herself.[80]

Lillian Hellman (1905–1984) was the best-known woman playwright of the 1930s, and her career extended to movies, screenplays, reportage, memoirs, and even the libretto for Leonard Bernstein's opera *Candide.* Hellman was born to a Jewish family in New Orleans, but moved to New York City while she was young. After attending New York University, she worked in publishing. In 1925, she married a press agent and writer, Arthur Kober, and they went to Hollywood, where she read scripts for MGM. In Hollywood she also met the detective novelist Dashiell Hammett, and divorced Kober. Although she and Hammett never married, they remained together until his death in 1961.

During the thirties, Hellman wrote two hit Broadway plays. *The Children's Hour* (1934) concerns two women teachers in a girls' school who are accused of lesbianism by a student, and whose lives are destroyed by the malicious gossip. The choice of subject shocked many critics in 1934, and Hellman stands as a bold pioneer for introducing it to the stage, even though the play now seems dated because of changes in public attitudes toward sexual orientation and same-sex couples. *The Little Foxes* (1939) is a more accomplished play, set in the Deep South around 1900, and combining a family drama with a fierce attack on capitalism. Its female protagonist, the villainous Regina, kills her husband by provoking a heart attack, and takes over control of her brothers' exploitative schemes. Hellman forcefully brings out the ways that this patriarchal society destroys women, who become either infantilized or hard and ruthless. Hellman was infuriated when reviewers compared her to Clare Boothe

Luce as if she were a mere "lady playwright." "We don't write the same way and we aren't interested in the same ends," she protested. "There is no possible basis for comparison except that we are women dramatists with successes to our credit."[81]

Hellman took an active part in antifascist campaigns, especially during the Spanish Civil War, and wrote an anti-Nazi play, *Watch on the Rhine,* in 1941. In the postwar years, Hammett, who had been a member of the Communist Party, was jailed for refusing to name names before the House Un-American Activities Committee, and Hellman herself pleaded the Fifth Amendment, famously stating, "I cannot and will not cut my conscience to fit this year's fashions." Although she was not jailed, she was blacklisted in Hollywood, and her screenwriting career abruptly ended. From this time forward, Hellman became an increasingly controversial figure. The widespread admiration for her refusal to betray her former colleagues was mitigated by charges that she blamed other leftists who agreed to testify more than she blamed the interrogators. Although she continued to write for the theater, she achieved her greatest fame as an author of memoirs, with *An Unfinished Woman* (1969), *Pentimento* (1973), and *Scoundrel Time* (1976). Soon, however, Hellman was accused of concealing her own dubious actions while indicting others, inventing stories to glorify herself, and hypocritically attempting to silence her critics. Her public clashes with the critic Diana Trilling, the journalist Martha Gellhorn, the psychiatrist Muriel Gardiner, and most notoriously the writer Mary McCarthy overshadowed her literary achievements, and by the end of her life, this scourge of capitalism had become a celebrity "legend," modeling a mink coat in a famous advertisement.

"Story belongs to the people"

One cultural contribution of the 1930s was the radio soap opera; daytime radio offered a rich choice of serial dramas about women, stories to brighten the lives of lonely housewives. Their shared theme, one historian notes, was women's strength in the face of male weakness. "The men in their lives were handsome but unreliable. They had affairs . . . they failed in business . . . or they were left helpless by blindness, amnesia, or some crippling trauma." Women had to step into the breach, save the family, and take over as breadwinners. These drastic solutions to female fantasies were deplored by male writers, as they had been in the days of Fanny Fern's *Ruth Hall*. James Thurber complained that "the man in the wheelchair has come to be the standard Soapland symbol," and William Faulkner described the era in Hollywood soaps and weepie movies as "the Kotex Age."[82]

The popular fiction of the thirties and even children's literature by women also provided resourceful women characters to overcome the anxieties of the decade, or told stories of survival in hard times. Laura Ingalls Wilder (1867–1957) began in 1932 to publish her fictionalized memoirs of homesteading as a girl with her beloved family in the woods of Wisconsin and the Dakota Indian Territory. *Little House in the Big Woods* (1932) and its sequels became favorites with children, teachers, and librarians. Marjorie Kinnan Rawlings (1896–1953) preferred to write for and about boys; *The Yearling* (1938), set in the backwoods of Florida, made her famous with its story of Jody Baxter, a capable and sensitive young boy who is forced to kill his pet deer after it destroys the family's precious crops, but who is so traumatized by his action that he runs away from home. He returns, though, no longer a "yearling," but matured by the experience.

Although the two legendary best sellers of the decade, *The Good Earth* (1931) and *Gone with the Wind* (1936), were worlds apart in plot and tone, they had deep similarities of feeling about women's endurance. While Pearl Buck was among the most open-minded and cosmopolitan of the women writers of the thirties, and Mitchell one of the most reactionary and provincial, both believed in the novel as a powerfully democratic form. In her speech accepting the Nobel Prize in 1938, Buck declared that "story belongs to the people. They are sounder judges of it than anyone else, for their senses are unspoiled and their emotions are free. No, a novelist must not think of pure literature as his goal . . . He is a storyteller in a village tent, and by his stories he entices people into his tent."[83]

Pearl Sydenstricker Buck (1892–1973) was what her biographer Peter Conn calls "an involuntary expatriate," who "had no home either in Asia or America." As Conn suggests, "if exile and displacement are the characteristic marks of modern experience, then a credible case can be made that Pearl Buck's life uniquely summarized the leading themes of her time." She had grown up as the only daughter of Southern Presbyterian missionaries stationed in China, and from childhood on, confronted two patriarchal cultures—her father's Christian disdain for women, and

China's traditional codes of male supremacy. Her father, Absalom Sydenstricker, was a harsh, intolerant man; Buck would later write that if he had been a Puritan, "he would have burned witches." His firm convictions of the divinely ordained subordination of women, she believed, stemmed from a "deep unconscious sex antagonism, rooted in no one knows what childhood experiences," and exacerbated by the obvious intelligence of his wife and daughter. "He could not bear better than another man a woman more clever than himself."[84] At the same time, she witnessed the oppression of Chinese women in all classes, the unending labor of peasant women in the fields, and the bound feet of daughters destined for arranged marriages and sexual slavery. In *The Good Earth*, fathers talk openly of surviving famine and drought by selling their daughters into servitude, and O-Lan, the female protagonist, half starving herself, commits infanticide when she bears a girl.

Buck grew up bilingual and bicultural. She was sent back to Virginia to be educated at Randolph-Macon Women's College, a place that seemed too small, intellectually undemanding, and isolated to her at the time, but that gave her a solid education. In 1917, she married an American agricultural economist, John Lossing Buck, and they returned to China to live in a rural province. Although the marriage lasted seventeen years, it was troubled from the start; Buck later described him as a person "who cannot for temperamental reasons be close to another human being."[85] Like her father, Lossing (as he was called) could not accept his wife as an equal partner, even though her fluency in Mandarin, which he could never learn to speak, was crucial for his research into Chinese farming methods.

In 1920, living in Nanking, Buck gave birth to her daughter Carol, who turned out to have an inherited metabolic disease, phenylketonuria, that led to severe mental retardation. By 1929, Buck felt compelled to place Carol in an institution in New Jersey, where she lived for the rest of her life. Although she visited her daughter frequently, and made generous contributions to the institution once she began to make money from her writing, Buck never came to terms with her guilt and grief. She kept Carol's existence a secret until the late 1940s, by which time she had adopted seven other children. When Buck began to write fiction and essays about the transformations of China in the twentieth century, her American publisher, Richard Walsh of the John Day Company, became first a friend, then a lover, and, after 1935, when she and Lossing finally divorced, her husband. Their long and happy relationship has been called "the most successful writing and publishing partnership in the history of American letters."[86]

While she was still living in China and married to Lossing, Buck wrote *The Good Earth*, drawing on her sympathy for the Chinese people and her knowledge of Chinese history to tell the life story of the illiterate farmer Wang Lung and his wife O-Lan, whom he buys as a slave. Written in a "formal, quasi-biblical rhetoric," the novel follows the economic vicissitudes, natural calamities, and political upheavals that make Wang Lung a kind of Chinese Job, and O-Lan a silent, unappreciated, and long-suffering victim of her gender and her class. By the end of the book, Wang Lung's sons, the new men of modern China, are educated and forward-looking, but cut off from their peasant roots, and attracted to the revolutionaries who will overthrow the emperor. The best-selling book in the United States in both 1931 and 1932, *The Good Earth* was nonetheless controversial among Chinese intellectuals for its portrayal of brutal poverty and injustice, and among the missionary community in China for its indifference to Christianity. In many respects, *The Good Earth* anticipated postcolonial novels like the Nigerian writer Chinua Achebe's *Things Fall Apart* (1958), which examined both the cruelty and superstition of non-Western cultures, and also their loss of tradition and dignity when taken over by Western colonialists. Conn suggests that the reasons for the novel's American success included its tale "of the suffering and endurance of farmers," and its celebration of "the traditional American value of simplicity," along with Buck's narrative skills.[87] When she won the Nobel Prize in 1938, however, the literary establishment was indignant, and Buck's Nobel Prize has become the standard example of the academy's poor critical judgment and political motives.

Margaret Mitchell (1900–1949) was brought up in Atlanta wanting to be a flirtatious Southern belle like Zelda Fitzgerald, but she was also the daughter of a women's suffrage activist who bribed her as a child to do serious reading. She spent her freshman year at Smith College, where she was preparing to study medicine, but was horrified and made a formal complaint to the dean when one of her classmates in a history seminar was black. Her mother died in the flu epidemic of 1918, and Mitchell had to return home to keep house for her father and brother; one critic thinks she was relieved to get away from the North.[88] For five years she worked as a reporter for the *Atlanta Journal*. Married in 1925 to the adoring John March (an earlier brief marriage to a bootlegger had been annulled), she quit her job and almost immediately began to suffer from an astonishing collection of real and imagined illnesses—arthritis of the ankle, suspected breast cancer, swollen hands, pleurisy. She started working at home on the epic novel that would become *Gone with the Wind,* doing vast amounts of research and reading Southern memoirs and histories of the Civil War brought home from the Atlanta library by her attentive husband.

As Helen Taylor points out, "for good or ill," *Gone with the Wind* is the "most globally known and celebrated text" about the Civil War.[89] Its commercial success was so phenomenal that it swamped other novels appearing at the same time, and exacerbated the sense of competition among Southern women writers. "Margaret Mitchell has got all the trade, damn her," Caroline Gordon (1895–1981) wrote to a friend when her own Civil War novel, *None Shall Look Back* (1937), foundered. "They say it took her ten years to write that novel. Why couldn't it have taken twelve?"[90] Gordon's book was a sober, almost documentary study of the horrors of war, written from a conservative Southern Agrarian perspective (she was married to the poet-critic Allen Tate). *Gone with the Wind,* on the other hand, has been condemned by some recent critics not only as romantic fluff, but also as a racist novel, with a "distorted sense of history," which "captures the hold of the Confederate cause better than any academic study," and shows Scarlett's "brutalization" alongside that of the soldiers.[91]

Mitchell's message, however, endured because it spoke to the universal uncertainties of the twentieth century as well as to the particular struggles of the Confederate past. Her mother had told her that with the Civil War, the seemingly secure world of the South "had exploded beneath them," and "my own world was going to explode under me, some day, and God help me if I didn't have some weapon to meet the new world."[92] American readers facing the rise of fascism in Europe could readily identify with fears of the world exploding around them. To them, *Gone with the Wind* brought hope; in the words of the critic Blanche Gelfant, it was "about the American thirties—about dispossession and loss, homelessness, hunger, the collapse of a society and its miraculous recovery."[93]

Whether they were writing red or black or pink, women's struggles in the 1930s came from private demons as well as political pressures. They were hampered by the men who jimmied their way into their lives, by their own failures of confidence, and by their multiple obligations to be nice, to serve, and to be good comrades. But the broadening of their literary horizons during the decade, and their battles to tell their stories gave them strong weapons to meet the new world they would face in the decade ahead.

15

The 1940s: World War II and After

n most surveys of American literature, one period comes to an end before World War II and another starts right after it, but little is said about the period from 1941 to 1945, the years of the war itself. World War II, the *Columbia Literary History of the United States* declares, "was a kind of literary hiatus, a pause between artistic generations."[1] Yet as I've shown before in the Civil War and World War I, the official hiatus or gap between generations usually means that men were in combat, and not publishing important work, while women were on the home front, writing, but invisible.

America's entry into World War II after Pearl Harbor brought women into the war effort as writers as well as laborers. Alongside the familiar wartime icon of Rosie the Riveter, baring her muscles and ready to pitch in for American defense, was another icon, Rosie the Writer—the war correspondent, war poet, best-selling novelist, and keeper of morale. Americans had asked for war poets, and women had responded: "a newly respected figure, the war poet as woman," writes Susan Schweik, "took her place next to the soldier in the photographic frontispiece and the tables of contents of war poetry collections."[2] Some reviewers thought that the war had inspired women to write poetry. In 1944, Louise Bogan observed that "an unusually large number of books written by women have appeared at the beginning of the fall season," and wondered whether the war might be the reason.[3] Yet women poets who addressed the war felt conflicted and uneasy about the validity of their contributions. "I hated the very idea of war," the poet Jane Cooper (1924–2007) remembered, ". . . yet obviously I was excited and absorbed by it, and also I felt guilty because I had not participated in any direct way, only through association. And how could you write except from experience? Men were acting and fighting; women were at home, waiting for their letters. Perhaps . . . this was one of the true problems of women writers at that time."[4] Women poets who did not address the war felt anxious, too. Writing to her editor at Houghton Mifflin in 1945, Elizabeth Bishop worried whether the "fact that none of these poems deal directly with the war, at a time when so much war poetry is being published, will . . . leave me open to reproach."[5]

Covering the War and Competing with Men

For the most daring women, the war offered opportunities to experience the challenge, excitement, and intensity of action. In the Civil War, women had been nurses; in World War I, they drove ambulances. When Alice Bradley Sheldon (1915–1987), who would later write science fiction under a male pseudonym in the 1970s, wanted to join the Women's Army Corps, her mother objected. "If I were a man, would you dissuade me from enlisting?" Sheldon asked. "This is one of the greatest occasions in life, a total war."[6] Her arrival at the training camp in Des Moines in 1942 was "an awakening, seeing for the first time in my life a world of women—women glimpsed through doors of canteens offices barracks kitchens guard-posts—women plowing through the black mud into the pools of light—women in uniform, looking as though they owned the place—and owning it!"[7] Although *The New Yorker* published her first short story, an accolade for twentieth-century American writers akin to publication in the *Atlantic Monthly* the century before, Sheldon felt cramped and dissatisfied by the range and expectations of women's writing. In her journal in 1945, she wrote, "I find, in all the writings of women, a strange muffled quality, as if the living word, as it left the lips, had been hastily suppressed and another substituted, one which would conform to some pattern imposed from without."[8]

Martha Gellhorn's novel *A Stricken Field* (1940) described the harsh and brutal lives of Jewish refugees in Prague. Determined to get back to Europe as a war correspondent, Gellhorn was in London in the winter of 1944, scheming to be in on the Allied invasion of France. Stowing away on a Red Cross hospital ship, she witnessed the D-Day landings on Omaha Beach, came ashore with the ambulance team, and helped care for the wounded. Gellhorn's final dispatches from the war came from Dachau, where she accompanied the U.S. Army in April 1945. The experience was a trauma that permanently destroyed her sense of optimism and faith in justice. "It is as if I walked into Dachau and there fell over a cliff," she wrote later. "I know I have never again felt that lovely, easy, lively hope in life which I knew before, not in life, not in our species, not in our future on earth."9

Internment and the Japanese-American Experience

In the United States, over 110,000 Japanese-Americans were sent to internment camps to prevent collusion with the enemy. As Hisaye Yamamoto (1921–) has explained, "It is an episode in our collective life which wounded us more painfully than we realize. I didn't know myself what a lump it was in my subconscious until a few years ago when I watched one of the earlier television documentaries on the subject . . . To my surprise, I found the tears trickling down my cheeks and my voice squeaking out of control, as I tried to explain to my husband and children why I was weeping."10 Nisei women, second-generation Japanese-Americans, had been developing their own literary communities before the war, and when Yamamoto was sent to Poston, Arizona, for three years, she began her literary career writing for the camp newspaper.11

After the war, she went to work for a black newspaper in Los Angeles, expanding her understanding of race, and began to publish her short stories in major magazines. Frank about female sexuality and the threat of sexual abuse, Yamamoto also conveyed the tensions between mothers and daughters, the trauma of the camps, and the problems of writing for women of her generation. In "Seventeen Syllables" (1949), the teenaged Rosie Hayashi is impatient with her quiet and traditional mother's pseudonymous career as writer of haiku for a Japanese newspaper in San Francisco. Under the name "Ume Hanazono" ("brief flowering tree"), Mrs. Hayashi has a second imaginative life outside their Southern California farm, apart from her hard work and unsympathetic husband. When the haiku editor of the newspaper arrives to tell her she has won a contest and gives her the prize of a Hiroshige print, Mr. Hayashi is enraged. He smashes the picture with an ax and burns it. For the first time, Rosie's mother confesses her story to her daughter: in Japan, she had become pregnant by a man forbidden to marry her, had lost the baby, and had accepted an arranged marriage in America. The dead son would have been seventeen, like the syllables of a haiku poem. The central character of "The Legend of Miss Sasagawara" (1950) is also a poet, driven mad by loneliness and family obligation.

Jim Crow, Chicago, and the African-American Experience

For black women writers, the forties were a continuation of racial segregation, and economic hardship. Margaret Walker (1915–1998) grew up in Birmingham, Alabama; she knew the Jim Crow South "and what it was to step off the sidewalk to let a white man pass." All her life, she felt that the "sordid and ugly world . . . keeps me on a battlefield, at war."[12] Walker went to Chicago to study at Northwestern University in the 1930s, became active in the Federal Writers' Project, and fell in love with Richard Wright.[13] Steeped in the proletarian literary tradition, she had "attended classes and lectures at the workers' school on dialectical materialism, Marxism-Leninism, art and society, the proletarian novel, and proletarian poetry."[14] In 1942, she received an M.A. in creative writing from the Writers' Workshop at the University of Iowa, and published her first volume of poems, *For My People*, which won the Yale Series of Younger Poets Award. Walker did not write about the war, but about African-American culture, which she treated in "prophetic" poems, jazz ballads, and sonnets.[15] As she recalled, the book had actually been rejected by Yale three times, but had finally been recalled and published because of the intervention of Stephen Vincent Benét, who "felt they were refusing purely on the basis of race."[16]

Walker and Gwendolyn Brooks (1917–2000) became friends in the Chicago Renaissance, a racially mixed artistic community that flourished on Chicago's South Side in the 1940s. Brooks had started to write poetry as a young girl growing up in Chicago, and had already had a number of poems published in the *Chicago Defender*. She published her first book of poems, *A Street in Bronzeville*, in 1945.[17] More thematically diverse than Walker's collection, the book combined portraits and vignettes of the lives of residents of a South Side black ghetto with a superbly crafted twelve-sonnet sequence called "Gay Chaps at the Bar," which looked at black servicemen in the war.[18] Measured, deeply felt, technically sophisticated, tonally haunting, *A Street in Bronzeville* was widely and enthusiastically reviewed by black and white poets, and Brooks won a number of awards and fellowships for her work.

The rivalries that tormented and divided white women writers, who felt that they were all competing for the very limited resources, acceptance, recognition, and honors available to women, affected black women writers as well. Walker felt that Brooks had somehow outdone her: "It was ironic that all the forces that had dealt negatively with my work dealt positively with Gwendolyn Brooks's work . . . First, Gwen won a poetry prize at Northwestern. That never happened to me . . . Second, after we broke up and our friendship ended, [Richard Wright] helped Gwen. I'm certain that Gwen got published at Harper because Wright was there."[19]

Brooks's second book, *Annie Allen* (1949), made it clear, however, that she deserved to prevail. Dedicated to Edward Bland, a black soldier who had been killed in Germany in 1945, and who had belonged to Brooks's poetry workshop, it was actually about an ordinary black woman, a paradigmatic figure of her generation, whose life is changed by the war. Ambitious in its conception, skilled, and finely executed, *Annie Allen* has three parts: "Notes from the Childhood and the Girlhood," "The Anniad," and "The Womanhood." "The Anniad," the central poem in the book, boldly claimed Homeric epic significance for the tale of its heroine. The book won the Pulitzer Prize, but black critics were troubled by its technical difficulty and elitism. By the end of the century, black feminist critics also challenged Brooks's initial acceptance of stereotypes of female passivity and domesticity. By the 1960s, however, Brooks herself was radicalized by the black power movement and the idea of the black aesthetic, and had moved away from traditional Western poetic forms to write in a style based on the black idiom, jazz, and blues.

The American Literary Canon in the 1940s

The forties began with disparaging critical assessments of the American female literary tradition. Herbert Ross Brown's *The Sentimental Novel in America* (1940) linked female authorship with undemanding female readership, and chose passages to demonstrate the incompatibility of the literary interests of women and men. Fred Lewis Pattee's *The Feminine Fifties* (1940) displayed extensive knowledge of women's writing, but caricatured its concerns and placed it below serious literary attention. Then, in 1941, F. O. Matthiessen's *American Renaissance* excluded women altogether. The rise of the New Criticism in the academy also had the effect of marginalizing women's writing. In its founding studies, *Understanding Poetry* (1938), by Cleanth Brooks and Robert Penn Warren, and John Crowe Ransom's *The New Criticism* (1941), this school of literary theory advocated strict attention to the poetic text itself, rather than historical or biographical context. In the late 1940s, when Jane Cooper lived in Princeton, she noticed that "work by women was still sparsely represented in contemporary poetry anthologies . . . Somehow I had absorbed out of the New Critical air . . . that women have trouble managing traditional meters with authority and verve and also can't handle long lines."[20] By the end of the decade, the fifty-four male editors (and one woman editor) of the *Literary History of the United States* (1948) identified democracy, mobility, progress, and independence as the essential characteristics of "the American way of life." Seeking great writers who embodied these themes, they found very few women, and even fewer African-Americans.

Yaddo

Yet other doors were opening to let women in during the forties. Perhaps owing to the absence of men and shortage of male applicants, women writers won the support of Guggenheim Fellowships, publishing contracts, and prolonged stays at Yaddo, the artists' colony in Saratoga Springs, New York. Opened in 1926 on a four-hundred-acre estate bequeathed by the wealthy Trask family, Yaddo was built around a fifty-five-room Victorian mansion, with a baronial dining hall, a rose garden and arboretum, and outlying studios and adjoining residences. It also hosted numerous painters, composers, and writers who were refugees from Nazi Europe. As Eudora Welty described it in the summer of 1941, "Yaddo was in the old, rural, comfortably settled part of New York State west of Albany . . . The estate was private and well-guarded, though its gardens were, at that innocent time, open to the public. The artists came for their summer at Yaddo solely by invitation. Elizabeth Ames gave her life to being its director—a woman of Quaker-like calm and decisiveness; she was beautiful and to some extent deaf. She stood ready for crises."[21] Ames had the final say with the board on who would be invited to visit; the "talents and creative works in progress" of the applicants "were usually subordinate to Mrs. Ames's personal opinion regarding the prospective guest's character, and . . . apparent compatibility with others."[22]

While the majority of Yaddo residents in the forties still were men, including Langston Hughes, Alfred Kazin, and Newton Arvin, Ames sought out women artists, and the estate was probably the first literary community in which women lived and worked together. Communal living, however, did not necessarily create an idyllic sisterly enclave, let alone a feminist utopia. The women writers in residence at Yaddo, including Carson McCullers, Flannery O'Connor, Katherine Anne Porter, Agnes Smedley, Jean Stafford, Margaret Walker, and Eudora Welty, had arguments as well as alliances. Such tensions were not unusual, according to Ames, who recalled that "over the years the female artists at Yaddo always got along better with the men than with each other"; women writers "are usually not very tolerant of each other. They're temperamental."[23] In fact, many arguments were political, and the most explosive event at Yaddo during the decade occurred in 1949, when Robert Lowell, then married to Elizabeth Hardwick, began a campaign to have Agnes Smedley ousted as a Communist spy, and also tried unsuccessfully to get Ames fired for sheltering her. Temperamental and political or not, women writers found Yaddo an important refuge from domestic responsibilities, loneliness, and exclusion.

MEMBER OF THE WEDDING—CARSON MCCULLERS

A female enfant terrible who dressed like an adolescent boy, Carson Smith McCullers (1917–1967) spent a great deal of time at Yaddo in the forties and fifties. When she made her first visit in the summer of 1941, McCullers was already "New York's new literary darling," famous for her precocious debut novels, *The Heart Is a Lonely Hunter* (1940) and *Reflections in a Golden Eye* (1941). Reviews had called her "the most exciting new talent of the decade."[24] As a young girl in Columbus, Georgia, Lula Carson Smith (she dropped her first name in her early teens) had trained to be a concert pianist; she was also an insatiable reader of the Russian novelists, in addition to the Brontës, Melville, Katherine Mansfield, Eugene O'Neill, and D. H. Lawrence. In "How I Began to Write," McCullers described her awakening as a writer in the winter of 1935: "The family rooms, the whole town, seemed to pinch and cramp my adolescent heart. I longed for wanderings. I longed especially for New York . . . and New York was the happy *mise en scène* of that first novel I wrote when I was fifteen. The details of the book were queer: ticket collectors on the subway, New York front yards—but by that time it did not matter for already I had begun another journey . . . the marvelous solitary region of simple stories and the inward mind."[25]

In this passage, McCullers sounds like Paul, the provincial adolescent artist desperate for beauty in Willa Cather's "Paul's Case." She understood at an early age that she was bisexual: "By the time I was six I was sure that I was born a man."[26] She was also politically and racially aware; Fort Benning was only nine miles from Columbus, and during the thirties she was "passionate about the European situation, zealous in her attack on fascism and Nazism, and indignant at racism and what she considered the gross mistreatment of blacks" in the South.[27] At the age of seventeen, she left Georgia to go to New York, intending to study music at Juilliard; but, according to legend, lost her pocketbook with all her money on the subway, and worked at odd jobs in addition to studying creative writing at Columbia and NYU instead.

Her first novel, *The Heart Is a Lonely Hunter,* was set in a small town "in the middle of the deep South," where "the summers always were burning hot," most of the population worked in the cotton mills, and "in the faces along the streets there was the desperate look of hunger and of loneliness." For McCullers, the South was hell's kitchen, and her characters were always yearning to be in a place where the snow allows clearness of mind, and they can find "spiritual integration with something greater than themselves."[28] Her main characters, all loners and outsiders, were types who would reappear in different forms in all of her fiction: Mick Kelly, the boyish, isolated, and creative adolescent girl; Jake Blount, the social radical; Dr. Benedict Mady Copeland, the black doctor who plans to lead a march of "more than one thousand Negroes in this county" to Washington to protest their oppression; and John Singer, the deaf-mute, who suffers for them all. *Reflections in a Golden Eye,* set on an army base, was written in the grotesque and sometimes lushly macabre genre that became known as Southern Gothic, and featured a murder, a woman who goes mad and mutilates herself, and a homoerotic triangle. McCullers dedicated the novel to Anne-Marie Clarac-Schwarzenbach, a glamorous Swiss artist she had met through Erika Mann and W. H. Auden, and for whom she had left her husband, Reeves McCullers, a Georgia army corporal and would-be writer. After her divorce, McCullers lived in Brooklyn Heights in a house shared by such diverse fellow artists as Richard Wright and Gypsy Rose Lee; she also spent a month at the Bread Loaf Writers' Conference in Vermont, with Louis Untermeyer, Eudora Welty, and Wallace Stegner, who remembered her as drinking straight gin out of water glasses.[29]

Her reputation for heavy drinking, bohemian wildness, perversity of imagination, and physical fragility, as well as precocity and literary genius, preceded her at Yaddo, and she was the focus of much gossip and many anecdotes. In 1943, Jean Stafford found her "by no means the consumptive dipsomaniac I'd heard she was," but very "strange."[30] Caroline Gordon wrote cynically to Stafford that summer, too: "McCullers, being slated to die before she's thirty, would evidently not be much help even if she were congenial. Maybe that hovering early death is part of her charm."[31] The charm did not work on Katherine Anne Porter, who became the prime target of McCullers's obsessive adoration. McCullers followed her around like a stalker, pledged her undying love, and threw herself on the floor across Porter's threshold, but Porter received these gestures coolly—"I merely stepped over her and continued on my way to dinner."[32] Despite her chaotic personal life, McCullers managed to complete a novella, *The Ballad of the Sad Café* (not published until 1951), remarried Reeves, who was serving in Europe, and wrote several short stories.

McCullers made her third visit to Yaddo in the summer of 1945, when it was still "operating on a wartime basis, with food supplies—especially meat—difficult to get in quantities." The mansion was closed, and guests ate their meals in the garage and slept in the outlying buildings. Nevertheless, McCullers, who had an open invitation to visit, finished the seventh and final draft of *The Member of the Wedding* at the end of August. Ames stayed up half the night reading it, and in the morning told a trembling McCullers, "You have done it, my dear."[33] She dedicated the novel to Ames when it came out in 1946.

The Member of the Wedding, her finest book, is both a semiautobiographical story of a young girl's coming-of-age and a novel about the war. Set in a small town in Georgia, it begins during the emotionally turbulent week that twelve-year-old Frankie Addams spends waiting for the wedding of her brother. This week, at the end of August 1944, coincides with the liberation of Paris and the coming end of the war in Europe. Frankie has been overwhelmed and confused by the war: "Frankie read the war news in the paper, but there were so many foreign places and the war was happening so fast that sometimes she did not understand. It was the summer when Patton was chasing the Germans across France. And they were fighting, too, in Russia and Saipan. She saw the battles and the soldiers. But there were too many different battles, and she could not see in her mind the millions and millions of soldiers all at once." Her idolized brother Jarvis is a soldier, stationed in Alaska, and she "wanted to be a boy and go to the war as a Marine. She thought about flying aeroplanes and winning gold medals for bravery. But she could not join the war."

She is even too young to give blood to the Red Cross, and "Frankie felt mad with the world and left out of everything. The war and the world were too fast and big and strange."

Having grown four inches in a single year, Frankie also feels estranged from her own body, has cut her hair into a crew cut, and worries that she will end up as a freak in the sideshow at the Chattahoochee Exposition, where she has seen the Giant, the Fat Lady, the Midget, the Wild Nigger (some said he was "just a crazy colored man from Selma"), the childlike Pin Head, and worst of all, the Half-Man, Half-Woman. She "was afraid of all the Freaks, for it seemed that they looked at her in a secret way . . . as though to say: we know you." Frankie's companions are a bit freakish, too—her younger cousin John Henry West, who plays with dolls; and the black housekeeper, Berenice Sadie Brown, who has one blue glass eye, replacing an eye gouged out by an abusive husband. Berenice, however, is a visionary maternal figure who articulates McCullers's utopian dream of a world beyond race, outcasts, freaks, and war, where "there would be no separate colored people . . . but all human beings would be light brown color with blue eyes and black hair. There would be no colored people and no white people to make the colored people feel cheap and sorry all through their lives." As someone who knows about pain and death, Berenice sees no glory in war; in her dream there would be "no stiff corpses hanging from the Europe trees, and no Jews murdered anywhere."

Frankie, who is completely sexually innocent, wishes that "people could change back and forth from boys to girls whichever way they felt like and wanted." She fixates on her brother's wedding as her opportunity to escape freakishness and loneliness, and to stop being "an unjoined person," an outsider who "belonged to no club and was a member of nothing in the world." She convinces herself that she will be able to join Jarvis and his bride, Janice, and live with them forever. Of course the wedding is humiliating and catastrophic. When the couple get ready to leave for their honeymoon, she gets into the car with her suitcase and has to be "hauled and dragged" away, crying "Take me! Take me!"

By October, Frankie has turned thirteen, and made the transition from androgyny to adolescence. The brief electric summer of Frankie's discontent, though, is also the last time when she will be able to share Berenice's double vision. When Frankie grows up, she also outgrows her feelings of easy intimacy with black people. Her new best friend and idol, Mary Littlejohn, is a girl Berenice regards as "lumpy and marshmallow-white," and Berenice gives "quit notice," and moves away to live with her own kin. John Henry dies horribly of meningitis. Growing up, for McCullers, means giving up the sense of identification with the sensitive and the visionary, and although Frankie survives, it is not a happy ending.

With the help of her friend Tennessee Williams, McCullers turned *The Member of the Wedding* into a play, which opened on Broadway in 1950 with Ethel Waters as Berenice, and ran for over a year, followed by a long national tour and a movie. McCullers made a great deal of money, although she suffered from an increasing number of serious and debilitating illnesses, including rheumatic fever, an infected jaw, pleurisy, breast cancer, several strokes, and a heart attack. Fame did not comfort her; she drank more and more heavily, and grew increasingly waspish about women rivals as she grew older, especially when she thought they were imitating her; Flannery O'Connor, she sniped, had "learned her lesson well," and Harper Lee was "poaching on my literary preserves." McCullers's final novel, *Clock Without Hands* (1960), was another book about alienated Southerners, which recycled motifs and images from her earlier work, including an embittered black man with blue eyes; but she had lost her creative energy. Flannery O'Connor opined that it was the worst book she had ever read. By the end of the 1950s, McCullers was an invalid who took to dressing entirely in white, like Emily Dickinson, giving interviews from her wheelchair dressed in white nightgowns and tennis shoes.[34] She was only fifty when she died. Louis Untermeyer had called her "the *fleur du mal*" and "predicted that she would die young," but outliving her talent may have been a more terrible fate.[35]

THE MOUNTAIN LION—JEAN STAFFORD

Jean Stafford (1915–1979) got to Yaddo in the summer of 1943. Stafford's life and career are such textbook illustrations of the worst-case tribulations of the talented woman writer in mid-century America—from unsympathetic family, to unstable genius husband, to alcoholism, mental breakdown, physical illness, and alienation of all her friends—that Joyce Carol Oates memorably called one study of her a "pathography." Yet Stafford fought to the end against the perception that being born female had anything to do with her trials, and was a fierce opponent of women's liberation. Her difficulties began with her family. She was born in Covina, California, the youngest of four children, but both her birth and her femaleness were unwelcome. Her father had hoped for another son. A would-be writer of "Thud and Blunder" Westerns who called himself "Jack Wonder" or "Ben Delight," he had lost the family's considerable fortune in bad investments, and let his wife support him while he spent his days in his basement "yarn factory," obsessively and hopelessly writing an endless book on government deficit spending. He was always reminding Jean that he had wanted a boy, and once clumsily gave her a boy's haircut. Stafford's mother and siblings were no more welcoming. When she was born, her brother Dick said, "She's alright, I guess, but I wish she'd been a dog." Although she adored Dick, he had little interest in playing with a girl, and was outraged when she wore his outgrown Boy Scout shirt. "Having that on a girl," he declared, "is like dragging the American flag in the dirt." Her two older sisters were conventional girls, and she also despised her mother's genteel housewifeliness. For a while Stafford kept a cruel notebook of her mother's pious bromides and folksy clichés. Later she would say that "for all practical purposes," she had left home at the age of seven. Overall, biographer Charlotte Goodman concludes, she felt "unwanted, unloved, and unprotected by her family."[36]

The family moved to Colorado in 1922, and as she grew older, Stafford expressed her discomfort with her body and her gender through anorexia, cross-dressing, and self-mutilation. The family called her a "problem feeder"; her sisters teased her about reducing pills, diets, and rubber underwear. She cut her high-school picture out of the yearbook because it made her look too fat. Like Willa Cather, she liked to dress as a boy, and had her picture taken wearing her father's suit and hat; in high school a friend described her as looking "like a boy with a dress on."[37]

During her undergraduate years at the University of Colorado, Stafford gamely made the most of her social opportunities. Indeed, one has to admire the sheer amount of perversity, high drama, heavy drinking, and self-destruction she managed to wrest out of a Rocky Mountain education. She modeled in the nude for art students, took up Catholic mysticism, and participated in a ménage à trois with lesbian undertones that ended in the suicide of its femme fatale leader, Lucy McKee Cooke. For much of her life, Stafford struggled unsuccessfully to novelize this dramatic bohemian experience.

Besides the partying, Stafford received encouragement for her work from a woman professor, Irene McKeehan, whose impeccable suits and medievalist scholarship offered her first adult model of the woman intellectual. It was largely McKeehan's example that persuaded Stafford to go to Heidelberg in 1936 as a graduate student in Anglo-Saxon and philology. She hoped to go on to Harvard to study, but instead had to take a job teaching English composition to the women at Stephens Junior College in Missouri. There she felt awkward and shabby, and retaliated with sneers at her "pretty, featherheaded" students with "rumps like a kitchen stove."[38] In her writing, she conscientiously apprenticed herself to male models, and wrote in a stilted, affected prose very different from her journals and letters to male friends, where she created various self-mocking female personae—"Bessie Barnstable" or "Florence Nightgown"—who wrote in an exaggerated jocular backwoods slang. Yet Stafford also realized that scathing mockery of women could not free her from the need to confront problems of sexuality and creativity in her own life and work. She was beginning to ask herself why women could not seem to separate the emotional from the aesthetic. "Why is it that a woman cannot write a book like *A Portrait of the Artist,*" she asked a friend. "I mean why it is that her experiences cannot be like those of a man."[39]

Nonetheless, she saw her priorities as feminine, traditional, and domestic, rather than literary and professional: "I want children, I want a house. I want to be a faithful woman. I want these things more than I want my present life of a writer."[40] Stafford maintained this traditional hierarchy of values throughout her life, although she would never have children. At a Colorado Writers' Conference in 1937, she met Robert Lowell, only twenty-one and still a Harvard undergraduate. He courted her intensely through the mails, and in December 1938, she went to visit him in Boston. While they were riding in his father's Packard, Lowell went into a rage at her refusal to marry him, and crashed the car into an embankment. He was unhurt (the court later convicted him with driving while intoxicated), but Stafford sustained massive injuries to her skull, nose, and jaw that required five painful operations to repair. After the accident, she would always look battered, her eyes teary and "permanently welled-up." As Lowell's friend Blair Clark remarked, "There was about a 25 percent reduction of the aesthetic value of her face."[41] The precision of this figure reflects widely held attitudes toward the market value of female beauty and its implicit contrast to the value of women's intelligence and art. Stafford felt herself marked by the accident as someone violated and damaged. She wrote about the experience in her harrowing short story "The Interior Castle" (1946), using images from the mystical visions of St. Teresa of Avila. Awaiting the surgeon whose scalpel will repair her "crushed and splintered nose," the heroine is in a state of terror about the invasion and pillaging of her brain, "her treasure whose price he, no more than the nurses, could estimate."

Although she had previously resisted Lowell's advances, describing him to a friend as "an uncouth, neurotic, psychopathic murderer-poet," Stafford married him not long after the accident, declaring that "he does what I have always needed to have done to me and that is that he dominates me." In the 1940s, they moved to Baton Rouge, Louisiana, where he was taking classes with Robert Penn Warren at Louisiana State University, and she was a secretary for Cleanth Brooks and Allen Tate at the *Southern Review.* "My retrogression is steady," she wrote to a friend, "now I'm a secretary. And will the next be a telephone operator or will I be the receptionist in a city laundry?"[42] Meanwhile, Lowell became a fanatical convert to an ascetic and sexless Catholicism. She went to church with him every day, did all the housework, supported them both with her earnings, and typed his poems over and over every time he changed a word.

Yaddo was a luxurious respite from her domestic chores and anxieties, but she quarreled with the other guests, particularly McCullers ("the most irritating of all") and Margaret Walker, who "loathes Allen's criticism and thinks Ransom is impossible" and used "her black skin as a weapon." She liked Elizabeth Ames, but not "this rarified atmosphere with the vibrations of these tragic lives . . . I suppose I am on the verge of some nervous crackup."[43] At the end of the summer, when she returned home, the marriage had entered a new and even more difficult phase. Although he had previously made some efforts to enlist, the day before he was due to be inducted on September 7, 1943, Lowell wrote a letter directly to President Roosevelt declaring that he would not serve because the war would leave Europe at the mercy of the Soviet Union and international Communism. Lowell's friends were appalled, and he himself was arrested and sentenced to the federal prison in Danville, Connecticut, for draft evasion; he served five months and then was paroled to finish his sentence mopping floors as a hospital orderly. In September 1944, three days before the publication of Stafford's novel *Boston Adventure,* Lowell's chapbook of poems, *Land of Unlikeness,* was published by a small Massachusetts press. "I can't tell you how glad I am his book came first," Stafford told friends.[44] Her book, though, was a best seller and a critical favorite, while his was a small printing and ignored. As a friend later observed, "Jean made a great mistake in becoming a success before

her husband did . . . I can imagine he made Jean pay for this a bit."[45]
He did.

By 1945, both Lowells were getting on with their writing. Stafford won
a Guggenheim Fellowship to finish her second novel, *The Mountain Lion*,
and Robert completed his first major book, *Lord Weary's Castle*. In the
summer of 1946, they bought a house in Damariscotta, Maine, with her
royalties from *Boston Adventure*, and invited their friends to stay, an experience she described in her short story "An Influx of Poets," which
appeared in *The New Yorker* in 1978. As the narrator Cora dryly recounts,

> *Every poet in America came to stay with us . . . At night, after supper,*
> *they'd read from their own works until four o'clock in the morning,*
> *drinking Cuba Libres. They never listened to one another; they were*
> *preoccupied with waiting for their turn. And I'd have to stay up and*
> *clear out the living room after they went soddenly to bed—soddenly, but*
> *not too far to lose their conceit. And then all day I'd cook and wash the*
> *dishes and chop the ice and weed the garden and type my husband's*
> *poems and quarrel with him.*

Like the poet-husband in the story, Lowell had an affair with one visitor, Gertrude Buckman, and the marriage ended that fall. Stafford had a
complete breakdown and went into the Payne Whitney Clinic in New
York for almost a year. From the hospital she wrote to Lowell in anguish:
"In your letter you say that you hope I will be recognized as the best novelist of my generation. I want you to know now and know completely
that that would mean to me absolutely *nothing*."[46]

If not the best novel of the 1940s, *The Mountain Lion* (1947) is a very
fine book indeed, a classic of childhood rage and bewilderment told in a
superbly controlled colloquial prose.[47] Growing up with their widowed
mother and older sisters in a genteel Covina, California, ten-year-old
Ralph Fawcett and his eight-year-old sister Molly are close companions,
who seem equally vulnerable and "feminine." They are both skinny,
runny-nosed, precocious, and nearsighted, and both suffer from bad
nosebleeds. Their lives change, however, when they start spending the
summers with their uncle Claude at his ranch in Colorado, which
Stafford presents from Ralph's point of view as a welcome transition to a
totally masculine environment: "Ralph thought of the house in Covina
with all its flurry of objects, little vases and boxes on little gilt tables and
whatnots hanging in the corners; and then thought of the big, bare

rooms of the ranch where the furniture was heavy and solid as if it were nailed to the floor and the only small things were catalogues from L. L. Bean and Montgomery Ward, boxes of buckshot, fly-books, and odd bits of leather and metal."

At the ranch, Ralph throws away his glasses, learns to ride and shoot, and observes the "robust and perpetual birth of the farm creatures." As he enters adolescence, he feels more ashamed of and distant from Molly, who does not feel at home in either place, does not believe in happiness, wants to become a writer, and is so naïve about sex that she announces she intends to marry her brother. She hates and denies her female body: "For the most part, she was not conscious of her body . . . Molly thought of herself as a long wooden box with a mind inside." She fights physical change, wraps herself in tight flannel bindings, and becomes anorexic: "If she ever got fat, she thought, she would lock herself in a bathroom and stay there until she died." Molly is also given to dramatic acts of self-mutilation; she runs a sewing-machine needle through her finger, and deliberately burns her hand with acid.

During the summer when she is twelve and Ralph is fourteen, they have an encounter with a mountain lion at the ranch, which is a rite of passage for Ralph, and a repudiation of all that is shamefully feminine and vulnerable in him, but fatal for Molly. Although Frankie survives her traumatic period as a would-be member of her brother's wedding, Molly has to be sacrificed. "The symbols are apparent," Stafford told her friend Cecile Starr, "though I didn't know what they meant at the time I wrote."[48] In the 1972 paperback edition, she added an evasive "Author's Note" about the time of the novel's composition, ending, "Poor old Molly! I loved her dearly and I hope she rests in peace." On the back cover was a photograph of Stafford, taken by her editor Robert Giroux, standing next to the lion cage at the zoo.

Stafford's fiction appeared regularly in *The New Yorker* over the next few years. Before anorexia, bulimia, and other eating disorders became epidemic, she was writing about them in short stories like "The Echo and the Nemesis" (1950), in which Ramona Dunn says, "I ought to hate myself for eating so much," and burns herself with a cigarette to punish herself for eating twelve cherry tarts. Her last novel, *The Catherine Wheel* (1952), came out when she was only thirty-six. Once again, as she explained, she had tried to create a heroine "with a male mind in which there is such and such a compartment for literature and such a one for love, but in the end she will be faced with the realization that a woman's mind can never be neatly ordered and every experience is tinged by every other one."[49]

Stafford's second marriage, to the editor Oliver Jensen, had quickly failed; and a brief happy third marriage to the journalist A. J. Liebling did not help her drinking or writing. When Liebling died in 1963, Stafford went into a long period of deterioration. She quarreled with her editors and publishers; her bouts of hospitalization increased; she flaunted her eccentricities and indulged her capacity for reactionary rudeness. She found it harder and harder to write fiction; between 1959 and her death in 1979, she published only five stories, and made her living as a reviewer and journalist. When Stafford's *Collected Stories* appeared in 1970, however, she received the Pulitzer Prize. She was glad to have it; however, she may have felt that it was overdue, and that she deserved the recognition.

By the 1970s, though, Stafford's chief pleasure seemed to be venomous attacks on the absurdities of the women's movement. "Fem Lib," she wrote in 1970, can "give a body the pip bad enough to call in the doctor."[50] A series of loyal women friends and editors—Evelyn Scott, Caroline Gordon, Katharine White, Eve Auchincloss—had offered nurturance and support for her writing. Even so, Stafford never had much respect for women or for herself; she was unable to finish her most autobiographical novels, "In the Snowfall" and "A Parliament of Women." In 1976, a stroke left her with aphasia and unable to speak. As her biographer Ann Hulbert concludes, "it was an all-too-fittingly scripted fate for a woman who had come to feel there was nothing very good to say about the world. Or, perhaps even more to the point, for a woman who was full of frustrated anger at her inability to find imaginative verbal form for her vision . . . [and] unfit to talk."[51]

A SHELTERED LIFE—EUDORA WELTY

Unlike McCullers, Porter, Stafford, and other women writers who sojourned at Yaddo in the 1940s, Eudora Welty (1909–2001) was considerate, levelheaded, single, and sober.[52] She was born in Jackson, Mississippi, where she went to public schools, graduating at age sixteen and winning the title of "Best All-round Girl." Her affectionate family could afford to send her away to college, first to Mississippi State College for Women for two years, and next to the University of Wisconsin, where she graduated in 1929. Welty then attended the Business School of Columbia University for a year, to study advertising. When her father died in 1931, she returned to Jackson, and took a series of jobs as a journalist for the local radio station, which had been established by her father's company, and then for local newspapers. From 1933 to 1935, she traveled around the state for federal agencies, including the WPA, taking brilliant pictures of poor black people in the Delta and using the camera to take her to places where nice white Southern girls were forbidden to enter. In general, however, neither the artistry nor the documentary value of her work was appreciated until much later, when two books of her photographs were published as *One Time, One Place: Mississippi in the Depression* (1971) and *Photographs* (1989). Meanwhile, she published her first short story, "Death of a Traveling Salesman," in *Manuscript* in 1936. She quickly began appearing regularly in other little magazines, like *Prairie Schooner* and *Accent,* and especially *Southern Review,* which published six of her stories.

When she arrived at Yaddo in the summer of 1941, Welty was preparing her first collection, *A Curtain of Green,* for publication. Yaddo was a retreat but not an oasis. That summer, "the company was in great part European. Elizabeth Ames had come to the aid of many artists who no longer had homes and were seeking refuge and a place to carry on their work. Our evening was indeed operatic, but it wasn't about the arts; it was about politics."[53] Katherine Anne Porter, who became a close friend, was among the most articulate and passionate of the group.

Ironically, Porter's introduction to *A Curtain of Green* stressed Welty's innocence of both radical politics and creative writing courses. Indeed, her introduction transformed the relatively sophisticated Welty into "a holy vestal of inexperience, with no personal history to mention, and no use for the wider world."[54] Porter also made veiled references to Welty's superiority to other women writers of the period; she "will never have to go away and live among the Eskimos or Mexican Indians" (like Cather?); "she need not follow a war and smell death to feel herself alive" (like Herbst and Gellhorn?); "she shall not even have to live in New York in order to feel that she is having the kind of experience . . . proper to a serious author" (like Stafford?).

A Curtain of Green was a vigorous debut, containing several of Welty's most original stories, and displaying her sharp ear for raucous and sometimes bawdy Southern language. In "Petrified Man," she was one of the first writers to use women's gossipy conversations in the setting of the beauty parlor. While the story involves a traveling freak show, where the customers and beauticians have seen twin fetuses in a bottle, two "African" pygmies, and a petrified man whose innards are turning to stone, these grotesque images are less about women's sense of freakishness and physical unease than metaphors for stunted and perverted hearts. "Powerhouse," a story that Welty wrote after a Fats Waller concert, was bowdlerized by the *Atlantic Monthly* when it was first published, to get rid of the raunchy lyrics of "Hold Tight, Mama," and has not held up as well. According to Lorrie Moore, "Reading 'Powerhouse' today is uncomfortable and baffling." While Welty intended it to honor Fats Waller, "it is so off-puttingly laced with racial clichés that it may have difficulty being understood as Welty . . . would have it be: as an *hommage* deliberately constructed from the white prejudice all black musicians faced."[55]

Welty was exceptionally productive in the 1940s. She did live in New York, working as an editor at *The New York Times Book Review,* where she wrote reviews about "battlefield reports from North Africa, Europe, and the South Pacific" under the male pseudonym "Michael Ravenna" at the behest of an editor who "suggested that a lady reviewer from the Deep South might not be the most authoritative critic of the accounts of . . . far-flung campaigns."[56] She was also corresponding with a beloved friend, John Robinson, during his military service in Africa and Italy. Another collection of her stories, *The Wide Net,* came out in 1943, followed by her first novel, *Delta Wedding* (1946), and further stories in *The Golden Apples* (1949). In the 1950s, along with Louise Bogan and Carson McCullers, Welty was elected to the National Institute of Arts and Letters, and published *The Ponder Heart* (1954), which became a hit Broadway play. With its gabby narrator, Edna Earle Ponder, and its hotel Beulah, the novel made fun of the Southern tradition of Augusta Evans, and its "dense sentences," according to one critic, "are often long enough to do justice to Evans herself."[57]

From *Delta Wedding* on, however, she was facing censure from critics like Diana Trilling about her avoidance of the racial problems of the South and her patronizing treatment of black characters.[58] In essays including "Place in Fiction" (1956) and "Must the Novelist Crusade?" (1965), Welty defended herself by citing the example of another white Mississippi novelist, William Faulkner, as an example of the inner truth of the imagination and the writer's call to create art rather than journalism. There was a notable exception, however, to Welty's relative silence on bigotry and racial hatred in the South. On June 11, 1963, the night of the murder of Medgar Evers in Jackson, she wrote a ferocious first-person narrative, "Where Is the Voice Coming From?" from the point of view of Evers's killer, exposing his evil and stupidity. (The actual murderer would not in fact be arrested and convicted for decades.) A much more conventional book about poor white country folks in Mississippi, *Losing Battles* (1970), was her first best seller, and her tragic masterpiece, *The Optimist's Daughter* (1972), won the Pulitzer Prize. By that time she had become an American national treasure, beloved as much for the sweet-old-lady persona she cultivated as for her fiction. President Jimmy Carter presented her with the Medal of Freedom, and Americans wondered why she never got a Nobel Prize. In 1973, she said in an interview, "All my life I've been opposed to such things as racism and injustice and cruelty."[59] Still, Welty's charm and kindness allowed her to get away with very conservative public comments, as in a 1973 interview with Alice Walker. Over glasses of iced tea, she sweetly told Walker that she didn't understand contemporary black poetry, found the women's movement "hilarious," and had never troubled to meet Langston Hughes whose poetry she dearly "loved."[60]

In her memoir, *One Writer's Beginnings* (1984), a series of lectures she was invited to give at Harvard, Welty acknowledged that she had had a sheltered life, but "a daring life as well. For all serious daring starts from within."[61] After Welty's death, however, more criticism began to surface. Claudia Roth Pierpont challenged the admission of Welty to the "national pantheon as a kind of favorite literary aunt—a living example of the best that a quaint and disappearing Southern society still has to offer." In Pierpont's view, after her first stories, Welty made her Southerners ever more innocent, comical, and endearing. Her books were "morally simplified," and "racial tensions" were "absent because no one in the author's field of vision, white or black, questions his or her given place; kindly employers and loyal servants are bound by ties of steadfast loyalty." She had acquired the aura of "a kind of Eleanor Roosevelt of literature."[62] In a broader context, Nadine Gordimer revered Welty as the greatest American short-story writer of all time, and believed that they shared similar cultural backgrounds as white women growing up in segregated and unjust societies. Gordimer, however, became a lifelong opponent of South African apartheid, while Welty took a different path. If she had lived in chaotic, rebellious Johannesburg instead of in the relatively protected enclave of Jackson, Mississippi, Gordimer speculated, she "might have turned those incredible powers of hers more outward— she might have written more, she might have tackled wider subjects."

Welty, she believed, was "not forced by circumstances to come to grips with something different."[63]

Such a historical argument would not have persuaded Margaret Walker, who spent the years from 1946 to 1979 teaching at Jackson State University, where two black student demonstrators were shot in May 1970, and certainly did not see Jackson as a calm oasis in the civil rights storm. Yet Walker, too, praised Welty's treatment of black characters, calling her a writer who "sees race superseded by humanity, and . . . values the human spirit above everything else."[64] Welty's writing will endure, I believe, for its accurate observation, faultless dialogue, psychological insight, humor, and narrative construction, but it will continue to be reread in terms of its historical and social context.

On the Street—Ann Petry

Black women novelists of the mid-century did not have the choice of allowing "humanity" to supersede "race," although some also led sheltered lives in middle-class white or racially mixed communities. Ann Petry (1908–1997) was born in Old Saybrook, Connecticut, where her father owned drugstores, and she studied pharmacy at the University of Connecticut. After her marriage in 1938, she worked as a journalist in New York for ten years. Petry wrote about the mean streets of Harlem in her first novel, *The Street* (1946), influenced by the naturalistic style of Richard Wright and James O'Farrell. Her heroine Lutie Johnson tries to create a home and earn a living in Harlem during the war, and to protect her little son from delinquency and despair. As the critic Mary Helen Washington argues, however, the novel of social protest and naturalism Petry had inherited emphasized racial conflicts between black and white men, rather than "the deeply felt realities of women's lives: their relationship with their families, their own suppressed creativity, and their conflicts with black men and patriarchy." This tradition impeded Petry's vision, as she turns away from Lutie's experience and emotions at key moments to concentrate on male characters, and uses a young man at the end to represent hope for the future.[65]

Lutie is doubly victimized—by white racism and by black male lust and indolence. She must work and leave her son alone at home because white folks will give black women jobs as domestics, but will not hire black men. On the other hand, "the men get out of the habit of working," and "go off, move on, slip away, and find new women. Find younger women." Poverty is also a factor in her oppression, she realizes; she is trapped in a cage of circumstances. Petry combines all of these forces in the symbol of "the street," an urban space of ugliness, coldness, crime, greed, and hate contrasted to the warmth and intimacy of the home, and the freedom and beauty of nature. In an interview with *The Crisis,* she described the importance of the urban environment in shaping black experience: "In *The Street* my aim is to show how simply and easily the environment can change the course of a person's life . . . I try to show why the Negro has a high crime rate, a high death rate, and little or no chance of keeping his family unit intact in large Northern cities."[66]

In addition to her political zeal, Petry was a poetic writer, who invested "the street" with the sinister qualities of a gothic villain, an "evil father and a vicious mother," that sucks children into its corruption. Lutie does her best to make a home that will be a sanctuary from the street, but despite her intelligence and effort, she is unable to save her son: "What possible good has it done," she wonders bitterly, "to teach people like me to write?" In a final paragraph, tonally very different from the style of her naturalist mentors, Petry suggests that art can offer a solace as well as a call to arms:

> The snow fell softly on the street. It muffled sound. It sent people scurrying homeward, so that the street was soon deserted, empty, quiet. And it could have been any street in the city, for the snow had laid a delicate film over the sidewalk, over the brick of the tired, old buildings, gently obscuring the grime and the garbage and the ugliness.[67]

The Street won the Houghton Mifflin Literary Fellowship, and Petry went on to write two more novels and a collection of short stories that demonstrated her versatility. *Country Place* (1947) was set in suburban Connecticut, where she had grown up. Narrated by a white druggist, George Fraser, it depicted small-town New England rather than Harlem. *The Narrows* (1953) described an interracial love affair between a black man and a white woman, in the black community of Monmouth, Connecticut, during the McCarthy era. The protagonist, Lincoln "Link" Williams, grows up on another symbolic street, one "so famous, or so infamous, that the people who lived in Monmouth rarely ever referred to it, or the streets near it, by name; it had become an area, a section, known variously as The Narrows, Eye of the Needle, The Bottom, Little Harlem, Dark Town, Niggertown—because Negroes had replaced those other earlier immigrants, the Irish, the Italians, and the Poles." Such symbolically named streets and mythic dark districts would reappear in the fiction of Toni Morrison and Gloria Naylor a few decades later. Petry's efforts to grow as writer did not, unfortunately, secure her reputation. Her first-rate short stories, set in New England and published as *Miss Muriel and Other Stories* (1971), deserve much more attention, especially "The Migraine Workers," with its male protagonists.

The Living Was Easy—Dorothy West

Dorothy West (1907–1998) grew up in a prosperous black household in Boston, where her father was a fruit merchant known as the Black Banana King. She attended Boston's prestigious Girls' Latin School and Boston University, and the family spent its summers in Oak Bluffs, the resort area of Martha's Vineyard claimed by the black elite. In 1926, having won an award for her short story "The Typewriter," West went to New York and became the youngest member of the Harlem Renaissance. She recalled that "I went to the Harlem Renaissance and never said a word. I was young and a girl so they never asked me to say anything."[68] The experience certainly broadened her horizons all the same. In 1929, she went to London for three months as an extra in *Porgy and Bess,* and in 1931, traveled to the Soviet Union with Langston Hughes and others to make a film about black Americans. In the 1930s in Boston, West started a magazine, *Challenge,* dedicated to publishing the prose and poetry of New Negro writers, but by the fall of 1937, Richard Wright and others had taken over the editorial board and set up a *New Challenge,* with a Marxist mission to oppose "fascism, war, and general reactionary policies." Unhappy about this direction, West ended the publication.

In *The Living Is Easy* (1948), West drew on her own childhood to explore the consciousness of the black middle class, and of privileged black children who nonetheless identify with white beauty. At Christmas, the girls in the family all get dolls: "Mine looks like me except her blue eyes," one says blissfully, in another foreshadowing of Toni Morrison's novel. West returned to Oak Bluffs, and spent almost fifty years there working on a local newspaper before she published her second novel, *The Wedding* (1994). Like McCullers's *The Member of the Wedding* and Stafford's *The Mountain Lion,* the book shows the effects of encountering adult sexuality on a preadolescent girl, but adds the complexities of race and intermarriage.

Best Sellers

Sales of mass-market fiction in the 1940s were bolstered by the development of the paperback book, and commercial publishing in the United States remained strong. Sally Benson's *Junior Miss* (1941) and *Meet Me in St. Louis* (1942) portrayed sweet, spunky American girls. Maureen Daly's *Seventeenth Summer* (1942) inaugurated the romance novel for teenagers. Betty Smith's *A Tree Grows in Brooklyn* (1943) described the hard times of an impoverished Irish-American family in Williamsburg. The Seattle chicken farmer's wife in Betty MacDonald's *The Egg and I* (1945), disturbingly racist about Native Americans for a twenty-first-century reader, was countered in the same year by the idyllic Quaker families of Jessamyn West's *Friendly Persuasion*. In 1947, Laura Z. Hobson (1900–1986), the daughter of Russian Jewish activists in New York, exposed American anti-Semitism in *Gentleman's Agreement,* which became an Oscar-winning movie starring Gregory Peck in 1948.

The blockbuster novel of the forties was Kathleen Winsor's *Forever Amber* (1944), which had plot similarities to *Gone with the Wind*—a civil war, a dashing blockade runner, a tigerish heroine named for a color, and the contrast between a corrupt society and its slaves and servants—but was set in Restoration England rather than Georgia. Nevertheless, American women readers identified with headstrong, beautiful, resilient Amber St. Clare, an English country girl who rises to become one of the mistresses of Charles II. Sales were helped by scandal over the novel's matter-of-fact sexual content. Winsor always professed to be puzzled by the fuss. "I only wrote two sexy passages," she said, "and publishers took both of them out. They put in ellipses instead. In those days, you could solve everything with an ellipse."[69]

Amber, the illegitimate offspring of nobility who is raised as a village girl by adoptive parents, is a heroine of enormous intelligence and resourcefulness, as well as beauty and sexual force—what Winsor calls "a kind of warm luxuriance, something immediately suggestive . . . of pleasurable fulfillment." During the ten-year period of the book, from 1660 to 1670, she takes full advantage of every opportunity to climb out of poverty and find independence, love, and fortune. At sixteen, seduced, made pregnant, and abandoned by her great love, the Cavalier

Lord Bruce Carlton, Amber ends up in Newgate prison, where she is taken under the wing of the pirate Black Jack Mallard. He gets her out of prison and sets her up with the bawd Mother Red-Cap in Whitefriars, who arranges for her baby to be farmed out, and launches her as an actress at the Kings Theatre. When Black Jack is arrested and hanged, Amber soon finds a rich new keeper, Rex Morgan, and when he dies in a duel, she marries an elderly city merchant, Samuel Dangerfield.

Meanwhile, Carlton has become a privateer, going back and forth between London and Jamaica, and he returns to tell her that he plans to settle in Virginia: "America is a country that's still young and full of promise, the way England hasn't been for a thousand years. It's a country that's waiting to be made by the men who'll dare to make it—and I intend getting there while I can help make it my way." Amber is devastated, but Dangerfield's death leaves her a rich widow, and she continues to hope that on Carlton's next visit to London she can persuade him to marry her. When he finally returns, it is the end of June 1665, and the largest and last epidemic of the black plague has hit London. In a stretch of thrilling narrative, Winsor describes a deserted London, in which Amber, a red cross marked on her door, stays by Carlton's side and nurses him through the plague. Winsor used Defoe's *Journal of the Plague Year* as a source of historical detail, and also showed her literary gifts in the creation of a cast of grotesque and Dickensian plague nurses, Mrs. Spong and Mrs. Maggot, parasites who rob and poison their helpless patients. As Camus would do in his existentialist novel *The Plague* (1947), where the disease is a symbol of fascism, Winsor made pestilence a metaphor for the corruption, cruelty, and decadence of Restoration London.

Amber is compassionate and brave, but she is finally defeated by the sickness of class division and inherited patriarchal status. Although she has saved his life, Carlton insists that he cannot lower himself to marry Amber, and he returns to Virginia. For the rest of the novel, Amber is an increasingly reckless survivor, who has a fling with King Charles and sells herself cynically to other men until she becomes a duchess. Carlton marries an exquisite Jamaican heiress, Corinna; but at the end of the novel, tricked by her enemies at court into believing her rival is dead, Amber sets sail for the New World to find him once again.

Surprisingly, Kathleen Winsor (1919–2003) was an American from Minnesota, who had never been to London and had re-created the panorama of Restoration England from exhaustive scholarly research. Her first husband, Robert Herwig, whom she married in 1936 when she was an undergraduate at the University of California at Berkeley, had done his senior thesis on Charles II. For five years, while he was away serving as a Marine lieutenant, she studied the period, reading almost four hundred books, and writing six drafts of the novel, running to almost thirteen thousand pages.[70] A beautiful brunette, whose looks, rival novelists lamented, played too large a role in her literary promotion, Winsor married not only early but often. After a divorce from Herwig in 1946, she wed the celebrity bandleader Artie Shaw, and then two other husbands, both lawyers.

Winsor's literary celebrity did not last. The end of *Forever Amber* hints at a "sequel not yet written," but she never wrote *Amber in America*. In 1950, however, Winsor published a sharp autobiographical novel, *Star Money*, which suggested her awareness of Amber's feminist energy and of the social obstacles to creative and active women. Winsor's alter ego, the beautiful Shireen Delaney, born in 1918, has been writing romances since she was eight years old, with titles like "A Girl's Right," and "The Carnival Kid." When her husband, Ed Farrell, goes overseas with the Navy, she writes a historical novel called *The Falcon*, dealing with an Englishwoman who has committed a crime (like Moll Flanders) and goes to Jamaica around 1700 to start her life anew. The novel is a huge best seller, what her agent calls "the Battle of the Sexes, in Technicolor and fancy-dress." Although *Star Money*, as *The New Yorker* pointed out, entertainingly described the "booby traps awaiting a beautiful bookworm with money in the bank and a husband overseas," lightning did not strike again, and it was not a hit.[71] As Shireen complained in the book, audacious women writers had to expect critical mockery. "How many geniuses do you suppose there'd have been if men had spent twelve hours a day peeling potatoes and changing diapers? And anyway, it's men who decide what genius is. And not only that, but society *expects* a man to get out and do something . . . but we don't expect that of women . . . and in fact we tell her she'll get into all kinds of trouble and furthermore be a hopeless neurotic."[72]

Postwar America: Back to the Home

While the years 1941 to 1945 gave women opportunities to work outside the home, and gave them psychological and social encouragement to do so, after the war, they had to be forced back into domesticity, in order to make room for the returning male veterans and to rebuild the population. Science and popular culture colluded in the effort to make this retreat palatable, extolling the joys of cooking, housekeeping, and child-raising, while threatening women who wanted to retain their salaries and independence with neurosis and damaged families. In the first edition of *Baby and Child Care* (1946), Dr. Benjamin Spock declared that "useful, well-adjusted citizens are the most valuable possession a country has, and good mother care during early childhood is the best way to produce them. It doesn't make sense *to let* mothers go to work." As if this were not enough, in 1947, psychiatrist Ferdinand Lundberg and a stern-looking Barnard College sociologist named Marnyia Farnham diagnosed American women as *Modern Woman: The Lost Sex,* neurotically driven to compete with men, and thus dissatisfied and harmful to themselves and their children.

Despite the efforts to label venturesome and ambitious women as damaged and destructive, strong women retained their appeal as heroines. Fay Kanin's play *Goodbye, My Fancy,* a hit of the 1948–49 season, featured such a woman in Agatha Reed, a congresswoman who returns to her alma mater Good Hope College to receive an honorary degree. "Good Hope" was an obviously ambiguous metaphor for the future of American women, a future dramatized as Agatha's choice between two suitors—the college president, who offers her a gracious auxiliary role (even a women's college must have a male president); and a war correspondent who urges her to run for the Senate. Agatha chooses to marry the journalist, keep up her hope of freedom and recognition for women, and honor the tradition of the college. She also insists on showing a grimly realistic war documentary to the undergraduates; these young women cannot be shielded from or deceived about the world they will inherit. Joan Crawford, far from the softest and most feminine of the Hollywood stars, played Agatha in the popular movie. In a journal entry from July 1950, a high school girl in suburban Boston, Sylvia Plath, wrote about her identification with *Goodbye, My Fancy,* which left her "wanting, in a juvenile way, to be like the heroine, a reporter in the trenches, to be loved by a man who admired me, who understood me as much as I understood myself."[73]

Such dreams were up against the images in the women's magazines, the "slicks" beloved of Plath and other American women readers. After the war, they "printed virtually no articles except those that serviced women as housewives, or described women as housewives." An editor of the *Ladies' Home Journal* told Betty Friedan that "if we get an article about a woman who does anything adventurous, out of the way, something by herself, you know, we figure she must be terribly aggressive, neurotic." American women were "not interested in politics, life outside the United States, national issues, art, science, ideas, adventure, education, or even their own communities, except where they could be sold through their emotions as wives and mothers."[74] In 1949, the *Ladies' Home Journal* carried out their agenda by publishing a feature story on Edna St. Vincent Millay, called "Poet's Kitchen." It showed Millay cooking and baking for her husband in the kitchen of her country home. "Now I expect to hear no more about housework's being beneath anyone," the author chided her readers, "for if one of the greatest poets of our day can find beauty in simple household tasks this is the end of the old controversy."[75] Since Millay, whose husband died later that year, was by then subsisting on wine, morphine, Seconal, and liver extract, prepared by her nurse, this propaganda piece seems especially ghoulish and fake. Millay's last letter, written the night before she broke her neck falling downstairs in October 1950, was a set of instructions to the housekeeper not to set the iron too high.[76]

16

The 1950s: Three Faces of Eve

n 1957, *The Three Faces of Eve,* a psychological case study about the shy housewife Eve White, her sexy double, Eve Black, and their happily adjusted composite, Jane, enthralled American readers. Overtly telling the story of one woman, it covertly hinted that American women in general were placid, contented, domestic, well groomed, and involved in togetherness on the surface, but churning with unspeakable desires underneath. This message coincided with other elements in the culture, as women artists of the fifties sought shocking images of their angry and rebellious inner selves. Diane Arbus began her career as a fashion photographer for *Glamour* magazine, but preferred to take pictures of outcast, forbidden subjects rather than beautiful models. With her camera as a shield, Arbus entered the urban underworld off-limits to respectable women, and photographed drag queens, circus people, the aged, lesbians, mental patients, retarded children, nudists, and giants. She represented her own three faces in her celebrated photograph of triplets. "Triplets remind me of myself when I was an adolescent," she explained, "lined up in three images: daughter, sister, bad girl, with secret lusting fantasies, each one with a tiny difference."[1]

Elite and popular fiction of the 1950s reproduced these images as well, emphasizing the splits and divisions in women's lives. The mask of the dutiful daughter could conceal the lustful temptress; behind the mask of the studious sister might be the outcast, freak, or witch. The critic Ellen Moers was the first to point out the similarities between Arbus and Carson McCullers: "not only the subject matter but the tone . . . recalls McCullers: the cold intimacy, the fear which suggests . . . the haunted and self-hating self."[2] By the 1950s, the female gothic was having a revival. Women's writing in that decade was obsessed with freaks, multiples, monsters, gigantism, and obesity. The traditional images of a heroine trapped in a gothic house, particularly apt in the postwar period when American women were repeatedly told that they were designed and destined to find fulfillment inside the home, took on additional meaning as these houses came to symbolize the female body, and the destiny of pregnancy, childbirth, and maternity.

The first face of the American Eve was the good girl, the happy housewife and contented mother. In the 1950s, the average age of marriage for American women had fallen to twenty, and was still falling. Percentages of women entering the professions had dropped from the 1930s, although three times as many girls were going to college. And sociologists and home economists had reported that American women were "spending as many, or even more, hours a day on housekeeping as women thirty years before, despite the smaller, easier-to-care-for homes, and . . . the fact that they had seven times as much capital equipment in housekeeping appliances."[3]

Indeed, the fifties marked a new phase in women's domestic destiny. In the nineteenth century, women were keeping house; at the beginning of the twentieth century, they were involved in homemaking and domestic science; by mid-century they were housewives. As Betty Friedan would argue, after the war

> *housewifery had to expand into a full-time career. Sexual love and motherhood had to become all of life, had to use up, to dispose of women's creative energies. As this began to happen, each labor-saving appliance brought a labor-demanding elaboration of housework. Each scientific advance that might have freed women from the drudgery of cooking, cleaning, and washing, thereby giving her more time for other purposes, instead imposed new drudgery, until housework not only expanded to fill the time available, but could hardly be done in the available time.*[4]

Doctors had even diagnosed a syndrome called "housewife's fatigue," requiring treatment with tranquilizers; Robert Lowell called the decade "the tranquillized Fifties."

Housewifery had become women's default identity, as Shirley Jackson's quasi-comic dialogue in *Life Among the Savages* (1953) neatly demonstrated. Arriving at the hospital to have her third child, Jackson answers the admitting nurse's questions:

"Age?" she asked. "Sex? Occupation?"
"Writer," I said.
"Housewife," she said.
"Writer," I said.
"I'll just put down housewife," she said.

"Housewife," an early poem by Anne Sexton, explored the Freudian implications of the standard terminology: "Some women marry houses." The woman was the wife of the house, wedded to it, bound to it. Caring for it was like the obsessive cleansing, purification, and care of her own female body, scrubbing away its dirt and impurity, its signs of sexuality and procreation. Being born into this body, obliged to tend it endlessly, a woman was part of the cycle of maternity whether she wished to be or not. On an even more mythic and anthropological level, the work of the housewife, like the body of the housewife, was an endless struggle against contamination.

Eve's second face was the intellectual and artist, often portrayed as a misfit, loner, or freak. Both in their personal lives and their writing, women in the fifties depicted intelligence, studiousness, erudition, and literary vocation as defeminizing to the point of deformity. Their heroines are mercilessly punished for their intellectual hubris. "You'll never get a boyfriend," Helen Brown in Gwendolyn Brooks's *Maud Martha* (1953) smugly warns her studious younger sister, "if you don't stop reading those books."

The 1950s offered intellectual women very little in the way of a supportive community. In the beginning of the twentieth century, women's colleges, especially Vassar and Bryn Mawr, had offered a bastion of professional encouragement. The feminist society Heterodoxy was also an environment where women writers could meet other artists and professionals. In the 1930s, the Communist Party, despite its aesthetic dogmas, had offered a sustaining network for some radical women. And in the 1940s, Yaddo was a sanctuary for women writers despite their quarrels and rivalries. Although only a small number of women, mainly on the East Coast, had access to these communities, they were symbolic alternatives. But in the 1950s, women's colleges, too, were paternalistic, restrictive, and male-dominated. At Bryn Mawr, students were required to bring tea sets and forbidden to drive or stay out late without male companions. At Radcliffe, Adrienne Rich recalled, "I never saw a single woman on a lecture platform, or in front of a class, except when a woman graduate student gave a paper on a special topic . . . Women students were simply not taken seriously."[5] Feminism was out of style, and women writers tended to be isolated in their rooms, homes, and marriages.

Without a feminist analysis of competition between women, aspiring women writers and intellectuals in the 1950s were battling for recognition by men, and antagonistic to each other. They yearned for the approval and endorsement of the *Partisan Review* as their nineteenth-century counterparts had yearned for the *Atlantic Monthly.* Acceptance by the *Partisan Review* was a crucial rite of literary initiation into the world of New York intellectuals, although the group allowed membership to only a few token women—the "Dark Ladies," as they were christened by Norman Podhoretz. Their fantasies of rejection inspired a love-hate relationship with the magazine. In Shirley Jackson's first novel, *Hangsaman* (1951), the heroine's vain and obnoxious father writes criticism for the *Passionate Review.* As late as 1968, in Joyce Carol Oates's novel *Expensive People,* one Moe Malinsky, a "professional intellectual" and radical editor of *The Transamerican Quarterly,* addresses the ladies' book club on the hypocrisy, greed, snobbery, and artificiality of American society while gobbling down smoked oysters, and bragging of being introduced to Princess Margaret. With its articles on Soviet economic growth and open letters to "our young friends of the New Left," the novel's narrator opines, "the magazine gives you a general frontal headache."

The third face of women in the fifties was the bad girl, who could be promiscuous, lesbian, or simply sexually passionate. Postwar views of female sexuality, the social historian Miriam G. Reumann explains, "often relied on an opposition between 'good' and 'bad' women, defined as sexually chaste versus sexually active."[6] In her journals from the 1950s, Sylvia Plath stressed her frustration with the sexual double standard, its insistence that women be passive and asexual, and the burdens these views imposed on women's desires. "I can only lean enviously against the boundary and hate, hate, hate the boys who can dispel sexual hunger freely without misgiving and be whole, while I drag from date to date in soggy desire, always unfulfilled."[7] Several of Plath's boyfriends, and even her lovers, were alarmed and threatened by her sexual overtures; good women were supposed to be passive and inert, "doing nothing whatever except being duly appreciative and allowing nature to take its course," as some psychiatrists recommended.[8]

When Alfred Kinsey's *Sexual Behavior in the Human Female* went on sale on September 14, 1953, it challenged American attitudes about women's normal sexual desire and its expression, and received massive coverage in the press. Kinsey's research showed that American women had "far more sexual drive than they had ever been given credit for." Almost half had had premarital sex; 11 percent had been attracted to women as well as men, and 2 to 6 percent were exclusively homosexual. Curiously, *Life* magazine turned to an older generation of mass-market women novelists for comments on the report. Kathleen Norris (1879–1966) had written ninety-three romantic best sellers about American women; she was "nauseated" by the Kinsey Report, and was sure the women who had participated in the surveys were not decent. Fannie Hurst, however, still feisty at sixty-eight, thought it would "lead to better understanding between the sexes."[9]

Housewives and Mothers

Fiction by American women in the 1950s combined the themes of domesticity, creativity, and sexuality in a wide variety of permutations. *Maud Martha,* one of the most subtle and finely crafted novels of the decade, and the only novel by the poet Gwendolyn Brooks, followed the story of a poor black Chicago housewife, in a form like that of Virginia Woolf's *Mrs. Dalloway,* but suffused with anger against racism, war, and the daily small tragedies of black women's lives. Told in thirty-four short sections, some almost vignettes, the novel takes Maud Martha Brown Phillips from the age of seven to her forties. On the surface the story of the dutiful daughter and contented housewife, *Maud Martha* is actually about anger and despair. Brooks begins with Maud Martha's childhood point of view, her grandmother's death, and her self-consciousness and sense of cultural inferiority when a white child comes to play. But what is just as destructive to her sense of self is the family's preference for her older sister Helen, "the pretty one," the thin one, the one with light skin, good hair, and dainty hands. Maud knows she is "much smarter" than Helen, but she knows that "Helen was still the ranking queen . . . even with their father—their mother—their brother. She did not blame the family. It was not their fault. She understood . . . They were enslaved, were fascinated, and they were not at all to blame."[10] In her presentation of Maud and Helen as two faces of the black woman at mid-century, Brooks followed the path of Jessie Fauset and Nella Larsen, and anticipated the theme of the rival sisters that would be taken up by the next generation of black women writers, especially Alice Walker.

Maud marries a grocery clerk, Paul Phillips, a black man trying to be accepted by the middle class. In one especially poignant chapter, he takes her to a "white" movie theater, where they feel excited but self-conscious and uncomfortable. She feels just as ill at ease, however, when they go to the Annual Foxy Cats Dawn Ball, and he leaves her to dance with lighter-skinned women. Their kitchenette apartment, like the room of Gilman's "The Yellow Wall-paper," soon feels like a haunted prison where

> she was becoming aware of an oddness in color and sound and smell around her, the color and sound and smell of the kitchenette building. The color was gray, and the smell and sound had taken on a suggestion of the properties of color, and impressed one as gray, too. The sobbings, the frustrations, the small hates, the large and ugly hates, the little pushing-through love, the boredom, that came to her from behind those walls . . . via speech and scream and sigh—all these were gray.

"Gray clay" is her private image for an undignified death, the fading of all individuality. Maud Martha has no great ambitions for herself; she "did not want to be a 'star.' To create—a role, a poem, picture, music, a rapture in stone: great. But not for her." Still, she asks herself, "What, *what*, am I to do with all of this life?" Brooks later acknowledged that the novel had its genesis in this question.

The novel appeared the year after Ralph Ellison won the National Book Award for *Invisible Man*. Ellison, who generally turned down invitations to help other black writers, declined to blurb *Maud Martha* as well.[11] While Brooks's novel quickly went out of print, James Baldwin's first novel, *Go Tell It on the Mountain* (1953), about the coming-of-age of a young black man, entered the canon of African-American literature.[12] The critic Mary Helen Washington has pointed out that neither reviewers nor readers in the 1950s seemed to notice that *Maud Martha* was "a novel about bitterness, rage, self-hatred, and the silence that results from suppressed rage," as well as sexism and racism. Even the form of the book, in its short discontinuous vignettes, reinforces the heroine's silence and passivity; Brooks leaves Maud "frozen in an enigmatic pose" that "denies her any expression of her real feelings." As she grows from girlhood to womanhood, Maud "seems to have become an accomplice in her own impotence." While she has artistic insights and aspirations, she allows herself to be stifled by the role of housewife without any real protest. Washington asks whether Brooks had some ambivalence herself toward heroic women: the heroes of her poems are all men, and even in *Annie Allen,* she was unable to give her central figure the "power, integrity or magnificence of her male figures."[13] In her autobiography, Brooks acknowledged that "much in the story was taken out of my own life, and twisted, highlighted, or dulled, dressed up or dressed down."[14]

In 1955, however, Brooks published a more feminist story called "The Rise of Maud Martha," which she intended to be the first chapter of a sequel to the novel. Like Kate Chopin's "Story of an Hour," it reveals the heroine's feelings of liberation when her husband dies. On the way back from Paul's funeral with her annoying mother-in-law, Maud suddenly realizes that she "could actually feel herself rising. She felt higher and more like a citizen—of what? A road was again clean before her. She held the destinies of herself and of her children in her individual power—it was up to her." In an interview, Brooks explained that she had intended to send Maud to Africa, and let her find her own identity and vocation.[15] But the sequel was never written; by the 1960s, Brooks had undergone her own conversion experience to the black power movement.

The Dollmaker (1954), by Harriette Simpson Arnow (1908–1986), has been called "a portrait of the artist as mother."[16] Arnow was inspired by European naturalists like Hardy and Zola, and by American gritty realists, including Rebecca Harding Davis and Edith Kelley.[17] To the young girl growing up in Wayne County, Kentucky, writing was an obsession, as natural to her as "knitting and crocheting are to other women." She trained to be a teacher, but longed to write a novel about the Kentucky miners, even though she suspected "it may be the kind of thing that would have to be done by a man."[18] She taught for a few years, then boldly resigned her post and moved to Cincinnati, where she worked as a waitress and tried to become a writer. Her short stories, published in little magazines and, in 1936, the *Southern Review,* won attention for their "terse, evocative prose" and "shocking violence."[19] The same year, she published her first novel, the autobiographical *Mountain Path* (1936), about a young schoolteacher, which Alfred Kazin praised for its "spiritual indignation." Married to the journalist Harold Arnow, Harriette moved with him to Detroit; they had two children.

Arnow was fascinated by the changing lives of Cumberland hill folk. "I was aware that nothing had been written on the Southern immigrants, of what was actually happening to them and their culture, of how they came to the cities for the first time in the 1920s, leaving their families behind," she said in an interview. "I began writing during the depression which had sent hill people back home again. And then, as I was still writing during the Second War, I witnessed the permanent move the men made by bringing their wives and children with them to the cities. With that last migration, hill life was gone forever, and with it, I suppose, a personal dream of community I'd had since childhood."[20]

The Dollmaker, which spent thirty-one weeks on the best-seller list, tells the story of Gertie Nevels, a giantess of a woman, who moves with her children from the Kentucky hills to wartime Detroit when her husband takes a job in a factory. Beginning with a stunning scene in which Gertie performs an emergency tracheotomy on her infant son, and climaxing with the heart-wrenching death of her little daughter Cassie Marie, the novel maintains its hold on the reader and its grim and relentless pace. With a surname that is close to "novels," Gertie is a would-be artist, but she is forced by poverty to abandon her dream of becoming a sculptor. Instead she splits up the fine piece of cherrywood she has been saving for a figure of Christ, and carves little dolls, in a tale of diminishment and defeat.

Gertie Nevels makes a final cameo appearance as a strange woman known as "The Primitive" in Arnow's last novel, *The Weedkiller's Daughter* (1970), but Arnow's social histories of Appalachia and the other work she published after the fifties were much less widely read than *The Dollmaker.* Joyce Carol Oates was the most important of the American women novelists Arnow influenced. "Gertie is an 'artist,' " Oates wrote in an essay on the book, but she is a "primitive, untheorizing, inarticulate artist; she whittles out figures that are dolls or Christs, figures of human beings not quite human, but expressive of old human dreams. She is . . . so real that one cannot question her existence." Overall, Oates concluded, while she had read greater novels, she could think "of none that have moved me more, personally, terrifyingly, involving me in the solid fact of life's criminal exploitation of those who live it."[21] When Oates wrote her own trilogy of novels about Detroit in the 1960s and 1970s, Arnow was an important progenitor.

Intellectuals

Mary McCarthy (1912–1989) could be considered as an intellectual of the 1930s, a writer of the 1940s, or an activist of the 1960s and 1970s; but her literary career peaked in the 1950s.[22] Orphaned in the flu epidemic of 1918, McCarthy and her brothers were raised by pious Catholic relatives, and she was educated in a Seattle convent, experiences she described and mythologized in *Memories of a Catholic Girlhood*. She always wrote as a theological moralist, albeit an agnostic one. But despite her religious background, her elite intellectual formation at Vassar, where her class-mates included Elizabeth Bishop and Muriel Rukeyser, and her leftist political formation with the *Partisan Review,* and; later, with the second-wave feminists and antiwar protesters, McCarthy never fit comfortably into any of these cultural categories. Already having lost her virginity by the time she went to Vassar in 1929, she was too sexual and antiauthori-tarian for the Catholics, too serious and political for the society girls, too chic and fashion-conscious for the feminists, too frivolous for the politi-cos. In the 1930s and 1940s, she had been the Dark Lady of the *Partisan Review,* although the editors, Philip Rahv and William Phillips, very much serious "men of the Thirties," regarded her as "a Twenties figure," a bourgeois "good-time girl." They gave her the job of drama critic because "they thought the theater was of absolutely no consequence."[23]

Her literary inclination was for satire, where she exercised her cutting wit (reviewers always used surgical metaphors, such as scalpel, blade, or knife, for her fictional style) against herself as much as any of her other characters. Finally, though, there was a misfit between McCarthy's somber times and her high-spirited style, which may have accounted for what Larissa MacFarquhar calls the "strange failures of her novels." She was "a delightfully vicious and lighthearted eighteenth-century satirist of manners," born, through some dreadful mix-up at the heav-enly registrar," into an age "preoccupied with Stalin, the Holocaust, and Vietnam."[24]

McCarthy's first efforts at fiction came at the insistence of her second husband, the critic Edmund Wilson, who shut her up in a room for three hours and ordered her to write a story. Paradoxically, during the time in her life when she was most dominated by a man, McCarthy began to cre-ate a new image for American women. Her confident motto, ironically spoken by the deluded autobiographical heroine of *The Company She*

Keeps (1942), was taken from Chaucer's Criseyde: "I am myn owene woman, wel at ease." In the opening story, "Cruel and Barbarous Treatment," the heroine, on her way to Reno for a divorce, is mercilessly exposed as self-dramatizing, vain, and competitive. The whole process of the affair, the announcement to the husband, the coming out to friends, and the divorce, demands "the glare of publicity," and has to be regularly revived with fresh gossip. "It was not, in the end, enough to be a Woman with a Secret, if to one's friends one appeared to be a woman without a secret."[25]

In 1950, McCarthy wrote a caustic essay on American women's magazines that dismissed much of the women's fiction of the time as merely fashionable. *Harper's Bazaar* and *Mademoiselle* were publishing fiction by such writers as Eudora Welty, Carson McCullers, and Jean Stafford, whose decadent "preoccupation with the décor of sorrow, sexual aberration, insanity, and cruelty," McCarthy pronounced, was promoted as enthusiastically as "a new silhouette, a new coiffure, a new young designer."[26] Indirectly, McCarthy was declaring her own literary credo, in favor of realism. She had slight regard as well for her academic colleagues when she taught at Bard and Sarah Lawrence. In *The Groves of Academe* (1952), she delivered an astringently funny novel about higher education and the Left. At progressive Jocelyn College, a whining humbug of a professor, Henry Mulcahy, loses his job and spreads the rumor that he is being fired because he was once a member of the Communist Party. His faculty friends fight for his reinstatement, although they become increasingly uneasy about his story. Indeed, they discover that the odious Mulcahy was never a Communist at all.

Understandably, a novel mercilessly satirizing left-wing political correctness and hypocrisy in the midst of the time of the (other) McCarthy hearings, infuriated her comrades on the Left. McCarthy despised her senatorial namesake and his "anti-American" activities, considered going to law school to fight him, and tried for several years to found a magazine of cultural criticism to oppose his values. Yet her attraction to satire was even stronger than her political allegiances, and she used her friends, lovers, and husbands as fictional fodder in *The Oasis* (1949) and *A Charmed Life* (1955) in ways that seemed disloyal and venomous. Indeed, McCarthy had a perverse and contrarian streak that drove her to speak up unwisely, to confess too much about herself, to recklessly humble male egos, often in public.[27] For a woman writer to appear heartless in the 1950s was even more damning in the eyes of male critics than being all heart in the 1850s. They regarded her nervously as "an ogress, booted and spurred," or at best, "a Valkyrie maiden . . . bearing the body of some dead hero across her saddle."[28] A writer for *Life* magazine called her "a lady with a switchblade," always "cold, steely, merciless."[29]

McCarthy's *Memories of a Catholic Girlhood* (1957) was not only the most critically admired book she published during the fifties, but also the one that seemed to redeem her from charges of heartlessness. She had assembled a group of childhood memoirs written for *The New Yorker* and added italicized "postscripts" on their accuracy or fictionality, reconsidering events and motives more searchingly. Critics such as W. T. Scott in the *New York Herald Tribune* and Victor Lange in *The New Republic* found a more compassionate and implicitly, more feminine, writer to praise.[30] Moreover, aside from being a kinder and gentler work than her novels, *Memories of a Catholic Girlhood* was McCarthy's most insightful and artful book of the fifties, a major influence on the genre of women's autobiography that developed in the second half of the century.

A Dutiful Daughter?—Flannery O'Connor

Mary Flannery O'Connor (1925–1964)—like Carson McCullers, she dropped her first name for one more androgynous when she began to publish—was another Catholic daughter and ardent intellectual, an experimental, modernist writer in contrast to McCarthy's realism. Despite her early death (from lupus) and her consequently small body of work—two novels, thirty-one short stories, a book of essays, and a collection of letters—she has been ranked with the greatest American writers of the twentieth century. Furthermore, O'Connor, whose fiction was grotesque, violent, savagely comic, tough and unemotional, escaped the charges of coldness and heartlessness that dogged McCarthy.

While McCarthy may be more famous now for her personal life than for her fiction, "less read than read about,"[31] O'Connor's fiction is intensely read, studied, and written about, while her life remains mysterious. Only one biography of O'Connor has appeared, and there are still many gaps in what we know about her affiliations and friendships. On the critical side, there is an ongoing battle between those who regard her as primarily a Catholic writer of complex theological arguments about salvation, and those who view her work from a feminist perspective. O'Connor's Catholicism, which she wrote about in her letters as well, offers many literary critics a tempting guidebook of exegesis for her brutal and bloody fiction. Alice Walker, who grew up in a family of black sharecroppers very close to the O'Connor farm, Andalusia, in Milledgeville, Georgia, reports an anecdote she heard from a student of Eudora Welty's: "Wherever we reached a particularly dense and symbolic section of one of O'Connor's stories, she would sigh and ask, 'Is there a Catholic in the class?' "[32]

In a perceptive critical study written just a few years after O'Connor's death, Josephine Hendin suggested a very different approach, emphasizing the "tension between [O'Connor's] disparate selves"—"the perfect daughter who lives on in her mother's memory," and the "more enigmatic writer of those strange and violent tales."[33] Because of her lupus, O'Connor was forced to live with her mother all her adult life until her death at thirty-eight. She was among the American women writers of the fifties who confronted matrophobia, or the fear of becoming one's mother. Hating one's mother was the prefeminist enlightenment of the fifties, as women writers attempted to resolve their sense of freakishness and anger by exorcising what Adrienne Rich called "the victim in ourselves, the unfree woman, the martyr."[34]

O'Connor showed a precocious flair for writing, and after graduating from the Georgia State College for Women, she attended the writers' workshop at the University of Iowa. Her first short story, "The Geranium," was published when she was only twenty-one. In 1947, she spent seven months at Yaddo, during a period when the colony was small, and completed four chapters of a novel, which were published in leading magazines—the *Partisan Review, Mademoiselle,* and the *Sewanee Review. Wise Blood* (1952) included these chapters and told the story of a war veteran, Hazel Motes, who returns home to Georgia as the prophet of a new religion, the Church Without Christ. After murdering a rival prophet, Motes blinds himself and embraces a suicidal asceticism. By the time the book came out, however, O'Connor had suffered her first attack of lupus, although she did not learn the true diagnosis for some time. She was forced to give up her independent life, and return home to accept her dependence on "the loving but dictatorial care" of her mother in the small Georgia town of Milledgeville. There she continued to read, especially in the field of Catholic theology; to write; and to correspond with literary friends including Robert Lowell, Robert Giroux, and Caroline Gordon.

The year 1955 was a momentous time for O'Connor. Her acclaimed collection of short stories, *A Good Man Is Hard to Find,* was published and positively, if obtusely, reviewed. "Highly unladylike," *Time* magazine noted, while the *Saturday Review* opined that "the gal can really write . . . and she places herself in the first rank of this country's younger women writers." At the same time, her lupus worsened, and she had to use crutches. She was forced to come to terms with the permanent circumscription of her life and the impossibility of marriage. Her friend Sally Fitzgerald has written that O'Connor fell in love in 1955 with Erik Langkjaer, a young Dane who worked for her editor Harcourt Brace. In O'Connor's mind, and according to Fitzgerald, marriage would have created a religious dilemma, since her strict Catholic beliefs would have ruled out birth control, while pregnancy would have been dangerous and possibly fatal to her health. In fact, Langkjaer married someone else and there is no evidence that he reciprocated O'Connor's love, but Fitzgerald speculates that "this anguishing disappointment brought O'Connor to the realization that her personal fulfillment would lie in other areas of achievement."[35] On the other hand, Jean Cash argues that O'Connor had no interest in marriage at all, and that although she was also corresponding with the bisexual woman writer Maryat Lee in the late 1950s, she "never actively pursued either a heterosexual or a homosexual relationship."[36] O'Connor's second novel, *The Violent Bear It Away* (1960), affirmed her reputation, but her illness became increasingly severe, and she died in August 1964. *Everything That Rises Must Converge,* her final collection of short stories, was published posthumously in 1965.[37]

A number of critics have interpreted O'Connor's career and her writing as a series of responses to and compromises with being a woman writer in the chivalrous South. In a study of O'Connor's manuscripts at Georgia College, most still unpublished, Katherine Hemple Prown concludes that "in order to fashion herself as a serious writer worthy of critical attention traditionally denied 'lady writers' of the South, she radically altered her fictional landscape. Banishing female characters, silencing female voices, and redirecting her satirical gaze from men to women, O'Connor reshaped her work to appeal to a literary and critical community built on the gender-based and racial hierarchies that traditionally characterized southern culture."[38] In early manuscripts of *Wise Blood,* for example, women characters play major roles, and female sexuality is treated positively; these characters were excised or diminished, and by the time she wrote *The Violent Bear It Away,* she "had all but abandoned her early interest in female characters." Prown argues that O'Connor used shock, the grotesque, deformity, and mutilation to align herself with serious male artists and to distinguish herself from the genteel women writers whom eminent Southern poets and critics of the fifties—the Fugitives and Agrarians, including Allen Tate and John Crowe Ransom—accused of dominating nineteenth-century Southern literary culture. In order to understand O'Connor's attitudes toward gender and race, Prown maintains, we need to see them as efforts "to create the illusion of conformity" to the dominant and influential male values of her region and era.[39] Thus O'Connor distanced herself from both the bodies and the minds of her female characters, and avoided any open confrontation with the racism of her culture. Other critics have stressed O'Connor's ties to the "modern Female Gothic," her predilection for "the imagery of self-hatred," and the ferocity of her need to shock and jolt her readers into awareness.[40]

"Good Country People," one of O'Connor's greatest stories, is about the hostility a thirtyish intellectual daughter feels toward her naïve and controlling mother, the bewilderment the mother feels toward her daughter, and the contempt the narrator feels for them both. Mrs. Hopewell spends a lot of time complaining to her friend Mrs. Freeman about her daughter Joy, a hulking thirty-two-year-old blonde with a Ph.D. in philosophy, who has legally renamed herself "Hulga." Hulga has a wooden leg (her leg was shot off in a hunting accident when she was ten), and stumps around in a yellow sweatshirt with a faded picture of a cowboy on a horse—scarcely the pretty and popular Southern belle her mother had yearned for. "When she looked at Joy . . . she could not help but feel that it would have been better if the child had not taken the Ph.D." The Freemans are Mrs. Hopewell's tenant farmers, housekeeper and hired man, but she prides herself on their being "good country people" rather than white trash; the two women converse in an inspired and hilarious litany of clichés. Hulga, by contrast, prides herself on her atheism and her intelligence; except for her weak heart, she tells herself, she "would be far from these red hills and good country people. She would be in a university lecturing to people who knew what she was talking about." When another country character, a young Bible salesman named Manley Pointer, asks her out for a picnic, she feels superior to him even when he is kissing her: "Her mind, clear and detached and ironic anyway, was regarding him from a great distance, with amusement but with pity." Nonetheless, Joy-Hulga is sexually and intellectually humiliated by this ignorant con man, who steals her wooden leg, and taunts her with her pretensions: "I'll tell you another thing, Hulga . . . you ain't so smart. I've been believing in nothing ever since I was born."

O'Connor professed herself much amused by the Signet paperback of *A Good Man Is Hard to Find,* which had a lurid cover illustration of "Good Country People," with "a lecherous-looking gent grabbing for a disheveled looking lady in a pile of straw, pitchfork to the side, suit-case full of whiskey behind."[41] Still, it's hard to accept such quibbles or disclaimers of sexual intent from a writer who named the gent in question "Manley Pointer," and depicted with such zesty self-hatred the metaphorical rape of a disabled woman somewhat like herself.

Along with debates about O'Connor's attitudes toward sexuality and gender are even more bitter debates over her attitude toward race. While some call her a racist who used the word "nigger" in both her fiction and her letters, refused to entertain James Baldwin in her home, and made flippant remarks about integration in her correspondence with more liberal friends, her defenders can also cite an interview she gave in 1963, where she gave her fullest statements about integration in the South. "White people and colored people are used to milling around together in the South, and integration only means that they are going to be milling around together in a few more places." A few months later, she added that "it requires considerable grace for two races to live together . . . it can't be done without a code of manners based on mutual charity."[42]

O'Connor's descriptions of her black characters may be offensive by twenty-first-century standards, but she is equally pitiless toward her white characters and their pretensions. In her dazzling last story before her death, "Revelation," O'Connor gives an account of the awakening of a bigoted and sanctimonious white hog farmer, Ruby Turpin, who accompanies her husband, Claud, to the doctor's office. Observing the other patients in the waiting room with some distaste, she sorts them mentally into categories of class and race. At the top of her list is a "well-dressed grey-haired lady"; then a fat acned girl in her late teens, "scowling into a book called *Human Development*"; then a white-trash woman in bed slippers and a yellow sweatshirt (apparently the nadir of ladylike attire in O'Connor's eyes), her lips stained with snuff; and finally a colored delivery boy. Encouraged, she thinks, by the "pleasant" and respectable gray-haired lady, Mrs. Turpin happily airs her racist views and patronizes the ugly girl, who turns out be named Mary Grace, and who goes to Wellesley and "just keeps right on studying." Enraged, Mary Grace leaps up and attacks her physically. Mrs. Turpin stares into her "fierce brilliant eyes . . . 'What you got to say to me?' she asked hoarsely, and held her breath waiting, as for a revelation." Mary Grace addresses her: "Go back to hell where you came from, you old wart-hog." The insult is both crudely funny and painfully unexpected; and ridiculous and intellectually limited though she is, Mrs. Turpin is shaken out of her complacencies. That night, back home with Claud, she has her revelation:

> *a vast, swinging bridge extending upward from the earth through a field of living fire. Upon it a vast horde of souls were tumbling toward heaven. There were whole companies of white-trash, clean for the first time in their lives, and bands of black niggers in white robes, and battalions of freaks and lunatics shouting and clapping and leaping like frogs. And bringing up the rear of the procession was a tribe of people whom she recognized at once as those who, like herself and Claud, had always had a little of everything and God-given wit to use it right.*

To boil this rich and resonant story down to a statement about race, purgatorial visions, or Southern ideals of genteel ladyhood is to deprive O'Connor of her unique flavor and hard-earned art.

Bad Girls

Shirley Jackson (1916–1965) wore many faces, as a best-selling novelist; happy wife of a distinguished literary critic; and cheerful mom who published comic stories about her big messy Vermont house and her four mischievous children in American women's magazines. Behind these smiling public masks, however, Jackson was a bad girl, a desperately unhappy, angry woman who became morbidly obese, addicted to alcohol and tranquilizers, and so severely agoraphobic that in the months before her death at age forty-nine, she could not even leave her room. These multiple selves were revealed in a remarkable and frightening series of novels, so central to the nightmares and contradictions of American women of the period that the critic Linda Wagner-Martin calls the 1950s "the decade of Jackson."[43] One of the most sophisticated crafters of fiction during the decade, with work compared during her lifetime to Poe and James, she has long been neglected by most critics of American literature.

The overweight, unkempt, Hulga-ish daughter of a slender and socially ambitious mother, Jackson had a long-standing fascination with witchcraft and Satanism, especially as modes of revenge and escape. During the fifties, she wrote a book on the Salem witch trials, and she often described herself to journalists as someone who enjoyed dabbling in spells. As an undergraduate at Syracuse University, she published one of her first stories, about suicide, which attracted the attention of Stanley Edgar Hyman, an intense Jewish intellectual from Brooklyn. Hyman married her in 1940 against the wishes of both sets of parents. The Hymans sat shiva (the Jewish ritual mourning for the dead); the Jacksons just stayed away; but both sides became reconciled to the marriage when their first grandchild, Laurie, was born in 1942. To his relief, Stanley Hyman was classified 4-F during the war (he bragged that he "had the organs of a much older man.").[44] He got a job at *The New Yorker* and brought home literary friends for weird dinners cooked by Jackson, who dyed her meals with food coloring and served visitors blue steak and red potatoes. She was also beginning to show signs of agoraphobia—"a virtual hermitress," one friend called her. In an unpublished story from this period, the heroine, Mrs. Van Corn, "had not been out of the house in seven months. She could walk perfectly well . . . she was not particularly afraid of subways or taxis; she was not pregnant, sick, or discouraged . . . she liked staying inside."[45]

In 1945, with Jackson pregnant with their second child, the Hymans moved to North Bennington, Vermont, where Stanley had a job teaching in the college. They bought an enormous old house, which Jackson "kept" in a state of squalor and creative disarray; the rooms reeked of cat pee and the refrigerator was full of moldy little jars of nameless decaying leftovers.[46] Jackson's sister-in-law later charged that she rarely even washed her children's hair.

Shirley Jackson was not an easy woman to live with, but while many American women writers had to pacify and submit to selfish husbands, Stanley Edgar Hyman must have been one of the most difficult. Intellectually, they were an excellent match. Hyman was a stimulating critic and a shrewd editor. He pushed Shirley first toward Marxism (which she abandoned); then to the study of psychoanalysis and the split personality (which she used in two of her novels in the 1950s); and finally to the study of myth and ritual. Hyman also played a crucial role in editing, cutting, and revising the work of his friend Ralph Ellison, on what became the classic American novel *Invisible Man* (1952). Some in their circle would speculate that without Hyman's editorial advice, Ellison had been unable to craft a second novel from the thousands of inchoate pages he turned out over the next forty-some years. The poet Theodore Weiss, who knew them both, thought "Stanley Hyman was instrumental in helping Ralph pull the material together for *Invisible Man* . . . Hyman helped him find the shape of the book, trimmed it, and gave it form and order. On the second novel, he had no one to help him in the same way."[47]

Nonetheless, Hyman did not expect Ralph Ellison to do his housework, chauffeuring, child care, and cooking, while also earning most of the family's income. His editorial advice was offered to Ellison over brandy and cigars, without condescension or patronage. With Jackson, he was an opinionated and bullying mentor, as well as an exploitative husband. He adopted a role as the disciplinarian of her writing and put her on a strict schedule. He handled the marketing of her fiction, and dictated the personal statements on her book jackets. As one critic concludes, "at his best he was arrogant and contentious," at worst "malevolent and tyrannical." While he pushed her to write, he also resented her greater success, developed writing blocks in his own criticism, and was a compulsive womanizer who had numerous affairs with thinner, prettier students and let her know about them. According to his second wife, he saw himself as a destructive personality "with a highly developed instinct for the jugular."[48] He resented more established literary critics, and especially detested homosexuals.

But Jackson was attracted to Hyman's bullying, even to his hostility and exploitation. Like Mary McCarthy and, later, Sylvia Plath, she eroticized male dominance: "Every woman adores a Fascist," Plath would write in "Daddy." Although Jackson's friends found Hyman an obnoxious little tyrant, they also had to admit that she seemed to blossom under his control. He made connections with the literary and academic world in which she shared. After a careful cost analysis, he purchased a dishwasher with her royalties so that she would have more time to produce commercial fiction—washing the dishes himself was obviously unthinkable.

And Jackson wrote steadily. She first achieved fame with her short story "The Lottery," which was published in *The New Yorker* on June 26, 1948. She had written the story three weeks before, "on a bright June morning while I was pushing my daughter up the hill in her stroller." Her agent sent it to *The New Yorker,* and they accepted it immediately, asking only that the original date of the story—June 21, the summer solstice—be changed to June 27 to follow the date of publication. "The Lottery" has become one of the most celebrated and anthologized short stories of the twentieth century, although the audience response to it was initially negative. "Millions of people, and my mother had taken a pronounced dislike to me," Jackson wrote. Set in a small New England town like North Bennington, "The Lottery" is about ritual sacrifice and scapegoating. One person in the community is selected by lot each summer to be publicly stoned to death. Jackson made readers uncomfortable not only through the matter-of-fact violence of the story—even the victim's little son has his pebbles ready—but also through implicitly questioning American innocence after the war: Would we too be good Germans, going along with atrocity? She had witnessed anti-Semitism in Vermont, and it may have inspired the story. Jackson commented wryly on the sadism of the people who wrote to her: "People at first were not so much concerned with what the story meant; what they wanted to know was where these lotteries were held, and whether they could go there and watch."[49]

Jackson's novels in the 1950s were all in the genre of female gothic, and dealt with themes of matrophobia, madness, lesbianism, and murderous rage. Her first novel, *Hangsaman* (1951), created the template for fiction about a sensitive, suicidal young woman with psychic powers and sexual secrets. Natalie Waite (Weight?) is a college freshman who dreads becoming like her mother, bullied, diminished, and trapped in a kitchen. Her real antagonist, however, is her domineering and narcissistic father, Professor Arnold Waite, who tells her what to think, what to do, and what to write. Caught between the two, Natalie gradually lapses into schizophrenia. In *The Bird's Nest* (1954), Jackson produced a fictional version of *The Three Faces of Eve,* with a heroine, Elizabeth Richmond, who has multiple personality disorder, and an arrogant therapist (another of her many caricatures of Stanley Hyman), Dr. Victor Wright.

The Haunting of Hill House (1959) is a psychological ghost story in which lonely Eleanor Vance is invited by the anthropologist John Mortimer to join a party of people with psychic credentials in order to test out an allegedly haunted house. As Jackson succinctly introduces her, "The only person in the world she genuinely hated, now that her mother was dead, was her sister. She disliked her brother-in-law and her five-year-old niece, and she had no friends." Like the heroine of a short story by Mary Wilkins Freeman, Eleanor has spent her whole life caring for relatives, and is loveless, awkward, and homeless. She has been chosen because of a poltergeist incident after her father's death. At Hill House, she lies about her circumstances, but becomes attached to one of the guests, the glamorous Theodora. When Eleanor's psychological emanations have produced disturbing incidents in the house, the party breaks up, and she announces her wish to move in with Theodora, who callously rejects her: "Do you *always* go where you're not wanted?" Revealed as both the source of the haunting and a closet lesbian, Eleanor has no place to go, and suicide is her only option.

Published in 1962, *We Have Always Lived in the Castle* is Jackson's masterpiece, a stunning first-person narrative told by a female mass murderer. Long overlooked, the novel has been rediscovered in the twenty-first century by writers including Stephen King and Jonathan Lethem, and by feminist critics who read it as a perfectly constructed and haunting example of the female gothic.[50] Mary Katherine Blackwood, called "Merricat," her older sister Constance, and their senile uncle Julian are shunned and feared by the folk of their New England village, because it is believed that Constance poisoned her parents by putting arsenic in their tea. Acquitted for lack of evidence, Constance has become agoraphobic, and the Blackwoods keep house in their beautiful but decaying mansion. When a fortune hunter manages to insinuate himself into the household and court Constance, Merricat has to drive him away, and reading her narrative, we become aware of her passionate love for her sister, her violent imagination, and her rebellion against masculine dominance. She is a psychopathic killer who believes that she has one eye for day and another for night, and who has constructed an occult world of fetishes, familiars, and charms to protect herself against the painful reality of everyday life; but, as Darryl Hattenhauer trenchantly points out, she and the demure Constance are doubles. Behind her sweet façade, Constance has used "the dark Merricat to do her dirty work."[51] Shortly after completing the book, Jackson had a breakdown and went into a hospital for several months.

At the end of her life, Jackson "succumbed almost entirely to crippling doubt and fear, and . . . a squalid, unreasonable agoraphobia—a sort of horrible parody of the full-time homemaker's role she's assumed."[52] Her last, uncompleted novel, posthumously published as *Come Along with Me* (1968), told the story of a plus-size clairvoyant widow who decides to run away and create a new life under the name of "Angela Motorman." Mordant and angry, the novel prefigures the feminist revenge stories of the 1970s.

Pulp Queen

In her publicity pictures, Grace de Repentigny Metalious (1924–1964) looks unnervingly like Shirley Jackson's twin sister—stolid, heavy, hair pulled tightly back in a ponytail, dressed in jeans and a man's flannel shirt. *Peyton Place* (1956) was the most avidly read novel of the fifties, and Julian Messner, Inc., the small firm that had published it, tried to lure Shirley Jackson onto their list. Grace Metalious was a bad girl herself. Raised in a French-Catholic family in small-town New England, she was notorious as the rebel who drank and swore, and had to get married at eighteen. The marriage did not go well: "I did not like being regarded as a freak because I spent time in front of a typewriter instead of a sink," Metalious recalled. Her husband, a schoolteacher and principal, resented her writing and her nonconformity. In 1955, at the age of thirty, Metalious was living in a New Hampshire shack, feeding her three children lettuce and tomato sandwiches, and falling behind on her car payments. She was "broke, smelly, thirsty, exhausted, and desperate."[53] She had been writing a novel called "The Tree and the Blossom," using an image of female sexuality that had long since become a cliché. When editor Kitty Messner saw it, however, she immediately grasped its potential, bought it, and renamed it *Peyton Place*. When it appeared on September 24, 1956, it became an astounding best seller, and transformed Metalious's life. She made huge amounts of money from the book and the subsequent movie, had affairs with con men, and fought rumors that her husband, not she, had written the novel.

Metalious defied the unwritten laws against women's sexual frankness in fiction. *Peyton Place* is about an aspiring novelist, teenage heroine Allison MacKenzie, who is also a bad girl. The book includes an abortion scene, the hint of homosexuality, forbidden sexual trysts, steamy love scenes, and casual violence. *Peyton Place* was not obscene but it was explicit, and its picture of goings-on in a rural New Hampshire town shocked Metalious's neighbors in Manchester and Gilmanton, and titillated millions of American readers. "To a tourist these towns look as peaceful as a picture postcard," she told an interviewer, "but if you go beneath that picture . . . all kinds of strange things crawl out."[54] In *The New York Times Book Review*, Metalious was condescendingly described as "a pretty fair writer for a first novelist . . . with the Indian Summer air of an emancipated modern authoress who knows the earthy words and rarely stints to use them."[55] As Emily Toth remarks, " 'Authoress?' It might have been 1852."[56] Metalious died of cirrhosis of the liver in 1964.

American Women Poets in the 1950s

While the fiction of the fifties was original and bold, American poetry in the period is generally regarded as timid and academic. The term "fifties poem" is critical shorthand for the apolitical, tamely formal lyric in which poets like the staid Richard Wilbur excelled. Women were certainly publishing poetry in the fifties: they included Léonie Adams, Babette Deutsch, and Muriel Rukeyser in the older generation; rising poets May Swenson, Mona Van Duyn, Jean Garrigue, and Barbara Howe; and young poets Adrienne Rich, Anne Sexton, and Sylvia Plath, just starting out. Yet poetry was publicized, defended, and policed by male poets and critics as a masculine activity in which women performers were unwelcome at best. As Edward Brunner shows in his study *Cold War Poetry,* poetry by women was held up as the bad example of emotionalism and lack of discipline. In 1950s book reviews, Brunner writes, "female poets are perceived as bad girls—bad because they act upon their transgressive desire to be poets, a role that males best fill because of their ability to exert control over their emotions."[57] Women poets were reproved for their poor organizational skills, their intellectual inferiority, their emotional spontaneity; and praised for being deferential, unobtrusive, and asexual.

Some of these reviews and blurbs have become notorious examples of male condescension; W. H. Auden, for example, praised the poems in Adrienne Rich's first book, *A Change of World* (1951), by writing in his foreword that they were "neatly and modestly dressed, speak quietly but do not mumble, respect their elders but are not cowed by them, and do not tell fibs." In short, they were good-girl poems, as Rich herself was painfully aware. According to "Snapshots of a Daughter-in Law," a defiant major poem she wrote at the end of the decade, women poets had compromised; they had colluded, *faute de mieux,* with chivalrous and condescending criticism: "our mediocrities over-praised / . . . every lapse forgiven." But, she sardonically concluded, those women who resisted, who "cast too bold a shadow" or smashed "the mold straight off," faced stern punishments: "Solitary confinement; / Tear gas, attrition shelling." Not many women were eager for such treatment.

THE FAIRY GODMOTHER OF US ALL—MARIANNE MOORE

In 1951, at the age of sixty-four, Marianne Moore (1887–1972) won the Pulitzer Prize, the National Book Award, and the Bollingen Prize for her collected poems.[58] By this time Moore had become the Grandma Moses or Disney godmother of American poetry, the sweet white-haired lady who posed for photographers in a tricorn hat and black cape. Moore was hired in 1955 to suggest names for a new Ford automobile, and came up with a list out of poetic never-never land, including Pastelogram, Utopian Turtletop, and Pluma Piluma. The arch names encouraged Americans to think of poets as silly relics of another age, and poetry as stuff for old ladies and girls, as Mark Twain had warned them with his caricature of Miss Emmeline Grangerford in *Huckleberry Finn*. (To be fair, the car was eventually named the Edsel, so Moore could not have done much worse.)

A 1909 graduate of Bryn Mawr, Moore had started writing as a young woman. Her first book, *Poems,* was published in London in 1921, and an expanded version titled *Observations* appeared in the United States in 1924. Soon after she became the editor of *The Dial,* reviewed difficult books by modernist poets including Eliot, Steinbeck, and Pound, and moved to Brooklyn with her mother. For decades she published poems in little magazines, rewriting and reworking them in books at wide intervals, and spending years on a translation of the fables of La Fontaine. Denying having any artistic ambition, literary credo, or aesthetic theory, Moore colluded in the diminutive image that defined her in the *Literary History of the United States* (1948): "She is feminine in a very rewarding sense, in that she makes no effort to be major." Her most famous lines are the self-deprecating ones of "Poetry," a poem that she wrote in 1921, but revised and reduced regularly until 1967: "I, too, dislike it: there are things that are important beyond all / this fiddle." Nonetheless, she concluded in her most definitive artistic statement, real poets are those "literalists of the imagination" who "can present / for inspection, imaginary gardens with real toads in them."

By the 1950s, Moore's poetry provided a mid-century answer to the question posed by Louise Bogan—what can an old lady poet write about? The answer, it seemed, was animals, not necessarily toads, but unusual ones with strange names like the jerboa, porcupine, arctic ox, or pangolin; and baseball (she supported the Brooklyn Dodgers). Critics wondered whether she was hiding her own psychology behind her portraits of these exotic creatures and even seeking publicity with her fondness for the national pastime. Erudite and technically superb, incorporating quotations from newspapers as well as literature into her texts, Moore's poetry was deliberately impersonal. Variously described as armored and self-effacing, Moore has become a poet read mainly by other poets and academic critics.

THE POETRESS—ELIZABETH BISHOP

Elizabeth Bishop (1911–1979) met Marianne Moore in 1934. Soon afterward they went to the circus together, fed the elephants, and from Bishop's point of view, stored up "enough anecdotes to meditate on for years"; they remained close friends until 1970.[59] Moore mentored the younger Bishop, introducing her to editors and publishers, but also making many suggestions about revising her work, which Bishop fended off. Most comically, Moore had objections to "Roosters," one of Bishop's signature poems, which was first published in the *New Republic* in April 1941. Bishop got the idea from her wish to make fun of militarism and from watching roosters strutting about the barnyard in the morning, lording it over the hens "who leads hen's lives / of being courted and despised."

"Roosters" is now interpreted by feminist critics as a scathingly funny denunciation of masculinity. But Moore and her mother, who read it in draft, objected (we learn from Bishop's careful response) to the "rattle-trap" rhyme scheme, Bishop's use of rude colloquialisms like "water closet," and, amusingly, the title, which they thought in their innocence should be changed to the "more classical" "The Cock."[60] "Roosters" was included in Bishop's first book of poems, *North and South,* in 1946.

Bishop was a much bolder, more adventurous and varied poet than Moore. She had survived a troubled childhood, traditionally a propitious background for becoming a poet. Her father died while she was a baby, and when she was five years old, her mother was committed to a mental hospital. Bishop never saw her again. For the next three years she lived contentedly in Nova Scotia with her maternal grandparents, but then her father's parents took her to live with them in Worcester and Boston. "I had been brought back unconsulted and against my wishes to the house my father had been born in, to be saved from a life of poverty and provincialism," Bishop wrote in her memoir "The Country Mouse." "I found myself aging, even dying. I was bored and lonely with Grandma, my silent grandpa, the dinners alone . . . At night I lay blinking my flashlight off and on, and crying."[61] In an interview for the *Paris Review* in 1978, she commented that although she recovered when she was a teenager and went away to school, "I was always a sort of a guest, and I think I've always felt like that."[62]

In 1951, Bishop traveled to South America on a writing fellowship, developed an illness in Brazil, and while recuperating, fell in love with the Brazilian architect and socialite Lota de Macedo Soares. She decided to stay on and made a life in Brazil with Soares for the next fifteen years. Bishop's first book was reissued with her second, *A Cold Spring* (1955), and the double volume won the Pulitzer Prize. Involved in a happy lesbian relationship, and having distanced herself from the pressures of American publishing and marketing, Bishop nevertheless remained ambivalent about her identity as a woman poet. In 1956, she wrote jokily to her friend Robert Lowell that even "the best we have," Emily Dickinson, "does set one's teeth on edge a lot of the time . . . 'Woman' poet—no, what I'd like to be called now is *poetress* . . . I think it's a nice mixture of poet and mistress."[63]

Tragedy ended her relationship with Soares in 1967. They had quarreled and separated, and in September, an agitated and depressed Soares flew to New York to meet Bishop, and upon arriving, intentionally took an overdose of tranquillizers and died. Bishop was devastated by the suicide, another episode in her long history of losses. Nevertheless, she taught at Harvard for seven years, and continued to write. She won the National Book Award for her *Complete Poems* (1969), and in her final book, *Geographies III* (1977), published one of her most-quoted poems, the poignant villanelle "One Art," with its repeated ironic line, "the art of losing isn't hard to master." To the disappointment of feminist critics, Bishop became increasingly hostile to any gender-marked criticism: "Undoubtedly gender does play an important part in the making of any art," she wrote, "but art is art and to separate writings, paintings, musical compositions, etc, into two sexes is to emphasize values that are *not* art."[64]

Bishop's refusal to consider the relationship of gender to art separated her from the new generation of American women poets emerging in the 1950s. Gender was anything but incidental to Sylvia Plath and her contemporaries Adrienne Rich and Anne Sexton, who were also wives and mothers. They were starting out in a decade when both the feminine and the poetic models had to be overthrown. In the fifties, they were hardly apprentices—indeed, Rich and Plath were astonishingly precocious poets, while Sexton used every ounce of her strength and determination to catch up. But their 1950s were quite different from the decade of Moore and Bishop.

ANNE SEXTON, POET

From the beginning of her career, Anne Sexton (1928–1974) insisted on bringing hitherto taboo subjects from female experience into her work. No matter how harsh the male critical response, she continued to write about abortion, menstruation, sexuality, marriage, motherhood, and divorce. Hospitalized for acute depression and an attempted suicide after the birth of her second daughter, Sexton, who had married young, missed college, and worked only as a model, was encouraged to study and write by her young psychiatrist. While watching the British critic I. A. Richards lecturing on the sonnet on Boston educational television, Sexton decided that she could write a sonnet herself, and went on to write one every day for a month. Other experiments with verse forms, all praised by her doctor, followed; beginning with simple couplets and quatrains, she rapidly moved through a series of experiments with more demanding and advanced poetic forms, including acrostics and villanelles. By Christmas 1956, at the pivotal age of twenty-nine, she presented her mother with thirty-seven poems, from "the first year of Anne Sexton, Poet." In 1957, she began to sign poems she submitted for publication as "Anne Sexton," rather than "Mrs. A. M. Sexton." Only in April 1960, after she had been publishing her poems for three years, did Sexton identify herself on her tax return as "poet" rather than "housewife."

The tension between the housewife and the poet resonated in much of Sexton's early work. In a letter, she wrote, "I do not live a poet's life. I look and act like a housewife . . . But still my desk is a mess of letters to be answered, and poems that want to tear their way out of my soul and onto the typewriter keys. At that point, I am a lousy cook, a lousy wife, a lousy mother, because I am too busy struggling with the poem to remember that I am a normal (?) American housewife."[65] In the fall of 1958, Sexton was admitted to Robert Lowell's prestigious writing seminar at Boston University. Lowell had strong views about gender and writing: "He spent a good deal of time mulling over whether this or that poet was 'major' or 'minor,' and women were almost inevitably categorized as 'minor, definitely minor'—though he made an exception of Elizabeth Bishop."[66] While she was in the workshop, Sexton expressed her fear of "writing as a woman writes." She wanted to be a major poet, and that meant writing like a man.

THE POETESS OF AMERICA—SYLVIA PLATH

On March 29, 1958, twenty-six-year-old Sylvia Plath (1932–1963) wrote in her journal:

> *I think I have written lines which qualify me to be the Poetess of Amer-*
> *ica . . . Who rivals? Well, in history Sappho, Elizabeth Barrett Brown-*
> *ing, Christina Rossetti, Amy Lowell, Emily Dickinson, Edna St.*
> *Vincent Millay—all dead. Now: Edith Sitwell and Marianne Moore,*
> *the aging giantesses and poetic godmothers. Phyllis McGinley is out—*
> *light verse: she's sold herself. Rather: May Swenson, Isabella Gardner,*
> *and most close, Adrienne Cecil Rich—who will soon be eclipsed by these*
> *eight poems. I am eager, chafing, sure of my gift, wanting only to train*
> *and teach it.*[67]

In February 1959, Plath joined Lowell's workshop, and she and Sexton became friends, going out after class for drinks at the Ritz with the poet George Starbuck, who was Sexton's lover. "Being a poet in Boston is not so difficult," Sexton noted, "except that there are hordes of us living here."[68] Plath's life story has become legend. Born in Boston, the daughter of Otto Plath, a German-born professor who studied bumblebees, and Aurelia Schober Plath, who had been one of his students, Sylvia saw the crisis of her childhood as her father's death in 1940. Aurelia Plath did not remarry, but worked as a high-school teacher and then secretarial instructor, to support Sylvia and her younger brother, Warren. By diligence and sacrifice, she managed to educate Warren at Exeter and Harvard, and to send Sylvia, a brilliant student at Wellesley High School, to Smith on a scholarship in the fall of 1950.

Outwardly a golden girl of the fifties, with bleached-blond hair, astonishing numbers of boyfriends and dates, and academic, artistic, and even athletic gifts, Plath was internally driven and divided between her desires for the perfect mate and marriage, and her resolve to become an important poet and novelist. Aided by a number of older women, including her mother, her Smith professors, and the popular novelist Olive Higgins Prouty, who paid for her scholarship, she nonetheless saw these benefactors as sinister representatives of female destiny, whom she described in "The Disquieting Muses" (1957), based on a painting by Giorgio di Chirico, as "Nodding by night around my bed, / Mouthless, eyeless, with stitched bald head."[69]

At Smith, too, Plath won all the prizes and met the high expectations of her teachers. When she became a college guest editor at *Mademoiselle* in the summer of 1953, she asked to meet Shirley Jackson, who was unavailable (how Jackson would have dreaded being photographed for *Mademoiselle* with a group of pretty college girls!).[70] Instead she was assigned to interview five young male poets, including Richard Wilbur. While she was in New York, Julius and Ethel Rosenberg were executed as Communist spies, and Plath was horrified at the indifference of her fellow editors. When she returned to suburban Wellesley for the rest of the summer, she was already in the midst of a severe depression, and on August 24, 1953, she attempted suicide by swallowing a full bottle of sleeping pills and hiding in the crawl space under the first floor of her house. She was discovered unconscious two days later and taken to Newton-Wellesley Hospital. By mid-October, she was moved to McLean Hospital, where she remained until February 1954, the start of the spring term at Smith. Ironically, Plath's time in the hospital coincided with the furor over the Kinsey Report; its findings might have assuaged her sense of freakish sexuality. But with the help of a woman therapist, Ruth Buescher, she recovered, and was encouraged to pursue both sexual and creative fulfillment.

After graduating summa cum laude from Smith, Plath won a Fulbright scholarship to Cambridge University, where she met and married the English poet Ted Hughes. In the late 1950s, the Hugheses were in the United States; both had been teaching at Smith, traveling on fellowships, and working furiously on their poems. Plath, however, seemed to be stuck as a writer; always dependent on a thesaurus, endlessly revising, she had transferred much of her ambition to Hughes, and he was assigning subjects and exercises to help overcome her writing blocks. Even when Plath went to Yaddo in the fall of 1959, she was already married, pregnant with her first child, and very much in her husband's shadow. "I have no life separate from him, am likely to become a mere accessory," she wrote in her journal. "This place is a terrible nunnery for me." At Yaddo, Plath had a nightmare of being discovered by her brother about to go to bed with a man named "Partisan Review."[71]

SNAPSHOTS OF A DAUGHTER-IN-LAW—ADRIENNE RICH

The woman poet Plath saw as her most dangerous rival was Adrienne Rich (1929–), the wife at that time of the Harvard economist Alfred Conrad, the mother of three sons, and the winner of the Yale Younger Poets prize for *A Change of World* (1951). Reading about Rich's honors, Plath confessed, "Occasionally I retch quietly in the wastebasket."[72] Educated at Radcliffe College as a promising young poet, Rich had viewed Moore and Bishop as women poets who "kept human sexual relationships at a measured and chiseled distance." Moore was "maidenly, elegant, intellectual, discreet."[73]

For Rich, the fifties were a period of constriction and compromise. She was isolated from other women in general, and from women poets in particular: "These were the fifties, and in reaction to the earlier wave of feminism, middle-class women were making careers of domestic perfection . . . I have a sense that women didn't talk to each other much in the fifties—not about their secret emptiness, their frustrations."[74] She recalled that she had been dissatisfied with her second book of poems, *The Diamond Cutters* (1955), "as mere exercises for poems I hadn't written," but that the book had been praised as "graceful"; if she was unhappy, it "could only mean that I was ungrateful, insatiable, perhaps a monster." By the time she met Sexton and Plath, in the summer of 1959, she felt "that I had either to consider myself a failed woman or a failed poet or try to find some synthesis by which to understand what was happening to me."[75] She felt "very competitive" with Sexton, who had a book coming out, and was "such a knockout" to boot. Plath asked her about combining motherhood and writing, and she gave a vaguely encouraging reply, but "what I wanted to tell her was 'Don't try,' because I was in such despondency; I'd just had my third child, I was thirty, and I felt that in many ways my life was over, that I would never write again. I couldn't foresee a future different from the past two years of raising children and being almost continuously angry."[76]

In 1958, Rich began to write "for the first time, directly about experiencing myself as a woman. The poem was jotted in fragments during children's naps, brief hours in a library, or at 3 a.m. after rising with a wakeful child . . . Over two years I wrote a 10-part poem called 'Snapshots of a Daughter-in-Law,' in a longer, looser mode than I'd ever trusted myself with before." Recalling the composition over a decade later, Rich felt that the poem "was too literary, too dependent on allusion; I hadn't found the courage yet to do without authorities, or even to use the pronoun 'I.' "[77] "Snapshots of a Daughter-in-Law" is about a daughter's relationship to her mother, and a woman writer's relationship to her tradition. The mother, to whom the poem is addressed, is an aging Louisiana belle out of *The Awakening*, her mind, "moldering like wedding-cake," playing a nostalgic Chopin prelude. But the daughter, "nervy, glowering," is going mad in her domestic confinement and her creative paralysis. She hears male voices from the past warning her of the futility of women's creative effort, and angry women's voices from the past, Wollstonecraft and Dickinson. Meanwhile, she makes coffee and wipes the teaspoons with which she is truly measuring out her life, and shaves her legs "until they gleam like petrified mammoth-tusk." This striking image, as if a woman were a fossilized extinct creature, was also the first time such feminine grooming had been considered worthy of poetic mention. The serious woman writer for whom Rich called would have to be very different, unwilling to enact male fantasies of the feminine, and "more merciless to herself than history."

Lesbian Literature of the 1950s

At Yaddo in 1959 with Ted Hughes, Sylvia Plath observed the lesbian writers in residence with curiosity and some envy: "The old admiration for the strong, if Lesbian, woman. The relief of limitation as a price for balance and surety."[78] Elizabeth Bishop's sexuality was known to her friends, but never made public in her lifetime. Adrienne Rich would not fully acknowledge her lesbianism until the 1970s. During the fifties, however, an underground literature of lesbianism began to appear in cheap paperback novels that had begun to be popular in 1950 with the success of Pocket Books. In 1952, Patricia Highsmith, writing as "Claire Morgan," published her novel *The Price of Salt*. In 1955 in San Francisco, a pioneering lesbian rights organization, the Daughters of Bilitis, was founded, and launched its magazine *The Ladder*. In 1957, the first pulp novel by cult writer "Ann Bannon," *Odd Girl Out*, made its appearance. Bannon, whose real name is Ann Weldy (1932–), became known as the "Queen of Lesbian Pulp Fiction," but when she started her series, Weldy was a young housewife; during her twenty-seven-year marriage to an engineer, she had two children. When the marriage ended, Weldy went to graduate school, receiving a Ph.D. in linguistics from Stanford. She taught at Sacramento State College and eventually became associate dean of the College of Arts and Sciences. Weldy's introductions to her reissued novels *I Am a Woman* and *Journey to a Woman* describe the evolution of her fiction.[79]

YOUNG, GIFTED, BISEXUAL, AND BLACK—LORRAINE HANSBERRY

Aspiring young black women writers were also caught in the limbo of the 1950s. Lorraine Hansberry (1930–1965) was one of the most intellectual and sophisticated writers of her generation, as well as a political radical. Hansberry came from a prosperous academic family in Chicago, and spent two years at the University of Wisconsin. But she found her voice and vocation in Harlem in 1950, writing for *Freedom,* a progressive publication for African-Americans. When she read Simone de Beauvoir's *The Second Sex* (1953), Hansberry's innate sense of women's oppression found a theorist, and her marriage to Robert Nemiroff, a Jewish activist, brought her in touch with interracial activism and the early civil rights movement. Within a few years, though, Hansberry had revealed another of her secret selves, by joining the Daughters of Bilitis and publishing two letters in *The Ladder.* While she kept her bisexuality private, she ended her marriage.

Hansberry's first play, *A Raisin in the Sun,* opened on Broadway on March 11, 1959. The title came from Langston Hughes's poem—"What happens to a dream deferred? Does it dry up, like a raisin in the sun?" Set in the 1950s in Chicago, it dramatized the dreams of three generations of a working-class black family, the Youngers: to own a house, to start a business, to enter a profession. *Raisin* was a hit, won the New York Drama Critics Circle Award, and introduced a number of themes that other African-American writers would develop over the next decades.

Like Berenice in *The Member of the Wedding,* Hansberry's Lena Younger, the matriarch of the family, was a traditional figure of wisdom, patience, and belief in racial uplift and progress. Her children, however, spoke for an angrier new generation of black urban Americans. Walter Lee was one of the first young militants on the American stage. The rebellious Beneatha, who wants to be a doctor, was the first profession-ally ambitious black woman in the theater, and the first to identify with the romance of African culture, a theme Hansberry treated satirically on stage, but also explored in its connections to African-American revolu-tionary ideals. Made into a successful movie in 1961, *A Raisin in the Sun* reached a wide audience in the United States and abroad, and brought its author fame and visibility.

Sadly, the triumph of *A Raisin in the Sun* was the peak of Hansberry's career. In 1963, she was diagnosed with pancreatic cancer. Her last play, *The Sign in Sidney Brustein's Window* (1964), had a Jewish male protago-nist, to the anger of some black intellectuals who felt that she had deserted and betrayed their cause. Actors and playwrights in New York, however, including Paddy Chayevsky, Sammy Davis, Jr., and Mel Brooks, raised money to keep the play going. It finally closed after ninety-nine performances in January 1965, and Hansberry died the same night, at the age of thirty-four. After her death, Nemiroff, her literary executor, devoted himself to the preservation of her legacy, editing her essays and producing a play, *To Be Young, Gifted and Black,* based on her life and writing. Nevertheless, Hansberry's tragically early death deprived American women's literature at mid-century of one of its most gifted artists, and yet another face of Eve.

At the U.S. trade fair in Moscow in 1959, President Richard Nixon faced Russian premier Nikita Khrushchev in a model American kitchen, and told him that for Americans, "diversity, the right to choose, is the most important thing . . . We have many different manufacturers and many different kinds of washing machines so that the housewives have a choice."[80] Deciding whether to buy a Maytag or a GE washing machine, however, was hardly freedom of choice for women. In American women's writing, kitchens had always been an important setting; in "A Jury of Her Peers," all the action takes place in the kitchen, where masculine and feminine observations, judgments, and values silently clash. By the fifties, these settings became increasingly ironic and dark, whether Gwendolyn Brooks's cramped Chicago "kitchenette," the kitchen of a deserted house with its dusty table and two embalmed doughnuts in Shirley Jackson's *Life Among the Savages,* or the ladies' magazine Food Testing Kitchen in Sylvia Plath's *The Bell Jar,* where everyone gets ptomaine poisoning. If the kitchen was the only room of her own for the American Eve, the only space for women's self-expression, it was a prison, and women writers were due for a break.

17

The 1960s: Live or Die

he 1960s were a decade of tumultuous change in almost every aspect of American life. The black power movement, the Vietnam War and the antiwar movement, the plague of assassinations, the women's liberation movement, the counterculture and sexual revolution, the beginnings of protest for gay rights, transformed American society; and women writers, wherever they lived, however they voted, whatever their age or their personal involvement with these upheavals, could not avoid or escape transformation as well. In the 1960s, Gwendolyn Brooks had a conversion experience that led her to reject the first part of her career as "Negro" writing, and to redefine herself as a black writer. In the early sixties, she published two books of poems, *The Bean Eaters* (1960) and *Selected Poems* (1962). Then, at a black writers' conference at Fisk University in 1967, she met a younger group of male poets who galvanized her by asserting that "black poets should write as blacks, about blacks, and address themselves to blacks." Brooks left her publisher and took her subsequent work to small black presses; she dedicated herself to expressing "rage" in a form accessible to readers or listeners on street corners, in taverns, or in prisons. From having been a very intellectual, allusive writer, she became a populist one. In her 1972 memoirs, she explained her change of purpose: "My aim in my next future is to write poems that will somehow successfully 'call' all black people: black people in taverns, black people in alleys, black people in gutters, schools, offices, factories, prisons, the consulate; I wish to reach black people in mines, on farms, on thrones."[1] After her poetic rebirth, Brooks's work during the sixties, especially *In the Mecca* (1968), made stunning use of black language, music, and idiom.

White women poets were also experiencing a rebirth that coincided with the feminist awakening of the decade. Like rock music and the popular songs that accompanied, inspired, and put words to vast changes of feeling, women's poetry of the 1960s carried the messages and questions of the new generation. Poems expressed women's anger, passion, self-exploration and self-realization, and rebelled against traditional subjects and forms in a language that was graphic, urgent, subversive, and above all memorable. Never before, and never since, has American poetry been such an effective medium for social, political, and cultural transformation. For women who lived through it, the 1960s were the equivalent of the French Revolution for the British Romantic poets; like Wordsworth describing his youth in *The Prelude,* they felt charged with hope: "Bliss was it in that dawn to be alive."

Novels, however, are generally slower than poetry to react to historical change; they take a long time to gestate, write, and publish. While important and impressive novels by women appeared during the sixties, most looked back to earlier decades. Popular fictional genres of the 1960s reflected the sense that women's lives were restricted and repetitive, and there was more scope in writing for and about men. Susan Eloise Hinton (1948–) from Tulsa, Oklahoma, for example, published her first novel, *The Outsiders* (1967), under her initials, S. E. Hinton; it became "the best-selling young-adult novel of all time." Strongly influenced by Shirley Jackson, Hinton wrote about teenage boys, gangs, and misfits in Western high schools, and along with *Rumble Fish* (1968) and *Tex* (1979), created books that became cult classics on the page and the movie screen.[2] "I started using male characters just because it was easiest," Hinton explains on her website. "I was a tomboy, most of my friends were boys, and I figured nobody would believe a girl would write about my subject matter." Married, a mother, Hinton published her first adult book, *Some of Tim's Stories,* in 2007.[3]

Growing Up Female—Harper Lee

The decade began with the publication of Harper Lee's *To Kill a Mockingbird* (1960), which won the Pulitzer Prize, and had sold thirty million copies as of 2004. Respected by critics, and beloved by readers, it became one of the instant classics of the twentieth century. Like *Uncle Tom's Cabin* and *Gone with the Wind,* Lee's novel dealt with the grand triumvirate of American history—race, sexuality, and the South. Set in the 1930s, it anticipated the emotional and political fervor of the civil rights movement, and at the same time told a story of growing up female that resonated with the inchoate frustrations of women in the years leading up to the second wave of feminism.

The life of Nelle Harper Lee (1926–) sounds very much like that of Eudora Welty or Flannery O'Connor. One of four children, she grew up in Monroeville, Alabama, where her father, Amasa Coleman Lee, practiced law until his death in 1962. As a child, Nelle read everything she could get her hands on—not that much, she recalled, because "[b]ooks were scarce. There was nothing you could call a public library, we were a hundred miles away from a department store's book section." Instead, she and her childhood friends, who included Truman Capote, "began to circulate reading material among ourselves until each child had read another's entire stock. There were long dry spells broken by the new Christmas books, which started the rounds again."[4] She attended a women's college, Huntingdon, in Montgomery, where her classmates remembered her as a maverick, uninterested in clothes, dates, or manners: "Everything about her hinted at masculinity," another freshman recalled.[5] After a year, she transferred to the University of Alabama at Tuscaloosa, where she edited the campus humor magazine and wrote for literary publications. She was thinking about becoming a lawyer, like her father and older sister, and briefly tried studying law; but she soon decided to become a writer instead and moved to New York, where she worked as clerk for BOAC (predecessor to British Airways) and Eastern Airlines by day, and wrote at night.

On Christmas Day 1956, her friends Joy and Michael Brown invited her to open presents. He was a Broadway lyricist who had made a lot of money for a TV musical with Roddy McDowall. The couple's surprising and generous gift to her was a kind of private fellowship—a year off to write. As she explained to another friend, "The one stern string attached is that I will be subjected to a sort of 19th Century regimen of discipline: they don't care whether anything I write makes a nickel. They want to kick me into some kind of seriousness towards my talents."[6] Michael Brown also introduced her to the literary agent Annie Laurie Williams. Lee immediately quit her job, and by January 1957, she brought Williams the first fifty pages of a novel tentatively titled "Go Set a Watchman"; a week later she returned with a hundred pages more. By May, the novel, renamed "Atticus," was deemed ready to send out to publishers. She had already written over a hundred pages of a second novel, "The Long Goodbye."[7] (It has never appeared.)

The editors at J. B. Lippincott were impressed, but found the book patchy and awkwardly structured, so they sent her off to rewrite it, a process that eventually took three drafts and two and a half years. The money from the Browns ran out, and Harper had to make several trips back to Monroeville. She depended on her editor, Tay Hohof, for literary guidance, and Hohof also suggested that she use the name "Harper Lee." Originally, the story was told in the third person by the adult Jean Louise Finch, looking back at a momentous period in her childhood; in the second draft, the child Jean, nicknamed "Scout," told the story in the first person; and finally Lee blended the two voices, alternating between them in her narrative. Lippincott accepted the novel and scheduled it for publication in June 1960. While she was waiting for galleys, Lee accompanied Truman Capote to Kansas as a paid research assistant to help him write a long article for *The New Yorker* on a murder case, which became the nonfiction novel *In Cold Blood*. Capote, who appears in *Mockingbird* as the odd child and "pocket Merlin" from Mississippi, Dill Harris, also took the photograph of Lee for the book jacket, in which she is lying in the weeds in a stretched-out sweatshirt, her dark hair cropped like a boy's.

Set in the "tired old town" of Maycomb, Alabama, at the end of the Depression, *To Kill a Mockingbird* is based on a real rape trial in Monroeville in the 1930s, in which the black defendant was convicted and sentenced to death. For Lee, it was a prime example, along with the Scottsboro trial, of racial injustice in the Deep South.[8] *Mockingbird* is also a novel about a good man, the widowed lawyer Atticus Finch, who fights the bigotry and hatred of the town with reason, compassion, and courage. A black man, Tom Robinson, is falsely accused of the rape and beating of a young white woman, Mayella Ewell, and Atticus defends him. Although he knows that Tom has no chance of being acquitted by a white supremacist jury, and although he regards himself as a pacifist, Atticus stands up to the lynch mob that comes after Tom when he is awaiting trial in the local jail. If the novel has a weakness, it is the sanctification of Atticus, who is depicted as an Alabama Christ figure who understands and even forgives the racism of his white neighbors while he firmly opposes them.

The trial scene, which is at the center of the book, looks back to Glaspell's "Jury of Her Peers" in its representation of the disenfranchised black people in Maycomb and the whites who accuse and judge them. But Lee also introduces the themes of incest, child abuse, alcoholism, poverty, and loneliness into her trial. She describes the Ewells as a generic underclass, the ne'er-do-wells, more like Dickens's swarming illiterate London poor than Faulkner's degenerate Snopeses or O'Connor's scheming white trash.

> *Every town the size of Maycomb had families like the Ewells. No economic fluctuations changed their status—people like the Ewells lived as guests of the county in prosperity as well as in the depths of a depression. No truant officers could keep their numerous offspring in school; no public health officer could free them from congenital defects, various worms, and the diseases indigenous to filthy surroundings.*

The Ewells live in a cabin behind the town dump, amid refuse and squalor. In contrast, the "small Negro settlement" is tidy and homey, with "neat cabins," from which rise "delicious smells" of frying chicken and bacon, as well as squirrel, possum, and rabbit.

Yet amid the garbage and chaos, Mayella, the oldest daughter and surrogate mother, has managed to put out some red geraniums in "chipped-enamel slop jars." During the trial, we learn that Mayella is another victim, ignorant, "accustomed to strenuous labor," friendless, beaten by her father, probably sexually molested by him as well, and so desperate for affection that she risks making sexual advances to a kind black man. "It came to me," Scout thinks, "that Mayella Ewell must have been the loneliest person in the world," a pariah to both races, and yet when she accuses Tom Robinson, "probably the only person who was decent to her," she "looked at him as if he were dirt beneath her feet."

On a third level, *To Kill a Mockingbird* is a novel about the injustice of gender in the South, where the boys, like Scout's older brother Jem, have some images of noble manhood, but the girls, like Scout, seek vainly for models of strong women. Jem is a football-mad preadolescent male radical, whose angry protests against the Southern race and class system are countered but not quelled by the saintly tolerance of his father. Nonetheless, he knows that his father is both the most decent man and the best shot in Maycomb County. Scout, however, is surrounded by negative images of femininity, whether as oversexed, hypocritical, silly, or weak. Even when she goes to the black church, "as I had often met in my own church, I was confronted with the Impurity of Women doctrine that seemed to preoccupy all clergymen." The class-obsessed and genteelly racist white ladies of the Missionary Society diligently study the Mrunas of Africa, charitable objects who "put the women out in huts when their time came, whatever that was." Aunt Alexandra Finch and Miss Maudie Atkinson, a dignified neighbor, are intelligent women, but even Atticus accepts that women in Alabama cannot serve on juries (indeed, *Mockingbird* may have had something to do with their finally being granted that right in 1967). Scout is indignant but Atticus explains with a grin, "I guess it's to protect our frail ladies from sordid cases like Tom's. Besides . . . I doubt if we'd ever get a complete case tried—the ladies'd be interrupting to ask questions."

By 1963, Lee had made a great deal of money from the sales, movie versions, translations, and editions of *Mockingbird,* and was free to work on her next book. Her older sister Alice, a lawyer, handled her finances. She tried to avoid public engagements and interviews; in one of the last, in 1964, she spoke on a New York radio program, *Counterpoint,* about her longing to "leave some record of the kind of life that existed in a very small world," to chronicle the life of the small Southern town "because I believe there is something universal in this little world, something decent to be said for it, and something to lament in its passing." She hoped to "do this in several novels." In short, she concluded with joking false modesty, "All I want is to be the Jane Austen of Southern Alabama."9

But the other novels never appeared. Much like Ralph Ellison, forever promising to follow up *Invisible Man,* and meanwhile accepting honors and serving on distinguished committees, Lee kept busy in New York for a time after her great success. Ralph Ellison claimed in his later years that he had lost hundreds of pages of his second novel in a fire; Lee's sister spoke vaguely about the manuscript being stolen in a burglary in Monroeville. Literary history has not been kind to American writers who stopped writing or perpetually announced a book that never appeared, but Harper Lee escaped criticism by keeping modestly out of the public eye. Unlike Ellison, she did not pursue the luxury high life in New York; unlike Truman Capote, she did not betray her friends in print; unlike Tillie Olsen, she did not market herself as a victim of silencing. Nevertheless, Lee remained silent throughout the years of the civil rights movement, the Kennedy and King assassinations, and the women's liberation movement. She wrote a notable chronicle of her childhood, but could not take a character like Scout into adulthood and describe the changing South.

Progress in the Female Sphere—the Ship and the Group

In the early sixties, two other novels set in the 1930s became best sellers. Katherine Anne Porter's long-awaited *Ship of Fools* (1962) was critically acclaimed, and highly profitable; the movie sale was rumored to be half a million dollars. Not everyone was enthusiastic; in "*Ship of Fools* and the Critics," Theodore Solotaroff called it "the most sour and morbid indictment of humanity to appear in years." Josephine Herbst agreed— "I never saw a bunch of more unloving, irritable, touchy folks either on ship or land," she confided to Alfred Kazin—but she was mainly outraged by Porter's distortions of the politics of 1931, making the Germans "evil" and the only Jew on board a greedy stereotype. Herbst also disliked Porter's portrayal of sexually fastidious and frigid modern women.[10]

Mary McCarthy's *The Group* (1963) was more sexually up-to-date; indeed, it achieved renown for "Dottie Makes an Honest Woman of Herself," the chapter (originally published in the *Partisan Review*) in which one of its heroines gets fitted with a diaphragm. "It's about eight Vassar girls," McCarthy explained. "It was conceived as a kind of mock-chronicle novel. It's a novel about the idea of progress, really . . . seen in the female sphere . . . home economics, architecture, domestic technology, contraception, child-bearing; the study of technology in the home, in the playpen, in the bed."[11] *The Group* begins with the wedding of Kay, the McCarthy figure, to the actor Harald Petersen in 1933, and ends with her suicide and funeral just before Pearl Harbor. The members of the Group have gathered to bury her, and to protect her memory from the vicious slanders of Harald, now her ex-husband. Lakey, the aristocratic lesbian, returns from Europe with her lover the Baroness, and finally has her revenge on Harald by letting him think that she had also seduced Kay. "What a filthy lesbian trick," he declares in fury. ". . . No wonder you hid yourself abroad all these years. You ought to have stayed in Europe, where the lights were going out . . . You have no part of America!"

The Group pleased readers (apart from McCarthy's Vassar classmates) but angered critics, and divided its literary jury. Other women writers speculated on the hidden motives and meanings of the novel. "The semi-Mary protagonist gets killed again (suicide?)" Louise Bogan wrote to Ruth Limmer, "while her other half (rich, soignée, onto everything) turns out to have been a corrupt and corrupting *Lesbian,* all along."[12]

McCarthy's friend Elizabeth Hardwick wrote a funny and treacherous parody of the novel for *The New York of Review of Books* under the pseudonym "Xavier Prynne." Hardwick had sent McCarthy a letter of congratulations calling *The Group* "very rich," "wonderful," and "a tremendous accomplishment." When she discovered the truth, McCarthy was devastated, but eventually forgave Hardwick.[13] Even more cruelly, the editors assigned the review of the novel to Norman Mailer, who penned an eviscerating attack on McCarthy's obsession with detail—"a cold lava of anality"—and concluded that "she is simply not a good enough woman to write a major novel."[14] Moreover, McCarthy's affinity for a realist novel of facts, dates, and places, seemed dated to admirers of Faulkner, Nabokov, and the *nouveau roman*.

In the late sixties, McCarthy became an active protester against the war, going to Vietnam in 1967, and writing a six-part series for *The New York Review of Books*, later published as *Hanoi*. With her usual contrariness, she was impatient and bored by the women's liberation movement. "This whole myth about how different the world would have been if it had been female-dominated, about how there would have been no wars . . . seems a complete fantasy to me. I've never noticed that women were less warlike than men."[15] Of course, McCarthy measured all women by her own Amazonian personality. Although she would have called herself a pacifist, she had a warrior fascination and attraction to combat. In her last novel, *Cannibals and Missionaries* (1979), written after the murder of the Israeli athletes at the Olympics in Munich, she imagined a violent encounter between Palestinian terrorists and their hostages. In writing it, she gave close attention both to the exact configuration of airplanes, and the psychology of religious terrorists, which makes chilling reading today.

American Chronicler—Joyce Carol Oates

In contrast to Harper Lee, Joyce Carol Oates (1938–), who also began her career in the 1960s, went on to become an exceptionally, even uncannily, productive and versatile writer. Born in a working-class Catholic family, Oates was raised on a small farm in rural Millersport, New York. Lockport, where she was bused to school in the 1950s, was a small industrial town, bisected by the Erie Canal, and in her fiction and poetry, its many metal bridges over seething dark water are recurring images of sexual

temptation and danger. As a child, Oates read American and British classics, but neither in her reading nor in her life did she encounter strong
professional women, or daring women writers. Yet by the time she graduated from high school, Oates had determined to be a novelist, and she
found her own path almost unaided. As a brilliant undergraduate at
Syracuse University, and as a graduate student in English at the University of Wisconsin, she met hardly any female professors. At Wisconsin,
however, she met another graduate student, Raymond Smith; they married in 1961.

The next year the couple moved to Detroit, where Oates became the
second female faculty member at the Jesuit-run University of Detroit
(the first was a nun). She had begun to publish short stories as an undergraduate, and continued to write and experiment in that form. In 1966,
Oates published one of her most poignant and haunting stories, "Where
Are You Going, Where Have You Been?" Dedicated to Bob Dylan,
inspired by a real murder case reported in 1965, and located by Oates
in the "new morality" of the "transformational years" of the 1960s,
"Where Are You Going" is set in a teenage culture that sounds more like
the 1950s, with radio disc jockeys, drive-in restaurants, and shopping
plazas. The fifteen-year-old heroine, Connie, knows that her sexual flowering may be brief, and that like her mother, she, too, may end up shuf-
fling around in bedroom slippers with a silent husband to remind her of
the lost sweetness of love. All a girl can do, her abductor warns her, is
"be sweet and pretty and give in." In Oates's prefeminist female gothic,
neither sisterhood nor motherhood have any power; bonds between
women are weak, and even Connie's girlfriends are not important
enough to be named. As in traditional gothic fiction, Connie has no
mobility of her own and has to be driven places by her father, or
abducted by a hoodlum in a convertible in order to activate a plot.
Indeed, in several of Oates's stories and novels of the sixties, being able
to drive and having wheels is about as much liberation as her heroines
can imagine.

Ironically, Oates was living in the capital of the automobile industry,
and during a decade when it was undergoing racial and economic crises.
"Moving to Detroit . . . changed my life completely," she has said. "Living in Detroit, enduring the extraordinary racial tensions of that city . . .
made me want to write directly about the serious social concerns of our
time."[16] In the late sixties, she published three remarkable novels, *A Garden of Earthly Delights* (1967), *Expensive People* (1968), and *them* (1969). All

three were nominated for the National Book Award, and Oates won the award for *them* in 1970. As a group, the novels have been considered as a loosely connected saga of American class struggle in the twentieth century, and Oates boldly declared that they "were conceived . . . as critiques of America—American culture, American values, American dreams—as well as narratives in which romantic ambitions are confronted by what must be called 'reality.' "[17] This desire to map the whole of America had hitherto been a masculine ambition, and all three novels use male narrators, the male point of view, or masculine themes. Oates never used a male pseudonym, but she clearly identified with the passion, frustration, and energy of her heroes; we could even call the series "portraits of the woman artist as a young man." Like Flannery O'Connor, she wanted to be a great American writer, which in the terms of the era meant also to be a male one. Her interests in the destiny of women, the creative freedom of the woman writer, and the function of art itself, were muted in the novels, but always breaking through into the main texts.

A Garden of Earthly Delights is about pretty Clara Walpole, the daughter of migrant workers, whose elementary-school teacher calls her "white trash." Among its distinctions is Oates's freedom from the verbal constraints that had long beleaguered women writers. While American writers had only recently won the legal rights to use the full range of language, including obscenity, in fiction, Oates was far in advance of her contemporaries in rendering the real speech of her working-class characters. Oates's editors at Vanguard Press, she recalled, "were offended by the frequent profanities and crudeness . . . objecting particularly to Clara's speech. For even as a girl, Clara can be forcefully crude. Yet to me, such speech was more or less commonplace . . . overheard as adult and adolescent speech."[18] But ultimately she gave in to her editors' scandalized urging and reduced some of Clara's blue language.

Clara attaches herself to a series of men, first the drifter and a loner, Lowry, who likes his car, driving and "just to be in motion." He takes her away from her family and leaves her pregnant in upstate New York. In her most self-determining act, Clara seduces a prosperous married businessman, Curt Revere, and persuades him that he has fathered her child. In the first sign of Clara's new sense of control, Revere teaches her to drive and buys her "a little yellow coupe." Clara has wheels but nowhere to go, and she imagines that her infant son Swan will grow up to live out her fantasies: "He's going by train and by airplane / All around the world," she croons to the sleeping baby. Swan, a doomed artist manqué, dominates the last part of the book, but in 2002, Oates rewrote it to give her heroine more complexity. She added details about Clara trying to copy the styles of movie stars, and taking on the characteristics of the iconic Blonde, the vehicle and victim of American cultural fantasies.

Oates's most documentary novel, *them,* contrasted the experiences of Maureen Wendall and her brother Jules, growing up in inner-city Detroit, the children of a worker on the Chrysler assembly line. Like Clara, Maureen is frantic to escape, but as a girl, she has no way to earn money or get away. In contrast, Jules, partly modeled on Julien Sorel of Stendhal's *The Red and the Black,* understands that even at his weakest he has more power than a woman. "A woman in a car only appears to be in control!" he thinks as a teenager. "Inside, her machinery is as wobbly and nervous as the machinery of her car." One of Jules's first jobs is playing messenger boy for a petty gangster who sends him out to buy a Cadillac, and gives him a gun.

The novel ends with the Detroit riots of 1967, an apocalyptic scene of twitchy self-important white radicals, black looters, and police as out of control as everyone else. Although it has been remembered as Oates's strongest and most explicit statement about race, *them* actually has less to say about race than many of her subsequent stories, novels, and plays. A "novel of Detroit," which deals with the violence of urban unrest, it is nonetheless limited by Oates's separation as a woman from black and masculine popular culture in the 1960s, including sports and Motown. As she later explained, in the sixties she did not "feel empowered to write about blacks."[19] Over the next decades, Oates would feel increasingly empowered to write about both masculinity and race.

Anne Sexton—the Birth of the Poet

In Anne Sexton's personal narrative of her career, she had been reborn as a poet in 1957–58, on the brink of her thirtieth birthday, as a result of breakdown, psychotherapy, and the discovery of poetic language and form. As she told the story, "It was a kind of rebirth at twenty-nine." According to her biographer Diane Middlebrook, "like a goddess from an egg, motherless and fatherless, the poet bursts into history as a completely new being . . . Leaving the domestic world composed of infant-parent dynamics, she burst into the cosmos of poetic art."[20] The problem Sexton faced in the 1960s was whether she could construct a new life from this new identity. Anne Sexton's first book of poems, *To Bedlam and Part Way Back,* based on her experiences in a Massachusetts mental hospital, was published on April 22, 1960, with a blurb from Robert Lowell. It received enthusiastic reviews: "a mental breakdown, pictured with a pitiless eye and clairvoyant sharpness," wrote *The New York Times.* From Brazil, Elizabeth Bishop wrote to Robert Lowell that she found the poems "good in spots," although less impressive than the more controlled confessional muse of Lowell's *Life Studies.* "I feel I know too much about her . . . I like some of the really mad ones best."[21]

One of the maddest of the mad poems was "Her Kind." In it, Sexton identified with the New England witch. Shirley Jackson was one of her literary models; she had read that Jackson wrote "like a witch with broomstick dipped in adder's blood," and felt, "God damn it, that's what I want them to say about me."[22] The poem begins with a powerful claim of kinship between the woman poet and the "posessed witch" as social and sexual outcasts because of their powers. In the conclusion, Sexton compares herself with the witch about to be tortured and burned at the stake, and makes a defiant assertion of dedication to her strange art:

> *A woman like that is not ashamed to die.*
> *I have been her kind.*

Was the witchcraft of poetry a survival tool or a death wish? Sexton played both the survivor and the martyr in her packed poetry readings, where she would make a slow entrance from the back of the room in a long red dress, diamond rings flashing on her bony fingers as she chain-smoked through a series of poems beginning with "Her Kind." One account of these readings praises Sexton as a sixties performance artist: "She would read, in her marvelous, throaty, classy voice, harrowing accounts of insanity and loss . . . She was very much a poet of her time."[23] However, Sexton's close friend Maxine Kumin, another Boston poet, hated them: "They were so melodramatic and stagey . . . I hated the way Annie pandered to an audience."[24] While all Sexton's readings were ordeals for which she painfully psyched herself up with pills and gin, they were also an intentional exhibition of wounds, a freak show, as she herself acknowledged.

In 1961–62, Sexton and Kumin were among the first group to benefit from the newly founded Radcliffe Institute, a residential program for "intellectually displaced women" whose careers had been interrupted by

family obligations and who wanted to pursue research or artistic work.
Despite her commitment to poetry, Sexton was still defining herself in
terms of the great male tradition. When *Harper's* asked her to contribute
to a special issue on "The American Female" in spring 1962, Sexton
wrote that "the best compliment a female poet could receive is that 'she
writes like a man.' " Her views began to change when Tillie Olsen joined
the Radcliffe scholars that year and gave a seminar on "The Death of the
Creative Process," which would eventually become her book *Silences*. It
educated Sexton about the self-inflicted damages of writers of both
sexes.[25] Sexton also was reassured to learn that Olsen shared her love for
Sara Teasdale and Edna St. Vincent Millay, women poets who had
become so unfashionable as to be pariahs.

In fall 1962, Sexton published *All My Pretty Ones*, a much more daring
and explicitly female book than *To Bedlam and Part Way Back*. Middlebrook describes it as "the work of a mature artist," which "displayed as
well the full range of subjects she was to write about: mental illness, sexual love, spiritual anguish."[26] Also among the subjects was abortion, and
the surgery Sexton had undergone for a benign ovarian cyst; in "The
Operation," she summoned up the memory of her mother's death from
cancer, and her dread as she herself lay in the hospital "Clean of the
body's hair / . . . smooth from breast to leg." This was much too strong
for the squeamish James Dickey, who charged in *The New York Times Book
Review* that "it would be hard to find a writer who dwells more insistently on the pathetic and disgusting aspects of bodily experience." But
women poets were impressed; Sexton had letters from May Swenson,
Denise Levertov, and Elizabeth Bishop ("harrowing, awful, very real—
and very good").[27] She sent a copy to Sylvia Plath, who sent a letter of
thanks for the book: "It is superbly masterful, womanly in the greatest
sense." In a BBC interview Plath also praised Sexton's "wonderfully
craftsmanlike poems" about "private and taboo subjects."[28]

Plath—the Death of the Poet

Plath had undergone more than one rebirth, beginning with her suicide
attempt just before her twenty-first birthday, and her miraculous recovery in the early 1950s. In its aftermath, she, too, had undergone psychotherapy, had come to understand her love-hate relationship with her
mother, and had reimagined herself as the literary daughter of Yeats and

Woolf. A second rebirth was her marriage to Ted Hughes, her poetic double—a courageous alliance that required Plath to give up her ideals of the prosperous partner she had internalized in years of dating well-groomed, middle-class, professional American family men, and to place a bet on a rough genius who had no intention of taking a job or settling down. But, rapidly, she became competitive with Hughes, or rather, transferred her poetic ambitions to him. Susan Van Dyne notes that she ceded him her place in her pantheon of great modernist writers, alongside Yeats, and beamed with pride when his first book was accepted by Faber, and he was photographed with Eliot, Auden, Louis MacNeice, and Stephen Spender. "As she watched their mantle unequivocally descend on Ted, Plath could claim a relation to this male literary history only by marriage."[29]

The early sixties, however, had seemed like the start of a new life for Plath. In January 1960, Heinemann in London accepted her first, much-worked-over, book of poems, *The Colossus*. As soon as the contract was signed, Hughes recalled, Plath had a kind of poetic breakthrough. "She started again, though with a noticeable difference . . . she seemed more relaxed about it." While previously she had obsessed about putting her poems together into a book, and finding exactly the right title for the whole thing, "she made no attempt to find an anxious mothering title for the growing brood, over the next two years, until she was overtaken by the inspiration that produced the poems of the last six months of her life."[30] The birth of their two children, Frieda and Nicholas, gave her hope that she could combine the roles of poet and mother, indeed, that motherhood would enrich her writing. The family had moved to Devon, created a home in the countryside.

When Plath discovered in June 1962 that Hughes was having an affair, her new life shattered, but the poems came with unprecedented rapidity and volcanic ferocity. After she left Hughes in October 1962, and moved back to London with their children, she wrote twenty-five poems in a single month, sometimes several in a single day. In the week preceding her thirtieth birthday, she wrote eight poems, concluding with "Ariel" on October 27, the day itself. For Plath, too, turning thirty was a threshold, a deadline for fame. And despite her anguish and rage, she recognized the quality of what she was producing. "I am a genius of a writer," she told her mother on October 16; "I have it in me. I am writing the best poems of my life; they will make my name."[31] She was also thinking about suicide, almost as an alternative to art. In "Lady Lazarus," she reconciled the two extremes by declaring that if her name could not be made in poetry, it could be made in death, through the art of dying, which she did "exceptionally well."

The poems of this period, especially "Daddy," which established an entirely new voice and tone for American women's poetry, and embodied women's rejection of patriarchal mythologies in the sixties, are now famous, although editors were not so quick to see her genius; *The New Yorker,* among other magazines, turned several of the poems down.

Of the astonishing October creations, the sequence of five poems Plath wrote consecutively from October 3 to October 8, which are known as the "Bee Poems," stand out both for their originality and for their relationship to the American female literary tradition. Plath had a family connection to bees; her father, Otto Plath, had been an entomologist at Boston University, and had published a standard work on *Bumblebees and Their Ways.* In an earlier poem, "The Beekeeper's Daughter" (1959), she had written about him as the "maestro of the bees." When she moved to Devon with Hughes, her midwife had introduced her to beekeeping, and she had gone to bee meetings with the local villagers. Back in London, she wrote to her mother, she had decorated her bedroom in yellow, white, and black—"bee colors." The poems focus on the queen bee, surrounded by her workers and drones, the symbol of female power, fertility, and mastery; and on the woman poet, the keeper of the bees, who identifies with the queen in the cycle of her life, death, and rebirth. In "Stings," this identification is made explicit. The queen is old, her "wings torn shawls, her long body / robbed of its plush—." The poet is not yet a queen; she is demoralized and beaten down, but she is not a drudge either, "Though for years I have eaten dust / And dried plates with my dense hair." Still, she has the chance to escape from her "wax house," and to reclaim her supremacy: "I / Have a self to recover, a queen." In the final poem of the sequence, "Wintering," the bees are hibernating, and "They have got rid of the men."

"Will the hive survive?" she asks, and answers that they will; they are already flying, "they taste the spring." In the table of contents she drew up for the book that became *Ariel,* Plath put this poem at the end. The Bee Poems are packed with references to classic and contemporary American literature. "The Bee Meeting" puns on the grove of hawthorn trees, and the black veil, like Nathaniel Hawthorne's short story; the poet's fear of the veiled villagers who seem to be conducting some murderous ritual suggests Shirley Jackson's "The Lottery." Above all, Plath revises and reverses Emily Dickinson and other American women writers who had traditionally written about flowers and bees, and made the male bees, rather than the queen, mobile, sexual, and dangerous.

That cold winter, however, Plath was falling back into a severe depression. On February 11, 1963, she committed suicide. Three days after her death, the *Times Literary Supplement* published four of the last poems: "Poppies in July," "Contusion," "Kindness," and "Edge." Anne Sexton learned of Plath's death on February 12, when it was reported in the Boston newspapers. She helped the minister of the Unitarian church in Wellesley organize a memorial service, but when the news spread that Plath was a suicide, Sexton told her psychiatrist that "Sylvia Plath's death disturbs me. Makes me want it too. She took something that was mine, *that* death was mine!" That tone of competition and self-pity mars the poem she wrote on the occasion, "Sylvia's Death." In Diane Middlebrook's words, "It was as if Sylvia Plath, the savvy rival, had leapfrogged right over Sexton's project of becoming famous, in which the fantasied finale was to be a well-publicized suicide. By this singular move, Plath had once and for all reversed their positions as senior and junior in the ranks of poetry."[32] Still, grief about Plath's death overshadowed the publication of Betty Friedan's highly publicized and revelatory study of *The Feminine Mystique* on February 19. When Maxine Kumin managed to read Friedan's book, she felt an instant sense of excitement and recognition; she wrote to Sexton that she had "been all but unable to put down FEM MYSTIQUE. Am mad for the message. Yes yes yes."[33] For Plath, alas, the message came too late.

The Bell Jar: A 1960s Jury of Her Peers

In the ten years after her death, Plath's final poems and her novel, *The Bell Jar*, appeared in the United States. She had finished the novel under the auspices of the Eugene F. Saxton Fellowship, affiliated with Harper and Row, and had sent the manuscript to the Saxton committee, which included two Harper editors, in late 1962. But the editors, both women, thought the novel was "disappointing, juvenile, and overwrought." So Plath gave it instead to her British publisher, William Heinemann; she claimed to be relieved that it would not be published in the United States because its transparently autobiographical references would hurt her friends and family. *The Bell Jar* came out in London on January 14, 1963, under the pseudonym "Victoria Lucas." Although the handful of reviews it received were positive, Plath was crushed and dismayed by their brevity. She had hoped for an instant success that would launch her into commercial fiction. By July 1963, Sexton had managed to obtain a copy of *The Bell Jar* ordered from a London bookstore, and read it avidly.

Although Plath herself disparaged it as a potboiler, *The Bell Jar* is an accomplished, penetrating, and darkly funny novel about the breakdown and recovery of a young woman artist. Set in 1953, "the summer they electrocuted the Rosenbergs," *The Bell Jar* is very much a novel about the fifties. Plath's first-person narrator, Esther Greenwood, undergoes several trials for the un-American activities of intellectualism, resistance to marriage and motherhood, and the desire to become a poet. First she is tried by ladies' magazine values, when she becomes a guest editor at *Ladies' Day*, as Plath had been at *Mademoiselle*. As one critic observes, "the magazine becomes for Esther a kind of tribunal, a College Board on female identity, questions of career, and . . . femininity."[34] Second, she is tried by the social organization of the suburb and its "motherly breath," offering up witnesses of proper domesticity and maternity. There she asks herself, "Why was I so unmaternal and apart?" The answers, she knows, are the warnings and her own fears of the absolute conflict of maternity and creativity: "After I had children I would feel differently, I wouldn't want to write poems anymore. I began to think that maybe it was true that when you were married and had children it was like being brainwashed, and afterward you went about numb as a slave in some private, totalitarian state." Finally, she has a breakdown, attempts suicide, and is tried by medicine, psychiatry, and hospitalization. She witnesses the medicalization of childbirth; the psychiatric policing and role reinforcement of therapy; the rewards (independence) and punishments (shock treatment) of mental hospitals. "I wasn't crippled in any way," Esther protests. "I just studied too hard. I didn't know when to stop."

While other American women novelists from Sarah Orne Jewett to Jean Stafford and Shirley Jackson had explored the psychology of women's eating disorders, Plath made the binge and the purge potent metaphors of female desire and purification. *The Bell Jar* is freighted with scenes in which female characters pay for their unfeminine appetites and sexuality by vomiting (as after the *Ladies' Day* luncheon); or in which Esther expresses her attraction and disgust through its terminology (in the mental hospital, when another patient, the lesbian Joan Gilling, tells Esther she likes her, Esther replies, "Frankly, Joan, you make me puke"); and in which, finally, she is purged of her unnatural and un-American behaviors through electroshock treatment: "all the heat and fear purged itself." Esther's survival at the novel's end comes at the price of Joan's suicide—the execution of the bad girl of the 1950s who wanted to use her mind, was not afraid to experiment with her sexuality, and felt tenderness rather than rivalry toward another woman. Although it was not published in the United States until 1971, when it became the great best seller Plath had always hoped for, *The Bell Jar* was by then already known to many American readers.

With the publication of *Ariel* in Britain in 1965, and the United States in 1966, Plath's fame as a poet was assured, and the Plath legend of the American female genius tormented, betrayed, and abandoned by a Heathcliff-like British poet-philanderer, was launched. Hughes had not followed the instructions Plath had left at her death about the order of the poems, and not until their daughter, Frieda, published an edition in 2004 was the text restored according to her plan.[35] Yet Plath's impact transcended any particulars of publication, nationality, or gender. *Ariel,* Diane Middlebrook concludes, ranks with *The Waste Land* "as one of the masterpieces of twentieth-century poetry in English, in having found a poetic mode that is the perfect medium of its culturally significant content, and that conveys an instantly recognizable subjectivity, one that matters to readers."[36]

Plath was a hard act to follow. In two books of poems in the late 1960s, *Live or Die* (1966) and *Love Poems* (1969), Anne Sexton continued to startle and inspire women readers, and to shock and appall male critics. "Menstruation at Forty," "In Celebration of My Uterus," "The Ballad of the Lonely Masturbator," "The Addict," and "The Breast" were both daring in their subject matter and dazzling in their metaphoric inventiveness. *Love Poems* was daring in other ways; Sexton wrote about an affair from the point of view of the "other woman," who is temporary, "part time," an object; when the fling is over, "he places her, / like a phone, back on the hook." In "For My Lover, Returning to His Wife," she ended: "As for me, I am a watercolor, / I wash off." Nonetheless, in her poem "Live," Sexton had listed herself on the side of survival and hope: "I say Live, Live because of the sun, / The dream, the excitable gift."

Other American women poets were also demanding a reclamation of their dreams. "And our dreams," wrote Denise Levertov (1923–1997) in "Hypocrite Women" (1967), "with what frivolity we have pared them / like toenails, clipped them like the ends of split hair." By decade's end, they were calling for a new kind of writing that would abandon the masks of feminine decorum and tell the whole truth about the gender and the nature of things. In "The Poem as Mask" (1968) Muriel Rukeyser declared: "No more masks! No more mythologies!" But Sexton finally chose death and mythologies, taking her life in 1974. The future of women's poetry, Adrienne Rich avowed at a memorial service for Sexton, could not be in "self-trivialization, contempt for women, misplaced compassion, addiction." It could not be in suicide: "We have had enough suicidal women poets, enough suicidal women, enough of self-destructiveness as the sole form of violence permitted to women."[37] For the 1970s, women writers would need the will to change.

18

The 1970s: The Will to Change

n 1971, Adrienne Rich published her eagerly awaited sixth book of poems, *The Will to Change*, which marked a shift in consciousness from protests against victimization, to the assertion of feminist will in political, spiritual, aesthetic, and sexual transformation. "Snapshots of a Daughter-in-Law" had warned that women writers who "cast too bold a shadow" faced "solitary confinement, / tear gas, attrition shelling." Now Rich wrote a poem called "Tear Gas," which defied attacks on feminist self-assertion and proclaimed the sexual solidarity of women: "The will to change begins in the body not in the mind."

In a talk called "When We Dead Awaken: Writing as Re-Vision," Rich defined the coming decade as a decade of awakening: "It's exhilarating to be alive in a time of awakening consciousness; it can also be confusing, disorienting, and painful," she declared. ". . . The sleepwalkers are coming awake, and for the first time this awakening has a collective reality; it is no longer such a lonely thing to open one's eyes." Women writers had a new world to create: "Women can no longer be primarily mothers and muses for men: we have our own work cut out for us."[1] By 1976, living with the Jamaican-American writer Michelle Cliff (1946–), Rich had willed herself to change, asserting her identity as a radical lesbian, a Jew, an antiracist, and, by the 1980s, a Marxist.

American feminism exploded in the 1970s, as women expressed optimism and determination about the possibilities for change in relations between women and men, and women and society. With wide public attention paid to Kate Millett's *Sexual Politics*, Robin Morgan's *Sisterhood Is Powerful*, and Shulamith Firestone's *The Dialectic of Sex* in 1970, feminism "filtered into virtually every area of U.S. life."[2] In academia, feminist scholars began to seek out and recover lost American women writers and texts. The recoveries of the decade began with Toni Cade Bambara's anthology *The Black Woman* (1970) and continued with the Feminist Press edition of Charlotte Perkins Gilman's "The Yellow Wallpaper" and the reprinting of "A Jury of Her Peers" in 1973. In 1975, in the first issue of the feminist journal *Signs,* the historian Carroll Smith-Rosenberg published "The Female World of Love and Ritual," a tremendously influential account of the friendships and cultural values growing out of the separate spheres of nineteenth-century American women. Nina Baym's *Woman's Fiction* (1978) analyzed 130 novels by American women published between 1830 and 1870. As Baym declared, "We thought of this lost work as a legacy, an inheritance that had been denied us. We took it for granted that the women we rediscovered would delineate an admirable, specifically female literary tradition, through which we ourselves would find strength and inspiration."[3]

Feminist literary criticism also began to appear in the 1970s. *The Female Imagination* (1975) by Patricia Meyer Spacks and *Literary Women* (1976) by Ellen Moers offered wide-ranging hypotheses about Anglo-American and European women novelists and poets. My first book, *A Literature of Their Own* (1977), considered nineteenth- and twentieth-century English women novelists, and outlined a three-phase trajectory of women's writing, which moved from imitation to resistance and then to self-discovery. *The Madwoman in the Attic* (1979), by Sandra M. Gilbert and Susan Gubar, analyzed classic women's texts of the nineteenth century as coded repudiations and revisions of the male literary tradition, gendered versions of what Harold Bloom had called the great writer's "anxiety of influence." Post-structuralist feminist critics, who believed women struggled against the symbolic order of language itself; socialist-feminist critics, who saw class as the major problem; lesbian-feminist critics who stressed sexual identity; and African-American feminist critics, who argued on behalf of a black women writers' literary tradition and history, created a sense of excitement and urgent debate that reinvigorated literary studies overall.

Both American women writers and feminist critics were challenged to find the will to change. For writers, feminism promised the end of second-class status, critical denigration, and self-censorship. It meant the legitimization of their creativity; no longer would women have to seek permission to write from parents, teachers, or husbands. Toni Morrison observed that when she started to write, "it looked like a male preserve . . . It's almost as if you needed permission to write. When I read women's biographies and autobiographies, even accounts of how they got started writing, almost every one of them had a little anecdote that told about the moment someone gave them permission to do it."[4] No longer would women writers would have to censor themselves in order to avoid offending traditional conventions of femininity. But would they now have to censor themselves to meet feminist conventions and shibboleths? Would being expected to deliver an "authentic" women's art be as damaging as being forbidden to deliver it? And was second-wave feminism a transitional stage leading to full self-expression for women, or another ideology limiting writers to a woman's preserve? These were the questions American women writers were urgently asking in the 1970s. For critics, feminism offered a new territory of women's writing to explore and map.

Feminism and Fiction

Scholars and literary historians have identified a number of overlapping genres associated with 1970s feminism. Katherine B. Payant sees the dominant form of popular fiction as the "*bildungsroman* or novel of the development of a young protagonist coming into conflict with society and finally taking her place." She cites books by Anne Roiphe, Alix Kates Shulman, Francine du Plessix Gray, Marge Piercy, Mary Gordon, and Marilyn French.[5] Lisa Maria Hogeland argues that the "most important form for feminist writers in the 1970s . . . was what I call the consciousness-raising novel," tracing a woman's understanding of her personal history in shared and political feminist concerns. Hogeland adds to the list novels by Kathy Acker, Lisa Alther, Rita Mae Brown, and Joanna Russ.[6] Gayle Greene defined the most significant form of women's writing during the decade as "feminist metafiction," novels in which "the protagonist looks to the literary tradition for answers about the present, speculates about the relation of 'the forms' to her life and her writing, seeks an 'ending of her own' which differs from the marriage or death to which she is traditionally consigned, and seeks freedom from the plots of the past." Among these metafictionists, Greene included Joan Didion, Gail Godwin, and Judith Rossner.[7]

All the feminist critics looking at the 1970s agree that Erica Jong's *Fear of Flying* (1973), which both fit and exceeded these genres and defied the restrictions on women's verbal range, sexual candor, and narrative voice, was a key book of the decade. "*Fear of Flying* was a declaration of independence," Jong herself said in an interview in 1974, using the classic metaphor of American women's protest. "It was a counterphobic book."[8] A alumna of Barnard who had done graduate study in eighteenth-century English literature at Columbia, Jong (1942–) began her literary career as a poet, but it was the publication of *Fear of Flying* that made her famous. As she explained in her introduction to the fifteenth-anniversary edition, the book connected with the spirit of the times: "Something new was beginning to happen. Women were starting to write about their lives as if their lives were as important as men's."[9] Yet at the same time that *Fear of Flying* addressed women's lives, it also spoke to men. As Christopher Lehmann-Haupt noted with surprise in *The New York Times*, "I can't remember ever before feeling quite so free to identify my own feelings with those of a female protagonist—which would suggest that Isadora Wing . . . is really more of a person than a woman."[10] John Updike and Henry Miller were among the first enthusiasts of the book, and contributed to its literary status.[11] In an interview in *Playboy*, Jong commented that "men and women do face similar problems, like those Isadora faced: the difficulty of separating oneself from one's family, of achieving a sense of adulthood; the dilemma of wanting to be sexually free and yet grounded in a safe, secure relationship."[12]

First of all, *Fear of Flying* was a female bildungsroman, a book about a married, twenty-nine-year-old Jewish-American woman poet from Manhattan. Named by her mother, another frustrated artist, for Isadora Duncan and Zelda Fitzgerald, Jong's heroine Isadora Zelda Wing believes that she must choose between creativity and maternity. Literary history seems to hold only two options for women writers: those "timid in their lives and only brave in their art," or those "severe, suicidal, strange." With few female role models, Isadora obsessively reads *The New Yorker*, her "shrine since childhood," and tries to write novels with male narrators. "No 'lady writers' subjects for me. I was going to have battles and bull fights and jungle safaris. Only, I didn't know a damn thing about battles and bull fights and jungle safaris (and neither do most men). I languished in utter frustration, thinking that the subjects I knew about were 'trivial' and 'feminine'—while the subjects I knew nothing of were 'profound' and 'masculine.' " At last, with the encouragement of her German psychoanalyst, Isadora determines to overcome her fear and "fly"—which to Jong means to express sexuality, independence, creativity, honesty, and passion. Leaving her husband, she sets off on a passionate odyssey around Europe with a Laingian therapist named Adrian Goodlove, inspired as much by Nabokov, Joyce, and Henry Miller as by Colette or Anaïs Nin. When they get to Paris, however, she sees a sign scrawled under a highway bridge: "Femmes! Libérons-nous!" Isadora's consciousness has been raised. When Adrian dumps her, she is frightened and angry, but she is also determined not to succumb to the fate of so many women artists before. "Whatever happened, I knew I would survive it. I knew, above all, that I'd go on working." In writing *Fear of Flying,* Jong herself determined, however, not to let her heroine "crawl back to her husband," or "get killed in a car crash" or "have a baby"—all the conventional endings for intelligent women in fiction who aspire to be artists. Above all, her heroine would refuse to kill herself.[13] In this respect, she was writing feminist metafiction, rewriting the endings and revising the plots of the past.

The Black Women's Renaissance

African-American literary critics also have accentuated the importance of the 1970s as a pivotal decade for black women writers. Selwyn Cudjoe describes the period as the moment when African-American women writers distanced themselves from their male counterparts, concentrated on their own experiences, and portrayed themselves as "autonomous subjects."[14] Maya Angelou (1928–) published three volumes of autobiography, *I Know Why the Caged Bird Sings* (1970), *Gather Together in My Name* (1974), and *Singin' and Swingin'* (1976). Toni Cade Bambara (1939–1995) edited two important collections of short stories, as well as publishing *Gorilla, My Love* (1972), her own stories about a young black girl. Nikki Giovanni and Audre Lorde were writing protest poems. Ntozake Shange (1948–), who had changed her name from Paulette Williams and concealed her education at Barnard and the University of Southern California "as an act of protest against her Western roots," created controversy in the black community with her hit play *For Colored Girls Who Have Considered Suicide / When the Rainbow is Enuf* (1976) and its negative portrayal of black men.[15]

Cudjoe sees the "outpouring of writings" during the decade as the "culmination of a number of factors at the end of the sixties"—the problematic nationalism of the black power movement; the social and economic pressures on black urban centers; "the rise of the feminist movement" and "increasing tensions in black male-female relations."[16] The Nigerian Chinua Achebe's important fiction, especially *Things Fall Apart* (1958), had presented an image of a traditional patriarchal African culture that proved compelling to African-American male novelists. As Toni Morrison recalled, in the 1960s, black male radicals had written "a lot of protest literature that was very strong and very flagellant," while "women were given secondary positions and there was some sort of romance about how the relationship between men and women worked in Africa. They talked of great harems. It was very funny but they took it quite seriously and the women agreed, in the interests of nation-building, for a while . . . So there were very strong sexist elements in that movement."[17] Black women writers were also urging each other to "get businesslike about the business of writing . . . to study marketing, distributing, printing."[18] They were becoming a professional cadre at the same time that they were exploring the lives of black girls and women, using the language of the black vernacular, and revisiting decades of black history.

A FEMALE PRESENCE—TONI MORRISON

Toni Morrison (1931–) has been the most honored and admired black woman writer in American history. Born Chloe Anthony Wofford in Lorain, Ohio, she was a precocious reader who graduated from high school with honors, and attended Howard University, where she changed her name to the more pronounceable "Toni." In 1955, she received a master's degree in English from Cornell with a thesis on suicide in the novels of Virginia Woolf and William Faulkner. While teaching in Washington, she married a Jamaican architect, Harold Morrison, and had two sons. The marriage ended in divorce, and Morrison moved to New York as an editor at Random House.

Morrison was working in that job when she started to feel the need for a literature by and about black women:

> The works of Richard Wright, Ralph Ellison, and James Baldwin . . .
> were not talking to me. There was some editorial address going on as
> though they were clarifying something for other men, or maybe white
> people . . . I know now that what I was longing for was a female pres-
> ence, not a female character but a female voice. There was an attitude
> and a gaze that I wanted to read through. So, since I wanted it so des-
> perately, I created it.[19]

The Bluest Eye (1970) begins with a passage from a Dick-and-Jane primer, repeated three times in a diminishing type size, the words run together so that they became a mocking chant of white middle-American normality: "hereisthefamilymotherfatherdickandjane . . . theyareveryhappy." In her first two pages, Morrison had brought the modernist stream-of-consciousness voice that introduced James Joyce's *Portrait of the Artist as a Young Man* into the ironic postmodernist seventies, and the contexts of multiracial America. The protagonists of her novel are young black girls in her hometown of Lorain, Ohio, in the fall of 1941, just before the United States entered the war. In what has become a famous line, the narrator, nine-year-old Claudia MacTeer, begins, in an italicized prologue, *"Quiet as it's kept, there were no marigolds in the fall of 1941. We thought, at the time, that it was because Pecola was having her father's baby that the marigolds did not grow."* In her afterword to a 1993 edition of the novel, Morrison explained that "quiet as it's kept" was a phrase from her childhood, meaning "Shh, don't tell anyone else" and "No one is allowed to know this."[20] It refers to a secret, and to intimate conspiracy. This tone of intimacy and tenderness pervades a text in which violent and tragic events take place.

Claudia MacTeer, her sister Frieda, and their friends have absorbed their notions of beauty and worth from white culture, especially the white baby dolls they have played with all their lives: "Adults, older girls, shops, magazines, newspapers, window signs—all the world had agreed that a blue-eyed, yellow-haired, pink-skinned doll was what every child treasured." The most popular, most admired black girl in the school, Maureen Peal, has the lightest skin. Claudia and Frieda live in a house, although it is "cold and old"; they have a mother and a father, although "adults do not talk to us—they give us orders." The most damaged family in the community is the Breedloves, Cholly, Pauline, and their daughter Pecola. They are "outdoors," homeless and evicted, and Pecola is sent by the county to stay with the MacTeers for a few days until her family is rehoused. The darkest, poorest, least-loved of the girls—she even calls her mother "Mrs. Breedlove"—Pecola feels that she also is the ugliest, and she prays for blue eyes: "If she looked different, beautiful, maybe Cholly would be different and Mrs. Breedlove too. Maybe they'd say, 'Why look at pretty-eyed Pecola. We mustn't do bad things in front of these pretty eyes.' "

The novel is divided into four seasons, beginning with autumn, and as the year goes on, Pecola's life gets worse. Morrison provides glimpses of her home, in which her mother showers affection on a little blond girl she is paid to care for, while treating her own daughter with cruel indifference. We get a lengthy and wrenching flashback of Cholly Breedlove's young manhood in Georgia and his abuse by a white gang, who force him to have sex with his girlfriend in public. Pecola has entered a premature and wounding menarche—"that's ministratin," Frieda tells her; ". . . it just means you can have a baby." In a devastating scene, narrated from Cholly's point of view, he rapes his daughter. Pregnant, beaten by her mother for her "sin," Pecola is expelled from school and becomes even more of a pariah. In the spring, she finds a storefront preacher, half-crazed himself, who takes pity on her: "Of all the wishes people had brought him—money, love, revenge—this seemed to him the most poignant and the one most deserving of fulfillment. A little black girl who wanted to rise out of the pit of her blackness and see the world with blue eyes." He promises to give her blue eyes.

The final section of the book, "Summer," is narrated by a grown-up Claudia, who tells how the baby died and Pecola went mad:

> You can see her even now, once in a while. The birdlike gestures are worn away to a mere picking and plucking her way between the tire rims and the sunflowers, between Coke bottles and milkweed, among all the waste and beauty of the world—which is what she herself was. All of our waste, which we dumped on her and which she absorbed. And all of our beauty, which was hers first and which she gave to us.

The soaring prose and deep compassion of this passage have been ongoing elements of Morrison's fiction. In *The Bluest Eye,* she extended her compassion even to Cholly: "I want you to look at him and see his love for his daughter and his powerlessness to help her pain. By that time his embrace, the rape, is all the gift he has left."[21]

The Bluest Eye remains Morrison's most finely achieved novel to date, because it combines sophisticated symbolism and literary craft with a clear, strongly plotted, and heartbreaking story. It was, however, too sophisticated for its first reviewers and readers. "With very few exceptions," Morrison notes in her afterword, "the initial publication of *The Bluest Eye* was like Pecola's life: dismissed, trivialized, misread." Nevertheless, she rapidly published two more novels in the 1970s, *Sula* (1973) and *Song of Solomon* (1977). *Sula* is about the deep friendship between Nel Wright and Sula Peace in a black community in the town of Medallion,

Ohio. *Song of Solomon* is more surreal, making use of techniques from Latin American magical realism to tell the story of black culture in the United States. Although it had a male protagonist, Morrison readily embraced the category of "black woman writer." In an interview with the African-American feminist critic Claudia Tate, Morrison explained that "the original definitions of me as a black woman writer were an attempt to reduce the area about which I wrote, to ghettoize me, and I was very forceful in turning that around. Now I insist on being identified as a black woman writer because those are the sensibilities out of which I write." She was convinced as well that "there's an enormous difference in the writing of black and white women. Aggression is not as new to black women as it is to white women. Black women seem able to combine the nest and the adventure. They don't see conflicts in certain areas as do white women. They are both safe harbor and ship; they are both inn and trail. We, black women, do both." Yet she also insisted that race was more important than gender: "I feel as deeply compassionate for males as I do females, and racism is always uppermost in my mind."[22]

LEAVING HOME—ALICE WALKER

Alice Walker (1944–) was the eighth child in a family of sharecroppers in Eatonton, Georgia, most celebrated as the birthplace of Joel Chandler Harris and "Uncle Remus," and near Flannery O'Connor's home in Milledgeville. Walker's brothers and sisters all tried to escape the low expectations and Jim Crow laws of the South; her sister Mamie became an academic specialist on colonialism, and traveled in Europe, South America, and Africa. Walker remembered her reading *Hamlet*, reciting ballads, and singing African songs, but also that her parents "had been badly burned in their experience with . . . Mamie . . . They'd made a lot of sacrifices for her to get an education. Then when she came home, she criticized the way they lived, the way they talked, what they didn't know. It seemed like she looked down on them."[23] At the same time, she knew, "we were so poor, so dusty and sunburnt . . . Only later, I realized that sometimes (perhaps), it becomes too painful to bear—seeing your home and family—shabby and seemingly without hope—through the eyes of your new friends and strangers."[24] The psychological tension between leaving home and betraying one's past would inform much of Walker's writing, first in a poem about Mamie ("For My Sister Molly Who in the Fifties"), and then in more subtle splittings and projections of her own conflicting emotions onto fictional sisters. .

Despite losing the sight of one eye in a childhood accident, and feeling "ugly and disfigured," Walker was recognized and rewarded for her precocious intelligence and literary gifts, and encouraged by her family.[25] With the help of scholarships, Walker attended Spelman College in Atlanta and then Sarah Lawrence, where she read Tolstoy, Turgenev, Dostoevsky, and García Márquez, alongside contemporary African novelists. In the summer of 1965, she traveled to Kenya to work with the Experiment in International Living, and to visit her roommate's family in Uganda; when she returned to school, she was pregnant from a rendezvous with a white lover who was in the Peace Corps, the first of her many interracial relationships. Walker was depressed and almost suicidal in her distress over the pregnancy, and her college friends raised money to pay for an abortion. The poets Jane Cooper and Muriel Rukeyser also mentored and supported Walker at Sarah Lawrence; Rukeyser gave her money to rent an apartment in New York after graduation, and introduced her to her own literary agent, Monica McCall, who helped Walker meet important writers including Langston Hughes.

In the mid-sixties, Walker left New York and moved to Mississippi to work for the NAACP. There she met and married Mel Leventhal, a Jewish civil rights lawyer. They lived warily as an interracial couple in Jackson, where their daughter, Rebecca, was born in 1969, and where Walker taught at Jackson State College and Tougaloo, won numerous grants and fellowships, and educated herself in the history of black women's writing, beginning with Zora Neale Hurston's *Their Eyes Were Watching God*. "I am still amazed," she wrote, ". . . that it speaks to me as no novel, past or present, has ever done; and that the language of the characters, that 'comical nigger dialect' that has been laughed at, denied, ignored, or 'improved' so that white folks and educated black folks can understand it, is simply beautiful. Here is enough self-love in that one book—love of community, culture, traditions—to restore a world. Or create a new one."[26] In the 1970s, Walker made an expedition to put a headstone on Zora Neale Hurston's unmarked grave, calling her "a genius of the South." Hurston would remain the most magical of the precursors, or spirit-ancestors, as Walker called them, who inspired her writing. In 1979, she edited a collection of Hurston's works, *I Love Myself When I Am Laughing . . . and Then Again When I Am Looking Mean and Impressive*.

The Third Life of Grange Copeland (1970), Walker's first novel, offered a realistic description of the world of a family of black Georgia sharecroppers. *Revolutionary Petunias* (1973), a collection of poems titled in honor of her mother's garden, was even more successful; it was nominated for a National Book Award. When the prize was awarded to Adrienne Rich for *Diving into the Wreck* (1973), Rich refused to accept it as an individual, and instead received it along with Walker and Audre Lorde, "in the name of all the women whose voices have gone and still go unheard in a patriarchal world . . . We symbolically join here in refusing the terms of patriarchal competition."

But women had to face matriarchal competition as well. Walker's teacher Muriel Rukeyser was upset by Walker's failure to acknowledge her white mentors, and perhaps also by envy of her young protégée's fame. In response to Walker's claims of rediscovering Zora Neale Hurston, she wrote, "Zora was helped . . . by white women. It's much more interesting, the truth . . . You were helped at Sarah Lawrence in comparable ways." Walker retorted sharply: "There is in me, for better or worse,—an absolute hatred of having to feel beholden to anyone. What is given should be given and forgotten the next day, I think. Have you ever considered how like a beggar I felt in all those days when you were 'helping' me? How it felt . . . to have to depend on people who had no concept of poverty that they did not get from visits to it?"[27] The quarrel between Walker and Rukeyser, which led to the rupture of their friendship, was a microcosm of the quarrels between black and white women in the feminist movement, with one side expecting camaraderie if not gratitude, and the other resenting matronage as much as patronage.

Walker did thank Rukeyser and Cooper in her dedication to her first collection of short stories, *In Love and Trouble: Stories of Black Women* (1973), along with Hurston, Larsen, and Jean Toomer. The most significant of these stories was "Everyday Use" (1973), in which she once more used the two-sisters theme to contrast the black woman who stays within the Southern black community and the intellectual who moves out into a cosmopolitan interracial world. The younger sister, Maggie, has been terribly scarred in a house fire; she stays at home with her mother. The older sister, Dee, is brighter and more confident; she is a sophisticated black nationalist who has changed her name to "Wangero Leewanika Kemanjo," and comes home spouting Swahili to claim her heritage in the form of "folk art"—the worn benches made by her father, the butter churn whittled by an uncle, and her grandmother's pieced quilts, which she intends to display on a wall. The mother, however, who has always been intimidated by Dee's worldliness, decides to give the quilts to Maggie, who cannot speak glibly about the quilt as a priceless artifact, but understands its history, knows how to quilt herself, and will put it to everyday use.

The story was also Walker's version of the debate over the aesthetic judgment of women's art, another "jury of her peers," in which she argued that a jury of black women can best judge the artistry of the marginal or unlettered. The metaphor of quilting, standing for black female nonverbal creativity and cultural heritage, connected to the revival of quilting around the Bicentennial, and the many museum exhibits devoted to the American quilt aesthetic and tradition. Nonetheless, the story is more ambiguous and conflicted than readers in the 1970s could see. The name given to Alice Walker by her African friends in Kenya was "Wangero," a name she used for herself in her first book of poems, *Once* (1969).[28] The fire that disfigures Maggie recalls Walker's comments about her family "being burned" by Mamie, and at the same time the author's own childhood accident. In an interview with Mary Helen Washington, Walker acknowledged that she had split her own identity between the three women in the story, the sustaining older woman, the abiding sister, and the autonomous sister who "wants to go out into the world and see change and be changed." As Washington astutely comments, Walker is most closely identified with Dee/Wangero, the autonomous sister, who is also an artist:

> *Walker shows that the quiltmaker, who has female precursors and female guidance, has an easier relationship with her art than the "deviant" female who finds herself outside of acceptable boundaries. Unlike quilt-making and garden-making, and even blues singing, which are a part of women's traditions, the writing of fiction is still done under the shadow of men, without female authority . . . "Everyday Use" tells a different, more threatening tale of the woman writer's fears, of the difficulty of reconciling home and art, particularly when the distance from home has been enlarged by education, by life among the "gentlefolk," and by literary reputation.*[29]

In her second novel, *Meridian* (1976), Walker moved from the realism of her earlier fiction to a more experimental style of vignettes and episodes, to tell the story of a young black woman in the 1960s. Meridian Hill drops out of high school to raise her child, but wins a scholarship to genteel Saxon College for Women in Atlanta, a hostile portrait of Spelman, influenced as well by Nella Larsen's Naxos College in *Quicksand*. Meridian gives her child away for adoption, a theme to which Walker would return in later novels, and joins the civil rights movement. In one of her campaigns, Meridian demonstrates against the Jim Crow policies that restrict entrance to a carnival to "Negro Day." Walker gives a contemporary twist to the traditional American women's trope of the freak show by having her heroine stand before a mummified white woman, "dead for twenty-five years, preserved in life-like condition." This sideshow attraction is all that remains of the Southern lady of romantic mythology.

Violence, Rape, and the Female Gothic

In 1975, Susan Brownmiller's best-selling study *Against Our Will* politicized the act of rape and analyzed it as a threat that kept all women "in a constant state of intimidation."[30] Rape became a significant theme in women's novels in the 1970s as well, with the rapist both a reflection of real male violence against women and the projection of imaginary female violence, the extreme externalized form of an anger that women had just begun to imagine and explore.[31] Many of these novels by white women boldly explored fantasies and fears about race that would be unacceptable, politically incorrect, in feminist writing twenty years later. Stories about fear of rape and male violence could be screens or masks for fears about racial conflict in a decade following race riots in American cities like Newark, Detroit, Washington, and Los Angeles. Was the outcry against rape about a female fantasy or a male social problem? Was it about male lust or male pathology? A problem for the psychoanalyst or the police? About gender or about race?

For black women writers, rape was a divisive and explosive issue. In *The Bluest Eye,* Toni Morrison had refused to condemn the troubled black man who rapes his daughter. Ntozake Shange's play, and Michele Wallace's angry condemnation of *Black Macho* (1979), brought on furious accusations of race treason. Alice Walker entered the fray with a collection of short stories, *You Can't Keep a Good Woman Down* (1981), which took on the issues of abortion and pornography as well as rape. In "Advancing Luna—and Ida B. Wells," Walker awkwardly attempted to contextualize contemporary criminal rape in the antilynching activism of Wells in the 1890s. A liberal white woman, Luna, is raped by a black man, but does not report the crime and even reconciles with him. The black woman narrator is outraged by the whole story because black women are much more likely to be rape victims than white women. Reviewers were unsympathetic to what Katha Pollitt called Walker's "confused welter of thoughts and feelings about interracial rape."[32]

White women writers made use of psychoanalysis and the techniques of the female gothic genre to discuss the fear of rape. Isadora Wing, in *Fear of Flying*, is intrepid about her sexual escapades, but also harbors a fear of the violent male intruder, which her many psychoanalysts have told her was an oedipal fantasy. She connects this fear with anxiety about writing and punishment for her cultural transgression: "I knew the man under my bed was partly my father . . . The fear of the intruder is the wish for the intruder. I thought of all my sessions with Dr. Happe in which we had spoken of my night terrors. I remember my adolescent fantasy of being stabbed or shot by a strange man. I would be sitting at my desk writing and the man would always attack me from behind." For Isadora, a Jew in Germany, the imagined intruder is also the Nazi. In fiction, the rapist/intruder could assume any form of the oppressor.

Jane Clifford, the heroine of Gail Godwin's novel *The Odd Woman* (1974), is no Isadora Wing; she is an English professor who teaches Romantic and Victorian literature at a university in the Midwest. Godwin (1937–), too, has an academic background; born in Birmingham, Alabama, she received a Ph.D. from the University of Iowa in 1971, and taught at Iowa and the University of Illinois. Jane is not a poet, but she is the first heroine of American women's writing to teach a course on "Women and Literature," and she chooses George Gissing's Victorian novel *The Odd Women* (1893) because of its "unrelenting pessimism. It was one of the few nineteenth-century novels she could think of in which every main female character who was allowed to live through the last page had to do so alone." Despite exposure to this bleak precursor, Jane has trouble freeing herself from her attachment to a married suitor. Terrified at the prospect of being alone, in her fantasies and nightmares, she also fixates on the spectre of the "Enema Bandit," a particularly nasty sexual predator haunting her campus, who embodies the gothic lover she still wants to order her to obey his commands.

Looking for Mr. Goodbar (1975) by Judith Rossner (1935–2005) dramatized a disturbing and unconscious collusion between male killer and female victim. Set in the singles scene of New York bars, the novel is about the tragically ironic intersection of male and female destinies and needs. The heroine, Terry Dunn, cannot bear to have a man spend the night, because she feels claustrophobic, as she did when she had a childhood operation for scoliosis (she still limps) and was strapped down. The killer, Gary Cooper White, needs to spend the night because he is on the run, exhausted, and uncertain of his masculinity. These characters fatally collide, because both the woman and the man are looking for "Mr. Goodbar," the omnipotent will to control. After the murder, White discovers that he is limping; some kind of psychosexual exchange has occurred. In *The Sea-Change* (1976), by Lois Gould (1932–2002) this transference was carried to its extremes and connected to anxieties about race. The heroine, Jessie Waterman, is tied up, raped, and robbed by an intruder she calls "B.G."—Black Gunman. During Hurricane Minerva, at her beach house, she gradually becomes B.G., who is both her demon lover and her own repressed violence and racism. We can't be sure whether either the rape or the hurricane happened or was a fantasy.

With *Wonderland* (1971), Joyce Carol Oates also moved deeper into gothic territory. Her hero, Jesse Vogel, is the only survivor of his family's massacre by his deranged father; through the help of various adoptive parents and mentors, he becomes a neurologist who is fascinated by and drawn to the freakish, the grotesque, and the monstrous. *Wonderland* ends with Jesse's daughter Michelle—Shelley, or "Shell," as she calls herself—running away with a counterculture guru. Jesse sets out to rescue her from a commune on Yonge Street in Toronto—an ironically hellish haven for the drugged young. As soon as Oates had finished the novel, she felt dissatisfied with its ending, in which Jesse takes his emaciated daughter out on a boat in Lake Ontario. "I think it is a very dark, relentless work, and I wonder if you might not be receptive to a modified ending?" she wrote to her editor at Vanguard. She did not want to "end with a small boat drifting out helplessly to sea . . . it had to end with a gesture of demonic-paternal control." In the new ending, Jesse "rescues" Shelley, but of course she is once again forced into the role of the gothic heroine, dependent on male intervention. As Oates herself observed, "In retrospect, it seems that Shelley Vogel was crying out for a novel of her own, a story that was not a mere appendage of her father's; but this was a novel that I could not, or would not write."[33] She would go on to write those novels of female destiny and agency in the 1980s and after.

Diane Johnson (1934–) grew up in Moline, Illinois, attended the University of Utah, and published two novels in the 1960s, *Fair Game* (1965) and *Loving Hands at Home* (1968), the latter a satiric study of marriage customs among the Mormons and a young wife who breaks away. Johnson received her doctorate from Berkeley in 1968, with a dissertation on the Victorian novelist George Meredith, and taught at the University of California at Davis until 1987. *Lesser Lives* (1972), her biography of Meredith's wife, Mary Ellen, was nominated for the National Book Award; she also wrote a biography of Dashiell Hammett. During the 1970s, she came to public attention as a novelist with three books set in California: *Burning* (1971), "about despair . . . and people creating terrible types of illusion" in Los Angeles; *The Shadow Knows* (1974); and *Lying Low* (1978), about radicals hiding out.[34] According to Larry McCaffery, "the images which dominated her fiction during the '70s—images of apocalypse, insanity, paranoia, misdirected passion which can suddenly flare into violence—are images which speak to us all of the nature of contemporary American life."[35]

·The Shadow Knows* (1974) was the seventies' most subtle and terrifying study of female vulnerability and the malign anonymous threats of modern life. It is still underestimated, only sporadically in print, and absent from most critical discussion. The title alludes to the popular American radio serial of the 1940s and 1950s called *The Shadow*, about the detective Lamont Cranston, whose eerie laugh accompanied the famous opening question: "Who knows what evil lurks in the hearts of men? The Shadow knows!" Johnson's heroine, N. Hexam (we never learn her full first name, but she sounds like a witch), is a pale, thin, divorced mother of four, living in a housing project in Sacramento, California. With her lives Ev, a black woman who cares for the children while N. goes to graduate school in structural linguistics. N. is having an affair with a married man who may have abandoned her; she may be pregnant and has had an IUD put in to induce an abortion. N. thinks someone is trying to kill her and she may be right. She is surrounded by potential killers, both those she knows and anonymous assailants; threatening messages and signs are left on her doorstep. She is full of guilt.

According to Johnson, *The Shadow Knows* was about "race relations, the evil in human nature, and social fear," not only of violence against women, but also of race riots and urban conflicts. It was intended as "a novel about fear, about how things were between blacks and whites in the early 1970s." It was also "about persons on the fringe; they happen to be women, and what happens to them is meant to be particular to America in the seventies."[36] These women on the fringe are N.'s doubles, the opposites of her white-skin privilege, her fastidiousness, her intellectuality, her class. Ev, the maid, is victimized, poor, abused, self-hating. As Johnson writes in the novel, Ev's lovers "slash and beat . . . and steal from her." She values herself so little that she often burns and cuts herself, and is scarred like "the vandalized statue of a great Nubian queen." Indeed, Ev dies mysteriously, possibly of acute pancreatic cancer, possibly killed by the neighborhood vandal.

Another marginal woman, so bizarre and fantastic as to seem N.'s Jungian shadow, Animus/Anima, or Other, is Osella, an enormously fat, crazed ex-nursemaid who has been making threatening phone calls, accusing N. of witchcraft and promiscuity. She is a giant, a "sort of super-female," like the Venus of Willendorf, all breasts and hips, a specter of the mammy, the earth mother, the man-eater. N. goes to see Osella perform as a stripper at the Club Zanzibar, the heart of darkness, where she "wore little trunks of purple satin and nothing else but a gold armlet around the expanses of her upper arm—a brilliant stroke, a rather Egyptian, goddess-like adornment calling to mind one of those frightening and horrifying fertility goddesses with swollen bodies and timeless eyes and the same engulfing infinitely absorbing quality Osella radiated now." In her size, madness, sexuality, and race, Osella is the stereotyped embodiment of female appetite and desire, the surreal opposite of the repressed middle-class white woman intellectual, N. (Nada?).

Is N. simply racist, paranoid, or neurotic? She tells the story, and she may not be telling the truth, although Johnson has said in an interview that she intended N. as "a reliable narrator and the events more or less real, and the fear certainly real."[37] At the end of the novel, N. is indeed raped by a mysterious assailant, an event Johnson treats as a fate better than death. She has commented that "the rape scene was meant to be a final symbol of ambiguity and everybody's complicity in evil. I wrote that last scene lightly, before my consciousness was raised about the political implications of rape."[38] After reviewing Brownmiller's *Against Our Will* in *The New York Review of Books,* Johnson told another interviewer that she now realized a woman who was raped "would feel angry, resentful, vengeful, guilty—a whole bunch of things which N. in *The Shadow Knows* doesn't feel. And maybe now that I've read Susan Brownmiller, I would not have had the book end that way."[39]

Johnson's half recantation was emblematic of the political pressures of 1970s feminism for literary women, inspiring but also restrictive. When she and her husband, a noted doctor, began spending much of their time abroad, especially in Paris, her fiction moved from American themes to international ones, leading up to a trio of poised and insightful novels of manners about American women living in Paris, *Le Divorce* (1997), *Le Mariage* (2000), and *L'Affaire* (2003). These are accomplished narratives with parallels to the ironic social worlds of Edith Wharton. But none has reached the level of imagination, daring, shock, and memorability of *The Shadow Knows*.

The Will to Change the Future—Science Fiction

The 1970s produced an explosion of speculative and allegorical fiction, as the genre of the feminist utopia was recast in the scientific and political terms of the women's liberation movement. Many women began to write utopian and dystopian novels, including Dorothy Bryant's *The Kin of Ata Are Waiting for You* (1971), Ursula Le Guin's *The Dispossessed* (1974), Joanna Russ's *The Female Man* (1975), and Marge Piercy's *Woman on the Edge of Time* (1976). Some of the novels explored such fantasies of the radical women's movement as male and female responsibility for children; in Piercy's vision of a futuristic utopian commune, Mattapoisett, the children are raised by three volunteer "co-mothers" of both sexes; men even lactate and breast-feed infants. In Ursula Le Guin's novel *The Dispossessed*, subtitled "An Ambiguous Utopia," a utopian society of total sexual equality is contrasted with a patriarchal society in which women are totally subordinate, allowed to be only sex objects or servants. Le Guin (1929–), a science fiction writer primarily interested in ecology, ethnography, and the environment, movingly explored the attractions and comforts of the paternalist society, and the kinds of problems that might arise in an egalitarian system.

In her essay "What Can a Heroine Do? Or Why Women Can't Write" (1972), Joanna Russ connected dystopia and dispossession to American literary history. "Women in twentieth-century American literature," she argued, "seem pretty much limited to either Devourer/Bitches or Maiden/Victims." For women writers wanting to use female protagonists, the available plots seemed limited to the love story. On the other hand, if a woman writer "stuck to male myths with male protagonists . . . she falsifies her position both artistically and humanly; she is an artist creating a world in which persons of her kind cannot be artists."[40] The dilemma seemed inescapable in the early 1970s; as Russ wrote,

"Every woman . . . I know has had in some way to give up being female (this means various things) in order to be a scholar, or intellectual, or even artist."[41] Her proposed solution was to write about the future, in science fiction: "Women cannot write—using the old myths. But using new ones?—"[42]

THE TIME TRAVELER—JAMES TIPTREE, JR.

Among the most intriguing writers of futuristic science fiction in the late 1960s and early 1970s was James Tiptree, Jr. Like other cult writers of the period, such as Thomas Pynchon and J. D. Salinger, Tiptree was a mysterious recluse. No one had ever met him, although he corresponded with many other science fiction writers, including Russ and Le Guin. Rumors circulated that he was a CIA spy or a government scientist. Some fans even speculated that "Tip," who wrote so sympathetically about female characters and feminist themes, might be a woman, although science fiction writers themselves found such an idea impossible to believe. "There is something ineluctably masculine about Tiptree's writing," Robert Silverberg asserted, and compared Tiptree's "lean, muscular, supple" style to Hemingway's.[43] Tiptree received wide attention, excellent sales, and the highest awards in the science fiction field, the Hugo and Nebula prizes.

Everyone was shocked in 1976 when Tiptree was outed as Alice Bradley Sheldon, a married, sixty-one-year-old woman who had been a CIA analyst, a painter, an air force intelligence officer, and a research psychologist and professor with a Ph.D. Readers of *Astounding* and other science fiction magazines were astounded indeed to learn that the macho writer about guns and war was "an old lady in Virginia."[44] But Sheldon (1915–1987) was an important figure in American literary history, whose strange story illuminates the age-old debate about the differences between the male and female literary voice, the mysteries of sexuality, gender, and their impact on the imagination. Out of her double, Tiresian life, she testified to the felt differences of writing as a man and writing as a woman—differences of power, morality, agency, and freedom.

It was not until the mid-1960s, after the launch of the space program, the Vietnam War, and the counterculture, including the women's liberation movement, that Alice Sheldon began to turn her private visions into the genre of science fiction stories. At the age of fifty-one, while she was finishing her dissertation in psychology and living in McLean, Virginia, she began to submit her work to magazines. She took her pseudonym from a jar of jam she saw at Giant Foods, and made Tiptree a man. If, as Sandra Gilbert and Susan Gubar would memorably declare in *The Madwoman in the Attic* (1979), "the pen is a symbolic phallus," Sheldon claimed it and made it the enabling fiction of her art: "Tiptree was 'magical' manhood, his pen my prick. I had through him all the power and prestige of masculinity."[45] Behind the mask of Tiptree, she was free-wheeling, uninhibited, daring, and bold. She created a Tiptree who shared her own experiences—in Africa, in World War II, in military intelligence—and her pessimism about the environment. She made him a self-described hermit, solitary and alienated from the public side of a literary career, as well as a sensitive, sexy, hard-drinking outdoorsman. Like Willa Cather, Sheldon had found her inspiration in colonial adventure stories, especially by Kipling and Conrad, which she would later transpose into the language of technology and space. "All of what I know about short-story writing and plotting came from Kipling," she later said.[46] The political, racial, cultural, and sexual themes of imperial quest romance, with its hearts of darkness and troubled narrators, influenced her own use of science fiction to explore the turbulent issues of 1960s American society.

Tiptree's first important story was "The Last Flight of Dr. Ain" (1969). In a future obsessed by viral contagion, Dr. Charles Ain (C. Ain) is a scientist traveling by a very circuitous route to a conference where he announces that he has created a virulent strain of leukemia that will kill all humans, but spare animals. He thinks that he has destroyed humanity in order to save the planet, but the story also hints that the earth—Gaea—is the real destroyer. Told in the deadpan style of a police investigation, the story is an impossible narrative like Gilman's "Yellow Wall-paper"—if humanity has been wiped out, who is reporting these events? With its metaphysical riddles, elegant exposition, and surprise ending, "The Last Flight of Dr. Ain" attracted a great deal of attention in the science fiction community, and soon Tiptree was being invited to contribute to magazines.

As the women's liberation movement became a national force, Sheldon's concerns about evolution, reproduction, sexuality, and gender began to enter her writing. Under her real name, she joined the National Organization for Women, and subscribed to *Ms. Magazine*. Meanwhile, Tiptree's stories became more angry and critical of male violence, aggression, and lust, getting him a reputation as a genuine male feminist. Hogeland calls "The Women Men Don't See" "the most elegant 'invisible woman' story of the decade," revising Ralph Ellison's famous novel to suggest that gifted women are invisible to the male observers who see them only as "female blurs."[47] By the mid-1970s, Sheldon/Tiptree's double life had begun to fray. After she was revealed as a woman, Sheldon declared herself proud of what she had accomplished. "Tiptree, by merely remaining unchallenged for eleven years, had shot the stuffing out of male stereotypes of women writers."[48] She retired Tiptree's signature and stopped writing, but she continued to feel possessed by him. "He had a life of his own. He would do things and he would not do other things, and I didn't have much control over him. But I wasn't faking it, really . . . I never calculated a masculine persona."[49] In creating Tiptree, Sheldon had channeled her fullest self, both the feminine and the masculine aspects of her personality. She felt diminished, inauthentic, and exposed without him.

After a period of silence, she began to write novels, stories, and essays as a woman. But even her most loyal admirers admit that the results were didactic or superficial, and she acknowledged how much "Tiptree's existence opened me to unknown possibilities of power."[50] In May 1987, dealing with her husband's severe illness after years of depression and psychotherapy, Sheldon killed him and then took her own life. She had a long history of suicidal threats, and left instructions for her lawyers that made clear that the suicide pact was carefully planned. Despite her own tragic ending, Sheldon/Tiptree's challenge to women writers who followed was to seize their possibilities for moral and aesthetic power, without needing to create a male persona in order to do so.

Activists

The political upheavals of the seventies drew many women writers into protest movements, and activist women responded quickly to women's liberation as well. Grace Paley (1922–2007) insisted that storytellers must first be story hearers, open to all narratives of suffering and survival.[51] Born in the Bronx, daughter of Russian Jewish parents, she attended classes at Hunter College and NYU. In 1942, she married Jess Paley, then a soldier and later a cameraman and filmmaker. For two years, they lived in various U.S. Army camps. By 1951, they had two children. She began to write fiction in the mid-fifties: "I needed to speak in some inventive way about our female and male lives in those years . . . I was a woman writing at the early moment when small drops of worried resentment and noble rage were secretly, slowly building in the second wave of the women's movement." In an interview in 1980, she described her subject as "the dark lives of women." Paley's first book of stories was *The Little Disturbances of Man* (1959), warmly praised by Philip Roth for "a language of new and rich emotional subtleties." For the next fifteen years, however, she raised her children, taught creative writing, and was a political activist, protesting the Vietnam War, traveling to North Vietnam, Chile, and Moscow, and participating in antinuclear demonstrations on the White House lawn. In 1971, she divorced Paley, and in 1972, she married the writer Robert Nichols.

In Paley's second collection, *Enormous Changes at the Last Minute* (1974), eleven of the seventeen stories included women without husbands. Many of the stories centered on the character Faith Darwin, Paley's alter ego, and "a modern woman whose openness to life disposes her to have affairs with men who often let her down. Her closest relationships are with other women . . . In the story 'A Conversation with My Father,' her father wishes also that Faith would write fiction with a beginning, middle and definite ending. But Faith counters with an explanation of her stories which might be Paley's own credo."[52] She insists that life continues beyond the confining plots of tragedy or comedy; she hates plot, "because it takes all hope away. Everyone, real, or invented, deserves the open destiny of life."[53]

In 1976, Maxine Hong Kingston (1940–) became the first Asian-American woman writer to appear on the front page of *The New York Times Book Review* with her book *The Woman Warrior: Memoirs of a Girlhood Among Ghosts,* an autobiography that was also a retelling of the Chinese legend of Fa Mulan. A graduate of Berkeley who had been active in the antiwar movement, Kingston introduced a new era of ethnic American women's writing, which made cultural hybridity its central theme. While her second-generation Chinese-American heroine feels silenced by having to speak two languages, and by her ethnic difference in American society, Kingston herself felt empowered as a writer by her bilingualism: "My hands are writing English, but my mouth is speaking Chinese. Somehow I am able to write a language that captures the Chinese rhythms and tones and images, getting that power into English. I am working in some kind of fusion language."[54]

Dissenters

Not all women writers in the 1970s identified with the women's move-ment, and several major novelists of the decade disagreed with it, had other priorities, or were ambivalent and conflicted about its meaning for their work. For some, feminism and solidarity with other women writ-ers seemed unimportant or a luxury in the context of more urgent social and political problems. Others resented being thrown together without regard to their differences of purpose, subject, or style. And stereotypes of the woman writer were often so belittling that one can understand a writer's wish to escape them. When a landmark work of feminist liter-ary criticism, *Literary Women: The Great Writers* by Ellen Moers, came out in 1976, Anne Tyler reviewed it with misgivings. "There is no room in these theories for the woman as mere individual . . . It's my personal feel-ing that only a portion of my life—and almost none of my writing life—is affected by what sex I happen to be." A few months later, however, she wrote elsewhere that she was "torn in two directions" by having children and would "often wonder what it would be like to live all alone in a shack by the sea and work 23 hours a day."[55]

One celebrated dissenter, Joan Didion (1934–), was born in Sacra-mento, California, and began to write as a child. She attended Berkeley, and then moved to New York to work at *Vogue*. There she married the writer John Gregory Dunne, and in 1966, they adopted a daughter, Quin-tana Roo.[56] These details of her life became familiar to many thousands of readers when both Dunne and their now-grown daughter died within months of each other; Didion's book about the tragedy and her efforts to cope with it, *The Year of Magical Thinking* (2005), became an inter-national best seller. By the 1970s, Didion was already well known as a novelist, journalist, and essayist, as well as a screenwriter. Her first novel, *Run River* (1963), was set in California and centered on the hero-ine's abortion, as did her second California novel, *Play It as It Lays* (1970). Maria Wyeth, a wan and depressed minor actress, discovers that on her own, without the sheltering identity of her husband, a Hollywood director, she is no one. The abortionist's sadism ("Hear that scraping, Maria? . . . That should be the sound of music to you. Don't scream, Maria, there are people next door") is not much different from the bru-tality of an actor who finds out after he has mistreated her that she is the wife of a powerful man: "Just hold on, cunt . . . You never told me who you were." Didion's third novel, *A Book of Common Prayer* (1977), featured another numb and victimized heroine, but she insisted that her books were not "women's novels," and that her heroines "don't really have specifically women's problems; they have rather more general problems." The abortion scene in *Play It as It Lays,* she explained, was merely "a narrative strategy."[57]

In 1972, Didion fiercely attacked the women's movement in an essay for *The New York Times Book Review* that attracted a great deal of attention. On one hand, Didion accused feminists of narcissism, ignorance, and sloth. With regard to women's writing, she declared that "fiction has certain irreducible ambiguities . . . for fiction is, in most ways, hostile to ideology." On the other hand, Didion described her own sense of "what it is to be a woman" in stark and gothic terms: "the irreconcilable difficulty of it,—that sense of living one's deepest life underwater, that dark involvement with blood, and birth and death."[58] Two years later, when she was interviewed by Linda Kuehl for the *Paris Review* (1974), Didion summarized the disadvantages of being a woman writer as she had observed them: "A man who wrote novels had a role in the world, and he could play that role, and do whatever he wanted behind it. A woman who wrote novels had no particular role. Women who wrote novels were quite often perceived as invalids . . . Novels by women tended to be described, even by their publishers, as sensitive."[59] Influenced mainly by James and Hemingway, Didion saw herself as a stylist but also as a tough adventurer. A woman writer in those roles had to gamble, had to play it as it lays. Didion's edgy, paranoid vision of California reflected her own sense of risk.

Cynthia Ozick (1928–), one of the most significant novelists who emerged during the 1970s, was the most intellectually formidable of the dissenters. The daughter of Russian Jewish immigrants in New York, Ozick was educated at NYU and then at Ohio State, where she received an M.A., and at Columbia, where she attended Lionel Trilling's graduate seminar, and planned to write a dissertation on Henry James. Instead, she married, had a daughter, and turned to writing fiction. In essays she published in the 1970s, Ozick both exposed the sexism and family pressure she encountered as a woman writer, and distanced herself from the women's movement and feminism. When she started her career, she recalled, she thought of herself as a writer, like James, Flaubert, and Proust, but her relatives saw her as "a childless housewife, a failed woman." Her first published novel, *Trust* (1966), which took her six years to write, was divided into four sections: "America," "Europe," "Birth," and "Death." She had intended it as a book about American history, and she believed it "contained everything—the whole world." She had deliberately made her female narrator an unnamed emotionless observer "because I was afraid to be pegged as having written a 'woman's novel.' Nothing was more certain to lead to that than a point-of-view seemingly lodged in a woman, and no one takes a woman's novel seriously." Of course, the result was not what she had hoped. Infuriatingly for her, *The New York Times Book Review* titled its review in July 1966, "Daughter's Reprieve," and claimed that the book was about the narrator's problem in defining "herself as a woman."[60]

In 1977, in an important essay, "Literature and the Politics of Sex: A Dissent," published in *Ms. Magazine,* Ozick differentiated between the "classic" feminism of equality with which she identified and the new feminism of difference which signaled that "all writing women possess . . . an instantly perceived common ground." In her view, the notion that women writers had a separate psychology, body of ideas, or body of experience was a "myth-fed condition of segregation that classical feminism was created to bring an end to." Instead, Ozick insisted, "When I write, I am free. I am, as a writer, whatever I wish to become. I can think myself into a male, or female, or a stone, or a raindrop, or a block of wood, or a Tibetan, or the spine of a cactus." While feminists were arguing that the emphasis on being a woman writer was a temporary strategy, Ozick was skeptical. Accepting the category of "woman writer," she felt, would "be transmogrified into a new truth," and would oblige "artists who are women . . . to deliver a 'woman's art,' as if ten thousand other possibilities, preoccupations, obsessions, were inauthentic, for women, or invalid, or worse yet, lyingly evasive."[61]

These are legitimate concerns, and no one ever articulated them better than Ozick. Yet how could she reconcile her experience in the literary marketplace with her conviction of imaginative freedom? And didn't her fear of writing a "woman's novel" show how completely she had been taught to despise it? Was it necessary for women to pass as men, like James Tiptree, to get serious critical attention? In the 1980s, women writers and theorists began to suggest answers to these questions, exploring the effects of self-hatred on women's artistic autonomy, making clearer distinctions between the androgyny and imaginative freedom of the solitary creative artist, and discussing the pressures and stereotypes that came with a professional career as a writer, the need to engage with a marketplace, and the politics of literary reception.

In the 1970s, Ozick turned to writing about the Holocaust and its shadow in American Jewish culture in *The Pagan Rabbi and Other Stories* (1971) and *Bloodshed and Three Novellas* (1976). But interestingly, she also began to publish the hilarious fables of the life of Ruth Puttermesser, a Jewish woman intellectual in New York, which would eventually be gathered as *The Puttermesser Papers* (1997). Despite her anxieties, Ozick's reputation as one of the outstanding postmodernist Jewish-American writers of her generation did not turn out to be in conflict with her use of a female point of view.

19

The 1980s: On the Jury

In the 1980s, women fully joined the literary juries of the United States, as writers, critics, reviewers, publishers, anthologists, and historians, contributing to the verdicts, and challenging the laws. No longer dependent on judgments that denied them representation, women writers felt empowered collectively and individually by the support of women readers, the attention of women scholars, and the impact of feminist activists. American feminist criticism had made the study of women's writing its priority, and writers as well as critics were thinking about women's history and tradition, and asserting their place in the American literary pantheon.

A new confidence and assertiveness marked American women's attitudes toward their position as professional writers. Whereas Cynthia Ozick had bemoaned the sexist treatment of her early fiction, and worried about women's liberation impinging on her creative freedom, Joyce Carol Oates, in *(Woman) Writer* (1988), firmly distinguished between the genderless world of the imagination and the deeply gendered world of publishing and reception. "The woman who writes is a writer by her own definition," Oates concluded, "but a *woman* writer by others' definition. The books she writes are assemblages of words but her sexual identity is not thereby dissolved or transcended, unless she writes under a male pseudonym and keeps her identity secret." Moreover, the "(woman) writer who imagines herself assimilated into the mainstream of literature, the literature of men, is surely mistaken, given the evidence of centuries, and the ongoing, by now perplexing, indifference of male critics to female effort." The (woman) writer should not deceive herself about her relative position in the literary world, but she should accommodate the problem "with resilience, with a sense of humor, with stubbornness, with anger, with hope."[1] During the 1980s, Oates published a trilogy that reimagined nineteenth-century American gothic novels (*Bellefleur*, 1980; *A Bloodsmoor Romance*, 1982; *Mysteries of Winter-thurn*, 1984); two novels about women in contemporary academia (*Solstice*, 1985, and *Marya*, 1986); and a book of poems called *Invisible Woman* (1982). *A Bloodsmoor Romance* combined plot elements from Alcott's *Little Women* and Hawthorne's *Blithedale Romance* in a magical imagining of possibilities and fantasies for American women.[2] In *Solstice*, Oates wrote for the first time about a passionate friendship between two women, one a painter whose Byronic dash, seductiveness, and commanding personality recalled Susan Sontag.

Yet at the same time that she was writing more directly about feminine experience, Oates was asserting her right to deal with the most violent and masculine subject matter. In the 1980s, Oates also became an expert on classic boxers of the American past. Her short story "Golden Gloves," from the collection *Raven's Wing* (1986), about a failed amateur boxer who cannot confront his wife's pregnancy, compared masculine contest to the heroism of childbirth. Her book *On Boxing* (1987) even won the respect of Norman Mailer. *(Woman) Writer* includes essays on Mike Tyson and on test-driving the Ferrari Testarossa. Boxing, Oates explained, is "a reading of American experience, unsentimentalized and graphic"; it also "ritualizes violence, primarily male violence, to the degree to which violence becomes an aesthetic principle."[3]

If violence was both American and aesthetic, American women writers needed to find ways to deal with it, and this was among the unstated literary projects of the 1980s and 1990s. In the popular genre of crime and detective fiction, women both appropriated and subverted conventions, creating female private detectives who are conventionally feminine on the outside, but also hard-boiled professionals who do not flinch from violence, get beaten up in the pursuit of their jobs, and even enjoy a gunfight. Among the women detectives who started to appear in the 1980s was Kinsey Millhone, the twice-divorced Californian who first appeared in Sue Grafton's *A Is for Alibi* (1982), when she was still getting used to her role: "The day before yesterday I killed someone, and the fact weighs heavily on my mind." V. I. (Victoria Iphigenia) Warshawski from Chicago made her debut in Sara Paretsky's *Indemnity Only* (1982) with the motto "I'm a woman and I can look out for myself." Paretsky (1947–) had become a writer to speak to the American condition. She grew up

> in the Fifties, in eastern Kansas . . . in a time and place where we girls
> knew our inevitable destiny was marriage, where only bad girls had sex
> beforehand—and then reaped our inevitable punishment. I grew up the

*only girl in a household of boys, where my parents—eccentric outsiders
in a Protestant and Republican landscape when it came to religion or
civil rights—conformed rigidly in their sexual politics . . . I grew up
barely able to speak above a whisper, so fearful I was of the criticism
that dogged almost anything I said or did.*

Paretsky escaped from that milieu in 1966, going to Chicago to do
community service work in black neighborhoods on the South Side. She
was so galvanized by the experience that she began to write "about ordinary people, whose lives, like mine, were filled with the anomie that
comes from having no voice, no power." Still, it was twelve more years
before she had the courage to try to sell her work.[4] Having received a
Ph.D. in history and an M.B.A. from the University of Chicago, she
turned to crime and detective fiction after years of reading Raymond
Chandler, in whose work she had noticed that "it's a woman who presents herself in a sexual way who is responsible for everything that goes
wrong . . . So I wanted a woman who could be a whole person, which
meant that she could be a sexual person without being evil." Paretsky's
heroine is sexual and political: "she came of age in the antiwar movement and the civil rights movement of the 60s and 70s. Her mother
was a World War II refugee from fascist Europe; all that shaped her
personality."[5]

In 1986, Paretsky and other women mystery writers formed an organization called Sisters in Crime to combat the "marginalization of novels
by women," which they saw had a shorter time in print and a much
smaller likelihood of being reviewed. As Paretsky explained, "libraries
with restricted budgets would buy works by men, because, as one librarian put it, women will read books by men, but men won't read those by
women." Tracking book reviews and creating their own *Books in Print*
to take to bookstores and libraries, the women helped build a large literary market for their work.[6] Less directly, they legitimized the idea
that women could take on the most extreme and disturbing aspects of
American society. Alaskan writer Dana Stabenow (1952–) won an Edgar
Award for her mystery novel *A Cold Day for Murder* (1992), which introduced her Aleut detective Kate Shugak, working in the Alaska wilderness. Stabenow credited her mother for success and her intrepid
heroines:

*I grew up believing I could do anything because my mother showed me
how. She could bake bread, shoot and skin and butcher a moose, shoot,*

*pluck and cook ducks, help maintain and run a boat, count fish, fool the
Fish and Game, skin a mink and tan its hide, homeschool me the year
we trapped . . . and survive three disastrous marriages.*[7]

In more elite literary genres as well, women writers had more visibility and assurance. For the first time, three women dramatists, Beth Hen-
ley, Marsha Norman, and Wendy Wasserstein, won the Pulitzer Prize in
the 1980s, almost as many as had won it in the previous sixty years put
together.[8] In "The Language of the Brag" (1980), the poet Sharon Olds
(1942–) described childbirth as an epic "American achievement," and
claimed her rightful place in the heroic pantheon of American poets:

> *I have done what you wanted to do, Walt Whitman,*
> *Allen Ginsburg, I have done this thing,*
> *I and the other women this exceptional*
> *Act with the exceptional heroic body,*
> *This giving birth, this glistening verb,*
> *And I am putting my proud American boast*
> *Right here with the others.*

Sandra M. Gilbert and Susan Gubar's groundbreaking *Norton Anthology of Literature by Women: The Tradition in English* (1985) was a literary
event that transformed the teaching of literature at all levels, and raised
fundamental questions about the history of women's writing and the
desirability of its achieving an internal canon. Almost 2,500 pages of
closely printed text, and including works by 148 writers from England,
the United States, Canada, Australia, and other Anglophone countries,
the anthology had as its goal, as the editors said in their preface,
"to define the ways in which the female imagination has struggled to
articulate visions and revisions of a literature energized by female consciousness, impelled by female creativity, and empowered by female
community." At first, however, some American women writers were
ambivalent about the book or even hostile to it. According to Oates, the
publication of the "monumental" volume "had the perhaps unantici-
pated effect of polarizing women writers into two contending camps:
those who denied the claims of gender and those who acknowledged
them."[9] A tiny number of women writers refused to have their work
included, and others reviewed the book harshly, prompting gossip that
they were angry that they had *not* been included.

Yet over time, the *NALW* had a clear impact on individual women writers and the trajectory of American women's literary history. Ursula Le Guin (whose short story "Sur," about a women's polar expedition, was in the original edition) read it "from cover to cover. It was a bible for me. It taught me that I didn't have to write like an honorary man anymore, that I could write like a woman and feel liberated in doing so."[10] In January 1985, Le Guin published her first feminist fable, "She Unnames Them," in *The New Yorker*. In her brief tale, Le Guin was commenting on the 1970s fascination with "unnaming"—shedding the terms of slavery and colonialism as a prerequisite to literary autonomy—and applying it to the situation of women's writing. Feminist critics had stressed that the Western poetic tradition derived from Genesis and *Paradise Lost*, in which Adam is given the power of naming creation. According to Margaret Homans in *Women Writers and Poetic Identity* (1980), Adam thus "participates in the invention of language," while "Eve only repeats something that she has been told and that she perhaps does not fully believe in." The American poetic tradition deriving from Emerson, Homans went on, envisions and enshrines the poet as a male Adamic figure, the namer and the speaker, while "Eve, and women after her, have been dislocated from the ability to feel that they are speaking their own language."[11] In "She Unnames Them," "she" is Eve, who returns to Adam all the names, taxonomies, and identities he has bestowed on the animals, and lets them name themselves. Finally, she gives back her own name, although Adam, who is tinkering in the garden, scarcely listens to what she is saying or notices when she leaves. No longer named in Adam's language, or defined in opposition to him, she is free to discover her own name and new words, which must be "as slow, as new, as single, as tentative, as the steps I took going down the path away from the house, between the dark-branched tall dancers motioning against the winter shining." As Le Guin explained, "At the end of the story, she has no words left. She's so close to the animals that she feels vulnerable and afraid, yet full of new desire to touch, smell, and eat."[12]

Housekeeping

Housekeeping (1980), by Marilynne Robinson (1943–), was a significant novel of the eighties that examined classic forms and formulas of American writing, and raised issues of women's relationship to language, nature, and spirituality. The descendant of pioneers who had arrived in Idaho in covered wagons, Robinson wanted to draw attention to the far West as an overlooked site of American history and culture. In "My Western Roots," she observed that "Idaho society at that time at least seemed to lack the sense of social class which elsewhere makes culture a system of signs and passwords, more or less entirely without meaning except as it identifies group and subgroup. I think it is indifference to these codes in westerners that makes easterners think they are without culture."[13] Educated at Pembroke College of Brown University, and at the University of Washington, where she received a Ph.D. for a dissertation on Shakespeare, Robinson was also drawn to nineteenth-century American literature, and "was particularly impressed with the use of metaphor in all the great ones—Melville, Dickinson, Thoreau. It seemed to me that the way they used metaphor was a highly legitimate strategy for real epistemological questions to be dealt with in fiction and poetry."[14]

Housekeeping is a haunting, metaphoric novel about two kinds of women—those women in the tradition of Anne Sexton's "Housewife," or Shirley Jackson's novels about agoraphobia, who like to keep their houses and to stay in their own rooms, however small, dark, and poor; and those less visible women, in the tradition of fairy tale, science fiction, and utopian narrative, who cannot be housekeepers or be kept in their houses. Robinson traces three generations of women in the imaginary Idaho town of Fingerbone, which is surrounded by mountains and next to a dark lake. The narrator, Ruth, and her sister, Lucille, are passed from one family caregiver to another; their father abandons them in Seattle; their mother brings them back to their grandmother in Fingerbone, and immediately drives her car off a cliff; the grandmother dies, leaving them in the care of two maiden great-aunts, and finally, their aunt Sylvie Fisher, a wanderer and transient, comes back to keep house for them. But Sylvie's housekeeping is like something out of a gothic fairy tale. "Sylvie talked a great deal about housekeeping. She soaked all the tea towels for a number of weeks in a tub of water and bleach. She emptied several cupboards and left them open to air, and once she washed half the kitchen ceiling and a door. Sylvie believed in stern solvents, and most of all in air. It was for the sake of air that she opened doors and windows, though it was probably through forgetfulness that she left them open. It was for the sake of air that on one early splendid day she wrestled my grandmother's plum-colored davenport into the front yard, where it remained until it weathered pink." Gradually Sylvie begins to hoard tin cans, piles of women's magazines, newspapers, paper bags; the windows in the house are broken, and the floors are littered with bits of dead birds killed by her cats. Ruth and Lucille react differently to this environment; Lucille, who wants only to be a normal teenage girl, goes off to live with her Home Ec teacher, while Ruth, who has become a rebel and outsider, runs away with Sylvie, who fakes their death so they will not be followed. Ruth and Sylvie escape into nature from the deadly domesticity of Fingerbone, and they also escape marriage, motherhood, and restriction by men, but the price they pay is cutting themselves off entirely from family and community.

Is *Housekeeping* a feminist novel? As Cornelia Nixon commented in an interview with Robinson, part of its phenomenal success "was due to the contemporary burgeoning of feminist literary theory and the creation of Women's Studies Programs, which embraced the book as a feminist statement about women's generational influences on each other and women's spirituality, which often is seen as including pantheistic elements rather than conforming to any conventional church doctrine."[15] Robinson herself has said, "I am a great admirer of the Women's Movement and I think everyone, not just women, is deeply indebted to it. But I wanted to write a book about women that was not a feminist book. It seems to me, in a way, that is the ultimate feminism. When you can actually put aside that category and write about women, but not as if you were writing about people who are some minor or special strain in the species rather than being simply human."[16] In another interview, she noted, "It's very hard for me to describe how I think about *Housekeeping* in terms of gender. One reason all the characters are female is because I think of them as being intrinsically one character, which is female. One of the reasons those characters, or that character, is female is because I was imagining a Western landscape, which people from the outside have always imagined as being deeply masculine in its essence. I didn't experience it that way at all, growing up there."[17] In many respects, Robinson has acknowledged, *Housekeeping* was influenced by Melville and other nineteenth-century metaphoric American writers, and was a kind of response to *Moby-Dick:* "I thought that if I could write a book that had only female characters that men understood and liked, then I had every right to like *Moby-Dick*." She was proud that the novel was "as well received by men as by women."[18]

Housekeeping has become almost a cult novel among feminist critics, but there is wide disagreement about how it should be interpreted. Most critics understand *Housekeeping* as a "narrative of feminist freedom" celebrating the escape of Ruth and Sylvie, although others see it as a contribution to "the literature of trauma," the story of two psychologically damaged women.[19] In my view, *Housekeeping* offers American Eves, who reject the conventions of domesticity, counterparts to the American male artist, an Adamic figure who entered nature and refused to be domesticated. As James Maguire sums up, "In leaving open the doors of her family's house, in leading her nieces into the woods, and in living the life of a transient, Sylvie shows Ruth the tenuousness and arbitrariness of social boundaries and how often habits have the effect of keeping one from recognizing the reality that all human beings are, ultimately, transients in life."[20] *Housekeeping* won numerous awards, but Robinson wrote only nonfiction for twenty-four years before publishing her second novel, *Gilead* (2004), which chronicled the spiritual battles of a Midwestern Congregationalist minister, John Ames; the book was warmly received and won the Pulitzer Prize.

Anne Tyler (1941–) also wrote fiction about breaking away from domestic routine and the operations of grace, in a more realistic mode than Robinson's. While Tyler had begun to publish her fiction about the American family in the 1960s, the eighties were her breakout decade, with the novels *Morgan's Passing* (1980), *Dinner at the Homesick Restaurant* (1982), *The Accidental Tourist* (1985), and *Breathing Lessons* (1988) all winning critical acclaim, prize nominations, and literary awards, as well as a following of devoted readers. Educated in Russian studies at Duke and Columbia, and married to an Iranian psychiatrist, Tyler set most of her fiction around the north-south divide of her home in Baltimore. Running away from claustrophobic marriages, families, and homes, her characters re-create new families and utopian communities in unexpected forms, where everyone can find his or her special kind of regional comfort food. Tyler's brilliant imagining of sanctuaries and spiritual rebirth reached its most memorable statement in *Saint Maybe* (1991), a novel in which she invented a very American and very pragmatic religion, The Church of the Second Chance. As its minister, Reverend Emmett sums up its credo, "Jesus remembers how difficult life on earth can be . . . he helps you with what you can't undo. But only after you've tried to undo it." Praying for forgiveness is meaningless, but sinners can have a second chance at grace and redemption if they "offer reparation—concrete, practical reparation." Ian Bedloe, Tyler's hero, must make enormous reparations and sacrifices to atone for the harm he caused his brother's family, but in Tyler's narrative theology, he is at best Saint Maybe, an ordinary man doing his best in difficult circumstances. "People changed other people's lives every day of the year," Tyler concludes. "There was no call to make such a fuss about it."

Born in the U.S.A.—Minimalism

The American short story enjoyed unprecedented scrutiny and prestige in the eighties, and several women writers made their reputation in this genre. Raymond Carver, a beloved writer who achieved canonical status without ever publishing a novel, was probably most responsible for the revived interest in the short story, and in the pared-down realist form of minimalism. In contrast to the allusive, experimental techniques of post-modernist American fiction writers like Donald Barthelme, Carver believed that "it is possible, in a poem or short story, to write about commonplace things and objects using commonplace but precise language, and to endow those things—a chair, a window curtain, a fork, a stone, a woman's carring—with immense, even startling power."[21] In the introduction to his 1987 anthology of American short-story masterpieces, coedited with Tom Jenks, Carver described the fiction of the eighties as a return to realism, to "fiction that approximates life—replete with recognizable people, and motive, and plot and drama."

Coming from very different regions and backgrounds, with lives and interests singularly unlike Carver's, several women writers nonetheless adopted Carver's intimate, economical, and understated style to talk about female experience and the American dream. Some also protested against the label of minimalism. Amy Hempel (1951–), a resident of San Francisco who had moved east and become a student and protégée of Carver's editor, Gordon Lish, at Columbia in 1982, won critical respect for the spare, meticulous stories of her debut collection *Reasons to Live* (1985). In her most-anthologized story, "In the Cemetery Where Al Jolson Is Buried," the narrator used anxiety about a San Francisco earthquake (a metaphor in much of her early writing) to evade the more immediate fear that she is unable to support her dying friend. Hempel called herself a miniaturist, telling an interviewer, "I work small, concise, precise."[22]

Another miniaturist, Ann Beattie (1947–), made her reputation as the chronicler of the prolonged adolescence and shallow angst of the American suburban generation that came of age in 1970—the baby-boom or Woodstock generation. She resisted this label: "I do not wish to be a spokesperson for my generation," she told an interviewer in 1985. But she acknowledged that the generation and her characters had much in common. "A lot of people from my generation got the idea that they were free agents pretty early on. And then I think that the war in Vietnam made people make choices that were either terrible compromises to them or scared them to death, or that embarrassed them, and . . . the political upheaval made people want to grab on to a life pretty fast. And I think that they did it too young and they did it on the defensive. And it often didn't work."[23] Between 1974 and 1985, Beattie published thirty-five short stories in *The New Yorker.* Her two novels, *Falling in Place* (1980) and *Love Always* (1985), and her volume of short stories, *The Burning House* (1982), also seemed to reflect the sensibility of troubled urban characters, who are aware of contemporary painting and photography, and who see popular culture as a metaphor for their genders and identities. In "The Burning House," a man tells his unhappy wife, "Let me tell you something. All men—if they're crazy . . . if they're gay . . . even if they're just six years old . . . Men think they're Spider-Man and Buck Rogers and Superman. You know what we all feel inside that you don't feel? That we're going to the stars."

Self-Help—Lorrie Moore

Lorrie Moore (1957–) began to publish in the mid-eighties, when the minimalism of Raymond Carver and his disciples had peaked. In an essay on the American short story, Vince Passaro described short fiction post-1985 as "more various, more successfully experimental, more urbane, funnier, and more bitterly ironic than that written in the Hemingway tradition. It is also more idiosyncratic in its voices, less commercial, and more expansive in its approach to the requirements of art."[24] Passaro ranked Moore among the best and most innovative writers of the period. Educated at St. Lawrence University and in Cornell University's creative writing program, Moore was only twenty-six when her first book, *Self-Help* (1985), was accepted for publication. Among its most notable stories was "How to Be an Other Woman," written in the second person imperative, and combining deadpan humor with pathos; Moore anticipated the cultural obsession with single women that would lead to *Sex and the City,* in a voice that was surprising and fresh: "Cut up an old calendar into weeklong strips. Place them around your kitchen floor, a sort of bar graph on the linoleum, representing the number of weeks you have been a mistress: thirteen. Put X's through all the national holidays." In other stories, however, such as "What Is Seized," Moore dealt with darker subject matter, the daughter's reconstruction of the disintegration of her parents' marriage, and her mother's decline into alcoholism and madness, offered as a story of becoming a writer. In her subsequent writing, especially the dazzling *Birds of America* (1998), with its unforgettable central story about a baby with a kidney tumor, "People Like That Are the Only People Here," Moore's writing became more profound and tragic without losing its immediacy and wit.

In Country—Vietnam

By the late 1970s and into the 1980s, American writers and filmmakers had begun to deal with Vietnam and its aftermath, and the dedication of the Vietnam Veterans Memorial in 1982 also focused attention on the ways that the war would be remembered. Dozens of harrowing novels, memoirs, and histories appeared throughout the decade, as well as angry, personal films about the soldier's experience, including *Platoon* (1986) and *Full Metal Jacket* (1987). While the majority of these works were written by men who had served as fighters or journalists, a few American women writers also wrote fiction about Vietnam, novels that were very different from those written by women in the Civil War or the two world wars. Women had usually concentrated on telling the story of noncombatants on the home front, but Jayne Anne Phillips (1952–) and Bobbie Ann Mason (1940–) felt free to write from male perspectives and to imagine the soldier's war.

Phillips had published a book of short stories, *Black Tickets* (1979), which Carver had praised. Nonetheless, she insisted that she was not a minimalist: "I feel strongly that . . . the material dictates form rather than the other way around . . . there are other things that I've done that are very lyrical."[25] In *Machine Dreams* (1984), she wrote a complex and luminous novel detailing the history of a representative American family, the Hampsons, from World War II to the aftermath of the Vietnam War. Narrated by all the members of the family, the father Mitch, the mother Jean, the daughter Danner, and the son Billy, *Machine Dreams* also includes letters and dreams—combat dreams, post-traumatic stress dreams, dreams of the moon landing, and the Vietnam draft lottery that will determine the fate of so many young men: "Hundreds of days of white balls tumbling in a black sphere, silent and very slow, moving as though in accordance with physical laws. A galaxy of identical white planets. No sun." These machine dreams, in which human freedom and also gender equality are overwhelmed by the mechanical forces of war, climax in Danner's last dream, in which she and her younger brother, a soldier reported missing in action, are walking through a forest as children, until Billy disappears. "She can only hear him, farther and farther behind her, imitating with a careful and private energy the engine sounds of a plane that is going down. War-movie sounds. *Eeee-yoww, ack-ack-ack.* So gentle it sounds like a song, and the song goes on softly as the plane falls, year after year, to earth."

For *In Country* (1985), her novel about the post-Vietnam generation, Bobbie Ann Mason used an epigraph from Bruce Springsteen: "Nowhere to run, ain't got nowhere to go." The novel, she has explained, "takes place in the summer of 1984, when . . . Springsteen's . . . album was playing everywhere. With its themes of pain and loss and searching, it was like a soundtrack . . . By that time, America was beginning to emerge from its amnesia about the war."[26] When she began the novel, Mason had experienced all the traditional self-doubts of women writing about war. "I was intimidated by the notion of writing about Vietnam vets . . . I didn't feel confident . . . plunging intimately into the complex subject of a soldier's memories. I even wondered if I—as a woman—had right to tell his story." But as she read Vietnam memoirs and visited the Vietnam Veterans Memorial, Mason grew to feel that the war "is every American's story."[27]

Her eighteen-year-old heroine Samantha Hughes, the daughter of a soldier killed in Vietnam, buys *Born in the U.S.A.* en route from Kentucky to see the Vietnam Veterans Memorial in Washington. "On the cover, Bruce Springsteen is facing the flag, as though studying it, trying to figure out its meaning." The songs of Springsteen and the sound track from the Vietnam War movie *Apocalypse Now* (1978) form a counterpoint to Sam's journey in country, trying to come to terms with her lost father and the losses of the war. Toward the end of the novel, Sam reads her father's diary from Vietnam, preserved but probably unread by his parents, and is sickened by his account of killing. She runs away to a Kentucky swamp in an attempt to experience something like jungle survival herself: "If men went to war for women, and for unborn generations, then she was going to find out what they went through . . . If the U.S.A. sent her to a foreign country, with a rifle and heavy backpack, could she

root around in the jungle, sleep in the mud, and shoot at strangers? How
did the Army get boys to do that?" The swamp experience provides few
answers, but Sam finds a sense of commonality at the Vietnam Memorial, an ending that is emotional and "feminine," in contrast to the very
nihilistic Vietnam fictions of American male novelists of the war. While
reviewers acclaimed Mason's reconstruction of the war and its effects on
the American psyche, critics later noticed that the novel was a coming-of-
age story, which "looks at the sudden fluidity, beginning in the Sixties, in
our concepts of what it means to be masculine or feminine."[28]

Mason was born on a farm outside Mayfield in western Kentucky, a
region in which most of her fiction is set, but her academic training had
taken her far from regionalist writing. In 1972, she received a Ph.D. in
English from the University of Connecticut; her dissertation on Nabokov became her first published book. She has said that it took her almost
a decade to break away from her training as a critic, and to "learn how to
write from scratch: no amount of studying literature prepared me for
knowing how a story is coaxed out of the imagination."[29] Mason's first
book of fiction, *Shiloh and Other Stories* (1982), included sixteen stories, all
in the present tense, and packed with references to popular culture, television, and rock music. The title story "Shiloh" is about the disintegration of a marriage, told from the perspective of the husband, a truck
driver named Leroy Moffitt. Injured in an accident, he is at home doing
crafts and even needlework, while his wife, Norma Jeane, is taking body-
building classes and adult-education courses. Married at eighteen when
Norma Jeane got pregnant, they lost their son to sudden infant death
syndrome at a drive-in movie, and have never really been able to talk
about it. In a last-ditch effort to rescue the marriage, he takes her on a
trip to the Civil War park at Shiloh, where 3,500 soldiers died; but it is too
late to start over; as Leroy dimly understands, "the real inner workings
of a marriage, like most of history, have escaped him." With Leroy wondering if their breakup was "one of those women's lib things," "Shiloh"
was the most-anthologized short story of the 1980s, but more didactic
and explicit than Mason's work would grow to be.

Multiculturalism

Multiculturalism appeared initially as part of the culture wars that raged
in the 1980s, political and academic battles over cultural and racial diver-

sity in the university humanities curriculum. To its defenders, multiculturalism stood for the enriching inclusion of women, minorities, and the
many ethnic, racial, and immigrant cultures that have made up the history of the United States. To its antagonists, however, it was the threatening substitution of relative cultural values and fragmented minority
identities for an unquestioned sense of cultural norms and hierarchies,
and a cohesive American character. Played out in the headlines and on
the nightly news, multiculturalism was never a literary movement, school
of writing, or technique; and those writers who were identified with it
stressed the enormous differences among the wide spectrum of groups
under its rubric. Nevertheless, the eighties witnessed an explosion of literature by women writers identifying themselves with minorities and
hybrid cultures—Mexican-American, Asian-American, Arab-American,
and many others in addition to African-American. These writers invented
narratives that looked at generational conflicts, particularly between
mothers and daughters; the difficulties and disadvantages of assimilation
to the American mainstream; and the conflicts of being educated artists, bicultural and bilingual, writing from both the literary traditions of
the dominant culture and the spiritual claims and deep mythologies
of the subculture.

Feminist literary critics in the eighties were challenging the idea of a
unified community of black, white, and Latina American women. *This
Bridge Called My Back: Writings by Radical Women of Color* (1981), edited by
Chicana feminists Gloria Anzaldúa (1942–2004) and Cherríe Moraga
(1952–), and Anzaldúa's *Borderlands/La Frontera* (1987), directed attention
to Hispanic and Mexican women living on the geographical and sexual
borders of American culture. Deborah McDowell's "New Directions for
Black Feminist Criticism" (1980) called for "rigorous textual analysis" of
black women's writing based on a thorough knowledge of African-
American literature.[30] *Black Women Novelists: The Development of a Tradition* (1980), by Barbara Christian (1943–2000), the first African-American
woman to be tenured at Berkeley, was followed by her essay collection,
Black Feminist Criticism (1985), and then by Hazel Carby's historical study,
*Reconstructing Womanhood: The Emergence of the Afro-American Woman
Novelist* (1987), which examined the development of black women novel-
ists and activist writers at the turn of the century, including Pauline
Hopkins and Anna Julia Cooper. Toward the end of the decade, the
Schomburg Library of Nineteenth-Century Black Women Writers pub-
lished thirty volumes of African-American women's poetry, fiction, and

prose, a significant part of the "project to resurrect, explicate, and canonize the Afro-American women's literary heritage."[31]

Sandra Cisneros (1954–) grew up in Chicago, but her family made frequent trips back to Mexico, and she recalled that "because we moved so much, and always in neighborhoods that appeared like France after World War II—empty lots and burned-out buildings—I retreated inside myself." After graduating from Loyola University, Cisneros attended the University of Iowa Writers' Workshop, where she discovered the writing of the French philosopher Gaston Bachelard on the poetics of houses, and realized that her own poetic and cultural space was not a house but a third-floor flat. Dedicated "A las mujeres/To the women," with an author's note that described Cisneros as "nobody's mother and nobody's wife," *The House on Mango Street* (1984) was composed of forty-five first-person narrative vignettes from the point of view of Esperanza Cordero, a Chicana girl who lives in a crowded run-down house that is "small and red with tight steps in front and windows so small you'd think they were holding their breath." Like Frankie, Molly, Maud Martha, Claudia, Sam, and other heroines of women's coming-of-age stories, Esperanza tells stories to escape, and dreams of "a house of my own," bigger than a room of one's own, a space free of domination and drudgery, "not a man's house. Not a daddy's . . . My books and my stories . . . Only a house quiet as snow, a space for myself to go, clean as paper before the poem." As one of the first Chicana writers to be accepted by the mainstream, Cisneros expressed her sense of responsibility: "I'm trying to write the stories that haven't been written. I feel like a cartographer. I'm determined to fill a literary void."[32]

Amy Tan (1952–) grew up rebelling against her strict, formidable, and eccentric Chinese-born mother, Daisy, and against her dual identity as a first-generation Chinese-American girl in California. These conflicts were exacerbated by her dramatic childhood; when Amy's father and older brother died from brain cancer, Daisy Tan took Amy and her remaining brother, John, to Europe to escape evil spirits, and they were educated at an elite secondary school in Montreux, Switzerland. Returning in the 1970s to California, where she studied English and linguistics at San Jose State College and began a doctorate at Berkeley, Tan read widely in American literature, but never encountered women or minorities. "I didn't question that it could be any other way," she recalled. ". . . I didn't even imagine there was such a thing as an Asian-American woman writer."[33] In 1984, she married a tax lawyer, Louis DeMattei; she also discovered that her mother had been married in China to an abusive husband, and had fled to California on the eve of the revolution, leaving her three small daughters behind. In 1987, Tan and her husband traveled to China to meet two of her half sisters; by then she written the interrelated short stories that form the novel based on her mother's life and the lives of other Chinese immigrant mothers and their American-born daughters.

The Joy Luck Club (1989) sold four million copies, and stayed on the best-seller list for most of the year. As Katherine Payant sums up, it was a paradigmatic novel of generations of immigrant women and their daughters, offering a narrative model that would be replicated by other multicultural and hybrid women writers. "Set in pre-World War II China and California in the 1950s and 1980s, *The Joy Luck Club* explores the antagonistic, yet achingly tender, feelings of Chinese-American mothers and daughters for each other. On the one hand, it deals with immigrant women who must struggle to understand their daughters' new language, who fear for their girls' freedom, and who live through their daughters' accomplishments. It shows equal sympathy with their Americanized daughters . . . Though the novel is particularly meaningful to readers of first-generation immigrant parentage, Tan speaks to all contemporary women struggling for understanding with mothers who have lived such different lives from themselves."[34] Tan attributed her success to transformations in the literary curriculum and the emergence of American women writers; when she had started reading fiction again in 1985, she had read O'Connor, Welty, Walker, Tyler, and younger writers including Amy Hempel and Louise Erdrich, and "found that I enjoyed their sensibilities, their voices, and what they had to say about the world . . . Now I kept reading, day and night, until I couldn't stop myself from *writing.*"[35]

Bharati Mukherjee (1940–) came to the United States from Calcutta for graduate study at the University of Iowa, where she received a Ph.D. in comparative literature in 1969, and married a Canadian writer, Clark Blaise. Teaching in Canada and then at Berkeley, she also began to write stories and novels about immigrants and the mixing of Eastern and Western cultures. In the 1980s, Mukherjee published four books: *An Invisible Woman* (1981), which used a metaphor from Ralph Ellison's classic novel about black men in America; *Darkness* (1985), short stories about the effects of racism; *The Middleman and Other Stories* (1988), which won the National Book Critics Circle Award; and a novel, *Jasmine* (1989), about the tragic oppression of a young Hindu woman. By this point, Mukherjee had come to see herself as "an American writer of Indian origin," rather than an "Indian-American writer." "I write in the tradition of immigrant experience rather than nostalgia and expatriation," she told an interviewer. ". . . I am saying that the luxury of being a U.S. citizen is for me that I can define myself in terms of things like my politics, my sexual orientation or my education . . . not in terms of my ethnicity or my race."[36]

Louise Erdrich (1954–) grew up in Wahpeton, North Dakota, one of seven children of devout Catholic teachers in a government school for Native American children, in which her maternal grandfather, a Turtle Mountain Chippewa, had been educated. Like many American women writers, she was a precociously gifted child, who began to write very young, encouraged by her German father and her French-Ojibwa mother. At Dartmouth in 1972, she began to write seriously. "It was the first year they allowed women in, and the first year they had a Native American program. It changed my life." As Erdrich has recalled, she was learning to read back through her literary mothers, as well as through her Chippewa culture. "Every female writer starts out with a list of other female writers in her head. Mine includes, quite pointedly, a mother list," the names of women writers who had children, since "it is only now that mothers in any number have written literature."[37] She was also influenced by reading Faulkner, Cather, Marilynne Robinson, and Bobbie Ann Mason, and developed an understanding of the importance of place in a contemporary sense that included suburbs, popular culture, even brand names. "A writer must have a place . . . to love and be irritated with. One must experience the local blights, hear the proverbs, endure the radio commercials, through the close study of a place, its people and character, its crops, paranoias, dialects, and failures, we come closer to our own reality . . . Location is where we start."[38]

In 1981, after receiving a master's degree in creative writing from Johns Hopkins, Erdrich married Michael Dorris, a novelist and the director of the Dartmouth program. Before her thirtieth birthday, she published her first novel, *Love Medicine* (1984), interrelated stories about fifty years in the lives of three generations of Chippewa families, narrated by seven different characters. With accolades from Toni Morrison and Angela Carter as well as Philip Roth, who called it "a masterpiece, written with spellbinding authenticity," *Love Medicine* won the National Book Critics Circle Award, and in 1993, Erdrich issued a new edition with four new chapters as well as revisions. She continued to chronicle Native American families in North Dakota in *The Beet Queen* (1986), *Tracks* (1988), and *The Bingo Palace* (1994).[39]

The Darker Sister

One of the most important developments in American women's writing in the 1980s was the emergence of the darker sister. In a celebrated poem of the Harlem Renaissance, Langston Hughes had asserted his right to join the American literary canon:

> *I too, sing America.*
> *I am the darker brother.*

Fifty years later, a series of critically acclaimed, historically significant, formally innovative, and immensely popular books by black American women writers won international attention. These novels both shared the formal literary concerns of eighties American writing, and brought something new to it. According to Henry Louis Gates, Jr., "the popularity of black women's literature . . . stems from the compelling blend of realistic and lyrical narrative modes," plus "the sheer energy that accompanies the utterance of a new subject matter" and "a resounding new voice, one that is at once black and female, replete with its own shadings and timbres, topoi and tropes."[40] Three exceptional African-American women novelists, Alice Walker, Gloria Naylor, and Toni Morrison, had a powerful impact on American fiction in the decade. Other writers who contributed to a growing body of literature by women of color were the novelists Sherley Anne Williams (1944–1999), Gayl Jones (1949–), and Andrea Lee (1953–), the poet Rita Dove (1952–), and the Caribbean novelist Jamaica Kincaid (1949–).

ALICE WALKER: *THE COLOR PURPLE*

Alice Walker's collection of essays *In Search of Our Mothers' Gardens: Womanist Prose* (1983) brought the ideas of black feminist criticism to a wide readership. In her classic feminist essay *A Room of One's Own* (1928), Virginia Woolf imagined what might have happened if Shakespeare had a sister, as extraordinarily gifted as himself, "as adventurous, as imaginative, as agog to see the world as he was," but born into the wrong body at the wrong time. A female Shakespeare, she concluded, would have run away to London, become the mistress of an actor, become pregnant, and killed herself, without ever writing a word. It would not have been possible for a woman to write the plays of Shakespeare "in the age of Shakespeare." Now Walker imagined an African-American equivalent— a great black woman writer born a slave or in poverty. These, she wrote, were the "women who might have been Poets, Novelists, Essayists, and Short-Story-Writers (over a period of centuries), who died with their real gifts stifled within them." For Walker, Phillis Wheatley was the real-life black parallel to Woolf's imaginary Elizabethan genius who died before she could even begin to realize her promise. Walker suggested, in effect, that in the age of Hawthorne and Whitman, no black woman could have written the novels of Hawthorne or the poems of Whitman. Walker also defined a nonseparatist but unique black feminism she named "woman-ism," which incorporated bisexuality, spirituality, and political strug-gle, and presented itself as deeper, richer, and stronger than its white counterpart. As she boldly concluded, "Womanist is to feminist as pur-ple is to lavender."[41] In its hardcover edition, the book had a purple binding, and the dust jacket featured a purple photograph of Walker.

Walker had made purple the symbol of African-American woman-hood in her novel *The Color Purple* (1982), which inaugurated a decade of major fiction by African-American women writers. *The Color Purple* is an epistolary novel, combining the letters of two black sisters from rural Georgia in the early 1900s, Nettie and Celie, and also touching on taboo themes of estrangement between black women and men, bisexuality, sexual abuse, and incest. Celie is the brutalized sister, raped by the man she believes is her father, forced to give up her children for adoption, and sold into a marriage in which she is beaten, exploited, and deprived. Nettie, the more educated sister, escapes, joins the black missionary movement in Africa, and eventually marries the widowed missionary she accompanies. Her letters describe an African village and tribe, the Olinka. By the end of the novel, however, as the sisters are reunited, Celie has traveled the furthest into self-knowledge and mastery.

The novel was especially admired for Walker's poetic use of black English; the friendless and despairing Celie begins by writing to God, in an almost illiterate black folk idiom. Nettie's African letters, withheld from Celie by her oppressive husband, "Mr.," appear suddenly in the middle of the book; there has never been a genuine correspondence between the sisters, and Nettie writes a pedantic and flat formal English. Beginning with the review by Mel Watkins for *The New York Times*, many critics found Nettie's letters "lackluster and intrusive."[42] Although

Walker intended Nettie's experience of Africa to parallel Celie's experience of the rural South, the novel, viewed as a realist narrative, is full of gaps.[43] Indeed, Bell Hooks sees Celie's letter writing itself as "one of the most fantastical happenings" in the book, adding to the temporal implausibilities of the classic epistolary novel the illiteracy and oppression of the protagonist: "Oppressed, exploited as laborer in the field, as worker in the domestic household, as sexual servant, Celie finds time to write—this is truly incredible." Moreover, if Celie is as illiterate as her letters suggest, "she would not be able to comprehend Nettie's words."[44] The novel's fairy-tale ending, in which the cruel husband Mr. becomes a kindly partner, Celie forms a happy lesbian liaison with his mistress Shug Avery, and "the disparate members of Celie's extended family come together, as if drawn by a cosmic magnet," defies "the most minimal demands of narrative probability."[45] Nettie and her family return to Georgia after they have been reported drowned at sea; Celie inherits property that makes her independent; and they all have a celebration on that most symbolic day of American literature, the Fourth of July.

Indeed, *The Color Purple* is far from being a straightforward realist narrative, and despite its apparent simplicity, use of dialect, and authorial attributions to the spirits of Walker's African ancestors, it is an intricately crafted text that incorporates references to a wide variety of historical and literary sources. First of all, it is a historical novel: Celie's story begins in 1906, when she is fourteen, and ends in 1942, when she is about fifty. Walker acknowledges that "I knew *The Color Purple* would be a historical novel, and thinking of this made me chuckle. In an interview, discussing my work, a black male critic said he'd heard I might write a historical novel someday, and went on to say, in effect, Heaven protect us from it. The chuckle was because, womanlike (he would say) my 'history' starts not with the taking of lands, or the births, battles, and death of Great Men but with one woman asking another for her underwear."[46] Walker had done research on black Americans in the African missionary movement before 1920, in Liberia, Sierra Leone, South Africa, and Congo. The novel's references to "Aunt Althea" describe Althea Brown Edmiston, one of the first African-American missionaries. Shug Avery knows Bessie Smith; at the end of the novel, a young black man is in the Army about to be sent to France, Germany, or the Pacific. While the influence of Zora Neale Hurston in the novel is strong and visible, Walker was also influenced by black male literary models, including Chinua Achebe's African classic, *Things Fall Apart* (1958), Alex Haley's best-selling account of slavery, *Roots* (1976), and *The Autobiography of Malcolm X* (1964), ghostwritten by Haley. With its imaginary Olinka culture, a compendium of uplifting traditions and patriarchal bias, *The Color Purple* undercut the romanticism of Africa and highlighted its limitations for girls and women. Walker's version of black history emphasized fruits as well as roots, female communities as well as male warrior-heroes.

The reception of the novel in the 1980s is a revealing example of the complexity of literary juries by the end of the twentieth century. Feminist critics acclaimed it for its portrait of black female solidarity and creative bonding, represented by the metaphor of the Sister's Choice quilt that Celie creates from the torn fragments of clothing in her female community. Whoopi Goldberg played Celie in the hit movie version of *The Color Purple,* directed by Steven Spielberg, which came out in 1985. But many black men were enraged by the book and its portrayal of black men. The novelist Ishmael Reed, who made a personal crusade out of attacks on black feminist writers, lambasted the novel as "a sentinel book exposing the depth and intensity of hatred of black men in this country."[47] Although *The Color Purple* won the Pulitzer Prize in 1983, its support on the jury came from two white male writers, while the chairwoman, Midge Decter, preferred two pedestrian books by men.[48] Meanwhile, readers kept the novel on *The New York Times* best-seller list for over a year, and it went on to sell millions of copies around the world.

GLORIA NAYLOR: BLACK FEMINIST METAFICTION

Trained in literary study, with an M.A. degree in African-American studies from Yale, Gloria Naylor (1950–) wrote novels that revised the classical Western literary canon from a feminist perspective. Born in New York to sharecroppers who had gone north in search of opportunity, Naylor was a gifted child who read Ellison, Austen, Dickens, the Brontës, Baldwin, and Faulkner at an early age. Between graduating from high school and attending Brooklyn College, she had worked as a missionary for the Jehovah's Witnesses in New York and in the South, and become familiar with Southern black folklore. By 1983, studying at Yale, she had discovered black women writers, especially Morrison's *The Bluest Eye.* "It said to a young black woman, struggling to find a mirror of her worth in this society, not only is your story worth telling but it can be told in words so painstakingly eloquent that it becomes a song."[49]

In her early fiction, Naylor brought her sense of religious mission and morality to bear on the conditions of contemporary black American life, linking her novels together with recurring characters who play marginal or walk-on roles in one, and central roles in the next. Naylor's first book, *The Women of Brewster Place* (1983), told the stories of seven black women who live in an inner city housing complex—Mattie Michael, Ella Mae Johnson, Lucelia Louise Turner, Cora Lee; a lesbian couple, Lorraine and Therese; and Kiswana Browne, née Melanie, the radical daughter of middle-class black parents from suburban Linden Hills, who has idealistically, if naïvely, changed her name and dropped out of college to be "in the streets with my people, fighting for equality and a better community." In 1998, Naylor revisited the streets in *The Men of Brewster Place*, picking up the story from the perspective of the sons. Kiswana is the link to Naylor's second novel, *Linden Hills* (1985), in which she uses the concentric residential circles of a black middle-class suburb to structure parallels with circles of hell in *The Inferno*. At the center, or ninth circle, where Dante placed traitors and betrayers like Cain and Judas, is Luther Nedeed, a real-estate dealer and mortician who exploits the greedy materialism of this striving community and the status hunger of the inhabitants.

Naylor's most ambitiously conceived and imaginatively complex novel of the decade, *Mama Day* (1988), takes a woman who was an eccentric old aunt with hoodoo powers just visiting in *Linden Hills,* and makes her a serious protagonist on her own soil. The novel is set in a fictional black island community, Willow Springs, in the real Sea Islands along the coast of Georgia and South Carolina. For two centuries, the Sea Islands have been the home of descendants of slaves·from Barbados and West Africa, speaking a special dialect called Gullah. Charlotte Forten Grimke had gone there to teach after the Civil War; Louisa May Alcott had wanted vainly to teach there as well; and during the Harlem Renaissance, the black educator Lucy Laney had urged African-American writers to travel to the Sea Islands to "study the Negro in his original purity."[50] Naylor made rich use of the Sea Islands' indigenous culture, which she had seen during her stint as a missionary; but through the devices of magical realism, she placed it in the literary framework of *The Tempest.* Bharati Mukherjee, one of the first reviewers of the novel, saw that "*Mama Day* has its roots in *The Tempest.* The theme is reconciliation, the title character is Miranda, and Willow Springs is an isolated island where, as on Prospero's isle, magical and mysterious events come to pass. As in *The Tempest,* one story concerns the magician Miranda Day . . . and her acquisition, exercise, and relinquishment of magical powers."[51]

As we have seen, *The Tempest* had been a touchstone for American women writers since Margaret Fuller, Harriet Beecher Stowe, and Louisa May Alcott; it had reappeared in the 1950s and 1960s in the work of Sylvia Plath, as *Ariel* indicates. In the 1980s, *The Tempest* became a paradigmatic reference for radical male writers, who used it in a critique of colonialism and imperialism, and claimed Caliban, the dark native who rebels against being enslaved by white invaders, as a symbol of revolution. Naylor saw its possibilities as a revolutionary text for women, with Miranda, a woman making her own brave new world, as its leader. Mama Miranda Day can bring the hurricane and conjure spirits. She can bring lovers together or torment them; she can invoke or break a curse; she can create life and raise the dead. Her power comes from her African heritage, and from her ancestor Sapphira Wade, a conjure woman brought to the island as a slave in 1823, who married her owner and persuaded him to deed the island to her and his other slaves. In Naylor's version, Willow Springs becomes not only Prospero's island, but also the black mother's garden, the space of black female creativity celebrated by Alice Walker.

TONI MORRISON: MAGICAL REALISM AND UNSPEAKABLE THINGS SPOKEN

Magical realism combined realistic narrative with supernatural or surreal events. A style invented in, and identified with, Latin America, especially the work of Gabriel García Márquez, it was first taken up by European writers, including Salman Rushdie and Günter Grass, to represent the absurd and monumental shifts of modern life. Because magical realism implicitly resisted official and linear political history, it also appealed to women writers as a way of subverting the standard narratives that had excluded them. Women writers were also drawn to the structures of late Shakespearean romance. The pastoral settings of these plays, their tragicomic resolutions, and their social and ethical metamorphoses could provide structural parallels for the magical transformations in character and relationships that stand out in the women's fiction of the eighties.[52]

In "Unspeakable Things Unspoken: The Afro-American Presence in American Literature," a lecture at the University of Michigan in October 1988, Toni Morrison described the impact of race on American literature as the "unspeakable thing" in historical scholarship, and used her own writing to ask what makes black writing black. A key element, she argued, was vernacular and coded language. In her early novels, like *Sula,* she explained, she had provided "transitional passages for the white reader" which framed and introduced black expressiveness. But in *Beloved* (1987), she had dispensed with these stage directions, and immersed the white reader in black culture from the first sentence: "124 was spiteful. Full of a baby's venom. The women in the house knew it and so did the children." "It is abrupt and should appear so," Morrison declared. "No native informant here. The reader is snatched, yanked, thrown into an environment completely foreign, and I want it as the first stroke of the shared experience that might be possible between the reader and the novel's population. Snatched just as the slaves were from one place to another, from any place to another, without preparation and without defense."[53]

Morrison based *Beloved* on the pre–Civil War case of Margaret Garner. A slave in Kentucky in the 1850s, Garner was the mother of a son through a marriage to Robert Garner, a slave on a neighboring plantation, and three mulatto children probably conceived with her owner. In January 1856, the Garner family escaped to Cincinnati, Ohio, but were recaptured by slave catchers. Robert had a gun and wounded one of the marshals who came to take them; Margaret killed her two-year-old daughter Mary with a butcher knife rather than have her reenslaved. She wounded the other children as well, and had been ready to kill them and herself when she was overpowered. Although Ohio authorities tried to extradite her for a murder trial, in which they expected her to be pardoned, Garner was sent back to Kentucky and moved around by her owner, who sold her to a plantation in New Orleans, where she died of typhoid in 1858. Frances Harper wrote a poem about the case, "Slave Mother: A Tale of Ohio" (1859), which presented Garner as a tragic heroine, a "modern Medea," as the artist Thomas Satterwhite Noble titled his painting commemorating the event. Harper evokes Garner's motives in her quatrains:

> I will save my precious child
> From their deadly threatened doom,
> I will hew their path to freedom
> Through the portals of the tomb.

Although she had read about the Garner case, Morrison made clear that she had not done extensive research for *Beloved*, and was certainly not writing a historical novel. She was less interested in facts and documents than in what she called memory: "Memory (the deliberate act of remembering) is a form of willed creation. It is not an effort to find out the way it really was—that is research. The point is to dwell on the way it appeared and why it appeared in that particular way."[54] What does this statement mean? Does it mean that truth is irrelevant and "memory" is another word for inventing a past that is commensurate with the ideologies of the present? Some of Morrison's critics have written approvingly of such an interpretation, crediting Morrison with the invention of "a black aesthetic of remembering."[55] I think it is more accurate to see Morrison as finding what is most human and hopeful in individual behavior, even under the brutal conditions of slavery, and refusing to claim total victimization for her characters. These people must be portrayed with interior lives and moral choices for which they accept consequences. Just as American Jews revisiting the history of the Holocaust needed to confront the entire range of behaviors by European Jews, so, too, African-Americans needed to examine not only the heroic resistance of those who fought slavery, but also the daily lives, family bonds, and personal choices of those who simply endured it. For many readers, Morrison's dedication of *Beloved* to "Sixty Million and more," an estimate of those who died in the Middle Passage or in slavery, also invokes the six million Jewish dead of the Holocaust.[56]

Morrison's treatment of the Garner case is tragic and unsparing. Sethe, the mother, has saved her unnamed daughter from slavery through murder, but has also committed a terrible crime that must haunt her and her family forever. Morrison does find mythic, literary, and ethnographic precedents for Sethe's act. In the novel's present of 1873, infanticide has a historical and racial meaning: just as Sethe's mother "threw away" all the infants she bore to white rapists during the Middle Passage, in keeping with African traditions about evil spirits, so, too, in the village Achebe described in *Things Fall Apart,* the tribe's religion commands it to throw away its twins. The story of Medea is another classical source for infanticide. But these parallels cannot assuage or excuse Sethe's guilt. Divided into three sections, the novel explores three stages of Sethe's coming to terms with her past through ritual and reconstruction. In part one, Paul D, another slave from the Kentucky plantation Sweet Home, comes to Ohio to tell his story, while Beloved, the ghost of the murdered daughter who has been haunting the house as a spirit, returns as a mysterious young woman. In part two, Sethe relives her history with all its suffering and shame. In part three, with the help of her daughter Denver and the women of the community, she exorcises Beloved, and is able to heal herself. At the end of the novel, in a poetic coda, Morrison acknowledges both the need and the cost of African-American repression of the trauma of slavery: "It was not a story to pass on," not a story of pride, but an "unpleasant dream during a troubling sleep." Yet the story of slavery, or rather of the humanity of the men and women who endured it, must be remembered through art.

In a number of details, Morrison's story has connections to the traditions of American women's writing. Several scholars have pointed to resemblances to *Uncle Tom's Cabin,* in the use of domestic architecture and in the gothic subplot.[57] In one scene that picks up on the imagery of the circus in women's writing, Sethe and Paul D take Denver, the surviving daughter, to the carnival on Colored Thursday, where she sees "whitepeople loose: doing magic, clowning, without heads or with two heads, twenty feet tall or two feet tall; weighing a ton, completely tattooed, eating glass, swallowing fire, spitting ribbons, twisted into knots, forming pyramids, playing with snakes and beating each other up." As in Jewett's *Deephaven,* the myths of gender and race on display are undermined by social reality and recognition. "When Wild African Savage shook his bars and said wa wa, Paul D told everybody he knew him back in Roanoke." In a fascinating but usually overlooked part of the story suggesting the bonds of womanhood that transcend race, Sethe is temporarily rescued on the banks of the Ohio River by a young white woman named Amy Denver, an indentured and abused servant who is also running away, and who helps Sethe give birth to her daughter, named Denver since the murdered baby will be known as "beloved" (aimée).[58] Finally, *Beloved* is also Morrison's contribution to the insistence on a jury of her peers. Who can judge the action of Margaret Garner? "I had gone about a quarter of the way through before I realized that the only person really in a place to judge the woman's action would be the dead child . . . at last the mother got the opportunity to explain or argue or defend."[59]

As these novels were appearing during the eighties, black feminist critics were also calling attention to the exclusion of black women writers from the American canon and from the institutions and anthologies that constructed it. "What we have to recognize," Mary Helen Washington argued, "is that the creation of the fiction of tradition is a matter of power, not justice, and . . . that power has always been in the hands of men—mostly white but some black."[60] In other words, black women had been kept off the literary juries, and now they demanded their power. On January 24, 1988, forty-eight black writers and critics, both men and women, including Alice Walker and Maya Angelou, wrote to *The New York Times Book Review* to decry the nonrecognition of Toni Morrison's *Beloved* in the 1987 American literary awards. Morrison won the Pulitzer Prize for *Beloved* in 1988.

Whether the attainment of literary power for women would mean a better distribution of literary justice, or a continuing struggle for turf, possession, and supremacy was a question the next decade would address. The most important change of the 1980s, however, was that the impact of feminist criticism and the attention paid to women's writing meant that all reviewers and critics, male and female, had a better understanding of the symbolic codes, genealogies, and traditions of women's writing, and were better readers of its texts. Emphasis was shifting from a definition of "peers" as "other women" to a more complex, diverse understanding of what constituted a peer. Having women writers judged primarily by other women was much too constricted, and the notion of a universal womanhood or sisterhood, unmarked by differences of race, religion, age, region, sexual orientation, and political affiliation, seemed like an outdated utopian fantasy. In the courts, lawyers were developing elaborate systems of jury selection that attempted to influence verdicts with demographically matched jurors. But in the culture, having a jury of one's peers was coming to be a matter of broad intellectual credentials and informed understanding, rather than a matter of identical sex, race, or creed.

Wendy Steiner, who wrote about contemporary American fiction in 1988 for the *Cambridge History of American Literature,* confessed eleven years later that the experimental male superstars of the decade seemed less interesting, while the novels of the "traditional" women writers had grown in stature and beauty. In the mid-1980s, Steiner recalled, postmodernist writers like John Barth had regarded contemporary women's writing as "premodern," old-fashioned. By the end of the century, however, these writers, including Toni Morrison, Ursula Le Guin, Louise Erdrich, Alice Walker, Marilynne Robinson, and Gloria Naylor, were "utterly compelling," whereas the postmodernists seemed "tedious and self-indulgent."[61] With women critics like Steiner added to the juries, judgments of women's literary significance were shifting and laws of influence were being challenged.

20

The 1990s: Anything She Wants

s they approached the twenty-first century, American women writers had traversed the three stages of feminine, feminist, and female writing, and had moved into the fourth stage: free. Asked why she rarely chose to write about women, Annie Proulx replied, "Writers can write about anything they want, any sex they want, any place they want."[1] No longer constrained by their femininity, women were free to think of themselves primarily as writers, and subject to the same market forces and social changes, the same shifts of popular taste and critical fashion, the same vagaries of talent, timeliness, and luck, as men. In a decade fraught with questions of national identity, they were challenged to define themselves as Americans. The symbols that had been part of a women's culture unreadable by men, from the patchwork quilt to the woman warrior, had become part of the common lexicon of all Americans. Moreover, women's power to judge did not appear to mean a new kind of critical tyranny. By the 1990s, as Mark Shechner wrote, women novelists were "under no obligation to gratify a meddlesome sisterhood any more than to mollify a scandalized patriarchy, but only, as artists, to express and please themselves."[2]

In a moment of high significance in 1993, Toni Morrison became the second American woman writer, after Pearl Buck, and the first African-American, to win the Nobel Prize. In her Stockholm lecture, Morrison told a story in the tradition of the American Sibyl:

Once upon a time there was an old woman. Blind. Wise.

In the version I know the woman is the daughter of slaves, black, American, and lives alone in a small house outside of town. Her reputation for wisdom is without peer and without question. Among her

people she is both the law and its transgression. The honor she is paid
and the awe in which she is held reach beyond her neighborhood to
places far away; to the city where the intelligence of rural prophets is
the source of much amusement.

By the end of the century, Morrison was by no means a rural prophet; she had reached that peak of literary veneration at which she became the sibyl and priestess. Her majestic face alone was sufficient adornment for the covers of her books, and took its place alongside Hawthorne, Poe, Twain, Hemingway, and Roth as an American icon. The honor accorded to Morrison surely raised the cultural standing of women's writing in general as well as bringing about the canonization of her own work.

The Literary Market

One of the most dramatic aspects of the changed environment for women writers was the feminization of the literary market. American women had long been a significant presence among readers and buyers, but in the 1990s, editors, publishers, and booksellers publicly acknowledged that women dominated the book market. On one side, editors at major publishing houses saw "an absolute burgeoning of first-rate women writers," and an audience demand for strong women characters from authors of both sexes. People in the book business, *The New York Times* reported (March 17, 1997), believed that women bought between 70 percent and 80 percent of all fiction. Carla Cohen, one of the owners of the independent bookstore Politics and Prose in Washington, D.C., commented that "we have fiction on one side of the store and then history and politics and biography on the other side . . . It's like the bride and groom at the wedding. People part when they come in the door," with women heading for fiction. A survey for the American Booksellers Association, however, showed that women were the majority of buyers of nonfiction as well. And while Oprah Winfrey's powerful book club selected both male and female authors to recognize, her access to a female target audience was unmatched by any comparable media targeted at men.

Was the feminization of the literary market a good thing or a bad thing? Unquestionably, women's writing profited from the combination of aesthetic freedom and audience interest. At the same time, however, having a commercial advantage had always worked against women writers when it came to critical assessment. Furthermore, there was risk of literature itself being downgraded to a feminized pursuit, with reading a suitable hobby for housewives, and an appropriate and unthreatening cultural concern for First Ladies. New media in television, video, and the emerging juggernaut of the Internet transformed and globalized cultural circulation and delivery, creating competition with print media and redefining national boundaries. Along with other demographic and cultural shifts in the 1990s, new media marginalized some traditional literary genres and promoted new ones.

Poetry was among the genres losing its cultural ground and emotional grip. From the ladies' annuals of the 1850s to the defiant declarations of the 1960s, poetry had once spoken directly to the hearts of women readers and carried the searing messages of revolutionary social change. But by the 1990s, there seemed to be many more women writing or teaching poetry than reading and buying it. Poetry in general had moved into the academy, and despite huge amounts of money given to support poetry journals, and enormous literary prizes for individuals keeping the po-biz afloat, even in universities few people other than specialists could name the titles of books by contemporary poets, or the titles of individual poems, let alone quote them. In a special issue of the journal *Contemporary Literature* on "American Poetry in the 1990s," critics described the tone of 1990s lyric as nostalgic, elegiac, autumnal, obsessed with loss and decline, a tone often associated with writing at the end of a century, but in this case, connected by the poets to the failure of poetry itself.[3] To be sure, many esteemed and award-winning women poets, including Louise Glück, Jorie Graham, Marilyn Hacker, Rita Dove, Lisel Mueller, Mary Oliver, Mary Jo Salter, and Rachel Hadas, and the Language poets, Lyn Hejinian, Susan Howe, and Fanny Howe, held prestigious teaching appointments and published in *The New Yorker* as well as in little magazines. Scholars continued to argue about twenty-first-century modernism versus postmodernism, and the presence of women in the avant-garde; but the era when women's poetry was urgent and shattering, the blood jet, as Sylvia Plath had called it, seemed past.

Still, there were exceptions, and new Plaths arising and facing tragic ends. Reetika Vazirani (1962–2003) was born in India, but came to the United States as a child, and was only six when her father committed suicide. She went to Wellesley to study science, but Derek Walcott encouraged her writing, and by the 1990s, she had embarked on a poetic career, traveling on a fellowship to the Far East, and winning the Barnard New Women's Poetry Prize in 1995 with *White Elephants,* published the following year. These were poems about the experience of dislocation, immigration, and hybridity, the impossible ironies of creating a new self as a woman artist in a new country. By the late 1990s, Vazirani was in a relationship with the poet Yusef Komunyakaa, then teaching at Princeton University. Their son, Jehan, was born in 2000, and Vazirani's career seemed to be going well; another book, *World Hotel,* came out in 2002. These poems are much more contemporary, gripping, and personal; one outstanding semi-villanelle, "It's Me, I'm Not Home," tells about a failing relationship recorded on an answering machine:

> *It's late in the city and I'm asleep.*
> *You will call again? Did I hear*
> *(please leave a message after the beep)*

In the summer of 2003, deeply depressed and house-sitting for friends in Washington, Vazirani killed herself and her child. She left behind a nearly completed manuscript, which has not yet been published. An electrifying poet too soon extinguished, she joined a terrible sisterhood of American women poets.

Extreme Gothic

One notable phenomenon of women's writing in the 1990s was the extreme female gothic—gory novels and terrifying memoirs, as if an unflinching confrontation with the bloodiest chambers of the body were the initiation rite into the boys' club of contemporary fiction and art. Competing with popular slasher movies about screaming women threatened by psychopathic killers, Susanna Moore's novel *In the Cut* (1995) and A. M. Homes's *The End of Alice* (1996) offered grisly cautionary tales of independent girls and young women living at the edge of urban gender boundaries, who are pursued, punished, and carved up by men with sharp phallic weapons. Joyce Carol Oates also experimented with this genre in *Black Water* (1992), a monologue of the consciousness of a drowning young woman modeled on Mary Jo Kopechne; in *Zombie* (1995), based on the gruesome homosexual murders of Jeffrey Dahmer in Milwaukee; and in her genre fiction (under the pseudonym "Rosamond Smith") about murderous sisters, psychopathic sons, and the uneasy collusion of vampire and victim. In essays and reviews, Oates examined the true-crime literature of serial killers and the anguish of their families. Frequently criticized for the violence of her imagination, and for the perception that violence is the default mode of conflict resolution in her fiction, Oates has always responded that violence and psychopathology are part of the contemporary world, subjects a serious writer must explore.

Women's memoirs of the 1990s told stories of brutality, poverty, promiscuity, child abuse, incest, and breakdown, often with jaunty humor and tough pride in survival—Dorothy Allison's *Bastard out of Carolina* (1992), Susanna Kaysen's *Girl, Interrupted* (1993), Mary Karr's *The Liars' Club* (1995), Elizabeth Wurtzel's *Prozac Nation* (1994), and Kathryn Harrison's *The Kiss* (1997). *Lucky* (1999), Alice Sebold's memoir of being raped as a college freshman, was followed by her best-selling novel of 2002, *The Lovely Bones,* narrated from heaven by a raped dead girl, in a combination of the gothic with the post–Civil War theological utopias of Elizabeth Stuart Phelps.

Of course, in the hands of a major novelist, the most sensational topics taken from the tabloids could yield important fiction. Oates's *Blonde* (2000), which rewrote the life and suicide of Marilyn Monroe as classic American female tragedy, was one of the finest novels of the 1990s. In writing about Monroe, Oates took on a subject that crisscrossed almost every important strand of mid-century American culture—sports, religion, literature, theater, politics, and, of course, the Hollywood dream machine, with a huge cast of real and imagined characters. Structuring her novel in five parts, like Shakespearean tragedy, Oates presented the Blonde as the princess both exalted and doomed by her beauty and sexuality, a figure of fairy tale and myth, but also a living product of the American century.

From Chick Lit to Chica Lit

Paradoxically, as women became free to choose their own subjects and to explore all territories, the publishing phenomenon of chick lit returned female experience and "women's fiction" to prominence. Chick lit was a genre that had its formal start with the English novelist

Helen Fielding's *Bridget Jones's Diary* (1996), a witty contemporary updating of Jane Austen's *Pride and Prejudice* with a flawed but lovable heroine. Chick lit rapidly became a lucrative marketing opportunity in the United States as well, featuring single women in their twenties and thirties facing issues of dieting, insecurity, disappointing relationships with men, and uncertainties about sexual mores and monogamy, although in the nineties, the happy endings of these stories also needed to include career success, and the resolution of generational and sibling conflict as well as marriage. As the genre evolved, however, it produced many variations. Christian chick lit deplored premarital sex, drinking, and conspicuous consumption, and stressed the daily presence of faith; black, Asian, Indian, Latina, and Chicana spin-offs foregrounded the specific concerns and pressures facing young women from those ethnic, racial, and religious subgroups, along with their common identities as Americans.

American chick lit has been both more problem-based and more politically aware than its British sister. Jodi Picoult (1966–), a Princeton graduate who had published ten novels by the age of thirty-seven, drew on a wide range of American social problems in her books, including euthanasia, teen suicide, rape, and Munchausen syndrome by proxy. In her eighth novel, *Salem Falls* (2001), Picoult reimagined Arthur Miller's *The Crucible*. In the novels of Jennifer Weiner (1970–), another Princeton graduate and journalist, the heroines live out fantasies and fairy tales. In her first novel, *Good in Bed* (2001), the writer protagonist Cannie Shapiro returns from the hospital, where she has given birth to her illegitimate premature baby, to find a new apartment, exquisitely decorated in butter yellow and with pinkish-white antique furniture by her fairy godmother, a munificent movie star who is also buying her screenplay, while her selfish ex-boyfriend is weeping with remorse, and her whole dysfunctional family is waiting on her hand and foot. But the city of Philadelphia in which Weiner's heroines reside has homelessness, poverty, illness, and madness as well. *Good in Bed* was written during the Clinton-Lewinsky scandal, and its mordant view of the diet industry and women's self-hating desperation to be thin bears the marks of that cultural moment of fat jokes and media cruelty. "The message came through loud and clear," Weiner explained in a Readers' Club Guide. A woman with a body like Lewinsky's was "not worthy of respect . . . not worthy of love . . . not even really worthy of lust."

Terry McMillan (1951–), a professor of creative writing at the University of Arizona who had edited *Black Ice* (1990), an anthology of contem-

porary African-American writing, had her first blockbuster novel with
Waiting to Exhale (1992), which followed four professional black women
in their thirties in their quest for love. Waiting to Exhale signaled a new
phase in black women's writing at the opposite end of the literary spectrum from the work of Toni Morrison, but reflecting the confidence in a
black female readership that came from economic progress. McMillan's
characters read Essence, but, as the critic-novelist Darryl Pinckney
pointed out in a review in The New York Review of Books, she does not
condescend to them, or worry about choosing topics "that are covered
every week on the Oprah Winfrey Show." McMillan's popular novels, set
in Phoenix, marked a shift from black literature of the ghetto. In
Phoenix, McMillan's women "are far from the black neighborhoods
of fiction that depended on messages of social consciousness. The
extended black family is contained in long-distance phone calls, and
political consciousness consists of being annoyed that Arizona has no
Martin Luther King Day." While it is easy to make fun of the women's
materialism and the formulas of chick lit, Pinckney insists, "the urban
story was largely the black man's story . . . and perhaps the black
woman's story should be seen as a part of a more general reaction
against this writing that identified black culture as a problem and the
ghetto as a symbol of the pathological. Celebrating the richness of black
life has made a comeback . . . and this revival emphasizes survival, conti-
nuity, family feeling—the woman's story."[4]

Alisa Valdes-Rodriguez (1969–) headed a group of writers including
Mary Castillo (1974–) and Sofia Quintero (1969–)who addressed the specific concerns of women in the Latina community. A musician and journalist who grew up in Albuquerque, New Mexico, Valdes-Rodriguez
made her literary debut with The Dirty Girls Social Club (2003), which was
published in both English and Spanish. The story of six ambitious Latina
friends who met at Boston University and reunite in their late twenties,
the novel started a trend of Latina women's fiction which earned her the
title of "the godmother of Chica lit." With other categories developing
to take on the situation of older women, whether single, widowed, or
divorced (hen lit), the experience of mothers (mom lit), and the ups and
downs of women's friendships, often in novels based on book clubs, the
1990s equivalent of the quilting bee, chick lit, however controversial or
trivializing its terminology, seemed likely to stay around for some time.

Typical Americans: Women Writers and Hybridity

The casual cultural mix of popular women's fiction in the 1990s showed the impact of ideas about multicultural change and ethnic cross-fertilization that were also affecting novelists at other points in the literary spectrum. Immigrant writing in the United States had gone through cycles of gratitude, displacement, resentment, anger, and protest. In critical literary theory, the concept of postcolonialism had outlined power differences between colonialist and the colonized, while theories of race and class mapped the inevitable opposition of reigning cultural elites and marginalized newcomers. By the 1990s, with the postmodern concept of hybridity, a much more positive, even celebratory literature of generational change and cultural interaction took over. Women novelists from a wide variety of locales and hyphenated national origins, as well as second-generation daughters of immigrant parents, stressed their contributions to the American experience rather than their distance or alienation from it. Julia Alvarez (1950–), writing about the Dominican Republic in *How the García Girls Lost Their Accents* (1991), Jhumpa Lahiri (1967–), writing about second-generation Indian-Americans, and Min Jin Lee (1969–), writing about Korean-Americans, were among the novelists who analyzed the American dream as citizens and contributors. Lahiri's collection of short stories, *Unaccustomed Earth* (2008), won both critical acclaim and best-seller status, while Lee's novel *Free Food for Millionaires* was selected by many critics as one of the top ten novels of 2007.

Gish Jen (1955–), who began to publish her work in the 1990s, is representative of this new hybrid generation. Growing up in suburban Scarsdale, New York, and educated at Harvard and the Iowa Writers' Workshop in the early 1980s, before the rise of multiculturalism, Jen assumed that "Asian-American writers would never be published in a mainstream publication. It was really clear to us that nobody was interested in us."[5] But in her fiction, she addressed the changing status of Asian-Americans, and defined her own status as an American novelist. Her first book, *Typical American* (1991), centered on Ralph Chang, a Chinese-American immigrant who makes himself into a middle-class American despite homesickness and racism. Jen followed it with a novel about Chang's American-born teenage daughter Mona. In the very funny, semiutopian coming-of-age novel, *Mona in the Promised Land* (1996), whose title plays off a long tradition of Jewish-American immigrant writing, the adolescent heroine is at a new stage of ethnic identity, renaming and self-creation. Mona owes something to McCullers's Frankie and Harper Lee's Scout, but her friends are Jewish or black, with skin colors from "gingerbread" to "cream" and "papaya." In their own enclave, they exchange food, music, games, and politics. Mona converts to Judaism, and in the final pages of the novel, discusses with Aunt Theresa the possibility of changing her name when she marries her high-school sweetheart Seth Mandel:

> "To Mandel?" says Theresa, surprised. "No more women's lib? . . ."
> "No, no. To Changowitz," says Mona. "I was thinking that Seth would change his name too."

In the promised land, girls can change their names, their religions, their nationalities. "I do struggle with the Asian-American thing," Jen told an interviewer. "I don't mind it being used as a description of me, but I do mind it being used as definition of me." Although she is not Jewish, and is married to an Irish-American, she took pride in writing so knowledgeably about Jewish-American culture that even Cynthia Ozick was impressed.[6]

Rewriting the Great American Novel

Women writers in the nineties also became interested in reimagining classic American literature from a female perspective. Susan Sontag (1933–2004) had long been famous as an intellectual, political activist, and literary theorist, but (in the tradition of Wharton and Cather) she had rejected any affiliation with the women's movement, lesbian and gay rights, American literature, or women's writing.[7] From her adolescence in Southern California, when she made a pilgrimage with a friend to pay tribute to Thomas Mann, then an elderly resident of Pacific Palisades, Sontag had identified with European high culture. Living in Paris in the late fifties, she admired another expatriate, Djuna Barnes, and then published two clever but arid experimental novels, *The Benefactor* (1963) and *Death Kit* (1967), with male protagonists.

In the 1990s, however, Sontag gave up intellectual essays and avant-garde styles, and returned to fiction and drama. *The Volcano Lover* (1992), which became an unexpected best seller, confronted the lives of women through a nineteenth-century intellectual heroine, Eleanora de Fonseca. In *Alice in Bed* (1993), she explicitly confronted the tradition of American women's writing. "Alice" is both Alice in Wonderland and Alice James, Henry James's brilliant and neurotic sister, who died of breast cancer at the age of forty-three. *Alice in Bed* brings together Alice James, Margaret Fuller, and Emily Dickinson in a surreal tea party. While she had once described writing as a field in which women would encounter few problems, Sontag suggested that Alice James was an American equivalent of the thwarted female genius Virginia Woolf imagined in *A Room of One's Own*. The play, she explained, was about "the all too common reality of a woman who does not know what to do with her genius, her originality, her aggressiveness, and therefore becomes a career invalid." More generally, it is a play about "the grief and anger of women" which she had "been preparing to write all my life."[8] In her last novel, *In America* (2000), Sontag echoed Cather in writing about a European diva, the Polish actress Maryna Zalewka, who emigrates to the United States and reinvents herself as "Marina Zalenska," the tragedy queen of the American stage. At first idealistic about her art, Maryna reconciles herself to the opportunities and commerical self-fashioning of America, choosing her career over love and finally blurring the boundaries between the subversive and the sentimental.

Sena Jeter Naslund's *Ahab's Wife: or, The Star-Gazer* (1999) began with the author's desire to write about "a woman's quest for a spiritual or philosophical stance." Rereading Melville and Twain with her daughter, Naslund (1942–) "thought about how *Huckleberry Finn* and *Moby-Dick* are often described as the great American novel, so I asked myself what these books have in common. They're both quest stories, quests over water, in fact. Both deal with friendships between men of different races. These *are* great subjects. But neither book had any important women characters in it. This made me suspicious of the canon. It implied that if you're going to write the great American novel, you're going to have to leave out women, an unsettling idea."[9]

Drawing upon a few brief passages in *Moby-Dick* where Ahab refers to his wife and child, Naslund constructed Una, Ahab's wife, who begins the novel by saying: "Captain Ahab was neither my first husband nor my last." As *The New York Times Book Review* commented, Naslund had "fashioned from this slender rib not only a woman but an entire world . . . a deep and wayward creature, undaunted by convention, whose descriptions are dense with a languid and sensuous interest in the world." Una is both Ahab's partner and lover, and an adventurer in her own right, who disguises herself as a cabin boy and goes to sea, where she deals with whaling, shipwreck, and survival. Naslund also decided that "if I was going to write an epic novel of this historic period, I couldn't not deal with the issue of slavery."[10] She invents the character of Susan, a pregnant slave Una helps to escape across the frozen Ohio River, as in *Uncle Tom's Cabin*. Unlike Eliza, however, Susan returns to the Southern plantation to get her mother, who has been cruelly punished for her daughter's escape, and she herself is branded and gives birth to her own daughter in slavery. Naslund includes Morrison's *Beloved* among the fourteen books most important to the creation of her novel.[11]

Andrea Barrett (1954–) grew up on Cape Cod, and studied biology and zoology before she became a novelist. As a girl, she recalled, she "wanted to be Darwin in a skirt, wandering through the Galápagos."[12] But slowly she began to understand that she could write fiction about scientific exploration and discovery, based on historical materials. Her fiction has included stories about Mendel, Darwin, the exploration of the Arctic, the mapping of the Himalayas, epidemics, and disasters. Barrett published four books during the 1990s: *The Middle Kingdom* (1991), *The Forms of Water* (1993), *Ship Fever* (1996), and *The Voyage of the Narwhal* (1998), all interrelated short stories and novellas constructed out of letters and journals as well as narrative. In some respects, Barrett fictionalizes episodes from the history of science, but she also re-creates these epic narratives from the perspective of women. Some are wives ashore: "To not include the women back at home would have been to write the nineteenth-century version of it," she told an interviewer; "the boys go out on the boat, the boys find stuff, the boys come home, the boys are heroes. I couldn't see the point in replicating that story." In other tales, Barrett invents the life histories of failed or successful women scientists, like the Marburg sisters in *Ship Fever*. "When I think about all the obvious things we all take for granted, as feminists," she explains, "the things that are open to us now, then I become interested, inevitably, in times when nothing could be taken for granted."[13] In the nineties, intellectual women novelists, including Francine Prose (1947–), Amy Bloom (1953–), and Lionel Shriver (1957–), were both stretching the boundaries of fiction and often taking a satirical or unsentimental look at feminism, maternity, and romance.

Beyond Women's Writing in the 1990s—Jane Smiley

Just as Willa Cather and Edith Wharton at the beginning of the twentieth century considered themselves outside the traditional categories of "women's writing," so Jane Smiley and Annie Proulx, at the end, developed as writers beyond gender and genre. Both write easily from either a male or female perspective, specialize in down-and-dirty American pastimes and occupations like hog farming, horse breeding, or rodeo, and present themselves as writers who have lived both male and female lives, not because of sexual orientation (both have been married, divorced, and are mothers) but because of fate, height, personality, or necessity. "I think partly because I'm 6'2,'" Smiley told an interviewer, "I live in a slightly different world from most women."[14] Proulx comments that

> I always wanted a brother and liked the things that men did; when I was growing up women didn't go skiing, or hiking, or have adventurous canoe trips, or any of that sort of thing. I felt the lack of a brother who I imagined could introduce me to the vigorous outdoor activities that my sisters were not particularly interested in. If you live in a woman's world and that's all there is, the other side of the equation looks pretty interesting . . . I find male characters interesting. Because much of my writing is set in an earlier period, they do things that women could not appropriately do.[15]

Jane Smiley (1949–) is prominent among the nineties women novelists who defied gender limitation, but also imagined women as protagonists of mythic American fiction. Smiley grew up in Saint Louis, graduated from Vassar, and spent a year on a medieval architectural dig in England. During her first marriage, she completed a graduate degree in Old Norse at the University of Iowa and then won a Fulbright to spend a year in Iceland. Although many American women writers in the 1980s and 1990s had graduate degrees, Smiley took one of the most indirect routes to writing fiction. Her early fiction included *The Greenlanders* (1988), a saga about the fourteenth century with an Amazonian Icelandic heroine, Sigrid Bjornsdottir, a woman not unlike herself. Smiley is also a brilliant literary critic, who has written books on Dickens and on the novel as a genre, arguing that the novel is an inherently democratic form that celebrates the individual.

Smiley's novel *A Thousand Acres* (1991) reimagined and updated *King Lear* through the lens of the fashionable nineties obsession with recovered memory of childhood sexual abuse. Iowa farmer Larry Cook divides his property between his two eldest daughters, Ginny and Rose, cutting out his favorite daughter, Caroline. Ginny narrates the novel, so we tend to identify with her, although she is based on the evil sister Goneril. The still more malicious sister Rose, based on Shakespeare's Regan, suggests to Ginny that the sisters were the victims of incestuous childhood rape, and the family is destroyed.

Even more controversial than *A Thousand Acres,* however, was an essay Smiley published in *Harper's* in 1996, which sharply criticized Mark Twain, praised Harriet Beecher Stowe, and argued that "the canonization of a very narrow range of white, Protestant, middle-class male authors . . . has misrepresented our literary life." "To invest *The Adventures of Huckleberry Finn* with 'greatness,' " she asserted, "is to underwrite a very simplistic and evasive view of what racism is." The racial brotherhood most critics see in the novel, she argued, is fraudulent: "Neither Huck nor Twain takes Jim's desire for freedom at all seriously; that is, they do not accord it the respect that a man's passion deserves. The sign of this is that not only do the two never cross the Mississippi to Illinois, a free state, but they hardly even consider it." In contrast, she argued, Stowe's *Uncle Tom's Cabin* treats racism seriously and ends tragically. "If 'great' literature has any purpose," Smiley concluded, "it is to help us face up to our own responsibilities instead of enabling us to avoid them once again by lighting out for the territory."[16]

Readers were outraged by Smiley's claims, and *Harper's* received more letters than it ever had for an article. One charged that if Smiley herself tried to write such a book it would be "three hundred bore-me-slack-jawed sermons from the high pulpit of a hundred years' hindsight."[17] Smiley rose to the challenge in *The All-True Travels and Adventures of Lidie Newton* (1998), a novel set in 1855 with a feisty heroine who is a combination of Huck Finn and Harriet Beecher Stowe. Lidie is the youngest, tallest, and plainest of thirteen daughters in an Illinois family, a strong girl who can ride, fish, swim, and walk as well as a man. She marries a New England abolitionist and helps him smuggle Sharp rifles (known as "Beecher's Bibles") to Kansas Territory, a battleground where Free Staters clash with proslavery activists. This is the "Bleeding Kansas" of John Brown's broadsword massacre of proslavers at Pottawatomie Creek, and the site of violent clashes over the Fugitive Slave Act of 1850. Lidie nevertheless shares the cult of domesticity common to American women of the period, expressed in epigraphs from Catherine Beecher's best-selling advice treatise, *Domestic Economy for Young Women at Home.* "The adventure is for the men, my dear," a friend warns her. "That's the way of it here in the west." But when Lidie's husband is murdered by proslavers, she has to fend for herself. Cross-dressing as a man and calling herself "Lyman Arquette," Lidie sets out to hunt down and kill the men who shot her husband.

Dressing like a man, however, is not a magical transformation. Lidie has to face her ambivalence, timidity, and even cowardice when she avoids the pleas of a slave child, and loses her nerve about confronting her husband's killers. She blames her femininity, for "the west was full of men, and the stories of men, who confronted bullies." Moreover, Lidie begins to realize that she has not thought out the question of slavery but has simply adopted her husband's views. In the most powerful and convincing part of the book, she tests her courage and develops her own ideas, then resumes female dress and helps Lorna, a runaway slave who has been separated from her husband and who refused to bear children for the institution of slavery. For Smiley, this plot cannot have a happy ending. The women are captured by bounty hunters, Lorna is sold downriver, and Lidie goes to jail, but is finally released and makes her way back North.

Lidie Newton is certainly not a boring compendium of sermons, but it is not a humorous picaresque adventure either. Smiley uses her heroine to pose intractable moral dilemmas about slavery, abolitionism, and the Civil War. In Kansas, the Free Staters rescue a slave woman in a raid, but let her get away from them. "Whether they should have liberated her had they found her was a matter of rather hot debate—more tempers flared over this question than over any other element of the encounter." Some of the men think they should have given her freedom; others think they have no right to do so unless they also accept responsibility for her. Lidie says, "You might have asked the woman what she wanted to do." In the end, she stands by the idea that each person must decide her own destiny: "Even abolitionists knew more about how and why to chop down the slavery tree than they ever knew about what to do with its sour fruit."

Rewriting the Western—Annie Proulx

In her prizewinning novels, and especially in her astounding short stories about Wyoming, E. Annie Proulx (1935–), more than any other American woman writer, has claimed male territory as her own. She writes about cowboys, ranchers, and drifters in ways that seem natural and unforced, and puts her version of the American West next to that of Cormac McCarthy. Raised in Connecticut, the eldest of five sisters, Proulx attended Colby College and the University of Vermont, and received an M.A. from Concordia University, where she also passed her oral exams for a Ph.D. on European economics, with a minor in Chinese history, before dropping out in 1975. She married three times, and had four children. In the early 1980s, she was living in an isolated town in Vermont, supporting herself and her family through freelance journalism, including six how-to books on subjects from grape growing to *Walkways, Walls and Drives* (1983). Using the name E. A. Proulx, she also wrote about hunting and fishing for a men's magazine, and in 1988, at the age of fifty-three, published her first collection of short stories, *Heart Songs*.

Like Jewett and Wharton, Proulx initially thought of herself as a short-story writer rather than a novelist. She also had strong feelings about improper or sentimental subjects for short stories, as she explained in her introduction to *The Best American Short Stories* (1997): "Too many were formulaic: sensitive girls or sensitive ex-cons set against someone ill, or old, or handicapped, or peculiar; mawkish urban and suburban love affairs; college students at intro-to-life summer jobs; the sensitive watcher-child observing mother's or father's adultery; insensitive kids making fun of sensitive kids of different ethnicity."[18] Proulx sounds very much like the young Willa Cather denouncing sentimental lady writers a century before.

She found, however, that her first novel, *Postcards* (1992), was surprisingly easy to write, spacious after so much cramping. With her second novel, *The Shipping News* (1994), critics began to pay attention; it won a Pulitzer Prize and a National Book Award. In *Accordion Crimes* (1996), written "during two years of disruption and uprooting that included the deaths of my mother and several relatives and a friend," Proulx used the accordion as a metaphor for the American immigrant experience. "It was small, light, inexpensive. You could play music on it easily. Even as an amateur you could work out some sort of recognizable tune. You could carry some of your culture with you," she told an interviewer.[19]

Proulx returned to the short-story form, and achieved her greatest literary distinction, after she moved to Wyoming in 1995 and began to write postmodern Westerns. In *Close Range* (1999), she published eleven stories that mingle gritty naturalism, magical realism, local color, and gender crossing, to talk about love and death. "The Bunchgrass Edge of the World" rewrites one kind of Grimm fairy tale, the frog prince; the frog in this case is a talking green John Deere 4030 tractor, crooning love to hefty Ottaline Touhey, one of the few heroines in the stories. Ottaline suffers from "minstrel problems," she's "the size of a hundred-gallon propane tank," and likes a good bull sale, where "scrotal circumference is damn important." The tractor is determined to win her: "There's girls fell in love with tractors all over the country. There's girls married tractors." But Ottaline is immune to his charms.

Another kind of grim fairy tale, "Brokeback Mountain," was first published in *The New Yorker* in 1998, a year before a gay university student, Matthew Shepard, was killed in Laramie. Proulx had sensed the seething anxiety and potential violence about homosexuality beneath the rough macho jokes of ranchers. "I had been visiting a number of ranches and every ranch has some old guy who has been there forever and is single and is pretty nice but a quiet fellow. And you hear a lot of rough talk in bars about fags." In the story, two young men herding sheep for the summer to make a few extra bucks unite in a passionate sexual partnership. Although Ennis and Jack separate, marry, and meet only infrequently during their lives, their affair is not only erotic but tender, for each "the single moment of artless, charmed happiness in their separate and difficult lives." Its memory sustains Ennis after Jack dies in a roadside "accident" he knows was really a gay lynching. Directed by the Taiwanese filmmaker Ang Lee, *Brokeback Mountain* became a surprisingly successful and Oscar-winning movie.

Proulx's understanding of the West and the Western genre is radically antiheroic, as she explained in *The Guardian* in 2005: "The heroic myth of the American west is much more powerful than its historical past. To this day, the great false beliefs about cowboys prevail: that they were— and are—brave, generous, unselfish men; that the west was 'won' by noble white American pioneers and staunch American soldiers fighting the red Indian foe; that frontier justice was rough but fair; and that everything in the natural world from the west bank of the Missouri to the Pacific ocean was there to be used by human beings to further their wealth." In reality, "women in the west boiled down to emigrant wives and female children on their way to Oregon and California over the dusty trails; frontier school teachers; the wives that ranchers, cowboys, store-keepers and army officers went back east to marry and bring west; and at the bottom of the ladder, prostitutes and squaws." The last frontier of this mythic West was the rodeo, "the west's own contribution to sport. (There is Indian rodeo, too, a separate world from the white cowboy shows, as is women's rodeo and gay rodeo.) Rodeo, once an exhibition of a buckaroo's riding and ranch-work skills, has devolved into show business and has itself become a stand-alone myth."[20]

In one of her unforgettable rodeo stories, "The Mud Below," Proulx demythologizes this world, too. "Rodeo's full of Jesus freaks," a cowboy named Pearl tells his little brother. "And double and triple sets of brothers. All kinds of Texas cousins. There's some fucking strange guys in it. It's a magic show sometimes, all kinds of prayers and jujus and crosses and amulets and superstitions. Anybody does anything good, makes a good ride, it's not them, it's their mystical power connection helping them out." As she writes in her acknowledgments, "the elements of unreality, the fantastic and improbable, color all of these stories, as they color real life. In Wyoming not the least fantastic situation is the determination to make a living ranching in this tough and unforgiving place."

In *Fine Just the Way It Is* (2008), Proulx turned to write about the female side of the great divide—the harsh lives of female homesteaders, housewives, and daughters in the tough and unforgiving Wyoming territory. "Them Old Cowboy Songs," set in 1885 on the frontier, tells the story of a teenage husband and wife, Archie and Rose McLaverty, who come to grief trying to fight poverty, isloation, and the cruel landscape. When Archie goes off cowboying and leaves pregnant Rose behind, she bears a dead baby in a long bloody labor alone in their cabin. Rose manages to bury the child, but as she is bleeding to death, she hears the coyotes digging up the corpse. In the cowboy songs Archie loves, "the green grass comes and the wild rose blooms," and pioneers were survivors who "founded ranch dynasties," but in reality, Proulx reminds us, many homesteaders "had short runs and were quickly forgotten." The masterly final story, "Tits-Up in a Ditch," is set in the present. Dakotah Lister escapes from a teenage marriage to become an MP in Iraq, where she falls in love with another woman, but ends up severely wounded, bereaved, and trapped back home. Dakotah comes to see the Wyoming country, with its "romantic heritage of the nineteenth-century ranch," as a tragic place, another graveyard of the American dream, where every woman had suffered, and "every ranch . . . had lost a boy, lost them early and late."

Toward the Future

Literary America began as a tough and unforgiving place, where women like Anne Bradstreet and Mary Rowlandson contended with hardship, deprivation, and death in a fantastic and improbable setting, and were consumed by the even more fantastic determination to write truthfully about their emotions and experiences. From its inception, women's writing in America has incorporated the unconventional along with the predictable, the transgressive and rebellious alongside genteel feminine conformity. Rowing against wind and tide, as Harriet Beecher Stowe described herself, American women writers persisted in leaving their record on shore and in wilderness.

By the 1990s, however, the idea of a literary tradition had changed. Globalization transformed the once-monumental sense of a national identity and a national literature. People questioned whether any literature could be uniquely "American," and whether any tradition could trace a pure lineage, unmarked by outside influences. At the same time, age-old beliefs in innate divisions between masculinity and femininity, between men's and women's writing, had dissolved. American women writers were regarded as part of the mainstream, and American women readers, critics, and literary historians were on the juries. Indeed, an African-American woman—Oprah Winfrey—was among the most powerful advocates of great literature that is international, multiracial, and open to writers of both sexes. By September 11, 2001, when the twentieth century ended for Americans, women's writing as a separate literary tradition, as a definition rather than a description, had reached the end of its usefulness. The woman writer, as an individual, could define and express herself.

But to many critics, the glorious role of American women's writing in creating the American tradition remained secondary at best, and invisible at worst. Without a sense of this neglected literary history, scholars still wrote about the literature of the Civil War or the Cold War, the Transcendentalists or the Beat Generation, the American intellectual scene or the avant-garde, without including women. Lacking a coherent and orderly tradition, what literary historians call "a definitive, unmistakable, and powerful heritage,"[21] women writers continued to be left in obscurity, while feminist scholars continued to wonder why they had been forgotten. I have written this work to establish that heritage.

Throughout the book, I have investigated what a literary "peer" might mean with regard to American women's writing. A peer is not a clone. Reading women's literature sympathetically and fairly is not simply a matter of being a woman reader. Nor must the reader exactly reproduce the writer's nationality, race, religion, ethnicity, region, sexual orientation, or age, in order to be a suitable respondent. A literary peer is a reader who is willing to understand the codes and contexts of literary writing. But in addition, I believe, a peer must be willing to assume the responsibility of judging. A peer is not restricted to explaining and admiring; quite the contrary. Some feminists argue against evaluating or comparing works by women writers, and some claim that to judge and rank women's literature is a betrayal of sisterhood, because all critical judgments are subjective and biased by cultural norms. Yet we need literary history, critical judgments, even a literary canon, as a necessary step toward doing the fullest justice to women's writing. Only in this way can we ensure its inclusion in our national literary heritage and ensure that women writers now and in the future may speak freely on their own terms. In the twenty-first century, no history of American literature that excludes their voices can be complete.

Acknowledgments

Charlotte Perkins Gilman wrote in her autobiography, "To California, in its natural features, I owe much. Its calm sublimity of contour, richness of color, profusion of flowers, fruit, and foliage, and the steady peace of its climate were meat and drink to me." I began the intensive reading for this book at the Munger Research Center at the Huntington Library in San Marino, California, a magnificent library in a beautiful garden with one of the world's great collections of pre-twentieth-century American literature. My first thanks go to Director Roy Ritchie and the staff at the Huntington, especially Susie Krasnoo. Michael Johnson, Sarah Hanley, Malcolm Rohrbaugh, Elaine Tyler May, and Laura Stevens were fellow Fellows who made many useful suggestions and always provided stimulating companionship. The early stages of my research and travel to other libraries in the United States were funded by an Andrew W. Mellon Foundation Emeritus Fellowship; I am grateful to the administration at Princeton University for nominating me for this award and to the Mellon Foundation for granting it, and providing support for initial research assistance from Princeton graduate students Briallen Hopper and Jules Hurtado and Harvard graduate student Adena Spingarn.

My thanks to Elaine Markson in New York and Derek Johns in London, literary agents and enthusiastic supporters who believed that I could finish this book, and my brilliant editors: LuAnn Walther, her assistants Gautam Hans and Florence Lui, and, above all, the eagle-eyed Holly Webber at Knopf; and Lennie Goodings and her able team at Little, Brown.

As ever, I owe the deepest thanks to the support, advice, and expertise of my husband, English Showalter: "If ever wife was happy in a man, / Compare with me, ye women, if you can."

Notes

In order to keep notes to a minimum, I have not
provided them in cases where the text makes the source
clear or a work exists in many different editions.

Introduction

1. For an examination of the legal issues in the real case and Glaspell's interpretation of them, see Patricia L. Bryan, "Stories in Fiction and in Fact: Susan Glaspell's *A Jury of Her Peers* and the 1901 Murder Trial of Margaret Hossack," *Stanford Law Review* 49 (July 1997): 1293–1364; and for a fascinating study of the Hossack murder and trial, see Patricia L. Bryan and Thomas Wolf, *Midnight Assassin: A Murder in America's Heartland* (Iowa City: University of Iowa Press, 2005).

2. Moses Coit Tyler, *A History of American Literature,* vol. 1: 1607–1676 (New York: G. P. Putnam's Sons, 1879).

3. William P. Trent et al., eds., *The Cambridge History of American Literature* (New York: Macmillan, 1917–18), "Preface" and 285. "Mrs. Carl Van Doren" was the brilliant Irita Van Doren, who by the 1930s was the editor for the Sunday "Books" supplement of the *New York Herald Tribune.*

4. See Carolyn L. Karcher, *The First Woman in the Republic: A Cultural Biography of Lydia Maria Child* (Durham, N.C.: Duke University Press, 1994), 608; Cheryl E. Torsney, *Constance Fenimore Woolson: The Grief of Artistry* (Athens: University of Georgia Press, 1989), 7; Faith Jaycox, "Regeneration through Liberation: Mary Austin's 'The Walking Woman' and Western Narrative Formula," *Legacy* 6 (1989): 5–12; Robert Penn Warren, "Elizabeth Madox Roberts: Life Is from Within," *Saturday Review,* March 9, 1963.

5. See, for example, Matthew Hutson, "Unnatural Selection," *Psychology Today,* March / April 2007.

6. For example, see David Perkins, *Is Literary History Possible?* (Baltimore: Johns Hopkins University Press, 1992).

7. Emory Elliott, editor of *The Columbia Literary History of the United States* (1988), in a letter to Annette Kolodny, quoted in Kolodny, "The Integrity of Memory: Creating a New Literary History of the United States," *American Literature* 5 (May 1985): 274.

8. Susan K. Harris, " 'But Is It Any Good?' Evaluating Nineteenth-Century American Women's Fiction," in *The (Other) American Traditions: Nineteenth-Century Women Writers,* ed. Joyce W. Warren (New Brunswick, N.J.: Rutgers University Press, 1993), 277.

9. "Borrowed Light," in Fanny Fern, *Ruth Hall and Other Writings,* ed. Joyce W. Warren (New Brunswick: Rutgers University Press, 1986), 252.

10. Elaine Showalter, *A Literature of Their Own: British Women Novelists from Brontë to Lessing* (1977), rev. ed. (Princeton, N.J.: Princeton University Press, 1999), 13, 36.

11. Perkins, *Is Literary History Possible?,* 17.

1. A New Literature Springs Up in the New World

1. Joseph R. McElrath, Jr., and Allan P. Robb, eds., *The Complete Works of Anne Bradstreet* (Boston: Twayne, 1981), xii–xiii.
2. Adrienne Rich, "The Tensions of Anne Bradstreet" (1966), in *Lies, Secrets and Silence: Selected Prose, 1966–1978* (New York: Norton, 1979), 32. See also Jeannine Hensley, ed., *The Works of Anne Bradstreet* (Cambridge, Mass.: Harvard University Press, 1967); Elizabeth Wade, *Anne Bradstreet: The Tenth Muse* (New York and Oxford: Oxford University Press, 1971); Pattie Cowell, *Women Poets in Pre-revolutionary America, 1650–1775: An Anthology* (Troy, N.Y.: Whitson Publishing Company, 1981); and Charlotte Gordon, *Mistress Bradstreet: The Untold Life of America's First Poet* (New York: Little, Brown, 2005).
3. Gordon, *Mistress Bradstreet*, 194–95.
4. Ibid., 251, 253.
5. Kathryn Zabelle Derounian-Stodola, "Introduction" to *Women's Indian Captivity Narratives* (New York: Penguin, 1998), 5.
6. Ibid.
7. Because the Puritans used a different calendar, this date is incorrect; it was 1676.
8. Laurel Thatcher Ulrich, *Good Wives: Image and Reality in the Lives of Women in Northern New England, 1650–1750* (New York: Vintage, 1991), 229.
9. Ibid., 228.
10. Ibid., 227–28.
11. Christopher Castiglia, *Bound and Determined: Captivity, Culture-Crossing, and White Womanhood from Mary Rowlandson to Patty Hearst* (Chicago: University of Chicago Press, 1996), 4, 201 n. 4, 114.

2. Revolution. Women's Rights and Women's Writing

1. Paula Bernat Bennett discusses these periodical writings in her important book *Poets in the Public Sphere: The Emancipatory Project of American Women's Poetry, 1800–1900* (Princeton, N.J.: Princeton University Press, 2003), 6–7.
2. Linda K. Kerber, *Women of the Republic: Intellect and Ideology in Revolutionary America* (Chapel Hill, N.C.: University of North Carolina Press, 1980).
3. Timothy Alden of Newark Academy in New Jersey, quoted ibid., 214.
4. Kerber, *Women of the Republic*, 278.
5. Judith Sargent Murray, "Desultory Thoughts Upon the Utility of Encouraging a Degree of Self-Complacency especially in Female Bosoms," in *Selected Writings of Judith Sargent Murray*, ed. Sharon M. Harris (New York and Oxford: Oxford University Press, 1995), 44–48.
6. Sharon M. Harris, *American Women Writers to 1800* (New York and Oxford: Oxford University Press, 1996), 241.
7. Kate Davies, "Revolutionary Correspondence: Reading Catharine Macaulay and Mercy Otis Warren," *Women's Writing* 13 (March 2006): 84. On Mercy Otis Warren, see Jeffrey Richards, *Mercy Otis Warren* (New York: Twayne, 1995); Rosemarie Zagarri, *A Woman's Dilemma: Mercy Otis Warren and the American Revolution* (New York: Harlan Davison, 1995); and Kate Davies, *Catharine Macaulay and Mercy Otis Warren: The Revolutionary Atlantic and the Politics of Gender* (Oxford: Oxford University Press, 2005).
8. Quoted in Davies, "Revolutionary Correspondence," 75–76.
9. Harris, *American Women Writers to 1800*, 243.

10. "Observations on the Tragedies of Mrs. Warren," in Harris, *American Women Writers to 1800,* 377–80.

11. See Amelia Howe Kritzer, *Plays by Early American Women, 1775–1850* (Ann Arbor: University of Michigan Press, 1995), 6–7.

12. Cookie Roberts, *Founding Mothers* (New York: Perennial, 2005), 253.

13. Henry Louis Gates, Jr., "Foreword: In Her Own Write," *Schomburg Library of Nineteenth-Century Black Women Writers* (New York and Oxford: Oxford University Press, 1988), x.

14. Henry Louis Gates, Jr., *The Trials of Phillis Wheatley* (New York: Perseus Books, 2003), 19–20.

15. Ibid., 22.

16. Ibid., 5.

17. *London Morning Post,* September 13, 1773.

18. See Gates, *The Trials of Phillis Wheatley,* 71–86.

19. Ibid., 71, 89–90.

20. June Jordan, "The Difficult Miracle of Black Poetry in America," *Massachusetts Review* 27 (Summer 1986): 262.

21. *The Gleaner,* (Boston: I. Thomas and E. T. Andrews, 1798), 3:189.

22. See Cathy N. Davidson, *Revolution and the Word: The Rise of the Novel in America* (New York: Oxford University Press, 1986), 30–31. After William Godwin's 1797 biography of his wife, which revealed her sexual relationships, Wollstonecraft ceased to be accepted as a respectable model for American women.

23. April 22, 1796, in *Extracts from the Journal of Elizabeth Drinker,* ed. Henry D. Biddle (Philadelphia: J. B. Lippincott, 1889), 285.

24. *Weekly Museum,* 1795; quoted in Bennett, *Poets in the Public Sphere,* 44.

25. *The Gleaner,* 1:15.

26. *The Gleaner,* 88:711.

27. *The Gleaner,* 40:327.

28. *The Gleaner,* 96:763.

29. Amelia Howe Kritzer, "Introduction" to *Plays by Early American Women, 1775–1850* (Ann Arbor: University of Michigan Press, 1995), 15.

30. See Sharon M. Harris, "Introduction" to *Selected Writings of Judith Sargent Murray* (New York and Oxford: Oxford University Press, 1995), xxxiii.

31. Elias Nason, *Memoir of Mrs. Susanna Rowson* (Albany: Joel Mansell, 1870), chap. VII.

32. Cathy N. Davidson, "Introduction" to Susanna Rowson, *Charlotte Temple* (New York and Oxford: Oxford University Press, 1986), xi–xii.

33. Ibid., xvii.

34. Susanna Rowson, *Exercises in History, Chronology, and Biography* (Boston: Richardson and Lord, 1822).

35. "A Lady of Massachusetts" [Hannah Foster], *The Boarding School* (Boston: J. P. Peaslee, 1798).

36. Quoted in Davidson, *Revolution and the Word,* 39.

3. Their Native Land

1. Sarah J. Hale, "Introduction" to *Woman's Record* (New York: Harper & Brothers, 1855).

2. John Greenleaf Whittier, "Biographical Introduction" to *Letters of Lydia Maria Child,* ed. H. W. Sewall (Boston: Houghton Mifflin, 1830).

3. Catharine Maria Sedgwick, *Hope Leslie*, ed. Mary Kelley (New Brunswick, N.J.: Rutgers University Press, 1987), 6.

4. E. C. Embury, "Essay on American Literature," *The Ladies' Companion* 9 (1838): 83–85.

5. Carolyn L. Karcher, *The First Woman in the Republic: A Cultural Biography of Lydia Maria Child* (Durham, N.C.: Duke University Press, 1994), xi; and Edgar Allan Poe, "The Literati of New York," quoted in Sandra Zagarell, "Introduction" to Caroline Kirkland, *A New Home, Who'll Follow?* (New Brunswick, N.J.: Rutgers University Press, 1990), xi.

6. Patricia Oker, *Our Sister Editors: Sarah J. Hale and the Tradition of Nineteenth-Century American Women Editors* (Athens: University of Georgia Press, 1995), 6.

7. Karcher, *The First Woman*, 60.

8. Ibid., 66.

9. Sarah J. Hale, *Ladies' Magazine*, March 1829, 143, in Oker, *Our Sister Editors*, 140.

10. Aleta Feinsod Cane and Susan Alves, eds., *American Women Writers and the Periodical, 1837–1916* (Iowa City: University of Iowa Press, 2001), 3.

11. Ann Stephens, *Portland Magazine*, October 1834, 1, in Oker, *Our Sister Editors*, 18.

12. Ann Stephens, "Women of Genius," *Ladies' Companion* 11 (1839): 89–90.

13. Melissa J. Homestead, "Behind the Veil? Catharine Sedgwick and Anonymous Publication," in *Catharine Maria Sedgwick: Critical Perspectives*, ed. Lucinda Damon-Bach and Victoria Clements (Boston: Northeastern University Press, 2003), 27.

14. Mary E. Dewey, ed., *Life and Letters of Catharine M. Sedgwick* (New York: Harper & Brothers, 1872), 150.

15. Cooper's first novel, *Precaution*, published in 1820, had also been modeled on Austen.

16. Catharine M. Sedgwick, *A New-England Tale, and Miscellanies* (New York: G. P. Putnam, 1852), 27, 62, 28.

17. See Ole Munch-Pedersen, "Crazy Jane: A Cycle of Popular Literature," *Eire-Ireland* 14 (1979): 56–73; and Elaine Showalter, *The Female Malady* (New York: Pantheon, 1985), 11–14.

18. Catharine M. Sedgwick, *Redwood: A Tale* (New York: E. Bliss and A. White, 1824), 179; *The Linwoods, or, "Sixty Years Since" in America* (New York: Harper & Brothers, 1935), 87.

19. Alexander Cowie, *The Rise of the American Novel* (New York: The American Book Company, 1948), 205.

20. Catharine M. Sedgwick, *Hope Leslie*, ed. Carolyn Karcher (New York: Penguin, 1998), 3.

21. Karcher, *The First Woman*, 35.

22. Cowie, *Rise of the American Novel*, 205.

23. *North American Review*, April 1828, 403–20.

24. Mary Kelley, *The Power of Her Sympathy: The Autobiography and Journal of Catharine Maria Sedgwick* (Boston: Massachusetts Historical Society, 1993), 286.

25. Kelley, *Power of Her Sympathy*, 122, 123, 127.

26. Catharine M. Sedgwick, "Cacoethes Scribendi," in *Tales and Sketches* (New York: Carey, Lea and Blanchard, 1835), 165–81.

27. Susan S. Williams, *Reclaiming Authorship: Literary Women in America, 1850–1900* (Philadelphia: University of Pennsylvania Press, 2006), 23–24.

28. See Karen Woods Weierman, "A Slave Story," in Damon-Bach and Clements, *Catharine Maria Sedgwck*, 133.

29. Ibid.

30. Dewey, *Life and Letters*, 249–50.

31. Sedgwick, *The Linwoods*, 271.

32. Equivalent to about $1,500,000 today, as measured by the consumer price index, or $13,700,000 as measured by the unskilled wage, according to http://www .measuringworth.com.

33. Karcher, *The First Woman*, 13.

34. Lydia Maria Child, *Selected Letters, 1817–1880*, ed. Milton Meltzer, Francine Krasno, and Patricia G. Holland (Amherst: University of Massachusetts Press, 1982), 506.

35. Karcher, *The First Woman*, xiii.

36. Ibid., 1.

37. Ibid., xiii, 16–17.

38. Cowie, *Rise of the American Novel*, 178.

39. [John Gorham Palfrey], *North American Review*, April 1821, 466–88.

40. Karcher, *The First Woman*, 20–21.

41. Ibid., 101.

42. Ibid., 321, 324.

43. Ibid., 35.

44. Lydia Maria Child, "Concerning Women," *Independent*, July 15, 1869, quoted ibid., 22.

45. Lydia Maria Child, *Hobomok*, ed. Carolyn L. Karcher (New Brunswick, N.J.: Rutgers University Press, 1986), 6.

46. Lydia Maria Child, *The First Settlers of New-England, or Conquest of the Pequods, Narragansets and Pokanokets: As Related by a Mother to Her Children and Designed for the Instruction of Youth* (Boston: Munroe and Francis, 1829), 13–14.

47. Karcher, *The First Woman*, 27.

48. See Helen Gray Cone, "Women in American Literature," *Century* 40 (1890): 923.

49. Karcher, *The First Woman*, 136.

50. Ibid., 473.

51. See Laura L. Mielke, "Sentiment and Space in Lydia Maria Child's Native American Writings, 1824–1870," *Legacy* 21 (2004): 172–92.

52. Lydia Maria Child, "To Charles Sumner," in *Selected Letters*, 493–97.

53. Karcher, *The First Woman*, 507.

54. Elizabeth Stuart Phelps, *Chapters from a Life* (Boston: Houghton Mifflin, 1896), 182.

55. Caroline Kirkland to John S. Hart, January 18, 1851, Cornell University Library, quoted in Zagarell, "Introduction," xv.

56. "Mrs. Mary Clavers" [Caroline Kirkland], *A New Home—Who'll Follow?* (New York: C. S. Francis, 1840), 194, 175.

57. Poe, "The Literati of New York," quoted in Zagarell, "Introduction," xi.

58. Caroline Kirkland to Rufus Griswold, January 21, 1843, Detroit Public Library, quoted in Zagarell, "Introduction," xvii.

59. Malcolm Bradbury and Richard Ruland, *From Puritanism to Postmodernism: A History of American Literature* (New York: Penguin, 1992), 65.

4. Finding a Form

1. Nathaniel Hawthorne, "A Select Party," in *Mosses from an Old Manse*, Centenary Edition, ed. William Charvat et al. (Columbus: Ohio State University Press, 1974), 66.

2. Margaret Fuller, *Woman in the Nineteenth Century* (London: H. G. Clarke, 1845).

3. Belle Gale Chevigny, *The Woman and the Myth: Margaret Fuller's Life and Writings* (Old Westbury, N.Y.: The Feminist Press, 1976), 63.
4. Jeffrey Steele, ed., *The Essential Margaret Fuller* (New Brunswick, N.J.: Rutgers University Press, 1992), 347.
5. Ibid., xxv.
6. Chevigny, *The Woman and the Myth*, 43–44.
7. Ibid., 57.
8. Alexander E. Jones, "Margaret Fuller's Attempt to Write Fiction," *Boston Public Library Quarterly* 6 (1954): 67–73.
9. Robert N. Hudspeth, ed., *The Letters of Margaret Fuller* (Ithaca, N.Y.: Cornell University Press, 1984), 3:199 n. 4. My discussion of Fuller here draws on my comments in "Miranda's Story," in *Sister's Choice: Tradition and Change in American Women's Writing* (Oxford: Clarendon Press, 1995), 25–32.
10. Chevigny, *The Woman and the Myth*, 279.
11. Margaret Fuller Ossoli, *At Home and Abroad*, ed. Arthur B. Fuller (New York: The Tribune Association, 1869), 420.
12. See Larry J. Reynolds and Susan Belasco Smith, "Introduction" to Margaret Fuller, *These Sad But Glorious Days: Dispatches from Europe, 1846–1850* (New Haven, Conn.: Yale University Press), 1991.
13. Cynthia J. Davis, "What 'Speaks in Us': Margaret Fuller, Woman's Rights, and Human Nature," in *Margaret Fuller's Cultural Critique: Her Age and Legacy*, ed. Fritz Fleischmann (New York: Peter Lang, 2000), 43.
14. Nina Baym, "The Rise of the Woman Author," in *Columbia Literary History of the United States*, ed. Emory Elliott (New York: Columbia University Press, 1988), 297.
15. Paula Bennett, "Introduction" to *Nineteenth-Century American Women Poets: An Anthology* (Oxford: Blackwell, 1998), xxxv.
16. Cheryl Walker, *The Nightingale's Burden: Women Poets and American Culture Before 1900* (Bloomington: Indiana University Press, 1982), xxvi.
17. Edgar Allan Poe, "Mrs. Sigourney—Mrs. Gould—Mrs. Ellet," *Southern Literary Messenger*, December 1835, 112.
18. William Michael Rossetti, *The Poetical Works of Felicia Hemans* (London, 1873), xxvii; and Letitia Landon, "Stanzas on the Death of Mrs. Hemans," both quoted in Isobel Armstrong, *Victorian Poetry: Poetry, Aesthetics, Politics* (London: Routledge, 1996).
19. Thomas Wortham, "William Cullen Bryant and the Fireside Poets," in *Columbia Literary History of the United States*, 279.
20. Bennett, "Introduction," xxxvi.
21. Sarah J. Hale, *Ladies Magazine*, March 1829, 143.
22. Armstrong, *Victorian Poetry*, 324.
23. Quoted in Walker, *The Nightingale's Burden*, xxxv.
24. For details about some of these relationships, see the essays in Shirley Marchalonis, ed., *Patrons and Protégées: Gender, Friendship, and Writing in Nineteenth-Century America* (New Brunswick, N.J.: Rutgers University Press, 1988).
25. Rufus Wilmot Griswold, *The Female Poets of America* (Philadelphia: Carey and Hart, 1849), 7.
26. Quoted ibid., 372.
27. See Joanne Dobson, "Sex, Wit, and Sentiment: Frances Osgood and the Poetry of Love," *American Literature* 65 (December 1993): 631–48.
28. Bennett, *Nineteenth-Century America Women Poets*, 24.

29. Lydia H. Sigourney, *Letters of Life* (New York: D. Appleton, 1867), 176.

30. On Mrs. Sigourney, see Patricia Crain, "Lydia Huntley Sigourney," in *Encyclopedia of American Poetry: The Nineteenth Century,* ed. Eric L. Haralson (Chicago and London: Fitzroy Dearborn Publishers, 1998), 381–84.

31. Sigourney, *Letters of Life,* 27, 57, 268, 40.

32. Ann Douglas Wood, "Mrs. Sigourney and the Sensibility of the Inner Space," *New England Quarterly* 45 (June 1972): 166.

33. David Bonnell Green, "William Wordsworth and Lydia Huntley Sigourney," *New England Quarterly* 37 (December 1964): 527–31.

34. Gordon S. Haight, *Mrs. Sigourney: The Sweet Singer of Hartford* (New Haven, Conn.: Yale University Press, 1930), 65, 58.

35. Sigourney, *Letters of Life,* 359–69.

36. Nina Baym, *Feminism and American Literary History: Essays* (New Brunswick, N.J.: Rutgers University Press, 1992), 59.

37. Sigourney, *Letters of Life,* 237.

38. Ibid., 327.

39. Quoted in Eric Wollencott Barnes, *The Lady of Fashion: The Life and the Theatre of Anna Cora Mowatt* (New York: Scribner's, 1954), 111–12.

40. In the 1990s, there were two productions, one in New York Off-Off Broadway and one at the American University in Washington, D.C.

41. Anna Cora Mowatt, *Autobiography of an Actress; or, Eight Years on the Stage* (Boston: Ticknor, Reed, and Fields, 1853), 216.

42. Helen Gray Cone, "Woman in American Literature," *Century* 40 (1890): 922.

5. Masterpieces and Mass Markets

1. Fred Lewis Pattee, *The Feminine Fifties* (New York: D. Appleton-Century Company, 1940), viii, 51, 67.

2. F. O. Matthiessen, *The American Renaissance* (New York and London: Oxford University Press, 1941), vii, ix.

3. Ibid., xi.

4. David S. Reynolds, *Beneath the American Renaissance: The Subversive Imagination in the Age of Emerson and Melville* (New York: Knopf, 1988), 387.

5. Creamer was in her fifties when she wrote her first novel. She went on to publish three other novels about women's rights. See Nina Baym, "Introduction" to *Delia's Doctors; or, A Glance Behind the Scenes* (Urbana and Chicago: University of Illinois Press, 2003).

6. Michael Davitt Bell, "Women's Fiction and the Literary Marketplace," in *Cambridge History of American Literature* (New York: Cambridge University Press, 1995), 2:76.

7. Richard Ruland and Malcolm Bradbury, *From Puritanism to Postmodernism: A History of American Literature* (New York: Penguin, 1991), 368.

8. Pattee, *The Feminine Fifties,* 38.

9. Joyce W. Warren, "Subversion Versus Celebration: The Aborted Friendship of Fanny Fern and Walt Whitman," in *Patrons and Protégés: Gender, Friendship, and Writing in Nineteenth-Century America,* ed. Shirley Marchalonis (New Brunswick, N.J.: Rutgers University Press, 1988), 65.

10. Ibid., 79–85.

11. *Putnam's Monthly: A Magazine of American Literature, Science, and Art,* February 1853.

12. Frances M. Whitcher, *The Widow Bedott Papers* (New York: J. C. Derby, 1856), 29.

13. Paula Bernat Bennett, "Phoebe Cary," in *Nineteenth-Century American Women Poets: An Anthology* (Oxford: Blackwell, 1998), 95.

14. Julia Ward Howe, *Reminiscences, 1819–1899* (Boston: Houghton Mifflin, 1988), 47–48.

15. Ibid., 47–49.

16. Mary H. Grant, *Private Woman, Public Person: An Account of the Life of Julia Ward Howe* (Brooklyn, N.Y.: Carlson Publications, 1994), 33.

17. Anne E. Boyd, *Writing for Immortality: Women Writers and the Emergence of High Literary Culture in America* (Baltimore: Johns Hopkins University Press, 2004), 27.

18. Gary Williams, *Hungry Heart: The Literary Emergence of Julia Ward Howe* (Amherst: University of Massachusetts Press, 1999), 229n.

19. Ibid., 75.

20. It survives in manuscript fragments at Harvard, and was edited by Gary Williams: *The Hermaphrodite* (Lincoln: University of Nebraska Press, 2005).

21. Valarie H. Ziegler, *Diva Julia: The Public Romance and Private Agony of Julia Ward Howe* (New York: Trinity, 2003), 186 n. 56.

22. See James D. Wallace, "Hawthorne and the Scribbling Women Reconsidered," *American Literature* 62 (1990): 218.

23. Williams, *Hungry Heart*, 136.

24. Howe, *Reminiscences*, 436.

25. Williams, *Hungry Heart*, 156.

26. Wallace, "Hawthorne and the Scribbling Women Reconsidered," 218.

27. Grant, *Private Woman*, 110.

28. Williams, *Hungry Heart*, 175.

29. Boyd, *Writing for Immortality*, 30.

30. *North American Review*, April 1857, 567–68.

31. Charlotte Forten [Grimke], *Journal*, ed. Brenda Stevenson, Schomburg Library, (New York and Oxford: Oxford University Press, 1988), 220.

32. Judith Fetterley, ed., *Provisions: A Reader from 19th-Century American Women* (Bloomington: Indiana University Press, 1985), 262.

33. Some critics have read the story as racist; see ibid., 267. I think the meanings are much more complex.

34. Alfred Bendixen, "Introduction" to Harriet Prescott Spofford, *The Amber Gods and Other Stories* (New Brunswick, N.J.: Rutgers University Press, 1989), x.

35. James H. Matlack, "The Literary Career of Elizabeth Barstow Stoddard" (Ph.D. diss., Yale University, 1968), 560.

36. Sherwood Bonner, *Like unto Like* (1878), with "Introduction" by Jane Turner Censer (Columbia: University of South Carolina Press, 1997), 52.

37. *Putnam's Monthly*, October 1854, in Nina Baym, *Novels, Readers, and Reviewers: Responses to Fiction in Antebellum America* (Ithaca, N.Y.: Cornell University Press, 1984), 31–32.

38. Bell, "Women's Fiction and the Literary Marketplace," 77.

39. Reynolds, *Beneath the American Renaissance;* Lawrence Buell says that only 26 percent of novels before the war were written by women in New England. See Buell, *New England Literary Culture: From Revolution Through Renaissance* (Cambridge: Cambridge University Press, 1986), 377.

40. Nathaniel Hawthorne, *The Centenary Edition of the Works of Nathaniel*

Hawthorne, ed. William Charvat et al. (Columbus: Ohio State University Press, 1987), 17:161.

41. Nina Baym, "Women's Novels and Women's Minds: An Unsentimental View of Nineteenth-Century American Women's Fiction," *Novel* 31 (Summer 1998): 335–36.

42. Fetterley, *Provisions,* 25.

43. Joanne Dobson, "Reclaiming Sentimental Literature," *American Literature* 69 (June 1997): 266.

44. Nina Baym, *Woman's Fiction: A Guide to Novels By and About Women in America, 1820–1870,* 2nd ed. (Urbana: University of Illinois Press, 1993), 11, 19, 49.

45. Jane Tompkins, *Sensational Designs: The Cultural Work of American Fiction, 1790–1860* (New York and Oxford: Oxford University Press, 1985), 124–25.

46. For example, see Rosemary Garland Thompson, "Crippled Girls and Lame Old Women: Sentimental Spectacles of Sympathy in Nineteenth-Century American Women's Writing," in *Nineteenth-Century American Women Writers: A Critical Reader,* ed. Karen Kilcup (Oxford: Blackwell, 1998), 128–45.

47. Thomas H. Johnson, ed., *The Letters of Emily Dickinson* (Cambridge, Mass.: Belknap Press, 1960), 1:82.

48. Elaine Showalter, *Sister's Choice: Tradition and Change in American Women's Writing* (Oxford: Clarendon Press, 1991), 148–49.

49. Matlack, "The Literary Career of Elizabeth Barstow Stoddard," 207.

50. Joan Hedrick, *Harriet Beecher Stowe: A Life* (New York and Oxford: Oxford University Press, 1995), 195.

51. Judith A. Roman, *Annie Adams Fields: The Spirit of Charles Street* (Bloomington: Indiana University Press, 1990), 51.

52. Grace Greenwood, "Heart Histories," in *Greenwood Leaves* (Boston: Ticknor, Reed, and Fields, 1852), 60.

53. Austin Phelps, "Memorial," in *The Last Leaf from Sunny Side* (Boston: Philips, Sampson, 1853), 60.

54. Elizabeth Stuart Phelps, *Chapters from a Life* (Boston: Houghton Mifflin, 1896), 12.

55. Boyd, *Writing for Immortality,* 28.

56. Pattee, *The Feminine Fifties,* 53.

57. John Seelye, *Jane Eyre's American Daughters* (Newark: University of Delaware Press, 2005), 28.

58. Forten [Grimke], *Journal,* 220.

59. *Louisa May Alcott: Her Life, Letters, and Journals,* ed. Ednah D. Cheney (Boston: Roberts Brothers, 1889; rpt. New York: Gramercy Books, 1995), 65.

60. For the definitive critical account of this phenomenon, see Sandra M. Gilbert and Susan Gubar, *The Madwoman in the Attic: The Woman Writer and the Nineteenth-Century Literary Imagination* (New Haven, Conn.: Yale University Press, 1979).

61. Maria McIntosh, *Woman in America: Her Work and Her Reward* (New York: D. Appleton & Co., 1850), 136–37.

62. On Blake, see Grace Farrell, *Lillie Devereux Blake: Retracing the Erased* (Amherst: University of Massachusetts Press, 2003).

63. Reynolds, *Beneath the American Renaissance,* 399.

64. Mary Clemmer Ames, *A Memorial of Alice and Phoebe Cary* (New York: Hurd and Houghton, 1873), 19.

65. Reynolds, *Beneath the American Renaissance,* 393.

66. Ibid., 392.

67. Laura Curtis Bullard, *Christine; or, Woman's Trials and Triumphs* (New York: DeWitt and Davenport, 1856), 27.

68. Marion Harland [Mary Virginia Hawes Terhune], *Marion Harland's Autobiography: The Story of a Long Life* (New York: Harper & Brothers, 1910), 485. On Terhune, see Elizabeth Moss, *Domestic Novelists in the Old South: Defenders of Southern Culture* (Baton Rouge: Louisiana State University Press, 1992).

69. See Mary Kelley, *Private Woman, Public Stage* (New York and Oxford: Oxford University Press, 1984), 133.

70. Harland [Terhune], "How 'Alone' Came to Be," in *Marion Harland's Autobiography,* chap. 23.

71. Terhune, quoted by Kate Sanborn, *Our Famous Women* (Hartford, Conn.: A. D. Worthington and Co., 1886), 628.

72. Harland, *Alone* (Richmond, Va.: A. Morris, 1854), 17, 18.

73. Ibid., 116.

74. Harland [Terhune], *Marion Harland's Autobiography,* 452.

75. Terhune, *Moss-side* (New York: Derby and Jackson, 1857), 179.

76. Ibid., 334.

77. "Mary Virginia Terhune," *The New York Times,* June 2, 1922, 24.

78. Kelley, *Private Woman, Public Stage,* 280.

79. Harland [Terhune], *Marion Harland's Autobiography,* 285; William Perry Fidler, *Augusta Evans Wilson, 1835–1909* (Tuscaloosa: University of Alabama Press, 1951), 8.

80. Augusta Jane Evans, letter of July 30, 1860, in Elizabeth Fox-Genovese, "Introduction" to *Beulah* (Baton Rouge: Louisiana State University Press, 1992), xxi.

81. Anne Goodwyn Jones, *Tomorrow Is Another Day: The Woman Writer in the South, 1859–1936* (Baton Rouge: Louisiana State University Press, 1981), 70.

82. Naomi Z. Sofer, *Making the "America of Art": Cultural Nationalism and Nineteenth-Century Women Writers* (Columbus: Ohio State University Press, 2005), 75.

83. On Evans and *Beulah,* see Baym, *Woman's Fiction,* 276–96; Jones, *Tomorrow Is Another Day,* 51–92; and Moss, *Domestic Novelists of the Old South.*

84. Fidler, *Augusta Evans Wilson,* 48, 54.

85. Evans, *Beulah,* 325, 331.

86. Anna B. Warner, *Susan Warner* (New York: Putnam's, 1909), 264.

87. Ibid.

88. Pattee, *The Feminine Fifties,* 57.

89. Helen Hunt Jackson to Henry Root, January 1852, quoted in Kate Philips, *Helen Hunt Jackson: A Literary Life* (Berkeley: University of California Press, 2003), 71.

90. Tompkins, *Sensational Designs,* 593.

91. See Kelley, *Private Woman,* 219.

92. Library of Congress, January 19, 1894, in Amy E. Hodick, "E.D.E.N. Southworth," quoted in *Nineteenth-Century American Women Writers: A Bio-Bibliographical Critical Sourcebook,* ed. Denise Knight (Westport, Conn.: Greenwood Press, 1997), 369.

93. Lyde Cullen Sizer, *The Political Work of Northern Women Writers and the Civil War, 1850–1872* (Chapel Hill: University of North Carolina Press, 2000), 52.

94. E.D.E.N. Southworth, *The Deserted Wife* (Philadelphia: T. B. Peterson, 1855), 90, 21.

95. Robert Bonner, 22 October 1856, in Joanne Dobson, introduction to *The Hidden Hand* (New Brunswick, N.J.: Rutgers University Press, 1988), xvi.

96. Moss, *Domestic Novelists of the Old South*, 17.

97. Fanny Fern, *New York Ledger*, November 17, 1860, in Joyce Warren, *Fanny Fern: An Independent Woman* (New Brunswick, N.J.: Rutgers University Press, 1992), 1.

98. Warren, *Fanny Fern*, 93.

99. Fanny Fern, *A New Story Book*, 8, quoted ibid., 102–3.

100. Elizabeth Stoddard, *Daily Alta*, October 1854; Gail Hamilton, *A New Atmosphere* (Boston: Ticknor and Fields, 1865), 53, quoted in the groundbreaking essay on Fern by Ann D.[ouglas] Wood, "The 'Scribbling Women' and Fanny Fern: Why Women Wrote," *American Quarterly* 23 (Spring 1971): 17.

101. Grace Greenwood, "Fanny Fern—Mrs. Parton," in *Eminent Women of the Age*, ed. James Parton (Hartford: S. M. Bettes, 1868), 74.

102. Linda Huf, *A Portrait of the Artist as a Young Woman* (New York: Frederick Ungar, 1983), 26, 31.

103. Sizer, *Political Work of Northern Women Writers*, 59.

104. Susan Belasco Smith, "Introduction" to Fanny Fern, *Ruth Hall* (New York: Penguin, 1997), xxxviii.

105. Hawthorne to Ticknor, April 24, 1854, *Centenary Edition*, 18:53.

106. Wood, "The 'Scribbling Women,' "24.

107. *New York Ledger*, December 1857, in Warren, *Fanny Fern*, 306.

6. Slavery, Race, and Women's Writing

1. Charles Frederick Briggs, "Uncle Tomitudes," *Putnam's*, January 1853, 98.

2. See, for example, Charles Dudley Warner, *Atlantic Monthly*, July 1896.

3. Helen Gray Cone, "Woman in American Literature," *Century* 40 (October 1890).

4. Henry Louis Gates, Jr., "Introduction" to *The Annotated Uncle Tom's Cabin* (New York: Norton, 2006), xi.

5. Harriet Beecher Stowe to Eliza Cabot Follen, December 16, 1852, in *Uncle Tom's Cabin: Norton Critical Edition* (New York: Norton, 1994), 413–14.

6. Joan Hedrick, *Harriet Beecher Stowe: A Life* (New York and Oxford: Oxford University Press, 1994), 119.

7. Ibid., 138.

8. Ibid., 139.

9. Mary Kelley, *Private Woman, Public Stage* (New York and Oxford: Oxford University Press, 1984), 249.

10. Bruce Kirkham, *The Building of Uncle Tom's Cabin* (Knoxville: University of Tennessee Press, 1977), 66–67.

11. Edmund Wilson, *Patriotic Gore: Studies in the Literature of the American Civil War* (New York: Norton, 1994), 5, 6.

12. Ellen Moers, *Literary Women* (New York: Doubleday, 1976), 36–40.

13. Grace King, *Memories of a Southern Woman of Letters* (New York: Macmillan, 1932), 76–78.

14. *Antifanaticism* (1853), by Martha Haines Butt; *Eoline* (1860), by Mrs. V. G. Cowdin; *Aunt Phillis's Cabin* (1852), by Mary H. Eastman; *The Ebony Idol* (1860), by Mrs. G. M. Flinders; *Liberia* (1853), by Sarah J. Hall; *The Planter's Northern Bride* (1854), by Caroline Lee Hentz; *The Lofty and the Lowly* (1853), by Maria Jane McIntosh; *The North and South* (1852), by Caroline E. Rush; and *The Black Gauntlet* (1860), by Mary Howard Schoolcraft.

15. Jamie Stanesa, "Caroline Lee Whiting Hentz, 1800–1856," *Legacy* 13 (1996): 135.

16. Caroline Lee Hentz, *The Planter's Northern Bride* (Philadelphia: T. B. Peterson, 1854), 104.

17. Caroline L. Karcher, *The First Woman in the Republic: A Cultural Biography of Lydia Maria Child* (Durham, N.C.: Duke University Press, 1994), 385, 387.

18. Hedrick, *Harriet Beecher Stowe*, 258.

19. Harriet Beecher Stowe, *Dred*, ed. Robert S. Levine (New York: Penguin, 2000), 198.

20. See Gail K. Smith, "Reading with the Other: Hermeneutics and the Politics of Difference in Stowe's *Dred*," *American Literature* 69 (1997): 310.

21. Hedrick, *Harriet Beecher Stowe*, 260–61.

22. *Westminster Review* 10 (October 1856): 571–73.

23. Harriet Beecher Stowe, *The Minister's Wooing* (New York: Library of America, 1982), 541, 642, 643, 566.

24. Harriet Beecher Stowe to George Eliot, April 15, 1869, in *Kindred Hands: Letters on Writing by British and American Women Authors, 1865–1935*, ed. Jennifer Cognard-Black and Elizabeth MacLeod Walls (Iowa City: University of Iowa Press, 2006), 26.

25. See Franny Nudelman, *John Brown's Body: Slavery, Violence, and the Culture of War* (Chapel Hill: University of North Carolina Press, 2004), 167.

26. For a positive view of Brown, see David S. Reynolds, *John Brown, Abolitionist* (New York: Vintage, 2006).

27. In *Frederick Douglass's Paper*, February 3, 1854; see Frances Smith Foster, ed., *A Brighter Coming Day: A Frances Ellen Watkins Harper Reader* (Old Westbury, N.Y.: Feminist Press, 1990), 57.

28. See letter to John Brown, November 25, 1859, in Foster, *A Brighter Coming Day*, 49–50; and "The Triumph of Freedom," *Anglo-African Magazine* 2 (1860): 21–23.

29. For a case from the 1890s, see Holly Jackson, "Identifying Emma Dunham Kelley: Rethinking Race and Authorship," *PMLA* 122 (May 2007): 728–41.

30. See John Blassingame, *The Slave Community: Plantation Life in the Antebellum South* (New York and Oxford: Oxford University Press, 1972).

31. See Harriet A. Jacobs, *Incidents in the Life of a Slave Girl, Written by Herself*, ed. Jean Fagan Yellin, enlarged ed. (Cambridge, Mass.: Harvard University Press, 2000); and Jean Fagan Yellin, *Harriet Jacobs: A Life* (New York: Basic Books, 2004).

32. Hedrick, *Harriet Beecher Stowe*, 248–49.

33. See Jean Fagan Yellin, "Written by Herself: Harriet Jacobs' Slave Narrative," *American Literature* 53 (November 1981): 479–86.

34. Henry Louis Gates, Jr., "Introduction" to Harriet E. Wilson, *Our Nig* (New York: Vintage Books, 1983), lii.

35. P. Gabrielle Foreman and Reginald Pitts, "Introduction" to Harriet E. Wilson, *Our Nig* (New York: Penguin, 2005), xxv.

36. Alice Walker, back cover of Vintage edition of *Our Nig*, 1983.

37. Barbara A. White, " 'Our Nig' and the She-devil: New Information About Harriet Wilson and the 'Bellmont' Family," *American Literature* 65 (March 1993): 19–52.

38. Foreman and Pitts, "Introduction" to *Our Nig*, xxiii, liii.

39. For a detailed account of the publishing history of the book, see Elaine and English Showalter, "Every Single One Matters," *London Review of Books*, June 27, 2005.

40. Hollis Robbins, *In Search of Hannah Crafts: Critical Essays on "The Bondwoman's Narrative,"* ed. Henry Louis Gates, Jr., and Hollis Robbins (New York: Basic Civitas, 2004), 74.

41. Celeste Marie Bernier and Judie Newman, *"The Bondwoman's Narrative:* Text, Paratext, Intertext, and Hypertext," *Journal of American Studies* 39 (2005): 147–65.

7. The Civil War

1. "War and Literature," *Atlantic Monthly,* June 1862.

2. In the twentieth century, in *The Unwritten War: American Writers and the Civil War* (Oxford: Oxford University Press, 1973), 328, Daniel Aaron declared that the war was "not so much unfelt as unfaced."

3. Alice Fahs, *The Imagined Civil War: Popular Literature of the North and South, 1861–1865* (Chapel Hill: University of North Carolina Press, 2001), 5.

4. Nathaniel Hawthorne to Horatio Bridge, February 13, 1862, Bowdoin College Library, quoted in James H. Matlack, "The Literary Career of Elizabeth Barstow Stoddard" (Ph.D. diss., Yale University, 1968), 218.

5. *The New York Times,* July 21, 1862, 3.

6. Fahs, *The Imagined Civil War,* 19.

7. Ibid., 20.

8. See Patricia R. Hill, "Writing Out the War: Harriet Beecher Stowe's Averted Gaze," in *Divided Houses: Gender and the Civil War,* ed. Catherine Clinton and Nina Silber (New York and Oxford: Oxford University Press, 1992), 260–82.

9. Elizabeth Young, *Disarming the Nation: Women's Writing and the American Civil War* (Chicago: University of Chicago Press, 1999), 19.

10. Mary Terhune to Virginia Eppes Dance, 1851, quoted in Elizabeth Moss, *Domestic Novelists of the Old South: Defenders of Southern Culture* (Baton Rouge: Louisiana State University Press, 1992), 150.

11. Robert J. Scholnick, *E. C. Stedman* (Boston: Twayne, 1977), 28.

12. Drew Gilpin Faust, "Altars of Sacrifice: Confederate Women and the Narratives of War," in *Divided Houses,* 171.

13. Ibid., 178.

14. Fahs, *The Imagined Civil War,* 67.

15. Faust, "Altars of Sacrifice," 175, 176.

16. *Louisa May Alcott: Her Life, Letters, and Journals,* ed. Ednah D. Cheney (Boston: Roberts Brothers, 1889; rpt. New York: Gramercy Books, 1995), 88.

17. September 1867, in Judith A. Roman, *Annie Adams Fields: The Spirit of Charles Street* (Bloomington: Indiana University Press, 1990), 54.

18. See Lyde Cullen Sizer, *The Political Work of Northern Women Writers and the Civil War, 1850–1872* (Chapel Hill: University of North Carolina Press, 2000), 219–21; and Karen Tracey, *Plots and Proposals: American Women's Fiction, 1850–1890* (Urbana and Chicago: University of Illinois Press, 2000), 132–47.

19. Fahs, *The Imagined Civil War,* 33.

20. Quoted in Aaron, *The Unwritten War,* 240.

21. Julia Ward Howe, *Reminiscences, 1819–1899* (Boston: Houghton Mifflin, 1988), 273–74.

22. Ibid., 273–75.

23. Rebecca Harding Davis, "The Civil War," in *Rebecca Harding Davis: Writing Cultural Autobiography,* ed. Janice Milner Lasseter and Sharon M. Harris (Nashville, Tenn.: Vanderbilt University Press, 2001), 73.

24. On Rebecca Harding Davis, see Jean Pfaelzer, *Parlor Radical: Rebecca Harding Davis and the Origins of American Social Realism* (Pittsburgh: University of Pittsburgh Press, 1996); and Jean Pfaelzer, ed., *A Rebecca Harding Davis Reader* (Pittsburgh: University of Pittsburgh Press, 1995).

25. Obituary for Davis in Phelps, "Stories That Stay," *Century* 8 (November 1910): 119.

26. Judith Fetterley, ed., *Provisions: A Reader from 19th-Century American Women* (Bloomington: Indiana University Press, 1985), 8.

27. For a comparison of Davis and Phelps, see Lisa A. Long, "The Postbellum Reform Writings of Rebecca Harding Davis and Elizabeth Stuart Phelps," in *The Cambridge Companion to Nineteenth-Century American Women's Writing,* ed. Dale Bauer, and Philip Gould (Cambridge: Cambridge University Press, 2001), 266, 271.

28. Lasseter and Harris, *Rebecca Harding Davis*, 5.

29. Rebecca Harding Davis to Annie Fields, in Pfaelzer, *Davis Reader,* 121.

30. See Donald Dingledine, ed., *Waiting for the Verdict* (Albany, N.Y.: NCUP, Inc., 1995).

31. *Nation,* November 21, 1867, 221–22.

32. Lasseter and Harris, *Rebecca Harding Davis,* 137.

33. Ibid., 36–52.

34. Alcott, *Her Life, Letters, and Journals,* 103.

35. Ibid., 110.

36. Elaine Showalter, "Introduction" to *Alternative Alcott* (New Brunswick, N.J.: Rutgers University Press, 1988).

37. See Young, *Disarming the Nation,* 69.

38. Ibid., 76.

39. "Frank Leslie," whose real name was Henry Carter, was an Englishman who immigrated to the United States in 1848 as an engraver and printer, and became a publishing mogul. By the 1860s, he owned papers specializing in scandals, crimes, natural disasters, and Civil War battle scenes.

40. LaSalle Corbett Pickett, in Madeline Stern, ed., *Critical Essays on Louisa May Alcott* (Boston: G. K. Hall, 1984), 42.

41. For the story of one researcher trawling old periodicals for republication profit, see Beth Rucker, "Panning for Literary Gold at the Public Library," *Washington Post,* December 27, 2005, C4.

42. Judith Fetterley, "*Little Women:* Alcott's Civil War," *Feminist Studies* 5 (Summer 1979): 369–83.

43. Joy Wittenberg, "Excerpts from the Diary of Elizabeth Oakes Smith," *Signs* 9 (1984): 537.

44. Young, *Disarming the Nation,* 95.

45. Abigail Ann Hemblin, "Louisa May Alcott and the Racial Question," *University Review* 37 (1971): 307–13.

46. This novel, *The Long Love Chase,* remained among Alcott's papers at Harvard University until it was finally published in 1998.

47. In her 2005 Pulitzer Prize–winning novel *March,* Geraldine Brooks follows Mr. March to the war and shows his horror and disillusionment. "There is union at last," he concludes, "a united states of pain." Mrs. March visits him at Blank Hospital and realizes that he has done what men "have ever done to women: march off to empty glory and hollow acclaim and let the women pick up the pieces" ([New York: Penguin, 2006], 211).

48. See Fetterley, "Alcott's Civil War."

49. Jo March's influence certainly lasted through the twentieth century. Gloria Steinem named Jo March as her sole role model; another feminist wrote that "I was sitting at a restaurant table with three other women academics of approximately my generation and our talk turned to earliest models of ideal readers. Simultaneously we all blurted out the same confessions: 'My model was Jo March.'" See Ann Romines, "Nineteenth-Century Reading and Twentieth-Century Texts: The Example of Laura Ingalls Wilder," *Legacy* 15 (1998): 23.

50. Augusta Jane Evans to L. Virginia French, in *Alabama Historical Quarterly* 3 (1941): 65–67.

51. Augusta Jane Evans to Janie Tyler, March 14, 1862, in William Perry Fidler, *Augusta Evans Wilson, 1835–1909* (Tuscaloosa: University of Alabama Press, 1951), 88.

52. Kate Phillips, *Helen Hunt Jackson: A Literary Life* (Berkeley: University of California Press, 2003), 147.

53. Ellen Weinauer and Robert McClure Smith, "Introduction: Crossing Can(n)on Street," in *American Culture, Canons, and the Case of Elizabeth Stoddard*, ed. Smith and Weinauer (Tuscaloosa: University of Alabama Press, 2003), 8; and Susan K. Harris, *Nineteenth-Century American Women's Novels: Interpretive Strategies* (Cambridge and New York: Cambridge University Press, 1990), 153.

54. Sandra A. Zagarell and Lawrence Buell, "Biographical and Critical Introduction," in Elizabeth Stoddard, *The Morgesons and Other Writings*, ed. Zagarell and Buell (Philadelphia: University of Pennsylvania Press, 1984), xi.

55. On Stoddard, see ibid.; Matlack, "The Literary Career of Elizabeth Barstow Stoddard"; and Anne E. Boyd, *Writing for Immortality: Women Writers and the Emergence of High Literary Culture in America* (Baltimore: Johns Hopkins University Press, 2004), 7.

56. Smith and Weinauer, *American Culture, Canons and the Case of Elizabeth Stoddard*, 6–7.

57. Matlack, "The Literary Career of Elizabeth Barstow Stoddard," 56.

58. Aaron, *The Unwritten War*, 151.

59. Elizabeth Stoddard, January 1856, quoted in *The Morgesons*, ed. Zagarell and Buell, 323.

60. Matlack, "The Literary Career of Elizabeth Barstow Stoddard," 114–15.

61. Bayard Taylor (1825–1878) was a poet, journalist, travel writer, and diplomat.

62. Elizabeth Stoddard, *California Daily Alta*, October 22, 1854. Fredrika Bremer was a Scandinavian novelist whose work was very popular in the United States.

63. Matlack, "The Literary Career of Elizabeth Barstow Stoddard," 372.

64. Quoted in Aaron, *The Unwritten War*, 150.

65. Ibid., 152.

66. Zagarell and Buell, "Biographical and Critical Introduction," xix.

67. Letter of June 22, 1865, in *The Morgesons*, ed. Zagarell and Buell, 337.

68. Boyd, *Writing for Immortality*, 141.

69. Ibid., 2.

70. Lawrence Buell, "Will Stoddard Endure?" in Smith and Weinauer, *American Culture, Canons, and the Case of Elizabeth Stoddard*, 265–69.

71. Matlack, "The Literary Career of Elizabeth Barstow Stoddard," 601.

72. Ibid., 470.

73. Wendy Martin, "Emily Dickinson," in *Columbia Literary History of the United States*, ed. Emory Elliott (New York: Columbia University Press, 1988), 609.

74. See Judith Farr, *The Gardens of Emily Dickinson* (Cambridge, Mass.: Harvard University Press, 2005), for a study of Dickinson's work in botany and the relationship between flowers and writing in her poetry.

75. See Paula Bennett, *Emily Dickinson: Woman Poet* (Iowa City: University of Iowa Press, 1990), 173.

76. All quotations from Dickinson's poems are to the numbered poems in R. W. Franklin, ed., *The Poems of Emily Dickinson: Reading Edition* (Cambridge, Mass.: Belknap Press of Harvard University Press, 1999). Numbers are indicated in the text.

77. Martin, "Emily Dickinson," 610.

78. Aaron, *The Unwritten War,* 355.

79. *Poems of Emily Dickinson,* 1230 (1871).

80. Thomas H. Johnson, ed., *The Letters of Emily Dickinson* (Cambridge, Mass.: Belknap Press, 1958), 1:380.

81. Martin, "Emily Dickinson," 610.

82. John Carey, *What Good Are the Arts?* (London: Faber and Faber, 2005), 231–32.

83. See Sarah E. Gardner, *Blood and Irony: Southern White Women's Narratives of the Civil War, 1861–1937* (Chapel Hill: University of North Carolina Press, 2004).

84. First published in *The Independent,* 1910. For Piatt, see *Palace-burner: The Selected Poetry of Sarah Piatt,* ed. Paula Bernat Bennett (Urbana: University of Illinois Press, 2001).

85. Drew Gilpin Faust, "Introduction" to Augusta Jane Evans, *Macaria; or, Altars of Sacrifice* (Baton Rouge: Louisiana State University Press, 1992), xxvi.

86. Moss, *Domestic Novelists,* 218.

87. Faust, "Altars of Sacrifice," 198.

88. Augusta Jane Evans, *St. Elmo,* ed. Diane Roberts (Tuscaloosa: University of Alabama Press, 1992).

89. Roberts, "Introduction" to ibid., v.

90. The books have recently been rediscovered by Christian fundamentalists in the United States and are vigorously marketed as texts for homeschooling little girls. On their website, the publishers of the Elsie novels praise them as "a fictional series that exalts the name of Jesus while demonstrating inspiring, virtuous womanhood."

91. Mrs. Furness, "Our Soldiers," *Atlantic Monthly* 13 (March 1864): 364.

92. Fanny Fern, *Ruth Hall and Other Writings,* ed. Joyce W. Warren (New Brunswick, N.J.: Rutgers University Press, 1986), 342.

93. *Harper's* 28 (January 1864): 238, 239.

94. Elizabeth Stuart Phelps, *Chapters from a Life* (Boston: Houghton Mifflin, 1896), 97–98.

95. Ibid., 98.

96. From *Three Spiritualist Novels,* ed. Nina Baym (Urbana: University of Illinois Press, 2000), 11.

97. Phelps, *Chapters from a Life,* 90–91.

98. Edmund Wilson, "Introduction" to *Patriotic Gore: Studies in the Literature of the American Civil War* (New York: Norton, 1994), xxiii.

99. Gary Williams, *Hungry Heart* (Amherst: University of Massachusetts Press, 1999), 212–13.

100. Laura E. Richards and Maud Howe Elliott, *Julia Ward Howe, 1819–1910* (Boston: Houghton Mifflin, 1915), chap. 14.

101. Elizabeth Cady Stanton, Susan B. Anthony, and Matilda Joslyn Gage, *The History of Woman Suffrage* (New York: Fowler & Wells, 1882), 2:23.

8. The Coming Woman

1. See Bettina Friedl, ed., *On to Victory: Propaganda Plays of the Woman Suffrage Movement* (Boston: Northeastern University Press, 1987). Ariana Randolph Wormeley Curtis (1833–1922) and her husband, Daniel Sargent Curtis (1825–1908), are the likeliest authors of the play, which was published anonymously in 1868 and went through twenty-three editions over the next twenty years.

2. Elizabeth Stuart Phelps, "The True Woman," *The Independent,* October 12, 1871, 1.

3. Emanie Sachs, *"The Terrible Siren": Victoria Woodhull (1838–1927)* (New York: Harper, 1928), 298.

4. In 1869, Howe and Lucy Stone led the formation of the American Woman Suffrage Association when its members separated from the National Association of Elizabeth Cady Stanton and Susan B. Anthony. From its first issue in 1870, she edited and contributed to the *Woman's Journal.* This passage is quoted in Mary H. Grant, *Private Woman, Public Persona: An Account of the Life of Julia Ward Howe* (Brooklyn, N.Y.: Carlson Publications, 1994), 198.

5. Joan Hedrick, *Harriet Beecher Stowe: A Life* (New York and Oxford: Oxford University Press, 1995), 359.

6. Harriet Beecher Stowe to George Eliot, May 25, 1869, Berg Collection, New York Public Library.

7. Gail Hamilton, "A Battle of the Books," in *Gail Hamilton: Selected Writings,* ed. Susan Coultrap-McQuin (New Brunswick, N.J.: Rutgers University Press, 1992), 148.

8. Gail Hamilton to Henry James, Sr., March 1865, in *Gail Hamilton: Selected Writings,* 20.

9. David S. Reynolds, *Beneath the American Renaissance: The Subversive Imagination in the Age of Emerson and Melville* (New York: Knopf, 1988), 398.

10. Mary Angela Bennett, "Elizabeth Stuart Phelps" (Ph.D. diss., University of Pennsylvania, 1939).

11. Marietta Holley, *My Opinion and Betsy Bobbet's* (Hartford: American Publishing Company, 1872), v.

12. Reynolds, *Beneath the American Renaissance,* 401.

13. Grace Farrell, "Afterword," in Lillie Devereux Blake, *Fettered for Life* (New York: Feminist Press, 1996).

14. *Louisa May Alcott: Her Life, Letters, and Journals,* ed. Ednah D. Cheney (Boston: Roberts Brothers, 1889; rpt. New York: Gramercy Books, 1995), 69; and Louise Chandler Moulton, "Louisa May Alcott," in *Our Famous Women,* ed. Elizabeth Stuart Phelps (1883; rpt. Freeport, N.Y.: Books for Libraries Press, 1975), 49.

15. Louisa May Alcott, journal entry, February 1864, in *Her Life, Letters, and Journals,* 128.

16. Louisa May Alcott, *Work: A Story of Experience* (New York: Schocken, 1977), 1–2. In my discussion of Alcott, I have drawn upon my introduction to *Alternative Alcott* (New Brunswick, N.J.: Rutgers University Press, 1989).

17. Caroline Ticknor, *May Alcott: A Memoir* (Boston: Little, Brown, 1928), 263–64.

18. Charlotte Streifer Rubenstein, *American Women Artists* (New York: Avon, 1982), 79.

19. Stowe letters to George Eliot, May 11, 1872, and September 26, 1872, quoted in Marlene Springer, "Stowe and Eliot: An Epistolary Friendship," *Biography* 9, no. 1 (Winter 1986): 63, 75.

20. Stowe to Eliot, September 25, 1876, in *Kindred Hands: Letters on Writing by British*

and American Women Authors, 1865–1935, ed. Jennifer Cognard-Black and Elizabeth MacLeod Walls (Iowa City: University of Iowa Press, 2006), 30–32.

21. Phelps recalled that "for six disastrous weeks before this simple experience, I dwindled with terror, day and night; and I came to that audience of boys and girls as if they had been a den of tigers and I a solitary disabled gladiator, doomed at their claws." Elizabeth Stuart Phelps, *Chapters from a Life* (1896; rpt. Manchester, N.H.: Ayer Publishing, 1980), 254–55.

22. See George V. Griffith, "An Epistolary Friendship: The Letters of Elizabeth Stuart Phelps to George Eliot," *Legacy* 18 (2001): 94–100.

23. Elizabeth Stuart Phelps, *The Story of Avis,* ed. Carol Farley Kessler (New Brunswick, N.J.: Rutgers University Press, 1985), 246.

24. *The Nation,* May 27, 1877; and Griffith, "An Epistolary Friendship," 98.

25. Sherwood Bonner, *Like unto Like* (1878), with "Introduction" by Jane Turner Censer (Columbia: University of South Carolina Press, 1997), 48.

26. On Bonner, see also William L. Frank, *Sherwood Bonner* (Boston: G. K. Hall, 1976); Hubert Horton McAlexander, *The Prodigal Daughter: A Biography of Sherwood Bonner* (Baton Rouge: Louisiana State University Press, 1981); and *A Sherwood Bonner Sampler, 1869–1884,* ed. Anne Razey Gowdy (Knoxville: University of Tennessee Press, 2000).

27. Sherwood Bonner, diary entry, June 1869, in McAlexander, *The Prodigal Daughter,* 39.

28. See Kathryn McKee, "Writing Region from the Hub: Sherwood Bonner's Travel Letters and Questions of Postbellum U.S. Southern Identity," *Legacy* 22 (2005): 126–43.

29. Censer, "Introduction," xx.

9. American Sibyls

1. "Miss Woolson's *Anne,*" *The Century* 24 (1882): 636; Constance Fenimore Woolson, "To George Eliot," *New Century for Women,* May 20, 1876, 1.

2. Helen Barolini, *Their Other Side: Six American Women and the Lure of Italy* (New York: Fordham University Press, 2006), 95; *The Diary of Alice James,* ed. Leon Edel (New York: Dodd, Mead & Co., 1964), 40–41.

3. Thomas Higginson, "The Greek Goddesses," *Atlantic Monthly,* July 1869.

4. Sarah Orne Jewett to Annie Fields, quoted in Richard Brodhead, *Cultures of Letters: Scenes of Reading and Writing in Nineteenth-Century America* (Chicago: University of Chicago Press, 1994), 157.

5. Harriet Beecher Stowe, "Sojourner Truth: The Libyan Sibyl," *Atlantic Monthly,* April 1863, 473–81.

6. Stowe's account was followed in April 1863 by another version by the feminist activist Frances Dana Gage. The construction of Sojourner Truth as an American sibyl had its own contradictions and complexities; see Nell Painter, *Sojourner Truth: A Life, A Symbol* (New York and Oxford: Oxford University Press, 1996).

7. Esther Schor, *Emma Lazarus* (New York: Schocken, 2006), 259. See also Dan Vogel, *Emma Lazarus* (Boston: G. K. Hall, 1980); and Eve Merriam, *Emma Lazarus Rediscovered* (New York: Biblio Press, 1998).

8. Emma Lazarus to Ralph Waldo Emerson, December 17, 1874, in *Emma Lazarus: Selected Poems and Other Writings,* ed. Gregory Eiselein (Peterborough, Ont.: Broadview Press, 2002), 312.

9. E. C. Stedman, *Genius and Other Essays* (New York: Moffat, Yard, 1911), 265–66.

10. Schor, *Emma Lazarus,* 176.

11. Ibid., 187.

12. James Russell Lowell to Emma Lazarus, December 17, 1883, in Eiselein, *Selected Poems,* 318.

13. Schor, *Emma Lazarus,* 235.

14. Ibid., 259.

15. Some critics see these terms as interchangeable, but others have made distinctions between them, defining "local color" as a tourist's outside use of place as exotic, backward, or strange; and "regionalism" as an insider's affectionate view of the small town and the rural environment outside the cultural mainstream.

16. Ann Douglas Wood, "The Literature of Impoverishment: The Woman Local Colorists in America, 1865–1914," *Women's Studies* 1 (1972): 3–35.

17. See Brodhead, *Cultures of Letters,* 115–21.

18. Josephine Donovan, *New England Local Color Literature: A Woman's Tradition* (New York: Frederick Ungar, 1983), 7.

19. Judith Fetterley and Marjorie Pryse summarize these debates in their indispensable study, *Writing Out of Place: Regionalism, Women, and American Literary Culture* (Urbana and Chicago: University of Illinois Press, 2003), 204.

20. Cheryl Torsney, *Constance Fenimore Woolson: The Grief of Artistry* (Athens: University of Georgia Press, 1989), 9.

21. Fetterley and Pryse, *Writing Out of Place,* 34.

22. Cecelia Tichi, "Women Writers and the New Woman," in *Columbia Literary History of the United States,* ed. Emory Elliott (New York: Columbia University Press, 1988), 590, 598.

23. Karen L. Kilcup and Thomas S. Edwards, "Confronting Time and Change: Jewett, Her Contemporaries, and Her Critics," in *Jewett and Her Contemporaries: Reshaping the Canon,* ed. Kilcup and Edwards (Gainesville: University Press of Florida, 1999), 7.

24. Brodhead, *Cultures of Letters,* 169.

25. Rose Terry Cooke, "The West Shetucket Railroad," in Donovan, *New England Local Color Literature,* 8.

26. Fetterley and Pryse, *Writing Out of Place,* 324.

27. June Howard, "Introduction: Sarah Orne Jewett and the Traffic in Words," in *New Essays on* The Country of the Pointed Firs, ed. June Howard (Cambridge: Cambridge University Press, 1994).

28. *Letters of Sarah Orne Jewett,* 47.

29. Brodhead, *Cultures of Letters,* 163.

30. See Sarah Way Sherman, *Sarah Orne Jewett: An American Persephone* (Hanover, N.H.: University Press of New England, 1989), esp. 92–108.

31. Sarah Orne Jewett, *Novels and Stories* (New York: Library of America, 1994).

32. See especially Louis A. Renza, *"A White Heron" and the Question of Minor Literature* (Madison: University of Wisconsin Press, 1984).

33. Willa Cather, "Preface," in *Best Stories of Sarah Orne Jewett* (Boston: Houghton Mifflin, 1925).

34. Howard, "Jewett and the Traffic in Words," 3.

35. Sharon O'Brien, "Becoming Noncanonical: The Case Against Willa Cather," in *Reading in America,* ed. Cathy N. Davidson (Baltimore: Johns Hopkins University Press, 1989), 240–58.

36. Warner Berthoff, "The Art of Jewett's _Pointed Firs,_" reprinted in _Fictions and Events: Essays in Criticism and Literary History_ (New York: Dutton, 1971), 263.

37. Michael Davitt Bell, "Gender and American Realism: _The Country of the Pointed Firs,_" in Howard, _New Essays,_ 61.

38. Elizabeth Ammons, _Conflicting Stories: American Women Writers at the Turn into the Twentieth Century_ (New York and Oxford: Oxford University Press, 1991), 58, 52–53.

39. Marjorie Pryse, "Introduction" to _The Country of the Pointed Firs,_ ed. Mary Ellen Chase (New York: Norton, 1981).

40. See Amy Kaplan, "Nation, Region, and Empire," in _Columbia History of the American Novel,_ ed. Emory Elliott (New York: Columbia University Press, 1991).

41. See the essays by Ammons and Gillman in Howard, _New Essays._

42. Brodhead, _Cultures of Letters,_ 175.

43. _Letters of Sarah Orne Jewett,_ 247–50.

44. On Freeman, see Leah Blatt Glasser, _In a Closet Hidden: The Life and Work of Mary Wilkins Freeman_ (Amherst: University of Massachusetts Press, 1996); Edward Foster, _Mary E. Wilkins Freeman_ (New York: Hendricks House, 1956); Perry Westbrook, _Mary Wilkins Freeman_ (New York: Twayne, 1967); and Sandra A. Zagarell, "Introduction" to Mary E. Wilkins Freeman, _A New England Nun and Other Stories_ (New York: Penguin, 2000).

45. Glasser, _In a Closet Hidden,_ 18.

46. Fred Lewis Pattee, _Side-Lights on American Literature_ (New York: The Century, 1922), 206–7.

47. Donovan, _New England Local Color Literature,_ 119.

48. Quoted in Glasser, _In a Closet Hidden,_ 55.

49. Freeman returned to these images repeatedly in her fiction; in "Eglantina," for example, the virginal heroine does her needlework in the garden near a hive of bees; "she could hear their drowsy hum and see their winged flights to a great bed of pinks, wilting in the full blaze of the sunlight, and giving out a great, panting fragrance of spice and honey."

50. Quoted in Glasser, _In a Closet Hidden,_ 219.

51. Donovan, _New England Local Color Literature,_ 119.

52. _Letters of Sarah Orne Jewett,_ 81.

53. Edd Winfield Parks, _Charles Egbert Craddock_ (Chapel Hill: University of North Carolina Press, 1941), 119.

54. Fetterley and Pryse, _Writing Out of Place,_ 187–88.

55. Kate Phillips, _Helen Hunt Jackson: A Literary Life_ (Berkeley: University of California Press, 2003), 2.

56. Ibid., 58. For letter to her father, see http://www.coloradocollege.edu/library/SpecialCollections/Manuscript/HHJ1-1-18.html.

57. See Thomas Johnson, _The Poems of Emily Dickinson_ (Cambridge, Mass.: Belknap Press, 1955), 179.

58. _Scribner's,_ 1872, quoted in Phillips, _Helen Hunt Jackson,_ 36.

59. Phillips, _Helen Hunt Jackson,_ 225.

60. Ibid., 253.

61. Quoted by Michael Dorris, "Introduction" to Helen Hunt Jackson, _Ramona_ (New York: Signet, 2002), xi.

62. Phillips, _Helen Hunt Jackson,_ 35.

63. Originally Josephine Donna Smith, a descendant of the Mormon founder

Joseph Smith, Coolbrith was the daughter of a renegade Mormon woman who escaped from her polygamous marriage. Taking her mother's maiden name, she had settled in Oakland and became the librarian at the Oakland Free Library in 1873. From that small power base, she became one of the most influential literary figures of the region.

64. Phillips, *Helen Hunt Jackson,* 3.
65. Ibid., 261.
66. Jay B. Hubbell, "Some New Letters of Constance Fenimore Woolson," *New England Quarterly* 14 (December 1941): 732.
67. Joan Myers Weimer, "Introduction" to *Women Artists, Women Exiles: "Miss Grief" and Other Stories* (New Brunswick, N.J.: Rutgers University Press, 1988), xiv–xv.
68. Constance Fenimore Woolson to Paul Hayne, January 10, 1876, quoted ibid., xli n. 3.
69. Constance Fenimore Woolson to Edmund Stedman, October, 1, 1876, quoted ibid., xiii.
70. Constance Fenimore Woolson, *For the Major* (1883; rpt. New York: AMS Press, 1970), 9–10.
71. Carolyn Hall, "An Elaborate Pretense for the Major: Making Up the Face of the Postbellum Nation," *Legacy* 22 (2005): 144–57.
72. Constance Fenimore Woolson to Edmund Stedman, July 23, 1876, in Weimer, "Introduction," xviii.
73. Torsney, *Constance Fenimore Woolson,* 76–78.
74. Henry James, "An American and an English Novel," *The Nation,* December 21, 1876; quoted in Phillips, *Helen Hunt Jackson,* 208.
75. Elizabeth Stuart Phelps, *Chapters from a Life* (Boston and New York: Houghton Mifflin, 1896), 187.
76. Anne E. Boyd, "Anticipating James, Anticipating Grief," in *Constance Fenimore Woolson's Nineteenth Century,* ed. Victoria Brehm (Detroit: Wayne State University Press, 2001), 196.
77. Lyndall Gordon, *A Private Life of Henry James: Two Women and His Art* (New York: Norton, 1999).
78. John Carlos Rowe, *The Other Henry James* (Durham, N.C.: Duke University Press, 1998), 38.
79. Henry James, "Miss Constance Fenimore Woolson," *Harper's Weekly,* February 12, 1887, 114–15.
80. Weimer, "Introduction," xxxix.
81. See Sergio Perosa, *American Theories of the Novel, 1793–1903* (New York: New York University Press, 1985), 167, 165.

10. New Women

1. Carroll Smith-Rosenberg, *Disorderly Conduct: Visions of Gender in Victorian America* (New York: Knopf, 1985), 245–57.
2. Christine Stansell, *American Moderns: Bohemian New York and the Creation of a New Century* (New York: Henry Holt, 2000), 28.
3. See Martha H. Patterson, *Beyond the Gibson Girl: Reimagining the New American Woman* (Urbana and Chicago: University of Illinois Press, 2005).
4. See Nancy Cott, "Passionlessness: An Interpretation of Victorian Sexual Ideology," *Signs* 4 (1978): 236 n. 60.

5. Ann Heilmann, *New Woman Fiction: Women Writing First-Wave Feminism* (London: Palgrave, 2000), 8, 9, 67.

6. Frank Luther Mott, *A History of American Magazines, 1885–1905* (Cambridge, Mass.: Harvard University Press, 1957), 120.

7. Kerry Powell, *Women and Victorian Theatre* (Cambridge: Cambridge University Press, 1997), 150–51.

8. Elizabeth Robins Collection, Fales Library, New York University.

9. Kerry Powell, "Oscar Wilde, Elizabeth Robins, and the Theatre of the Future," *Modern Drama* 37 (1994): 232.

10. "The Short Story," *Atlantic Monthly*, February 1892, 261.

11. Bliss Perry, "The Short Story," in *A Study of Prose Fiction* (Boston and New York: Houghton Mifflin, 1902), 300–334.

12. Elizabeth Stuart Phelps, *Chapters from a Life* (Boston: Houghton Mifflin, 1896), 263.

13. Charlotte Perkins Gilman, *The Living of Charlotte Perkins Gilman: An Autobiography* (1935; rpt. Madison: University of Wisconsin Press, 1991), 121.

14. Willa Cather, review of *The Green Carnation*, in *The Kingdom of Art: Willa Cather's First Principles and Critical Statements, 1893–1896*, ed. Bernice Slote (Lincoln: University of Nebraska Press, 1966), 390.

15. Helen Lefkowitz Horowitz, *The Power and Passion of M. Carey Thomas* (New York: Knopf, 1994), 286, 488 n. 23.

16. Emily Wortis Leider, *California's Daughter: Gertrude Atherton and Her Times* (Stanford, Calif.: Stanford University Press, 1991), 102.

17. Pauline Hopkins, "Higher Education of Colored Women," *Colored American Magazine* 5 (October 1902): 447.

18. Frances W. Harper, *Iola Leroy; or, Shadows Uplifted* (Boston: Beacon Press, 1987).

19. Pauline E. Hopkins, "Preface" to *Contending Forces: A Romance Illustrative of Negro Life North and South* (New York and Oxford: Oxford University Press, 1988), 13–14.

20. Richard Yarborough, "Introduction" to Hopkins, *Contending Forces*, xxxi.

21. See Elaine Showalter, *Sexual Anarchy: Gender and Culture at the Fin de Siècle* (London: Virago, 1992), chap. 5.

22. Pauline Hopkins, *Of One Blood; Or, The Hidden Self* (New York: Washington Square Press, 2004).

23. Elizabeth Ammons, *Conflicting Stories: American Women Writers at the Turn into the Twentieth Century* (New York and Oxford: Oxford University Press, 1991), 85.

24. Yarborough, "Introduction," xlii, xliii.

25. Nan Bowman Albinski, "Utopia Reconsidered: Women Novelists and Nineteenth-Century Utopian Visions," *Signs* 13 (1988): 830–41.

26. Sandra M. Gilbert and Susan Gubar, *No Man's Land: Sexchanges* (New Haven, Conn.: Yale University Press, 1988), 2:38.

27. Eveleen Laura Knaggs Mason, *Hiero-Salem: The Vision of Peace* (1889), in *Daring to Dream: Utopian Stories by United States Women, 1836–1919*, ed. Carol Farley Kessler (Boston: Pandora Press, 1984), 142.

28. See Kate Douglas Wiggin, *My Garden of Memory: An Autobiography* (London: Hodder & Stoughton, 1924), 3.

29. See Pam McAllister, "Introduction" to Lois Waisbrooker, *A Sex Revolution* (Philadelphia: New Society Publishers, 1985), 3, 34–35.

30. Alice Ilgenfritz Jones went on to publish two more novels, *Beatrice of Bayou Teche* (1895), about a mixed-race woman of genius in New Orleans before the Civil War who is a gifted painter and opera singer; and *The Chevalier of St. Denis*

(1900). See Carol A. Kolmerten, "Introduction" to Alice Ilgenfritz Jones and Ella Merchant, *Unveiling a Parallel: A Romance* (Syracuse, N.Y.: Syracuse University Press, 1991); and Thomas A. Fick and Eva Gold, "Introduction" to Alice Ilgenfritz Jones, *Beatrice of Bayou Teche* (Bowling Green, Ky.: Bowling Green State University Press, 2001).

31. Barbara Will, "The Nervous Origins of the American Western," *American Literature* 70 (1998): 293–316.

32. Denise D. Knight, " 'All the Facts of the Case': Gilman's Lost Letter to Dr. Silas Weir Mitchell," *American Literary Realism* 37 (Spring 2005): 259–77.

33. Mary A. Hill, *Charlotte Perkins Gilman: The Making of a Radical Feminist, 1860–1896* (Philadelphia: Temple University Press, 1980), 167. On Gilman, see also Carol Farley Kessler, "Charlotte Perkins Gilman," in *Modern American Women Writers,* ed. Elaine Showalter (New York: Scribner's, 1991); Ann J. Lane, *To Herland and Beyond: The Life and Work of Charlotte Perkins Gilman* (New York: Pantheon, 1990); Denise D. Knight, ed., *The Abridged Diaries of Charlotte Perkins Gilman* (Charlottesville: University Press of Virginia, 1998); and Joanne Karpinski, ed., *Critical Essays on Charlotte Perkins Gilman* (Boston: G. K. Hall, 1991).

34. Hill, *Charlotte Perkins Gilman,* 132.

35. For the definitive history of the story, its text, and its publication, see Julie Bates Dock, *Charlotte Perkins Gilman's "The Yellow Wall-paper" and the History of Its Publication and Reception* (University Park: Pennsylvania State University Press, 1998).

36. H[enry] B[lackwell], review of "The Yellow Wall-paper," *Woman's Journal,* June 17, 1899, 187.

37. Charlotte Perkins Gilman, "Why I Wrote 'The Yellow Wall-paper,' " *The Forerunner* 4 (October 1913): 271, in Dock, *Charlotte Perkins Gilman's "The Yellow Wall-paper,"* 86.

38. See Joan Wylie Hall, "Ruth McEnery Stuart," *Legacy* 10 (1993): 47–56; and Helen Taylor, *Gender, Race, and Region in the Writings of Grace King, Ruth McEnery Stuart, and Kate Chopin* (Baton Rouge: Louisiana State University Press, 1989), 131–33.

39. Charlotte Perkins Gilman, *The Man-Made World; or, Our Androcentric Culture* (New York: Charlton, 1911), chap. 5.

40. Gertrude Atherton, *The Adventures of a Novelist* (New York: Blue Ribbon Books, 1932), 212–15.

41. Leider, *California's Daughter,* 5–6.

42. Ibid., 172.

43. See *The American Essays of Henry James,* ed. Leon Edel (New York: Vintage, 1956), 207.

44. Leider, *California's Daughter,* 104.

45. Cora Kaplan, "Introduction" to *Aurora Leigh and Other Poems by Elizabeth Barrett Browning* (London: Women's Press, 1978), 19.

46. Taylor, *Gender, Race, and Region,* 189.

47. Ibid., 105.

48. According to Etta Reid Lyles, the Exposition "served as a forum from which Julia Ward Howe and other Northern social reformers launched a Southern women's rights movement and created an unprecedented alliance between women of the North and South." See Melissa Walker Heidari, ed., *"To Find My Own Peace": Grace King in Her Journals, 1886–1910* (Athens: University of Georgia Press, 2004), xxxii.

49. Anne Goodwyn Jones, *Tomorrow Is Another Day: The Woman Writer in the South, 1859–1936* (Baton Rouge: Louisiana State University Press, 1981), 33.
50. Taylor, *Gender, Race, and Region,* 25.
51. Ibid., 23–24.
52. Ibid., 153.
53. Jones, *Tomorrow Is Another Day,* 128.
54. Heidari, *"To Find My Own Peace,"* xxvii. See also Robert Bush, "The Patrician Voice: Grace King," in *Literary New Orleans: Essays and Meditations,* ed. Richard S. Kennedy (Baton Rouge: Louisiana State University Press, 1992), 8–15.
55. In *Grace King of New Orleans,* ed. Robert Bush (Baton Rouge: Louisiana State University Press, 1973), 42.
56. Published May 31, 1885, *New Orleans Times-Democrat;* see Taylor, *Gender, Race, and Region,* 41.
57. Taylor, *Gender, Race, and Region,* 39.
58. Grace King to Warrington Dawson, March 15, 1906, in Bush, *Grace King of New Orleans,* 390.
59. Jones, *Tomorrow Is Another Day,* 99.
60. Ibid., 121.
61. Heidari, *"To Find My Own Peace,"* 40.
62. Kate Chopin, "Crumbling Idols," in *The Complete Works of Kate Chopin,* ed. Per Seyersted (Baton Rouge: Louisiana State University Press, 1969), 2:693.
63. Per Seyersted, *Kate Chopin: A Critical Biography* (New York: Octagon Books, 1980), 83. See also Emily Toth, *Kate Chopin* (New York: William Morrow; London: Century, 1990).
64. Kate Chopin, "Confidences," in *Complete Works,* 2:702.
65. Some of my remarks on Chopin are adapted from *Sister's Choice: Tradition and Change in American Women's Writing* (Oxford: Clarendon Press, 1991), chap. 4.
66. "Sibert" [Willa Cather], "Books and Magazines," *Pittsburgh Leader,* July 8, 1899, 6.
67. Seyersted, *Kate Chopin,* 196.
68. Gloria T. Hull, "Researching Alice Dunbar-Nelson: A Personal and Literary Perspective," *Feminist Studies* 6 (Summer 1980): 314–20.
69. Judith Fetterley and Marjorie Pryse, *American Women Regionalists, 1850–1910* (New York: Norton, 1992), 459. Alice Ruth Moore was Dunbar-Nelson's maiden name.
70. Ibid., 460.
71. Ammons, *Conflicting Stories,* 66–71.
72. See ibid.,62, and Gloria Hull, *Color, Sex, and Poetry: Three Women Writers of the Harlem Renaissance* (Bloomington: Indiana University Press, 1987), 64.
73. Ammons, *Conflicting Stories,* 71.
74. *Century* 30 (May 1885): 50–53.
75. Kate Phillips, *Helen Hunt Jackson: A Literary Life* (Berkeley: University of California Press, 2003), 268.
76. Ammons, *Conflicting Stories,* 70.
77. Edith Wharton, "The Valley of Childish Things, and Other Emblems," *Century* 52 (July 1896): 467–69.
78. Hermione Lee, *Edith Wharton* (London: Chatto and Windus, 2007), 160.
79. Ellen Glasgow, "A Woman of To-Morrow," *Short Stories* XIX (1895): 415–27.
80. Ellen Glasgow, *The Woman Within* (New York: Harcourt, Brace, 1954), 140.
81. Helen Gray Cone, "Woman in American Literature," *Century* 40 (October 1890): 921–30.

11. The Golden Morrow

1. Floyd Dell, *Homecoming* (New York: Farrar, 1933), 218.
2. Mabel Dodge Luhan, *Intimate Memories: The Autobiography of Mabel Dodge Luhan,* ed. Lois Rudnick (Albuquerque: University of New Mexico Press, 1999), 112.
3. See Elaine Showalter, *Inventing Herself: Claiming a Feminist Intellectual Heritage* (New York: Simon & Schuster, 2001), chap. 6.
4. For example, see Katherine Gerould, "The Newest Woman," *Atlantic Monthly* 109 (1912): 606–11.
5. Beatrice Hale, *What Women Want: An Interpretation of the Feminist Movement* (New York: Frederick A. Stokes, 1914), 122–23.
6. Elizabeth Robins, *Way-Stations* (New York: Dodd, Mead, 1913), 73.
7. Quoted in Christine Stansell, *American Moderns: Bohemian New York and the Creation of a New Century* (New York: Henry Holt, 2000), 231.
8. Mary Johnston, *Hagar* (Boston: Houghton Mifflin, 1913), 7.
9. Ibid., 211. For a detailed analysis and critique of Johnston's novel, see Martha H. Patterson, "Mary Johnston, Ellen Glasgow, and the Evolutionary Logic of Progressive Reform," in *Beyond the Gibson Girl: Reimagining the American New Woman, 1895–1915* (Urbana and Chicago: University of Illinois Press, 2005), 125–51.
10. Elizabeth Ammons, *Conflicting Stories: American Women Writers at the Turn into the Twentieth Century* (New York and Oxford: Oxford University Press, 1991), 123.
11. Marjorie Pryse, "Introduction" to Mary Austin, *Stories from the Country of Lost Borders* (New Brunswick, N.J.: Rutgers University Press, 1995), xvii.
12. Mary Austin, *Earth Horizon: An Autobiography* (Boston: Houghton Mifflin, 1932), 129.
13. Mary Austin, "Woman Alone," in *These Modern Women,* ed. Elaine Showalter (Old Westbury, N.Y.: Feminist Press, 1989), 78–85.
14. Mary Austin, "The Forward Turn," *The Nation,* July 20, 1927, 58.
15. Mary Austin, *A Woman of Genius,* ed. Nancy Porter (Old Westbury, N.Y.: Feminist Press, 1985).
16. Austin, *Earth Horizon,* 114.
17. Quoted in T. M. Pearce, ed., *Literary America: The Mary Austin Letters* (Westport, Conn.: Greenwood Press, 1979), 177.
18. Pryse, "Introduction," xxxv.
19. Quotations are from Gilman, *Herland* (New York: Pantheon, 1979).
20. Janet Malcolm, *Two Lives: Gertrude and Alice* (New Haven, Conn.: Yale University Press, 2007), 40.
21. Guy Reynolds, *Twentieth-Century American Women's Fiction* (New York: St. Martin's Press, 1999), 44.
22. Carl Van Vechten, "Introduction" to *Gertrude Stein: Three Lives* (New York: Modern Library, 1933). Van Vechten became Stein's literary executor; he also photographed her. See Bruce Kellner, "Baby Woojums in Iowa," *Books at Iowa* 26 (April 1977), http://www.lib.uiowa.edu/spec-coll/Bai/Kellner.htm.
23. Stein was equally complimentary about Wright's *Black Boy* (1945): "I do not think there has been anything like it since I wrote *Three Lives.*" Hemingway observed that Stein only spoke well of writers who had "written favorably about her work or done something to advance her career." Cited in Malcolm, *Two Lives,* 72–73.
24. Malcolm, *Two Lives,* 38.
25. See Sandra M. Gilbert and Susan Gubar, *No Man's Land: Sexchanges* (New

Haven, Conn.: Yale University Press, 1988); and Mary K. DeShazer, ed., *Longman Anthology of Women's Literature* (New York: Longman, 2001), 283.

26. Mabel Dodge, "Speculations, or Post-Impressionism in Prose," *Arts and Decoration* (March 1913), in *Critical Essays on Gertrude Stein,* ed. Michael J. Hoffman (Boston: Hall & Co., 1986), 27; Gertrude Stein, *Lectures in America* (Boston: Beacon Press, 1985), 177.

27. Emily Wortis Leider, *California's Daughter: Gertrude Atherton and Her Times* (Stanford, Calif.: Stanford University Press, 1991), 331–32.

28. Ibid., 333–34.

29. Ibid., 337.

30. Karen Ford, *Gender and the Poetics of Excess: Moments of Brocade* (Jackson: University Press of Mississippi, 1997).

31. Wayne Koestenbaum, "Stein Is Nice," *Parnassus* 20 (1995): 297–319.

32. Adelaide Morris, "H.D.," in *Modern American Women Writers,* ed. Elaine Showalter (New York: Scribner's, 1991), 95.

33. H.D., *End to Torment: A Memoir of Ezra Pound,* ed. Norman Holmes Pearson and Michael King (New York: New Directions, 1979), 18.

34. Susan Stanford Friedman, *Penelope's Web: Gender, Modernity, H.D.'s Fiction* (New York and Cambridge: Cambridge University Press, 1990), 39–48.

35. C. David Heymann, *American Aristocracy: The Lives and Times of James Russell, Amy, and Robert Lowell* (Boston: Dodd, Mead, 1980), 217.

36. Amy Lowell, "Why We Should Read Poetry," *Boston American,* May 3, 1914.

37. Amy Lowell, "Two Generations in American Poetry," *New Republic* 37 (1923): 1–3.

38. *The Complete Poetical Works of Amy Lowell,* 4th ed. (Cambridge, Mass.: Riverside Press, 1955).

39. Ardis Cameron, "Immigration," in *The Oxford Companion to Women's Writing in the United States,* ed. Cathy N. Davidson and Linda Wagner-Martin (New York and Oxford: Oxford University Press, 1995).

40. Werner Sollers, "Ethnic Modernism," in *Cambridge History of American Literature,* ed. Sacvan Bercovitch (Cambridge: Cambridge University Press, 2005), 6:411.

41. Ibid., 6:418.

42. Mary Antin, "The Lie," *Atlantic Monthly* (1913), quoted ibid., 6:424. See also ibid., 6:540, on Antin's views of Judaism.

43. On Zitkala-Ša, see Judith Fetterley and Marjorie Pryse in *American Women Regionalists, 1850–1910: A Norton Anthology* (New York: Norton, 1992).

44. Zitkala-Ša, "An Indian Teacher Among Indians," *Atlantic Monthly,* March 1900, 381–86.

45. The story appeared in *Everybody's Magazine.* See Carmen Burkle, "Multiculturalism and the New Woman in Early Twentieth-Century America," in *Feminist Forerunners: New Womanism and Feminism in the Early Twentieth Century,* ed. Ann Heilmann (London: Pandora, 2003), 58–75.

46. For an excellent account of Zitkala-Ša's dilemma, see Judith Fetterley and Marjorie Pryse, *Writing Out of Place: Regionalism, Women, and American Literary Culture* (Urbana: University of Illinois Press, 2003), 312–13.

47. Sui Sin Far, "Leaves from the Mental Portfolio of an Eurasian," *The Independent* 66 (January 1909): 132.

48. Ibid., 128.

49. Sollers, "Ethnic Modernism," 402.

50. Elin Diamond, "Drama," in *The Oxford Companion to Women's Writing in the United States.*

51. Yvonne Shafer, *American Women Playwrights, 1900–1950* (New York: Peter Lang, 1995).

52. Floyd Dell, *Homecoming,* quoted in C. W. E. Bigsby, ed., *Plays by Susan Glaspell* (Cambridge: Cambridge University Press, 1987), 1.

53. Susan Glaspell, *Lifted Masks and Other Works,* ed. Eric S. Rabkin (Ann Arbor: University of Michigan Press, 1993).

54. Susan Glaspell, *The Road to the Temple* (New York: Frederick A. Stokes, 1927), 235–36.

55. Laura Godwin, "Preface" to Susan Glaspell, *Fidelity* (London: Persephone Books, 1999), xv.

56. See Linda Ben-Zvi, *Susan Glaspell, Her Life and Times* (New York and Oxford: Oxford University Press, 2005), and Veronica Makowsky, *Susan Glaspell's Century of American Women* (New York and Oxford: Oxford University Press, 1993).

57. Linda Ben-Zvi, "Susan Glaspell's Contributions to Contemporary Women Playwrights," in *Feminine Focus: The New Women Playwrights,* ed. Enoch Brater (New York and Oxford: Oxford University Press, 1984), 152.

58. Ben-Zvi, *Susan Glaspell,* 187.

59. Makowsky, *Susan Glaspell's Century,* 115.

60. Karen Alkalay-Gut, *Alone in the Dawn: The Life of Adelaide Crapsey* (Athens: University of Georgia Press, 1988), 249. See also Alkalay-Gut, "Jean Webster," http://www.karenalkalay-gut.com/web.html; and Elaine Showalter, "Introduction" to Jean Webster, *Daddy-Long-Legs and Dear Enemy* (New York: Penguin, 2004), vii–xviii.

61. Anne L. Bower, *Epistolary Responses: The Letter in Twentieth-Century American Fiction and Criticism* (Tuscaloosa: University of Alabama Press, 1997), 99.

62. Eleanor H. Porter, *Pollyanna* (Boston: L. C. Page, 1913).

12. Against Woman's Writing: Wharton and Cather

1. Louis Auchincloss, "Introduction" to Edith Wharton, *A Backward Glance* (New York: Appleton-Century Company, 1934; rpt. New York: Scribner's, 1961), vii.

2. Wharton thought that Eliot's novels suffered from "cumbersome construction" and were "a continuous hymn to respectability." Cather objected to Eliot's "long dissertations" and her "constant intrusions."

3. Edith Wharton, *French Ways and Their Meaning* (New York: Appleton, 1919), 102.

4. Edith Wharton, *The Letters of Edith Wharton,* ed. R. W. B. Lewis and Nancy Lewis (New York: Scribner's, 1980), 124.

5. Wharton, *A Backward Glance,* 205.

6. Edith Wharton, "Life and I," unpublished manuscript in Beinecke Library, Yale University; quoted in Candace Waid, *Edith Wharton's Letters from the Underworld: Fictions of Women and Writing* (Chapel Hill: University of North Carolina Press, 1991), 5.

7. Wharton, *Letters,* 80.

8. Wharton, *A Backward Glance,* 51.

9. Ibid., 35.

10. R. W. B. Lewis, *Edith Wharton: A Biography* (New York: Harper & Row, 1979); Hermione Lee, *Edith Wharton* (London: Chatto and Windus, 2007), 78–80.

11. Wharton, *A Backward Glance,* chap. 6.

12. Ibid., 207–8. Marilyn French, however, is one critic who argues that Wharton's writing always remained secretive and illicit. See her introduction to *The House of Mirth* (New York: Berkley, 1981), xii.

13. Sigmund Freud, "Femininity," in *The Standard Edition of the Complete Psychological Works of Sigmund Freud,* ed. and trans. Alix and James Strachey (London: Hogarth Press, 1964), 22:134.

14. Elizabeth Ammons, *Edith Wharton's Argument with America* (Athens: University of Georgia Press, 1980), 3.

15. Edmund Wilson, "Justice to Edith Wharton," in *Edith Wharton: A Collection of Critical Essays,* ed. Irving Howe (Englewood Cliffs, N.J.: Prentice-Hall, 1962), 26–27.

16. Hermione Lee comments that while Rosedale has "complexity, even attractiveness," Wharton's private letters displayed a much cruder and more offensive "snobbery, racism, anti-Semitism, and antifeminism" (*Edith Wharton,* 607). Awareness of these attitudes, and views of their centrality to Wharton's outlook have begun to convert some of Wharton's critical admirers into detractors. See Jennie Kassanoff, *Edith Wharton and the Politics of Race* (Cambridge: Cambridge University Press, 2004).

17. Quoted in Cynthia Griffin Wolff, *A Feast of Words: The Triumph of Edith Wharton* (New York: Oxford University Press, 1977), 151.

18. Edith Wharton, "The Writing of Ethan Frome," Edith Wharton Collection, Yale Collection of American Literature, Beinecke Rare Book and Manuscript Library, box 32, folder 1010.

19. Wharton, *A Backward Glance,* 293–94.

20. Ibid. For a detailed comparison of *Ethan Frome* and *Wuthering Heights,* see Jean Blackall Frantz, "Imaginative Encounter: Edith Wharton and Emily Brontë," *Edith Wharton Review* 9 (Spring 1992): 9–11.

21. The critic Joseph X. Brennan notes that "the narrator who presents himself as an engineer in the realistic framework of the novel is actually a writer in disguise with the technical skill of a professional novelist . . . and his reconstruction of Ethan Frome's story, in view of what little he had to go by, is really no more than a brilliant fiction." Brennan, "Ethan Frome: Structure and Metaphor," *Modern Fiction Studies* 7 (Winter 1961): 348.

22. Owen and Donald Davis, *Ethan Frome,* with a foreword by Edith Wharton (Dramatists Play Service, [1936]), 14.

23. Edith Wharton to Charles Scribner, February 23, 1914, quoted in Alan Price, *The End of Innocence: Edith Wharton and the First World War* (New York: St. Martin's Press, 1996), 7.

24. Lee, *Edith Wharton,* 173.

25. Quoted in Deborah Lindsay Williams, *Not in Sisterhood: Edith Wharton, Willa Cather, Zona Gale, and the Politics of Female Authorship* (New York: Palgrave, 2001), 122.

26. Lee, *Edith Wharton,* 508.

27. Hermione Lee, *Willa Cather: A Life Saved Up* (London: Virago, 1989), 12.

28. Ibid., 13.

29. *The Kingdom of Art: Willa Cather's First Principles and Critical Statements, 1893–1896,* ed. Bernice Slote (Lincoln: University of Nebraska Press, 1966), 448.

30. Lee, *Willa Cather,* 3.

31. Sharon O'Brien, *Willa Cather: The Emerging Voice* (New York and Oxford: Oxford University Press, 1987), 6.

32. *The World and the Parish: Willa Cather's Articles and Reviews, 1893–1902*, ed. William M. Curton (Lincoln: University of Nebraska Press, 1970), 275.

33. Slote, *Kingdom of Art,* 406.

34. *Pittsburgh Leader,* July 8, 1899.

35. Slote, *Kingdom of Art,* 361.

36. Cather told a friend that she chose to have her work published by Knopf because she saw the young Alfred Knopf at concerts in the afternoon and felt an instant affinity with his choice of culture over business.

37. Katherine Anne Porter, "A Note," *The Troll Garden* (New York: New American Library, 1984).

38. *Letters of Sarah Orne Jewett,* ed. Annie Fields (Boston: Houghton Mifflin, 1911), 247–48.

39. Lee, *Willa Cather,* 89.

40. Slote, *Kingdom of Art,* 448.

41. Lee, *Willa Cather,* 108, 118.

42. Joan Accocella, *Willa Cather and the Politics of Criticism* (New York: Vintage, 2000), 2.

43. Lee, *Willa Cather,* 121.

44. Elizabeth Ammons, *Conflicting Stories: American Women Writers at the Turn into the Twentieth Century* (New York and Oxford: Oxford University Press, 1991), 128.

45. Deborah Carlin, *Cather, Canon, and the Politics of Reading* (Amherst: University of Massachusetts Press, 1992), 41.

46. Williams, *Not in Sisterhood,* 101.

47. Lee, *Willa Cather,* 624, 629.

48. Williams, *Not in Sisterhood,* 17.

49. Quoted in Susan Hegeman, "Taking Blondes Seriously," *American Literary History* 7 (Fall 1995): 525.

50. Accocella, *Willa Cather and the Politics of Criticism,* 25.

51. Ibid., 24.

52. *Ernest Hemingway: Selected Letters, 1917–1961,* ed. Carlos Baker (New York: Scribner's, 1981), 105.

53. She wrote twenty-nine chapters of the book, which was finished according to her notes by Marion Mainwaring in 1993.

54. See Judith Fetterley and Marjorie Pryse, *Writing Out of Place: Regionalism, Women, and American Literary Culture* (Urbana: University of Illinois Press, 2003), 44, 48.

13. You Might as Well Live

1. Dorothy Dunbar Bromley, "Feminist—New Style," *Harper's,* October 1927, 552–60.

2. Josephine Herbst, *The Starched Blue Sky of Spain and Other Memoirs* (Boston: Northeastern University Press, 1999), 66.

3. Elizabeth Ammons, *Conflicting Stories: American Women Writers at the Turn into the Twentieth Century* (New York and Oxford: Oxford University Press, 1991), 170; Linda Wagner, *Ellen Glasgow: Beyond Convention* (Austin: University of Texas Press, 1982), 22.

4. Susan Goodman, *Ellen Glasgow: A Biography* (Baltimore: Johns Hopkins University Press, 1998), 211.

5. See Julia Cluck, "Elinor Wylie's Shelley Obsession," *PMLA* 56 (September 1941): 841–60.

6. Mary Kinzie, ed., *A Poet's Prose: Selected Writings of Louise Bogan* (Athens, Ohio: Swallow Press, 2005), 139, 158.

7. Nancy Milford, *Savage Beauty: The Life of Edna St. Vincent Millay* (New York: Random House, 2001), 194.

8. William D. Drake, *Sara Teasdale: Woman and Poet* (New York: Harper & Row, 1979), 43.

9. Ibid., 73.

10. Ibid., 119.

11. Ibid., 140.

12. Ibid., 73, 119.

13. Van Wyck Brooks, *An Autobiography* (New York: Dutton, 1965), 376.

14. Stanley Olson, *Elinor Wylie: A Biography* (New York: Dial Press, 1979), 287.

15. William D. Drake, *The First Wave: Women Poets in America, 1915–1945* (New York: Collier Books, 1987), 92; *Letters of Virginia Woolf*, ed. Nigel Nicholson and Joanne Trautman (New York: Harcourt Brace Jovanovich, 1978), 3:279–80.

16. Thomas Wolfe, March 26, 1927, quoted in Olson, *Elinor Wylie*, 147.

17. Evelyn Helmick Hively, "Introduction" to *Selected Works of Elinor Wylie* (Kent, Ohio: Kent State University Press, 2005), xiii.

18. Olson, *Elinor Wylie*, 284.

19. Wylie's sister, Nancy Hoyt, wrote a memoir of her, *Elinor Hoyt: The Portrait of an Unknown Lady* (New York: Bobbs-Merrill, 1935).

20. Olson, *Elinor Wylie*, 286.

21. Ibid., 263.

22. "American Poetess Laureate" is from Sandra M. Gilbert and Susan Gubar, *No Man's Land: Letters from the Front* (New Haven, Conn.: Yale University Press, 1994), 3:67. Elizabeth Adkins, *Edna St. Vincent Millay and Her Times* (New York: Russell and Russell, 1964), 70.

23. Milford, *Savage Beauty*, 57.

24. Edmund Wilson, *The Shores of Light*, quoted ibid., 188.

25. Edna St. Vincent Millay, *The Harp-Weaver: and Other Poems* (New York: Harper & Brothers, 1923), and *American Poetry: A Miscellany*, ed. Louis Untermeyer (New York: Harcourt, Brace, 1922).

26. Gilbert and Gubar, *No Man's Land: Letters from the Front*, 3:77–78.

27. Ibid., 3:113.

28. Deborah Fried, "Andromeda Unbound: Gender and Genre in Millay's Sonnets," *Twentieth-Century Literature* 32 (1986): 17.

29. Elizabeth P. Perlmutter, "A Doll's Heart: The Girl in the Poetry of Edna St. Vincent Millay and Louise Bogan," *Twentieth-Century Literature* 23 (1977): 158.

30. Genevieve Taggard to Josephine Herbst, July 28, 1921, New York Public Library, in Drake, *The First Wave*, 174.

31. Genevieve Taggard, "Hawaii, Washington, Vermont," *Scribner's*, October 1934, 248. This memoir also appeared in revised form as the preface to *Calling Western Union* (New York: Harper & Brothers, 1936).

32. Taggard, "Hawaii, Washington, Vermont," 250.

33. Ibid., 251.

34. Genevieve Taggard, "Introduction" to *May Days* (New York: Boni and Liveright, 1925). For a fascinating discussion of the evolution of Taggard's ideas about "Everyday Alchemy," see Nancy Berke, *Women Poets on the Left* (Gainesville: University Press of Florida, 2001), 110–13.

35. Drake, *The First Wave*, 175.

36. Ibid., 177.

37. Elaine Showalter, ed., *These Modern Women: Autobiographies from the Twenties* (Old Westbury, N.Y.: Feminist Press, 1989), 66–67.

38. "Writers at Work," *Paris Review* (1956), in *The Portable Dorothy Parker*, ed. Marion Meade (New York: Penguin, 2006), 576.

39. Mary K. DeShazer, ed., *Longman Anthology of Women's Literature* (New York: Longman, 2001), 529.

40. Nora Ephron, *Crazy Salad* (New York: Knopf, 1976), 139.

41. Dorothy Parker, *Laments for the Living* (New York: Viking, 1930).

42. Marion Meade, "Introduction" to *The Portable Dorothy Parker*, xvii.

43. *The Letters of Edna St. Vincent Millay*, ed. Allan Ross MacDougal (New York: Harper, 1952), 173.

44. Elaine Showalter, *Sister's Choice: Tradition and Change in American Women's Writing* (Oxford: Clarendon Press, 1991), 111. See *What the Woman Lived: Selected Letters of Louise Bogan, 1920–1970*, ed. Ruth Limmer (New York: Harcourt Brace Jovanovich, 1973), 86.

45. Elizabeth Frank, *Louise Bogan: A Portrait* (New York: Knopf, 1985), 77. See also Limmer, *What the Woman Lived*.

46. Katha Pollitt, "Sleeping Fury," *Yale Review* 74 (Summer 1985): 600.

47. Louise Bogan, "Several Voices Out of a Cloud," in *The Blue Estuaries* (New York: Farrar, Straus & Giroux, 1968).

48. See Ann Douglas, *Terrible Honesty: Mongrel Manhattan in the 1920s* (New York: Farrar, Straus & Giroux, 1995); and Sandra M. Gilbert and Susan Gubar, *No Man's Land: The War of the Words* (New Haven, Conn.: Yale University Press, 1988).

49. See Elizabeth Francis, *The Secret Treachery of Words: Feminism and Modernism in America* (Minneapolis: University of Minnesota Press, 2002), xix.

50. Lola Ridge to Harold Loeb, July 11, 1922, quoted in Berke, *Women Poets on the Left*, 173 n. 16.

51. Bromley, "Feminist—New Style," 560.

52. George Hutchinson, *In Search of Nella Larsen: A Biography of the Color Line* (Cambridge, Mass.: Harvard University Press, 2006), 247.

53. Herbst, *Starched Blue Sky of Spain*, 84.

54. Ibid., 96.

55. The literature on the Sacco/Vanzetti case is huge. For an excellent recent study, see Bruce Watson, *Sacco and Vanzetti: The Men, The Murders, and The Judgment of Mankind* (New York: Viking, 2007).

56. Jerry Dickey, "The Expressionist Moment: Sophie Treadwell," in *The Cambridge Companion to American Women Playwrights*, ed. Brenda Murphy (Cambridge: Cambridge University Press, 1999), 70, 66.

57. Ibid., 72.

58. *The New York Times*, September 16, 1928.

59. Dickey, "The Expressionist Moment," 81.

60. Jerry Dickey and Miriam Lopez-Rodriguez, *Broadway's Bravest Woman: Selected Writings of Sophie Treadwell* (Carbondale: Southern Illinois University Press, 2006), 3.

61. Letter MS. 318 4/1, August 16, 1969, in Sophie Treadwell Collection, University of Arizona.

62. August Derleth, *Still Small Voice: The Biography of Zona Gale* (New York: Appleton-Century Co., 1940).

63. Zona Gale, *Miss Lulu Bett,* in *Plays by American Women, 1900–1930,* ed. Judith E. Barlow (New York: Applause, 1985), 161.

64. Patricia Schroeder, "Realism and Feminism in the Progressive Era," in *Cambridge Companion to American Women Playwrights,* 35.

65. Derleth, *Still Small Voice,* 117.

66. *The New Republic,* January 12, 1921.

67. Karen Knox, "Preface" to Dorothy Canfield Fisher, *The Home-Maker* (London: Persephone Books, 2004), ix.

68. Dorothy Goldman, "Introduction" to Dorothy Canfield Fisher, *Her Son's Wife* (London: Virago, 1986), x.

69. Ida H. Washington, *Dorothy Canfield Fisher* (Shelburne, Vt.: New England Press, 1982).

70. *Keeping Fires Night and Day: Selected Letters of Dorothy Canfield Fisher,* ed. Mark J. Madigan (Columbia: University of Missouri Press, 1993), 15.

71. The story was published in the university yearbook in 1894, and reprinted in a limited edition of thirty copies by Phoenix Book Shop in New York in 1931.

72. Letter of June 22, 1918, quoted in Alan Price, "Writing Home from the Front: Edith Wharton and Dorothy Canfield Fisher Present Wartime France to the United States, 1917–1919," *Edith Wharton Newsletter* 5 (Fall 1988): 1–8.

73. Fisher, *Letters,* 239; on Yezierska, see Louise Levitas Henriksen with assistance from Jo Ann Boydston, *Anzia Yezierska: A Writer's Life* (New Brunswick, N.J.: Rutgers University Press, 1988), 154, 155.

74. Henriksen, *Anzia Yezierska,* 134–35, 147.

75. Ibid., 152.

76. Laura Shapiro, *Perfection Salad: Women and Cooking at the Turn of the Century* (New York: Modern Library, 1986).

77. See Mary V. Dearborn, *Love in the Promised Land: The Story of Anzia Yezierska and John Dewey* (New York: Free Press, 1988).

78. Ibid., 3.

79. See Anzia Yezierska, *Hungry Hearts* (1920; London: Virago, 1987).

80. Ibid., 314.

81. Henriksen, *Anzia Yezierska,* 3–4.

82. Riva Krut, "Introduction" to Anzia Yezierska, *Hungry Hearts* (London: Virago, 1987), xx.

83. Cheryl A. Wall, *Women of the Harlem Renaissance* (Bloomington: Indiana University Press, 1995), 134.

84. See David Littlejohn, *Black on White: A Critical Survey of Writing by American Negroes* (New York: Viking, 1966), 50–51.

85. See Deborah E. McDowell, "Introduction" to Jessie Fauset, *Plum Bun* (London, Pandora Press, 1985), ix–xxiv.

86. See Jessie Fauset, *The Chinaberry Tree and Selected Writings* (Boston: Northeastern University Press, 1995).

87. Zona Gale, "Introduction" to *The Chinaberry Tree,* 74, 75.

88. Jessie Fauset, "Dark Algiers the White," *The Crisis,* April–May 1925, in *The Chinaberry Tree.*

89. Wall, *Women of the Harlem Renaissance,* 36.

90. Mary Helen Washington, "Nella Larsen: Mystery Woman of the Harlem Renaissance," *Ms.,* December 1980, 44–50.

91. George Hutchinson, *In Search of Nella Larsen: A Biography of the Color Line* (Cambridge, Mass.: Harvard University Press, 2006).

92. Ibid., 487.

93. Quoted ibid., 54.

94. Werner Sollers, "Ethnic Modernism," in *Cambridge History of American Literature,* ed. Sacvan Berkovitch (Cambridge: Cambridge University Press, 2005), 6:379.

95. Wall, *Women of the Harlem Renaissance,* 131.

96. See Hildegard Hoeller, "Race, Modernism, and Plagiarism: The Case of Larsen's 'Sanctuary,' " *African-American Review* 40, no. 3 (September 2006): 421–38. Beverly Haviland, cited in this essay, calls Larsen's plagiarism an "act of literary suicide."

97. Wall, *Women of the Harlem Renaissance,* 138.

98. Elizabeth Ammons, "Progressive Era Writing," in *Oxford Companion to Women's Writing in the United States.*

99. Lorine Livingston Pruette, in Showalter, *These Modern Women,* 73.

14. The Great Depression

1. George Hutchinson, *The Harlem Renaissance in Black and White* (Cambridge, Mass.: Belknap Press of Harvard University Press, 1995), 521 n. 170.

2. Louise Bogan, "Profiles: American Classic," *The New Yorker,* August 8, 1931.

3. Judith E. Barlow, "Introduction" to *Plays of American Women, 1930–1960* (New York and London: Applause, 2001).

4. Granville Hicks, "The Literary Caravan," *Modern Quarterly* 6 (Autumn 1932): 100.

5. Valerie Boyd, *Wrapped in Rainbows: The Life of Zora Neale Hurston* (New York: Scribner, 2003), 250.

6. See Darden Asbury Pyron, *Southern Daughter: The Life of Margaret Mitchell and the Making of* Gone with the Wind (Athens, Ga.: Hill Street Press, 2004), 335.

7. Willa Cather, paraphrased in Deborah Lindsay Williams, *Not in Sisterhood: Edith Wharton, Willa Cather, Zona Gale and the Politics of Female Authorship* (New York: Palgrave, 2001), 1.

8. Richard Ruland and Malcolm Bradbury, *From Puritanism to Postmodernism: A History of American Literature* (New York: Penguin, 1992), 394.

9. William Drake, *The First Wave: Women Poets in America, 1915–1945* (New York: Macmillan, 1987), 288.

10. See William Drake, *Sara Teasdale: Woman and Poet* (New York: Harper & Row, 1979).

11. Elaine Showalter, *Sister's Choice: Tradition and Change in American Women's Writing* (Oxford: Clarendon Press, 1991), 109.

12. Charlotte Nekola and Paula Rabinowitz, "Preface" to *Writing Red: An Anthology of American Women Writers, 1930–1940* (Old Westbury, N.Y.: Feminist Press, 1987), xii.

13. Mike Gold, "Go West, Young Writers," in *Mike Gold: A Literary Anthology,* ed. Michael Folsom (New York: International Publishers, 1972), 188.

14. Constance Coiner, *Better Red: The Writing and Resistance of Tillie Olsen and Meridel Le Sueur* (New York and Oxford: Oxford University Press, 1995), 35.

15. Mike Gold, September 1930, quoted ibid., 24.

16. Paula Rabinowitz, *Labor and Desire: Women's Revolutionary Fiction in America* (Chapel Hill: University of North Carolina Press, 1991), 80.

17. See Caroline Moorehead, *Martha Gellhorn: A Life* (London: Vintage, 2004), 168.

18. See Elizabeth Francis, *The Secret Treachery of Words: Feminism and Modernism in America* (Minneapolis: University of Minnesota Press, 2002), 117–18.

19. Richard A. Cordell, "After the Gilded Age," *Saturday Review of Literature,* March 5, 1939, 7.

20. Coiner, *Better Red,* 108.

21. Leslie J. Reagan, *When Abortion Was a Crime: Women, Medicine, and Law in the United States, 1867–1973* (Berkeley: University of California Press, 1997), chap. 5.

22. According to www.measuringworth.com, $200 in 1933 was equivalent to about $3,100 in 2006, measured by the consumer price index, or close to $9,000 measured by the unskilled wage.

23. Quoted in Elaine Hedges, "Introduction" to Meridel Le Sueur, *Ripening: Selected Work, 1927–1980* (Old Westbury, N.Y.: Feminist Press, 1982), 15.

24. Coiner, *Better Red,* 72.

25. Ibid., 87–89.

26. Ibid., 36.

27. Hedges, "Introduction," 15.

28. Rabinowitz, *Labor and Desire,* 114–20.

29. Coiner, *Better Red,* 86.

30. Ibid., 96.

31. Ibid., 139.

32. Elizabeth Hardwick, "Introduction" to Tess Slesinger, *The Unpossessed: A Novel of the Thirties* (New York: New York Review Books, 2002), viii.

33. Ibid., vii–ix.

34. Rabinowitz, *Labor and Desire,* 148–49.

35. See Janet Sharistanian, "Afterword" to Slesinger, *The Unpossessed,* 370–71.

36. Personal interview with Tillie Olsen, May 1970.

37. Deborah Rosenfelt, "From the Thirties: Tillie Olsen and the Radical Tradition," in *Feminist Criticism and Social Change,* ed. Judith Newton and Deborah Rosenfelt (New York: Methuen, 1985), 229. First published in 1981, Rosenfelt's article is still the best guide to Olsen's work.

38. Robert Cantwell, *The New Republic,* July 25, 1934.

39. Rosenfelt, "From the Thirties," 227.

40. Coiner, *Better Red,* 158–59.

41. Rosenfelt, "From the Thirties," 242.

42. Coiner, *Better Red,* 178.

43. On Olsen as a feminist icon, see Elaine Hedges and Shelley Fisher Fishkin, eds., *Listening to Silences: New Essays in Feminist Criticism* (New York and Oxford: Oxford University Press, 1994).

44. Myles Weber, *Consuming Silences: How We Read Authors Who Don't Publish* (Athens: University of Georgia Press, 2005).

45. Nancy Berke, *Women Poets on the Left: Lola Ridge, Genevieve Taggard, Margaret Walker* (Gainesville: University of Florida Press, 2001), 110.

46. Ibid., 89.

47. Coiner, *Better Red,* 3.

48. Josephine Herbst, "The Magicians and Their Apprentices," in *The Starched Blue Sky of Spain* (Boston: Northeastern University Press, 1999), 47, 49.

49. Elinor Langer, *Josephine Herbst* (Boston: Little, Brown, 1983), 37.

50. Ibid., 66.

51. Ibid., 68.

52. Ibid., 71–72.

53. Ibid., 120.

54. Winifred Farrar Bevilacqua, "An Introduction to Josephine Herbst," *Books in Iowa* 25 (1976): 3–20.

55. Rose C. Feld, "Miss Herbst's *Rope of Gold*," *The New York Times Book Review,* March 5, 1939, 6.

56. Langer, *Josephine Herbst,* 165.

57. Ibid., 232.

58. Katherine Anne Porter, "The Wooden Umbrella," *The Collected Essays and Occasional Writings of Katherine Anne Porter* (New York: Delacorte, 1970); and Josephine Herbst, "Miss Porter and Miss Stein," *Partisan Review* 15 (1948): 568–72.

59. Langer, *Josephine Herbst,* 317.

60. On Porter, see her *Collected Essays and Occasional Writings; The Collected Stories of Katherine Anne Porter* (New York: Harcourt Brace Jovanovich, 1979); and *Uncollected Early Prose of Katherine Anne Porter,* ed. Ruth M. Alvarez and Thomas F. Walsh (Austin: University of Texas Press, 1993).

61. Joan Givner, *Katherine Anne Porter: A Life* (New York: Simon & Schuster, 1982), 17.

62. From "Miranda's Story," in Showalter, *Sister's Choice;* also Wendy Martin, "Katherine Anne Porter," in *Modern American Women Writers,* ed. Elaine Showalter (New York: Scribner's, 1991), 281–94.

63. Givner, *Katherine Anne Porter,* 170.

64. Enrique Hank Lopez, *Conversations with Katherine Anne Porter* (Boston: Little, Brown, 1981), 203.

65. Barbara Thompson, "Katherine Anne Porter: An Interview," *Paris Review* 29 (Winter–Spring 1963).

66. See Arnold Rampersad's splendid biography, *Ralph Ellison* (New York: Knopf, 2007).

67. Janis P. Stout, *Katherine Anne Porter: A Sense of the Times* (Charlottesville: University Press of Virginia, 1995), 217.

68. Ibid., 264.

69. Shari Benstock, *Women of the Left Bank: Paris, 1900–1940* (London: Virago, 1987), 424.

70. Guy Reynolds, *Twentieth-Century American Women's Fiction* (New York: St. Martin's Press, 1999), 81.

71. Benstock, *Women of the Left Bank,* 429.

72. Boyd, *Wrapped in Rainbows,* 246, 310–11.

73. Ibid., 75.

74. Ibid., 109.

75. Reynolds, *Twentieth-Century American Women's Fiction,* 93.

76. Cheryl Wall, "Zorah Neale Hurston: Changing Her Own Words," in *Zora Neale Hurston: Critical Perspectives Past and Present,* ed. Henry Louis Gates, Jr., and K. A. Appiah (New York: Amistad, 1993), 89.

77. I have written in chapter 11 about Wright's admiration for Gertrude Stein. Another of his patrons was Dorothy Canfield Fisher, who, in her position as a judge for the Book-of-the-Month Club, wrote the introduction to their edition of *Black Boy* in 1940, comparing Wright to Dostoevsky. They corresponded for many years.

78. Claudia Roth Pierpont, *Passionate Minds: Women Rewriting the World* (New York: Knopf, 2000), 148.

79. Worth Tuttle Hedden, *The New York Herald Tribune Weekly Book Review,* October 10, 1948.

80. Susan Koppelman, "Introduction" to *The Stories of Fannie Hurst* (Old Westbury, N.Y.: Feminist Press, 2004), xi.

81. Barlow, "Introduction," xxvi.

82. Gail Collins, *America's Women* (New York: William Morrow, 2003), 350–52.

83. *Nobel Lectures, Literature, 1901–1967* (River Edge, N.J.: World Scientific, 1967).

84. Peter Conn, *Pearl S. Buck: A Cultural Biography* (New York: Cambridge University Press, 1996), 163, 20.

85. Ibid., 97.

86. Ibid., 112.

87. Ibid., 131–32.

88. Pierpont, *Passionate Minds,* 111.

89. Helen Taylor, "Women and Dixie: The Feminization of Southern Women's History and Culture," *American Literary History* 18 (2006): 847–60.

90. Sarah E. Gardner, *Blood and Irony: Southern Women's Narratives of the Civil War, 1861–1937* (Chapel Hill: University of North Carolina Press, 2004), 253.

91. Anne-Marie Slaughter, "War: A Reader's Guide," *New York Times Book Review,* December 17, 2007, 31.

92. Anne Goodwyn Jones, *Tomorrow Is Another Day: The Woman Writer in the South, 1859–1936* (Baton Rouge: Louisiana State University Press, 1981), 323.

93. Blanche H. Gelfant, *Women Writing in America* (Hanover, N.H.: University Press of New England, 1984), 172.

15. The 1940s: World War II and After

1. Wendy Steiner, "The Diversity of American Fiction," in *Columbia Literary History of the United States,* ed. Emory Elliott (New York: Columbia University Press, 1988), 871.

2. Susan Schweik, *A Gulf So Deeply Cut: American Women Poets and the Second World War* (Madison: University of Wisconsin Press, 1991), 4.

3. *The New Yorker,* quoted ibid., 3.

4. Jane Cooper, "Nothing Has Been Used in the Manufacture of This Poetry That Could Have Been Used in the Manufacture of Bread," in *Scaffolding: New and Selected Poems* (London: Anvil, 1984), 23–24.

5. Elizabeth Bishop to Ferris Greenslet, January 22, 1945, in Bishop, *One Art,* ed. Robert Giroux (New York: Farrar, Straus & Giroux, 1994), 125.

6. Julie Phillips, *James Tiptree, Jr.: The Double Life of Alice B. Sheldon* (New York: St. Martin's Press, 2006), 106.

7. Ibid., 109.

8. Ibid., 137–38.

9. Caroline Moorhead, *Martha Gellhorn: A Life* (London: Vintage, 2004), 284–85.

10. Hisaye Yamamoto, "I Still Carry It Around," *RIKKA* 3, no. 4 (1976): 11, quoted in King-Kok Cheung, "Introduction" to Yamamoto, *Seventeen Syllables and Other Stories* (New Brunswick, N.J.: Rutgers University Press, 2001).

11. On Yamamoto, see King-Kok Cheung, *Articulate Silences: Hisaye Yamamoto, Maxine Hong Kingston, Joy Kogawa* (Ithaca, N.Y.: Cornell University Press, 1993).

12. Maryemma Graham, "Introduction" to *On Being Female, Black, and Free: Essays by Margaret Walker, 1932–1992,* ed. Graham (Knoxville: University of Tennessee Press, 1997), xv.

13. See Claudia Tate, ed., *Black Women Writers at Work* (New York: Continuum, 1983), 194.

14. Nancy Berke, *Women Poets on the Left* (Gainesville: University Press of Florida, 2001), 125.

15. On Walker, see James Smethurst, *The New Red Negro: The Literary Left and African-American Poetry, 1930–1946* (New York and Oxford: Oxford University Press, 1999).

16. Tate, *Black Women Writers at Work,* 192.

17. Nellie Y. McKay, "Gwendolyn Brooks," in *Modern American Women Writers,* ed. Elaine Showalter (New York: Scribner's, 1991), 26. See also Harry B. Shaw, *Gwendolyn Brooks* (New York: Twayne, 1980); Keith D. Leonard, *The African-American Bardic Poet from Slavery to Civil Rights* (Charlottesville: University of Virginia Press, 2006); George E. Kent, *A Life of Gwendolyn Brooks* (Lexington: University Press of Kentucky, 1996).

18. Ann Folwell Stanford, "Gwendolyn Brooks," in the *Oxford Companion to Women's Writing in the United States,* ed. Cathy N. Davidson and Linda Wagner-Martin (New York and Oxford: Oxford University Press, 1995), 136.

19. Tate, *Black Women Writers,* 193.

20. Cooper, "Nothing Has Been Used," 25, 33.

21. Eudora Welty, "My Introduction to Katherine Anne Porter," in *Friendship and Sympathy: Communities of Southern Women Writers,* ed. Rosemary M. Magee (Jackson: University Press of Mississippi, 1992), 124–26.

22. Virginia Spencer Carr, *The Lonely Hunter: A Biography of Carson McCullers* (Athens: University of Georgia Press, 2003), 214.

23. Ibid., 157.

24. Ibid., 97.

25. *Mademoiselle* (1948), quoted ibid., 39

26. Virginia Spencer Carr, "Introduction" to *Collected Stories of Carson McCullers* (Boston: Houghton Mifflin, 1987), ix.

27. Carr, *The Lonely Hunter,* 84.

28. McCullers's outline for *The Heart Is a Lonely Hunter,* quoted in Cheryl B. Torsney, "Carson McCullers," in *Modern American Women Writers,* 174.

29. Carr, *The Lonely Hunter,* 112.

30. Ann Hulbert, *The Interior Castle: The Art and Life of Jean Stafford* (New York: Knopf, 1992), 167.

31. Caroline Gordon to Jean Stafford, undated but probably summer 1943, McFarlin Library, University of Tulsa, Caroline Gordon Papers, box 1, folder 1.

32. Carr, *The Lonely Hunter,* 157.

33. Ibid., 257, 259.

34. Ibid., 433, 476.

35. Josyane Savigneau, *Carson McCullers: A Life* (Boston: Houghton Mifflin, 2001), 74.

36. Charlotte Margolis Goodman, *Jean Stafford: The Savage Heart* (Austin: University of Texas Press, 1990), 1, 11, 15. See also Hulbert, *The Interior Castle;* and David Roberts, *Jean Stafford: A Biography* (Boston: Little, Brown, 1988).

37. See Elaine Showalter, "I Wish She'd Been a Dog," *London Review of Books,* February 7, 1991, 14–15.

38. Goodman, *The Savage Heart,* 61.

39. Hulbert, *The Interior Castle,* 81.

40. Ibid., 89.

41. Goodman, *The Savage Heart*, 91.
42. Hulbert, *The Interior Castle*, 88, 99, 114.
43. Ibid., 167; and Goodman, *The Savage Heart*, 131.
44. Roberts, *Jean Stafford*, 261.
45. Wilfrid Sheed, quoted ibid., 269.
46. Hulbert, *The Interior Castle*, 215.
47. See Susan J. Rosowski, "Molly's Truthtelling, or Jean Stafford Rewrites the Western," in *Reading the West: New Essays on the Literature of the American West*, ed. Michael Kowalewski (Cambridge and New York: Cambridge University Press, 1996), 157–76.
48. Hulbert, *The Interior Castle*, 197.
49. Ibid., 81.
50. Jean Stafford, "Topics: Women as Chattels, Men as Chumps," *The New York Times*, May 4, 1970, 24.
51. Hulbert, *The Interior Castle*, 372.
52. On Welty, see Suzanne Marrs, *Eudora Welty: A Biography* (New York: Harcourt, 2005); and Ann Waldron, *Eudora Welty: A Writer's Life* (New York: Anchor, 1998).
53. Welty, "My Introduction to Katherine Anne Porter," 124–26.
54. Claudia Roth Pierpont, *Passionate Minds: Women Rewriting the World* (New York: Knopf, 2000), 159.
55. Lorrie Moore, "A Pondered Life," *The New York Review of Books*, September 21, 2006.
56. Candace Waid, "Eudora Welty," in *Modern American Women Writers*, 371.
57. Diane Roberts, "Introduction" to Augusta Evans, *St. Elmo* (Tuscaloosa: University of Alabama Press, 1992), xx n. 4.
58. Pierpont, *Passionate Minds*, 163.
59. Waid, " Eudora Welty," 374.
60. Alice Walker, "Eudora Welty: An Interview," *Harvard Advocate*, 1973, reprinted in *Friendship and Sympathy*, 154–63.
61. Eudora Welty, *One Writer's Beginnings* (Cambridge, Mass.: Harvard University Press, 1984), 104.
62. Pierpont, *Passionate Minds*, 103.
63. *Conversations with Nadine Gordimer*, ed. Nancy Topping Bazin and Marilyn Seymour (Jackson: University Press of Mississippi, 1990), 139.
64. Margaret Walker, "A Brief Introduction to Southern Literature," in *Friendship and Sympathy*, 34.
65. Mary Helen Washington, *Invented Lives: Narratives of Black Women, 1860–1960* (New York: Anchor, 1987), 298–99.
66. Interview with James Ivy, *The Crisis* 53 (February 1946): 48–49.
67. Ann Perry, *The Street* (Boston: Beacon Press, 1985), 389, 436.
68. Washington, *Invented Lives*, 344.
69. Eric Homberger, "Kathleen Winsor," *Guardian*, June 4, 2003.
70. Winsor's notes and drafts are at the Ransom Humanities Research Center at the University of Texas; the book itself is a massive 972 pages.
71. *The New Yorker*, April 22, 1950.
72. *Star Money* (New York: Appleton-Century-Crofts, 1950), 184.
73. *The Unabridged Journals of Sylvia Plath, 1950–1962*, ed. Karen V. Kukil (New York: Anchor Books, 2000), 8.
74. Betty Friedan, *The Feminine Mystique* (1963; with new introduction, New York: Dell, 1984), 50.
75. Ibid., 423.

76. Nancy Milford, *Savage Beauty: The Life of Edna St. Vincent Millay* (New York: Random House, 2001), 508–9.

16. The 1950s: Three Faces of Eve

1. Patricia Bosworth, *Diane Arbus: A Biography* (New York: Knopf, 1984), 158, 217.
2. Ellen Moers, *Literary Women* (New York: Doubleday, 1976), 109.
3. Betty Friedan, *The Feminine Mystique* (1963; New York: Dell, 1984), 141.
4. Ibid., 240–41.
5. Adrienne Rich, "Taking Women Students Seriously," in *On Lies, Secrets, and Silence: Selected Prose, 1966–1978* (New York: Norton, 1979), 238.
6. Miriam G. Reumann, *American Sexual Character: Sex, Gender, and National Identity in the Kinsey Report* (Berkeley: University of California Press, 2005), 86.
7. Sylvia Plath, *The Unabridged Journals of Sylvia Plath,* ed. Karen V. Kukil (New York: Anchor, 2000), 81–82.
8. Reumann, *American Sexual Character,* 88.
9. Ibid., 95; and Deanna Paoli Gumina, *A Woman of a Certain Importance: A Biography of Katherine Norris* (Calistoga, Calif.: Illuminations Press, 2004), 279.
10. See Gwendolyn Brooks, *Maud Martha: A Novel* (Chicago: Their World Press, 1993), 34–35.
11. Arnold Rampersad, *Ralph Ellison* (New York: Knopf, 2007), 281.
12. Barbara Christian, *Black Feminist Criticism: Perspectives on Black Women Writers* (New York: Pergamon Press, 1985), 127–28.
13. Mary Helen Washington, " 'Taming All That Anger Down': Rage and Silence in the Writing of Gwendolyn Brooks," in *Invented Lives: Narratives of Black Women, 1860–1960* (New York: Doubleday, 1987), 387, 389, 391, 394, 396.
14. Gwendolyn Brooks, *Report from Part One* (Detroit: Broadside Press, 1972), 191.
15. Washington, *Invented Lives,* 395.
16. Glenda Hobbs, "A Portrait of the Artist as Mother: Harriette Arnow and *The Dollmaker,*" *Georgia Review* 33 (Winter 1979): 851–67.
17. On Harriette Arnow, see Wilton Eckley, *Harriette Arnow* (New York: Twayne, 1974); and Haeja K. Cheung, *Harriette Simpson Arnow: Critical Essays on Her Work* (East Lansing: Michigan State University Press, 1995).
18. Eckley, *Harriette Arnow,* 38.
19. Glenda Hobbs, "Harriette Arrow," in *Dictionary of American Biography* (Farmington Hills, Mich.: Gale Group, 1980), 6:308.
20. Barbara L. Baer, "Harriette Arnow's Chronicles of Destruction," *The Nation,* January 31, 1976, 117–20.
21. Joyce Carol Oates, in *Rediscoveries,* ed. David Madden (New York: Crown, 1971).
22. On Mary McCarthy, see Carol Brightman, *Writing Dangerously: Mary McCarthy and Her World* (New York: Clarkson Potter, 1981); Carol Gelderman, *Mary McCarthy: A Life* (New York: St. Martin's, 1988); Carol Gelderman, ed., *Conversations with Mary McCarthy* (Jackson: University Press of Mississippi, 1991); and Frances Kiernan, *Seeing Mary Plain: A Life of Mary McCarthy* (New York and London: Norton, 2000).
23. Elisabeth Niebuhr, "Interview with Mary McCarthy," *Paris Review* 27 (Winter–Spring 1962): 74.
24. Larissa MacFarquhar, "Group Therapy," *The New York Times,* March 26, 2000.
25. Mary McCarthy, *The Company She Keeps* (New York: Harvest, 2003), 8.
26. Mary McCarthy, "Up the Ladder from *Charm* to *Vogue,*" in *On the Contrary* (New York: Farrar, Straus & Giroux, 1961), 184, 186.

27. Mary Gordon, "A Novel of Terrorism," *The New York Times,* September 30, 1979.

28. William Barrett, *The Truants* (New York: Anchor, 1982), 48, 67.

29. Wendy Martin, "Mary McCarthy," in *Modern American Women Writers,* ed. Elaine Showalter (New York: Scribner's, 1991), 163.

30. Kiernan, *Seeing Mary Plain,* 435–36.

31. MacFarquhar, "Group Therapy."

32. Alice Walker, *In Search of Our Mothers' Gardens* (New York: Harvest, 1983), 56.

33. Josephine Hendin, *The World of Flannery O'Connor* (Bloomington: Indiana University Press, 1970), 4–5.

34. Adrienne Rich, *Of Woman Born: Motherhood as Experience and Institution* (New York: Norton, 1976).

35. Sally Fitzgerald, "Flannery O'Connor," in *The History of Southern Women's Literature,* ed. Carolyn Perry and Mary Louise Weaks (Baton Rouge: Louisiana State University Press, 2002), 408–9.

36. Jean W. Cash, *Flannery O'Connor: A Life* (Knoxville: University of Tennessee Press, 2002), 143.

37. On Flannery O'Connor, see Sally Fitzgerald, ed., *The Habit of Being: Selected Letters of Flannery O'Connor* (New York: Farrar, Straus & Giroux, 1979).

38. Katherine Hemple Prown, *Revising Flannery O'Connor: Southern Literary Culture and the Problem of Female Authorship* (Charlottesville: University Press of Virginia, 2001), 3.

39. Ibid., 15.

40. See Moers, *Literary Women;* Claire Kahane, "The Maternal Legacy: The Grotesque Tradition in Flannery O'Connor's Female Gothic," in *The Female Gothic,* ed. Juliann E. Fleenor (Montreal: Eden Press, 1983), 232–56.

41. Flannery O'Connor to William Sessions, October 11, 1956, in *The Habit of Being,* 178. I have my own tattered copy of the Signet edition, and Hulga also has a big bust, long red fingernails, and a bouffant hairdo.

42. Gerard Sherry, "An Interview with Flannery O'Connor," in *Conversations with Flannery O'Connor,* ed. Rosemary M. Magee (Jackson: University of Mississippi Press, 1987), 92–102.

43. Linda Wagner-Martin, *The Mid-Century American Novel, 1935–1965* (New York: Twayne, 1997), 107.

44. Judy Oppenheimer, *Private Demons: The Life of Shirley Jackson* (New York: Ballantine, 1988), 89.

45. Ibid., 109.

46. Ibid., 120.

47. Rampersad, *Ralph Ellison,* 538.

48. Darryl Hattenhauer, *Shirley Jackson's American Gothic* (Albany, N.Y.: State University of New York Press, 2003), 17.

49. Shirley Jackson, "Biography of a Story," in *Come Along with Me,* ed. Stanley Edgar Hyman (London: Michael Joseph, 1969), 211–24.

50. See Bernice M. Murphy, ed., *Shirley Jackson: Essays on the Literary Legacy* (Jefferson, N.C.: McFarland and Co., 2005).

51. Hattenhauer, *Shirley Jackson's American Gothic,* 117.

52. Jonathan Lethem, "Introduction" to Shirley Jackson, *We Have Always Lived in the Castle* (New York: Penguin, 2006).

53. Michael Callahan, "Peyton Place's Real Victim," *Vanity Fair,* March 2006.

54. See Emily Toth, *Inside Peyton Place: The Life of Grace Metalious* (Jackson: University Press of Mississippi, 1981), 123.

55. Carlos Baker, quoted ibid., 135–36.
56. Toth, *Inside Peyton Place,* 145–46.
57. Edward Brunner, *Cold War Poetry* (Urbana: University of Illinois Press, 2001), 84. Brunner argues that Rosalie Moore, V. R. Lang, and Katherine Hoskins were underrated women poets of the 1950s.
58. On Marianne Moore, see Charles Molesworth, *Marianne Moore: A Literary Life* (New York: Atheneum, 1990); and Laurence Stapleton, *Marianne Moore: The Poet's Advance* (Princeton, N.J.: Princeton University Press, 1990).
59. Elizabeth Bishop, *One Art: Letters,* ed. Robert Giroux (New York: Farrar, Straus & Giroux, 1994), 23.
60. Ibid., 96–97.
61. Anne Agnes Colwell, American National Biography Online, http://www.anb.org/articles/16/16-01885.html.
62. Elizabeth Squires, interview with Elizabeth Bishop, *Paris Review 80* (Summer 1981): 74–75.
63. Bishop, *One Art,* 33.
64. In Sandra M. Gilbert and Susan Gubar, eds., *Norton Anthology of Literature by Women,* 3rd ed. (New York: Norton, 2007), 2:618.
65. Suzanne Juhasz, "Anne Sexton," in *Modern American Women Writers,* 309–20.
66. Diane Wood Middlebrook, *Anne Sexton* (London: Virago, 1991), 93.
67. *The Unabridged Journals of Sylvia Plath,* ed. Karen V. Kukil (New York: Anchor, 2000), 360.
68. Anne Sexton to Carolyn Kizer, in Middlebrook, *Anne Sexton,* 56.
69. Plath commented on this poem on a BBC radio broadcast, quoted in David Craig Austin, "Sylvia Plath," in *Modern American Women Writers,* 271.
70. Linda Wagner-Martin, *Sylvia Plath: A Biography* (New York: Simon & Schuster, 1987), 97.
71. Plath, *Unabridged Journals,* 524–25, 529.
72. Wagner-Martin, *Sylvia Plath,* 118.
73. Adrienne Rich, "When We Dead Awaken: Writing as Re-Vision," in *Adrienne Rich's Poetry,* ed. Barbara Charlesworth Gelpi and Albert Gelpi (New York: Norton, 1975), 91, 94.
74. Ibid., 95.
75. Adrienne Rich, "Introduction" to *The Diamond Cutters* (New York: Harper & Brothers, 1955), 42.
76. Middlebrook, *Anne Sexton,* 111.
77. Rich, "When We Dead Awaken," 97.
78. Plath, *Unabridged Journals,* 524–25.
79. See Katherine V. Forrest, ed., *Lesbian Pulp Fiction* (San Francisco: Cleis Press, 2005).
80. See Elaine Tyler May, "Containment at Home: Cold War, Warm Hearth," in *American Identities,* ed. Lois P. Rudnick et al. (New York: Wiley-Blackwell, 2005), 66.

17. The 1960s: Live or Die

1. Gwendolyn Brooks, *Report from Part One: An Autobiography* (Detroit: Broadside Press, 1972), 183.
2. Dale Peck, " 'The Outsiders': 40 Years Later," *The New York Times Book Review,* September 23, 2007, 31.

3. See http://www.sehinton.com.

4. "A Letter from Harper Lee," *O, The Oprah Magazine*, July 2006, 151–52.

5. Charles J. Shields, *Mockingbird: A Portrait of Harper Lee* (New York: Henry Holt, 2006), 77.

6. Ibid., 26.

7. Ibid., 115.

8. The defendant, Walter Lett, who insisted he was innocent, had a schizophrenic breakdown while awaiting execution and was sent to the state mental hospital, where he died a few years later. See ibid., 118–20.

9. Ibid., 240–41.

10. Elinor Langer, *Josephine Herbst: The Story She Could Never Tell* (Boston: Little, Brown, 1984), 312–13.

11. Mary McCarthy, *Paris Review* 27 (Winter–Spring 1962): 62.

12. Frances Kiernan, *Seeing Mary Plain: A Life of Mary McCarthy* (New York: Norton, 2000), 519.

13. Ibid., 520, 524, 526. Hardwick's authorship was publicly revealed in obituaries after her death on December 4, 2007.

14. Ibid., 521.

15. Carol Gelderman, *Mary McCarthy: A Life* (New York: St. Martin's Press, 1988), 307.

16. Greg Johnson, *Invisible Writer: A Biography of Joyce Carol Oates* (New York: Dutton, 1998), 151.

17. Joyce Carol Oates, "Afterword" to *Expensive People* (New York: Modern Library, 2006), 221.

18. Johnson, *Invisible Writer*, 145.

19. Christopher Bigsby, *Writers in Conversation* (Norwich, U.K.: EAS Publishing, 2000), 301.

20. Diane Wood Middlebrook, *Anne Sexton: A Biography* (New York: Houghton Mifflin, 1991), 65.

21. Ibid., 125.

22. Ibid., 160.

23. Diane Wood Middlebrook and Diana Hume George, "Introduction" to *The Selected Poems of Anne Sexton* (Boston: Houghton Mifflin, 1988), xi.

24. Middlebrook, *Anne Sexton*, 306.

25. Diane Middlebrook, "Circle of Women Artists: Tillie Olsen and Anne Sexton at the Radcliffe Institute," in *Listening to Silences: New Essays in Feminist Criticism*, ed. Elaine Hedges and Shelley Fisher Fishkin (New York and Oxford: Oxford University Press, 1994), 17–22.

26. Middlebrook, *Anne Sexton*, 188.

27. Ibid., 174.

28. Diane Middlebrook, *Her Husband: Hughes and Plath—a Marriage* (New York: Viking, 2003), 189.

29. Susan R. Van Dyne, *Revising Life: Sylvia Plath's Ariel Poems* (Chapel Hill: University of North Carolina Press, 1993), 21.

30. Ted Hughes, "Introduction" to *The Collected Poems: Sylvia Plath* (New York, HarperPerennial, 1992), 14.

31. Sylvia Plath to Aurelia Plath, October 16, 1962, in *Letters Home: Correspondence, 1950–1963*, ed. Aurelia Schober Plath (New York: Harper & Row, 1975), 468.

32. Middlebrook, *Anne Sexton*, 201.

33. Ibid., 195.

34. Pat McPherson, *Reflecting on* The Bell Jar (London: Routledge, 1991), 6.

35. Sylvia Plath, *Ariel: The Restored Edition,* ed. Frieda Hughes (New York: Harper-Collins, 2004).

36. Middlebrook, *Her Husband,* 227.

37. Adrienne Rich, "Anne Sexton, 1928–1974," in *On Lies, Secrets, and Silence: Selected Prose, 1966–1978* (New York: Norton, 1979), 122.

18. The 1970s: The Will to Change

1. Quoted in Nina Baym, "Revising the Legacy of 1970s Feminist Criticism," in *Constance Fenimore Woolson's Nineteenth Century,* ed. Victoria Brehm (Detroit: Wayne State University Press, 2001), 98.

2. Lisa Maria Hogeland, *Feminism and Its Fictions: The Consciousness-Raising Novel and the Women's Liberation Movement* (Philadelphia: University of Pennsylvania Press, 1998), 1.

3. Baym, "Revising the Legacy of 1970s Feminist Criticism," 21.

4. Toni Morrison, *The Paris Review Interviews,* ed. Philip Gourevitch (New York: Picador, 2007), 367–68.

5. Katherine B. Payant, *Becoming and Bonding: Contemporary Feminism and Popular Fiction by American Women Writers* (Westport, Conn.: Greenwood Press, 1993).

6. Hogeland, *Feminism and Its Fictions.*

7. Gayle Greene, "Ambiguous Benefits: Reading and Writing in Feminist Meta-fiction," in *Anxious Power: Reading, Writing, and Ambivalence in Narrative by Women,* ed. Carol J. Singley and Susan Elizabeth Sweeney (Albany: State University of New York Press, 1993), 315.

8. Elaine Showalter and Carol Smith, "An Interview with Erica Jong," *Columbia Forum* (Winter 1975), in *Conversations with Erica Jong,* ed. Charlotte Templin (Jackson: University Press of Mississippi, 2002), 34.

9. Charlotte Templin, *Feminism and the Politics of Literary Reputation: The Example of Erica Jong* (Lawrence: University Press of Kansas, 1995), 29.

10. Christopher Lehmann-Haupt, "Books of the Times: Nuances of Women's Liberation," *The New York Times,* November 6, 1973.

11. Templin, *Feminism and the Politics of Literary Reputation,* 28–29.

12. Gretchen McNeese, "Interview with Erica Jong," *Playboy,* September 1975, 61–78, 202.

13. Showalter and Smith, "An Interview with Erica Jong," 27.

14. Selwyn R. Cudjoe, "Maya Angelou: The Autobiographical Statement Updated," in *Reading Black, Reading Feminist,* ed. Henry Louis Gates, Jr. (New York: Meridian, 1990), 282–83.

15. Claudia Tate, ed., *Black Women Writers at Work* (New York: Continuum, 1983), 149.

16. Cudjoe, "Maya Angelou," 284.

17. Christopher Bigsby, *Writers in Conversation* (Norwich, U.K.: EAS Publishing, 2000), 252.

18. Toni Cade Bambara, in Tate, *Black Women Writers at Work,* 38.

19. Bigsby, *Writers in Conversation,* 250–89.

20. Toni Morrison, "Afterword" to *The Bluest Eye* (New York: Plume, 1994).

21. Morrison, in Tate, *Black Women Writers at Work,* 125.

22. Ibid., 122, 253, 254.

23. Evelyn C. White, *Alice Walker: A Life* (New York: Norton, 2004), 61–62.

24. Alice Walker, in *Interviews with Black Writers,* ed. John O'Brien (New York: Live-right, 1973), 79–80.

25. Ibid., 185–212.

26. White, *Alice Walker,* 251.

27. Ibid., 273.

28. Barbara T. Christian, "Introduction" to Alice Walker, *Everyday Use* (New Brunswick, N.J.: Rutgers University Press, 1994), 13.

29. Mary Helen Washington, "An Essay on Alice Walker," in *Everyday Use,* 101–3.

30. Jean Stafford, herself a victim of violence, was apoplectic about Brownmiller's "screed," which she ranted against in "Brownmiller on Rape: A Scare Worse than Death," *Esquire* 84 (November 1975): 50, 52.

31. Some of this discussion draws on Elaine Showalter, "Rethinking the Seventies: Women Writers and Violence," *Antioch Review* 39 (Spring 1981): 156–70; and Elaine Showalter, *Sister's Choice: Tradition and Change in American Women's Writing* (Oxford: Clarendon Press, 1991), 141–43.

32. Quoted in White, *Alice Walker,* 330.

33. Oates, "Afterword" to *Wonderland* (New York: Modern Library, 2006).

34. Larry McCaffery, *Anything Can Happen: Interviews with Contemporary American Novelists* (Urbana: University of Illinois Press, 1983), 205.

35. Ibid., 200.

36. Ibid., 202.

37. Quoted in "Diane Johnson," in *Women Writers Talking,* ed. Janet Todd (New York: Holmes & Meier, 1983), 125.

38. McCaffery, *Anything Can Happen,* 213.

39. Constance Carey, interview with Diane Johnson, *San Francisco Review of Books* 1 (June 1976): 17.

40. Joanna Russ, "What Can a Heroine Do?" in *Feminist Literary Theory and Criticism,* ed. Sandra M. Gilbert and Susan Gubar (New York: Norton, 2007), 200–11.

41. Julie Phillips, *James Tiptree, Jr.: The Double Life of Alice B. Sheldon* (New York: St. Martin's Press, 2006), 90.

42. Russ, "What Can a Heroine Do?" 211.

43. Robert Silverberg, "Introduction" to James Tiptree, Jr., *Warm Worlds and Otherwise* (New York: Ballantine, 1975), quoted in Phillips, *James Tiptree, Jr.,* 2.

44. Alice B. Sheldon, "A Woman Writing Science Fiction," in *Meet Me at Infinity: The Uncollected Tiptree,* ed. Jeffrey D. Smith (New York: Tom Doherty Associates, 2000), 391.

45. Phillips, *James Tiptree, Jr.,* 422.

46. Ibid., 44.

47. Hogeland, *Feminism and Its Fictions,* 136.

48. Michael Swanwick, "Introduction" to James Tiptree, Jr., *Her Smoke Rose Up Forever* (San Francisco: Tachyon Publications, 2004), xii.

49. Nancy S. Gearhart and Jean W. Ross, "Alice Hastings Bradley Sheldon," in *Contemporary Authors* (Detroit: Gale, 1983) 108:443–50.

50. Phillips, *James Tiptree, Jr.,* 381.

51. On Paley, see Anne Hiemstra, "Grace Paley," in *Modern American Women Writers,* ed. Elaine Showalter (New York: Scribner's, 1991), 259–65; and Mark Krupnick, "Grace Paley," *The Guardian,* August 24, 2007, 44.

52. Krupnick, "Grace Paley."

53. See "Where Life Happens: Remembering Grace Paley," in *Pen America: A Journal for Writers and Readers* 8 (2008): 211–17.

54. Maxine Hong Kingston, "After the Fire," interview by Miel Alegre and Dave Weich, http://www.powells.com/authors/kingston.html.

55. Anne Tyler, "Women Writers: Equal but Separate," *The National Observer,* April 10, 1976, 2; and "Because I Want More than One Life," *Washington Post,* August 15, 1976, G1, G7.

56. On Didion, see Joan Zseleczky, "Joan Didion," in *Modern American Women Writers,* 71–80.

57. Linda Kuehl, "Interview with Joan Didion," *Paris Review* 74 (Fall–Winter 1974): 19.

58. Joan Didion, "The Women's Movement," *The New York Times Book Review,* July 30, 1972, reprinted in *The White Album* (New York: Simon & Schuster, 1979), 116–17.

59. Kuehl, "Interview with Joan Didion," 8.

60. Cynthia Ozick, "We Are the Crazy Lady and Other Feisty Feminist Fables," *Ms.,* Spring 1972, 40–44.

61. Cynthia Ozick, "Literature and the Politics of Sex: A Dissent" and "Justice to Feminism," in *Art and Ardor: Essays by Cynthia Ozick* (New York: Knopf, 1983), 284–90.

19. The 1980s: On the Jury

1. Joyce Carol Oates, "Woman Writer: Theory and Practice," in *(Woman) Writer: Occasions and Opportunities* (New York: Dutton, 1988), 22–32.

2. See Judith Wynne, "Profile of a Prolific Writer: Joyce Carol Oates," *Sojourner,* March 7, 1983, 4; and Elizabeth Lennox Keyser, "*A Bloodsmoor Romance:* Joyce Carol Oates's Little Women," *Women's Studies* 14 (1988): 211–24.

3. Oates, "Blood, Neon, and Failure in the Desert," in *(Woman) Writer,* 264–67.

4. Sara Paretsky, in *Writers on Writing: Collected Essays from* The New York Times, ed. John Darnton (New York: Times Books, 2002).

5. Linda Richards, "Interview with Sara Paretsky," http://www.januarymagazine.com/profiles/paretsky.html.

6. Sara Paretsky, "Introduction" to *Sisters on the Case: Celebrating Twenty Years of Sisters in Crime,* ed. Paretsky (New York: Penguin, 2007).

7. Dana Stabenow, *Alaska Women Write: Living, Laughing, and Loving on the Last Frontier* (Kenmore, Wash.: Epicenter Press, 2003), 176–77.

8. Laurin Porter, "Contemporary Playwrights/Traditional Forms," in *Cambridge Companion to American Women Playwrights,* ed. Brenda Murphy (Cambridge: Cambridge University Press, 1999), 195.

9. Joyce Carol Oates, "(Woman) Writer: Theory and Practice," in *(Woman) Writer,* 30.

10. Jonathan White, "Coming Back from the Silence: Interview with Ursula Le Guin," *Whole Earth Review,* Spring 1995.

11. Margaret Homans, *Women Writers and Poetic Identity* (Princeton, N.J.: Princeton University Press, 1980), 31, 32.

12. White, "Coming Back from the Silence."

13. Marilynne Robinson, "My Western Roots," in *Old West–New West: Centennial Essays,* ed. Barbara Howard Meldrum (Moscow: University of Idaho Press, 1993), 165–72.

14. Thomas Schaub, "An Interview with Marilynne Robinson," *Contemporary Literature* 35 (1994): 231–51.

15. Cornelia Nixon, "Talk with Marilynne Robinson," in *The Believer Book of Writers Talking to Writers,* ed. Vendela Vida (San Francisco: Believer Books, 2005), 277.

16. James H. Maguire, "Marilynne Robinson," *Dictionary of Literary Biography 206: Twentieth-Century American Western Writers,* ed. Richard H. Cracroft (Farmington, Mich.: The Gale Group, 1999), 251–60.

17. Marilynne Robinson, Iowa Writers' Workshop Newsletter, 1993, quoted in *Postmodern American Literature,* ed. Paula Geyn, Fred G. Leebron, and Andrew Levy (New York: Norton, 1998), 489.

18. Nixon, "Talk with Marilynne Robinson," 280.

19. Christine Caver, "Nothing Left to Lose: *Housekeeping'*s Strategic Freedoms," *American Literature* 68 (March 1996): 111–37.

20. Maguire, "Marilynne Robinson."

21. Raymond Carver, "On Writing," in *Fires: Essays, Poems, Stories* (New York: Vintage, 1989), 24.

22. Jo Sapp, "An Interview with Amy Hempel," *Missouri Review* 16 (1993): 75–95.

23. Mervyn Rothstein, "Ann Beattie's Life After Real Estate," *The New York Times,* December 30, 1985.

24. Vince Passaro, "Unlikely Stories," *Harper's,* August 1999, 81.

25. Jayne Anne Phillips, in Sarah Anne Johnson, *Conversations with American Women Writers* (Hanover, N.H.: University Press of New England, 2004), 188.

26. Bobbie Ann Mason, "Frequently Asked Questions," in *In Country* (New York: HarperPerennial, 2005), 11.

27. "A Note from Bobbie Ann Mason," in *In Country,* 5.

28. Ellen A. Blais, "Gender Issues in Bobbie Ann Mason's *In Country," South Atlantic Quarterly* 56 (1991): 107.

29. John D. Kalb, "Bobbie Ann Mason," *Dictionary of Literary Biography,* 173:118–31.

30. Deborah E. McDowell, "New Directions for Black Feminist Criticism," in *The New Feminist Criticism,* ed. Elaine Showalter (New York: Pantheon, 1985), 193.

31. Henry Louis Gates, Jr., "Introduction" to *Reading Black, Reading Feminist: A Critical Anthology,* ed. Gates (New York: Meridian, 1990), 6–7.

32. Sandra Cisneros, *Publishers Weekly,* March 29, 1991.

33. Amy Tan, *The Opposite of Fate* (New York: G. P. Putnam's, 2003), 318.

34. Katherine B. Payant, *Becoming and Bonding: Contemporary Feminism and Popular Fiction by American Women Writers* (Westport, Conn.: Greenwood Press, 1993), 68.

35. Tan, *The Opposite of Fate,* 319.

36. Nicholas A. Basbanes, "Bharati Mukherjee," quoted in Shilpi Pradhan, http://www.english.emory.edu/Bahri/Mukherjee.html.

37. Louise Erdrich, "Rose Nights, Summer Storms: Lists of Spiders and Literary Mothers," in *Louise Erdrich's* Love Medicine: *A Casebook,* ed. Hertha Sweet Wong (New York and Oxford: Oxford University Press, 2000), 221.

38. Louise Erdrich, "Where I Ought to Be," in *Louise Erdrich's* Love Medicine, 49.

39. On Louise Erdrich, see Lorena Laura Stookey, *Louise Erdrich: A Critical Companion* (Westport, Conn.: Greenwood Press, 1999); and Louise Erdrich, *Love Medicine,* new and expanded version (New York: HarperPerennial Modern Classics, 2005).

40. Gates, "Introduction," 2.

41. Alice Walker, *In Search of Our Mothers' Gardens: Womanist Prose* (New York: Harcourt Brace Jovanovich, 1983).

42. Deborah E. McDowell, " 'The Changing Same': Generational Connections and Black Women Novelists," in Gates, *Reading Black, Reading Feminist*, 104.

43. See Molly Hite, "Romance, Marginality, and Matrilineage: *The Color Purple* and *Their Eyes Were Watching God*," in Gates, *Reading Black, Reading Feminist*, 430.

44. Bell Hooks, "Writing the Subject: Reading *The Color Purple*," in Gates, *Reading Black, Reading Feminist*, 466.

45. Ibid., 452.

46. Alice Walker, "Writing *The Color Purple*," in *In Search of Our Mothers' Gardens*, 355–56.

47. Quoted in Evelyn C. White, *Alice Walker: A Life* (New York: Norton, 2004), 364.

48. See ibid., 353–57.

49. Gloria Naylor, "A Conversation" with Toni Morrison, *The Southern Review* 21 (July 1985): 568.

50. See Henry Louis Gates, Jr., *The Signifying Monkey: A Theory of Afro-American Literary Criticism* (New York and Oxford: Oxford University Press, 1988), xxiv, 175.

51. *The New York Times Book Review*, February 21, 1988, cited in Elaine Showalter, *Sister's Choice: Tradition and Change in American Women's Writing* (Oxford: Clarendon Press, 1991), 38–39, from which some of this discussion is taken.

52. Molly Hite suggests this connection in Gates, *Reading Black, Reading Feminist*; I believe it applies more generally to 1980s women writers.

53. Morrison, "Unspeakable Things Unspoken," *Norton Anthology of Literature by Women*, 2:1010, 1018, 1024.

54. Quoted in Ashraf H. A. Rushdy, "Daughters Signifyin(g) History: The Example of Toni Morrison's *Beloved*," in *Toni Morrison's Beloved: A Casebook*, ed. Nellie Y. McKay and William L. Andrews (New York and Oxford: Oxford University Press, 1999), 37.

55. Rushdy, "Daughters Signifyin(g) History," 38.

56. Morrison has never said specifically what the figure of "Sixty Million" refers to, but many American critics have pointed out the connection to the Holocaust. See Naomi Mandel, " 'I make the ink': Identity, Complicity, 60 Million and More," *Modern Fiction Studies* 48 (Fall 2002): 561–613.

57. See Lori Askeland, "Remodeling the Model Home in *Uncle Tom's Cabin* and *Beloved*," in *Toni Morrison's Beloved: A Casebook*, 159–78.

58. See Nicole B. Coonradt, "To Be Loved: Amy Denver and Human Need—Bridges to Understanding in Toni Morrison's *Beloved*," *College Literature* 32, no. 4 (Fall 2005): 168–87.

59. Christopher Bigsby, *Writers in Conversation* (Norwich, U.K.: EAS Publishing, 2000), 250–89.

60. Mary Helen Washington, "The Darkened Eye Restored," in Gates, *Reading Black, Reading Feminist*, 32.

61. Steiner, "Look Who's Modern Now," *The New York Times Book Review*, October 10, 1999, 18.

20. The 1990s: Anything She Wants

1. Ellen Kanner, "After the Pulitzer Prize–winning *Shipping News*, a Story of the Immigrant Experience," interview with Annie Proulx, August 31, 1997, http://www.bookpage.com/9606bp/fiction/accordioncrimes.html.

2. Mark Shechner, "Until the Music Stops: Women Novelists in a Post-feminist Stage," *Salmagundi* 113 (Winter 1997): 220–38.

3. See Willard Spiegelman, "The Nineties Revisited," *Contemporary Literature* 42 (Summer 2001): 233.

4. Darryl Pinckney, "The Best of Everything," *The New York Review of Books,* November 4, 1993, 33–37.

5. Beth Potier, "Gish Jen, American," *Harvard Gazette Archives,* http://www .hno.harvard.edu/gazette/2002/01.24/11-gishjen.html.

6. Gish Jen, in *Conversations with American Women Writers,* ed. Sarah Anne Johnson (Hanover, N.H.: University Press of New England, 2004), 93.

7. On Sontag, see Carl Rollyson and Lisa Paddock, *Susan Sontag: The Making of an Icon* (New York: Norton, 2000); Sohnya Sayers, *Susan Sontag: The Elegiac Modernist* (New York: Routledge, 1990); and Elaine Showalter, *Inventing Herself: Claiming a Feminist Intellectual Heritage* (New York: Simon & Schuster, 2001).

8. Susan Sontag, *Alice in Bed* (New York: Farrar, Straus & Giroux, 1993).

9. Seta Jeter Naslund, in Johnson, *Conversations with American Women Writers,* 158, 159.

10. Ibid., 160.

11. Sena Jeter Naslund, "P.S. Insights, Interviews & More," in *Ahab's Wife* (New York and London: HarperPerennial, 2005), 13.

12. Andrea Barrett, *PBS NewsHour* interview, November 8, 1996.

13. Andrea Barrett, in Johnson, *Conversations with American Women Writers,* 13.

14. Marcelle Thiebaux, "An Interview with Jane Smiley," *Publishers Weekly,* April 1, 1998, 65–66.

15. Katie Bolick, "A Conversation with Annie Proulx," http://www.theatlantic .com/unbound/factfict/eapint.htm.

16. Jane Smiley, "Say It Ain't So, Huck," *Harper's,* January 1996, 61.

17. Anson J. Cameron, letter to the editor, *Harper's,* April 1996, 7. See also Jim O'Loughloin, "Off the Raft: *Adventures of Huckleberry Finn* and Jane Smiley's *The All-True Travels and Adventures of Lidie Newton,*" *Papers on Language & Literature* 43 (Spring 2007): 205–23.

18. Annie Proulx, "Introduction" to *Best American Short Stories 1997* (Boston: Houghton Mifflin, 1997), xvii.

19. Kanner interview.

20. Annie Proulx, "How the West was Spun," *The Guardian,* June 25, 2005.

21. Richard Ruland and Malcolm Bradbury, *From Puritanism to Postmodernism: A History of American Literature* (New York: Viking, 1991), 368.

Index